LEGAL RESPONSES TO TERRORISM

Wayne McCormack

Professor of Law
S.J. Quinney College of Law
University of Utah

LCCN#: 2005925234

ISBN#: 0–8205–6381–1

Editorial Offices
744 Broad Street, Newark, NJ 07102 (973) 820-2000
201 Mission St., San Francisco, CA 94105-1831 (415) 908-3200
701 East Water Street, Charlottesville, VA 22902-7587 (804) 972-7600
www.lexis.com

(Pub.03211)

PREFACE

I have spent my career teaching constitutional law and civil liberties. I have litigated many cases against government agencies. I do not want government controlling my life.

I have two teenage sons. I cannot imagine anyone more fervent to have a safe environment in which my children can grow and learn. I understand the importance of public safety.

Like most people, I find my desires occasionally to be in tension. That is one reason why this course has been so engaging for me.

In 1997, I was assigned to coordinate the involvement of the University of Utah with the 2002 Olympic Winter Games, which involved me heavily with security planning alongside professionals from such agencies as the Department of Justice and Secret Service. I cannot emphasize enough the extraordinary professionalism of the men and women involved in security planning for that event. As life on this campus intensified from September 2001 to February 2002, I told many groups that my fondest hope was to wake up on the morning after the Closing Ceremonies and think "What was the big deal?" And that's exactly how it transpired.

From the perspective of a lawyer involved in security planning, I then grew more and more interested in the role of law in dealing with the threat of terrorism. At that same time, Americans first became aware that military options could exist alongside prevention and law enforcement in the tools available for dealing with terrorism. The three modes of response are not the same, each has benefits and limits, and it will be difficult to find the proper balance among them. This book is about balance. The terrorist needs to be stopped, people need to be protected, and people need freedom. And, yes, some disaffected potential terrorists have legitimate grievances or needs but those are mostly beyond the scope of this book.

This book is in the traditional mode of law school coursebooks, albeit with some emphasis from my own preferences. Specifically, I prefer to put explanatory information up front before the court opinions and then to limit sharply the number of questions and further information following each of the cases. The questions in the notes are meant to raise serious issues for class discussion. For similar reasons, I have limited the amount of reference to secondary source material in an effort to avoid interrupting the flow of the readings, while providing a list of "Selected Readings" at the end of each chapter.

The statutes and treaties necessary for the course are located in the Appendix. I will try to maintain a web site with updates and some of the more lengthy materials, such as government reports, that are not appropriate for reprinting in a hard-copy book. For similar reasons, the book attempts to provide background for current breaking issues, such as the prisoner abuse scandals, but does not purport to be a mechanism for tracking the latest events. Following those developments with a daily news service, either in print or online, will make the course even more engaging for everyone.

ACKNOWLEDGMENTS

David Schwendiman of the U.S. Attorney's Office in Utah has co-taught this course with me for two years, at least to the extent that he has been available from duties that have taken him to Greece, Bangladesh, the Maldives, Bahrain, Vietnam, and elsewhere. Dave is the quintessential professional, in constant pursuit of the "Rule of Law" through equal attention to public safety and individual rights. Jeff Breinholt of the Counterterrorism Section of the Justice Department has made guest appearances in the class, has provided ideas and updates on a number of matters in this field, and provided extraordinarily helpful comments on a draft of this book. Needless to say, the gaps and errors in this book are mine alone.

A number of people attempted to educate me to the demands of security planning while ensuring that the University of Utah remained an academic institution open to the public and vibrant with avenues for discourse during the 2002 Games. On the public safety front, I want to acknowledge primarily Chief Ben Lemmon and Sergeant Kent Curtis of the University of Utah Police Department, and Sergeant Kirk Middaugh of the Utah Highway Patrol. The facilities and event management team at the University worked incredible hours to accommodate the needs of the event while keeping the needs of an academic institution foremost: Dan Adams, Norm Chambers, Pieter van der Have, Gwen Springmeyer, and Randall Turpin. My thanks to these capable people are not just on my own behalf but that of the entire University community for their brilliant managing of those events, especially considering the context of the times.

This book is dedicated to my sons Bradley and Kevin, with hope that they may experience a peaceful world in which to live and grow.

Reprinted by Permission:

Douglas E. Streusand, *What Does Jihad Mean?*, MIDDLE EAST QUARTERLY (September 1997), *http://www.ict.org.il/articles/jihad.htm*

TABLE OF CONTENTS

Chapter 1

INTRODUCTION:
DEFINITIONS & STRUCTURES

The word "terrorism" evokes many images for each person who hears it. Perhaps the only consistent themes are that no image is positive and all are violent. A single mention of the word might set my mind loose on a kaleidoscopic rampage from Munich Olympic Village, to the Achille Lauro, to a masked gunman in the cockpit of an airplane in Athens, to guerillas in the jungles of Colombia, to a sidewalk café bomb in Spain, and ultimately to fully loaded airplanes flying into the World Trade Center Towers.

Notice that other themes could be lurking in the list above. All but the last incident occurred outside the United States. Most, but not all, involved Middle Eastern Islamist fundamentalists. Many were linked to demands for a Palestinian or Basque homeland, or a radical Colombian regime. Very few involve people such as Timothy McVeigh who acted out of sheer malice for his home government. Some of these themes are probably red herrings. When faced with conduct to which we want to respond, the human mind naturally wants to define that conduct so that we can distinguish it from what is acceptable behavior. But searching for a definition within the chaotic nature of terrorism could send us on a series of wild goose chases. (The mixing of metaphors in this paragraph is intentional to emphasize that chaotic events can cause chaotic thinking, which can lead in turn to unfortunate responses.)

The dominant purposes of this course are to determine what should be the appropriate responses of the United States and the international community to international terrorism. To what extent can criminal prosecutions do the job? Is military action a legitimate or appropriate response? If so, what are the rules of warfare, and how do they apply to U.S. citizens or residents? To what extent is government "spying" on citizens or residents necessary and to what extent must it be restricted?

An important starting point is to reduce some of the confusion surrounding the term "terrorism" itself.

§1.01 UNDERSTANDING TERRORISM

The one consistent theme in terrorism is violence against civilians. But not all violence against civilians is considered terrorism, most is simply criminal conduct. Some violence against civilians committed by official representatives of a government would be considered a war crime or genocide under international law, but it might also be considered terrorism.

[A] DEFINING TERRORISM

One question we will ask repeatedly is "what difference does the terrorist label make in legal parlance?" Three common elements can be isolated in most actions labeled as terrorism: the terrorist appears in civilian clothing, attacks civilian targets, and blends back into civilian populations. But many people classify state-uniformed "death squads" and the like as terrorist activities. And many experts will not call an action terrorism unless the perpetrator has some kind of political motivation. So the lines can get very fuzzy very quickly.

The U.S. Department of State is mandated by federal law, 8 USC § 1189, to designate "foreign terrorist organizations" based on three criteria: that it is a foreign organization, that it engages in terrorist activity, and that its terrorist activity threatens the security of U.S. nationals or the national security of the U.S. The definition of terrorism used for this purpose is that contained in a separate statute which requires an annual report to Congress of terrorism developments, 22 U.S.C. § 2656f(d):

> premeditated, politically motivated violence perpetrated against noncombatant targets by subnational groups or clandestine agents.

Similarly, the federal criminal code defines terrorism in 18 U.S.C. § 2331 as

> violent acts or acts dangerous to human life that are a violation of the criminal laws [and] appear to be intended
>
> (i) to intimidate or coerce a civilian population;
> (ii) to influence the policy of a government by intimidation or coercion; or
> (iii) to influence the policy of a government by mass destruction, assassination, or kidnapping.

Another definition used in the criminal code is at 18 U.S.C. § 2332b:

> an offense that
> (A) is calculated to influence or affect the conduct of government by intimidation or coercion, or to retaliate against government conduct; and
> (B) is a violation of [one or more of 39 listed criminal offenses].

Various authors have provided their own definitions. "Terrorism is the deliberate and systematic murder, maiming, and menacing of the innocent to inspire fear for political ends." CHRISTOPHER HARMON, TERRORISM TODAY 1 (2000).

"[T]errorism, . . is simply the contemporary name given to, and the modern permutation of, warfare deliberately waged against civilians with the purpose of destroying their will to support either political leaders or policies that the agents of such violence find objectionable." CALEB CARR, THE LESSONS OF TERROR 6 (2003).

Heymann describes terrorism as combining elements of crime and armed combat. It is different from normal crime because of its purposes (crime is usually motivated by greed, jealousy, anger, or power) and different from legitimate combat because of its clandestine and unauthorized character. His definition of terrorism thus is "an illegal form of clandestine warfare that is carried out by a sub-state group to change the policies, personnel, structure, or ideology of a government, or to influence the actions of another part of the population – one with enough self-identity to respond to selective violence." PHILLIP HEYMANN, TERRORISM AND AMERICA 9 (1998).

Terrorism is the "peacetime equivalent of war crimes: acts that would, if carried out by a government in war, violate the Geneva Convention." ALEX P. SCHMID & RONALD D. CRELINSTEN, WESTERN RESPONSES TO TERRORISM 13 (1993).

The international community has been edging ever closer to defining and outlawing terrorism. Although numerous UN Security Council resolutions have condemned terrorism, international conventions create commitments to eliminate certain practices such as bombing or aircraft piracy without attempting to define terrorism. For example, the Convention for Suppression of Terrorist Financing states that a person

> commits an offence within the meaning of this Convention if that person by any means, directly or indirectly, unlawfully and wilfully, provides or collects funds with the intention that they should be used or in the knowledge that they are to be used, in full or in part, in order to carry out:
>
> (a) An act which constitutes an offence within the scope of and as defined in one of the treaties listed in the annex; or
>
> (b) Any other act intended to cause death or serious bodily injury to a civilian, or to any other person not taking an active part in the hostilities in a situation of armed conflict, when the purpose of such act, by its nature or context, is to intimidate a population, or to compel a Government or an international organization to do or to abstain from doing any act.

An ad hoc Committee of the General Assembly has been at work since 1996 on a draft Comprehensive Convention Against Terrorism, in which the working definition is this:

> Any person commits an offence within the meaning of this Convention if that person, by any means, unlawfully and intentionally causes
>
> (a) Death or serious bodily injury to any person; or
>
> (b) Serious damage to public or private property, including a place of public use, a State or government facility, a public transportation system, an infrastructure facility or the environment; or
>
> (c) Damage to property, places, facilities, or systems referred to in paragraph 1(b), resulting or likely to result in major economic loss
>
> when the purpose of the conduct, by its nature or context, is to intimidate a population, or to compel a Government or an international organization to do or abstain from doing any act.

From this welter of definitions, at least we can delineate some common features. Generally, a terrorist

1. is a civilian or subnational group who

2. uses violence

3. against civilians

4. for political motivations.

The first element, civilian or clandestine status, is relevant because such persons may blend back into civilian populations, thus making it difficult if not impossible to attack them without endangering other civilians. Members of a

Definition of terrorism

uniformed official agency may claim authority of the nation and may be acting pursuant to military orders, in which case their actions are proscribed by the laws of war or other international law, and most observers would not use the label of terrorism for their actions; some commentators nevertheless insist that officially sanctioned violence against civilians is still terrorism even when committed by uniformed troops.

The fourth element, political motivation, at first glance could seem irrelevant to the question of whether someone is deliberately targeting civilians with violence. The motivation, however, may distinguish the terrorist from the ordinary serial murderer, although again there are many instances in which the distinction can become blurred. Another relevance of this distinction may be relevant if international law attempts to distinguish between crimes against humanity or genocide (which may lack a discernible political motivation) and some future definition of terrorism. We will explore these topics in more depth below.

[B] DESCRIBING THE TERRORIST GROUPS

The most famous (or infamous) terrorist groups active in the world today are al Qaeda, Hezbollah and its related groups, FARC (Revolutionary Armed Forces of Colombia), ETA (Basque Fatherland and Liberty – Spain), and Aum Shinrikyo (Japan). The IRA (Irish Republican Army) and Shining Path (Peru) arguably have cooled their level of activity over the past several years. Other groups come and go. The purely political ideologues of the 1960s and 1970s, such as the Red Brigade (Brigate Russo – Italy) and Baader-Meinhoff (Germany) have all but disappeared.

As of April 2004, the State Department designated 37 "Foreign Terrorist Organizations" (FTO) (*http://www.state.gov/s/ct/rls/pgtrpt/2003/31711.htm*) and provided background information on 40 "Other Terrorist Groups." Designation as an FTO carries at least these legal consequences:

1. It is a crime to knowingly provide material support or resources to a designated FTO.
2. Representatives and certain members of a designated FTO can be denied visas or excluded from the United States.
3. U.S. financial institutions must block funds of designated FTOs and their agents and must report suspicious transactions to the U.S. Department of the Treasury.

You should read (at least glance through) the descriptions in both lists to get a sense of the activities of the organizations that the U.S. Government considers to be most active in the world today. Questions for discussion after reading these descriptions will be:

1. How would you classify these groups for ease of discussion?

   a. by political affiliations, such as Marxist, nationalist, reactionary?

   b. by religious affiliation or motivation?

   c. by region of the world?

2. How many are Islamist? Latin American?

4. How many seek an independent government for their homeland?

5. What are their funding sources?

Christopher Harmon, a faculty member at the Marine Corps Command and Staff College, contends that "Terrorism is always political, even when it also evinces other motives, such as the religious, the economic, or the social. . . . If terrorism is best defined by its calculated abuse of the innocent for political purposes, there is reason to survey the political objectives which prompt such actions by militants of the modern day." He describes organizations with political agendas of anarchism, communism, neofascism, national separation, religion, and pro-state terrorism. With this variety of political motivations, can we even conclude that political objectives are a defining characteristic of terrorism? Harmon concedes that "Individual terrorists may find the clandestine struggle so appealing that it almost becomes an end in itself, a way of life. But while such nihilism is present by degrees in anyone willing to maim and murder the innocent, it is a mistake to think that nihilism, rather than purpose, is the essence of the typical contemporary terrorist organization."

political motivations

N. nihilism

Why do motivations matter? One answer is that motivation may distinguish the terrorist from the common criminal or serial killer. With this in mind, how would you characterize Theodore Kaczynski, the Unabomber? The Unabomber Manifesto decried technology and the industrial society, proposing a revolution that would smash the factories and even burn the books to prevent future regeneration of technology, but was he organized enough to warrant being treated as a terrorist rather than mere psychopath? Most authors consider Timothy McVeigh to be a terrorist because he acted out of malice for the government, but there is no known indication that he had an alternative in mind that would qualify as a political agenda.

What distinguishes the "terrorist" from the ordinary street criminal with ties to an international criminal organization? Take, for instance, a murder committed on the streets of an American city by a drug dealer who knows in some vague way that his livelihood is linked to a well-organized and well-funded cartel in Colombia or Afghanistan. Is this an act of terrorism? Is it an act of war? Is the U.S. justified in invading Colombia because there are organized criminals there who carry out violence on U.S. civilians? This has been the theme of at least two recent movies, both carrying the message that U.S. involvement in Colombia would be permissible only with the permission of the Colombian government, certainly the correct answer under international law.

On the global stage, what distinguishes Jose Padilla from Timothy McVeigh? Padilla was arrested deplaning at O'Hare Airport upon his return from Afghanistan with at least hopes of setting off bombs in the U.S.; he was first brought before a grand jury in New York but then transferred to military custody in South Carolina. Setting aside the procedural issues raised in his habeas corpus petitions, a more fundamental question is why he should be treated any differently from any other criminal such as McVeigh. Both apparently were motivated by extreme hatred for the U.S. government, both were planning mass civilian casualties at governmental centers. Padilla was in league with foreign citizens, but what does this signify? How do we distinguish him from alleged Mafiosi, or drug dealers in league with Colombian cartels?

International law and organizations are creating cooperative efforts to deal with the transborder aspects of large criminal organizations without promoting intrusion into the internal affairs of any one nation. The United Nations has two principal agencies active in the field of counter-terrorism. The UN Office on Drugs and Crime is charged with coordinating efforts with respect to organized crime as well as terrorism. Its principal mandate is the Convention Against Transnational Organized Crime. "In the new global age, borders have opened up, trade barriers have fallen and information speeds around the world at the touch of a button. Business is booming – and so is transnational organized crime. Fortunes are being made from drug trafficking, prostitution, illegal firearms and a host of other cross-border crimes. Every year, organized crime groups launder huge amounts of money in illegal proceeds. These large criminal groups often mimic legitimate business by forming multinational alliances to extend their reach and push up profits."

Islamist fundamentalist groups have taken center stage in the global concern with terrorism over the past 30 years, but they neither invented terrorism nor are the only purveyors of it today. The term "fundamentalist" can be taken to refer either to a desire to return to basic fundamentals or to a belief that the adherent is caught up in a cosmic struggle between good and evil. Many fundamentalists will share these and more characteristics. For a good summary of the concept of fundamentalism, see

http://religiousmovements.lib.virginia.edu/nrms/fund.html

It is worth recalling that fundamentalist beliefs have spawned terrorist activities in many centuries, including the Spanish Inquisition and conflicts in Northern Ireland, and have contributed to other reigns of terror such as the KKK. For an excellent depiction of fundamentalism in the three principal monotheistic religions, see KAREN ARMSTRONG, THE BATTLE FOR GOD (2000).

[C] WHAT PRODUCES A TERRORIST?

"Who Becomes a Terrorist and Why" is the name of a study conducted by the staff of the Library of Congress in 1999 (LC Study), attempting to determine from the available literature whether a psychological profile could be built of the typical terrorist. Although some gross generalizations were available, the basic conclusion was that profiling a terrorist would not make it possible to pick out the terrorist from a crowd. Identifying the terrorist is not the only reason for studying the psychology. Another desirable goal would be to find mechanisms of dissuading vulnerable young people from entering the trade. Study of the terrorist phenomenon with a sympathetic eye to understanding may eventually yield results in both prevention and response.

The orderly and systematic analysis of terrorist motivation could provide valuable clues about strategies for responding to terrorism in terms of both protection and mitigation activities (antiterrorism) and for direct action involving preemption, interdiction, or retribution (counter-terrorism).

Thomas F. Ditzler, *Malevolent Minds: The Teleology of Terrorism*, in Fathali Modhaddam & Anthony Marsella, UNDERSTANDING TERRORISM 188 (2004).

Terrorist foot-soldiers tend to be in their twenties while the leaders are somewhat older (nothing surprising in that), about 80% are male (although the LC Study goes on at some length about the single-mindedness and ferocity of the few women terrorists), and most feel that they have a political injury (perhaps ethnic or religious in nature) to redress. Obviously, there are millions of oppressed males in their twenties who do not turn to terrorism, so a further question is what psychological forces can combine to produce the violence of terrorism.

From a psychological standpoint, there are a number of hypotheses about why someone turns to terrorism. The three cited in the LC Study are labeled frustration-aggression, negative identity, and narcissistic rage. What the hypotheses share are that an individual with either very low self-esteem or highly inflated views of self (and often these are found in the same person) may be so frustrated with society that violence seems the only method of releasing the pressure on his psyche. The LC Study cautions against making too much of this type of oversimplified psycho-profile.

"[T]he terrorist is not diagnosably psychopathic or mentally sick. Contrary to the stereotype that the terrorist is a psychopath or otherwise mentally disturbed, the terrorist is actually quite sane, although deluded by an ideological or religious way of viewing the world. . . . A member who exhibits traits of psychopathy or any noticeable degree of mental illness would only be a liability for the group." Nevertheless, it is possible to generalize that terrorist groups attract persons who are "action-oriented, aggressive persons who are stimulus-hungry and seek excitement." As the study points out, this description could apply to many persons who go into law enforcement; there are even people who enter more sedentary professions and seek their adrenaline rushes from rock-climbing or snow-boarding.

Despite these claims, there are many people who believe the modern terrorist is bent simply on killing for the sake of killing. After the school massacre at Breslan, Russia, one commentator said that terrorists were damaging many of their own causes. "But that's the idea. Because the death cult is not really about the cause it purports to serve. It's about the sheer pleasure of killing and dying." David Brooks, *Death Cult on the Fringe of the Muslim World Is Beyond Reason*, NY TIMES A23 (Sept. 7, 2004). Maybe it would be as difficult to generalize about the psychological condition of those who commit terrorist acts as it would be to generalize about the psychology of any other form of criminal behavior. Nevertheless, any glimmer of understanding the terrorist psychology should be helpful in crafting responses to it.

One factor that is often emphasized is the religious fanaticism of many recent terrorists. Some authors link this with the increasing fatality levels of the past two decades. In the 1970s and 1980s, the prevailing belief was that "Terrorists want a lot of people watching, not a lot of people dead." The LC Study then notes a new trend in the 1990s, "the emergence of religious fundamentalists and new religious groups espousing the rhetoric of mass-destruction terrorism." (*Id*. at 6)

"The actions of terrorist organizations are based on a subjective interpretation of the world rather than objective reality." It is possible that the emergence of religion-based interpretations of reality ease the leaders' ability to instill fervor and lack of remorse in their followers.

A predominant characteristic of terrorists is the belief that they are right. Most report feeling no remorse over killing innocent civilians, including children, because it was the right thing to do. At least, that is, until they are confronted with pictures or descriptions of the lives of those they have killed. Because the psychological profiling excludes psychopaths or sociopaths, the speculation is that this lack of remorse can be instilled by consistent "brainwashing" emphasizing the wrongs that have been done to the ethnic or religious group with which the terrorist group identifies. Many terrorists will be disaffected from society before they contact a terrorist group. At first, the newcomer may be just curious or seeking like-minded comrades. Over time, the iteration of deeply felt injustices links the novitiate into taking further steps. Usually, full membership will require training and tests, perhaps even to the point of killing before full induction.

The terrorist's background and personal makeup can be combined to think of the "psychosocial" setting of the terrorist's worldview. This permits analyzing the worldview itself for a number of purposes. For example, to consider the likelihood that a terrorist organization may negotiate, we might look to this matrix developed from the analyses of Bruce Hoffman of the RAND Corporation:

Motivation	Context	Negotiate?
Rational	Political	High
Psychological	Personal	No
Cultural	Group	No

Ditzler at 201.

In this framework, the rational terrorists with specific political objectives may "sound a lot like legitimate military authorities planning an operation or even business executives developing an advertising campaign" except that they choose illegal means of targeting civilian populations to accomplish their goals. One might expect to be able to negotiate compromises with such a group because the weighing of costs and benefits is part of the formulation of their strategy, and obtaining partial benefits at reduced costs may look attractive. One aspect to which we in the West must be alert is that our rationality may be different from the rationality of someone from another setting. For example, it may be perfectly rational for either an Israeli or Palestinian to sabotage peace negotiations by an extreme act if the actor does not like any of the proposed solutions for a peaceful settlement.

For Hoffman's "psychological" terrorist with a personal orientation to the world, "the impetus to commit acts of violence is often related to a profound sense of failure or inadequacy for which the perpetrator may seek redress through revenge." This person may possess elements of what many of us would think of as psychosis, although the LC Study insists that no terrorist group would trust the psychotic to be a member. This may be the category in which we could differentiate most cleanly between the terrorist and the criminal. The "lone wolf" seeking to ameliorate some deep personal pain does not easily fit the common-sense definition of terrorist because he or she is not acting pursuant to the direction of, or in complicity with, an organized group. Timothy McVeigh to many people is a terrorist, but without a group identity he does not represent an ongoing threat that will continue after his capture. The psychological terrorist may, on the other hand, be part of a group that represents a significant threat. "For these terrorists, the attraction to terrorism is typically based on the psychic benefits of group affiliation." And what if the whole group is bound to terrorism as a way of life?

> Hoffman noted that if these groups achieve any meaningful progress toward their espoused goals, they often adopt increasingly radicalized positions characterized by increasingly nonachievable goals. The development of these goals may become necessary for the organization, because the attainment of true success would threaten their continuing need to exist.

Ditzler at 202. Assuming that these observations are accurate, then it is easy to see why this category gets a "will not negotiate" rating in the Hoffman chart.

The third category is the "culturally motivated" terrorist with a strong "group" identity. "According to Hoffman, the motivation for these groups to commit violent acts typically derives from an almost primordial fear of cultural extermination or the loss of cultural identity." Ditzler concentrates on religious fundamentalists in this category and finds again an extreme lack of ability or willingness to negotiate. "In a world of absolute truth . . . there is no room for dissent and no room for theological doubt." "In this worldview, the failure to respond to the utmost of one's ability would be tantamount to an acceptance of damnation." Racial/ethnic/cultural groups without the overlay of religion could be viewed in similar light with examples ranging from Nazi Germany through the Serbian atrocities in Kosovo and Hutu-Tutsi atrocities in Rwanda.

If the "cultural" group were to achieve an autonomous homeland, would the group then be persuaded to give up the terrorist methodology? Authors differ on this issue, some asserting that the successful terrorist will produce a tyrannical regime. Nevertheless, the group presumably would have no further incentive to attack transnationally so to some extent there would be a type of negotiated settlement in place. If that were to happen, then the chart might be revised to reflect a type of "negotiation" with the "cultural" terrorist, who then takes on many of the characteristics of a "political" terrorist.

[D] FINAL THOUGHTS ON UNDERSTANDING TERRORISM

No human can ever completely understand the motivations and character of another human being. Even harder is attempting to understand the motivations and character of a group of people, each of whom may come into an enterprise with unique expectations and assumptions. This section has emphasized the importance of coming to some minimal understanding of the motivations of terrorists and terrorist organizations for several reasons. First, in many definitions of terrorism, motivation is itself a critical factor. Second, the more one knows the thought patterns of an adversary, the better one is equipped to confront that adversary. For example, understanding some of the cultural background and motivations of a terrorist may be critically important to interrogation of a captive, a factor that we will consider in the final chapter of this book when we think about torture. Finally, considering the motivations and expectations of a terrorist organization may lead to some modifications of foreign policy that would alleviate the tensions motivating some terrorist acts.

Some psychiatrists and philosophers would say that "Motivation is a stream with many tributaries," meaning that any single act may be prompted by many motivating factors. In this context, the political motivation of a terrorist may be either pre-hoc or post-hoc, motivated by the past or motivated to the future. The political motivation may come from anger and frustration with what has happened in the past and thus could not be addressed, if at all, by anything other than an abject apology or reparations, neither of which is likely to be politically viable in the face of continued violence. Or the motivation may be forward looking, such as a set of objectives that could be addressed by hard-headed negotiation in an international setting. Once again, it is important to realize that one individual is likely to carry multiple motivations and that a group is even more complex.

§ 1.02 INTERLOCKING GOVERNMENTAL CONTROLS

Our next task is to understand the framework of responses available to us. There is an interlocking set of "communities" devoted to public safety within government today. Similarly, there are interlocking legal controls or restraints that operate both on the individual or group who contemplates terrorist action and on the government agencies attempting to respond. Although the political world and the popular press tend to lump all responses to terrorism together under the heading of "counter-terrorism," that label is more appropriately used for prosecutorial and military-type responses while preventive measures are more aptly characterized as "anti-terrorism." The difference corresponds roughly to prevention versus reaction.

[A] STRUCTURE OF U.S. PUBLIC SAFETY

The U.S. government, unlike many governments in history or even in the world today, has divided and separated various units which deal with aspects of public safety. The three principal divisions with which we will be concerned are protective services, law enforcement, and the military. In a rather loose or rough sense, their functions could be thought to form a spectrum of prevention, prosecution, and warfare. There are many other agencies involved in public safety, primarily those that deal with public health and response to emergencies.

The division of public safety into different units could be analogized to how individuals deal with their own home safety. Think about the steps you take to guard against intrusions on your own space. First, you lock your doors. This is a phenomenon of relatively recent vintage itself, and there are many societies in the world today that still do not have locking doors. If this is not enough, and you have the money, you install an electronic security system, and maybe you have that system wired to call armed guards at a signal of intrusion, or maybe you even go so far as to build a gated community with guards at the entrance. All these are progressive steps of increasingly aggressive preventive measures that you can take on your own or in conjunction with immediate neighbors. Second, if you have been the subject of an intrusion, you may want to apprehend and punish the intruder. In early stages of society, this might have been done by the individual acting alone, but for many centuries this function has been turned over to law enforcement agencies. Whether the purpose is to disempower the specific intruder or to deter others, punishment is the province of communal groups. Finally, if the community feels threatened as a group by some outside group, it may move to the level of armed conflict between politically defined groups. Again, in more "primitive" societies these conflicts were often less deadly and widespread than is likely to be the case today, but the concept of an organized military response that operates across more or less defined borders between recognized political groups is ancient.

These three steps reflect roughly the three divisions of prevention, enforcement, and military action. Each stage carries not only its own culture and modes of operation, but it also is constrained by a set of limiting rules. The civil liberties implications of prevention (such as limits on demonstrations or searching persons entering an airport) may differ somewhat from the civil liberties aspects of criminal law enforcement. The limitations on military action are among the most elusive of legal concepts because they arise rather infrequently and because the enforcement mechanisms for those limits themselves are somewhat tenuous.

At the state or local level, "public safety" agencies typically are thought to consist of police, fire, and emergency medical services. These are the groups that are assembled to plan and coordinate response to minor emergencies, such as an urban fire or a multi-car crash. When a major event is contemplated, however, whether a planned event such as a Super Bowl, or a natural disaster such as an earthquake or hurricane, other agencies must be brought to the table. Managers of the utility and infrastructure systems, transportation coordinators, public health agencies, and medical care providers all become part of any team that is planning for a major event. The Federal Emergency Management Agency (FEMA) was created in 1979 and charged with developing, coordinating, and funding emergency management using both federal and state resources to plan for response to either human-triggered or natural disasters and emergencies.

The principal federal civilian agencies devoted to combating terrorism, other than the intelligence agencies, are three. The lead prosecutorial office is the Counterterrorism Section of the Criminal Division, Department of Justice, which relies on the investigative services of the FBI. In the Department of State, the lead is taken by its Office of the Coordinator for Counterterrorism, and in the Department of Treasury by the Office of Terrorism and Financial Intelligence.

[B] THE INTELLIGENCE COMMUNITY

Because intelligence services have been somewhat difficult for the public to understand, because they came in for heavy criticism following 9/11, and because a "major reorganization" is underway, a quick discussion of the structure of the Intelligence Community (IC) of the United States is in order. By both Executive Order and statute, the Intelligence Community is defined as consisting of the eight intelligence agencies within the Department of Defense (DIA, NSA, NRO, NIMA, and the IA's of the four uniformed services), the CIA, and portions of five executive departments (State, Treasury, Homeland Security, Energy, and FBI).

Until recently, under the National Security Act, 50 U.S.C. § 401 *et seq.*, the CIA was formally the lead agency for coordination of all intelligence. The reality, of course, is that coordination of such secretive organizations is not easy to achieve from what would be viewed as a co-equal agency. In practice, each President has had preferences with regard to which agency he or she will consider the most reliable and thus the strongest within that particular administration. *See* 9/11 COMMISSION REPORT at 86. For that reason, Presidents have tended to rely on the National Security Council and National Security Advisor to bring vertical pressure or control to the IC. The informal power structures thus remain within the political choices of the President. Amendments to the IC structure in 2004, including creation of a Director of National Intelligence, may or may not affect the actual operation of the IC.

The Intelligence Community has its own website. The definition page describes the general mission and links to documents such as the National Security Act and Executive Order 12333.

> The IC is a federation of executive branch agencies and organizations that work separately and together to conduct intelligence activities necessary for the conduct of foreign relations and the protection of the national security of the United States. These activities include:
>
> - Collection of information needed by the President, the National Security Council, the Secretaries of State and Defense, and other Executive Branch officials for the performance of their duties and responsibilities;
> - Production and dissemination of intelligence;
> - Collection of information concerning, and the conduct of activities to protect against, intelligence activities directed against the U.S., international terrorist and international narcotics activities, and other hostile activities directed against the U.S. by foreign powers, organizations, persons, and their agents;
> - Special activities;
> - Administrative and support activities within the U.S. and abroad necessary for the performance of authorized activities; and
> - Such other intelligence activities as the President may direct from time to time

http://www.intelligence.gov/1-definition.shtml

There are many interesting assessments available on the internet of the U.S. Intelligence effort. In 1996, there was a presidential review of intelligence operations that resulted in enhancing the role of the Defense Department. The Federation of American Scientists did an analysis of the IC budget following the 1996 review. Although the details of the number of personnel and actual dollar amounts are secret, FAS extrapolated from public information to reach some estimates for each agency. *http://www.fas.org/irp/commission/budget.htm*

Some important features can be observed from a quick glance at that analysis. The National Security Agency, with almost 40,000 employees, spent about $4 billion in 1996. That is less than $100,000 per employee for the agency that has all the high-tech electronic communications intercepts and code-breaking gadgetry. By contrast, the National Reconnaissance Office, with very few employees, spent more than $6 billion working through a variety of independent contractors to run a variety spy satellites and mapping programs. Neither of these agencies is involved in placing agents on the ground or running infiltration operations.

About 80% of the total intelligence budget of the U.S. is in the Defense Department, which first emphasized technological intelligence to track and identify military targets and then shifted that technology to monitoring communications traffic. That factor, plus budget cuts at the end of the Cold War, plus the fact that most CIA personnel were trained in the ways of Soviet intelligence rather than the distinctly different culture of terrorist organizations, all combined by the late 1990s to leave the U.S. less than adequately prepared to infiltrate or monitor terrorist organizations. FINAL REPORT OF THE NATIONAL COMMISSION ON TERRORIST ATTACKS UPON THE UNITED STATES [hereafter 9/11 COMMISSION REPORT or 9/11 REPORT] 86-91.

On 9/11, Jane's (the primary private analyst of military capability) published a statement regarding the "chronic underfunding of HUMINT" in the U.S. intelligence community:

> One possible contributing factor to this failure of the intelligence and security system could be the lack of resources the U.S. has devoted to human intelligence (HUMINT) capabilities throughout the past decade. While national technical means continued to receive high levels of funding for . . . eavesdropping technologies, human-based intelligence capabilities have withered. Areas such as analysis, linguist skills, cultivation of agent networks, and "tradecraft" . . . have suffered a lack of resources of late. This shortfall has been exacerbated by the growing demand that increased emphasis on technical intelligence has placed on the people who must process the vast amounts of resulting data and prioritise it.

http://www.janes.com/security/international_security/news/jdw/jdw01091 1_1_n.shtml

The 9/11 Commission also commented, somewhat less bluntly, on the impact of the Cold War on U.S. intelligence resources:

> During the Cold War, intelligence agencies did not depend on seamless integration to track and count the thousands of military targets – such as tanks and missiles – fielded by the Soviet Union and other adversary states. Each agency concentrated on its special mission, acquiring its own information and sharing it via formal, finished reports. The Department of

Defense had given birth to and dominated the main agencies for technical collection of intelligence.

9/11 REPORT at 407. The Commission commented that the end of the Cold War also meant budget cuts, that the CIA had become highly risk averse and had no personnel trained for infiltrating terrorist organizations, and that the "intelligence community's confederated structure left open the question of who really was in charge of the entire U.S. intelligence effort." *Id.* at 93.

The Commission made specific recommendations addressing the structure of the Intelligence Community:

> The United States has the resources and the people. The government should combine them more effectively, achieving unity of effort. We offer five major recommendations to do that:
>
> - unifying strategic intelligence and operational planning against Islamist terrorists across the foreign-domestic divide with a National Counterterrorism Center;
> - unifying the intelligence community with a new National Intelligence Director;
> - unifying the many participants in the counterterrorism effort and their knowledge in a network-based information-sharing system that transcends traditional governmental boundaries;
> - unifying and strengthening congressional oversight to improve quality and accountability; and
> - strengthening the FBI and homeland defenders.

Id. at 399-400 (*http://www.9-11commission.gov/report/911Report_Ch13.htm*)

When bills were introduced in Congress to implement these recommendations, political controversy arose over whether the new NID would have full budgetary and personnel control over the existing units within the Department of Defense. The Commission's recommendation for a Director of National Intelligence to sit above the Director of Central Intelligence was designed to relieve the DCI of some of the office's conflicting job descriptions by assuming overall coordination of the Intelligence Community. On December 17, 2004, Congress passed a bill incorporating most elements of the Commission recommendations. The DNI is to have some degree of involvement with the funding and deployment of intelligence resources in the Department of Defense, and also to have consultation authority with domestic agencies such as the FBI. National Security Intelligence Reform Act of 2004, Pub. L. 108-458.

Addressing the issues of human intelligence directly, Congress had this to say in section 101(b) of the Act:

> It is the sense of Congress that
>
> (1) the human intelligence officers of the intelligence community have performed admirably and honorably in the face of great personal dangers;
> (2) during an extended period of unprecedented investment and improvements in technical collection means, the human intelligence capabilities of the United States have not received the necessary and

commensurate priorities;

(3) human intelligence is becoming an increasingly important capability to provide information on the asymmetric threats to the national security of the United States;

(4) the continued development and improvement of a robust and empowered and flexible human intelligence work force is critical to identifying, understanding, and countering the plans and intentions of the adversaries of the United States; and

(5) an increased emphasis on, and resources applied to, enhancing the depth and breadth of human intelligence capabilities of the United States intelligence community must be among the top priorities of the Director of National Intelligence.

On a more substantive plane, the Commission's recommendation to "unify across the foreign-domestic divide" would run counter to the mandate of EO 12333 issued by President Ronald Reagan on Dec. 4, 1981. The key elements of the "foreign-domestic divide" were summarized in this statement of the CIA:

Collection within the United States of foreign intelligence not otherwise obtainable shall be undertaken by the FBI or, when significant foreign intelligence is sought, by other authorized agencies of the Intelligence Community, provided that no foreign intelligence collection by such agencies may be undertaken for the purpose of acquiring information concerning the domestic activities of United States persons.

http://www.cia.gov/cia/information/eo12333.html#2.3

EO 12333 was based on some of the work of the so-called "Church Commission," which held hearings and issued reports from 1973-1976 primarily on the activities of the CIA. Although a major focus of the recommendation for a foreign-domestic divide was the protection of civil liberties of U.S. persons, another aspect was the belief that the accumulation of too much power in one place could make that agency inefficient by reducing the need for it to justify its actions to other agencies.

These are critical issues for the structure and control of intelligence gathering, which will in turn dictate legal arguments over the validity of investigatory techniques. Therefore, lawyers concerned with national security and civil liberties issues will need to monitor these political arguments closely.

As lawyers involved in various ways in the struggle against terrorism, we must be aware of the difficulties of gathering reliable intelligence about terrorist groups and their actions. These difficulties raise many issues, including

1. If military action in another country should be contemplated, as in the instances of Afghanistan and Iraq, what confidence level will you demand for intelligence data on which invasions might be based?

2. If it were decided that the use of deadly force against a known terrorist were appropriate, what confidence level would you demand before sending out a team to kill such a person? (Mossad experienced serious fallout from killing a person that they mistakenly believed to be the leader of the Munich Olympic incident.)

3. Preventive security measures, such as screening at airports or special events, necessarily rise and fall with the level of threat reported at any time by the intelligence community. What level of intrusion into the privacy of citizens and visitors are you willing to endure to regulate security measures? (And bear in mind that tightening our borders can result in "reprisal" difficulties at entry points into other countries.)

4. What level of intelligence data should we be willing to share with other countries? and under what restrictions?

[C] THE INTERNATIONAL FRAMEWORK

The previous section looked at the communities which provide the basic mechanisms for response to terrorism within the United States. The U.S. as a whole, however, is part of a larger community, the international body of law that is developing with respect to terrorism.

"One person's terrorist is another's freedom fighter." For many years, this deceptively ominous statement stalled the world's debates over outlawing terrorism. As numerous authors have pointed out, this is an almost silly argument because universal law criminalizes attacks on civilian populations without regard to the political motivations of the actor. The difficulty is not whether there could be justification for an attack on civilians because legally there cannot be, but the nations of the world have been at odds for decades over the definition of terrorism and whether it constitutes a crime under international law. The difficulty is not in justifying violence against civilians but more in determining by what process to respond to an attack against civilians, a question that usually depends on the degree of affiliation by the actor with a nation-state or "sub-national" organization.

For our purposes, the UN has been the stage on which a number of conventions regarding terrorism have been adopted. The UN Office on Drugs and Crime says that its "Global Programme against Terrorism . . . , working closely with the Counter-Terrorism Committee of the Security Council, provides technical assistance to Member States and promotes international cooperation against terrorism." UNODC lists 12 International Conventions dealing with terrorism. Most of the conventions call on member states to criminalize terrorist acts (usually defined as violence which cuts across national borders without military authority) and require extradition or trial of alleged perpetrators. *See http://untreaty.un.org/English/Terrorism.asp.* On the UN's role generally, see JANE BOULDEN & THOMAS G. WEISS, TERRORISM AND THE UN: BEFORE AND AFTER SEPTEMBER 11 (2004).

The UN Security Council Counter-Terrorism Committee was established following adoption of Sec. Council Resolution 1373, which condemned the acts of 9/11 and expressed that the Security Council "decides . . . that all states shall . . . take the necessary steps to prevent the commission of terrorist acts" and "shall ensure that . . . terrorist acts are established as serious criminal offences in domestic laws." Res. 1373 is the first directive of a UN agency requiring that member states take affirmative steps with regard to terrorism. The Security Council claims the power to direct action by declaring that "such acts constitute a threat to international peace and security." One troubling problem is that the Resolution does not define "terrorism" and only refers obliquely to the only existing UN definition, which is found in the Convention of Financing of Terrorism.

The United Nations Sixth (Legal) Committee has been debating a Draft Comprehensive Convention on International Terrorism since 1997. The principal components of the Convention would require that all signatories criminalize terrorist acts and agree to prosecute or extradite alleged perpetrators found within their borders. This is the same mechanism found in the prior Conventions dealing with air piracy, bombings, and financing of terrorism. The central statement of prohibited conduct is:

Article 2

Any person commits an offence within the meaning of this Convention if that person, by any means, unlawfully and intentionally, does an act intended to cause:

(a) Death or serious bodily injury to any person; or

(b) Serious damage to a State or government facility, a public transportation system, communication system or infrastructure facility with the intent to cause extensive destruction of such a place, facility or system, or where such destruction results or is likely to result in major economic loss;

when the purpose of such act, by its nature or context, is to intimidate a population, or to compel a Government or an international organization to do or abstain from doing any act.

In some versions of the draft, the last clause is printed at the end of, as if part of, subsection (b). If placed there, then (a) would stand alone without a requirement of political motivation and thus cover virtually any act of violence.

The Lawyer's Committee on Nuclear Policy reports the 2001 deliberations of the Sixth Committee in these terms:

The Coordinator, Richard Rowe (Australia), reported that the outcome of the treaty would depend heavily on the decision for Article 18 on the exemption of armed forces from the scope of the treaty. Rowe proposed a draft that he prepared at the end of the October 2001 session, which exempted the activities of "armed forces . . . inasmuch as they are governed by other rules of international law." Meanwhile, the Organization of the Islamic Conference proposed changes, which would exempt the activities of "parties during an armed conflict, including in situations of foreign occupation . . . in conformity with international law." The OIC wants to ensure that the "armed struggle against foreign occupation . . . shall not be considered a terrorist crime," and [to] prevent certain oppressed groups, like the Palestinians, from being more criminalized under the treaty than a state's armed forces.

http://www.lcnp.org/global/terrorismconvention.htm

International law, as found from custom as well as from the various conventions regarding use of force, has given rise to a heading of "universal jurisdiction" for any nation to prosecute offenses against the law of nations. This power was first used in relation to piracy and slave trade, but it could be a source of law with regard to terrorism as well.

In addition to these steps, the UN has been an integral part of prosecuting war crimes and genocide. It formed ad hoc tribunals for the trial of crimes committed in Rwanda and Yugoslavia. At the same time, it promoted the drafting and eventual adoption of the International Criminal Court, a multinational body asserting jurisdiction over offenses against the law of nations in the categories of war crimes, crimes against humanity, and genocide. The ICC would not be expected to assert jurisdiction over an act of terrorism unless it formed part of a "systematic and continuous" pattern by a state actor.

Thus, international law is becoming an increasing presence in regard to the behavior of persons formally affiliated with a nation-state (a state actor) and is promoting cooperation and assistance among the nations for dealing with non-state-actors such as terrorists and drug lords. All of these issues and developments will be given more extensive treatment in later chapters.

SELECTED READINGS

General Readings on Terrorism:

- LIBRARY OF CONGRESS, WHO BECOMES A TERRORIST AND WHY (1999).
- FATHALI M. MOGHADDAM & ANTHONY J. MARSELLA (EDS.), UNDERSTANDING TERRORISM (2004).
- CALEB CARR, THE LESSONS OF TERROR (2002).
- JESSICA STERN, THE ULTIMATE TERRORISTS (1999).
- CHRISTOPHER C. HARMON, TERRORISM TODAY (2000).
- PHILLIP B. HEYMANN, TERRORISM AND AMERICA (1998).
- BRUCE HOFFMAN, INSIDE TERRORISM (1998).

Books Particular to al Qaeda:

- ROHAN GUNARATNA, INSIDE AL QAEDA (2002).
- JOHN COOLEY, UNHOLY WARS (2002).

Islamic Law and Democracy:

- NOAH FELDMAN, AFTER JIHAD (2003).
- M. CHERIF BASSIOUNI, THE ISLAMIC CRIMINAL JUSTICE SYSTEM (1982).
- M. Cherif Bassiouni & Gamal M. Badr, *The Shari'ah: Sources, Interpretation, and Rule Making*, 1 UCLA J. ISLAMIC & NEAR E.L. 135 (2002).
- Khaled Abou El Fadl, *Constitutionalism and the Islamic Sunni Legacy*, 1 UCLA J. ISLAMIC & NEAR E.L. 67 (2002).
- Michael S. Doran, *The Saudi Paradox*, 83 FOREIGN AFFAIRS 35 (2004).

Chapter 2

AL QAEDA AND RELATED PROSECUTIONS

Very few Americans had anything more than hazy impressions about terrorist organizations prior to 9/11. Through the 1970s and 1980s we knew that a variety of Palestinian organizations, such as the PLO and Hamas, were active and had replaced the more ideological leftist organizations of the 1960s and early 1970s. Most of us still did not consider these organizations to be a significant threat on our soil even after the first World Trade Center bombing in 1993 and attacks on U.S. installations in Lebanon and Somalia. After U.S. embassies in Kenya and Tanzania were bombed in 1998, Americans gradually started becoming aware of a more significant and well-organized international regime of terrorist organizations. Before we turn to U.S. prosecutions of members of those organizations, we should get a general view of the organizational structures as they relate to the law of conspiracy.

§ 2.01 TERRORIST CELLS AND CONSPIRACY LAW

Conspiracy classically is defined as "a combination of two or more persons to achieve an unlawful object or to achieve a lawful object by unlawful means." In the context of terrorism, this definition raises intriguing possibilities right from the start.

The most successful terrorist organizations carefully hide the "cells" from each other. Consider a normal business-style organization chart:

In the classic business enterprise, members of the various departments feed information to their managers who then share it with the CEO and other managers to make the entire enterprise flow as smoothly as possible. The employees in a department will know as much or as little about the activities of employees in other departments as their managers have time or inclination to share, plus whatever information is shared in informal settings such as meetings, social occasions, or rumor mill. If an investigator, say a journalist doing a story on the company, asks questions about how an employee's work fits into the overall business plan, the employee may draw upon both fact and rumor to provide as complete a picture as possible.

In a clandestine operation, it becomes important that the members of each "department," usually known as "cells," know as little as possible about each other. This is so that an investigator who manages to capture or "turn" one cell member will not thereby be able to learn anything about the other cells.

Everyone who has ever read a spy novel will recognize that the Lieutenants will even insulate themselves from the cell members by a series of "cutouts," anonymous or pseudonymous individuals who themselves know nothing of either the cells or the lieutenants. In a highly sophisticated operation such as al Qaeda or the Medellin Cartel of the 1980s, only the ruling elite or inner circle will know each other. This is why it has seemed so important to the U.S. to locate the al Qaeda leadership. But the classic hierarchical model is not fully adequate to describe this type of operation., and as we will discuss below, it is not necessarily true that "cutting off the head" will cause the "body to die."

In 1929, the British courts promulgated the metaphor of "wheels" and "chains" to describe two distinct types of conspiracy: "There may be one person . . . round whom the rest revolve. The metaphor is the metaphor of the centre of a circle and the circumference. There may be a conspiracy of another kind, where the metaphor would be rather that of a chain; A communicates with B, B with C, C with D, and so on to the end of the line of conspirators." *Rex v. Meyrick and Ribuffi*, 21 Crim. App. R. 94 (1929); *see* Jerome Campane, *Chains, Wheels, and the Single Conspiracy, Pt. I*, FBI LAW ENFORCEMENT BULL. p. 24 (Aug. 1981) and Pt. II p. 24 (Sept. 1981); Note, *Federal Treatment of Multiple Conspiracies*, 57 COLUM. L. REV. 387 (1975).

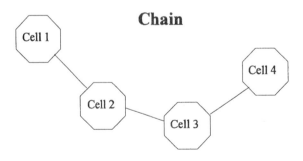

Chain

Assume that Cell 4 has been successful in carrying out a terrorist act. Cell 1 provided money with which Cell 2 purchased materials, which Cell 3 assembled and delivered to a designated place for Cell 4 to use in the act. All of this was orchestrated by the elite group outside the chain. Nobody else had any idea of the identity of the members of Cell 4 or their precise plans. Can the members of the other cells be prosecuted for conspiracy?

Wheel

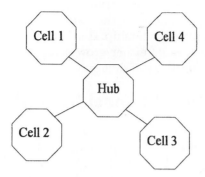

In the wheel model, the question is whether each of the spokes of the wheel may be involved in a single conspiracy with each other even though they do not know each other's identity. In the chain, persons far removed from each other because of the presence of intermediaries may similarly be engaged in a single conspiracy. The element of secrecy in clandestine schemes was recognized by the U.S. Supreme Court when it declared that "the law rightly gives room for allowing the conviction of those discovered upon showing sufficiently the essential nature of the plan and their connections with it, without requiring evidence of knowledge of all its details or the participation of others." *Blumenthal v. United States*, 332 U.S. 539, 551 (1947).

There are limits, both constitutional and otherwise, on the application of these models. In *Kotteakos v. United States*, 328 U.S. 750 (1946), the hub of the conspiracy dealt with each of the spokes separately. The Supreme Court acknowledged that the person at the hub may have thought of the entire enterprise as a single scheme, but without something more to tie the individual transactions together (a rim around the spokes), "there was no drawing of all together in a single, overall comprehensive scheme." A wheel may have spokes each of which itself is a chain (the "chain-wheel"). In *United States v. Perez*, 489 F.2d 51 (5th Cir. 1973), the defendants were involved in multiple instances of fake traffic accidents in which doctors and lawyers concocted fraudulent reports for submission to insurance companies. Each chain included several persons (one driver and a pedestrian or two drivers and a passenger, doctor, lawyer, and "recruiter" who set up each accident), each chain of which reported back to the central organizer. The court considered that none of the participants could rationally have believed that the scheme would work if there were not others out doing the same thing because otherwise the risks would not be worth the payoff to professionals such as the doctors and lawyers. This inference of knowledge was sufficient to form a rim around the spokes to complete the wheel.

In the electronic world, we have developed another metaphor for exchange of information and services. We are growing accustomed to the language of "networks," and this is convenient for describing a more fluid type of organizational structure.

In this structure, cells are free to communicate with others and to move money or weapons or training services among various cells. The loose configuration means that a cell can change location or the nature of its operations without needing clearance from a central leadership. It also means that if one cell were eliminated, then the network could either grow a replacement cell or call on another cell to perform the functions of that one.

Multi-Channel Network

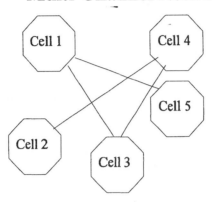

We will read three terrorism conspiracy cases, two of which involve the New York cells responsible for the first World Trade Center bombing and various other criminal plots. You might try to diagram the structure of these "conspiracies" to see how well they conform to the models, an exercise which will then be useful in assessing whether it is fair to introduce evidence of activity by one person when the other "co-conspirators" had no idea who he was or what he was doing. At what point does the evidence get too far removed from the inferential knowledge of each defendant? or becomes overwhelmingly lopsided in light of what a particular defendant should have known?

§ 2.02 WORLD TRADE CENTER I

The first bombing of the World Trade Center, claimed by the "Islamic Group" of Sheikh Abdel Rahman ("the blind Sheikh" of Brooklyn) occurred in February 1993 and resulted in three separate prosecutions. Ramzi Yousef, the alleged mastermind of that specific incident, fled the U.S. but was brought back after capture in Pakistan for trial on other charges (see p. 166 below). The four defendants in the *Salameh* case below were tried for various levels of involvement in a conspiracy to "bomb structures used in interstate commerce" and related charges. Sheikh Rahman and a number of others were then prosecuted for somewhat more peripheral connections to this incident and for a more broad-reaching charge of "seditious conspiracy" consisting of "levying war against the United States."

Conspiracy cases consistently refer to the concept of vicarious liability known as the Pinkerton Doctrine. *Pinkerton v. United States*, 328 U.S. 640 (1946) established several propositions regarding the law of conspiracy. One of the most important is the proposition that a person may be convicted of conspiracy without knowing the details of what others are planning to do. Agreement to commit a *category* of offence may produce liability for all members of the conspiracy when any one of the members commits an overt act of the type contemplated. "An overt act of one partner may be the act of all without any new agreement specifically directed to that act."

Pinkerton also confirms that conspiracy is an offense separate and apart from the "substantive" crimes contemplated. Thus, there is no double jeopardy involved in prosecution for the agreement as well as for the criminal act. And, thirdly, conspiracy is an inchoate offense that is punishable even if no physical harm ever occurs to a victim. "For two or more to confederate and combine together to commit or cause to be committed a breach of the criminal laws, is an offense of the gravest character, sometimes quite outweighing, in injury to the public, the mere commission of the contemplated crime. It involves deliberate plotting to subvert the laws, educating and preparing the conspirators for further and habitual criminal practices. And it is characterized by secrecy, rendering it difficult of detection, requiring more time for its discovery, and adding to the importance of punishing it when discovered."

UNITED STATES v. SALAMEH
152 F.3d 88 (2d Cir. 1998)

Before MESKILL, MCLAUGHLIN, and CALABRESI, Circuit Judges.

PER CURIAM:

Following a lengthy jury trial, defendants were convicted of various crimes related to the bombing of the World Trade Center Complex in New York City. Defendants now appeal, asserting a congeries of arguments. For the reasons that follow, we affirm the judgment of the district court but remand for re-sentencing and decline to exercise jurisdiction over certain post-trial motions pending before the district court.

BACKGROUND

On April 24, 1992, Ahmad Mohammad Ajaj departed from his home in Houston, Texas, and traveled to the Middle East to attend a terrorist training camp, known as "Camp Khaldan," on the Afghanistan-Pakistan border. There he learned how to construct homemade explosive devices. During his time in Pakistan, Ajaj met Ramzi Ahmed Yousef. Together the two plotted to use their newly acquired skills to bomb targets in the United States.

In the fall of 1992, after formulating a terrorist plan, Ajaj and Yousef traveled to New York under assumed names. Ajaj carried with him a "terrorist kit" that he and Yousef had assembled in Pakistan. The kit included, among other things, handwritten notes Ajaj had taken while attending explosives courses, manuals containing formulae and instructions for manufacturing bombs, materials describing how to carry-off a successful terrorist operation, videotapes advocating terrorist action against the United States, and fraudulent identification documents.

On September 1, 1992, Ajaj and Yousef, using false names and passports, arrived at John F. Kennedy International Airport in New York. At customs, INS inspectors discovered that Ajaj's passport had been altered and, consequently, they searched his belongings. Upon discovery of the "terrorist kit," Ajaj became belligerent. The INS seized Ajaj's "terrorist kit" and placed him under arrest. Ajaj was later indicted in the United States District Court for the Eastern District of New York for passport fraud. He pled guilty and was sentenced to six months' imprisonment.

During Ajaj's encounter with the INS inspectors, he denied that he was traveling with Yousef, who proceeded unmolested to the secondary inspection area where he presented an Iraqi passport and claimed political asylum. Yousef was arrested for entering the United States without a visa. Eventually he was released on his own recognizance.

Once in New York, Yousef assembled a team of trusted criminal associates, including Mohammed Salameh, Nidal Ayyad, Mahmoud Abouhalima and Abdul Rahman Yasin. Together, the conspirators implemented the bombing plot that Ajaj and Yousef had hatched overseas. Ayyad and Salameh opened a joint bank account into which they deposited funds to finance the bombing plot. Some of that money was later used by Salameh to rent a storage shed in Jersey City, New Jersey, where the conspirators stored chemicals for making explosives. Yousef also drew on that account to pay for materials described in Ajaj's manuals as ingredients for bomb making.

The first target of the conspirators' plot was the World Trade Center. Ayyad used his position as an engineer at Allied Signal, a large New Jersey chemical company, to order the necessary chemical ingredients for bomb making, and to order hydrogen tanks from ALG Welding Company that would enhance the bomb's destructive force. Abouhalima obtained "smokeless powder," which the conspirators used to make explosives. Smokeless powder, and all the other chemicals procured by the conspirators for the bomb, were stored in the shed rented by Salameh.

Abouhalima helped Salameh and Yousef find a ground floor apartment at 40 Pamrapo Avenue in Jersey City. The apartment fit the specifications in Ajaj's manuals for an ideal base of operations. In the 40 Pamrapo apartment, Abouhalima, Salameh, Yousef and Yasin mixed the chemicals for the World Trade Center bomb, following Ajaj's formulae. Abouhalima also obtained a telephone calling card, which the conspirators used to contact each other and to call various chemical companies for bomb ingredients.

During this entire period, although Ajaj remained incarcerated, he kept in telephone contact with Yousef. By doing so, Ajaj stayed abreast of the conspirators' progress in carrying out the terrorist plot and attempted to get his "terrorist kit" into Yousef's hands. Because Ajaj was in jail and his telephone calls were monitored, Ajaj and Yousef spoke in code when discussing the bomb plot.

On February 23, 1993, Salameh rented a yellow van at DIB Leasing, a Ryder dealership in Jersey City. The conspirators loaded their homemade bomb into that van. On February 26, 1993, the conspirators drove the bomb-laden van into a below-ground parking lot on the B-2 level of the World Trade Center Complex and, using a timer, set the bomb to detonate. At 12:18 p.m., the bomb exploded, killing six people, injuring over a thousand others, and causing hundreds of millions of dollars in damage.

After the explosion, Ayyad took credit for the bombing on behalf of the conspirators by, among other things, writing an anonymous letter to the New York Times explaining that the attack was undertaken in retaliation for American support of Israel. The letter threatened future terrorist "missions."

Ayyad's letter

Immediately after the bombing, Yousef, Abouhalima and Yasin fled the country. Abouhalima was apprehended in Egypt prior to the trial and turned over to federal agents by Egyptian authorities, but Yousef and Yasin remained fugitives. Salameh arranged to flee as well, but was arrested the day before he planned to depart when he made the ludicrous mistake of going back to the Ryder truck rental office to get his rental deposit back. On March 1, 1993, Ajaj completed his term of imprisonment on the passport fraud conviction and was released. Approximately one week later, on March 9, Ajaj was taken into government custody on an INS detainer.

In September 1993, Ayyad, Abouhalima, Ajaj, Salameh, Yousef and Yasin were indicted in the United States District Court for the Southern District of New York (Duffy, J.), on various charges relating to their participation in the plot to bomb the World Trade Center. Yousef and Yasin were still fugitives at the time of trial. [Yousef was captured in Pakistan on or about February 8, 1995. He was tried and convicted in 1997. As of March 2005, Yasin remains a fugitive. He is an interesting character who may have severed his connections with terrorist organizations while living in Iraq for the last decade. *See* http://www.trackingthethreat.com/content/entities/ent1007.html]

Indictment

The trial lasted six months and involved over 1000 exhibits and the testimony of more than 200 witnesses. The defendants were convicted on all counts and each was sentenced to 240 years' imprisonment. Defendants now appeal their convictions and sentences, raising a variety of issues.

Convicted

I. SUPPRESSION MOTIONS

A. Motions to Suppress Materials Seized from Ajaj

1. Ajaj's Motion

Ajaj claims that Judge Duffy should have suppressed the terrorist materials seized from him at Kennedy Airport. He maintains that the materials were obtained and then held pursuant to an illegal grand jury subpoena. Ajaj's argument has no merit.

On October 6, 1992, Ajaj pled guilty in the United States District Court for the Eastern District of New York (Raggi, J.) to one count of passport fraud. After the guilty plea, Judge Raggi ordered the government to return Ajaj's belongings or to come forward with a reason for failing to do so.

On December 22, 1992, an Assistant United States Attorney for the Eastern District of New York served a grand jury subpoena on Ajaj calling for production of many of the terrorist materials seized at Kennedy Airport. Although the subpoena purported to be a subpoena *ad testificandum*, it was accompanied by a *duces tecum* rider that specified the materials Ajaj was ordered to produce. When Ajaj's counsel in the passport fraud case inquired whether the subpoena really sought Ajaj's testimony as well as the evidence listed in the rider, the government explained that the subpoena sought only the specified evidence. Ajaj did not move to quash the subpoena.

After Ajaj learned that the government was planning to introduce the terrorist materials in the World Trade Center bombing trial, he moved to suppress the materials held pursuant to the grand jury subpoena. Ajaj argued that the subpoena was illegal since: (1) Ajaj could not have been under investigation when the subpoena was issued because it was issued after the completion of the passport fraud case but before the World Trade Center was bombed; and (2) the subpoena was a subpoena *ad testificandum*, not a subpoena *duces tecum*. Judge Duffy denied Ajaj's motion to suppress, finding that the use of the subpoena was proper. Ajaj renews his claim on appeal.

It is "improper for the government to use a grand jury subpoena 'for the sole or dominant purpose of preparing for trial.'" *United States v. Sasso,* 59 F.3d 341, 351 (2d Cir. 1995). However, "where there [is] some proper dominant purpose for the postindictment subpoena . . . the government is not barred from introducing evidence obtained thereby."

Ajaj failed to present any proof that the government misused the grand jury subpoena. He maintains that the subpoena had no legitimate purpose because in December 1992, when the subpoena was issued, his passport fraud prosecution was over and the World Trade Center had not yet been bombed. He therefore posits that he could not have been under investigation when the subpoena was issued and therefore that the sole purpose of the subpoena was to circumvent Judge Raggi's order for the return of the materials.

The government presented evidence that demonstrated a proper purpose for the grand jury subpoena. It consisted primarily of an affidavit from the Assistant United States Attorney who prepared the subpoena, explaining that the materials seized from Ajaj were used in a joint FBI-NYPD investigation of terrorism. The affidavit further noted that the subpoena was not connected to the Eastern District passport fraud case. This evidence established that the subpoena had a proper purpose.

2. Abouhalima's Motion

Judge Duffy admitted some of the materials seized from Ajaj into evidence against all the defendants. Abouhalima argues that the admission of Ajaj's terrorist materials violated Federal Rule of Evidence 403, and his rights under the First Amendment of the Constitution.

a. Rule 403

The trial judge admitted the following terrorist materials seized from Ajaj into evidence against all the defendants: (1) a videotape of the bombing of an American embassy which also provided instruction on how to make explosives and timing devices; (2) Ajaj's handwritten notebooks on how to make explosives (including urea nitrate) and improvised weapons; (3) a videotape containing a chemistry lesson on manufacturing explosives; (4) manuals on catalysts, detonators and other bomb ingredients; (5) a document entitled "Facing the enemies of God – terrorism is a religious duty and force is necessary," which urged acts of terrorism against the enemies of Islam; and (6) a book entitled "Rapid Destruction and Demolition," which described the destruction of buildings and contained a formula for using explosives to accomplish this end.

In addition, Judge Duffy admitted copies of: (1) "Facing the enemies of God"; and (2) "Rapid Destruction and Demolition" that were recovered from Abouhalima's residence. The copy of "Rapid Destruction and Demolition" found in Abouhalima's residence bore his fingerprint on the page containing the formula for destroying buildings with explosives. Abouhalima argues that Judge Duffy should not have admitted these terrorist materials because they were highly prejudicial and lacked probative value. He is incorrect.

Under Rule 403, relevant evidence may be excluded when its probative value is "substantially outweighed by the danger of unfair prejudice, confusion of the issues, or misleading the jury, or by considerations of undue delay, waste of time, or needless presentation of cumulative evidence." A district court is obviously in the best position to do the balancing mandated by Rule 403. We will second-guess a district court "only if there is a clear showing that the court abused its discretion or acted arbitrarily or irrationally." To avoid acting arbitrarily, the district court must make a "conscientious assessment" of whether unfair prejudice substantially outweighs probative value.

Although it does not bear directly on the charged elements of a crime, evidence offered to prove motive is commonly admitted. In addition, evidence that provides background information necessary to the jury's understanding of the nature of the conspiratorial agreement properly is admitted "to furnish an explanation of the understanding or intent with which certain acts were performed."

Where a defendant is a member of a conspiracy, all the evidence admitted to prove that conspiracy, even evidence relating to acts committed by co-defendants, is admissible against the defendant.

The record amply demonstrates that Judge Duffy made a "conscientious assessment" of the proffered evidence and properly determined that unfair prejudice did not substantially outweigh the probative value of these materials. Before admitting any materials, Judge Duffy scrupulously reviewed each item and heard extensive argument from counsel. Having heard both sides, Judge Duffy excluded a number of the materials seized from Ajaj as unduly prejudicial. The materials that were admitted established the existence of the conspiracy to bomb American targets and demonstrated the defendants' intent and motivation to use violence to protest American foreign policy in the Middle East.

For example, the documents seized from Ajaj provided instruction on: (1) constructing bombs; (2) mixing explosives; and (3) using bombs to destroy buildings. Specific pages of these materials contained formulae for the same explosives that were used to construct the World Trade Center bomb, and Ajaj's and Yousef's fingerprints were found on those pages. Moreover, traces of those same explosives were found in the homes of, and on objects linked to, Yousef, Abouhalima, Salameh and Ayyad. Thus, the terrorist materials provided circumstantial proof of a connection among the conspirators and their familiarity with bomb making and the use of explosives.

In addition, the copies of "Facing the enemies of God," and "Rapid Destruction and Demolition," that were recovered from Abouhalima's residence linked the conspirators. The copy of "Rapid Destruction and Demolition" seized from Abouhalima bore his fingerprint on the page containing the formula for destroying buildings with explosives. Under the circumstances, the fact that Ajaj and Abouhalima both possessed the same documents was probative of their relationship as co-conspirators.

The materials possessed by both Ajaj and Abouhalima bristled with strong anti-American sentiment and advocated violence against targets in the United States. These same themes were expressed in a letter attributed to another co-conspirator, Ayyad, that was sent to the New York Times in the aftermath of the bombing. The materials, in addition to establishing a link between the co-conspirators, evidenced the conspiracy's motive and intent to bomb targets in the United States. In addition, the materials provided the jury with background and "an explanation of the understanding or intent with which certain acts were performed."

Furthermore, the materials had probative value in light of their similarity to the actual bombing. As Judge Duffy recognized, one videotape admitted in evidence showed a man driving a truck into a building that was flying an American flag. The building was then demolished in an explosion. The videotape thus closely resembled the actual events at the World Trade Center and provided further evidence of motive and intent.

The sulphurous anti-American sentiments expressed in the terrorist materials no doubt threatened to prejudice the jury against the defendants. However, Judge Duffy did not abuse his discretion by concluding that the significant probative value of this evidence was not substantially outweighed by the danger of unfair prejudice.

b. First Amendment

Abouhalima argues also that the admission of Ajaj's terrorist materials violated Abouhalima's First Amendment rights. Ajaj's possession of the terrorist materials, Abouhalima contends, was used as the basis for an inference that Abouhalima and the other conspirators engaged in criminal acts. It is difficult to comprehend this argument since it is beyond cavil that "the First Amendment . . . does not prohibit the evidentiary use of speech to establish the elements of a crime or to prove motive or intent." Neither Ajaj nor Abouhalima was prosecuted for possessing or reading terrorist materials. The materials seized from Ajaj were used appropriately to prove the existence of the bombing conspiracy and its motive. Moreover, any prejudicial effect they might have had was ameliorated by the trial court's instruction that mere possession of the literature is not illegal and that the defendants' political beliefs were not on trial.

B. Motion to Suppress Contents of the Storage Shed

At trial, the government introduced homemade nitroglycerine and large quantities of bomb making ingredients seized from a storage shed (the "Shed"), at the Space Station storage facility in Jersey City (the "Space Station"). Salameh argues that Judge Duffy should have suppressed this evidence. Salameh is wrong.

On March 5, 1993, a Magistrate Judge in the District of New Jersey issued a search warrant for the Shed. Probable cause for the warrant was based upon an affidavit of FBI Special Agent Eric Pilker.

Before trial, Salameh moved to suppress the evidence from the Shed on the ground that Pilker's affidavit did not establish probable cause for the search. Salameh also requested a hearing to test alleged misstatements in Pilker's affidavit. Judge Duffy denied the motion to suppress as well as the requested hearing, finding that: (1) Salameh lacked standing to contest the search; (2) there was probable cause for the search warrant; and (3) even if the warrant was not supported by probable cause, the search was proper because it was conducted in good faith reliance on the search warrant. Because we agree that there was both probable cause and good faith, we need not and do not address the standing argument.

1. Probable Cause

In deciding whether probable cause exists for a search warrant, a judge must determine whether "there is a fair probability that contraband or evidence of a crime will be found in a particular place." "Only the probability, and not the prima facie showing, of criminal activity is the standard of probable cause." In assessing the proof of probable cause, the government's affidavit in support of the search warrant must be read as a whole, and construed realistically.

Pilker's affidavit in support of the search warrant stated that an explosion had occurred at the World Trade Center, and that an FBI explosives expert had determined that it was caused by a bomb. The affidavit also related that the expert knew from examining an auto part recovered at the crime scene that the part belonged to whatever vehicle carried the bomb. Using the part's vehicle identification number, investigators traced it to a yellow Ford Econoline 350 van registered in Alabama to the Ryder Truck Rental Company and leased by Mohammad Salameh from a rental office in Jersey City for a one-week period beginning three days before the explosion.

Elsewhere in the affidavit, Pilker related that a Space Station employee informed the FBI that storage shed number 4344 was under lease to "Kamil Ibrahim." The employee told the FBI that on February 25, 1993, one day before the bombing, he observed "Kamil Ibrahim," along with other males, making numerous trips to the Shed using a yellow Ryder van. Moreover, the same Space Station employee stated that on March 4, 1993, less than one week after the bombing, he entered the Shed and observed containers marked "sulfuric acid," "nitric acid" and "urea." A forensic chemist at the Bureau of Alcohol, Tobacco and Firearms informed the FBI that those three substances could be combined to produce a powerful bomb.

Finally, the affidavit described that, when renting the Ryder van, Salameh had given a telephone number that belonged to someone named Jodie Hadas at 34 Kensington Avenue, Apt. 4, in Jersey City. When investigators searched that apartment on March 4, 1993, they found tools, wiring and manuals concerning antennae, circuitry and electromagnetic devices. A law enforcement bomb technician advised the FBI that these items indicated that a bomb maker lived in that apartment.

Cumulatively, this evidence provided ample probable cause to believe that the Shed contained evidence of the World Trade Center bombing.

II. PROCEDURAL MOTIONS

A. Abouhalima – Severance

Abouhalima argues that the district court deprived him of a constitutionally fair trial by denying his pretrial motion for a severance. Specifically, Abouhalima first claims that absent severance, he was harmed by the admission and the subsequent "spillover" effect of "holy war" literature and video tapes that were seized from Ajaj at Kennedy Airport in September 1992 [the six items listed above].

Next, Abouhalima argues that through the joinder, he was prejudiced by Salameh's closing argument, where Salameh purportedly asserted a defense antagonistic to his own. In this regard, as part of his defense, Abouhalima refused to concede either that a bomb had caused the World Trade Center explosion, or that he had any association with Yousef. Salameh, on the other hand, conceded not only the existence of a bomb, but argued that he was an unwitting dupe of Yousef, who had masterminded the bombing. Because the government had characterized Yousef as Abouhalima's close associate, Abouhalima avers that Salameh's summation undermined his defense of not knowingly participating in the conspiracy.

We find no basis for reversal. "There is a preference in the federal system for joint trials of defendants who are indicted together." "It would impair both the efficiency and the fairness of the criminal justice system to require . . . that prosecutors bring separate proceedings, presenting the same evidence again and again, requiring victims and witnesses to repeat the inconvenience (and sometimes trauma) of testifying, and randomly favoring the last-tried defendants who have the advantage of knowing the prosecution's case beforehand." *Richardson v. Marsh,* 481 U.S. 200, 210 (1987).

1. Ajaj's Holy War Materials

The admission of Ajaj's "holy war" materials did not result in prejudicial spillover as to Abouhalima. Therefore, the district court did not err in denying severance. A defendant's claim that he was prejudiced by the admission of evidence at a joint conspiracy trial is insupportable when the evidence would have been admissible against him in a separate trial alone as a member of the conspiracy. "Prejudice" occurs in joint trials when proof inadmissible against a defendant becomes a part of his trial solely due to the presence of co-defendants as to whom its admission is proper. This is an unlikely occurrence when all the defendants are charged under the same conspiracy count.

In the present case, Ajaj and Abouhalima were alleged to have participated in a common plan or scheme and were tried under the same conspiracy count. As we have already discussed in connection with co-appellant Ayyad, the materials seized from Ajaj at Kennedy Airport were properly admitted as background evidence to establish the nature and scope of the conspiracy and to establish the motive and intent of the conspirators, namely, a desire to use violence to effect change in American foreign policy in the Middle East. Additionally, the materials were admissible to link Abouhalima to the conspiracy, as two of the terrorist publications seized from Ajaj were identical to the publications found in Abouhalima's apartment. Because each of the items would have been admitted against Abouhalima had he been tried alone, they were properly admitted against Abouhalima in the joint trial and there is no prejudicial "spillover." Consequently, Abouhalima has not shown that the district court erred in denying his pretrial motion for a severance, let alone an abuse of discretion and a miscarriage of justice.

2. Salameh's Summation

We find no prejudice to Abouhalima arising from Salameh's summation. "'Mutually antagonistic' or 'irreconcilable' defenses may be so prejudicial in some circumstances as to mandate severance." In order to make a showing of "mutually antagonistic" or "irreconcilable defenses," the defendant must make a factual demonstration that "acceptance of one party's defense would tend to preclude the acquittal of [the] other." However, "mutually antagonistic defenses are not prejudicial per se. Moreover, Rule 14 does not require severance even if prejudice is shown; rather, it leaves the tailoring of the relief to be granted, if any, to the district court's sound discretion." *Zafiro v. United States*, 506 U.S. 534, 538-39 (1993) (where two co-defendants both claim they are innocent and each accuses the other of the crime, district court did not err in denying motion for severance).

Throughout the trial in this case, all four defendants challenged the government's case without attempting to accuse one another. Unlike Abouhalima, during summation Salameh abandoned his trial strategy of disputing that a bomb had caused the explosion and argued that he was nothing more that an unwitting dupe of Yousef, who had masterminded the bombing. While the defense asserted by Salameh was, in the end, inconsistent with Abouhalima's defense, at no time did Salameh argue or suggest that Abouhalima was involved in the bombing, or directly contradict Abouhalima's defense strategy. Salameh and Abouhalima both claimed to be innocent of the charges and neither's claim of innocence required the jury to find the other guilty.

B. Abouhalima – Involuntariness of Statement

Abouhalima made two incriminating remarks during his post-arrest interview. Specifically, shortly after being taken into United States' custody [in Egypt], Abouhalima was informed that he was under arrest for his participation in the World Trade Center bombing. Once FBI agents advised him of his constitutional rights, they interviewed him about the apartment at 40 Pamrapo. During the interview, Abouhalima asked an officer whether he knew an individual by the name of "Rashid." Yousef's nickname was "Rashed." Abouhalima also corrected an FBI agent's pronunciation of "Pamrapo."

Abouhalima now argues that we should direct the district court on remand to reconsider Abouhalima's motion to suppress his post-arrest remarks. Specifically, Abouhalima asserts that his comments were given involuntarily and without a valid Miranda waiver because they followed ten days of incarceration and torture in Egypt.

In the present case, while it is reasonable that Egyptian incarceration and torture, if true, would likely weaken one's mental state, one's mental state does not become part of the calculus for the suppression of evidence unless there is an allegation that agents of the United States engaged in some type of coercion. Because Abouhalima does not contend that federal agents either mentally or physically coerced his remarks during that interrogation, there is no basis for inquiry into a possible constitutional violation. "Only if we were to establish a brand new constitutional right – the right of a criminal defendant to confess to his crime only when totally rational and properly motivated – could respondent's present claim be sustained." *Colorado v. Connelly,* 479 U.S. 157, 166 (1986).

C. Elements of the Charged Conspiracy

Abouhalima next assails the district court's denial of his request to charge concerning the intent required to be convicted of the conspiracy. Specifically, in Abouhalima's request to charge, he averred that, based on the conspiracy as charged in the indictment, the government was required to prove specific knowledge and intent to bomb the World Trade Center. The district court disagreed and instead instructed the jury that for purposes of unlawful intent, the object of the conspiracy "is not restricted to a particular building." Abouhalima argues that the district court's instruction was error because it invited the jury to convict him without finding the mental element of the crime charged. Furthermore, Abouhalima asserts that the indictment's repeated references to the World Trade Center and the government's repeated references to that complex during opening statements and summation required the government to prove a specific conspiracy to bomb the World Trade Center.

It is well settled that the essential elements of the crime of conspiracy are: (1) that the defendant agreed with at least one other person to commit an offense; (2) the defendant knowingly participated in the conspiracy with the specific intent to commit the offenses that were the objects of the conspiracy; and (3) that during the existence of the conspiracy, at least one of the overt acts set forth in the indictment was committed by one or more of the members of the conspiracy in furtherance of the objectives of the conspiracy.

The indictment does not charge the defendants with conspiring to bomb the World Trade Center. The indictment alleges that the defendants conspired "to commit offenses against the United States." Four objectives of the conspiracy, each a separate bombing violation, are alleged as follows: (i) to bomb buildings used in or affecting interstate and foreign commerce, (ii) to bomb property and vehicles owned by the United States, (iii) to transport explosives interstate for the purpose of bombing buildings, vehicles, and other property, and (iv) to bomb automobiles used in interstate commerce. The World Trade Center bombing is not listed as an object of the conspiracy, but merely as one of 31 overt acts alleged to have been committed in furtherance of the conspiracy. Consequently, because the World Trade Center bombing is not alleged as an objective of the conspiracy, the district court did not err in refusing to charge the jury that specific knowledge and intent was required with respect to that bombing.

Consistent with the indictment, the government argued to the jury that the defendants engaged in a conspiracy to bomb buildings, vehicles and property in the United States and the World Trade Center bombing was one act committed in furtherance of the overall conspiracy.

Aside from the unprecedented nature of Abouhalima's argument, those multiple references to the World Trade Center bombing were due to the fact that most of the substantive crimes charged in the indictment stemmed from that bombing. In any event, the proof at trial demonstrated that the conspiracy encompassed considerably more than just the bombing of the World Trade Center, including: (1) the existence of additional chemicals recovered from the Shed after the bombing; (2) the modified timing device found in Ayyad's home; and (3) Ayyad's continuing attempts to procure additional explosive chemicals after the bombing. The most definitive proof of the broad scope of the conspiracy and the defendants' intent to commit additional bombings after the World Trade Center was the letter sent to the New York Times claiming responsibility for the bombing and the similar draft letter retrieved from an erased file on Ayyad's computer disk, both of which speak to future acts of terrorism.

The government is not required to demonstrate that the defendant agreed to all of the conspiracy's objectives, as long as the defendant shared "some knowledge of the [conspiracy's] unlawful aims and objectives."

III. SUFFICIENCY OF THE EVIDENCE

Ajaj

Ajaj argues that the government presented insufficient evidence to establish his guilt on the counts for which he was convicted. As an initial matter, Ajaj argues that the government failed to prove his membership in the conspiracy that bombed the World Trade Center. Ajaj contends that the government's evidence fails to prove that Ajaj agreed to the "essential nature of the plan," that is, to bomb a populated structure in an urban area. In the alternative, Ajaj argues that his incarceration before the construction and detonation of the World Trade Center bomb constituted a withdrawal from the conspiracy as a matter of law, shielding him from criminal liability for the offenses later committed by his co-conspirators.

With respect to the conviction under Count One for conspiracy, the government's argument at trial that Ajaj not only agreed to the essential nature of the plan but was one of the conspiracy's architects enjoyed solid evidentiary support. The government established that in April 1992, Ajaj surreptitiously traveled from the United States to Pakistan to attend Camp Khaldan, a terrorist training camp. Ajaj, once in the Middle East, made contact with Yousef and they together plotted to bomb targets in the United States. The presence of both of their fingerprints in the terrorist manuals indicated that Ajaj and Yousef studied the materials, assimilating knowledge that Yousef later applied directly to the construction of the World Trade Center bomb.

The government demonstrated that after completing their training, Ajaj and Yousef jointly prepared to enter the United States illegally. Ajaj and Yousef carefully created false identities for themselves in the names of "Khurram Khan" and "Azan Mohammad," respectively. They collected false passports, identification cards and bank, education and medical records to support their false identities.

Ajaj's participation in the conspiracy continued even after his incarceration on the passport fraud conviction. Ajaj stayed abreast of the conspiracy's progress through telephone conversations with Yousef. The government's evidence went far beyond proving Ajaj's mere association with terrorists and suspicious circumstances. The possibility that the government's evidence at trial is subject to alternative inferences consistent with Ajaj's innocence does not vitiate the reasonableness of the jury verdict

Abouhalima

Abouhalima argues that the evidence presented at trial does not support a finding that he was a participant in the conspiracy to bomb the World Trade Center, but instead shows only that he knew the other defendants in this case and was present when they were taking some of the actions that furthered the conspiracy. Contrary to Abouhalima's claims, however, the government presented more than enough evidence from which the jury could have concluded beyond a reasonable doubt that Abouhalima was a knowing member of the conspiracy and was guilty, either directly or on a *Pinkerton* theory, on all of the substantive counts with which he was charged.

First, there was testimony that Abouhalima helped Salameh and Yousef find the apartment at 40 Pamrapo. And the evidence that 40 Pamrapo was intended to and did serve as a bomb factory was strong. The apartment had bluish stains on the walls and rust on the inside door knob and hinges of the back bedroom door, both consistent with the fumes generated by mixing explosives such as urea nitrate and nitroglycerine. Most important, samples of these two chemicals were found in scrapings taken from various items in the apartment.

Second, a receipt entered into evidence showed that Abouhalima was the purchaser of a refrigerator that bore Yousef's fingerprint and contained traces of nitroglycerine.

Third, there was testimony that, in the weeks preceding the bombing, Abouhalima, a limousine driver, made several unsuccessful attempts to secure the use of a van from his employer.

Fourth, one of Abouhalima's dress shoes, recovered from his apartment after the bombing, was found to have a burn that contained high levels of sulfate ions.

Fifth, in addition to the shoe, a copy of "Rapid Destruction and Demolition" was discovered at Abouhalima's home. Abouhalima's fingerprint was recovered from a page in this publication providing a formula for making explosives that could be used to destroy buildings.

Sixth, there was evidence that Abouhalima purchased a can of "Hodgdon" brand smokeless powder, a substance similar to that used in the detonator of the bomb planted at the World Trade Center.

Seventh, the government offered telephone records for a calling card that belonged to Abouhalima. These revealed that Abouhalima was in frequent contact with the other defendants. Moreover, the card was used to make various calls to chemical companies and garden supply stores.

Eighth, a gas station attendant identified Abouhalima as the driver of a Lincoln Town Car (to which Abouhalima had access in the course of his employment as a limousine driver) that accompanied the Ryder van carrying Salameh and Yousef (and presumably also the bomb) early in the morning of the day on which the bomb was detonated. The attendant stated that Abouhalima paid to fill the gas tanks of both vehicles.

Finally, on the day following the bombing, Abouhalima made arrangements to flee the country. On March 2, 1993, leaving his family behind, Abouhalima traveled from the United States to the Sudan without any luggage and with only a one-way ticket. The jury was entitled to infer consciousness of guilt from the facts surrounding this flight.

All of this evidence was more than sufficient, when taken together, to establish beyond a reasonable doubt that Abouhalima was a knowing and active participant in the conspiracy to bomb the World Trade Center; that he, himself, committed at least some of the substantive offenses in the indictment; and, to the extent that he did not directly participate in the substantive acts, that he was nonetheless liable under the *Pinkerton* doctrine.

NOTES AND QUESTIONS

1. Why did the prosecution bother to charge a conspiracy to bomb buildings other than the WTC? Understanding terrorism investigations will be aided by articulating how prevention of future violence relates to investigation and prosecution of completed offenses. This will become an explicit topic when we come to investigation of terrorist financing.

2. Ajaj was served with a grand jury subpoena for materials in his possession after his plea on the passport fraud and before the WTC bombing. As the next case shows, an FBI investigation of the Brooklyn groups was underway at this time but the FBI had severed relations with their main informant within the group. The subpoena was issued just six weeks before the WTC bombing. A grand jury subpoena is not reviewed by a judge unless the recipient moves to quash. When we consider some of the controversy over FISA Court orders under the PATRIOT Act amendments, the presence of grand jury subpoenas as an option will be relevant.

3. The Ajaj materials were introduced into evidence against all defendants. They were highly inflammatory, but the court holds their prejudicial character did not outweigh their probative value on motive and intent. Why does the jury need to know about motive? How does showing motive differ from showing that a person has a bad attitude?

4. The discussion of the motion to suppress seized evidence displays some of the forensic techniques of law enforcement. Government spends millions of dollars on tracing minute details of a completed crime. Again, it will be helpful to articulate how pursuing the details of a completed crime relates to prevention of future harm. Any bombing incident will present you with an opportunity to reflect on this connection.

5. What do you think of the almost cavalier treatment of alleged torture of Abhouhalima at the hands of Egyptian agents? The practice of obtaining a captive from a foreign nation informally rather than through extradition is known as rendition. It is one of the principal tools in the investigative arsenal as nations attempt to cooperate in the suppression of terrorism. Should U.S. courts be more sensitive to potential abuses in these situations?

6. Finally, the *Salameh* opinion provides details of an investigation that should be borne in mind for future cases. The plot in this case is connected to the Rahman case that we consider next. Ramzi Yousef, who figures prominently in the WTC bombing, was later captured after a series of bombings in the Phillipines and returned to the U.S. for trial on air piracy charges unrelated to the WTC plot. His prosecution is considered below at p. 166.

UNITED STATES v. RAHMAN
189 F.3d 88 (2d Cir. 1999)

[Editor's Note: This opinion is quite lengthy. The factual summary is reprinted here in some detail because it shows the methods of operation for a terrorist plot, for government infiltration of the group, and for subsequent investigation. Thus, it will serve as a referent for future discussions of investigative techniques.]

Before: NEWMAN, LEVAL, and PARKER, Circuit Judges.

CONTENTS

PER CURIAM:

INTRODUCTION

These are appeals by ten defendants convicted of seditious conspiracy and other offenses arising out of a wide-ranging plot to conduct a campaign of urban terrorism. Among the activities of some or all of the defendants were rendering assistance to those who bombed the World Trade Center, see *United States v. Salameh,* 152 F.3d 88 (2d Cir. 1998) (affirming convictions of all four defendants), planning to bomb bridges and tunnels in New York City, murdering Rabbi Meir Kahane, and planning to murder the President of Egypt. We affirm the convictions of all the defendants. We also affirm all of the sentences, with the exception of the sentence of Ibrahim El-Gabrowny, which we remand for further consideration.

BACKGROUND

Defendants-Appellants Sheik Omar Abdel Rahman, El Sayyid Nosair, Ibrahim El-Gabrowny, Clement Hampton-El, Amir Abdelgani ("Amir"), Fares Khallafalla, Tarig Elhassan, Fadil Abdelgani ("Fadil"), Mohammed Saleh, and Victor Alvarez (collectively "defendants") appeal from judgments of conviction entered on January 17, 1996, following a nine-month jury trial in the United States District Court for the Southern District of New York (Michael B. Mukasey, District Judge).

The defendants were convicted of the following: seditious conspiracy (all defendants); soliciting the murder of Egyptian President Hosni Mubarak and soliciting an attack on American military installations (Rahman); conspiracy to murder Mubarak (Rahman); bombing conspiracy (all defendants found guilty except Nosair and El-Gabrowny); attempted bombing (Hampton-El, Amir, Fadil, Khallafalla, Elhassan, Saleh, and Alvarez); two counts of attempted murder and one count of murder in furtherance of a racketeering enterprise (Nosair); attempted murder of a federal officer (Nosair); three counts of use of a firearm in relation to a crime of violence (Nosair); possession of a firearm with an obliterated serial number (Nosair); facilitating the bombing conspiracy by shipping a firearm in interstate commerce and using and carrying a firearm in relation to a crime of violence (Alvarez); two counts of assault on a federal officer (El-Gabrowny); assault impeding the execution of a search warrant (El-Gabrowny); five counts of possession of a fraudulent foreign passport, and one count of possession with intent to transfer false identification documents (El-Gabrowny).

I. The Government's Case

At trial, the Government sought to prove that the defendants and others joined in a seditious conspiracy to wage a war of urban terrorism against the United States and forcibly to oppose its authority. The Government also sought to prove various other counts against the defendants, all of which broadly relate to the seditious conspiracy. The Government alleged that members of the conspiracy (acting alone or in concert) took the following actions, among others, in furtherance of the group's objectives: the attempted murder of Hosni Mubarak, the provision of assistance to the bombing of the World Trade Center in New York City on February 26, 1993, and the Spring 1993 campaign of attempted bombings of buildings and tunnels in New York City. In addition, some members of the group were allegedly involved in the murder of Rabbi Meir Kahane by defendant Nosair.

The Government adduced evidence at trial showing the following: Rahman, a blind Islamic scholar and cleric, was the leader of the seditious conspiracy, the purpose of which was "jihad," in the sense of a struggle against the enemies of Islam. Indicative of this purpose, in a speech to his followers Rahman instructed that they were to "do jihad with the sword, with the cannon, with the grenades, with the missile . . . against God's enemies." Rahman's role in the conspiracy was generally limited to overall supervision and direction of the membership, as he made efforts to remain a level above the details of individual operations. However, as a cleric and the group's leader, Rahman was entitled to dispense "fatwas," religious opinions on the holiness of an act, to members of the group sanctioning proposed courses of conduct and advising them whether the acts would be in furtherance of jihad.

According to his speeches and writings, Rahman perceives the United States as the primary oppressor of Muslims worldwide, active in assisting Israel to gain power in the Middle East, and largely under the control of the Jewish lobby. Rahman also considers the secular Egyptian government of Mubarak to be an oppressor because it has abided Jewish migration to Israel while seeking to decrease Muslim births. Holding these views, Rahman believes that jihad against Egypt and the United States is mandated by the Qur'an. Formation of a jihad army made up of small "divisions" and "battalions" to carry out this jihad was therefore necessary, according to Rahman, in order to beat back these oppressors of Islam including the United States.

Although Rahman did not arrive in the United States until 1990, a group of his followers began to organize the jihad army in New York beginning in 1989. At that time, law enforcement had several of the members of the group under surveillance. In July 1989, on three successive weekends, FBI agents observed and photographed members of the jihad organization, including (at different times), Nosair, Hampton-El, Mahmoud Abouhalima, Mohammad Salameh, and Nidal Ayyad (the latter three of whom were later convicted of the World Trade Center bombing, shooting weapons, including AK-47's, at a public rifle range on Long Island. Although Rahman was in Egypt at the time, Nosair and Abouhalima called him there to discuss various issues including the progress of their military training, tape-recording these conversations for distribution among Rahman's followers. Nosair told Rahman "we have organized an encampment, we are concentrating here."

On November 5, 1990, Rabbi Meir Kahane, a former member of the Israeli parliament and a founder of the Jewish Defense League, gave a speech at the Marriot East Side Hotel in New York. Kahane was a militant Zionist, who advocated expelling Arabs from Israel. The content of this speech was a plea to American Jews to emigrate and settle in Israel. Nosair and possibly Salameh and Bilal Alkaisi, another member of the group, attended the speech. After the speech, as Kahane stood talking with the crowd, two shots were fired and Kahane was hit in the neck and chest.

Nosair, whom witnesses observed with a gun in hand immediately after the shooting, then ran toward the rear door of the room, trailed by one of the onlookers. At the door, 70-year-old Irving Franklin sought to impede Nosair's flight. Nosair shot Franklin in the leg, and fled the room. Outside the hotel Nosair encountered uniformed postal police officer Carlos Acosta. Acosta tried to draw his weapon and identify himself, but before he could fire, Nosair fired two shots at him. The first of these shots hit Acosta in the chest but was deflected into his shoulder by a bullet-proof vest he was wearing, and the second just missed Acosta's head. Despite being shot, Acosta returned fire, hitting Nosair in the neck. Nosair fell to the ground, dropping his weapon, a .357 caliber magnum revolver, at his side. Acosta recovered the weapon and detained Nosair. Ballistics testing showed that the weapon recovered from Nosair was the weapon that fired projectiles found in the room in which Kahane and Franklin had been shot, as well as in the area Acosta had been shot.

Subsequent to these events, law enforcement personnel executed search warrants for Nosair's home, car, and work lockers. Among the items seized in these searches was a handwritten notebook, in which Nosair stated that to establish a Muslim state in the Muslim holy lands it would be necessary:

> to break and destroy the morale of the enemies of Allah. (And this is by means of destroying) (exploding) the structure of their civilized pillars. Such as the touristic infrastructure which they are proud of and their high world buildings which they are proud of and their statues which they endear and the buildings in which they gather their heads (leaders).

While Nosair was at the prison ward of Bellevue Hospital following the shooting, Nosair stated in response to a question from a treating physician that he had no choice but to kill Kahane, and that it was his "duty." After Nosair was moved from Bellevue to Rikers Island, he began to receive a steady stream of visitors, most regularly his cousin El-Gabrowny, and also Abouhalima, Salameh, and Ayyad. During these visits, as well as subsequent visits once Nosair was at Attica,[3] Nosair suggested numerous terrorist operations including the murders of the judge who sentenced him and of Dov Hikind, a New York City Assemblyman, and chided his visitors for doing nothing to further the jihad against the oppressors. Nosair also tape recorded messages while in custody, including one stating:

> God the Almighty . . . will facilitate for the believers to penetrate the lines no matter how strong they are, and the greatest proof of that [is] what happened in New York. God the Almighty enabled His extremely brave people, with His great power, to destroy one of the top infidels. They were preparing him to dominate, to be the Prime Minister some day. They were preparing him despite their assertion that they reject his agenda . . . and that he is a racist.

---

[3] Nosair was eventually acquitted of the murder of Kahane in New York state court, but was found guilty of weapons charges, and was sentenced to a term of 7 1/3 to 22 years' imprisonment, and was transferred to Attica. The visits by members of the group continued when Nosair moved to Attica as did Nosair's calls to arms.

During Nosair's state trial in 1991, an FBI informant, Emad Salem, began to befriend various of Rahman's followers in an attempt to infiltrate the jihad organization.[4] At that trial, Salem met El-Gabrowny, Nosair's cousin, who was raising money to aid in Nosair's defense. Salem, accompanied by El-Gabrowny, also met with Nosair. El-Gabrowny introduced Salem as "a new member in the family."

As a result of these contacts, Salem traveled to Detroit with Rahman and others to attend a conference on the Islamic economy. During this trip, Salem, seeking to ingratiate himself to Rahman, informed Rahman of his prior service in the Egyptian military during the 1973 conflict with Israel. Rahman told Salem that this was not jihad because he had been paid to fight by an infidel government. Rahman also told Salem that he could make up for this, however, by assassinating Mubarak, a "loyal dog to the Americans."

Before the Nosair trial ended, Salem was invited for dinner at El-Gabrowny's house. During dinner, El-Gabrowny indicated he was concerned about being bugged by the FBI, turned up the television, and then discussed construction of high-powered explosives with Salem. Salem testified that after this dinner at El-Gabrowny's house, bombing became a frequent topic of conversation between them. By early 1992, Rahman had also welcomed Salem into the group. Rahman specifically praised Salem for attempting to restart paramilitary training with the group, noting that there would come a day when the training would be needed.

Mohammad Saad, the cousin of Sattar and a participant in the jihad group, developed a plan to get Nosair out of jail and confided the plan to Salem. Salem repeated the plan to El-Gabrowny, who cautioned them to slow down and await the outcome of Nosair's appeal. After being badgered by Nosair to take action, El-Gabrowny met with Salem and told him that he was in touch with "underground people" who could help them construct bombs. El-Gabrowny instructed Salem on the superiority of remote detonators rather than timers, describing to Salem how a remote detonator could assist in bombing Dov Hikind.

In June 1992 El-Gabrowny visited Nosair again in prison. Upon his return, he instructed Salem and Shinawy that Nosair wanted to see them. Salem testified that, when they made the visit, Nosair berated them for not proceeding with bombing plans and directed Shinawy to seek a fatwa from Rahman approving the bombings. On the way home from the visit, Shinaway told Salem that the planned operation would involve twelve bombs. Shinawy also explained that they would need guns in case they encountered police during the deployment, indicating that his source for firearms was Hampton-El.

Two days later Salem went to El-Gabrowny's house and found Shinawy already there. The three agreed that they would try to secure a "safehouse" for constructing bombs, and El-Gabrowny committed to attempt to obtain

---

[4] Salem was one of the Government's key witnesses at trial. The Government acknowledges that Salem is a braggart who often told tall tales of his past. However, by 1993 Salem was regularly tape recording his conversations with the group members and those tapes served to corroborate much of his testimony at trial.

detonators from Afghanistan. A few days later, Shinawy summoned Salem to the Abu Bakr Mosque where he introduced Salem to Hampton-El. Salem and Shinaway explained to Hampton-El that they were making bombs but that they were having trouble getting detonators. Hampton-El said that he had access to "ready-made bombs" for $900 to $1,000 apiece. He also offered to obtain a handgun for Salem. A few days later Shinaway gave Salem a handgun presumably from Hampton-El.

In early July 1992, a rift developed between Salem and the FBI, and it was agreed that Salem's undercover investigation would be terminated. To explain his disappearance, Salem told El-Gabrowny that he needed to go to Spain for a while to take care of a problem in his jewelry business.

In late 1992, the paramilitary training resumed, led by Siddig Ali and Hampton-El on weekends between October 1992 and February 1993. Defendants Amir and Fadil Abdelgani and Elhassan all participated in the training camp, as did Abdo Haggag, an Egyptian spy who testified for the Government during the trial. The purpose of the training was to teach the participants jihad tactics. There was talk that jihad was needed in Bosnia, and that some of the trainees might go there. [None of the trainees ever went to Bosnia.] As Siddig Ali later explained to Salem, the training was meant to prepare the trainees for jihad wherever it was needed. During training, Siddig Ali reported to Rahman, and Rahman offered his insights into the training.

In the midst of this training, Hampton-El sought detonators and "clean" guns from Garrett Wilson, a cooperating witness for the U.S. Naval Investigative Service, who testified for the Government at trial. Hampton-El explained that he wanted to train a group of people in "commando tactics" and discussed training techniques and bomb identification.

During this time, Ramzi Yousef (another compatriot who was later convicted of the World Trade Center bombing) arrived in the United States. Rahman was making numerous calls to overseas numbers, including a Pakistan number which Yousef had inscribed in a bomb making pamphlet. Rahman, Salameh, and Yousef also made several calls to the same number in Pakistan in November. Nosair, speaking with his wife from prison, said, "And what will happen in New York, God willing, it will be . . . because of my prayers."

In January 1993, Rahman appeared at a conference in Brooklyn, and voiced his beliefs in violent jihad. Rahman further stated that being called terrorists was fine, so long as they were terrorizing the enemies of Islam, the foremost of which was the United States and its allies. While building the World Trade Center bomb, the builders kept in close phone contact with El-Gabrowny and Rahman. Salameh and Yousef repeatedly called El-Gabrowny at home and at the Abu Bakr Mosque and Rahman at home. In December 1992 and January 1993, El-Gabrowny visited Nosair at Attica and later arranged for the World Trade Center bombers to visit Nosair in the weeks preceding the bombing (Abouhalima visited Nosair on January 2 and February 7, and Salameh visited him on February 13).

On February 24, 1993, Salameh rented a van to be used in the World Trade Center bombing. As identification, he used a New York license bearing his own name and El-Gabrowny's address. As Ayyad was making arrangements to purchase the hydrogen gas to be used in the World Trade Center bomb, he called El-Gabrowny. On February 26, 1993, the World Trade Center complex was bombed, causing six deaths and massive destruction.

On March 4, 1993, federal agents executed a search warrant for El-Gabrowny's home. Salameh's use of El-Gabrowny's address when renting the van used in the bombing provided the basis for the warrant. The warrant allowed a search for explosives and related devices. The search of El-Gabrowny's home revealed, among other things, stun guns and taped messages from Nosair urging fighting and jihad in response to the Jewish immigration to Israel. Just prior to executing the search warrant, the agents encountered El-Gabrowny as he left the building and then, seeing them, started back toward it. The agents stopped and frisked him. El-Gabrowny became belligerent and assaulted two agents. On his person, the agents found five fraudulent Nicaraguan passports and birth certificates with pictures of Nosair and his wife and children.

After the bombing of the World Trade Center, Salem again began working for the FBI as an informant. In March of 1993, President Mubarak was scheduled to visit New York. Certain members of Rahman's group saw this visit as an opportunity to assassinate him, in the words of Siddig Ali, "to execute the desire of the Sheik." Siddig Ali described the plan to Abdo Mohammed Haggag, an Abdel Rahman confidant who later cooperated with the Egyptian and United States authorities. Nothing came of this plan because Haggag secretly gave the Egyptian government information about the plot, and the New York part of Mubarak's trip to the United States was canceled.

Siddig Ali then proposed a new round of bombings. In late April 1993, he became friendly with Salem, who was, by that point, tape recording his conversations for the FBI. Salem agreed to assist Siddig Ali in putting together the bombs but stated that he would have no part in deploying them. After contemplating bombing a U.S. armory, Siddig Ali proposed bombing the United Nations complex. When initially discussing this plan with Salem, he stated that Rahman had approved the attack on the United Nations, and had called it not merely permissible, but a "must" and a "duty." Siddig Ali invited Salem to discuss these matters directly with Rahman, but reminded him that because of the surveillance, to use caution in so doing. Caution, as defined by Siddig Ali, included phrasing statements in a broad and general manner, and assuring that Rahman was insulated from active involvement in the plot.

Salem met with Siddig Ali again on May 12, pretending that he had surveyed locations for use as a bomb-making safehouse and that he had settled on a garage in Queens that was renting for $1,000 a month. This safehouse was actually rented by the FBI, and the FBI installed videocameras and surveillance equipment in the safehouse before members of the group began using it.

Taking Siddig Ali up on his earlier invitation, Salem had a private conversation with Rahman on the night of May 23, 1993. At the bidding of Siddig Ali, Salem began the conversation by pledging allegiance to Rahman. Salem then told Rahman that he and Siddig Ali were planning to "do a job." Salem explicitly asked Rahman about the United Nations. Rahman replied that bombing the

United Nations was "not illicit, however will be bad for Muslims." Rahman instead told Salem to "Find a plan, find a plan . . . to inflict damage on the American army itself." Salem then asked about a strike on the FBI headquarters in New York. Rahman told him to "wait for a while," and to "plan carefully."

Salem recounted this conversation to Siddig Ali, who stated that when he had discussed the United Nations issue with Rahman, Rahman had been in favor of the plan. Subsequently, in discussing the plan to bomb the United Nations with Hampton-El, Siddig Ali told him that he had received an "official fatwa" from Rahman regarding the plan. Siddig Ali also told Khallafalla and Amir Abdelgani the same thing, stating that Rahman's approval was necessary whenever one did something "basically unlawful," which would be wrong unless the "mission [was] under the flag of God and his messenger."

As a result of the failure of the plan to execute Mubarak, there was some speculation by members of the group that Siddig Ali was an informer. Siddig Ali and Salem conversed one day with Rahman about the issue. Rahman voiced his suspicions that Siddig Ali was the informer. Ironically, Salem secretly tape recorded this conversation for the Government. During the conversation, Rahman revealed that Abouhalima, one of the World Trade Center bombers, was supposed to have fled to Sudan, not to Egypt, where he was subsequently arrested after the bombing. After the discussion, Siddig Ali told Salem that Rahman had ordered that they be circumspect when discussing their plans with him so that he would not be incriminated.

On May 27, 1993, Siddig Ali introduced Salem to Amir Abdelgani and Fares Khallafalla near the Medina Mosque. The four then traveled to the safehouse where they discussed the bombing plans. At that time Siddig Ali indicated he wanted to bomb the United Nations and the Lincoln and Holland Tunnels. Siddig Ali outlined the proposed plan for three explosions five minutes apart, sometimes sketching on a piece of cardboard. The cardboard was later recovered at the safehouse.

Over the next few days, Siddig Ali and Amir Abdelgani (once accompanied by Salem) drove together to the Lincoln and Holland tunnels, the United Nations, and the Federal Building in Manhattan to scout the targets and examine traffic conditions. During one of these scouting trips, Amir suggested that they consider bombing the diamond district in Manhattan because that would be like "hitting Israel itself." At the United Nations, Siddig Ali noted that a bomb detonated at the entrance would topple the building. The men later gathered at the safehouse to discuss the operation.

On May 30, 1993, Hampton-El met with Siddig Ali and Salem at Hampton-El's safehouse, which he used for conducting business. Siddig Ali and Salem explained that they needed detonators, and Hampton-El said he would try to locate some for them. The three discussed the plan to blow up the United Nations and the tunnels. On June 4, 1993, Siddig Ali arranged to go with Salem to meet Mohammed Saleh. Siddig Ali explained to Salem that Saleh was an important supporter of jihad activities who might assist in the bombing campaign. Saleh was the owner of two gasoline stations in Yonkers, New York. During dinner at Saleh's house, Siddig Ali explained the bombing plan to Saleh, noting the different targets on a piece of paper. Salem was asked by Siddig Ali to eat the piece of paper once Siddig Ali felt that Saleh understood the plan. During dinner, Saleh agreed to help purchase military equipment.

Over the next few weeks, Siddig Ali brought Alvarez and Elhassan into the group. Various members of the group began to collect the items they believed were needed to prepare the bombs. The group also met frequently to refine the bombing plan. On June 13, 1993, Salem and Khallafalla purchased two timers for the bombs in Chinatown. On June 15 and 18, Hampton-El left messages for Siddig Ali indicating that he was still searching for detonators. On June 19, Amir Abdelgani, Khallafalla, Salem, Alvarez, and Siddig Ali met at Siddig Ali's house to discuss the details of the plan, including the number of people and bombs needed to carry it out. Siddig Ali indicated that they needed fertilizer, fuel, and stolen cars.

Amir, Alvarez, and Salem attempted on the evening of June 19 to buy stolen cars to deliver the bombs and to use as getaway cars during the bombing. Although they located a source for stolen cars, they did not have sufficient funds to purchase the cars. That same day, Elhassan met with a friend who was an engineer to discuss the feasibility of blowing up the tunnels and to determine where the weakest points of the tunnels were located.

On June 21, 1993, the group met at the Mosque and drove to the safehouse. Amir, Siddig Ali, and Elhassan discussed a method of communicating at the tunnels so that both of them would blow up at the same time, and planned their escapes after the bombing. Amir and Siddig Ali advised everyone that, if they were caught, not to talk until their lawyers were present. That evening Alvarez tried again, unsuccessfully, to obtain cars for the operation.

On June 22, 1993, after buying five 55-gallon steel barrels from a Newark drum business, Siddig Ali and Amir went to Saleh's gas station to get fuel for the bombs. Saleh agreed over the phone to provide the fuel. Belhabri, Saleh's employee, filled two of the drums with $140 worth of diesel fuel. Saleh agreed to keep two of the empty barrels in his garage. Siddig Ali and Amir did not pay for the fuel, but Belhabri made out a receipt on which he recorded the license plate of the van. Siddig Ali wrote a phony signature on the receipt.

The next day, June 23, Amir returned to Saleh's gas station with Fadil to fill the remaining three 55-gallon drums with diesel fuel. They met Saleh who called his employee at the other station to tell him to wait for the two so that they could get fuel before the station closed. Amir called Siddig Ali and asked if he could tell Fadil the bombing plan since Amir thought that Fadil would eventually catch on. Siddig Ali gave him permission to tell Fadil. Amir and Fadil obtained fuel. When Belhabri wrote out a receipt, Amir objected and called Saleh who then told Belhabri not to put the license number on the receipt but just to write "Sudanese." Belhabri provided $151 worth of fuel. At the same time, Siddig Ali and Salem were purchasing more fertilizer for the bombs.

Later in the day, Alvarez gave Siddig Ali a 9mm semi-automatic rifle with an empty 25-round magazine. Siddig Ali and Salem took the gun from Alvarez's apartment in New Jersey to the safehouse. A little after 8 p.m. that evening, Amir and Fadil arrived at the safehouse with the fuel. Amir then washed down the van so that there would be no traces left of the fuel. For the next hour, Amir, Fadil, Siddig Ali, and Salem discussed the bombing plan. At one point, Fadil was asked whether he would participate, and he responded that he had to perform an Istikhara prayer (a prayer seeking divine intervention to guide one's decision in a course of action). After going to the Mosque to pray, Fadil met Elhassan and Alvarez, and they drove back to the safehouse.

Back at the safehouse, Amir began mixing the fuel and the fertilizer, and watched a videotape showing the tunnels that had been shot earlier in the day by Siddig Ali and Salem. Elhassan, Alvarez, and Fadil then returned, joined Amir, and began stirring the fuel and fertilizer together. They discussed the timers and the placement of bombs. At about 2 a.m. on the morning of June 24, FBI agents raided the safehouse and arrested the defendants, seizing the fuel and fertilizer mixture and the cardboard diagram Siddig Ali had periodically used to sketch the bombing plan.

A few hours before arrests were made at the safehouse, FBI agents arrested Saleh at his apartment in Yonkers. At FBI headquarters, Saleh denied having sold fuel to the men but said that Salem had come to his station demanding fuel on two occasions. About a week later on July 5, 1993, Saleh called one of his employees from prison and instructed him to tell Belhabri to destroy the two receipts documenting the fuel given to the Abdelganis and Siddig Ali. Saleh said that it would be "dangerous" for Belhabri if he failed to follow these instructions.

II. The Defense Case

The defendants presented their case for two months, calling 71 witnesses. Hampton-El, Elhassan, Alvarez, and Fadil Abdelgani each testified on his own behalf. The specific defenses put forth by the individual defendants will be set out below as they become relevant to particular claims on appeal. Siddig Ali, among others, was charged in the same indictment as the defendants but was not part of the trial because he pleaded guilty to all counts with which he was charged and cooperated, to a degree, with the Government.

III. Verdicts and Sentences

The jury trial in the case ran from January 9, 1995, to October 1, 1995. The jury returned verdicts finding defendants guilty on all submitted charges, except that Nosair and El-Gabrowny obtained not guilty verdicts on the Count Five bombing conspiracy charges. The defendants were sentenced as follows: Rahman and Nosair, life imprisonment; El-Gabrowny, 57 years; Alvarez, Hampton-El, Elhassan, and Saleh, 35 years; Amir Abdelgani and Khallafalla, 30 years; Fadil Abdelgani, 25 years.

DISCUSSION

I. Constitutional Challenges

A. Seditious Conspiracy Statute and the Treason Clause

Defendant Nosair (joined by other defendants) contends that his conviction for seditious conspiracy, in violation of 18 U.S.C. § 2384, was illegal because it failed to satisfy the requirements of the Treason Clause of the U.S. Constitution, Art. III, § 3.

Article III, Section 3 provides, in relevant part:

Treason against the United States, shall consist only in levying War against them, or in adhering to their Enemies, giving them Aid and Comfort. No Person shall be convicted of Treason unless on the Testimony of two Witnesses to the same overt Act, or on Confession in open Court.

The seditious conspiracy statute provides:

If two or more persons in any State or Territory, or in any place subject to the jurisdiction of the United States, conspire to overthrow, put down or to destroy by force the Government of the United States, or to levy war against them, or to oppose by force the authority thereof, or by force to prevent, hinder or delay the execution of any law of the United States, or by force to seize, take, or possess any property of the United States contrary to the authority thereof, they shall each be fined under this title or imprisoned not more than twenty years, or both.

18 U.S.C. § 2384.

Nosair contends that because the seditious conspiracy statute punishes conspiracy to "levy war" against the United States without a conforming two-witness requirement, the statute is unconstitutional. He further claims that because his conviction for conspiracy to levy war against the United States was not based on the testimony of two witnesses to the same overt act, the conviction violates constitutional standards.

It is undisputed that Nosair's conviction was not supported by two witnesses to the same overt act. Accordingly the conviction must be overturned if the requirement of the Treason Clause applies to this prosecution for seditious conspiracy. The plain answer is that the Treason Clause does not apply to the prosecution. The provisions of Article III, Section 3 apply to prosecutions for "treason." Nosair and his co-appellants were not charged with treason. Their offense of conviction, seditious conspiracy, differs from treason not only in name and associated stigma, but also in its essential elements and punishment.

Seditious conspiracy by levying war includes no requirement that the defendant owe allegiance to the United States, an element necessary to conviction of treason. *See* 18 U.S.C. § 2381 (defining "allegiance to United States" as an element of treason). Nosair nevertheless maintains that "the only distinction between the elements of seditious conspiracy under the levy war prong and treason by levying war is that the former requires proof of a conspiracy while the latter requires proof of the substantive crime."

Nosair's suggestion that the statutory definition of treason added the requirement of allegiance is mistaken. The reference to treason in the constitutional clause necessarily incorporates the elements of allegiance and betrayal that are essential to the concept of treason. The functions of the Clause are to limit the crime of treason to betrayals of allegiance that are substantial, amounting to levying war or giving comfort to enemies, and to require sufficiently reliable evidence. Treason, in other words, may not be found on the basis of mere mutterings of discontent, or relatively innocuous opposition. The fact that the Treason Clause imposes its requirements without mentioning the requirement of allegiance is not a basis for concluding that treason may be prosecuted without allegiance being proved. That any conviction for treason under the laws of the United States requires a betrayal of allegiance is simply implicit in the term "treason." Nosair was thus tried for a different, and lesser, offense than treason.

B. Seditious Conspiracy Statute and the First Amendment

Rahman, joined by the other appellants, contends that the seditious conspiracy statute is an unconstitutional burden on free speech and the free exercise of religion in violation of the First Amendment. First, Rahman argues that the statute is facially invalid because it criminalizes protected expression and that it is overbroad and unconstitutionally vague. Second, Rahman contends that his conviction violated the First Amendment because it rested solely on his political views and religious practices.

1. Facial Challenge

As Section 2384 proscribes "speech" only when it constitutes an agreement to use force against the United States, Rahman's generalized First Amendment challenge to the statute is without merit.

It remains fundamental that while the state may not criminalize the expression of views – even including the view that violent overthrow of the government is desirable – it may nonetheless outlaw encouragement, inducement, or conspiracy to take violent action. The prohibitions of the seditious conspiracy statute are much further removed from the realm of constitutionally protected speech than those at issue in *United States v. Dennis* and its progeny [*see* § 6.02 *infra*]. To be convicted under Section 2384, one must conspire to use force, not just to advocate the use of force. We have no doubt that this passes the test of constitutionality.

2. Application of Section 2384 to Rahman's Case

Rahman also argues that he was convicted not for entering into any conspiratorial agreement that Congress may properly forbid, but "solely for his religious words and deeds" which, he contends, are protected by the First Amendment. In support of this claim, Rahman cites the Government's use in evidence of his speeches and writings.

There are two answers to Rahman's contention. The first is that freedom of speech and of religion do not extend so far as to bar prosecution of one who uses a public speech or a religious ministry to commit crimes. Numerous crimes under the federal criminal code are, or can be, committed by speech alone [citing statutes based on conspiracy, procuring, or inducing]. All of these offenses are characteristically committed through speech. Notwithstanding that political speech and religious exercise are among the activities most jealously guarded by the First Amendment, one is not immunized from prosecution for such speech-based offenses merely because one commits them through the medium of political speech or religious preaching. Of course, courts must be vigilant to insure that prosecutions are not improperly based on the mere expression of unpopular ideas. But if the evidence shows that the speeches crossed the line into criminal solicitation, procurement of criminal activity, or conspiracy to violate the laws, the prosecution is permissible.

The evidence justifying Rahman's conviction for conspiracy and solicitation showed beyond a reasonable doubt that he crossed this line. His speeches were not simply the expression of ideas; in some instances they constituted the crime of conspiracy to wage war on the United States and solicitation of attack on the United States military installations, as well as of the murder of Egyptian President Hosni Mubarak.

Words of this nature – ones that instruct, solicit, or persuade others to commit crimes of violence – violate the law and may be properly prosecuted regardless of whether they are uttered in private, or in a public speech, or in administering the duties of a religious ministry. The fact that his speech or conduct was "religious" does not immunize him from prosecution under generally-applicable criminal statutes. *See [Empl. Div. of Oregon v.] Smith*, 494 U.S. 872, 879 (1990).

Rahman also protests the Government's use in evidence of his speeches, writings, and preachings that did not in themselves constitute the crimes of solicitation or conspiracy. He is correct that the Government placed in evidence many instances of Rahman's writings and speeches in which Rahman expressed his opinions within the protection of the First Amendment. However, while the First Amendment fully protects Rahman's right to express hostility against the United States, and he may not be prosecuted for so speaking, it does not prevent the use of such speeches or writings in evidence when relevant to prove a pertinent fact in a criminal prosecution. The Government was free to demonstrate Rahman's resentment and hostility toward the United States in order to show his motive for soliciting and procuring illegal attacks against the United States and against President Mubarak of Egypt.

Furthermore, Judge Mukasey properly protected against the danger that Rahman might be convicted because of his unpopular religious beliefs that were hostile to the United States. He explained to the jury the limited use it was entitled to make of the material received as evidence of motive. He instructed that a defendant could not be convicted on the basis of his beliefs or the expression of them – even if those beliefs favored violence. He properly instructed the jury that it could find a defendant guilty only if the evidence proved he committed a crime charged in the indictment.

III. Pretrial and Trial Challenges

    . . . .

D. Sufficiency of the Evidence

The following defendants challenge the sufficiency of the evidence on the following charges: Rahman challenges the sufficiency of the evidence on all counts of conviction; El-Gabrowny, Hampton-El, and Fadil Abdelgani challenge the sufficiency of the evidence supporting their seditious conspiracy convictions; Hampton-El and Alvarez contend that the proof supporting their attempted bombing convictions was insufficient; and Nosair attacks the sufficiency of the evidence supporting his three convictions for racketeering (the murder of Meir Kahane and the shootings of Irving Franklin and Carlos Acosta).

1. Standard of Review

[O]ne may be proven guilty of conspiracy even if one does not know all the other members or all the details of the conspiracy's operation. Once an unlawful agreement is shown, to show membership, the Government need provide only "some evidence from which it can reasonably be inferred that the person charged with conspiracy knew of the existence of the scheme alleged in the indictment and knowingly joined and participated in it."

2. Rahman

Rahman argues that the evidence presented by the Government was insufficient to support a conviction for any of the counts with which he was charged. Rahman asserts that he had limited contact with most of the other defendants, that he was physically incapable, due to his blindness, of participating in the "operational" aspects of the conspiracies, and that there was little direct evidence of his knowledge of many of the events in question. We find Rahman's claims unavailing.

a. Seditious Conspiracy and Bombing Conspiracy.

First, we find ample evidence in the record to support the jury's finding that there was indeed a conspiracy to "levy war" against the United States. While there is no evidence that Rahman personally participated in the performance of the conspiracy, when conspiracy is charged, the Government is not required to show that the defendant personally performed acts in its furtherance: it is sufficient for the defendant to join in the illegal agreement. The evidence showed that Rahman was in constant contact with other members of the conspiracy, that he was looked to as a leader, and that he accepted that role and encouraged his co-conspirators to engage in violent acts against the United States.

Although Rahman did advise against making the United Nations a bombing target because that would be bad for Muslims, he advised Salem to seek a different target (U.S. military installations) for the bombings, and to plan for them carefully. In that same conversation, he also warned Salem to be careful around Siddig Ali, who he suspected was a traitor. Rahman then sought out the traitor in his group, having a long discussion with Salem and Siddig Ali over who was the traitor. This evidence shows that a reasonable trier of fact could have found that Rahman was a member of the conspiracy and that he was in fact its leader.

As to the bombing conspiracy count, there is clear evidence to support a reasonable conclusion that there was a conspiracy of which Rahman was a member, and that the conspirators had taken overt acts "to effect the object" thereof. The conspirators had, among other things: (1) scouted the Lincoln and Holland Tunnels; (2) contributed rent for a place to make the bombs; (3)

purchased fuel oil, fertilizer, and timers from which to make the bombs; and (4) begun mixing the fuel and fertilizer.

b. Conspiracy and Solicitation to Murder Mubarak.

Rahman also claims that there is insufficient evidence to support his convictions for soliciting Salem, Siddig Ali, and Haggag, to murder Mubarak, and for being a member of a conspiracy to do such. Rahman had made clear to Siddig Ali that he wanted Mubarak killed, and had already issued a fatwa regarding such. Rahman told Haggag that killing Mubarak did not require an additional fatwa, and that Haggag and "the people with training" should carry out the assassination.

In furtherance of this conspiracy, Siddig Ali made contacts with an individual at the Sudanese mission to the UN seeking to get information regarding Mubarak's itinerary, and made plans for the assassination. In May 1993, both Haggag and Siddig Ali sought to take credit for proposing the plan when Rahman was questioning them over who was the traitor in the group.

c. Solicitation to Bomb a Military Installation.

With regard to the conviction for solicitation to bomb a military installation, the test is met again based on Rahman's status as leader of the group, combined with the fact that he specifically told Salem to target military bases. Thus a reasonable trier of fact could find Rahman guilty of such solicitation.

3. Nosair

Nosair argues that the evidence was insufficient to show that the murder of Kahane (or any of the specific charges levied under the RICO statute, including the attempted murder of Acosta and Franklin) was done with the statutorily required motive – to maintain or increase his position within a racketeering enterprise. Nosair bases his claim on a narrow construction of the term "Jihad Organization," which the indictment defined as being equivalent to the charged seditious conspiracy. Thus, Nosair claims that the murder of Kahane, a private Israeli citizen, could not further the goals of an organization whose primary purpose was to levy war on the United States. We find this reading of the indictment flawed. According to the indictment, the Jihad Organization, the RICO enterprise in question, was "opposed to nations, governments, institutions and individuals that did not share the group's particular radical interpretation of Islamic law," and an objective of this group was "to carry out, and conspire to carry out, acts of terrorism – including bombings, murders, and the taking of hostages – against various governments and government officials, including the United States government and its officials." Thus, the murder of Kahane did not "stray" from the purposes of the Jihad organization, and in fact was entirely consonant therewith.

Nosair, in a message taped from Rikers Island, stated "God the Almighty enabled His extremely brave people, with His great power, to destroy one of the top infidels." Nosair told his physician, in response to a question about the murder, "I had no choice, it was my duty." Nosair sought to use the murder to inspire his compatriots to take other action, thus using it to increase his position in the organization. Thus, a reasonable inference that the murder was in furtherance of his membership can be made, and his statement that it was his "duty" to murder Kahane leads to an inference that the murder was motivated by a desire to maintain or elevate his position in the organization.

4. Fadil Abdelgani

Fadil Abdelgani concedes that there was sufficient evidence for the jury to convict him of the conspiracy to bomb and attempted bombing charges. However, he alleges that there was not sufficient evidence to support the guilty verdict for seditious conspiracy for which he received twenty years' imprisonment. We disagree.

The Government persuasively counters that a jury could reasonably infer that Fadil knew of the group's overriding purpose of forcibly opposing the United States based on his participation in the 1992 training camp and on the time he spent with Amir and other group members in the safehouse on June 23 while the plot was discussed. Fadil's participation in the attempted bombing itself also justifies an inference that he agreed to forcibly oppose the United States; the bombing plan was to disable major commercial activity of the United States (by disabling the tunnels) and to hit at the Government itself by bombing the United Nations. Fadil's alleged lack of knowledge of Nosair or Rahman and the details of some of the other overt acts of the conspiracy is not fatal to the Government's position. The case law of this Court holds that to be guilty of conspiracy a defendant need not know every detail of the conspiracy or know of the identities of all of the other conspirators.

5. El-Gabrowny

El-Gabrowny claims there was insufficient evidence for the jury to convict him of seditious conspiracy. El-Gabrowny claims that the jury's verdict was based on circumstantial evidence and that he was simply found guilty "by association." The claim is unavailing. In his brief on appeal, El-Gabrowny focuses on the evidence that was not presented at trial and the acts in which he was not involved. El-Gabrowny notes that no tapes were produced in which he discusses plans to bomb buildings or any violent acts. He argues that he had nothing to do with the Kahane murder or the Spring 1993 bombing plots (during which time he was in prison).

El-Gabrowny routinely engaged in discussions with Salem about building bombs, and in June 1992 offered to attempt to obtain detonators from Afghanistan. He also indicated he would try to acquire a safehouse for the construction of bombs, and that he was in touch with "underground people" who could assist in a bombing. He was in constant contact with Nosair, and evidence seized from his house indicated that he shared Nosair's views on the duty to perform jihad. El-Gabrowny encouraged Salem and others to visit Nosair in prison at which time Nosair advocated that they begin jihad and plan to bomb buildings. El-Gabrowny frequently communicated with the World Trade Center bombers during the months, weeks, and days prior to the bombing. Salameh used El-Gabrowny's address on the driver's license that he used to rent the van that was used in the bombing. Upon his arrest, El-Gabrowny was carrying forged passports for Nosair and his family which were apparently meant to be used as part of the planned jailbreak of Nosair.

6. Alvarez

Alvarez claims that there was insufficient evidence to show a "substantial step" to support the attempted bombing charge. In this case, given the large number of steps taken by the defendants in preparation for the bombing, we find that they had moved beyond "mere preparation." The defendants had: recruited sufficient participants to carry out the plan; contributed money to rent a safehouse in which to build the bombs; reconnoitered the potential targets of the bombs, by driving through and videotaping the tunnels and discussing the structure of the tunnels with an engineer; purchased, or attempted to purchase, what they believed to be the necessary components for the bombs, including actually purchasing oil, fertilizer, timers, and barrels in which to mix the explosives; attempted to find stolen cars in which to carry the bombs; and obtained a submachine gun to assist in carrying out the plan. Given the nature and scope of the proposed plan, namely, that it was to be a coordinated explosion of massive bombs designed to destroy large targets, we believe that the defendants had moved beyond "mere preparation," and had in fact taken numerous "substantial steps" which were "strongly corroborative of their criminal purpose." We therefore reject Alvarez's claim.

7. Hampton-El

Hampton-El challenges the sufficiency of evidence against him on the seditious conspiracy and attempted bombing charges. As to both charges, he argues that he did not have the requisite intent. He asserts that the Government did not prove that he intended to "join Siddig Ali and his minions" to oppose the authority of the U.S. by force or to levy war against the U.S. nor did the Government prove that he specifically intended to bring about the bombing by aiding and abetting in the safehouse operation. [The Government did not seek to prove at trial that Hampton-El was guilty as a principal of the attempt.]

a. Seditious Conspiracy. At trial Hampton-El testified that he did not know any specifics of the operations of Siddig Ali, Salem, or the others, and that he "did not mean it," when he agreed to try to find detonators and weapons for them. We find sufficient evidence to support a finding of intent to join the conspiracy beyond a reasonable doubt based on the following evidence: Hampton-El co-led the shooting training in 1989 and the paramilitary training in 1992 of jihad group members, some of whom were involved in the World Trade Center bombing, and some of whom were involved in the spring 1993 bombing attempt; from 1989 to 1993, he was closely aligned with [others attempting to obtain detonators]; on May 30, 1993, he discussed the spring 1993 bombing plot with Siddig Ali and Salem, said the attack "takes a lot of courage," and agreed to try to find detonators for them; and he contacted Mustafa Assad after meeting with Siddig Ali and Salem, met with Assad who is known to have been a bomb builder, and then told Siddig Ali that his source was working on the request.

The jury was not obliged to accept Hampton-El's claim that after the May 30, 1993, meeting with Siddig Ali and Salem, he deliberately distanced himself from the bombing plan because he did not want to be involved in violence against the United States. In numerous phone calls to Siddig Ali after the meeting, several of which Hampton-El initiated, he assured Siddig Ali that he was continuing to look for detonators and that he expected to obtain them soon. Hampton-El also frequently called his source for the detonators, Assad, during this time period.

The evidence was sufficient to permit a jury to find beyond a reasonable doubt that Hampton-El was continuously involved with group members throughout the life of the conspiracy, that he actively sought out detonators for Siddig Ali and Salem, and that he joined in the seditious conspiracy to make war on the United States.

b. Attempted Bombing. The evidence was also sufficient to show that Hampton-El aided and abetted the attempt to bomb by his efforts to find detonators. To be found guilty as an aider and abettor, a defendant must know of the criminal venture, have joined the criminal venture, shared in it, and contributed to it by some act. [A] reasonable trier of fact could have found that Hampton-El did know of the scheme after the May 30, 1993, meeting at his apartment with Siddig Ali and Salem. At that time, Salem testified, and the intelligible portions of the tape corroborate, that Hampton-El was informed that they planned to bomb the United Nations and the tunnels, and that Hampton-El agreed to help find detonators. He then sought out the detonators. Thus, the jury's verdict finding Hampton-El guilty of attempted bombing was reasonable and supported by sufficient evidence.

E. Government Overinvolvement

Defendants Khallafalla and Saleh argue that their conviction violated the Due Process Clause by reason of the Government's "overinvolvement" in the conspiracy. According to defendants, the Government impermissibly lent direction, technical expertise, and critical resources to the bombing plot through Salem, an informant.[16] We reject this claim because the Government's conduct was within acceptable bounds.

The Supreme Court has suggested that in an extreme case, Government involvement in criminal activity might be "so outrageous that due process principles would absolutely bar the Government from invoking judicial processes to obtain a conviction." However, only Government conduct that "'shocks the conscience'" can violate due process. The paradigm examples of conscience-shocking conduct are egregious invasions of individual rights. *See, e.g.*, *Rochin [v. California]*, 342 U.S. at 172 (breaking into suspect's bedroom, forcibly attempting to pull capsules from his throat, and pumping his stomach without his consent). Especially in view of the courts' well-established deference to the Government's choice of investigatory methods, the burden of establishing outrageous investigatory conduct is very heavy.

The Government's behavior, and in particular the role of Salem, does not shock the conscience. Undercover work, in which a Government agent pretends to be engaged in criminal activity, is often necessary to detect criminal conspiracies. If such work is to succeed, the undercover agent must have

---

[16] Entrapment requires proof that the Government induced commission of the charged crime, and that the defendant lacked a predisposition to engage in such criminal conduct. The evidence at trial established that both Khallafalla and Saleh joined the conspiracy at the bidding of Siddig Ali. There was no Government inducement, and hence no entrapment.

"something of value to offer" the conspirators. Supplying such a resource "can hardly be said to violate" due process. In *Schmidt*, we found that United States Marshals did not violate due process when they posed as hit men, accepted a prisoner's solicitation to murder two guards during an escape, and then conducted a controlled breakout. In this case, Salem's contribution to the criminal conduct was proportionately far smaller: the defendants were already actively advancing a conspiracy, and they already had substantial resources and technical expertise. There is no evidence that the criminal conspiracy would have foundered without the Government's entry. The jihad organization had, after all, already bombed the World Trade Center without Salem's help. Moreover, as in *Schmidt*, the entry of the Government informant was intended not only to gather evidence, but also to prevent further death and destruction. Such conduct is not outrageous, and it does not violate due process.

NOTES AND QUESTIONS

1. The relationship between seditious conspiracy and treason will come up again when we consider prosecutions for "material support of terrorist organizations" and the constitutional right of association in Chapter 6. Why should treason be limited to those who "owe allegiance" to the United States and who would be considered to owe such allegiance? Does this cast a different light on controversies over the Pledge of Allegiance, such as religious objections to saying the Pledge, or is that a red herring?

2. The breadth of a conspiracy charge depends on how broadly the defendants can be shown to have agreed, either explicitly or tacitly. Only slightly tongue in cheek, can you imagine bringing every gang member in Los Angeles to trial for "conspiracy to intimidate the population of Los Angeles and thus to interfere with their rights to use public thoroughfares?" If that works, then how about sweeping in every kid wearing baggy pants and a black puffy jacket? Before you think your author is getting carried away with politically incorrect fantasy, look at the injunctions against gang-style loitering that were upheld in *Gallo v. Acuna*, 14 Cal. 4th 1090, 929 P.2d 596, 60 Cal. Rptr. 2d 277 (1997); and *City of New York v. Lenny Andrews, a/k/a Bloody Pimp,* 186 Misc. 2d 533, 719 N.Y.S.2d 442 (S. Ct. 2000).

Note on Islamic Law and Terminology

Salameh introduces the concepts of Jihad and fatwa to our study. As part of exploring appropriate responses to violence against civilian populations, it is natural to want to understand some of the motivations of those who engage in violence for political/ethnic/religious/cultural reasons. This Note is offered with great trepidation knowing that selective reading can cause gross misunderstanding of concepts that are central to the tenets of any faith system. To pursue the subject on your own, you can find much more simply by searching on the words "Shari'ah," "fatwa," or "jihad" on the web. It is also important to note that, although the acts of Islamist fundamentalists are a principal focus of terrorism concerns in the world today, these groups neither invented the technique nor have a monopoly on its use.

Shari'ah (sometimes transliterated as Shari'a) is the concept of Islamic law that corresponds to the Talmud in Hebrew law. Because neither Judaism nor Islam recognizes a separation of church and state, but rather purports to be a set of principles for all purposes, theological and behavioral principles are blended into a single code. Shari'ah is based on the Qu'ran (truth as revealed to the Prophet Muhammad), the Sunnah (words and deeds of the Prophet), and various secondary sources depending on the particular school of Shari'ah. It is promulgated and interpreted by jurists, persons with special training in the law who have created four distinct "schools" with slightly differing interpretations.

With respect to jihad, the following two pieces present competing views:

Islamic jurisprudence divides the inhabitants of Dar al-Harb (known as harbis) into two: People of the Book (Ahl al-Kitab) and polytheists. People of the Book, defined in the Qur'an as Christians, Jews, and Sabeans, have a distinct status in Muslim eyes because they follow a genuine – if incomplete – revelation from a genuine prophet. They may live undisturbed under Muslim rule so long as they accept a subordinate status (that of the dhimmi) which entails paying a tribute (jizya) and suffering a wide range of disabilities. As for polytheists, the law requires Muslims to offer them the choice of Islam or death, though this was rarely followed after the initial Muslim conquest of Arabia. Instead, Muslims generally treated all harbis as People of the Book. The jurists first sanctioned the inclusion of Zoroastrians in this category; Muslim conquerors of the Indian subcontinent extended it to Hindus as well, thereby effectively eliminating the category of polytheists.

The belief that jihad should continue until Dar al-Islam covers the entire world does not imply that the jurists expect Muslims to wage non-stop war. The Prophet Muhammad made a peace agreement with the Meccans in 630, the Treaty of Hudaybiya, and several of the early caliphs made peace treaties with the Byzantine Empire (some of which even required them to pay tribute to the Byzantines). Although there is no mechanism for recognizing a non-Muslim government as legitimate, the jurists built on these precedents to allow the negotiation of truces and peace treaties of limited duration. The jurists provide for military prudence, permitting the withdrawal of badly outnumbered or overpowered forces. And some jurists added an intermediate category, Dar al-`Ahd (Abode of Covenant) or Dar al-Sulh (Abode of Peace), for those countries where non-Muslim rulers govern non-Muslim subjects.

The jurists understand jihad not as an obligation of each individual Muslim but as a general obligation of the Muslim community. Only in emergencies, when Dar al-Islam comes under unexpected attack, do they expect all Muslims to participate in jihad warfare. Under normal circumstances, the failure of the community to fulfill the obligation of jihad is sinful; but an individual Muslim need not participate so long as other Muslims carry the burden. Shi`i writers make a further qualification, that offensive jihad is permissible only in the presence of the expected Imam – and thus not under current circumstances.

In contrast to this consensus view on a restricted doctrine of jihad, the prominent legal philosopher Ibn Taymiya (1268-1328) took a more activist position. He declared that a ruler who fails to enforce the Shari`a [Islamic law] rigorously in all its aspects, including the performance of jihad, forfeits his right to rule. A vigorous critic of the status quo, Ibn Taymiya strongly advocated, and personally participated in, jihad as warfare against the Crusaders and Mongols who occupied parts of Dar al-Islam. Ibn Taymiya developed his outlook by building on a long tradition of dissidents in Islamic history who directed jihad against rulers they deemed insufficiently Muslim, including the Kharijis of the seventh century and the Assassins of the eleventh century. Perhaps most important, he broke with the mainstream of Islam by his asserting that a professing Muslim who does not live by the faith is an unbeliever. Most jurists tolerated Muslim rulers who violated the Shari`a for the sake of the community, finding tyranny less bad than division or disorder, but Ibn Taymiya insisted on more. Ibn Taymiya and his associates are the most important intellectual precursors of contemporary Islamism.

Douglas E. Streusand, *What Does Jihad Mean?*, Middle East Quarterly (September 1997), http://www.ict.org.il/articles/jihad.htm

The Islamic Revolution of Iran continues its triumphant march, despite the enemies' plots, and this year (1985) the Islamic Republic of Iran celebrates the sixth anniversary of the victory of the Revolution on Feb. 10, 1979. On this day, after a centuries-long night, the sun of Islam rose again in all its resplendent glory, and this historic event is celebrated in the Islamic Republic during the course of the "Ten-Day Dawn Celebrations."

It is said about Christianity that it has the distinction of not having any rule governing war. We, on the other hand, say that Islam has the distinction of having the law of jihad. If we look closely, we see that in Christianity there is no jihad because it has nothing at all. By which I mean that there is no Christian structure of society, no Christian legal system, and no Christian rules as to how a society is to be formed, for these to contain a law of jihad. There is no substance in Christianity; it contains no more than a few moral teachings that form a set of advice such as "tell the truth", "do not tell lies", "do not gobble up the wealth of others", and so on. Such things do not call for jihad? Islam however is a religion that sees it its duty and commitment to form an Islamic state. Islam came to reform society and to form a nation and government. Its mandate is the reform of the whole world.

Such a religion cannot be indifferent. It cannot be without a law of jihad. In the same way, its government cannot be without an army. While the scope of Christianity is extremely limited, that of Islam is extremely wide. While Christianity does not cross the frontiers of advice, Islam is a religion which covers all the activities of human life. It has laws which govern the society, economic laws, and political laws. It came to organize a state, to organize a government. Once this done, how can it remain without an army? How can it be without a law of jihad?

Council for Ten-Day Dawn Celebrations, *Jihad: The Holy War of Islam and Its Legitimacy in the Quran, http://www.al-islam.org/short/jihad/*

In a similar vein, the term "fatwa" has different connotations to different adherents of Islam. In its most technical usage, it refers to a legal ruling by a religious lawyer or cleric with special qualifications to decide an issue. Because there is no central hierarchy or priesthood in Islam, however, various leaders can proclaim themselves qualified to issue fatwas. In the parlance of recent years, fatwas have been issued by various leaders for the purpose of calling on their followers to carry out violent acts against those who are thought to have committed a wrong against Islam. Sheikh Rahman and Osama bin Laden have both used the term in this fashion. Ayatollah Khomeini issued a fatwa, since declared inactive by the Iranian government, calling for the death of Salman Rushdie.

§ 2.03 THE EMERGENCE OF AL QAEDA

Among the many excellent depictions of the background of al Qaeda and Osama bin Laden, one of the most readable and accessible is the REPORT OF THE 9/11 COMMISSION. The underpinnings of U.S. support for the mujahadeen in Afghanistan and the subsequent coalescing of the remnants of those forces into al Qaeda is probably familiar to most students. The training and weapons supplied by the CIA to confront the Soviets went to groups many of whom endorsed one or more of the views that the Middle East should never have been broken into separate nations after World War I, that the Muslim world should be reunited into a single Caliphate, and that the secular governments of most Arab nations were aligned with the nations of the West who were responsible for all the difficulties of the Middle East. The philosophical and historical bases of these views can be traced to the writings of Sayyid Qutb, the spokesperson for the Muslim Brotherhood who was executed by Egypt in 1966. *See* RONAN GUNARATNA, INSIDE AL QAEDA 114 (2002).

Two short quotes make the basic point.

"When you decide to go to war against your current enemy, take a good, long look at the people behind you whom you choose as your friends, allies or mercenary fighters. Look well to see whether these allies already have unsheathed their knives – and are pointing them at your own back." JOHN K. COOLEY, UNHOLY WARS 226 (2002).

"To [many Muslim fundamentalists] the miracle victory over the Soviets was all the work of Allah – not the billions of dollars that America and Saudi Arabia poured into the battle, not the ten-year commitment of the CIA that turned an army of primitive tribesmen into techno-holy warriors. The consequence for America having waged a secret war and never acknowledging or advertising its role was that we set in motion the spirit of jihad and the belief in our surrogate soldiers that, having brought down one superpower, they could just as easily take on another." GEORGE CRILE, CHARLIE WILSON'S WAR 521-22 (2002).

In 1993, al Qaeda made its existence known with attacks on U.S. forces serving as part of a UN peace-keeping mission in Somalia. The "Embassy

Bombings" in Kenya and Tanzania on August 7, 1998 resulted in a wide-ranging conspiracy indictment in the Southern District of New York.

UNITED STATES v. BIN LADEN
(bill of particulars)
92 F. Supp. 2d 225 (S.D.N.Y. 2000)
MEMORANDUM AND ORDER

SAND, District Judge.

Defendants are charged with numerous offenses arising out of their alleged involvement with an international terrorist organization led by Defendant Usama Bin Laden ("Bin Laden"). Presently before the Court are four motions, filed by Defendants Wadih El Hage ("El Hage"), Mamdouh Mahmud Salim ("Salim"), Mohamed Sadeek Odeh ("Odeh"), and Khalfan Khamis Mohamed ("K.K. Mohamed") seeking an order compelling the Government to file a bill of particulars that is responsive to over 150 separate requests for information. For the reasons set forth below, those motions are granted in part and denied in part. The Government is ordered to file a bill of particulars, but that bill need only be responsive to those specific requests that we identify below.

I. BACKGROUND

The indictment presently before the Court charges the 15 named Defendants with 267 discrete criminal offenses. Eleven of the Defendants (all except Salim, Khaled Al Fawwaz ("Al Fawwaz"), Ali Mohammed, and El Hage) are charged with 229 counts of murder, as well as nine other substantive offenses[1], based on the August, 1998 bombings of the United States embassies in Nairobi, Kenya and Dar es Salaam, Tanzania. Defendant El Hage is charged with twenty counts of perjury before a federal grand jury and three counts of making false statements to special agents of the Federal Bureau of Investigation ("FBI").

Each of the Defendants is also charged with participating in at least five distinct criminal conspiracies; El Hage and Ali Mohamed are accused of participating in six. Although each conspiracy is charged under a different provision of the federal criminal code, the allegations overlap to a significant degree. The six conspiracies are, for the most part, alleged to have had the same four criminal objectives: (1) murder of United States nationals; (2) killing of United States military personnel serving in Somalia and on the Saudi Arabian peninsula; (3) killing of United States nationals employed at the United States Embassies in Kenya and Tanzania; and (4) concealment of the conspirators' activities through the use of front companies, false identity and travel documents, coded correspondence, and by providing false information to

---

[1] In a prior opinion, this Court ordered two of those substantive offenses (two counts of maiming) as well as two of the murder counts to be dismissed for lack of jurisdiction. See United States v. Bin Laden, 92 F. Supp. 2d [189] (S.D.N.Y. 2000). [The dismissed counts were based on the murder or maiming of persons other than U.S. nationals or employees on the embassy premises. The court merely held that §§ 114 & 1114 evidenced no congressional intent to claim U.S. jurisdiction for murder or maiming of a non-national by a non-national within a federal enclave overseas.]

authorities. All but one of the conspiracies are alleged to have been furthered by the commission of the same set of 144 overt acts.

In a section labeled, "Background," the Indictment explains that the charges arise out of the Defendants' alleged involvement with a vast, international terrorist network known as "al Qaeda," or "the Base." According to the Indictment, al Qaeda emerged in 1989, under the leadership of Bin Laden and his two chief military commanders, Defendant Muhammad Atef ("Atef") and the now-deceased, Abu Ubaida al Banshiri ("Abu Ubaidah"), replacing a predecessor organization known as "mekhtab al khidemat," or the "Services Organization." Members of al Qaeda "pledged an oath of allegiance (called a 'bayat') to Bin Laden and al Qaeda." The group was allegedly headquartered in Afghanistan from 1989 until 1991, at which time it re-located to the Sudan, ultimately returning to Afghanistan in 1996. According to the Indictment, al Qaeda functioned both on its own and in conjunction with other groups – such as the "al Jihad" organization in Egypt, Sheik Omar Abdel Rahman's "Islamic Group," the Iranian terrorist group, Hezballah, and the Sudanese National Islamic Front – that shared its strong opposition to the United States and a willingness to use violent, terrorist tactics in furtherance of their shared goals.

The Indictment's core factual allegations are set forth in a 31-page section that appears under the heading "Overt Acts." Without re-stating the entire litany of acts alleged therein, it is fair to say that the basic pattern that emerges is one in which al Qaeda, over a period of at least ten years, is said to have organized, financed, inspired, and generally facilitated a variety of violent attacks against United States personnel and property abroad. Some of the overt acts set forth in the Indictment, such as detonation of the explosives that destroyed the American embassies, are plainly violent acts in and of themselves. But many of the overt acts alleged consist of seemingly non-criminal conduct – such as writing letters, traveling, and engaging in business transactions – which, according to the Indictment, facilitated the violent attacks and thereby constitute overt acts in furtherance of the charged conspiracies.

A. The Organization

The Indictment alleges that beginning at least in 1989, al Qaeda established "training camps" and "guesthouses" in various areas around the world, including Afghanistan, Pakistan, the Sudan, Somalia, and Kenya. Al Qaeda members and the members of affiliated groups allegedly received military and intelligence training in those camps under the direction of Defendant Ali Mohamed and others. Defendant Salim allegedly managed some of the camps in Afghanistan and Pakistan.

The camps were allegedly operated under the auspices of a series of business established by Bin Laden, Salim, and others. The businesses were used to engage in activities such as purchasing land, warehouses, and equipment for the camps; and for transporting currency and weapons to al Qaeda members "in various countries throughout the world."

Assistance from American citizens was allegedly essential to al Qaeda's operation. Two of the Defendants, Ali Mohamed and El Hage, both American citizens, are accused of assisting the organization by traveling "throughout the

Western world to deliver messages and engage in financial transactions for the benefit of al Qaeda . . . ." According to the Indictment, Ali Mohamed and El Hage exchanged messages with each other, and with other co-conspirators, through letters and visits, regarding al Qaeda activities and the whereabouts of al Qaeda leaders.

B. The Fatwahs and Declarations of Jihad

In addition to providing military and intelligence training, obtaining weapons, establishing base camps, and coordinating the work of various members around the globe, al Qaeda allegedly facilitated violent attacks on United States interests by providing religious authority for those attacks. From time to time, according to the Indictment, Bin Laden would issue rulings on Islamic law, called "fatwahs," which purported to justify al Qaeda's violent activities. [The earliest bin Laden fatwas urged that U.S. military forces in Somalia and the Arabian Peninsula should be attacked.]

Finally, in February, 1998 Bin Laden issued another fatwah, eliminating the distinction between military and civilian personnel and stating that "Muslims should kill Americans – including civilians – anywhere in the world where they can be found." A few months later, in May, 1998, Bin Laden endorsed a fatwah characterizing the United States Army as "the 'enemies of Islam'" and declaring a "jihad" against the United States "and its followers." That same month, according to the Indictment, Bin Laden held a press conference, attended by Defendants Atef and Al-'Owhali, in which he reiterated his "intention to kill Americans."

C. The Violent Attacks

1. Somalia

Under the leadership of Defendants Atef, Fazul Abdullah Mohamed ("F.A. Mohamed"), Odeh, and the now deceased, Abu Ubaidah, al Qaeda allegedly provided military training and assistance in its camps to Somali tribes opposed to the UN peacekeeping mission in that country. On October 3 and 4, 1993, the Indictment alleges, those persons they trained "participated in an attack on United States military personnel serving in Somalia as part of Operation Restore Hope, which attack resulted in the killing of 18 United States Army personnel . . . ."

2. The East African Bombings

The Indictment includes roughly parallel allegations with respect to the bombings in Kenya and Tanzania. During the spring and early summer of 1998, al Qaeda members and other co-conspirators began to congregate in both Nairobi and Dar es Salaam. One of the first tasks for each group was to purchase a truck and make necessary alterations to prepare the truck for use with a bomb. Defendant Sheikh Ahmed Salim Swedan ("Swedan") is charged with purchasing both trucks, assisted in Nairobi by Msalam and assisted in Dar es Salaam by Defendant Ahmed Khalfan Ghailani ("Ghailani").

During the first week in August, final preparations were made. Defendants Al-'Owhali and F.A. Mohammed, along with Azzam, made those preparations at a villa in Nairobi; Defendants Fadhil, K.K. Mohamed, and Msalam, along with an unindicted co-conspirator identified only as "CS-2" made preparations in Dar es Salaam. On the night before the bombings, pursuant to the advice of an unidentified "al Qaeda member," Defendants Odeh, Msalam, and Ghailani left Nairobi under assumed names and traveled to Karachi, Pakistan. Early the next morning, claims of responsibility were sent by fax to London, England for further distribution by unidentified co-conspirators.

Finally, on August 7, 1998, separated in time by only ten minutes, the two bombs were detonated. In Nairobi, they were allegedly detonated by Azzam and F.A. Mohammed, accompanied by Al-'Owhali; in Dar es Salaam, they were detonated by an unindicted co-conspirator, identified by the Government as "Ahmed the German." In the immediate aftermath of the bombing, Defendant F.A. Mohammed allegedly cleaned out the villa in Nairobi where preparations had been made and traveled to the Comoros Islands.

Also in the aftermath of the bombing, Defendant El Hage – who had testified about al Qaeda before a federal grand jury upon his return to the United States from Kenya approximately one year earlier – was subpoenaed to appear before a federal grand jury investigating the bombings. On both occasions, El Hage was also interviewed by special agents of the FBI. The Indictment accuses Mr. El Hage of making a wide variety of false statements both to the FBI agents and to the grand jury, in both 1997 and 1998.

D. Procedural History

On September 16, 1998, following his testimony before the Grand Jury, Defendant El Hage was arrested by federal authorities. He was incarcerated pursuant to certain special conditions of confinement, which federal regulations authorize for particularly dangerous detainees. In this case, those conditions have included periods of solitary confinement, as well as severe restrictions on the Defendants' access to visitors and to the telephone. Defendants Odeh and Al-'Owhali were next brought into federal custody, and first appeared before the Court on October 8, 1998. Salim first appeared on December 21, 1998, after having been arrested in Germany on September 6, 1998. Ali Mohamed first appeared on May 27, 1999 and K.K. Mohamed was arraigned before this Court on October 8, 1999. Since being brought into federal custody, each of those Defendants has also been incarcerated pursuant to the particularly restrictive conditions described above.

The process of preparing for a trial in this case has been unusually protracted. The complexity of the charges, the voluminous discovery that needs to be exchanged, the location of many relevant documents and witnesses in various countries around the world, special procedures for handling classified material, the need to translate literally thousands of documents, and the potential availability of capital punishment for some of the Defendants have combined to require an extraordinary amount of work on the part of all parties involved. Despite everyone's best efforts, it is anticipated at this time that the earliest possible date that this case could be ready for trial is September 5, 2000 – almost two years after the first Defendant was brought into custody and incarcerated under restricted conditions. Trial of the guilt phase of this case, excluding jury selection and deliberation, is expected to last at least six months.

Four of the Defendants – El Hage, Salim, Odeh, and K.K. Mohamed – now move for an order requiring the Government to file a bill of particulars. Together, the Defendants have requested more than 150 specific items of information that they wish to be included in that bill. The Defendants contend that the filing of a bill of particulars responsive to those requests is necessary to permit them to prepare a defense and to prevent prejudicial surprise at trial. The Government, on the other hand, in addition to challenging the appropriateness of a bill of particulars that includes the types of information requested by the Defendants, contends that it need not file a bill of particulars because the extensive detail included in the Indictment, the voluminous discovery it has provided to date,[14] and the additional disclosures provided in its response to Mr. El Hage's bail application more than adequately apprise the Defendants of the charges that they must be prepared to answer.

[The court denied all but a few of the requests for more particular allegations.]

NOTES AND QUESTIONS

1. *United States v. Bin Laden (severance)*, 109 F. Supp. 2d 211 (S.D.N.Y. 2000). Six of the persons indicted in the Somalia attacks and Embassy bombings were slated to be tried jointly. Three (El Hage, Salim, and Ali Mohamed) called themselves the "non-bombing defendants" because they were charged only with conspiracy moved to sever their trials from the "bombing defendants" who were charged with both conspiracy and the substantive offenses. Their principal argument related to graphic photographs and details from the bombings that they claimed would not be admissible against them in a mere conspiracy trial. The judge responded:

The moving Defendants anticipate that the jury will erroneously consider the graphic bombing evidence against them even though it might be inadmissible. They argue that notwithstanding any cautionary instruction this Court might provide, the jurors will simply be unable to compartmentalize the evidence and consider it only against those Defendants as to whom it is admissible and they argue (somewhat differently) that, even if the jurors can compartmentalize the evidence, they will be so inflamed by the graphic bombing evidence that they will ignore what the moving Defendants claim is a relative lack of evidence establishing the existence of, and moving Defendants' participation in, the charged conspiracies. We are not convinced, at this stage of the case, that either form of anticipated prejudicial spillover is so likely as to constitute 'a serious risk' that the jury will not make 'a reliable judgment about guilt or innocence.' Multi-defendant trials are quite common in the federal system, and many involve evidence that is admissible against one

---

[14] To date, the Government has provided hundreds of thousands of pages of documents, dozens of audio and video tapes, transcripts and translations of these materials, hundreds of crime scene and other photographs, several dozen laboratory reports reflecting forensic tests of thousands of items and numerous other FBI Reports.

defendant, but not against another. Federal courts, quite routinely, have found juries able to follow and abide by appropriate cautionary instructions.

2. *United States v. El-Hage*, 213 F.3d 74 (2d Cir. 2000). El Hage was held in solitary confinement with very limited access to counsel, friends, or family. In response to his claims that he was a loyal U.S. citizen with a stable family and not a threat to flee, the Government produced affidavits regarding his involvement with the al Qaeda. "Defendant was one of Bin Laden's trusted associates, privy to al Qaeda's secrets and plans, served as Bin Laden's personal secretary, traveled on his American passport on Bin Laden's behalf, moved Bin Laden's money, and worked in Bin Laden's factories in the Sudan – factories which served as a cover for the procurement of chemicals and weapons."

Defendant Wadih El-Hage appeals from an order [denying] defendant's motion to be released on bail, his application for rescission or for substantial modification of the Special Administrative Measures (S.A.M.) of his confinement. Pretrial detention is authorized by statute. Under 18 U.S.C. § 3142(e) a person may be detained before trial if it is found that no condition or combination of conditions of an indicted defendant "will reasonably assure the appearance of the [defendant] . . . and the safety of any other person and the community." Due process limits how long an accused may be detained in prison without a trial. But exactly how long such detention may extend before violating due process limits – the issue we face on this appeal – has not been fixed in the law. The 30-33 months of pretrial detention served or contemplated to be served before the conclusion of a trial in this case is extraordinary, and justified only by the unprecedented scope of violence that the conspiracy of which defendant was allegedly a part inflicted on innocent victims, by the extraordinarily complex and difficult preparation needed to present this case, and, more particularly, because the lengthy delay in bringing defendant to trial may not be laid at the government's doorstep.

3. Several defendants in the "embassy bombing" case eventually pleaded guilty, offered differing levels of cooperation, and were sentenced to various terms in prison. El-Hage and three other defendants were convicted after trial and sentenced to life imprisonment. In failing to come to a unanimous recommendation for the death penalty, the jury noted that some of its members believed that life imprisonment was a worse punishment than death.

§ 2.04 9/11 AND FOLLOW-UP PROSECUTIONS

A great deal of political ink has been spilled over the question of whether the airplane "attacks" of 9/11 should have been foreseen and thwarted. Detailed investigations isolated 20 hijackers who planned to be on board the aircraft, but only 19 made it. The alleged "20th hijacker" is Zacarias Moussaoui, who was already in custody for visa violations and whose computer was not tapped into until after the incidents. One FBI agent in Phoenix had noticed the prevalence of young Arab males taking flying lessons without wanting to learn how to take-off or land. His memo was working its way through the system at the time of the incident. Several of the hijackers were on his list and had been admitted to the U.S. while also on "terrorist watch lists."

Some reports claim that as many as 500 al Qaeda members or operatives have been taken into U.S. custody since 9/11. So far as we know, there are only two persons alleged to have had close involvement with the 9/11 plots who are currently in custody in the U.S. One published report asserts that as many as 20 separate criminal cases have been built in Brooklyn around the activities of one government informant. Most of these prosecutions have been for providing material support to terrorist organizations through channeling of money abroad. *See* William Glaberson, *Behind Scenes, Informer's Path Led U.S. to 20 Terror Cases*, NY TIMES B1 (Nov. 18, 2004). According to this article, the informer attempted to set himself on fire in front of the White House.

The three most senior al Qaeda associates that the U.S. has admitted to holding are Khalid Sheikh Mohammed (aka KSM or Mukhtar), Riduan Isamuddin (aka Hambali), and Zein al Abideen Mohamed Hussein (aka Abu Zubaydah). Hambali and KSM both illustrate the inter-connectedness of alQaeda with other groups. Hambali was the leader of Jemaal Islamiya, worked closely with bin Laden until his capture in August 2003, and is credited with the bombing of the Bali night club in 2002.

Khalid (KSM) is widely regarded as the "mastermind" of the 9/11 plot as well as numerous other actions. He is the uncle of Ramzi Yousef, who was the mastermind of the 1993 WTC bombing working with the Sheikh Rahman group in New York. KSM was also involved with several other groups before affiliating with al Qaeda and claims to have maintained some autonomy by not "swearing allegiance to bin Laden." He was captured by Pakistani ISI forces on March 2, 2003 and turned over to U.S. authorities who have been interrogating him in an undisclosed location ever since. *Time* magazine reported on March 24, 2003 (*http://www.time.com/time/nation/article/0,8599,436061,00.html*):

> Mohammed's cooperation has improved investigators' understanding of al-Qaeda's command-and-control structure. Sources say he has explained that at any time, the organization has open-ended plans for as many as two dozen attacks – mostly ideas proposed by field operatives and sanctioned and financed by Osama bin Laden's inner circle.

The two alleged 9/11 conspirators in custody in the U.S. are Ali Saleh al-Maari and Zacarias Moussaoui. Al-Maari was originally charged in the civilian courts with having been part of the financial team for the plot, but his case was dismissed and he was confined to military detention without trial.

Moussaoui is the only person who has been charged in the U.S. with direct participation in the 9/11 attacks. He allegedly was to have been one of the hijackers but did not make the flight because he was already in custody for violations of immigration laws. He is charged with six conspiracy counts: to commit a terrorist act under 2332b, to commit air piracy, to destroy aircraft, to use weapons of mass destruction, to murder U.S. employees, and to destroy property. The tortured progress of attempting to bring his case to trial has gone on for almost three years, and he is not likely to be in front of a jury anytime soon. The essential difficulty is that the defendant is requesting access to witnesses who are in government custody but as to whom the government claims a national security need for secrecy. We will take up the problems of the Classified Information Procedure Act in the next chapter. For now, you should think generally about how to prosecute someone in this position.

Another alleged 9/11 conspirator, part of the "Hamburg cell," was tried and acquitted in a German court after both sides sought and were denied access to information from witnesses who were in U.S. custody at undisclosed locations.

The Lackawanna Six and Portland Seven are two alleged al Qaeda sleeper cells "broken up" in the year following 9/11. A few terrorist cells in Europe were raided and found with sufficient hard evidence such as explosives to make a basis for prosecution on conspiracy to commit specific crimes. Apparently, however, in neither the Lackawanna nor Portland cases were authorities able to find plans or materials for specific acts of violence in this country. The Portland Indictment alleges that members of the cell had trained with al Qaeda and were preparing to travel through Hong Kong to Afghanistan to take up arms on behalf of the Taliban against the U.S. The Lackawanna Complaint alleges only that members of the "cell" had trained in Al-Farooq and stayed at an al Qaeda safe house. There is nothing in the affidavit accompanying the charges that indicates any future plans other than the statement that two uncharged co-conspirators had communicated by e-mail with "information which law enforcement personnel interpret as referring to possible terrorist activity." Despite the lack of any information related to future plans, the Magistrate Judge granted most of the government's motion for detention without bail. The test for detention without bail is whether "by clear and convincing evidence" the defendant is a threat to the community or a flight risk. How does one prove or disprove a future event "by clear and convincing evidence?" Although granting the Government's petitions, Magistrate Schroeder in his bail decision says,

> We must never adopt an "ends justifies the means" philosophy by claiming that our Constitutional and democratic principles must be temporarily furloughed or put on hold in cases involving alleged terrorism in order to preserve our democracy. To do so would result in victory for the terrorists.

Some defense attorneys complained that guilty pleas were coercively tainted by the threat that the defendants could be subject to the "enemy combatant" designation and thus imprisoned without a trial. That prospect presumably would not be available after the Supreme Court decision in *Hamdi*, p. 492.

In the wake of 9/11, federal agencies were subjected to harsh criticism for failing to prevent the attacks. Breaking up terrorist cells would seem to be what the public and politicians want. But how does a federal agent know which of the thousands of tips and leads to follow? For that matter, how does an agency "break up a cell?" Should there be some proof that the Lackawanna defendants planned to do something? They pleaded guilty to going to an al Qaeda training camp while al Qaeda was a "designated foreign terrorist organization." Does this interfere with their rights of association under the first amendment? Should there be more required before we throw people into prison?

SELECTED READINGS

▶ Sam A. Schmidt & Joshua L. Dratel, *Turning the Tables: Using the Government's Secrecy and Security Arsenal for the Benefit of the Client in Terrorism Prosecutions*, N.Y.L.S.L. REV. 69 (2003) (article by defense counsel in the Embassy Bombing Case).

▶ ROHAN GUNARATNA, INSIDE AL QAEDA (2002).

▶ PHILLIP B. HEYMANN, TERRORISM, FREEDOM, AND SECURITY (2004).

▶ JOHN COOLEY, UNHOLY WARS (2002).

Chapter 3

TOWARD AN INTERNATIONAL LAW OF TERRORISM

There are at least three reasons why a study of legal responses to international terrorism must start with the international law of war and its offspring, international criminal law. One is that some aspects of terrorism essentially amount to illegal methods of warfare and can be treated as such by emerging criminal processes that enforce the "customs and law of war." Second, international criminal law dealing with widespread violence against civilians (genocide and crimes against humanity) has been spawned from international enforcement of the law of war, and instances of this behavior may prompt calls for international military action (most recently, for example, in the Sudan). The third reason is that some nations, particularly the U.S. following 9/11, use the language of war and envision the use of military force in responding to terrorism.

For all these reasons, we will spend some time with the law of war, then turn to international criminal enforcement and conventions regarding terrorism. The progression of legal concepts here flows from norms of behavior during time of warfare between nations, to international sanctions on atrocities committed during internal conflicts, to national and international sanctions on violence by civilians against civilians.

§ 3.01 INTERNATIONAL LAW OF ARMED CONFLICT

The rhetoric of a "war against terrorism" began immediately on September 11, 2001. It was difficult to argue against it at the time, although a few cautionary voices were heard. Some observers pointed out that military action against terrorist groups would not technically be a war and argued against immediate military action as a response. Others pointed out that this will be a war of ideas, not just weapons. Meanwhile, President Bush authorized the creation of military tribunals to deal with alleged terrorists under statutory authorization that allows military tribunals to punish violations of the "law of war." Thus, the laws and customs of war are very much a part of our study of responses to terrorism.

[A] THE LANGUAGE AND HISTORY OF WAR

In traditional international terms, it would not be possible for a nation to go to war with a group of individuals, criminal or otherwise. War traditionally is a status that exists between nations, not among individuals nor even between a nation-state and a group of individuals. Professor Paust says that the law of war applies in "armed conflict" with a "nation, state, belligerent, or insurgent group." The difference between the latter two is that the insurgent has not yet received "outside recognition by one or more states as a belligerent or a state." To the extent that insurgents gain enough power to move beyond the status of ordinary street criminals, then they may be engaged in an "armed conflict" with the state, but they do not partake of the protections of the law of war unless they organize and behave according to those rules. Jordan J. Paust, *War and Enemy Status After 9/11: Attacks on the Laws of War*, 28 YALE J. INT'L L. 325, 326 (2003).

Professor Feldman claims that the status of "war" is a bit more complicated than that. He notes that the distinction between "war" and "crime" has "practical consequences . . . for the pursuit and capture of international terrorists" because of

> a striking asymmetry: on the one hand, criminals generally may not be killed by their pursuers if they pose no immediate threat, but may be punished after capture; adversaries in war, on the other hand, may generally be killed in pursuit without giving quarter, but generally cannot be punished after they are captured.

Noah Feldman, *Choices of Law, Choices of War*, 25 HARV. J. L. PUB. POLICY 457 (2002). Professor Feldman distinguishes between war and crime on the basis of four criteria, which he calls the identity factor (status of the actor as a state or recognized group), provenance (whether action originates from within or outside the state), intent (whether the actor is challenging the very existence of the governing regime), and scale (the scope of violent action).

Generally speaking, in the international law regime discussed below, war must be defensive, carried out by persons identified by discernible insignia, and limited to military targets, sparing civilian populations to the extent possible. (The argument against the legality of nuclear weapons is that they can never be limited effectively to military targets without extensive destruction of human life. This is still under debate in the international community.)

Generally speaking, a terrorist is a person who clandestinely attacks civilian targets and blends back into a civilian population. Each of these three aspects defies the rules laid down by nations for the conduct of their affairs. We must be careful, however, not to use the language of war loosely because the "law of war" applies only in the context of "armed conflict," a term of art that refers to organized use of deadly force. Other law, primarily "international humanitarian law" (IHL) is developing from the law of war at least to govern "widespread and systematic" attacks on civilians.

The nations of the world have not agreed on a definition of terrorist because some maintain that these are the only methods for "freedom fighters" to strike at an oppressive regime. The counter-argument is that the striking of civilian targets is neither essential to the freedom fighter nor warranted by the customs and usages of war. Moreover, when an action is taken outside the person's home base, then even this justification could reach only the citizenry of an "oppressor" or "colonizing" nation. As the twentieth century drew to a close, systematic violence against civilians became more a matter of organized violence by national forces against minority or subservient civilian populations than a matter of violence by insurgents against the civilians of a perceived aggressor or colonizer. Examples of the former included Yugoslavia (Bosnia & Kosovo), Rwanda, Somalia, Darfur. An example of the latter would be Iraq in 2003-04. As a result of the shift in emphasis, most third-world countries came to the view that systematic violence against civilians should be condemned by the international community, and attention turned from the basic moral question to the technical definition.

[B] INTERNATIONAL LAW AND USE OF FORCE

1. Historical Introduction to the Law of War

International law applies to "armed conflict." In recent decades, commentators have been abandoning the term "war" because of the need to deal with undeclared conditions of combat. Many students will be tempted to believe that it is also an oxymoron to speak of international "law" because the rules to be followed appear to be simply whatever the strongest wish to apply to the weaker. More prosaically, the rules of etiquette are set by the 500 pound gorilla at the dinner table. There is some truth to this observation, but the complete picture is much more complex. Over the last 4000 years, norms have been written down, and in the last few hundred years those norms have come to receive increasing levels of enforcement in various settings.

The "law of war" flows from self-imposed limitations on the use of force that have been promulgated by every known civilization. "As early as the Egyptian and Sumerian wars of the second millennium B.C., there were rules defining the circumstances under which war might be initiated. Among the Hittites of the fourteenth century B.C., a formal exchange of letters and demands generally preceded hostilities." 1 LEON FRIEDMAN, THE LAW OF WAR: A DOCUMENTARY HISTORY 3 (1972). The Hebrew Torah, in the Book of Deuteronomy, written down somewhere around 500 BCE, contained mandates to spare noncombatants (with exceptions) and the "trees of the field." In China, Sun Tzu's *The Art of War*, also ca. 500 BCE, prohibited injury to a wounded enemy and exhorted leaders that "All the soldiers taken must be cared for with magnanimity and sincerity so that they may be used by us." The Hindu *Book of Manu*, ca. 200 CE, contained lengthy, detailed proscriptions on hidden or poisoned weapons as well as on treatment of prisoners.

The seminal written work for Western development was provided by St. Augustine in various letters and essays before and around the time of the fall of Rome in 410 CE. Augustine is best known for distinguishing between *jus ad bellum* (law of going to war) and *jus in bellum* (law during war). His two conditions for "just war" dictated by *jus ad bellum* were that it must be declared by a recognized authority and that it must be defensive (the origin of nonaggression). The three principal elements of *jus in bellum* he said to be sparing noncombatants, limitations of military necessity and proportionality, and protection of the means of human survival (water, trees, etc).

Over the course of European history, heavily influenced by the writings of Christian clergy, rules for the conduct of warfare became ever more elaborate. Rules of warfare during the medieval period were expressed mostly in the codes of chivalry. Then, at the dawn of the age of colonialism, as European nations came into contact with other cultures that they wished to subdue, writers began to elaborate the "laws and customs" by which these other cultures were to be approached. The principal architect of what is now the international law of war was HUGO GROTIUS, ON THE LAW OF WAR AND PEACE (1625). In this series of three books, Grotius, a Dutch lawyer, set out the requirements for lawful use of military force and the limitations on the use of force.

The cynical may view all these mandates, and the many departures from them over the centuries, as nothing but self-aggrandizing sentiments that could be followed or not as the military commanders and their sovereigns chose. Certainly, human history is rampant with unjustified use of force and with extreme cruelty and barbarity to both civilians and combatants. Nevertheless, there are self-interested reasons for imposing limitations. "A commander does not kill his prisoners because he does not want his own men slaughtered if they fall into an enemy's hands. Civilian populations should not be eliminated after they have been conquered since they can work for, pay tribute to, or be conscripted into, the victorious army. Unrestrained warfare would jeopardize reconciliation and make later trade and peaceful intercourse impossible." FRIEDMAN at 4. In addition, Friedman points out that evolving standards of civilization (to which we might add increasing levels of globalized trade) have added levels of conscience to the human tension between violence and peace. Philosophical norms eventually do find their way into enforceable norms of law.

Fourteen separate Conventions adopted at the Hague in 1907 committed signatory nations to a variety of limitations on the use of force. Hague I "Pacific Settlement of International Disputes" stated that "the Signatory Powers agree to use their best efforts to ensure the pacific settlement of disputes" and established a system of mediation and the Permanent Court of Arbitration for international disputes. Hague II "Laws and Customs of War on Land" stated that "In view of the High Contracting Parties, these provisions, the wording of which has been inspired by the desire to diminish the evils of war so far as military necessities permit, are destined to serve as general rules of conduct for belligerents in their relations with each other and with populations." The other Conventions established conditions for conduct of military operations in specific settings, established conditions for treatment of prisoners, and prohibited certain kinds of weapons. Although the Hague Conventions were treated with attitudes approaching contempt in the initiation and conduct of World War I, it was the rules of these conventions that ultimately became the bases for prosecutions after World War II for violations of the "laws and customs of war."

The most visible enforcement mechanisms of current international law are one set for nations and one for individuals. The United Nations Security Council enforces rules of nonaggression by calling on member states to invoke sanctions against any state that violates the UN Charter's prohibition on aggression. That there are obvious political dimensions to the decisions of the Security Council does not take away the facial legitimacy of those decisions.

The second set of enforcement mechanisms, applying the law of war to individuals, begins with war crimes trials following World War II. The United States tried some German spies and saboteurs in military courts. *Johnson v. Eisentrager,* 339 U.S. 763 (1950). The United States also conducted military trials for vanquished Japanese commanders accused of allowing their troops to violate the "laws and customs of war." *In re Yamashita*, 327 U.S. 1 (1946).

The genesis of international enforcement of the law of war was the Treaty of London and the resulting Nuremberg trials of high-ranking Nazi officials. The trials at Nuremberg were intended to import the processes of law onto the international scene for dealing with war crimes. Prior to that time, "victor's justice" had been meted out at the national level. Gerry J. Simpson, *War Crimes: A Critical Introduction*, TIMOTHY L.H. MCCORMACK & GERRY J. SIMPSON, THE LAW OF WAR CRIMES 5 (1997). The Nuremberg trials have been followed in more recent times by Ad Hoc Tribunals for Rwanda & Yugoslavia. *See* Christopher Blakesley, *Atrocity and Its Prosecution*, MCCORMACK & SIMPSON, THE LAW OF WAR CRIMES 189 (1997). These Tribunals are considered in § 3.02[B] below.

Until recently, the world held to a dichotomous distinction between the processes of warfare and those of the civilian criminal system. War was something that took place between nations, involved an effort to kill or capture enemy combatants, and thus provided no occasion for making considered judgments about the culpability of someone on the other side. The rules of engagement of a particular military action eliminate the soldier's need to inquire into the culpability of someone in uniform carrying arms. WILLIAM WINTHROP, MILITARY LAW AND PROCEDURE 778 (2d ed. 1920): "The State is represented in active war by its contending army, and the laws of war justify killing or disabling of members of the one army by those of the other in battle or hostile operations."

The exclusive focus on nation-state participation in international law has been modified by the emergence of additional organizations as world players, such as Regional Organizations (*e.g.*, NATO, EU, OAS) and Non Governmental Organizations (*e.g.*, Amnesty International, International Red Cross). Although these additional actors are participants in the development of international law, there are only a few instances of treaties that specifically recognize their role as legal actors.

More importantly, the lines between warfare and criminal processes have blurred because of changes in approach both by the enforcers of peace and the perpetrators of violence. The peacemakers have attempted to use processes patterned from criminal law to punish violations of respected rules of warfare, while the perpetrators of violence have acted on their own outside the confines of government and those same rules of warfare. The world's search for a new paradigm to deal with these phenomena has produced international commissions for prosecution of war crimes and is now engaged in defining responses to terrorism.

2. The Basics of "Armed Attack" and Aggression

The starting point for international law is similar to the rules regarding assault between individuals. If you use force against another, you must have a justification. UN Charter Art. 2(4) sets out the basic rule of nonaggression: "All Members shall refrain in their international relations from the threat or use of force against the territorial integrity or political independence of any state, or in any other manner inconsistent with the Purposes of the United Nations." Articles 39-50 give the Security Council authority to determine when a nation is committing aggression and to call on Member nations to employ sanctions, ranging from diplomatic and economic sanctions to the use of military force against the aggressor.

Justifications for the use of force are implied in Article 51, which states that "Nothing in the present Charter shall impair the inherent right of individual or collective self-defense if an armed attack occurs against a Member of the United Nations." Recognition of the right of self-defense calls into play a network of doctrines regarding response to threats, proportional reprisals, protection of nationals, humanitarian intervention, and dealing with insurgents or belligerents.

First, there is the question of what constitutes aggression sufficient to justify self-defensive reaction. "Armed attack" under Art. 51 seems to imply the obvious, incursion of armed invaders with full military equipment (planes, tanks, etc) in the uniforms of the invading country into the recognized borders of another nation. In this event, the invaded country can use whatever force is necessary to defend itself including, at least if it declares war, invading the offending country to take the offensive.

Short of the obvious level of armed attack, however, there are a host of lesser incursions that might trigger the right of self-defense. Blockade of a nation's ports is traditionally regarded as an act of war. An embassy is generally regarded as part of the sovereign territory of the guest nation so that an attack on the embassy is an act of war. Attacks on military ships on the high seas, and arguably attacks on merchant vessels as well, are acts of war. And minor border skirmishes may trigger the right of reprisal as part of self-defense, and there will inevitably be questions raised as to whether the incursions were actually undertaken on behalf of the neighboring state or were instead private actions (by "irregulars" or terrorists). In all these instances of "minor" acts of war, the defending nation is limited to responding to the extent necessary to defend itself and in proportion to the actions of the aggressor. These rules of necessity and proportionality may be more frequently observed than one might think, for the simple reason that escalation of the conflict is undertaken only at risk of triggering "total war," in which all the military-industrial apparatus of the enemy nation is arrayed in an effort to obliterate the defensive capability of the enemy.

The issues of "armed attack" and appropriate responses are explored in the opinions of the International Court of Justice in *Nicaragua v. United States*, 1986 ICJ 14, excerpted below.

Second, to what extent may a nation respond to a perceived threat before the other nation can strike? The United Nations has never adopted language that specifically addresses this issue, and in fact has refrained from defining the scope of self-defense to avoid the issue. Many observers believe that a majority of nations do not subscribe to the doctrine of anticipatory self-defense or preemptive strikes. Israel claimed anticipatory self-defense in its 1981 attack on an Iraq nuclear power plant, but skirted the issue in justifying its 1967 invasion of Egypt, Jordan, and Syria by claiming that other actions of those states essentially amounted to acts of war against Israel. The U.S. used a similar approach to justify its blockade of Cuba during the 1962 missile crisis by claiming that it was engaged in regional peacekeeping under Chapter VIII of the UN Charter. The U.S. has specifically invoked anticipatory self-defense with regard to Iraq, first in enforcing the "no-fly" zones by targeting Iraq installations that show "hostile intent" and then ultimately in the 2003 invasion based on reported stockpiles of weapons of mass destruction.

As one observer concluded prior to the 2003 invasion, "reluctance to rely on anticipatory self-defence even by the USA and Israel is not conclusive that they do not believe that it is legal, as it is natural for states to choose the strongest grounds to justify their claims, but it is strong evidence of the controversial nature of this justification for the use of force, as is the deliberate avoidance of the issue of the legality of anticipatory self-defence by the International Court of Justice in the Nicaragua case. States prefer to argue for an extended interpretation of armed attack and to avoid the fundamental doctrinal debate." CHRISTINE GRAY, INTERNATIONAL LAW AND THE USE OF FORCE 115 (2000).

Third, may one state invade the territory of another state to protect its nationals? The U.S. has claimed this right in its invasions of Panama (1989) and Grenada (1983), the hostage-rescue attempt in Iran (1980), and a few other instances. One of the most famous incidents of this type was the hostage rescue by Israeli forces at Entebbe in 1976. Grey points out that the pattern of allowing incursions into other states to rescue a nation's own citizens has been accepted by silence of the invaded state in most instances but that there is still not a widely accepted norm that would lead to the conclusion that this is a lawful practice. The options, however, are limited if the harboring state does not respond immediately to diplomatic demands.

Fourth, may one state or a collection of states invade another for humanitarian reasons? This rationale was probably unheard of until the late twentieth century. It has been the focus of a number of legal debates regarding the NATO intrusion into Kosovo, the most significant of which was expression of serious doubts about the matter by the International Court of Justice. In justifying invasion of Iraq in 2003, the Bush Administration repeatedly referred to the "brutal dictatorship" of Saddam Hussein as a political justification to the American people but did not seem to be arguing for humanitarian intervention as a matter of legal justification.

Fifth, and finally for our purposes, may a state invade the territory of another in pursuit of terrorists? The justification for U.S. invasion of Afghanistan in 2002 was that Afghanistan was "harboring" persons involved in the 9/11 attacks. Indeed, the links between al Qaeda and the Taliban may have been sufficient to consider one to be the agent of the other. Earlier justifications for limited strikes by Israel and the U.S. may have been more in the nature of "reprisals" than defensive actions. Most of those strikes were sharply limited by "necessity and proportionality" but they also seemed to be designed to punish the offending state. The UN Security Council in Resolution 188 stated in 1964 that it condemned reprisals in general.

Perhaps the closest corollary in international custom has been the use of military force to root out piracy and slave trading centers in the eighteenth and nineteenth centuries. There are several examples in recent decades of the U.S.

government's seizing drug lords and bringing them to trial in this country. In the cases of a few individuals seized in Mexico and brought to the U.S. for trial, U.S. agents did not engage in an "armed attack" but the Mexican government objected to the perceived interference in its internal affairs. In the case of Manuel Noriega, we justified our actions by claiming that the prior government of Panama was the legitimate government and we were carrying out their wishes.

The International Court of Justice has decided a handful of cases regarding the justifications for military invasion of another country. We will read the two most significant and then discuss the extent to which they shed light on our questions.

CASE CONCERNING MILITARY AND PARAMILITARY ACTIVITIES IN AND AGAINST NICARAGUA (NICARAGUA v. UNITED STATES OF AMERICA)
1986 I.C.J. 14

International Court of Justice
June 27, 1986

[Nicaragua filed a petition with the ICJ regarding U.S. support of groups, known collectively as the Contras, who were engaged in violent conflict with the leftist government of Nicaragua. The source of the conflict was the ouster of the prior Samosa regime and its replacement by the leftist Sandinista regime in 1979. The U.S. initially was friendly to the new regime but eventually began to support the rebel forces from bases in Costa Rica, Honduras, and El Salvador. The U.S. objected to the jurisdiction of the ICJ on the ground that issues of the legality of an armed conflict were within the exclusive jurisdiction of the UN Security Council, but the court held that customary international law could also be a source of law. The U.S. did not participate in the proceedings after that decision. Ultimately, the court found that the U.S. was not sufficiently in control of the Contras to the point that the U.S. could be found responsible for the acts of the Contras. This issue of control of a guerilla force is important to understanding the opinions of the International Criminal Tribunals for Yugoslavia and Rwanda, which in turn become part of the international response to acts of terrorism.

[The U.S. support, however, was held to constitute interference in the internal affairs of Nicaragua in violation of international law, and the U.S. actions in mining harbors of Nicaragua was a direct act of aggression. The principal questions after that were whether the U.S. could claim a right to assist Costa Rica, Honduras, or El Salvador in their defense against border actions of Nicaragua, a claim that was also rejected by the court. The self-defense issues are relevant to the issue of armed intervention by the U.S. into Afghanistan and Iraq as part of a response to terrorism.]

110. [W]hether the United States Government at any stage devised the strategy and directed the tactics of the contras depends on the extent to which the United States made use of the potential for control inherent in [the dependence of the Contras on U.S. aid]. The Court already indicated that it has

insufficient evidence to reach a finding on this point. It is *a fortiori* unable to determine that the contra force may be equated for legal purposes with the forces of the United States. This conclusion, however, does not of course suffice to resolve the entire question of the responsibility incurred by the United States through its assistance to the contras.

116. The Court does not consider that the assistance given by the United States to the contras warrants the conclusion that these forces are subject to the United States to such an extent that any acts they have committed are imputable to that State. It takes the view that the contras remain responsible for their acts, and that the United States is not responsible for the acts of the contras, but for its own conduct *vis-á-vis* Nicaragua, including conduct related to the acts of the contras. What the Court has to investigate is not the complaints relating to alleged violations of humanitarian law by the contras, regarded by Nicaragua as imputable to the United States, but rather unlawful acts for which the United States may be responsible directly in connection with the activities of the contras. The lawfulness or otherwise of such acts of the United States is a question different from the violations of humanitarian law of which the contras may or may not have been guilty. It is for this reason that the Court does not have to determine whether the violations of humanitarian law attributed to the contras were in fact committed by them.

[The Court examined two manuals allegedly authored and distributed by the CIA to the Contras. One was admittedly a CIA document but was somewhat ambiguous about the extent to which it promoted tactics such as torture or murder of civilians. The Court found that it could have had that effect.]

[Customary Law of Justification for Armed Conflict]

183. [T]he Court has next to consider what are the rules of customary international law applicable to the present dispute. . . . In this respect the Court must not lose sight of the Charter of the United Nations and that of the Organization of American States, notwithstanding the operation of the multilateral treaty reservation. Although the Court has no jurisdiction to determine whether the conduct of the United States constitutes a breach of those conventions, it can and must take them into account in ascertaining the content of the customary international law which the United States is also alleged to have infringed.

191. As regards certain particular aspects of the principle in question, it will be necessary to distinguish the most grave forms of the use of force (those constituting an armed attack) from other less grave forms. In determining the legal rule which applies to these latter forms, the Court can again draw on the formulations contained in the Declaration on Principles of International Law concerning Friendly Relations and Co-operation among States in accordance with the Charter of the United Nations (General Assembly resolution 2625 (XXV)). As already observed, the adoption by States of this text affords an indication of their *opinio juris* as to customary international law on the question. Alongside certain descriptions which may refer to aggression, this text includes others which refer only to less grave forms of the use of force. In particular, according to this resolution:

Every State has the duty to refrain from the threat or use of force to violate the existing international boundaries of another State or as a means of solving international disputes, including territorial disputes and problems concerning frontiers of States.

States have a duty to refrain from acts of reprisal involving the use of force.

Every State has the duty to refrain from any forcible action which deprives peoples referred to in the elaboration of the principle of equal rights and self-determination of that right to self-determination and freedom and independence.

Every State has the duty to refrain from organizing or encouraging the organization of irregular forces or armed bands, including mercenaries, for incursion into the territory of another State.

Every State has the duty to refrain from organizing, instigating, assisting or participating in acts of civil strife or terrorist acts in another State or acquiescing in organized activities within its territory directed towards the commission of such acts, when the acts referred to in the present paragraph involve a threat or use of force.

192. Moreover, in the part of this same resolution devoted to the principle of non-intervention in matters within the national jurisdiction of States, a very similar rule is found:

Also, no State shall organize, assist, foment, finance, incite or tolerate subversive, terrorist or armed activities directed towards the violent overthrow of the regime of another State, or interfere in civil strife in another State.

211. The Court has recalled above (paragraphs 193 to 195) that for one State to use force against another, on the ground that that State has committed a wrongful act of force against a third State, is regarded as lawful, by way of exception, only when the wrongful act provoking the response was an armed attack. Thus the lawfulness of the use of force by a State in response to a wrongful act of which it has not itself been the victim is not admitted when this wrongful act is not an armed attack. In the view of the Court, under international law in force today – whether customary international law or that of the United Nations system – States do not have a right of 'collective' armed response to acts which do not constitute an 'armed attack'.

[Application of Law to Facts]

227. The Court will first appraise the facts in the light of the principle of the non-use of force. What is unlawful, in accordance with that principle, is recourse to either the threat or the use of force against the territorial integrity or political independence of any State. For the most part, the complaints by Nicaragua are of the actual use of force against it by the United States. Of the acts which the Court has found imputable to the Government of the United States, the following are relevant in this respect:

- the laying of mines in Nicaraguan internal or territorial waters in early 1984;
- certain attacks on Nicaraguan ports, oil installations and a naval base.

These activities constitute infringements of the principle of the prohibition of the use of force, defined earlier, unless they are justified by circumstances which exclude their unlawfulness, a question now to be examined.

228. As to the claim that United States activities in relation to the contras constitute a breach of the customary international law principle of the non-use of force, the Court finds that, subject to the question whether the action of the United States might be justified as an exercise of the right of self-defence, the United States has committed a prima facie violation of that principle by its assistance to the contras in Nicaragua, by 'organizing or encouraging the organization of irregular forces or armed bands . . . for incursion into the territory of another State', and 'participating in acts of civil strife . . . in another State', in the terms of General Assembly resolution 2625 (XXV). In the view of the Court, while the arming and training of the contras can certainly be said to involve the threat or use of force against Nicaragua, this is not necessarily so in respect of all the assistance given by the United States Government. In particular, the Court considers that the mere supply of funds to the contras, while undoubtedly an act of intervention in the internal affairs of Nicaragua, as will be explained below, does not in itself amount to a use of force.

229. The Court must thus consider whether, as the Respondent claims, the acts in question of the United States are justified by the exercise of its right of collective self-defence against an armed attack. For the Court to conclude that the United States was lawfully exercising its right of collective self-defence, it must first find that Nicaragua engaged in an armed attack against El Salvador, Honduras or Costa Rica.

230. As regards El Salvador, the Court has found that between July 1979 and the early months of 1981, an intermittent flow of arms was routed via the territory of Nicaragua to the armed opposition in that country. The Court was not however satisfied that assistance has reached the Salvadorian armed opposition, on a scale of any significance, since the early months of 1981, or that the Government of Nicaragua was responsible for any flow of arms at either period. Even assuming that the supply of arms to the opposition in El Salvador could be treated as imputable to the Government of Nicaragua, to justify invocation of the right of collective self-defence in customary international law, it would have to be equated with an armed attack by Nicaragua on El Salvador. As stated above, the Court is unable to consider that, in customary international law, the provision of arms to the opposition in another State constitutes an armed attack on that State. Even at a time when the arms flow was at its peak, and again assuming the participation of the Nicaraguan Government, that would not constitute such armed attack.

231. Turning to Honduras and Costa Rica, the Court has also stated that it should find established that certain transborder incursions into the territory of those two States, in 1982, 1983 and 1984, were imputable to the Government of Nicaragua. Very little information is however available to the Court as to the circumstances of these incursions or their possible motivations, which renders it difficult to decide whether they may be treated for legal purposes as

amounting, singly or collectively, to an 'armed attack' by Nicaragua on either or both States.

232. The exercise of the right of collective self-defence presupposes that an armed attack has occurred; and it is evident that it is the victim State, being the most directly aware of that fact, which is likely to draw general attention to its plight. It is also evident that if the victim State wishes another State to come to its help in the exercise of the right of collective self-defence, it will normally make an express request to that effect. Thus in the present instance, the Court is entitled to take account, in judging the asserted justification of the exercise of collective self-defence by the United States, of the actual conduct of El Salvador, Honduras and Costa Rica at the relevant time, as indicative of a belief by the State in question that it was the victim of an armed attack by Nicaragua, and of the making of a request by the victim State to the United States for help in the exercise of collective self-defence.

233. The Court has seen no evidence that the conduct of those States was consistent with such a situation, either at the time when the United States first embarked on the activities which were allegedly justified by self-defence, or indeed for a long period subsequently. So far as El Salvador is concerned, it appears to the Court that while El Salvador did in fact officially declare itself the victim of an armed attack, and did ask for the United States to exercise its right of collective self-defence, this occurred only on a date much later than the commencement of the United States activities which were allegedly justified by this request.

234. As to Honduras and Costa Rica, they also were prompted by the institution of proceedings in this case to address communications to the Court; in neither of these is there mention of armed attack or collective self-defence.

235. There is also an aspect of the conduct of the United States which the Court is entitled to take into account as indicative of the view of that State on the question of the existence of an armed attack. At no time, up to the present, has the United States Government addressed to the Security Council, in connection with the matters the subject of the present case, the report which is required by Article 51 of the United Nations Charter in respect of measures which a State believes itself bound to take when it exercises the right of individual or collective self-defence. This fact is all the more noteworthy because, in the Security Council, the United States has itself taken the view that failure to observe the requirement to make a report contradicted a State's claim to be acting on the basis of collective self-defence.

237. Since the Court has found that the condition *sine qua non* required for the exercise of the right of collective self-defence by the United States is not fulfilled in this case, the appraisal of the United States activities in relation to the criteria of necessity and proportionality takes on a different significance. As a result of this conclusion of the Court, even if the United States activities in question had been carried on in strict compliance with the canons of necessity and proportionality, they would not thereby become lawful. If however they were not, this may constitute an additional ground of wrongfulness.

241. It appears to the Court to be clearly established first, that the United States intended, by its support of the contras, to coerce the Government of Nicaragua in respect of matters in which each State is permitted, by the principle of State sovereignty, to decide freely; and secondly that the intention of the contras themselves was to overthrow the present Government of Nicaragua. The Court considers that in international law, if one State, with a view to the coercion of another State, supports and assists armed bands in that State whose purpose is to overthrow the government of that State, that amounts to an intervention by the one State in the internal affairs of the other, whether or not the political objective of the State giving such support and assistance is equally farreaching. It is for this reason that the Court has only examined the intentions of the United States Government so far as they bear on the question of self-defence.

242. The Court therefore finds that the support given by the United States, up to the end of September 1984, to the military and paramilitary activities of the contras in Nicaragua, by financial support, training, supply of weapons, intelligence and logistic support, constitutes a clear breach of the principle of non-intervention. The Court has however taken note that, with effect from the beginning of the United States governmental financial year 1985, namely 1 October 1984, the United States Congress has restricted the use of the funds appropriated for assistance to the contras to 'humanitarian assistance'. There can be no doubt that the provision of strictly humanitarian aid to persons or forces in another country, whatever their political affiliations or objectives, cannot be regarded as unlawful intervention, or as in any other way contrary to international law.

252. These violations cannot be justified either by collective self-defence, for which, as the Court has recognized, the necessary circumstances are lacking, nor by any right of the United States to take counter-measures involving the use of force in the event of intervention by Nicaragua in El Salvador, since no such right exists under the applicable international law. They cannot be justified by the activities in El Salvador attributed to the Government of Nicaragua. The latter activities, assuming that they did in fact occur, do not bring into effect any right belonging to the United States which would justify the actions in question. Accordingly, such actions constitute violations of Nicaragua's sovereignty under customary international law.

256. It is also appropriate to recall the circumstances in which the manual of psychological operations was issued. When considering whether the publication of such a manual, encouraging the commission of acts contrary to general principles of humanitarian law, is unlawful, it is material to consider whether that encouragement was offered to persons in circumstances where the commission of such acts was likely or foreseeable. The Court has however found that at the relevant time those responsible for the issue of the manual were aware of, at the least, allegations that the behaviour of the contras in the field was not consistent with humanitarian law; it was in fact even claimed by the CIA that the purpose of the manual was to 'moderate' such behaviour. The publication and dissemination of a manual in fact containing the advice quoted above must therefore be regarded as an encouragement, which was likely to be

effective, to commit acts contrary to general principles of international humanitarian law reflected in treaties.

DISSENTING OPINION OF JUDGE SCHWEBEL

1. To say that I dissent from the Court's Judgment is to understate the depth of my differences with it. I agree with the Court's finding that the United States, by failing to make known the existence and location of the mines laid by it, acted in violation of customary international law (in relation to the shipping of third States); I agree that the CIA's causing publication of a manual advocating acts in violation of the law of war is indefensible; and I agree with some other elements of the Judgment as well. Nevertheless, in my view the Judgment misperceives and misconstrues essential facts – not so much the facts concerning the actions of the United States of which Nicaragua complains as the facts concerning the actions of Nicaragua of which the United States complains. It misconceives and misapplies the law – not in all respects, on some of which the whole Court is agreed, but in paramount respects: particularly in its interpretation of what is an 'armed attack' within the meaning of the United Nations Charter and customary international law; in its appearing to justify foreign intervention in furtherance of 'the process of decolonization'; and in nearly all of its holdings as to which Party to this case has acted in violation of its international responsibilities and which, because it has acted defensively, has not. And, I am profoundly pained to say, I dissent from this Judgment because I believe that, in effect, it adopts the false testimony of representatives of the Government of the Republic of Nicaragua on a matter which, in my view, is essential to the disposition of this case and which, on any view, is material to its disposition. The effect of the Court's treatment of that false testimony upon the validity of the Judgment is a question which only others can decide.

2. These are uncommonly critical words in a Court which rightly enjoys very great respect. Coming as they do from a Judge who is a national of a Party to the case, I am conscious of the fact that this opinion accordingly is long, not only for that reason but because the differences between the Court's views and mine turn particularly on the facts.

7. While United States pressure upon Nicaragua is essentially lawful, nevertheless questions about the legality of aspects of United States conduct remain. In my view, the fundamental question is this. Granting that the United States can join El Salvador in measures of collective self-defence (even if, contrary to Article 51 of the United Nations Charter, they were not reported to the United Nations Security Council, as, by their nature, covert defensive measures will not be), those measures must be necessary, and proportionate to the delicts – the actions tantamount to armed attack – of Nicaragua. And they must in their nature be fundamentally measures of self-defence.

8. By these standards, the unannounced mining by the United States of Nicaraguan ports was a violation of international law. That mining could affect and did affect third States as against whom no rationale of self-defence could apply in these circumstances. As against Nicaragua, however, the mining was no less lawful than other measures of pressure.

9. Are United States support of the contras and direct United States assaults on Nicaraguan oil tanks, ports and pipelines, as well as other measures such as intelligence overflights, military and naval manoeuvres, and a trade embargo, unnecessary and disproportionate acts of self-defence? I do not believe so. Their necessity is, or arguably is, indicated by recurrent, persistent Nicaraguan failure to cease armed subversion of El Salvador. To the extent that proportionality of defensive measures is required, in their nature, far from being disproportionate to the acts against which they are a defence, the actions of the United States are strikingly proportionate. The Salvadoran rebels, vitally supported by Nicaragua, conduct a rebellion in El Salvador; in collective self-defence, the United States symmetrically supports rebels who conduct a rebellion in Nicaragua. The rebels in El Salvador pervasively attack economic targets of importance in El Salvador; the United States selectively attacks economic targets of military importance, such as ports and oil stocks, in Nicaragua. Even if it be accepted, arguendo, that the current object of United States policy is to overthrow the Nicaraguan Government – and that is by no means established – that is not necessarily disproportionate to the obvious object of Nicaragua in supporting the Salvadoran rebels who seek overthrow of the Government of El Salvador. To say, as did Nicaraguan counsel, that action designed to overthrow a government cannot be defensive, is evident error, which would have come as a surprise to Roosevelt and Churchill (and Stalin), who insisted on the unconditional surrender of the Axis Powers.

NOTES AND QUESTIONS

1. The ICJ announced on Sept. 26, 1991, that Nicaragua had chosen to "discontinue" the proceedings. "The Sandinista regime and the Contras successfully concluded direct negotiations on a cease-fire in meetings held at Sapoá, Nicaragua, during June 1988. In February 1989, the five Central American presidents met once again in Costa del Sol, El Salvador, and agreed on a plan to support the disarming and dissolving of Contra forces in Honduras, as well as their voluntary repatriation into Nicaragua." Library of Congress, Country Studies, Nicaragua, *http://countrystudies.us/nicaragua/18.htm*.

2. One critical feature of the *Nicaragua* opinion is its holding that "the supply of arms and other support to [opposition] bands cannot be equated with armed attack." The concurring opinion of Judge Ruda elaborated further:

I fully agree with this statement and others made by the Court in the same sense. It does not mean, however, that assistance to rebels in another country could not be considered illegal under other rules of international law, such as the obligation not to intervene in the internal affairs of another State and to refrain in international relations from the threat or use of force.

3. The reasons for considering international law of armed conflict and international humanitarian law as part of the law of terrorism become more clear as the law develops through these international courts. Common Article 3 of the Geneva Conventions of 1949 is described in the *Nicaragua* opinion as setting out minimum standards of humanitarian law applying to armed conflicts of both international and non-international character. This provision became a focal point for the question of whether international law could be applied to authorize criminal punishment for some of the gross abuses occurring in the former Yugoslavia and Rwanda in the early 1990s. Because much of the behavior in those situations fits some of the classic definitions of "terrorism," the use of Common Article 3 as a source of criminal law may become important in a number of situations. Therefore, we will consider it more thoroughly in the context of the International Criminal Tribunals for Yugoslavia and Rwanda.

4. In November 1979, the United States filed a petition in the ICJ against Iran for allowing the seizure and continued detention of hostages from the U.S. Embassy in Tehran. On May 24, 1980, the ICJ issued its opinion holding that, even if the Government of Iran were not responsible for the initial seizure of the embassy and its personnel, it had an obligation under various international multilateral conventions on the protection of diplomatic and consular personnel to secure the release of those held hostage and to return control of the premises to the U.S. *http://www.icj-cij.org/icjwww/icases/iusir/iusir_ijudgment /iusir_iJudgment_19800524.pdf.* The U.S. exerted pressure on Iran by freezing assets of Iran held in the U.S., such as billions of dollars in U.S. financial institutions. Release of the hostages was finally secured on the last day of President Carter's administration through a complicated Executive Agreement that was the subject of domestic litigation in *Dames & Moore v. Regan*, 453 U.S. 654 (1981). There could be an apparent inconsistency in the U.S. position in the *Iran* and *Nicaragua* cases regarding the ICJ jurisdiction to interpret and enforce multilateral treaties. But the Iranian situation did not involve an ongoing state of armed conflict. Does this make ICJ jurisdiction dependent on whether the parties decide to resort to armed force to resolve their disputes?

5. Many of the violence-prone religious-cultural groups in the Third Millennium are formed around religious fundamentalism. Few of these groups have a motivation to control any particular territory, although driving all Westerners from Muslim lands could be counted as a political objective. Does lack of a motivation to control certain territory make these groups something other than "terrorist" in character? What is the point of a political motivation for our study?

6. As the ICJ indicates, although international conventions state commitments to peace and nonintervention, details of the Law of War are not found so much in explicit codes as in the writings of commentators. For some explications in recent times, see the "Additional Readings" at the end of this chapter.

CASE CONCERNING LEGALITY OF USE OF FORCE (YUGOSLAVIA v. BELGIUM) [NATO]
1999 I.C.J. 124

[Identical petitions were filed by Yugoslavia against each of the member nations of NATO. Yugoslavia made a "request for provisional measures," which is the rough equivalent of a motion for preliminary injunction.]

1. Whereas Yugoslavia defines the subject of the dispute as follows:

"The subject-matter of the dispute are acts of the Kingdom of Belgium by which it has violated its international obligation banning the use of force against another State, the obligation not to intervene in the internal affairs of another State, the obligation not to violate the sovereignty of another State, the obligation to protect the civilian population and civilian objects in wartime, the obligation to protect the environment, the obligation relating to free navigation on international rivers, the obligation regarding fundamental human rights and freedoms, the obligation not to use prohibited weapons, the obligation not to deliberately inflict conditions of life calculated to cause the physical destruction of a national group";

3. Whereas Yugoslavia states that the claims submitted by it to the Court are based upon the following facts:

The Government of the Kingdom of Belgium, together with the Governments of other Member States of NATO, took part in the acts of use of force against the Federal Republic of Yugoslavia by taking part in bombing targets in the Federal Republic of Yugoslavia. In bombing the Federal Republic of Yugoslavia military and civilian targets were attacked. Great number of people were killed, including a great many civilians. Residential houses came under attack. Numerous dwellings were destroyed. Enormous damage was caused to schools, hospitals, radio and television stations, cultural and health institutions and to places of worship. A large number of bridges, roads and railway lines were destroyed. Attacks on oil refineries and chemical plants have had serious environmental effects on cities, towns and villages in the Federal Republic of Yugoslavia. The use of weapons containing depleted uranium is having far-reaching consequences for human life. The above-mentioned acts are deliberately creating conditions calculated at the physical destruction of an ethnic group, in whole or in part. The Government of the Kingdom of Belgium is taking part in the training, arming, financing, equipping and supplying the so-called 'Kosovo Liberation Army'.

6. Whereas, in support of its request for the indication of provisional measures, Yugoslavia contends inter alia that, since the onset of the bombing of its territory, and as a result thereof, about 1,000 civilians, including 19 children, have been killed and more than 4,500 have sustained serious injuries; that the lives of three million children are endangered; that hundreds of thousands of citizens have been exposed to poisonous gases; that about one million citizens are short of water supply; that about 500,000 workers have become jobless; that two million citizens have no means of livelihood and are unable to ensure minimum means of sustenance; and that the road and railway network has suffered extensive destruction.

16. Whereas the Court is deeply concerned with the human tragedy, the loss of life, and the enormous suffering in Kosovo which form the background of the present dispute, and with the continuing loss of life and human suffering in all parts of Yugoslavia;

17. Whereas the Court is profoundly concerned with the use of force in Yugoslavia; whereas under the present circumstances such use raises very serious issues of international law;

18. Whereas the Court is mindful of the purposes and principles of the United Nations Charter and of its own responsibilities in the maintenance of peace and security under the Charter and the Statute of the Court;

19. Whereas the Court deems it necessary to emphasize that all parties appearing before it must act in conformity with their obligations under the United Nations Charter and other rules of international law, including humanitarian law;

48. Whereas, whether or not States accept the jurisdiction of the Court, they remain in any event responsible for acts attributable to them that violate international law, including humanitarian law; whereas any disputes relating to the legality of such acts are required to be resolved by peaceful means, the choice of which, pursuant to Article 33 of the Charter, is left to the parties;

49. Whereas in this context the parties should take care not to aggravate or extend the dispute;

50. Whereas, when such a dispute gives rise to a threat to the peace, breach of the peace or act of aggression, the Security Council has special responsibilities under Chapter VII of the Charter;

51. For these reasons,

THE COURT,

(1) By twelve votes to four,

Rejects the request for the indication of provisional measures submitted by the Federal Republic of Yugoslavia on 29 April 1999;

(2) By fifteen votes to one,

Reserves the subsequent procedure for further decision.

NOTES AND QUESTIONS

1. On December 15, 2004, the ICJ dismissed the various actions challenging the use of force by NATO nations in the Yugoslav conflict. It found that Serbia and Montenegro did not exist between 1992 and 2000, when they were admitted to the UN as a separate nation under the name of Yugoslavia. Therefore, there was no state party to appear before the court with regard to the time at which the armed intervention occurred. To Professor Eric Posner, this decision

> demonstrated just how incapable the court is of resolving disputes, and what little hope the new International Criminal Court has to do much better. First, there is no doubt that, in strictly legal terms, NATO's intervention violated international standards. . . . [T]he court was in an unenviable position: if it had held against the NATO states, they would surely have ignored the judgment. By holding in favor of these states, the court showed its irrelevance.

Eric A. Posner, *All Justice, Too, Is Local*, NY TIMES (Dec. 30, 2004).

2. The ICJ statement that it was "profoundly concerned with the use of force in Yugoslavia; whereas under the present circumstances such use raises very serious issues of international law" has become a focal point for debate over the propriety of humanitarian intervention without Security Council authorization. The "serious issues" included whether NATO could act without UN sanction. In fact, the European nations came under heavy criticism for delaying action while they engaged in a long debate over whether to intervene in the bloodshed and "ethnic cleansing" taking place in the republics of the former Yugoslavia. There was very little thought given at the time to seeking Security Council intervention, at least partly because it was not clear that the attempts of these republics to break away from Yugoslavia created an "international" dispute rather than a civil war (i.e., an armed conflict not of an international character).

3. Arguments over the validity of NATO's bombing campaign also were pursued through the forum of the International Criminal Tribunal for Yugoslavia (ICTY) established by the UN Security Council. The work of the ICTY will be considered in the next section. For now, it is enough to know that the Tribunal has criminal jurisdiction over war crimes committed during the conflict. To assess the assertion that the NATO bombing was illegal both in its inception and in its targeting decisions, the Prosecutor appointed a committee to review the available evidence. The Committee report included this statement regarding the legality of the bombing in its inception:

> Allegations have been made that, as NATO's resort to force was not authorized by the Security Council or in self-defence, that the resort to force was illegal and, consequently, all forceful measures taken by NATO were unlawful. These allegations justify a brief discussion of the *jus ad bellum*. In brief, the *jus ad bellum* regulates when states may use force and is, for the most part, enshrined in the UN Charter. In general, states may use force in self defence (individual or collective) and for very few other purposes. In particular, the legitimacy of the presumed basis for the NATO bombing campaign, humanitarian intervention without prior Security Council authorization, is hotly debated. That being said, . . . the crime related to an unlawful decision to use force is the crime against peace or aggression. While a person convicted of a crime against peace may, potentially, be held criminally responsible for all of the activities causing death, injury or destruction during a conflict, the ICTY does not have jurisdiction over crimes against peace.

> The *jus in bello* regulates how states may use force. The ICTY has jurisdiction over serious violations of international humanitarian law as specified in Articles 2-5 of the Statute. These are *jus in bello* offences.

> The precise linkage between *jus ad bellum* and *jus in bello* is not completely resolved. There were suggestions by the prosecution before the International Military Tribunal at Nuremberg and in some other post World War II war crimes cases that all of the killing and destruction caused by German forces were war crimes because the Germans were conducting an aggressive war. The courts were unreceptive to these arguments.

www.un.org/icty/pressreal/nato061300.htm at ¶ 30-32.

4. In early 2005, a similar dispute is raging over the responsibility of other nations or the United Nations to act in the "internal" bloodbath occurring in Darfur in the Sudan. European nations and the U.S. have condemned the Sudanese government for massive human rights violations, either actively or passively allowing unofficial groups to massacre civilians. From the UN perspective, one question is whether the situation amounts to a threat to "international peace and security" and another is whether it would be in the long-term interests of the world community to promote regional solutions to problems of this type. At this time, the African Union is taking the lead on attempting to promote ceasefire and humanitarian aid to the region. An excellent summary of the situation is provided by Human Rights Watch at *http://www.hrw.org/reports/2004/sudan0504/8.htm#_Toc71531715*

5. *Afghanistan.* Shortly after 9/11, U.S. intelligence agencies identified al Qaeda as the perpetrator of the incidents and identified the Taliban regime in Afghanistan as harboring and fostering the operations of the organization. The U.S. Congress adopted this resolution:

> That the President is authorized to use all necessary and appropriate force against those nations, organizations, or persons he determines planned, authorized, committed, or aided the terrorist attacks that occurred on September 11, 2001, or harbored such organizations or persons, in order to prevent any future acts of international terrorism against the United States by such nations, organizations or persons.

PUB. LAW 107-40 [S.J. Res. 23] (Sept. 18, 2001).

The resolution was widely understood at the time to refer primarily to Afghanistan although, only one week after the incidents, it was not entirely clear which countries could be found to have been involved. In passing this resolution, Congress declined to act on this proposed language: "Congress hereby declares that a state of war exists between the United States of America and any entity determined by the President to have planned, carried out, or otherwise supported the attacks against the United States on September 11, 2001."

There are two theories under which the U.S. invaded Afghanistan. One is that Afghanistan "harbored" terrorists to the extent that the terrorists became essentially the agents of that government, thus moving from the class of mere criminal to agents of war. Because those agents violated the rules of war by taking aggression, by striking civilian targets, and by blending back into civilian populations, other nations were justified in using military force to retaliate and prevent further attack.

The second theory harkens back to the piracy and slave trading of the eighteenth and nineteenth Centuries. "From the Halls to Montezuma to the shores of Tripoli" salutes the actions of Marines who rooted out pirate strongholds located in other nations. Other nations of the world were never called on to decide whether our actions were legitimate. Similarly, the European-American nations were in disarray over whether it was legitimate to strike militarily against slave depots and slave trading ships within the boundaries of other nations. Suffice to say that time and history are on the side of the victors in those cases. Today there is near, but not complete, consensus that it is permissible to make "surgical" incursions into another country to root out a pirate or slave trader to an extent that would not be permissible with a "mere" criminal.

There has been virtually no dissent from the proposition that the U.S. was within its rights under international law to invade Afghanistan for the purpose of disrupting the activities of al Qaeda. Afghanistan had refused to turn over those responsible for what could be considered an "armed attack" on the U.S., an obligation that would exist regardless of whether those persons could be considered agents of the government of Afghanistan. In the process, the invasion went further by toppling the Taliban regime and installing a new regime friendly to the West. Is "overthrow of the government" of another nation illegal in the absence of finding that that government had engaged in an "armed attack" against the U.S.? Recall the ICJ's statement that funding and support of an armed band is not itself an armed attack.

In this regard, also bear in mind the political and cultural fallout of the widespread characterization of the Taliban regime as brutal and despotic (women in particular were brutalized under its power). For those who applaud the humanitarian response of bringing some degree of liberty to Afghanistan, there are others who view the U.S. intrusion as part of an ongoing "Crusade" against Islam.

6. *Iraq.* By contrast to Afghanistan, the U.S. invasion of Iraq has brought widespread criticism. *See* Arthur Schlesinger, Jr., *The Making of a Mess*, 51 NY REVIEW OF BOOKS (Sept 23, 2004), *reviewing* JAMES MANN, RISE OF THE VULCANS: THE HISTORY OF BUSH'S WAR CABINET (2004) *and* JAMES BAMFORD, A PRETEXT FOR WAR: 9/11, IRAQ, AND THE ABUSE OF AMERICA'S INTELLIGENCE NETWORKS (2004).

The initial arguments for the invasion were (1) humanitarian intervention, on the basis that the Saddam Hussein regime was a brutal dictatorship committing multiple crimes against its own people, (2) self-defense, on the basis that Iraq was harboring elements of al Qaeda engaged in an ongoing campaign against western nations, and (3) preemptive self-defense, on the basis that Iraq was attempting to acquire weapons of mass destruction (WMD) and would allow them to be used against the U.S.

As events unfolded, it became apparent that the WMD justification was based on faulty intelligence. The al Qaeda connection also proved to be unlikely. It is likely that prior to the invasion, Osama bin Laden had some degree of hostility toward Saddam Hussein along with other "secular" Arab leaders, but Iraq had harbored Abu Musab al-Zarqawi who had been sentenced to death by Jordan for various terrorist activities. Zarqawi may or may not have had links to bin Laden prior to the invasion, and intelligence sources differed on whether he was an associate of or a rival to bin Laden. After the invasion, elements of groups linked to al Qaeda, particularly Zarqawi and his associates, concentrated in Iraq and become principals in some of the insurgent resistance. Zarqawi has subsequently declared himself to be in alliance with al Qaeda.

The third justification, humanitarian intervention, seems forbidden in the absence of at least multilateral action of the NATO-Yugoslavia variety or more formal UN Security Council action. The official U.S. position became difficult to discern in the partisan politics of the 2004 presidential campaign. The Bush campaign combined humanitarian intervention with the preemptive self-defense rationale and made an argument for "exporting democracy." The Kerry campaign promoted the view that armed force, outside of imminent self-defense, should be employed only if it passed a "global test."

Although doubts about the legality of the Iraq invasion persist in both the academic and popular press, a widespread acceptance seems to be emerging from a number of sources, both Government and NGO, that the international community should have some role to play in bringing freedom and democracy to oppressed peoples. *See* NOAH FELDMAN, AFTER JIHAD (2003). Whether this rhetoric could develop into a full-blown justification for armed intervention in the affairs of another nation will have to await further developments.

Finally, a number of critics have argued that one effect of the Iraq invasion was to reduce the resources applied to the effort to apprehend Osama bin Laden. *See* James Fallows, *Bush's Lost Year*, ATLANTIC MONTHLY 68 (Oct. 2004); Peter Bergen, *The Long Hunt for Osama*, ATLANTIC MONTHLY 88 (Oct. 2004).

§ 3.02 DEVELOPING INTERNATIONAL CRIMINAL LAW

International action to control violence comes in two forms. One is cooperation among states, traditionally consisting of extradition of alleged offenders by one state for trial in another, and in recent years emerging as codified agreements to cooperate in the detection, apprehension, and prosecution of offenders. The other, and much more recent, phenomenon is collective action in the form of supranational tribunals.

We will look at these in reverse order, however, to form a more logical progression leading toward both international and American law related to terrorism. One outgrowth of prosecution of war crimes at the end of World War II has been international tribunals for atrocities in "internal" conflicts that yield a number of legal principles regarding criminal responsibility for attacks on civilian populations. These developments parallel the establishment of an International Criminal Court. If there develops an international crime of terrorism, which could evolve from the crimes of humanitarian law, then a number of implications would follow from the traditional approaches that include extradition of offenders. Some of this possibility is hinted in the *Pinochet* case at the end of this chapter.

American students may find familiar themes in trial of an offender under state law compared with definition and prosecution of crimes by the federal government. If you think that Utah is to the U.S. as the U.S. is to international bodies, then some of the lessons of American federalism can be transported to the international scene. Of course, some significant differences make the analogy far less than perfect.

Starting with Nuremberg, the international community began to impose individual criminal sanctions for serious violations of the law of war, genocide, and crimes against humanity. The first effort of this type under United Nations auspices was establishment of the International Criminal Tribunal for the Former Yugoslavia in 1993, followed closely by the International Criminal Tribunal for Rwanda in 1994. The UN, working through its International Law Commission, promulgated a convention to create a permanent international tribunal for prosecution of crimes against the law of war, genocide, and crimes against humanity, now known as the International Criminal Court (ICC).

[A] WORLD WAR II "WAR CRIMES" TRIBUNALS

We start our reading with the Judgment of the International Military Tribunal created for the purpose of trying Nazi war criminals by the victorious parties after World War II. The Charter of the IMT was adopted through the Treaty of London as a project of the four victorious powers (U.S., Britain, France, USSR). It lists three categories of crimes: crimes against peace (aggression), war crimes, and crimes against humanity. The IMT conducted one trial, known generally as the Trial of Major War Criminals. In addition to the trial of major leaders, the four occupying forces adopted Control Council Law No. 10, which repeated the definition of crimes and authorized each military authority to conduct trials of lower-level Nazi officals. Under this order, the U.S. conducted 12 additional trials in Germany.

Excerpts from the Major War Crimes Trial appear below. On the assumption that you are familiar with the atrocities of the Nazi regime, the excerpts omit recitation of the atrocities themselves and the specific evidence with respect to each defendant. Twenty-two persons were indicted and tried by the tribunal (two more were indicted but not tried, one committed suicide and the other was too frail). Twelve were sentenced to death, three to life imprisonment, four to prison ranging from 10 to 20 years, and three were acquitted. Ten of the twelve sentenced to death were hanged on October 16, 1946. (Hermann Göring committed suicide just three hours before the hanging. Martin Bormann was tried in absentia and sentenced to death but it was later discovered that he had died.) Rudolf Hess was the controversial deputy to Hitler who flew to England in 1941, ostensibly to negotiate a peace without Hitler's approval; he was sentenced to life in prison and for decades was the only inmate of Spandau Prison in Berlin until his death at the age of 93 in 1987. The three persons acquitted at Nuremberg were sentenced by other courts to work camps. Conversely, Alfred Jodl was hanged but posthumously found by a German court to be not guilty of violating international law.

INTERNATIONAL MILITARY TRIBUNAL (NUREMBERG)

Nuremberg, 30th September and 1st October, 1946

THE PRESIDENT: The judgment of the International Military Tribunal will now be read. I shall not read the title and the formal parts.

JUDGMENT

On the 8th August, 1945, the Government of the United Kingdom of Great Britain and Northern Ireland, the Government of the United States of America, the Provisional Government of the French Republic, and the Government of the

Union of Soviet Socialist Republics entered into an Agreement establishing this Tribunal for the trial of War Criminals whose offences have no particular geographical location.

The Tribunal was invested with power to try and punish persons who had committed crimes against peace, war crimes and crimes against humanity as defined in the Charter

This Indictment charges the defendants with crimes against peace by the planning, preparation, initiation and waging of wars of aggression, which were also wars in violation of international treaties, agreements and assurances: with war crimes: and with crimes against humanity. The defendants are also charged with participating in the formulation or execution of a common plan or conspiracy to commit all these crimes. The Tribunal was further asked by the Prosecution to declare all the named groups or organisations to be criminal within the meaning of the Charter.

On the 17th November, 1945, the Tribunal decided to try the defendant Bormann in his absence under the provisions of Article 12 of the Charter. After argument, and consideration of full medical reports, and a statement from the defendant himself, the Tribunal decided on the 1st December, 1945, that no grounds existed for a postponement of the trial against the defendant Hess because of his mental condition. A similar decision was made in the case of the defendant Streicher.

The Trial [lasted 9 months and involved dozens of witnesses and thousands of documents].

Much of the evidence presented to the Tribunal on behalf of the Prosecution was documentary evidence, captured by the Allied armies in German army headquarters, Government buildings, and elsewhere. Some of the documents were found in salt mines, buried in the ground, hidden behind false walls and in other places thought to be secure from discovery. The case, therefore, against the defendants rests in a large measure on documents of their own making, the authenticity of which has not been challenged except in one or two cases.

Law of the Charter

The making of the Charter was the exercise of the sovereign legislative power by the countries to which the German Reich unconditionally surrendered; and the undoubted right of these countries to legislate for the occupied territories has been recognised by the civilised world. The Charter is not an arbitrary exercise of power on the part of the victorious nations, but in the view of the Tribunal, as will be shown, it is the expression of international law existing at the time of its creation; and to that extent is itself a contribution to international law.

The Signatory Powers created this Tribunal, defined the law it was to administer, and made regulations for the proper conduct of the Trial. In doing so, they have done together what any one of them might have done singly; for it is not to be doubted that any nation has the right thus to set up special courts to administer law. With regard to the constitution of the court, all that the defendants are entitled to ask is to receive a fair trial on the facts and law.

The Charter makes the planning or waging of a war of aggression or a war in violation of international treaties a crime, and it is therefore not strictly necessary to consider whether and to what extent aggressive war was a crime before the execution of the London Agreement. But in view of the great importance of the questions of law involved, the Tribunal has heard full argument from the Prosecution and the Defence, and will express its view on the matter.

It was urged on behalf of the defendants that a fundamental principle of all law – international and domestic – is that there can be no punishment of crime without a pre-existing law. "*Nullum crimen sine lege. Nulla poena sine lege.*" It was submitted that ex post facto punishment is abhorrent to the law of all civilised nations, that no sovereign power had made aggressive war a crime at the time the alleged criminal acts were committed, that no statute had defined aggressive war, that no penalty had been fixed for its commission, and no court had been created to try and punish offenders.

In the first place, it is to be observed that the maxim *nullum crimen sine lege* is not a limitation of sovereignty, but is in general a principle of justice. To assert that it is unjust to punish those who in defiance of treaties and assurances have attacked neighbouring states without warning is obviously untrue, for in such circumstances the attacker must know that he is doing wrong, and so far from it being unjust to punish him, it would be unjust if his wrong were allowed to go unpunished.

This view is strongly reinforced by a consideration of the state of international law in 1939, so far as aggressive war is concerned. The General Treaty for the Renunciation of War of 27th August, 1928, more generally known as the Pact of Paris or the Kellogg-Briand Pact, was binding on sixty-three nations, including Germany, Italy and Japan at the outbreak of war in 1939. The first two Articles are as follows:

> Article I: The High Contracting Parties solemnly declare in the names of their respective peoples that they condemn recourse to war for the solution of international controversies and renounce it as an instrument of national policy in their relations to one another.

> Article II: The High Contracting Parties agree that the settlement or solution of all disputes or conflicts of whatever nature or of whatever origin they may be, which may arise among them, shall never be sought except by pacific means.

The question is, what was the legal effect of this Pact? The nations who signed the Pact or adhered to it unconditionally condemned recourse to war for the future as an instrument of policy, and expressly renounced it. In the opinion of the Tribunal, the solemn renunciation of war as an instrument of national policy necessarily involves the proposition that such a war is illegal in international law; and that those who plan and wage such a war, with its inevitable and terrible consequences, are committing a crime in so doing.

But it is argued that the Pact does not expressly enact that such wars are crimes, or set up courts to try those who make such wars. To that extent the same is true with regard to the laws of war contained in the Hague Convention.

The Hague Convention of 1907 prohibited resort to certain methods of waging war. These included the inhumane treatment of prisoners, the employment of poisoned weapons, the improper use of flags of truce, and similar matters. Many of these prohibitions had been enforced long before the date of the Convention; but since 1907 they have certainly been crimes, punishable as offences against the laws of war; yet the Hague Convention nowhere designates such practices as criminal, nor is any sentence prescribed, nor any mention made of a court to try and punish offenders. For many years past, however, military tribunals have tried and punished individuals guilty of violating the rules of land warfare laid down by this Convention. In the opinion of the Tribunal, those who wage aggressive war are doing that which is equally illegal, and of much greater moment than a breach of one of the rules of the Hague Convention. In interpreting the words of the Pact, it must be remembered that international law is not the product of an international legislature, and that such international agreements as the Pact have to deal with general principles of law, and not with administrative matters of procedure. The law of war is to be found not only in treaties, but in the customs and practices of states which gradually obtained universal recognition, and from the general principles of justice applied by jurists and practiced by military courts. This law is not static, but by continual adaptation follows the needs of a changing world. Indeed, in many cases treaties do no more than express and define for more accurate reference the principles of law already existing.

The view which the Tribunal takes of the true interpretation of the Pact is supported by the international history which preceded it. In the year 1923 the draft of a Treaty of Mutual Assistance was sponsored by the League of Nations. In Article I the Treaty declared " that aggressive war is an international crime," and that the parties would "undertake that no one of them will be guilty of its commission." The draft treaty was submitted to twenty-nine States, about half of whom were in favour of accepting the text. The principal objection appeared to be in the difficulty of defining the acts which would constitute " aggression," rather than any doubt as to the criminality of aggressive war.

At the meeting of the Assembly of the League of Nations on the 24th September, 1927, all the delegations then present (including the German, the Italian and the Japanese), unanimously adopted a declaration concerning wars of aggression. The preamble to the declaration stated:

> The Assembly:
>
> Recognising the solidity which unites the community of nations;
>
> Being inspired by a firm desire for the maintenance of general peace;
>
> Being convinced that a war of aggression can never serve as a means of settling international disputes, and is in consequence an international crime.

All these expressions of opinion, and others that could be cited, so solemnly made, reinforce the construction which the Tribunal placed upon the Pact of Paris, that resort to a war of aggression is not merely illegal, but is criminal. The prohibition of aggressive war demanded by the conscience of the world, finds its expression in the series of pacts and treaties to which the Tribunal has just referred.

It is also important to remember that Article 227 of the Treaty of Versailles provided for the constitution of a special Tribunal, composed of representatives of five of the Allied and Associated Powers which had been belligerents in the first World War opposed to Germany, to try the former German Emperor "for a supreme offence against international morality and the sanctity of treaties." The purpose of this trial was expressed to be "to vindicate the solemn obligations of international undertakings, and the validity of international morality." In Article 228 of the Treaty, the German Government expressly recognised the right of the Allied Powers "to bring before military tribunals persons accused of having committed acts in violation of the laws and customs of war."

It was submitted that international law is concerned with the action of sovereign States, and provides no punishment for individuals; and further, that where the act in question is an act of state, those who carry it out are not personally responsible, but are protected by the doctrine of the sovereignty of the State. In the opinion of the Tribunal, both these submissions must be rejected. That international law imposes duties and liabilities upon individuals as well as upon States has long been recognised. In the recent case of *Ex Parte Quirin* (1942 317 U.S. 1), before the Supreme Court of the United States persons were charged during the war with landing in the United States for purposes of spying and sabotage. The late Justice Stone, speaking for the Court, said:

> From the very beginning of its history this Court has applied the law of war as including that part of the law of nations which prescribes for the conduct of war the status, rights and duties of enemy nations as well as enemy individuals.

It was also submitted on behalf of most of these defendants that in doing what they did they were acting under the orders of Hitler, and therefore cannot be held responsible for the acts committed by them in carrying out these orders. The Charter specially provides in Article 8:

> The fact that the defendant acted pursuant to order of his Government or of a superior shall not free him from responsibility, but may the considered in mitigation of punishment.

The provisions of this Article are in conformity with the law of all nations. That a soldier was ordered to kill or torture in violation of the international law of war has never been recognised as a defence to such acts of brutality, though, as the Charter here provides, the order may be urged in mitigation of the punishment. The true test, which is found in varying degrees in the criminal law of most nations, is not the existence of the order, but whether moral choice was in fact possible.

Law as to the Common Plan or Conspiracy

In the previous recital of the facts relating to aggressive war, it is clear that planning and preparation had been carried out in the most systematic way at every stage of the history.

Planning and preparation are essential to the making of war. In the opinion of the Tribunal aggressive war is a crime under international law. The Charter defines this offence as planning, preparation, initiation or waging of a war of aggression "or participation in a common plan or conspiracy for the accomplishment . . . of the foregoing." The Indictment follows this distinction. Count One charges the common plan or conspiracy. Count Two charges the planning and waging of war. The same evidence has been introduced to support both counts. We shall therefore discuss both counts together, as they are in substance the same. The defendants have been charged under both counts, and their guilt under each count must be determined.

The "common plan or conspiracy" charged in the Indictment covers twenty-five years, from the formation of the Nazi party in 1919 to the end of the war in 1945. The party is spoken of as "the instrument of cohesion among the defendants" for carrying out the purposes of the conspiracy the overthrowing of the Treaty of Versailles, acquiring territory lost by Germany in the last war and "lebensraum" in Europe, by the use, if necessary, of armed force, of aggressive war. The seizure of power by the Nazis, the use of terror, the destruction of trade unions, the attack on Christian teaching and on churches, the persecution of the Jews, the regimentation of youth – all these are said to be steps deliberately taken to carry out the common plan. It found expression, so it is alleged, in secret rearmament, the withdrawal by Germany from the Disarmament Conference and the League of Nations, universal military service, and seizure of the Rhineland. Finally, according to the Indictment, aggressive action was planned and carried out against Austria and Czechoslovakia in 1936-1938, followed by the planning and waging of war against Poland; and, successively, against ten other countries.

The Prosecution says, in effect, that any significant participation in the affairs of the Nazi Party or Government is evidence of a participation in a conspiracy that is in itself criminal. Conspiracy is not defined in the Charter. But in the opinion of the Tribunal the conspiracy must be clearly outlined in its criminal purpose. It must not be too far removed from the time of decision and of action. The planning, to be criminal, must not rest merely on the declarations of a party programme, such as are found in the twenty-five points of the Nazi Party, announced in 1920, or the political affirmations expressed in "Mein Kampf" in later years. The Tribunal must examine whether a concrete plan to wage war existed, and determine the participants in that concrete plan.

It is not necessary to decide whether a single master conspiracy between the defendants has been established by the evidence. But the evidence establishes with certainty the existence of many separate plans rather than a single conspiracy embracing them all. That Germany was rapidly moving to complete dictatorship from the moment that the Nazis seized power, and progressively in the direction of war, has been overwhelmingly shown in the ordered sequence of aggressive acts and wars already set out in this Judgment.

In the opinion of the Tribunal, the evidence establishes the common planning to prepare and wage war by certain of the defendants. It is immaterial to consider whether a single conspiracy to the extent and over the time set out in the Indictment has been conclusively proved. Continued planning, with aggressive war as the objective, has been established beyond doubt.

The argument that such common planning cannot exist where there is complete dictatorship is unsound. A plan in the execution of which a number of persons participate is still a plan, even though conceived by only one of them; and those who execute the plan do not avoid responsibility by showing that they acted under the direction of the man who conceived it. Hitler could not make aggressive war by himself. He had to have the co-operation of statesmen, military leaders, diplomats, and business men. When they, with knowledge of his aims, gave him their co-operation, they made themselves parties to the plan he had initiated. They are not to be deemed innocent because Hitler made use of them, if they knew what they were doing. That they were assigned to their tasks by a dictator does not absolve them from responsibility for their acts. The relation of leader and follower does not preclude responsibility here any more than it does in the comparable tyranny of organised domestic crime.

Count One, however, charges not only the conspiracy to commit aggressive war, but also to commit war crimes and crimes against humanity. But the Charter does not define as a separate crime any conspiracy except the one to commit acts of aggressive war. Article 6 of the Charter provides:

> Leaders, organisers, instigators and accomplices participating in the formulation or execution of a common plan or conspiracy to commit any of the foregoing crimes are responsible for all acts performed by any persons in execution of such plan.

In the opinion of the Tribunal these words do not add a new and separate crime to those already listed. The words are designed to establish the responsibility of persons participating in a common plan. The Tribunal will therefore disregard the charges in Count One that the defendants conspired to commit war crimes and crimes against humanity, and will consider only the common plan to prepare, initiate and wage aggressive war.

War Crimes and Crimes Against Humanity

The evidence relating to war crimes has been overwhelming, in its volume and its detail. It is impossible for this Judgment adequately to review it, or to record the mass of documentary and oral evidence that has been presented. The truth remains that war crimes were committed on a vast scale, never before seen in the history of war. They were perpetrated in all the countries occupied by Germany, and on the High Seas, and were attended by every conceivable circumstance of cruelty and horror. There can be no doubt that the majority of them arose from the Nazi conception of "total war," with which the aggressive wars were waged. For in this conception of "total war," the moral ideas underlying the conventions which seek to make war more humane are no longer regarded as having force or validity. Everything is made subordinate to the overmastering dictates of war. Rules, regulations, assurances and treaties all alike are of no moment, and so, freed from the restraining influence of international law, the aggressive war is conducted by the Nazi leaders in the most barbaric way. Accordingly, war crimes were committed when and wherever the Fuehrer and his close associates thought them to be advantageous. They were for the most part the result of cold and criminal calculation.

On some occasions, war crimes were deliberately planned long in advance. In the case of the Soviet Union, the plunder of the territories to be occupied, and the ill-treatment of the civilian population, were settled in minute detail before the attack was begun.

Similarly, when planning to exploit the inhabitants of the occupied countries for slave labour on the very greatest scale, the German Government conceived it as an integral part of the war economy, and planned and organised this particular war crime down to the last elaborate detail.

Other war crimes, such as the murder of prisoners of war who had escaped and been recaptured, or the murder of Commandos or captured airmen, or the destruction of the Soviet Commissars, were the result of direct orders circulated through the highest official channels.

The Tribunal proposes, therefore, to deal quite generally with the question of war crimes, and to refer to them later when examining the responsibility of the individual defendants in relation to them. Prisoners of war were ill-treated and tortured and murdered, not only in defiance of the well-established rules of international law, but in complete disregard of the elementary dictates of humanity. Civilian populations in occupied territories suffered the same fate. Whole populations were deported to Germany for the purposes of slave labour upon defence works, armament production and similar tasks connected with the war effort. Hostages were taken in very large numbers from the civilian populations in all the occupied countries, and were shot as suited the German purposes. Public and private property was systematically plundered and pillaged in order to enlarge the resources of Germany at the expense of the rest of Europe. Cities and towns and villages were wantonly destroyed without military justification or necessity.

Law Relating to War Crimes and Crimes Against Humanity

Article 6 of the Charter provides:

(b) War Crimes: namely, violations of the laws or customs of war. Such violations shall include, but not be limited to, murder, ill-treatment or deportation to slave labour or for any other purpose of civilian population of or in occupied territory, murder or ill-treatment of prisoners of war or persons on the seas, killing of hostages, plunder of public or private property, wanton destruction of cities, towns or villages. or devastation not justified by military necessity;

(c) Crimes against Humanity: namely, murder, extermination, enslavement, deportation, and other inhumane acts committed against any civilian population, before or during the war, or persecutions on political, racial or religious grounds in execution of or in connection with any crime within the jurisdiction of the Tribunal, whether or not in violation of the domestic law of the country where perpetrated.

As heretofore stated, the Charter does not define as a separate crime any conspiracy except the one set out in Article 6 (a), dealing with crimes against peace.

The Tribunal is of course bound by the Charter, in the definition which it gives both of war crimes and crimes against humanity. With respect to war crimes, however, as has already been pointed out, the crimes defined by Article 6, section (b), of the Charter were already recognised as war crimes under international law. They were covered by the Hague Convention of 1907, and the Geneva Convention of 1929. That violations of these provisions constituted crimes for which the guilty individuals were punishable is too well settled to admit of argument.

But it is argued that the Hague Convention does not apply in this case, because of the "general participation" clause in Article 2 of the Hague Convention of 1907. That clause provided:

> The provisions contained in the regulations (Rules of Land Warfare) referred to in Article 1 as well as in the present Convention do not apply except between contracting powers, and then only if all the belligerents are parties to the Convention.

Several of the belligerents in the recent war were not parties to this Convention.

In the opinion of the Tribunal it is not necessary to decide this question. The rules of land warfare expressed in the Convention undoubtedly represented an advance over existing international law at the time of their adoption. But the Convention expressly stated that it was an attempt "to revise the general laws and customs of war," which it thus recognised to be then existing, but by 1939 these rules laid down in the Convention were recognised by all civilised nations, and were regarded as being declaratory of the laws and customs of war which are referred to in Article 6 (b) of the Charter.

A further submission was made that Germany was no longer bound by the rules of land warfare in many of the territories occupied during the war, because Germany had completely subjugated those countries and incorporated them into the German Reich, a fact which gave Germany authority to deal with the occupied countries as though they were part of Germany. In the view of the Tribunal it is unnecessary in this case to decide whether this doctrine of subjugation, dependent as it is upon military conquest, has any application where the subjugation is the result of the crime of aggressive war. The doctrine was never considered to be applicable so long as there was an army in the field attempting to restore the occupied countries to their true owners.

With regard to crimes against humanity, there is no doubt whatever that political opponents were murdered in Germany before the war, and that many of them were kept in concentration camps in circumstances of great horror and cruelty. The policy of terror was certainly carried out on a vast scale, and in many cases was organised and systematic. The policy of persecution, repression and murder of civilians in Germany before the war of 1939, who were likely to be hostile to the Government, was most ruthlessly carried out. The persecution of Jews during the same period is established beyond all doubt.

To constitute crimes against humanity, the acts relied on before the outbreak of war must have been in execution of, or in connection with, any crime within the jurisdiction of the Tribunal. The Tribunal is of the opinion that revolting and horrible as many of these crimes were, it has not been satisfactorily proved that they were done in execution of, or in connection with, any such crime. The Tribunal therefore cannot make a general declaration that the acts before 1939 were crimes against humanity within the meaning of the Charter, but from the beginning of the war in 1939 war crimes were committed on a vast scale, which were also crimes against humanity; and insofar as the inhumane acts charged in the Indictment, and committed after the beginning of the war, did not constitute war crimes, they were all committed in execution of, or in connection with, the aggressive war, and therefore constituted crimes against humanity.

NOTES AND QUESTIONS

1. The Nuremberg Tribunal operated under a "statute" created by the Treaty of London, which defined three categories of crimes: aggression, war crimes, and crimes against humanity. Could the Nazi defendants have been held liable for war crimes with respect to offenses against their own citizens? If not, then how does the international community have power to punish them for crimes against humanity with regard to their own citizens? This theme will be a dominant subject in the cases below dealing with Yugoslavia and Rwanda.

2. The international interest in internal affairs, reflected in crimes against humanity, is similar to that of the international interest in terrorism. If the Nazi party rose to power on the basis of intimidation and violence in the streets of Germany, was it guilty from the beginning of terrorism? If so, was this a violation of international law? The realization that this kind of power and intimidation over one's own citizenry is an added impetus for protection of human rights and the interest of other nations in the internal affairs of an abusive regime.

3. The Nuremberg trials have been the subject of extensive commentary. A set of essays applying its principles in developing international criminal law is TIMOTHY MCCORMACK & GERRY J. SIMPSON, THE LAW OF WAR CRIMES (1997). *See also* OSCAR SCHACHTER, INTERNATIONAL LAW IN THEORY AND PRACTICE (1991).

4. In addition to the IMT and the trials in Germany under the auspices of the Control Council, additional military tribunals were convened to prosecute Italian, Yugoslav, and Japanese officials. One early activity of the United Nations (formed in 1945) was to monitor these proceedings through its War Crimes Commission, which reported that the U.S. conducted a total of 809 trials of war crimes. Other nations were engaged in similar trials, both in military courts and in ordinary civilian courts. The most controversial of these trials was that of General Yamashita who commanded the Japanese forces overrun by American troops in the Philippines.

IN RE YAMASHITA

327 U.S. 1 (1946)

Mr. Chief Justice STONE delivered the opinion of the Court.

[The Court had before it both an application for leave to file a petition for writs of habeas corpus and prohibition under the Court's original jurisdiction and a petition for certiorari to review an order of the Supreme Court of the Commonwealth of the Philippines, denying petitioner's application to that court for writs of habeas corpus and prohibition.

[Yamashita was the Commanding General of Japanese forces in the Philippines. He surrendered to U.S. forces on Sept. 3, 1945, was charged with violations of the law of war on Sept. 25, brought to trial on Oct 8, and convicted on Dec. 7 by a military commission of five Army officers. He was sentenced to death by hanging. His Army defense team of six lawyers brought petitions before both the Philippine courts and the Supreme Court.]

In *Ex parte Quirin*, we had occasion to consider at length the sources and nature of the authority to create military commissions for the trial of enemy combatants for offenses against the law of war. We there pointed out that Congress, in the exercise of the power conferred upon it by Article I, § 8, cl. 10 of the Constitution to "define and punish . . . Offenses against the Law of Nations," of which the law of war is a part, had by the Articles of War recognized the "military commission" appointed by military command, as it had previously existed in United States Army practice, as an appropriate tribunal for the trial and punishment of offenses against the law of war. Article 15 [now Article 21, 10 U.S.C. § 821, preserves the practice of trial by military commission or tribunal for violations of the "law of war"].

We further pointed out that Congress, by sanctioning trial of enemy combatants for violations of the law of war by military commission, had not attempted to codify the law of war or to mark its precise boundaries. Instead, by Article 15 it had incorporated, by reference, as within the preexisting jurisdiction of military commissions created by appropriate military command, all offenses which are defined as such by the law of war, and which may constitutionally be included within that jurisdiction. It thus adopted the system of military common law applied by military tribunals so far as it should be recognized and deemed applicable by the courts, and as further defined and supplemented by the Hague Convention, to which the United States and the Axis powers were parties.

Finally, we held in *Ex parte Quirin*, as we hold now, that Congress by sanctioning trials of enemy aliens by military commission for offenses against the law of war had recognized the right of the accused to make a defense. It has not foreclosed their right to contend that the Constitution or laws of the United States withhold authority to proceed with the trial. It has not withdrawn, and the Executive branch of the government could not, unless there was suspension of the writ, withdraw from the courts the duty and power to make such inquiry into the authority of the commission as may be made by habeas corpus.

The authority to create the Commission. An important incident to the conduct of war is the adoption of measures by the military commander, not only to repel and defeat the enemy, but to seize and subject to disciplinary measures those enemies who, in their attempt to thwart or impede our military effort, have violated the law of war. The trial and punishment of enemy combatants who have committed violations of the law of war is thus not only a part of the conduct of war operating as a preventive measure against such violations, but is an exercise of the authority sanctioned by Congress to administer the system of military justice recognized by the law of war. That sanction is without qualification as to the exercise of this authority so long as a state of war exists – from its declaration until peace is proclaimed. The war power, from which the commission derives its existence, is not limited to victories in the field, but carries with it the inherent power to guard against the immediate renewal of the conflict, and to remedy, at least in ways Congress has recognized, the evils which the military operations have produced.

No writer on international law appears to have regarded the power of military tribunals, otherwise competent to try violations of the law of war, as terminating before the formal state of war has ended. In our own military history there have been numerous instances in which offenders were tried by military commission after the cessation of hostilities and before the proclamation of peace, for offenses against the law of war committed before the cessation of hostilities.

The extent to which the power to prosecute violations of the law of war shall be exercised before peace is declared rests, not with the courts, but with the political branch of the Government, and may itself be governed by the terms of an armistice or the treaty of peace. Here, peace has not been agreed upon or proclaimed. Japan, by her acceptance of the Potsdam Declaration and her surrender, has acquiesced in the trials of those guilty of violations of the law of war. The conduct of the trial by the military commission has been authorized by the political branch of the Government, by military command, by international law and usage, and by the terms of the surrender of the Japanese government.

The Charge. Neither Congressional action nor the military orders constituting the commission authorized it to place petitioner on trial unless the charge preferred against him is of a violation of the law of war. The charge is that petitioner "unlawfully disregarded and failed to discharge his duty as commander to control the operations of the members of his command, permitting them to commit brutal atrocities and other high crimes against people of the United States and of its allies and dependencies, particularly the Philippines; and he . . . thereby violated the laws of war."

Bills of particulars allege a series of acts committed by members of the forces under petitioner's command, during the period mentioned. The first item specifies the execution of "a deliberate plan and purpose to massacre and exterminate a large part of the civilian population of Batangas Province, and to devastate and destroy public, private and religious property therein, as a result of which more than 25,000 men, women and children, all unarmed noncombatant civilians, were brutally mistreated and killed, without cause or trial, and entire settlements were devastated and destroyed wantonly and without military necessity." Other items specify acts of violence, cruelty and homicide inflicted upon the civilian population and prisoners of war, acts of wholesale pillage and the wanton destruction of religious monuments.

It is not denied that such acts directed against the civilian population of an occupied country and against prisoners of war are recognized in international law as violations of the law of war. But it is urged that the charge does not allege that petitioner has either committed or directed the commission of such acts, and consequently that no violation is charged as against him. But this overlooks the fact that the gist of the charge is an unlawful breach of duty by petitioner as an army commander to control the operations of the members of his command by "permitting them to commit" the extensive and widespread atrocities specified. The question then is whether the law of war imposes on an army commander a duty to take such appropriate measures as are within his power to control the troops under his command for the prevention of the specified acts which are violations of the law of war and which are likely to attend the occupation of hostile territory by an uncontrolled soldiery, and whether he may be charged with personal responsibility for his failure to take such measures when violations result. That this was the precise issue to be tried was made clear by the statement of the prosecution at the opening of the trial.

It is evident that the conduct of military operations by troops whose excesses are unrestrained by the orders or efforts of their commander would almost certainly result in violations which it is the purpose of the law of war to prevent. Its purpose to protect civilian populations and prisoners of war from brutality would largely be defeated if the commander of an invading army could with impunity neglect to take reasonable measures for their protection. Hence the law of war presupposes that its violation is to be avoided through the control of the operations of war by commanders who are to some extent responsible for their subordinates.

[The Hague Conventions] plainly imposed on petitioner, who at the time specified was military governor of the Philippines, as well as commander of the Japanese forces, an affirmative duty to take such measures as were within his power and appropriate in the circumstances to protect prisoners of war and the civilian population. This duty of a commanding officer has heretofore been recognized, and its breach penalized by our own military tribunals. A like principle has been applied so as to impose liability on the United States in international arbitrations.

We do not make the laws of war but we respect them so far as they do not conflict with the commands of Congress or the Constitution. There is no contention that the present charge, thus read, is without the support of evidence, or that the commission held petitioner responsible for failing to take measures which were beyond his control or inappropriate for a commanding officer to take in the circumstances.[4] We do not here appraise the evidence on which petitioner

---

[4] In its findings the commission took account of the difficulties "faced by the accused, with respect not only to the swift and overpowering advance of American forces, but also to errors of his predecessors, weakness in organization, equipment, supply, training, communication, discipline and morale of his troops," and "the tactical situation, the character, training and capacity of staff officers

was convicted. We do not consider what measures, if any, petitioner took to prevent the commission, by the troops under his command, of the plain violations of the law of war detailed in the bill of particulars, or whether such measures as he may have taken were appropriate and sufficient to discharge the duty imposed upon him. These are questions within the peculiar competence of the military officers composing the commission and were for it to decide.

The Proceedings before the Commission. The regulations prescribed by General MacArthur governing the procedure for the trial of petitioner by the commission directed that the commission should admit such evidence "as in its opinion would be of assistance in proving or disproving the charge, or such as in the commission's opinion would have probative value in the mind of a reasonable man," and that in particular it might admit affidavits, depositions or other statements taken by officers detailed for that purpose by military authority. The petitions in this case charged that in the course of the trial the commission received, over objection by petitioner's counsel, the deposition of a witness taken pursuant to military authority by a United States Army captain. It also, over like objection admitted hearsay and opinion evidence tendered by the prosecution. Petitioner argues as ground for the writ of habeas corpus, that Article 25 of the Articles of War prohibited the reception in evidence by the commission of depositions on behalf of the prosecution in a capital case, and that Article 38 prohibited the reception of hearsay and of opinion evidence.

We think that neither Article 25 nor Article 38 is applicable to the trial of an enemy combatant by a military commission for violations of the law of war. Petitioner, an enemy combatant, is . . . not a person made subject to the Articles of War, and the military commission before which he was tried, though sanctioned, and its jurisdiction saved, by Article 15, was not convened by virtue of the Articles of War, but pursuant to the common law of war. It follows that the Articles of War were not applicable to petitioner's trial and imposed no restrictions upon the procedure to be followed. The Articles left the control over the procedure in such a case where it had previously been, with the military command.

Petitioner further urges that by virtue of Article 63 of the Geneva Convention of 1929, he is entitled to the benefits afforded by the 25th and 38th Articles of War to members of our own forces. Article 63 provides: "Sentence may be pronounced against a prisoner of war only by the same courts and according to the same procedure as in the case of persons belonging to the armed forces of the detaining Power." Since petitioner is a prisoner of war, and as the 25th and 38th Articles of War apply to the trial of any person in our own armed forces, it is said that Article 63 requires them to be applied in the trial of petitioner. But we think examination of Article 63 in its setting in the Convention plainly shows that it refers to sentence "pronounced against a prisoner of war" for an offense

---

and subordinate commanders, as well as the traits of character of his troops." It nonetheless found that petitioner had not taken such measures to control his troops as were "required by the circumstances." We do not weigh the evidence. We merely hold that the charge sufficiently states a violation against the law of war, and that the commission, upon the facts found, could properly find petitioner guilty of such a violation.

committed while a prisoner of war, and not for a violation of the law of war committed while a combatant.

We cannot say that the commission, in admitting evidence to which objection is now made, violated any act of Congress, treaty or military command defining the commission's authority. From this viewpoint it is unnecessary to consider what, in other situations, the Fifth Amendment might require, and as to that no intimation one way or the other is to be implied.

We therefore conclude that the detention of petitioner for trial and his detention upon his conviction, subject to the prescribed review by the military authorities were lawful, and that the petition for certiorari, and leave to file in this Court petitions for writs of habeas corpus and prohibition should be, and they are

Denied.

Mr. Justice JACKSON took no part in the consideration or decision of these cases.

Mr. Justice MURPHY, dissenting.

The significance of the issue facing the Court today cannot be overemphasized. An American military commission has been established to try a fallen military commander of a conquered nation for an alleged war crime. The authority for such action grows out of the exercise of the power conferred upon Congress by Article I, § 8, cl. 10 of the Constitution to "define and punish . . . Offenses against the Law of Nations . . . ." The grave issue raised by this case is whether a military commission so established and so authorized may disregard the procedural rights of an accused person as guaranteed by the Constitution, especially by the due process clause of the Fifth Amendment.

The answer is plain. The Fifth Amendment guarantee of due process of law applies to "any person" who is accused of a crime by the Federal Government or any of its agencies. No exception is made as to those who are accused of war crimes or as to those who possess the status of an enemy belligerent. Indeed, such an exception would be contrary to the whole philosophy of human rights which makes the Constitution the great living document that it is. The immutable rights of the individual, including those secured by the due process clause of the Fifth Amendment, belong not alone to the members of those nations that excel on the battlefield or that subscribe to the democratic ideology. They belong to every person in the world, victor or vanquished, whatever may be his race, color or beliefs. They rise above any status of belligerency or outlawry. They survive any popular passion or frenzy of the moment. No court or legislature or executive, not even the mightiest army in the world, can ever destroy them. Such is the universal and indestructible nature of the rights which the due process clause of the Fifth Amendment recognizes and protects when life or liberty is threatened by virtue of the authority of the United States.

The failure of the military commission to obey the dictates of the due process requirements of the Fifth Amendment is apparent in this case. The petitioner was the commander of an army totally destroyed by the superior power of this nation. While under heavy and destructive attack by our forces, his troops committed many brutal atrocities and other high crimes. Hostilities ceased and he voluntarily surrendered. At that point he was entitled, as an individual protected by the due process clause of the Fifth amendment, to be treated fairly and justly according to the accepted rules of law and procedure. He was also entitled to a fair trial as to any alleged crimes and to be free from charges of legally unrecognized crimes that would serve only to permit his accusers to satisfy their desires for revenge.

A military commission was appointed to try the petitioner for an alleged war crime. The trial was ordered to be held in territory over which the United States has complete sovereignty. No military necessity or other emergency demanded the suspension of the safeguards of due process. Yet petitioner was rushed to trial under an improper charge, given insufficient time to prepare an adequate defense, deprived of the benefits of some of the most elementary rules of evidence and summarily sentenced to be hanged. In all this needless and unseemly haste there was no serious attempt to charge or to prove that he committed a recognized violation of the laws of war. He was not charged with personally participating in the acts of atrocity or with ordering or condoning their commission. Not even knowledge of these crimes was attributed to him. It was simply alleged that he unlawfully disregarded and failed to discharge his duty as commander to control the operations of the members of his command, permitting them to commit the acts of atrocity. The recorded annals of warfare and the established principles of international law afford not the slightest precedent for such a charge.

In my opinion, such a procedure is unworthy of the traditions of our people or of the immense sacrifices that they have made to advance the common ideals of mankind. The high feelings of the moment doubtless will be satisfied. But in the sober afterglow will come the realization of the boundless and dangerous implications of the procedure sanctioned today. No one in a position of command in an army, from sergeant to general, can escape those implications. Indeed, the fate of some future President of the United States and his chiefs of staff and military advisers may well have been sealed by this decision. But even more significant will be the hatred and ill-will growing out of the application of this unprecedented procedure.

War breeds atrocities. From the earliest conflicts of recorded history to the global struggles of modern times inhumanities, lust and pillage have been the inevitable by-products of man's resort to force and arms. Unfortunately, such despicable acts have a dangerous tendency to call forth primitive impulses of vengeance and retaliation among the victimized peoples. The satisfaction of such impulses in turn breeds resentment and fresh tension. Thus does the spiral of cruelty and hatred grow.

If we are ever to develop an orderly international community based upon a recognition of human dignity it is of the utmost importance that the necessary punishment of those guilty of atrocities be as free as possible from the ugly stigma of revenge and vindictiveness. Justice must be tempered by compassion rather than by vengeance. In this, the first case involving this momentous problem ever to reach this Court, our responsibility is both lofty and difficult. We must insist, within the confines of our proper jurisdiction, that the highest standards of justice be applied in this trial of an enemy commander conducted under the authority of the United States. Otherwise stark retribution will be free to masquerade in a cloak of false legalism. And the hatred and cynicism engendered by that retribution will supplant the great ideals to which this nation is dedicated.

This Court fortunately has taken the first and most important step toward insuring the supremacy of law and justice in the treatment of an enemy belligerent accused of violating the laws of war. Jurisdiction properly has been asserted to inquire "into the cause of restraint of liberty" of such a person. Thus the obnoxious doctrine asserted by the Government in this case, to the effect that restraints of liberty resulting from military trials of war criminals are political matters completely outside the arena of judicial review, has been rejected fully and unquestionably. This does not mean, of course, that the foreign affairs and policies of the nation are proper subjects of judicial inquiry. But when the liberty of any person is restrained by reason of the authority of the United States the writ of habeas corpus is available to test the legality of that restraint, even though direct court review of the restraint is prohibited. The conclusive presumption must be made, in this country at least, that illegal restraints are unauthorized and unjustified by any foreign policy of the Government and that commonly accepted juridical standards are to be recognized and enforced. On that basis judicial inquiry into these matters may proceed within its proper sphere.

At a time like this when emotions are understandably high it is difficult to adopt a dispassionate attitude toward a case of this nature. Yet now is precisely the time when that attitude is most essential. We live under the Constitution, which is the embodiment of all the high hopes and aspirations of the new world. And it is applicable in both war and peace. We must act accordingly. Indeed, an uncurbed spirt of revenge and retribution, masked in formal legal procedure for purposes of dealing with a fallen enemy commander, can do more lasting harm than all of the atrocities giving rise to that spirit. The people's faith in the fairness and objectiveness of the law can be seriously undercut by that spirit. The fires of nationalism can be further kindled. And the hearts of all mankind can be embittered and filled with hatred, leaving forlorn and impoverished the noble ideal of malice toward none and charity to all. These are the reasons that lead me to dissent in these terms.

Mr. Justice RUTLEDGE, dissenting.

Not with ease does one find his views at odds with the Court's in a matter of this character and gravity. Only the most deeply felt convictions could force one to differ. That reason alone leads me to do so now, against strong considerations for withholding dissent.

More is at stake than General Yamashita's fate. There could be no possible sympathy for him if he is guilty of the atrocities for which his death is sought. But there can be and should be justice administered according to law. In this stage of war's aftermath it is too early for Lincoln's great spirit, best lighted in the Second Inaugural, to have wide hold for the treatment of foes. It is not too early, it is never too early, for the nation steadfastly to follow its great constitutional traditions, none older or more universally protective against unbridled power than due process of law in the trial and punishment of men, that is, of all men, whether citizens, aliens, alien enemies or enemy belligerents. It can become too late.

The difference between the Court's view of this proceeding and my own comes down in the end to the view, on the one hand, that there is no law restrictive upon these proceedings other than whatever rules and regulations may be prescribed for their government by the executive authority or the military and, on the other hand, that the provisions of the Articles of War, of the Geneva Convention and the Fifth Amendment apply.

I cannot accept the view that anywhere in our system resides or lurks a power so unrestrained to deal with any human being through any process of trial. What military agencies or authorities may do with our enemies in battle or invasion, apart from proceedings in the nature of trial and some semblance of judicial action, is beside the point. Nor has any human being heretofore been held to be wholly beyond elementary procedural protection by the Fifth Amendment. I cannot consent to even implied departure from that great absolute.

It was a great patriot who said: "He that would make his own liberty secure must guard even his enemy from oppression; for if he violates this duty he establishes a precedent that will reach himself." 2 The Complete Writings of Thomas Paine (edited by Foner, 1945) 588.

NOTES AND QUESTIONS

1. Was it "fair" to hang General Yamashita for the actions of his troops if he really was unable to control them in the chaos of the Allied invasion? Did he perhaps bear some responsibility for years of propaganda that created the conditions of undisciplined patriotic fervor leading to this result?

2. Justices Murphy and Rutledge used strong language to express their outrage over the treatment of General Yamashita, while the more famous liberal Justices Douglas and Black were silent. Do you suspect that the Murphy and Rutledge reactions were prompted more by (1) military procedures, (2) the fairness of holding him responsible for the actions of his troops, or (3) the assertion of unilateral authority by the U.S. to execute a vanquished general? From the perspective of more than a half century later, and in the context of worldwide terrorism, what do you think of Justice Murphy's warning that vengeful action could create more fuel for a cycle of hate?

[B] INTERNATIONAL CRIMINAL TRIBUNALS FOR YUGOSLAVIA (ICTY) AND RWANDA (ICTR)

The International Criminal Tribunal for Yugoslavia was created by action of the UN Security Council in 1993, followed shortly by creation of the ICT for Rwanda in 1994. The ICTY is based in The Hague and ICTR in Arusha, Tanzania. Each has multiple Trial Chambers composed of panels of judges, but both share the same Appellate Chamber. The judges of all Chambers are elected by the General Assembly.

The "statutes" of the tribunals define the crimes to be adjudicated. There are some subtle differences between the two statutes, and the Tribunals struggle with what law applies in some of situations. A side-by-side comparison of the two statutes can be found on the website for this course. Both Tribunals have developed elaborate procedures for protection of witnesses and for translation of testimony.

There has been only one case fully tried in the ICTY as yet. This is the case of Dusko Tadic, a relatively obscure Serbian resident of Bosnia who is alleged to have participated in some of the brutalities as his Muslim and Croat neighbors were rounded up, imprisoned, and eventually either killed or expelled from the region as part of the ethnic cleansing of what dominant Serbian elements hoped would result in a Serbian addition to Yugoslavia. Because this is the first opinion of a tribunal instigated by the United Nations for war crimes, the Court goes into vast detail regarding the background of the incidents and the analysis of customary international law that creates individual criminal responsibility for atrocities against civilian populations. This background and analysis is part of what may become international criminal responsibility for terrorism, as it sets the stage for finding that targeting of civilians by an organized group, whether affiliated with a government or not, is a subject of customary international law and thus enforceable either by international tribunals or under the universal jurisdiction of individual states.

PROSECUTOR v. TADIC

Int'l Crim. Tribunal for Yugoslavia, Trial Chamber

1997

OPINION AND JUDGMENT

I. INTRODUCTION

3. The International Tribunal is governed by its Statute ("Statute"), adopted by the Security Council.

4. The Statute grants competence to prosecute persons responsible for serious violations of international humanitarian law committed in the territory of the former Yugoslavia since 1991. Subject-matter jurisdiction is stated in Articles 2 to 5 of the Statute to consist of the power to prosecute persons responsible for "grave breaches" of the Geneva Conventions of 1949 (Article 2), [violations of] the laws or customs of war (Article 3), genocide (Article 4), and crimes against humanity when committed in armed conflict (Article 5), which are beyond any doubt part of customary international law.

B. Procedural Background

9. The accused was charged with individual counts of persecution, inhuman treatment, cruel treatment, rape, wilful killing, murder, torture, wilfully causing great suffering or serious injury to body and health, and inhumane acts alleged to have been committed in the Republic of Bosnia and Herzegovina. The accused

was transferred to the International Tribunal on 24 April 1995, after the Federal Republic of Germany enacted the necessary implementing legislation for his surrender, and thereafter was detained in the United Nations detention unit in The Hague.

II. BACKGROUND AND PRELIMINARY FACTUAL FINDINGS

A. The Context of the Conflict

53. In order to place in context the evidence relating to the counts of the Indictment, especially Count 1, persecution, it is necessary to say something in a preliminary way about the relevant historical, geographic, administrative and military setting about which evidence was received.

1. Historical and Geographic Background

55. The area with which this trial is primarily concerned is north-western Bosnia and Herzegovina; more specifically, opstina (district) Prijedor, which includes the town of Prijedor and the town of Kozarac some 10 kilometres to its east.

56. For centuries the population of Bosnia and Herzegovina, more so than any other republic of the former Yugoslavia, has been multi-ethnic. For more than 400 years Bosnia and Herzegovina was part of the Ottoman Empire. Its western and northern borders formed the boundary with the Austro-Hungarian Empire or its predecessors; a military frontier along that boundary was established as early as the sixteenth century to protect the Hapsburg lands from the Ottoman Turks. The presence of this old military frontier is said to account for the presence there of much of its present-day Serb population, encouraged centuries ago to move into and settle on the frontier, forming there a loyal population base as a potential border defence force. The large Muslim population of Bosnia and Herzegovina owes its religion and culture, and hence its identity, to the long Turkish occupation, during which time many Slavs adopted the Islamic faith. The third ethnic population living in Bosnia and Herzegovina, also sizeable, are the Croats, living principally in the south-west adjacent to Croatia's Dalmatian coast. Since all three population groups are Slav it is, no doubt, inaccurate to speak of three different ethnic groups; however, this appears to be accepted common usage.

[Here the Court engages in a lengthy review of the history and religious-ethnic strife of the region. The Balkan region has been fractured for so many centuries that it has produced the term "balkanization" to refer to a situation in which various entities are competing for the same political spoils in a chaotic fashion. Geographically, the region runs from the border of Hungary in the north to the border of Greece in the south. It includes what are now known as Slovenia, Croatia, Yugoslavia (Serbia and Montenegro), Bosnia-Herzegovina, Albania, Bulgaria, and Macedonia.

[Over the centuries, the region has been the dividing line between eastern and western empires. In the West, these have included Rome, the Holy Roman Empire, and Austro-Hungarian Empire. From the east have come the Persian, Turkish and Ottoman Empires. Similarly, it has been the meeting point of religions: Roman Catholic, Eastern Orthodox, and Muslim.

[In biological or genetic terms, it is at least arguable that all the long-term population of the region are of a single Slavic background, but the inhabitants identify themselves as ethnic Serb, Croat, or Muslim (and others not relevant here) more along cultural than biologic lines. Indeed, surnames are common to all groups and only the Muslim given names are distinctive from the other groups. Thus, it would be difficult to identify someone as belonging to one or other group by appearance or name alone without knowing the person's family and cultural history.

[At the end of World War II, much of the region was unified in the republic of Yugoslavia under Marshal Tito allied to some extent with the Soviet Union. As dissatisfaction with the USSR grew during the 1960s and 1970s, Yugoslavia began to be viewed as almost an independent buffer between east and west. Without the common unifier (or common enemy) of communism, the various ethnic groups began to assert their claims for nationhood. With the breakup of the Soviet Union in 1989, all hell broke loose in the Balkans.

[In elections in 1990, separatist parties won in Slovenia, Croatia, and Bosnia-Herzegovina. Slovenia and Croatia immediately declared independence. That left the Serbian majority in Yugoslavia in control of the Yugoslav National Army (JNA) but without political control of the rebellious areas. Slovenia was allowed to go its way but Serb JNA forces attempted to subdue Croatia. In bitter fighting through 1991 & the first half of 1992, Serbian Yugoslavia managed to annex the most Serbian portions of Croatia but the JNA was repelled from the rest of what became a new nation-state. Moving back across the border into Bosnia-Herzegovina, the JNA was welcomed by the Serbian sympathizers in the northern part of that republic.

[The following acronyms are used throughout the Court's opinion:

[JNA = Yugoslav National Army

[SDS = Serbian political party of Bosnia-Herzegovina

[SDA = Muslim political party of B-H

[HDZ = Croat political party of B-H

[TO = Territorial Defense

[In northern Bosnia-Herzegovina, Serb citizens formed SDS provisional governments, allied with the JNA troops, and embarked on a program of "ethnic cleansing" of the region.]

147. Immediately upon its formation, the ARK Crisis Staff began to make decisions about the treatment of non-Serbs. The President of the ARK Crisis Staff [stated] that the largest percentage of non-Serbs acceptable in the territory designated as Greater Serbia was 2 percent. In order to secure this percentage he advocated on Radio Banja Luka a direct struggle, including the killing of non-Serbs. Similarly [another Serbian municipal official decided] not to allow any non-Serb women to give birth at Banja Luka Hospital. He also asserted that all mixed marriage couples should be divorced or that all mixed marriages should be annulled and that children of mixed marriages "were good only for making soap."

151. Generally the [non-Serb] men were taken to the Keraterm and Omarska camps and the women to the Trnopolje camp. For those held at camps in the area, the overwhelming majority of whom were non-Serbs, the situation was horrendous, with, as described below, brutal beatings, rapes and torture commonplace and the conditions of life appalling.

152. Whereas before the conflict opstina Prijedor contained approximately 50,000 Muslims and 6,000 Croats, only approximately 6,000 Muslims and 3,000 Croats remained after the cleansing and they endured very harsh conditions. They were required to perform dangerous and difficult work, had difficulties buying food, were harassed, and killings occurred on a continual basis.

154. After the take-over of Prijedor and the outlying areas, the Serb forces confined thousands of Muslim and Croat civilians in the Omarska, Keraterm and Trnopolje camps. The establishment of these camps was part of the Greater Serbia plan to expel non-Serbs from opstina Prijedor. Generally the camps were established and run either at the direction of, or in cooperation with, the Crisis Staffs, the armed forces and the police. During confinement, both male and female prisoners were subjected to severe mistreatment, which included beatings, sexual assaults, torture and executions. Members of paramilitary organizations and local Serbs were routinely allowed to enter the camps to abuse, beat and kill prisoners.

155. Perhaps the most notorious of the camps, where the most horrific conditions existed, was the Omarska camp. It was located at the former Ljubija iron-ore mine, situated some two kilometres to the south of Omarska village. The camp was in operation from 25 May 1992 until late August 1992 when the prisoners were transferred to Trnopolje and other camps. Omarska held as many as 3,000 prisoners at one time, primarily men, but also had at least 36 to 38 women. With little exception, all were Muslims or Croats. The only Serb prisoners sighted by any of the witnesses were said to have been there because they were on the side of the Muslims. The commander of the camp was Zeljko Meakic. The camp consisted of two large buildings, the hangar and the administrative building, and two smaller buildings, known as the "white house" and the "red house."

[Prisoners were regularly called out for interrogation, in the process of which many were severely beaten or killed.]

164. The calling-out of prisoners was not only for the purposes of interrogation. In the evening, groups from outside the camp would appear, would call out particular prisoners from their rooms and attack them with a variety of sticks, iron bars or lengths of heavy electric cable. Sometimes these weapons would have nails embedded in them so as to pierce the skin. On occasions knives would be used to slash a prisoner's body. The prisoners as a whole feared groups of men from outside the camp even more than they did the regular camp guards. These groups appeared to be allowed free access to the camp and their visits greatly increased the atmosphere of terror which prevailed in the camp. Frequently prisoners who were called out failed to return and witnesses who were their close relatives gave evidence that they had never been seen since, and were assumed to have been murdered.

165. Women who were held at Omarska were routinely called out of their rooms at night and raped. One witness testified that she was taken out five times and raped and after each rape she was beaten.

166. The white house was a place of particular horror. One room in it was reserved for brutal assaults on prisoners, who were often stripped, beaten and kicked and otherwise abused. Many died as a result of these repeated assaults on them. Prisoners who were forced to clean up after these beatings reported finding blood, teeth and skin of victims on the floor. Dead bodies of prisoners, lying in heaps on the grass near the white house, were a not infrequent sight. Those bodies would be thrown out of the white house and later loaded into trucks and removed from the camp.

167. The red house was another small building where prisoners were taken to be beaten and killed. When prisoners were required to clean the red house, they often found hair, clothes, blood, footwear and empty pistol cartridges. They also loaded onto trucks bodies of prisoners who had been beaten and killed in the red house.

[The Tribunal describes conditions and incidents at other camps in the region. In American courts, this evidence likely would have been excluded as prejudicial to the accused and not sufficiently connected to the offenses with which he was charged.]

C. The Accused

180. The accused, Dusko Tadic, was born on 1 October 1955 and grew up in Kozarac, living most of the time in the family home in the centre of the town. He came from a very prominent family of Serb ethnicity in Kozarac; his father was a decorated Second World War hero and well respected throughout the community.

181. Towards the end of 1990 or in the beginning of 1991 the accused opened a café in Kozarac, the Nipon café, attached to the family home on Marsala Tita Street in the centre of town. At first it was a popular bar visited by Muslims and Serbs alike from Kozarac and the surrounding area. Ninety percent of the inhabitants of Kozarac were Muslims prior to the conflict and the accused testified that most of his friends were Muslim.

185. The accused himself acknowledges that several Serbs and Muslims began to boycott his café in the belief that he wanted to "disturb relations between ethnic groups."

188. After the ethnic cleansing of Kozarac had been accomplished, the accused became the political leader of Kozarac. He became its representative to the Prijedor Municipal Assembly, which entrusted him with the task of re-establishing civilian control in Kozarac and he was in charge of population resettlement there.

III. FACTUAL FINDINGS

[The Court went into elaborate detail of witness testimony on the events in each paragraph of the Indictment. Given the chaotic nature of the times, it is not surprising that witnesses were confused and often unable to identify an assailant. Tadic, however, was known to many of the prisoners from prior life in town. This led to his being identified but also to some question of whether the identification was erroneously based on rumor or imagination. The specific incidents in which he was alleged to be involved included beatings of nine different prisoners, shooting of four civilians who were pulled out of a line of detainees in the street, and one particularly gruesome incident in which one prisoner was coerced into oral castration of another prisoner.

[The voluminous recitation of evidence is omitted, although it is worth emphasizing that Tadic maintained that his role was passive or even a tentative peacemaker. He insisted that he was not present at many of these events, and pointed out that he was fired from his municipal post for conflicts with the ruling SDS chiefs and eventually deserted from the military and fled to Germany.

[In brief, the Court found that Tadjic was present but not actively involved in many of the beatings, murders, and the sexual mutilation. Because bodies were disposed of in secrecy, the Court was unable to find beyond a reasonable doubt that persons who were beaten and disappeared had in fact died of their injuries, so the murder counts other than the shooting incident resulted in not guilty verdicts.

[U.S. students should note that the Court acts as fact-finder. There is no provision for jury in most continental systems, on which the procedure of the International Tribunal is based. The lengthy detailed recitation of evidence in the opinion may be similar to that of U.S. judges when making findings without a jury, but it is more technical in tone and structure than that of most U.S. judges. The structure of the opinion also reflects the "syllogistic" process of continental legal decisions.]

VI. APPLICABLE LAW

A. General Requirements of Articles 2, 3 & 5 of the Statute

B. Article 2 of the Statute

[The Geneva Conventions prohibit violence against "protected persons." Each of the four Conventions applies to a different category of "protected persons" (soldiers, naval personnel, prisoners of war, and civilians). A major legal question was presented by whether the inmates of the camps were harmed by forces of a party to an armed conflict other than the state of which they were nationals. If the camps were under the control of Yugoslavia, then the protected status would apply. If the camps were under control of persons of the same nationality as the inmates, then the matter would be one for domestic law. The situation thus was somewhat comparable to the question of whether the U.S. "controlled" the Contras in Nicaragua. The Court concluded on this issue that "since it cannot be said that any of the victims, all of whom were civilians, were at any relevant time in the hands of a party to the conflict of which they were not nationals, the accused must be found not guilty of the counts which rely upon" Article 2 of the ICTY Statute.]

C. Article 3 of the Statute

[All four of the Geneva Conventions contain what is known as "Common Article 3," a provision which applies in "armed conflict not of an international character." It requires that "persons taking no active part in the hostilities" be "treated humanely" without discrimination and defines certain prohibited acts, such as violence, torture, or hostage-taking.]

609. Article 3 of the Statute directs the Trial Chamber to the laws or customs of war, being that body of customary international humanitarian law [which] includes the regime of protection established under Common Article 3 applicable to armed conflicts not of an international character, as a reflection of elementary considerations of humanity, and which is applicable to armed conflicts in general.

617. For the purposes of the application of the rules of customary international humanitarian law contained in Common Article 3, this Trial Chamber finds, in the present case, that: (i) an armed conflict existed at all relevant times in relation to the alleged offences; (ii) each of the victims of the acts charged was a person protected by those provisions being a person taking no active part in the hostilities; and (iii) the offences charged were committed within the context of that armed conflict. Accordingly, the requirements of Article 3 of the Statute are met.

D. Article 5 of the Statute

618. The notion of crimes against humanity as an independent juridical concept, and the imputation of individual criminal responsibility for their commission, was first recognized in Article 6(c) of the Nürnberg Charter. The term "crimes against humanity," although not previously codified, had been used in a non-technical sense as far back as 1915 and in subsequent statements concerning the First World War and was hinted at in the preamble to the 1907 Hague Convention. Thus when crimes against humanity were included in the Nürnberg Charter, although it was the first technical use of the term, it was not considered a novel concept. Nevertheless a new category of crime was created.

623. [S]ince the Nürnberg Charter, the customary status of the prohibition against crimes against humanity and the attribution of individual criminal responsibility for their commission have not been seriously questioned. "It is by now a settled rule of customary international law that crimes against humanity do not require a connection to international armed conflict."

The meaning of "population"

644. The requirement in Article 5 of the Statute that the prohibited acts must be directed against a civilian "population" does not mean that the entire population of a given State or territory must be victimised by these acts in order for the acts to constitute a crime against humanity. Instead the "population" element is intended to imply crimes of a collective nature and thus exclude single or isolated acts which, although possibly constituting war crimes or crimes against national penal legislation, do not rise to the level of crimes against humanity. [T]he inclusion in Article 5 of the requirement that the acts "be 'directed against any civilian population' ensures that what is to be alleged will not be one particular act but, instead, a course of conduct." The purpose of this requirement was clearly articulated by the United Nations War Crimes Commission when it wrote that:

Isolated offences did not fall within the notion of crimes against humanity. As a rule systematic mass action, particularly if it was authoritative, was necessary to transform a common crime, punishable only under municipal law, into a crime against humanity, which thus became also the concern of international law. Only crimes which either by their magnitude and savagery or by their large number or by the fact that a similar pattern was applied at different times and places, endangered the international community or shocked the conscience of mankind, warranted intervention by States other than that on whose territory the crimes had been committed, or whose subjects had become their victims.

Thus the emphasis is not on the individual victim but rather on the collective, the individual being victimised not because of his individual attributes but rather because of his membership of a targeted civilian population. This has been interpreted to mean, as elaborated below, that the acts must occur on a widespread or systematic basis, that there must be some form of a governmental, organizational or group policy to commit these acts and that the perpetrator must know of the context within which his actions are taken, as well as the requirement that the actions be taken on discriminatory grounds.

649. A tangential issue, not at issue before this Trial Chamber, is whether a single act in and of itself can constitute a crime against humanity. This issue has been the subject of intense debate, with the jurisprudence immediately following the Second World War being mixed. The American tribunals generally supported the proposition that a massive nature was required, while the tribunals in the British Zone came to the opposite conclusion, finding that the mass element was not essential to the definition, in respect of either the number of acts or the number of victims and that "what counted was not the mass aspect, but the link between the act and the cruel and barbarous political system, specifically, the Nazi regime." Clearly, a single act by a perpetrator taken within the context of a widespread or systematic attack against a civilian population entails individual criminal responsibility and an individual perpetrator need not commit numerous offences to be held liable. Although it is correct that isolated, random acts should not be included in the definition of crimes against humanity, that is the purpose of requiring that the acts be directed against a civilian population and thus "[e]ven an isolated act can constitute a crime against humanity if it is the product of a political system based on terror or persecution."

E. Individual Criminal Responsibility

676. As noted in the *Justice* case [an American military trial of Nazi judges], knowledge and intent can be inferred from the circumstances [in that case, knowledge that the courts were being used in furtherance of Nazi racial objectives]. In the *Mauthausen* case, the United States Military Tribunal, after finding all 61 accused guilty, stated in its special findings that the state of the camp where detainees were murdered *en masse* in gas chambers "was of such a criminal nature as to cause every official, governmental, military and civil, and every employee thereof, whether he be a member of the Waffen SS, Allgemeine SS, a guard, or civilian, to be culpably and criminally responsible." This finding

was based on the determination that "it was impossible for a governmental, military or civil official, a guard or a civilian employee, of the Concentration Camp Mauthausen, to have been in control of, been employed in, or present in, or residing in, Mauthausen at any time during its existence, without having acquired a definite knowledge of the criminal practices and activities therein existing." Thus the court inferred knowledge on the part of the accused, and concluded that the staff of the concentration camp was guilty of the commission of a war crime based on this knowledge and their continued participation in the enterprise.

681. The remaining question for consideration is the amount of assistance that must be shown before one can be held culpable for involvement in a crime.

689. The Trial Chamber finds that aiding and abetting includes all acts of assistance by words or acts that lend encouragement or support, as long as the requisite intent is present. Under this theory, presence alone is not sufficient if it is an ignorant or unwilling presence. However, if the presence can be shown or inferred, by circumstantial or other evidence, to be knowing and to have a direct and substantial effect on the commission of the illegal act, then it is sufficient on which to base a finding of participation and assign the criminal culpability that accompanies it.

690. Moreover, when an accused is present and participates in the beating of one person and remains with the group when it moves on to beat another person, his presence would have an encouraging effect, even if he does not physically take part in this second beating, and he should be viewed as participating in this second beating as well. This is assuming that the accused has not actively withdrawn from the group or spoken out against the conduct of the group.

691. However, actual physical presence when the crime is committed is not necessary; just as with the defendants who only drove victims to the woods to be killed, an accused can be considered to have participated in the commission of a crime based on the precedent of the Nürnberg war crimes trials if he is found to be "concerned with the killing." However, the acts of the accused must be direct and substantial.

692. In sum, the accused will be found criminally culpable for any conduct where it is determined that he knowingly participated in the commission of an offence that violates international humanitarian law and his participation directly and substantially affected the commission of that offence through supporting the actual commission before, during, or after the incident. He will also be responsible for all that naturally results from the commission of the act in question.

VII. LEGAL FINDINGS

693. The Trial Chamber has held, by a majority, that the Prosecution has failed to prove beyond reasonable doubt that the victims of the acts alleged in the Indictment were protected persons under the provisions of the Geneva Conventions. Accordingly, as found by the Appeals Chamber, Article 2 of the Statute proscribing grave breaches of those Conventions is inapplicable; therefore, the evidence will be assessed by considering Article 3 of the Statute

and its invocation of Common Article 3 of the Geneva Conventions, and Articles 5 and 7, paragraph 1 of the Statute.

[The Tribunal then proceeds to discuss the law and facts again in relation to each of the 34 counts in the indictment, finding Tadic to have been present and supportive of a number of beatings, torture, and killings but not involved with others. With regard to persons who were beaten and never seen again, the court could not find beyond a reasonable doubt that they died of those wounds and thus acquitted on some charges of murder. With regard to mistreatment of dead bodies, the court decided that the statutes apply only to living persons.]

VIII. JUDGMENT

FOR THE FOREGOING REASONS, having considered all of the evidence and the arguments, THE TRIAL CHAMBER finds [the Accused guilty on 11 of the 34 counts in the indictment].

Note on "Protected Persons" and "Armed Conflict"

The discussion of who is protected under what circumstances is critical to our study of terrorism for several reasons. First, there is the question of whether clandestine actors can be held to have violated international law. Second, under what circumstances is a large-scale act of violence subject to the "law of war?" Third, by what constraints is a military force governed in its dealings with paramilitary or even less-organized groups, such as those engaged in resistance violence in Iraq? And, conversely, what law applies to those insurgents themselves?

The dilemma of what to do about loosely organized mob violence has been around for millennia. As mentioned before, the U.S. experience with the KKK presented a similar phenomenon in the sense that it was not clear in early stages that California had a sufficient interest in what occurred in Alabama to trigger federal oversight of occurrences that were "local" to the state where they were occurring. Even today, federal statutes dealing with racial violence hinge on jurisdictional factors such as depriving a person of the use of public facilities or exercising a right connected to the federal government. This is roughly corollary to the question of when the international community should take oversight of violence that is contained within one nation-state.

The Trial Chamber decided that the Geneva Conventions did not apply to the situation in Bosnia because the Serbian militias were not under the "effective control" of Serbian Yugoslavia and therefore the situation was not an "international armed conflict." As a result, the civilian victims would not be considered "protected persons" under the Conventions. The Prosecutor appealed from this ruling on the ground that the conflict was international in scope because the Bosnian Serb militias had a "demonstrable link" to the forces of Yugoslavia.

The Appeals Chamber approached this question by asking whether the Bosnian Serbs might be considered "lawful combatants" in the sense of the Convention on Prisoners of War. Under that Convention,

militias or paramilitary groups or units may be regarded as legitimate combatants if they form 'part of [the] armed forces' of a Party to the conflict

or 'belong' to a Party to the conflict and satisfy the other four requirements
.... It is clear that this provision is primarily directed toward establishing
the requirements for the status of lawful combatants. Nevertheless, one of
its logical consequences is that if, in an armed conflict, paramilitary units
'belong' to a State other than the one against which they are fighting, the
conflict is international and therefore serious violations of the Geneva
Conventions may be classified as 'grave breaches.'

This approach might seem a bit surreal if it meant that a paramilitary group
could avoid application of the Conventions to them by violating the laws and
customs of war. After creating this apparent conundrum, however, the Tribunal
explained that what it was seeking was a mechanism by which to hold states
accountable for the actions of irregulars.

> States have in practice accepted that belligerents may use paramilitary
> units and other irregulars in the conduct of hostilities only on the condition
> that those belligerents are prepared to take responsibility for any
> infringements committed by such forces. In order for irregulars to qualify
> as lawful combatants, it appears that international rules and State practice
> therefore require control over them by a Party to an international armed
> conflict and, by the same token, a relationship of dependence and allegiance
> of these irregulars *vis-á-vis* that Party to the conflict. These then may be
> regarded as the ingredients of the term "belonging to a Party to the
> conflict."

The Appeals Chamber thus considers that the Third Geneva Convention,
by providing in Article 4 the requirement of "belonging to a Party to the
conflict," implicitly refers to a test of control.

This conclusion, based on the letter and the spirit of the Geneva
Conventions, is borne out by the entire logic of international humanitarian
law. This body of law is not grounded on formalistic postulates. It is not
based on the notion that only those who have the formal status of State
organs, i.e., are members of the armed forces of a State, are duty bound both
to refrain from engaging in violations of humanitarian law as well as – if
they are in a position of authority – to prevent or punish the commission of
such crimes. Rather, it is a realistic body of law, grounded on the notion of
effectiveness and inspired by the aim of deterring deviation from its
standards to the maximum extent possible. It follows, amongst other things,
that humanitarian law holds accountable not only those having formal
positions of authority but also those who wield *de facto* power as well as
those who exercise control over perpetrators of serious violations of
international humanitarian law. Hence, in cases such as that currently
under discussion, what is required for criminal responsibility to arise is
some measure of control by a Party to the conflict over the perpetrators.

This approach means that the Geneva Conventions apply to paramilitary
units if they are under some degree of control by a state belligerent and do not
apply if those persons are acting on their own. The Prosecutor attempted to focus
the court on the nature of the perpetrators' activities rather than on the
connection with the State:

First, with a view to limiting the scope of the test at issue, the Prosecution has contended that the criterion for ascertaining State responsibility is different from that necessary for establishing individual criminal responsibility. In the former case one would have to decide whether serious violations of international humanitarian law by private individuals may be attributed to a State because those individuals acted as de facto State officials. In the latter case, one would have instead to establish whether a private individual may be held criminally responsible for serious violations of international humanitarian law amounting to "grave breaches." Consequently, it has been asserted, the *Nicaragua* test, while valid within the context of State responsibility, is immaterial to the issue of individual criminal responsibility for "grave breaches." The Appeals Chamber, with respect, does not share this view.

What is at issue is not the distinction between the two classes of responsibility. What is at issue is a preliminary question: that of the conditions on which under international law an individual may be held to act as a *de facto* organ of a State. Logically these conditions must be the same both in the case: (i) where the court's task is to ascertain whether an act performed by an individual may be attributed to a State, thereby generating the international responsibility of that State; and (ii) where the court must instead determine whether individuals are acting as de facto State officials, thereby rendering the conflict international and thus setting the necessary precondition for the "grave breaches" regime to apply. In both cases, what is at issue is not the distinction between State responsibility and individual criminal responsibility. Rather, the question is that of establishing the criteria for the legal imputability to a State of acts performed by individuals not having the status of State officials. In the one case these acts, if they prove to be attributable to a State, will give rise to the international responsibility of that State; in the other case, they will ensure that the armed conflict must be classified as international.

In other words, the Geneva Conventions apply to international armed conflicts, not to localized violence. If two rival gangs in Los Angeles are engaged in bloodshed without following the laws and customs of war, that is no business of the international community but is a problem to be dealt with by local authorities. If the United States Government is engaged in bloodshed against its own civilians, there may be sources of international humanitarian law that apply but not the Geneva Conventions (unless the situation rises to the level of a "Common Article 3" situation discussed later). In between these extremes, there is the possibility that one of the rival gangs is acting, as U.S. statutes put it, "under color of state law," in which case outsiders take an interest.

The Appeals Chamber continued:

[I]nternational law renders any State responsible for acts in breach of international law performed (i) by individuals having the formal status of organs of a State (and this occurs even when these organs act ultra vires or contra legem), or (ii) by individuals who make up organised groups subject to the State's control. International law does so regardless of whether or not the State has issued specific instructions to those individuals. Clearly, the rationale behind this legal regulation is that otherwise, States might easily shelter behind, or use as a pretext, their internal legal system or the lack of any specific instructions in order to disclaim international responsibility.

Despite the formalism of the European opinion style, there is a policy reality behind the Tribunal's position. If a rebel group is not playing by the rules, then the international community can leave them to the tender mercies of the government under attack and not take an interest in their behavior, at least insofar as the Geneva Conventions are concerned. In this situation, then the government need not be concerned about application of the Geneva Conventions to its treatment of the rebels.

In the Yugoslavia situation, however, the armed bands were not attacking the government but were attacking civilians, allegedly with government acquiescence. Thus, the real policy question is at what stage does the international community take an interest in this situation? The answer of the ICTY is "when the perpetrators are under the control of the State."

All of this, however, is limited to application of those Conventions that depend upon the existence of a state of "armed conflict." Absent "armed conflict," the government forces are still subject to other Conventions such as those dealing with torture. The next question is whether crimes against humanity and genocide have been sufficiently incorporated into customary international law that they can be applied to non-state actors.

Note on Crimes Against Humanity

Two additional grounds of appeal by the Prosecutor dealt with the Trial Chamber's reading of the Statute's definition of "crimes against humanity" to exclude both purely personal pursuits and actions not tinged with discrimination on the basis of race, sex, religion, or similar criteria.

The Trial Chamber held that a person does not commit a "crime against humanity" when acting for purely personal reasons separated from any "armed conflict" during which those actions occur. This is not exactly the same as a "color of law" argument, because it recognizes that even private persons are subject to the rules against commission of crimes against humanity. Although Tadic had been convicted for these crimes and thus the ruling had no bearing on the outcome, the Appeals Chamber nevertheless took up this issue as an "matter of general significance for the Tribunal's jurisprudence." (We can only wonder how vigorously did the Defence Team research and argue the opposite position?)

The Appeals Chamber decided that personal motivation is irrelevant to crimes against humanity. Even if the defendant were acting for reasons wholly unrelated to the armed conflict and even if there were no group-based discriminatory motivation behind those actions, the listed actions would still be criminal. The U.S. has faced this issue in its KKK statutes that criminalize conspiracies to deprive persons of civil rights and has imposed a group-based discriminatory intent requirement. The ICTY decision, however, must be read in light of the particular wording of its statute, which criminalizes certain actions when taken "in armed conflict . . . and directed against a civilian population."

Could Tadic have been considered a terrorist? Was he engaged in "armed conflict" subject to the laws and customs of war? or was he a civilian engaged in violence against fellow civilians? Should ordinary street thugs be subject to the processes of international criminal law? In the context of widespread civil unrest and bloodshed, perhaps so.

Both the Geneva Convention issue and the crimes against humanity issues were addressed by the Security Council in creating the Statute of the International Tribunal for Rwanda, to which we turn next.

PROSECUTOR v. AKAYESU

International Criminal Tribunal for Rwanda, Trial Chambre I

Case No. ICTR-96-4-T

JUDGEMENT

Rwanda is a small, very hilly country in the Great Lakes region of Central Africa. Before the events of 1994, it was the most densely populated country of the African continent (7.1 million inhabitants for 26,338 square kilometres) [about 100 miles square, slightly smaller than Maryland]. Ninety percent of the population lives on agriculture. Its per capita income is among the lowest in the world, mainly because of a very high population pressure on land.

[Colonial rule in the region began with Germany in 1897 and was taken over by Belgium in 1917. The native monarchy drew heavily on a type of caste system in which the Tutsi were like a nobility.]

The terms Hutu and Tutsi . . . referred to individuals rather than to groups. In those days, the distinction between the Hutu and Tutsi was based on lineage rather than ethnicity. Indeed, the demarcation line was blurred: one could move from one status to another, as one became rich or poor, or even through marriage. Both German and Belgian colonial authorities, if only at the outset as far as the latter are concerned, relied on an elite essentially composed of people who referred to themselves as Tutsi . . . . In the early 1930s, Belgian authorities introduced a permanent distinction by dividing the population into three groups which they called ethnic groups, with the Hutu representing about 84% of the population, while the Tutsi (about 15%) and Twa (about 1%) accounted for the rest. In line with this division, it became mandatory for every Rwandan to carry an identity card mentioning his or her ethnicity.

[Belgium attempted established a "provisional government" and granted self-governance to the country in 1961. Over the next three decades, sporadic outbreaks of violence resulted in thousands of deaths and large-scale emigration of Tutsis to neighboring countries. Some of those exiles formed armed rebel forces such as the RPF. Following several assassinations, a transitional government attempted to negotiate new arrangements but the President was killed in a plane crash in April 1994. The Rwandan military seized control of the government and several moderate leaders (both Tutsi and sympathetic Hutus) were killed. The Tutsi exile forces then started moving across the border and mass violence erupted. Reliable estimates indicate that between April and the end of June 1994, as many as 500,000 to 1,000,000 were killed, mostly Tutsi and their Hutu sympathizers. The principal Hutu perpetrators were the MRND paramilitary militia and its youth subsidiary, the Interahamwe.

[Jean Paul Akayesu, a Rwandan citizen who was bourgmestre of Taba commune (something like chief executive of a U.S. county), was brought to trial on charges of participating in the violence.

[The principal differences between the ICTY Statute and the ICTR Statute are that the latter omitted "violations of the laws or customs of war" but specifically included "serious violations of Common Article 3." Thus, the ICTR has jurisdiction over Common Article 3, genocide, and crimes against humanity.]

1. INTRODUCTION

6. The Amended Indictment [stated, among other things]:

12. As bourgmestre, Jean Paul AKAYESU was responsible for maintaining law and public order in his commune. At least 2000 Tutsis were killed in Taba between April 7 and the end of June, 1994, while he was still in power. The killings in Taba were openly committed and so widespread that, as bourgmestre, Jean Paul AKAYESU must have known about them. Although he had the authority and responsibility to do so, Jean Paul AKAYESU never attempted to prevent the killing of Tutsis in the commune in any way or called for assistance from regional or national authorities to quell the violence.

12A. Between April 7 and the end of June, 1994, hundreds of civilians (hereinafter "displaced civilians") sought refuge at the bureau communal. The majority of these displaced civilians were Tutsi. While seeking refuge at the bureau communal, female displaced civilians were regularly taken by armed local militia and/or communal police and subjected to sexual violence, and/or beaten on or near the bureau communal premises. Displaced civilians were also murdered frequently on or near the bureau communal premises. Many women were forced to endure multiple acts of sexual violence which were at times committed by more than one assailant. These acts of sexual violence were generally accompanied by explicit threats of death or bodily harm. The female displaced civilians lived in constant fear and their physical and psychological health deteriorated as a result of the sexual violence and beatings and killings.

12B. Jean Paul AKAYESU knew that the acts of sexual violence, beatings and murders were being committed and was at times present during their commission. Jean Paul AKAYESU facilitated the commission of the sexual violence, beatings and murders by allowing the sexual violence and beatings and murders to occur on or near the bureau communal premises. By virtue of his presence during the commission of the sexual violence, beatings and murders and by failing to prevent the sexual violence, beatings and murders, Jean Paul AKAYESU encouraged these activities.

14. The morning of April 19, 1994, following the murder of Sylvere Karera, Jean Paul AKAYESU led a meeting in Gishyeshye sector at which he sanctioned the death of Sylvere Karera and urged the population to eliminate accomplices of the RPF, which was understood by those present to mean Tutsis. Over 100 people were present at the meeting. The killing of Tutsis in Taba began shortly after the meeting.

15. At the same meeting in Gishyeshye sector on April 19, 1994, Jean Paul AKAYESU named at least three prominent Tutsis who had to be killed because of their alleged relationships with the RPF. Later that day, Juvénal Rukundakuvuga was killed in Kanyinya. Within the next few days, Emmanuel Sempabwa was clubbed to death in front of the Taba bureau communal.

19. On or about April 19, 1994, Jean Paul AKAYESU took 8 detained men from the Taba bureau communal and ordered militia members to kill them. The militia killed them with clubs, machetes, small axes and sticks. The victims had fled from Runda commune and had been held by Jean Paul AKAYESU.

20. On or about April 19, 1994, Jean Paul AKAYESU ordered the local people and militia to kill intellectual and influential people. Five teachers from the secondary school of Taba were killed on his instructions. The local people and militia killed them with machetes and agricultural tools in front of the Taba bureau communal.

30. In essence, the Defence case – insofar as the Chamber has been able to establish it – is that the Accused did not commit, order or participate in any of the killings, beatings or acts of sexual violence alleged in the Indictment. The Defence concedes that a genocide occurred in Rwanda and that massacres of Tutsi took place in Taba Commune, but it argues that the Accused was helpless to prevent them, being outnumbered and overpowered by one Silas Kubwimana and the Interahamwe. The Defence pointed out that, according to prosecution witness R, Akayesu had been so harassed by the Interahamwe that at one point he had had to flee Taba commune. Once the massacres had become widespread, the Accused was denuded of all authority and lacked the means to stop the killings.

31. The Defence claims that the Chamber should not require the Accused to be a hero, to have laid down his life – as, for example, did the bourgmestre of Mugina – in a futile attempt to prevent killings and beatings. The Defence alluded to the fact that General Dallaire, in charge of UNAMIR and 2,500 troops, was unable to prevent the genocide. How, then, was Akayesu, with 10 communal policemen at his disposal, to fare any better? Moreover, the Defence argue, no bourgmestre in the whole of Rwanda was able to prevent the massacres in his Commune, no matter how willing he was to do so.

3. GENOCIDE IN RWANDA IN 1994?

114. Even though the number of victims is yet to be known with accuracy, no one can reasonably refute the fact that widespread killings were perpetrated throughout Rwanda in 1994.

116. Consequently, in view of these widespread killings the victims of which were mainly Tutsi, the Chamber is of the opinion that the first requirement for there to be genocide has been met, the killing and causing serious bodily harm to members of a group.

117. The second requirement is that these killings and serious bodily harm, as is the case in this instance, be committed with the intent to destroy, in whole or in part, a particular group targeted as such.

118. In the opinion of the Chamber, there is no doubt that considering their undeniable scale, their systematic nature and their atrociousness, the massacres were aimed at exterminating the group that was targeted.

4. EVIDENTIARY MATTERS

151. The Interahamwe were the youth movement of the MRND. During the war, the term also covered anyone who had anti-Tutsi tendencies, irrespective of their political background, and who collaborated with the MRND youth.

5. FACTUAL FINDINGS

192. The Chamber finds that the allegations set forth in paragraph 12 cannot be fully established. The Accused did take action between 7 April and 18 April to protect the citizens of his commune. It appears that he did also request assistance from national authorities at the meeting on 18 April 1994. Accordingly, the Accused did attempt to prevent the killing of Tutsi in his Commune, and it cannot be said that he never did so.

193. Nevertheless, the Chamber finds beyond a reasonable doubt that the conduct of the Accused changed after 18 April 1994 and that after this date the Accused did not attempt to prevent the killing of Tutsi in the commune of Taba. In fact, there is evidence that he not only knew of and witnessed killings, but that he participated in and even ordered killings. The fact that on one occasion he helped one Hutu woman protect her Tutsi children does not alter the Chamber's assessment that the Accused did not generally attempt to prevent the killings at all after 18 April. The Accused contends that he was subject to coercion, but the Chamber finds this contention greatly inconsistent with a substantial amount of concordant testimony from other witnesses. It is also inconsistent with his own pre-trial written statement. Witness C testified to having heard the accused say to an Interahamwe "I do not think that what we are doing is proper. We are going to have to pay for this blood that is being shed,"a statement which indicates the Accused's knowledge of the wrongfulness of his acts and his awareness of the consequences of his deeds. For these reasons, the Chamber does not accept the testimony of the Accused regarding his conduct after 18 April, and finds beyond a reasonable doubt that he did not attempt to prevent killings of Tutsi after this date. Whether he had the power to do so is not at issue, as he never even tried and as there is evidence establishing beyond a reasonable doubt that he consciously chose the course of collaboration with violence against Tutsi rather than shielding them from it.

309. The Chamber finds that it has been proved beyond reasonable doubt that Akayesu released eight detained men of Runda commune whom he was holding in the bureau communal and handed them over to the Interahamwe. It has also been proved beyond reasonable doubt that Akayesu ordered the local militia to kill them. It has been proved beyond reasonable doubt that the eight refugees were killed by the Interahamwe in the presence of Akayesu. It has been proved beyond reasonable doubt that the eight refugees were killed because they were Tutsi.

313. The Chamber finds that it has been proved beyond reasonable doubt that on or about 19 April 1994, Akayesu ordered the local people and Interahamwe to kill "intellectual people." It has been proved beyond reasonable doubt that, after the killing of the refugees, Akayesu instructed the local people and Interahamwe near him at the bureau communal to "fetch the one who remains," a professor by the name of Samuel, and that consequent to this instruction, a

certain professor by the name of Samuel was brought to the bureau communal. It has been proved beyond reasonable doubt that Samuel was then killed by the local people and Interahamwe with a machete blow to the neck. The Chamber finds that it has been proved beyond reasonable doubt that teachers from the commune of Taba were killed pursuant to the instructions of Akayesu.

314. The Chamber finds that it has been proved beyond reasonable doubt that the teachers were killed because they were Tutsi.

359. On the basis of consistent evidence and the facts confirmed by the Accused himself, the Chamber is satisfied beyond a reasonable doubt that the Accused was present in Gishyeshye, during the early hours of 19 April 1994, that he joined the crowd gathered around the body of a young member of the Interahamwe militia, and that he took that opportunity to address the people. Furthermore, on the basis of consistent evidence, the Chamber is satisfied beyond a reasonable doubt that on that occasion, the Accused, by virtue of his functions as bourgmestre and the authority he held over the population, did lead the crowd and the ensuing proceedings.

361. With regard to the allegation that the Accused urged the population, during the said gathering, to eliminate the accomplices of the RPF, after considering the weight of all supporting and corroborative evidence, the Chamber is satisfied beyond a reasonable doubt that the Accused clearly called on the population to unite and eliminate the sole enemy: accomplices of the Inkotanyi. The Chamber is satisfied beyond a reasonable doubt that the Accused was himself fully aware of the impact of his statement on the crowd and of the fact that his call to wage war against Inkotanyi accomplices could be construed as one to kill the Tutsi in general.

452. On the basis of the evidence set forth herein, the Chamber finds beyond a reasonable doubt that the Accused had reason to know and in fact knew that sexual violence was taking place on or near the premises of the bureau communal, and that women were being taken away from the bureau communal and sexually violated. There is no evidence that the Accused took any measures to prevent acts of sexual violence or to punish the perpetrators of sexual violence. In fact there is evidence that the Accused ordered, instigated and otherwise aided and abetted sexual violence.

6. THE LAW

6.1 Cumulative Charges

461. In the amended Indictment, the accused is charged cumulatively with more than one crime in relation to the same sets of facts, in all but count 4. [ICT practice is to make sentences run concurrently for convictions based on the same facts.]

467. It is clear that the practice of concurrent sentencing ensures that the accused is not twice punished for the same acts. Notwithstanding this absence of prejudice to the accused, it is still necessary to justify the prosecutorial practice of accumulating criminal charges.

468. On the basis of national and international law and jurisprudence, the Chamber concludes that it is acceptable to convict the accused of two offences in

relation to the same set of facts in the following circumstances: (1) where the offences have different elements; or (2) where the provisions creating the offences protect different interests; or (3) where it is necessary to record a conviction for both offences in order fully to describe what the accused did. However, the Chamber finds that it is not justifiable to convict an accused of two offences in relation to the same set of facts where (a) one offence is a lesser included offence of the other, for example, murder and grievous bodily harm, robbery and theft, or rape and indecent assault; or (b) where one offence charges accomplice liability and the other offence charges liability as a principal, *e.g,*. genocide and complicity in genocide.

469. Having regard to its Statute, the Chamber believes that the offences under the Statute – genocide, crimes against humanity, and violations of article 3 common to the Geneva Conventions and of Additional Protocol II – have different elements and, moreover, are intended to protect different interests. The crime of genocide exists to protect certain groups from extermination or attempted extermination. The concept of crimes against humanity exists to protect civilian populations from persecution. The idea of violations of article 3 common to the Geneva Conventions and of Additional Protocol II is to protect non-combatants from war crimes in civil war. These crimes have different purposes and are, therefore, never co-extensive.

6.3. Genocide (Article 2 of the Statute)

6.3.1. Genocide

494. The definition of genocide, as given in Article 2 of the Tribunal's Statute, is taken verbatim from Articles 2 and 3 of the Convention on the Prevention and Punishment of the Crime of Genocide (the "Genocide Convention"). It states:

> Genocide means any of the following acts committed with intent to destroy, in whole or in part, a national, ethnical, racial or religious group, as such: (a) Killing members of the group; (b) Causing serious bodily or mental harm to members of the group; (c) Deliberately inflicting on the group conditions of life calculated to bring about its physical destruction in whole or in part; (d) Imposing measures intended to prevent births within the group; (e) Forcibly transferring children of the group to another group.

498. Genocide is distinct from other crimes inasmuch as it embodies a special intent, . . . "the intent to destroy, in whole or in part, a national, ethnical, racial or religious group, as such."

512. [T]he Chamber holds that a national group is defined as a collection of people who are perceived to share a legal bond based on common citizenship, coupled with reciprocity of rights and duties.

513. An ethnic group is generally defined as a group whose members share a common language or culture.

514. The conventional definition of racial group is based on the hereditary physical traits often identified with a geographical region, irrespective of linguistic, cultural, national or religious factors.

515. The religious group is one whose members share the same religion, denomination or mode of worship.

560. The mens rea required for the crime of direct and public incitement to commit genocide lies in the intent to directly prompt or provoke another to commit genocide.

6.4. Crimes against Humanity (Article 3 of the Statute)

565. Crimes against humanity are aimed at any civilian population and are prohibited regardless of whether they are committed in an armed conflict, international or internal in character.

567. The Chamber notes that, following the Nuremberg and Tokyo trials, the concept of crimes against humanity underwent a gradual evolution in the Eichmann, Barbie, Touvier and Papon cases.

568. In the *Eichmann* case, the accused, Otto Adolf Eichmann, was charged with offences under [Israeli] Nazi and Nazi Collaborators Law for his participation in the implementation of the plan known as the "Final Solution of the Jewish problem." The district court in the *Eichmann* case stated that crimes against humanity differs from genocide in that for the commission of genocide special intent is required. This special intent is not required for crimes against humanity. Eichmann was convicted by the District court and sentenced to death.

569. In the *Barbie* case, the accused, Klaus Barbie, who was the head of the Gestapo in Lyons from November 1942 to August 1944, during the wartime occupation of France, was convicted in 1987 of crimes against humanity for his role in the deportation and extermination of civilians. The French Court of Cassation, . . . held that:

> The fact that the accused . . . took part in the execution of a common plan to bring about the deportation or extermination of the civilian population during the war, or persecutions on political, racial or religious grounds, constituted not a distinct offence or an aggravating circumstance but rather an essential element of the crime against humanity, consisting of the fact that the acts charged were performed in a systematic manner in the name of a State practising by those means a policy of ideological supremacy.

577. Article 7 of the Statute of the International Criminal Court defines a crime against humanity as any of the enumerated acts committed as part of a widespread of systematic attack directed against any civilian population, with knowledge of the attack

578. The Chamber considers that Article 3 of the Statute confers on the Chamber the jurisdiction to prosecute persons for various inhumane acts which constitute crimes against humanity. This category of crimes may be broadly broken down into four essential elements, namely:

> (i) the act must be inhumane in nature and character, causing great suffering, or serious injury to body or to mental or physical health;
>
> (ii) the act must be committed as part of a wide spread or systematic attack;
>
> (iii) the act must be committed against members of the civilian population;

(iv) the act must be committed on one or more discriminatory grounds, namely, national, political, ethnic, racial or religious grounds.

6.5. Violations of Common Article 3 and Additional Protocol II (Article 4 of the Statute)

599. Pursuant to Article 4 of the Statute, the Chamber shall have the power to prosecute persons committing or ordering to be committed serious violations of Article 3 common to the four Geneva Conventions of 12 August 1949 for the Protection of War Victims, and of Additional Protocol II thereto of 8 June 1977. [Common Article 3 applies during "armed conflicts not of an international character."] These violations shall include, but shall not be limited to:

a) violence to life, health and physical or mental well-being of persons, in particular murder as well as cruel treatment such as torture, mutilation or any form of corporal punishment;

b) collective punishments;

c) taking of hostages;

d) acts of terrorism;

e) outrages upon personal dignity, in particular humiliating and degrading treatment, rape, enforced prostitution and any form of indecent assault;

f) pillage;

g) the passing of sentences and the carrying out of executions without previous judgment pronounced by a regularly constituted court, affording all the judicial guarantees which are recognised as indispensable by civilised peoples;

h) threats to commit any of the foregoing acts.

601. The four 1949 Geneva Conventions and the 1977 Additional Protocol I thereto generally apply to international armed conflicts only, whereas Article 3 common to the Geneva Conventions extends a minimum threshold of humanitarian protection as well to all persons affected by a non-international conflict, a protection which was further developed and enhanced in the 1977 Additional Protocol II. In the field of international humanitarian law, a clear distinction as to the thresholds of application has been made between situations of international armed conflicts, in which the law of armed conflicts is applicable as a whole, situations of non-international (internal) armed conflicts, where Common Article 3 and Additional Protocol II are applicable, and non-international armed conflicts where only Common Article 3 is applicable. Situations of internal disturbances are not covered by international humanitarian law.

619. The norms set by Common Article 3 apply to a conflict as soon as it is an "armed conflict not of an international character." An inherent question follows such a description, namely, what constitutes an armed conflict? The Appeals Chamber in the *Tadic decision on Jurisdiction* held "that an armed conflict exists whenever there is . . . protracted armed violence between governmental authorities and organized armed groups or between such groups within a State.

International humanitarian law applies from the initiation of such armed conflicts and extends beyond the cessation of hostilities until . . . in the case of internal conflicts, a peaceful settlement is reached."

625. It suffices to recall that an armed conflict is distinguished from internal disturbances by the level of intensity of the conflict and the degree of organization of the parties to the conflict. Under Additional Protocol II, the parties to the conflict will usually either be the government confronting dissident armed forces, or the government fighting insurgent organized armed groups.

626. The armed forces opposing the government must be under responsible command, which entails a degree of organization within the armed group or dissident armed forces. This degree of organization should be such so as to enable the armed group or dissident forces to plan and carry out concerted military operations, and to impose discipline in the name of a de facto authority. Further, these armed forces must be able to dominate a sufficient part of the territory so as to maintain sustained and concerted military operations. In essence, the operations must be continuous and planned. The territory in their control is usually that which has eluded the control of the government forces.

627. In the present case, evidence has been presented to the Chamber which showed there was at the least a conflict not of a international character in Rwanda at the time of the events alleged in the Indictment. It has been shown that there was a conflict between, on the one hand, the RPF, under the command of General Kagame, and, on the other, the governmental forces, the FAR.

631. The duties and responsibilities of the Geneva Conventions and the Additional Protocols, hence, will normally apply only to individuals of all ranks belonging to the armed forces under the military command of either of the belligerent parties, or to individuals who were legitimately mandated and expected, as public officials or agents or persons otherwise holding public authority or de facto representing the Government, to support or fulfil the war efforts.

634. Thus it is clear from the above that the laws of war must apply equally to civilians as to combatants in the conventional sense. Further, the Chamber notes, in light of the above dicta, that the accused was not, at the time of the events in question, a mere civilian but a bourgmestre. The Chamber therefore concludes that, if so established factually, the accused could fall in the class of individuals who may be held responsible for serious violations of international humanitarian law, in particular serious violations of Common Article 3 and Additional Protocol II.

7. LEGAL FINDINGS

[Akayesu was found not guilty of war crimes because there was not a sufficient connection between him and the government forces. He was found guilty of crimes against humanity for murder or aiding and abetting murder as to incidents at which he was present during a period of armed conflict. He was found guilty of genocide and incitement to genocide. He was found guilty of crimes against humanity on the basis of torture incidents in which detainees were interrogated with threats to their lives or with physical beating. He was found guilty of crimes against humanity on the basis of sexual violence which he either specifically instigated or which took place in the government compound while he was present. In all, he was convicted on 9 of 15 counts.]

NOTES AND QUESTIONS

1. If Akayesu is held responsible for murder and genocide based on his failure to "attempt to stop the killing," who else should be prosecuted on this basis? doctors? photographers and journalists? Belgian military officials? In the language of Anglo-American tort law, what gives rise to a duty to act? Harkening back to the *Yamashita* questions, is it fair to hold civilian leaders responsible for the acts of their citizens?

2. If "widespread and systematic" violence by civilians against fellow civilians is already criminal under international law, do we need a separate concept for terrorism? What would be the limits of the theories deployed in *Akayesu*?

3. Would it be genocide to try to kill all Republicans in the U.S.? what about all Baptists? The ICTR states that the concept applies to groups that are "permanent and stable," but it also says that ethnicity is based on cultural identity. In the current literature, it appears that ethnic identity is a matter of some degree of choice by each individual. If I am free to think of myself as American, or Irish-American, or English, could I also have the choice of thinking of myself as Armenian? Or is the identity more a matter of what others think you are, in which case it is not a matter of your own choice but someone else's?

4. You should recall the *Akayesu* case when we come to the "prisoner abuse scandal" of Abu Ghraib and Guantanamo.

[C] INTERNATIONAL CRIMINAL COURT

The Statute of the International Criminal Court went into effect on 1 July 2002 with 139 signatory nations. The statute creates a court for prosecution of individuals who commit crimes in four categories: aggression, genocide, crimes against humanity, or war crimes. There are definitional elaborations for each of these categories except for the crime of aggression. The applicable law is stated to be the Statute itself, plus "applicable treaties and the principles and rules of international law, including the established principles of the international law of armed conflict" and "general principles of law derived by the Court from national laws."

The United States initially signed the document on 31 December 2000 (during the last weeks of the Clinton administration) and then withdrew its consent during the Bush administration. The U.S. government sent the following communique to the UN on 6 May 2002:

> This is to inform you, in connection with the Rome Statute of the International Criminal Court adopted on July 17, 1998, that the United States does not intend to become a party to the treaty. Accordingly, the United States has no legal obligations arising from its signature on December 31, 2000. The United States requests that its intention not to become a party, as expressed in this letter, be reflected in the depositary's status lists relating to this treaty.

The ICC is still in its formative stages. *See http://www.icc-cpi.int/home.html.* In 2004, the Prosecutor opened investigations into two situations in Africa at the behest of the governments of Uganda and the Congo.

In a related development, some nations have specifically asserted "universal jurisdiction" over offenses against international law, such as war crimes. The Center for Constitutional Rights, an American NGO, filed a petition with the Federal Prosecutor in Germany seeking prosecution of Secretary of Defense Rumsfeld and others for the prisoner abuses at Abu Ghraib. *http://www.ccr-ny.org/v2/reports/report.asp?ObjID=TCRlT9TuSb&Content=471*

[D] EXTRADITION AND UNIVERSAL JURISDICTION

International Conventions related to terrorism all proceed on the following structure: state parties agree to criminalize certain behavior, to cooperate in the apprehension of persons who commit that behavior, and then either to extradite or prosecute an accused person. Extradition arises only by operation of treaties and not by operation of general customary international law, although there is some reason to expect this to change under increasing pressure of international regimes.

One reason that it is important for states to agree to criminalize the defined behavior is that extradition hinges on the principle of "dual criminality," which permits extradition only if the alleged conduct would be criminal in both the requesting and requested states. Dual criminality does not require identity of all elements of the crime or of procedures for adjudication, it requires only that the specific alleged conduct would be criminal in both jurisdictions. The next case involves an effort by Spain to extradite the former Chilean President from Britain to stand trial in Spain. It is not an international prosecution but an effort by one state to prosecute for crimes committed in another state. Part of the conceptual difficulty with this situation is the question of what law is the prosecuting state to enforce? Of course, the political difficulties of Britain in this instance were that it felt caught between the Spain and Chile.

Ex Parte PINOCHET UGARTE (No. 3)

[2000] 1 AC 147, [1999] 2 All ER 97 (HOUSE OF LORDS 1999)

[Spain applied for extradition of Pinochet to prosecute him for crimes allegedly committed while he was President of Chile. The lower court held that the offenses were not extraditable for lack of "dual criminality" and that Pinochet had immunity as a head of state when the offenses were committed. The government appealed to the House of Lords. The House held that Pinochet could be extradited only for acts committed after the date on which Chile ratified the Convention Against Torture in 1988. The House of Lords by tradition acts through an Appellate Committee of judges who each submits a separate opinion.]

LORD BROWNE-WILKINSON:

My Lords, as is well known, this case concerns an attempt by the Government of Spain to extradite Senator Pinochet from this country to stand trial in Spain for crimes committed (primarily in Chile) during the period when Senator Pinochet was head of state in Chile.

The facts

On 11 September 1973 a right-wing coup evicted the left-wing regime of President Allende. The coup was led by a military junta, of whom Senator (then General) Pinochet was the leader. At some stage he became head of state. The Pinochet regime remained in power until 11 March 1990 when Senator Pinochet resigned.

There is no real dispute that during the period of the Senator Pinochet regime appalling acts of barbarism were committed in Chile and elsewhere in the world: torture, murder and the unexplained disappearance of individuals, all on a large scale. Although it is not alleged that Senator Pinochet himself committed any of those acts, it is alleged that they were done in pursuance of a conspiracy to which he was a party, at his instigation and with his knowledge. He denies these allegations. None of the conduct alleged was committed by or against citizens of the United Kingdom or in the United Kingdom.

In 1998 Senator Pinochet came to the United Kingdom for medical treatment. The judicial authorities in Spain sought to extradite him in order to stand trial in Spain on a large number of charges. Some of those charges had links with Spain. But most of the charges had no connection with Spain. The background to the case is that to those of left-wing political convictions Senator Pinochet is seen as an arch-devil: to those of right-wing persuasions he is seen as the saviour of Chile. It may well be thought that the trial of Senator Pinochet in Spain for offences all of which related to the State of Chile and most of which occurred in Chile is not calculated to achieve the best justice. Our job is to decide two questions of law: are there any extradition crimes and, if so, is Senator Pinochet immune from trial for committing those crimes. If, as a matter of law, there are no extradition crimes or he is entitled to immunity in relation to whichever crimes there are, then there is no legal right to extradite Senator Pinochet to Spain or, indeed, to stand in the way of his return to Chile. If, on the other hand, there are extradition crimes in relation to which Senator Pinochet is not entitled to state immunity then it will be open to the Home Secretary to extradite him. The task of this House is only to decide those points of law.

On 16 October 1998 an international warrant for the arrest of Senator Pinochet was issued in Spain. On the same day, a magistrate in London issued a provisional warrant ("the first warrant") under section 8 of the Extradition Act 1989. He was arrested in a London hospital on 17 October 1998. On 18 October the Spanish authorities issued a second international warrant. A further provisional warrant ("the second warrant") was issued by the magistrate at Bow Street Magistrates' Court on 22 October 1998 accusing Senator Pinochet of [torture and conspiracy to commit torture between 1 January 1988 and December 1992, taking of hostages and conspiracy to take hostages between 1 January 1982 and 31 January 1992, and conspiracy to commit murder between January 1976 and December 1992].

Outline of the Law

In general, a state only exercises criminal jurisdiction over offences which occur within its geographical boundaries. If a person who is alleged to have committed a crime in Spain is found in the United Kingdom, Spain can apply to the United Kingdom to extradite him to Spain. The power to extradite from the United Kingdom for an "extradition crime" is now contained in the Extradition Act 1989. That Act defines what constitutes an "extradition crime." For the purposes of the present case, the most important requirement is that the conduct complained of must constitute a crime under the law both of Spain and of the United Kingdom. This is known as the double criminality rule.

Since the Nazi atrocities and the Nuremberg trials, international law has recognised a number of offences as being international crimes. Individual states have taken jurisdiction to try some international crimes even in cases where such crimes were not committed within the geographical boundaries of such states. The most important of such international crimes for present purposes is torture which is regulated by the International Convention against Torture and other Cruel, Inhuman or Degrading Treatment or Punishment. The obligations placed on the United Kingdom by that Convention (and on the other 110 or more signatory states who have adopted the Convention) were incorporated into the law of the United Kingdom by section 134 of the Criminal Justice Act 1988. That Act came into force on 29 September 1988. Section 134 created a new crime under United Kingdom law, the crime of torture. As required by the Torture Convention "all" torture wherever committed worldwide was made criminal under United Kingdom law and triable in the United Kingdom.

No one has suggested that before section 134 came into effect torture committed outside the United Kingdom was a crime under United Kingdom law. Nor is it suggested that section 134 was retrospective so as to make torture committed outside the United Kingdom before 29 September 1988 a United Kingdom crime. Since torture outside the United Kingdom was not a crime under U.K. law until 29 September 1988, the principle of double criminality which requires an Act to be a crime under both the law of Spain and of the United Kingdom cannot be satisfied in relation to conduct before that date.

Torture [and Universal Jurisdiction]

Apart from the law of piracy, the concept of personal liability under international law for international crimes is of comparatively modern growth. The traditional subjects of international law are states not human beings. But consequent upon the war crime trials after the 1939-45 World War, the international community came to recognise that there could be criminal liability under international law for a class of crimes such as war crimes and crimes against humanity. In the early years state torture was one of the elements of a war crime. In consequence torture, and various other crimes against humanity, were linked to war or at least to hostilities of some kind. But in the course of time this linkage with war fell away and torture, divorced from war or hostilities, became an international crime on its own: *see Prosecutor v. Furundzija*, International Criminal Tribunal for the Former Yugoslavia, Case No. IT-95-17/1-T 10.

Moreover, the Republic of Chile accepted before your Lordships that the international law prohibiting torture has the character of *jus cogens* or a peremptory norm, i.e. one of those rules of international law which have a particular status. In the *Furundzija* case, at paragraphs 153 and 154, the tribunal said:

Because of the importance of the values it protects, [the prohibition of torture] has evolved into a peremptory norm or *jus cogens*, that is, a norm that enjoys a higher rank in the international hierarchy than treaty law and even 'ordinary' customary rules. The most conspicuous consequence of this higher rank is that the principle at issue cannot be derogated from by states through international treaties or local or special customs or even general customary rules not endowed with the same normative force. . . . Clearly, the *jus cogens* nature of the prohibition against torture articulates the notion that the prohibition has now become one of the most fundamental standards of the international community. Furthermore, this prohibition is designed to produce a deterrent effect, in that it signals to all members of the international community and the individuals over whom they wield authority that the prohibition of torture is an absolute value from which nobody must deviate.

The *jus cogens* nature of the international crime of torture justifies states in taking universal jurisdiction over torture wherever committed. International law provides that offences *jus cogens* may be punished by any state because the offenders are "common enemies of all mankind and all nations have an equal interest in their apprehension and prosecution:"

But there was no tribunal or court to punish international crimes of torture. Local courts could take jurisdiction. But the objective was to ensure a general jurisdiction so that the torturer was not safe wherever he went. For example, in this case it is alleged that during the Pinochet regime torture was an official, although unacknowledged, weapon of government and that, when the regime was about to end, it passed legislation designed to afford an amnesty to those who had engaged in institutionalised torture. If these allegations are true, the fact that the local court had jurisdiction to deal with the international crime of torture was nothing to the point so long as the totalitarian regime remained in power: a totalitarian regime will not permit adjudication by its own courts on its own shortcomings. Hence the demand for some international machinery to repress state torture which is not dependent upon the local courts where the torture was committed. In the event, over 110 states (including Chile, Spain and the United Kingdom) became state parties to the Torture Convention. But it is far from clear that none of them practised state torture. What was needed therefore was an international system which could punish those who were guilty of torture and which did not permit the evasion of punishment by the torturer moving from one state to another. The Torture Convention was agreed not in order to create an international crime which had not previously existed but to provide an international system under which the international criminal – the torturer – could find no safe haven.

The Torture Convention

Article 1 of the Convention defines torture as the intentional infliction of severe pain and of suffering with a view to achieving a wide range of purposes "when such pain or suffering is inflicted by or at the instigation of or with the consent or acquiescence of a public official or other person acting in an official capacity." Article 2(1) requires each state party to prohibit torture on territory within its own jurisdiction and article 4 requires each state party to ensure that "all" acts of torture are offences under its criminal law. Article 2(3) outlaws any defence of superior orders. Under article 5(1) each state party has to establish its jurisdiction over torture (a) when committed within territory under its jurisdiction (b) when the alleged offender is a national of that state, and (c) in certain circumstances, when the victim is a national of that state. Under article 5(2) a state party has to take jurisdiction over any alleged offender who is found within its territory. Article 6 contains provisions for a state in whose territory an alleged torturer is found to detain him, inquire into the position and notify the states referred to in article 5(1) and to indicate whether it intends to exercise jurisdiction. Under article 7 the state in whose territory the alleged torturer is found shall, if he is not extradited to any of the states mentioned in article 5(1), submit him to its authorities for the purpose of prosecution. Under article 8(1) torture is to be treated as an extraditable offence and under article 8(4) torture shall, for the purposes of extradition, be treated as having been committed not only in the place where it occurred but also in the state mentioned in article 5(1).

State immunity

It is a basic principle of international law that one sovereign state (the forum state) does not adjudicate on the conduct of a foreign state. The foreign state is entitled to procedural immunity from the processes of the forum state. This immunity extends to both criminal and civil liability. State immunity probably grew from the historical immunity of the person of the monarch. In any event, such personal immunity of the head of state persists to the present day: the head of state is entitled to the same immunity as the state itself. The diplomatic representative of the foreign state in the forum state is also afforded the same immunity in recognition of the dignity of the state which he represents. This immunity enjoyed by a head of state in power and an ambassador in post is a complete immunity attaching to the person of the head of state or ambassador and rendering him immune from all actions or prosecutions whether or not they relate to matters done for the benefit of the state. Such immunity is said to be granted *ratione personae*.

The continuing partial immunity of the ambassador after leaving post is of a different kind from that enjoyed *ratione personae* while he was in post. Since he is no longer the representative of the foreign state he merits no particular privileges or immunities as a person. However in order to preserve the integrity of the activities of the foreign state during the period when he was ambassador, it is necessary to provide that immunity is afforded to his official acts during his tenure in post. If this were not done the sovereign immunity of the state could be evaded by calling in question acts done during the previous ambassador's time. Accordingly under article 39(2) the ambassador, like any other official of the state, enjoys immunity in relation to his official acts done while he was an official. This limited immunity, *ratione materiae*, is to be contrasted with the former immunity ratione personae which gave complete immunity to all activities whether public or private.

The question then which has to be answered is whether the alleged organisation of state torture by Senator Pinochet (if proved) would constitute an act committed by Senator Pinochet as part of his official functions as head of state. It is not enough to say that it cannot be part of the functions of the head of state to commit a crime. Actions which are criminal under the local law can still have been done officially and therefore give rise to immunity *ratione materiae*. The case needs to be analysed more closely.

I have doubts whether, before the coming into force of the Torture Convention, the existence of the international crime of torture as *jus cogens* was enough to justify the conclusion that the organisation of state torture could not rank for immunity purposes as performance of an official function. At that stage there was no international tribunal to punish torture and no general jurisdiction to permit or require its punishment in domestic courts. Not until there was some form of universal jurisdiction for the punishment of the crime of torture could it really be talked about as a fully constituted international crime. But in my judgment the Torture Convention did provide what was missing: a worldwide universal jurisdiction. Further, it required all member states to ban and outlaw torture. How can it be for international law purposes an official function to do something which international law itself prohibits and criminalises? Thirdly, an essential feature of the international crime of torture is that it must be committed "by or with the acquiesence of a public official or other person acting in an official capacity." As a result all defendants in torture cases will be state officials. Yet, if the former head of state has immunity, the man most responsible will escape liability while his inferiors (the chiefs of police, junior army officers) who carried out his orders will be liable. I find it impossible to accept that this was the intention.

For these reasons in my judgment if, as alleged, Senator Pinochet organised and authorised torture after 8 December 1988 [the date after which both Chile and the UK recognized torture as a crime wherever committed], he was not acting in any capacity which gives rise to immunity *ratione materiae* because such actions were contrary to international law, Chile had agreed to outlaw such conduct and Chile had agreed with the other parties to the Torture Convention that all signatory states should have jurisdiction to try official torture (as defined in the Convention) even if such torture were committed in Chile.

As to the charges of murder and conspiracy to murder, no one has advanced any reason why the ordinary rules of immunity should not apply and Senator Pinochet is entitled to such immunity.

For these reasons, I would allow the appeal so as to permit the extradition proceedings to proceed on the allegation that torture in pursuance of a conspiracy to commit torture was being committed by Senator Pinochet after 8 December 1988 when he lost his immunity.

LORD GOFF of Chieveley:

The central question in the appeal is whether Senator Pinochet is entitled as former head of state to the benefit of state immunity *ratione materiae* in respect of the charges advanced against him.

[I]f immunity *ratione materiae* was excluded [by the Torture Convention], former heads of state and senior public officials would have to think twice about travelling abroad, for fear of being the subject of unfounded allegations emanating from states of a different political persuasion. Preservation of state immunity is therefore a matter of particular importance to powerful countries whose heads of state perform an executive role, and who may therefore be regarded as possible targets by governments of states which, for deeply felt political reasons, deplore their actions while in office. But, to bring the matter nearer home, we must not overlook the fact that it is not only in the United States of America that a substantial body of opinion supports the campaign of the I.R.A. to overthrow the democratic government of Northern Ireland. It is not beyond the bounds of possibility that a state whose government is imbued with this opinion might seek to extradite from a third country, where he or she happens to be, a responsible Minister of the Crown, or even a more humble public official such as a police inspector, on the ground that he or she has acquiesced in a single act of physical or mental torture in Northern Ireland. The well known case of *Ireland v. United Kingdom* (1978) 2 E.H.R.R. 25 provides an indication of circumstances in which this might come about. [See Chapter 9 *infra*.]

Reasons such as these may well have persuaded possible state parties to the Torture Convention that it would be unwise to give up the valuable protection afforded by state immunity. Indeed, it would be strange if state parties had given up the immunity *ratione materiae* of a head of state which is regarded as an essential support for his immunity *ratione personae*. In practice state immunity is relevant in only two cases – where the offender is present in a third state, or where the offender is present in a state one of whose nationals was the victim, that state being different from the state where the offence was committed.

LORD HOPE of Craighead:

The crimes which are alleged in the Spanish request are murder on such a scale as to amount to genocide and terrorism, including torture and hostage-taking. The Secretary of State has already stated in his authority to proceed that Senator Pinochet is not to be extradited to Spain for genocide. So that part of the request must now be left out of account. But my impression is that the omission of the allegation of genocide is of little consequence in view of the scope which is given in Spanish law to the allegations of murder and terrorism.

Murder is a common law crime which, before it became an extraterritorial offence if committed in a convention country under section 4 of the Suppression of Terrorism Act 1978, could not be prosecuted in the United Kingdom if it was committed abroad except in the case of a murder committed abroad by a British citizen.

Section 134 of the Criminal Law Act 1988 did not come into force until 29 September 1988. But acts of physical torture were already criminal under

English law. Among the various offences against the person which would have been committed by torturing would have been the common law offence of assault occasioning actual bodily harm. A conspiracy which was entered into in England to commit these offences in England was an offence at common law.

However none of these offences, if committed prior to the coming into force of section 134 of the Criminal Justice Act 1988, could be said to be extraterritorial offences against the law of the United Kingdom as there is no basis upon which they could have been tried extraterritorially in this country. The effect of section 134 of the Criminal Justice Act 1988 was to make acts of official torture, wherever they were committed and whatever the nationality of the offender, an extraterritorial offence in the United Kingdom. The section came into force two months after the passing of the Act on 29 September 1988, and it was not retrospective. As from that date official torture was an extradition crime because it was an extraterritorial offence against the law of the United Kingdom.

DISPOSITION:

Appeal allowed to extent that extradition to proceed for offences of torture and conspiracy to torture occurring after 8 December 1988.

NOTES AND QUESTIONS

1. Lord Browne-Wilkinson states: "No one has suggested that before section 134 came into effect torture committed outside the United Kingdom was a crime under United Kingdom law." Why not? As Lord Hope states, torture and murder were crimes in the United Kingdom long before 1988. And dual criminality does not require that the requested nation assert extraterritorial jurisdiction over the alleged misconduct. So what would be the point of requiring that the requested nation criminalize conduct committed outside its borders? Lord Browne-Wilkinson's answer appears to be that the extraterritorial acts were not an extraditable crime because neither Spain nor the UK would have had jurisdiction until all three states ratified the Convention. Lord Hope's answer appears to be that the 1989 Act limited extradition to acts that would have been punishable in the UK, which acts committed in Chile would not have been until the 1988 Act proclaimed power to do so.

In other words, the problem is not whether the type of offense was a crime under English law, but whether the particular acts were punishable by both Britain and Spain. Murder and assault are not criminal under international jus cogens and thus not subject to universal jurisdiction, but torture is. In this sense, the Lords were struggling with the point in time at which torture became subject to either to universal jurisdiction or to the jurisdiction of Spain based on harms to its nationals. *See* DIANA WOODHOUSE, THE PINOCHET CASE (2000).

2. The issue of defining and criminalizing Torture will be explored again in Chapter 11 in the specific context of the "prisoner abuse" scandal arising from the aggressive interrogation of detainees in Iraq and Guantanamo. For now, it is enough to note that Lord Goff's concern about a third country's prosecution of a government official for torture based on policies of interrogation has borne fruit in the attempt to have Secretary Rumsfeld prosecuted by German authorities.

[E] INTERNATIONAL CONVENTIONS RELATED TO TERRORISM

The United Nations lists 12 separate Conventions dealing with terrorism. (*http://untreaty.un.org/English/Terrorism.asp*). The principal headings are aircraft crimes, protection of nuclear materials, hostage taking, and the most recent on financing of terrorism.

International concern over terrorism started with airplane hijackings in the 1960s. Although many of those incidents were just attempts by desperate persons to get "home" or conversely to flee to a perceived safer environment, some created dangerous situations as pilots were forced to divert their aircraft. These incidents also occasioned significant expense for the companies and countries involved. Even when the receiving country could make political mileage of the incident, it could prove costly. For example, if a hijacker diverted a plane from the U.S. to Cuba, the Cuban government would incur expenses in landing, refueling, and sending the plane on its way before it even experienced political costs associated with harboring someone who had committed what most countries would consider the crime of piracy.

As the phenomenon began to unfold, western nations enacted specific statutes criminalizing the offense of air piracy and attempted to extradite perpetrators. The host country, however, might be unwilling to extradite because it had promised safe haven to the hijacker as part of a deal in which the plane was allowed to land and the hijacker freed the crew and passengers. Reneging on that promise would then cause difficulties in future negotiations with hijackers. The first international treaty (convention) dealing with the issue attempted to meet the threat head-on by allowing the pilot ("aircraft commander") to subdue any person who threatened the safety of a flight. It also create an obligation on the part of a state to restore control of an aircraft to its crew and to send it on its way. Notably, however, the treaty specifically stated that "nothing in this Convention shall be deemed to create an obligation to grant extradition."

The attitude of the international community changed with the campaign of Palestinian hijackings beginning with El Al planes in 1968 and continuing through 1972 with hijackings of U.S. and British flag carriers. In some of those incidents, passengers and crew were killed. In most the hijackers were set free as part of negotiated deals, and in some instances the planes were blown up at the end of their usefulness. The 1970 Hague Convention dealing with aircraft hijacking and the 1971 Montreal Convention dealing with placing explosives on an airplane attempted to establish two central themes: signatory countries agreed to punish the proscribed offenses with "severe penalties" and a country having custody of an offender was required either to extradite or prosecute. (Almost as a sidenote, in order to define the offenses that were to be subject to "severe penalties," the Conventions described certain behaviors as criminal. Prior attempts to enact international criminal provisions had foundered, with the exception of the post-hoc definitions of war crimes in the Treaty of London.)

The 1972 Munich Olympics saw the kidnaping of the Israeli wrestling team and the botched rescue attempt at the Munich airport leaving 11 Israelis, 5 terrorists and one German policeman dead, much of which was displayed on international television. Then came the Achille Lauro, with the cold-blooded murder of a U.S. citizen in a wheelchair, and a series of kidnapings and murders of western diplomats in various African and Middle East countries. Two events prior to 9/11 touched U.S. interests or soil, the bombing of Pan Am 103 over Lockerbie, Scotland, and an attempted bombing of the World Trade Center, for which a number of associates of Osama bin Laden were convicted and bin Laden himself was indicted. The second millennium closed with a campaign of suicide bombings in Israel.

Meanwhile, the diplomatic wheels were turning out conventions: taking of hostages, piracy against maritime shipping, acts involving airports, control of nuclear devices and plastic explosives. Each of the conventions commits signatory nations to define the offenses as crimes within their own law, which in turn leads to a commitment either to extradite or to place the accused on trial. The loop is closed by stating that nobody can be tried if he or she has already been tried for the same offense unless the accusing nation finds that the first trial was essentially a sham.

No convention prior to the "Financing of Terrorism" in 1999 attempted to define terrorism. Instead, the conventions described "offenses" and committed signatory nations to criminalize those offenses. In many instances, there were exceptions to the description of offenses such as that the offense of placing an explosive on an aircraft did not apply to military or police aircraft. Another notable exception was that exploding a device in a public place did not constitute an offense under the convention if the perpetrator and victims were nationals of the same nation in which the acts occurred. It was only in these backhanded fashions that the international community addressed the phenomenon known as "terrorism."

In the Convention for the Suppression of Financing of Terrorism, it finally became necessary to define what the international community conceived to be terrorism:

Article 2

1. Any person commits an offence within the meaning of this Convention if that person by any means, directly or indirectly, unlawfully and wilfully, provides or collects funds with the intention that they should be used or in the knowledge that they are to be used, in full or in part, in order to carry out:

   a. An act which constitutes an offence within the scope of and as defined in one of the treaties listed in the annex; or

   b. Any other act intended to cause death or serious bodily injury to a civilian, or to any other person not taking an active part in the hostilities in a situation of armed conflict, when the purpose of such act, by its nature or context, is to intimidate a population, or to compel a Government or an international organization to do or to abstain from doing any act.

NOTES AND QUESTIONS

1. An apparently easy question that could provoke some much deeper thought is: What is a "situation of armed conflict" and why are persons engaged in it not protected by the Convention? Are the ordinary laws of war adequate for dealing with intentional harm to civilians during armed conflict?

2. What is the point of the mens rea requirement (purpose is to intimidate a population or coerce a government)? For that matter what is a population? What does it mean to describe the purpose of an act "by its nature or context?" Each of these points is discussed in the *Akayesu* opinion.

3. If a drug dealer lets it be known that his "troops" will conduct drive-by shootings in any neighborhood in which a snitch or informer might be living, is this terrorism?

4. With regard to the funding provision itself, do I commit an offense if I contribute money to an organization that is often described in the popular press as "having ties" or being the "political arm" of a group that does use violence? For example, Sinn Fein and the IRA. Or what about all the various factions of the PLO?

5. The U.S. Supreme Court held in *Buckley v. Valeo*, 424 U.S. 1 (1976), that contributing money to an election campaign is protected by the free expression clause of the First Amendment to the U.S. Constitution. In subsequent cases, this protection was extended to contributions to campaigns for political agenda other than partisan elections. The Court has also protected the freedom of association by which persons join organizations to carry out political objectives. Is there an argument that some of this activity could fall within the definition in the Convention yet also be protected by the U.S. Constitution? We will return to this question when we discuss U.S. statutes dealing with providing "material support" to terrorist organizations.

The Draft Comprehensive Convention on International Terrorism

The draft was proposed by India in 1996. It is significant that India would be the proponent because India is the leader of the Non-Aligned Movement. (India even refused to accept western aid following the December 2004 tsunami despite some criticism for that stance.) The draft has been in the process of review both by an ad hoc committee of the UN General Assembly and by the International Law Commission. To this date, no agreement has been reached, although the universal condemnation of terrorism by both General Assembly and Security Council appear to have taken away the thrust of the position that "one man's terrorist is another man's freedom fighter."

Despite unanimity on the condemnation of terrorism, there still remains some concern that an insurgent attacking only military targets of an occupying nation could be considered a terrorist and thus subject to international criminal sanctions and procedures. The difficulty is that the insurgent in that position would be considered a criminal under the law of the occupying force (e.g. the U.S. in Iraq), but the "developing" nations do not want to put that person in jeopardy of being apprehended and extradited or prosecuted by a third nation. The initial definition of terrorism in Article 2 is quite broad:

Article 2(1). Any person commits an offence within the meaning of this Convention if that person, by any means, unlawfully and intentionally, does an act intended to cause:

(a) Death or serious bodily injury to any person; or

(b) Serious damage to a State or government facility, a public transportation system, communication system or infrastructure facility with the intent to cause extensive destruction of such a place, facility or system, or where such destruction results or is likely to result in major economic loss;

when the purpose of such act, by its nature or context, is to intimidate a population, or to compel a Government or an international organization to do or abstain from doing any act.

The breadth of the definition, however, is ameliorated by the principal exclusion in Article 3:

This Convention shall not apply where the offence is committed within a single State, the alleged offender is a national of that State and is present in the territory of that State and no other State has a basis . . . to exercise jurisdiction . . . .

In addition, the obligations of the States Party to the Convention have a number of exclusions and limitations depending on their interest in or connection to the offense. The thrust of the controversy to this point has been whether to tighten the basic definition, rely on the exclusions and limitations, or undertake some combination of both.

SELECTED READINGS

Law of War:

- CHRISTINE GRAY, INTERNATIONAL LAW AND THE USE OF FORCE (2000).
- OSCAR SCHACHTER, INTERNATIONAL LAW IN THEORY AND PRACTICE (1991)
- RICHARD I. MILLER, THE LAW OF WAR (1975).
- MICHAEL HOWARD, GEORGE ANDROPOULOS & MARK SHULMAN, THE LAWS OF WAR (1994).
- TIMOTHY L.H. MCCORMACK & GERRY J. SIMPSON (EDS.), THE LAW OF WAR CRIMES (1997).
- INGRID DETTER DE LUPIS, THE LAW OF WAR (1987).
- Symposium, *The Changing Laws of War: Do We Need a New Legal Regime After September 11?* 79 NOTRE DAME L. REV. 1183 (2004).
- LEON FRIEDMAN, THE LAW OF WAR: A DOCUMENTARY HISTORY (1972).

International Criminal Law:

- LYAL S. SUNGA, THE EMERGING SYSTEM OF INTERNATIONAL CRIMINAL LAW (1997).
- CHRISTOPH SAFFERLING, TOWARDS AN INTERNATIONAL CRIMINAL PROCEDURE (2001).
- WILLIAM A. SCHABAS, AN INTRODUCTION TO THE INTERNATIONAL CRIMINAL COURT (2001).
- DIANA WOODHOUSE, THE PINOCHET CASE (2000).

Chapter 4

U.S. STATUTES & JURISDICTION

The story of U.S. involvement with terrorism really begins with the post-Civil War statutes aimed at the Ku Klux Klan. There are perhaps some lessons for the international community to be gained from the experience of U.S. federalism, and we will look at some of those developments later. For now, we will focus on the prosecutions and statutes involving "international terrorism" beginning with prosecutions of airplane hijackers and bombers in the 1980s.

§ 4.01 U.S. STATUTES RELATED TO TERRORISM

The U.S. passed statutes dealing with Aircraft Piracy and Hostage-Taking in response to, or in conjunction with, treaty obligations entered into during the 1970s. The Omnibus Diplomatic Security and Antiterrorism Act of 1986 produced what is now 18 U.S.C. § 2332, which sets penalties for murder or manslaughter in the case of anyone who "kills a national of the United States, while such national is outside the United States."

The first "material support" statute, 18 U.S.C. § 2339A, was adopted in 1994. The Antiterrorism and Effective Death Penalty Act of 1996 (AEDPA) produced what is now 18 U.S.C. § 2332b, "acts of terrorism transcending national boundaries" and the prohibition on material support to designated organizations in 18 U.S.C. § 2339B.

To become familiar with the statutory scheme, you should read and become familiar with the following principal statutes.

General Federal Criminal Law

There are ample federal statutes criminalizing actions such as murder, destruction of property, and other violent actions that touch federal interests. Because of U.S. constitutional limitations on the power of the federal government, all of these have some jurisdictional base that ties either to interstate commerce or to governmental interests. The basic civil rights criminal provisions are included for comparison.

18 U.S.C. §§ 1111, 1114, 1119 (Murder)

18 U.S.C. § 844 (Unlawful use of explosive materials)

18 U.S.C. §§ 242, 245 (Civil rights)

U.S. Statutes Based on Extraterritoriality and International Conventions

Many U.S. statutes carry their own statement of extraterritorial jurisdiction, while others refer to the general statement in section 7 of the Criminal Code. A number of other statutes carry out the obligation under international conventions to criminalize actions such as aircraft piracy regardless of where the event occurred.

18 U.S.C. § 7 (Extraterritorial jurisdiction in general)

18 U.S.C. § 32 (Destruction of aircraft – including threats)

18 U.S.C. § 2340 (Torture)

U.S. Statutes Referring to "Terrorism"

In recent years, attempts have been made to define crimes that are based on more general concepts of terrorism. The following are the principal U.S. statutes in this regard.

18 U.S.C. § 2331 (Terrorism Definitions)

18 U.S.C. § 2332 (Terrorist Homicide)

18 U.S.C. § 2332b (Terrorism Transcending National Boundaries)

18 U.S.C. § 2339A (Providing Material Support to Terrorists)

18 U.S.C. § 2339B (Providing Material Support to Terrorist Organizations)

Section 2332 (dealing with homicide of a U.S. national) states that "No prosecution for any offense described in this section shall be undertaken by the United States except on written certification of the Attorney General or the highest ranking subordinate of the Attorney General with responsibility for criminal prosecutions that, in the judgment of the certifying official, such offense was intended to coerce, intimidate, or retaliate against a government or a civilian population." If the concern was over diplomatic officials, why apply it to any U.S. national?

For that matter, why the need for a special statute applying to homicide of a U.S. national in the first place? On this issue, consider whether the United States could have a general statute punishing murder of anyone anywhere. Would international law prevent the U.S. from asserting adjudicative jurisdiction over the murder of a foreign national by a foreign national in a foreign country? To go further, what is the point of the AG certification of a political motivation for the crime? 18 U.S.C. § 1113 applies the same penalties to anyone who commits murder or manslaughter on an officer or employee of the U.S. government while in the course of his or her duties.

§ 4.02 EXTRATERRITORIAL JURISDICTION AND APPREHENSION OF DEFENDANTS

United States v. Yunis, is the earliest example in which the United States pursued and prosecuted an incident of international political terrorism taking place outside our borders. As you read *Yunis*, be alert to the multiple interactions between U.S. domestic law and customary international law, to the jurisdictional bases for prosecution in the United States, and to implications for investigation and enforcement of U.S. penal laws in incidents occurring abroad.

UNITED STATES v. YUNIS
288 U.S. App. D.C. 129; 924 F.2d 1086 (D.C. Cir. 1991)

MIKVA, Chief Judge:

Appellant Fawaz Yunis challenges his convictions on conspiracy, aircraft piracy, and hostage-taking charges stemming from the hijacking of a Jordanian passenger aircraft in Beirut, Lebanon. He appeals from orders of the district court denying his pretrial motions relating to jurisdiction, illegal arrest, alleged violations of the Posse Comitatus Act, and the government's withholding of classified documents during discovery. Yunis also challenges the district court's jury instructions as erroneous and prejudicial.

Although this appeal raises novel issues of domestic and international law, we reject Yunis' objections and affirm the convictions.

I. Background

On June 11, 1985, appellant and four other men boarded Royal Jordanian Airlines Flight 402 ("Flight 402") shortly before its scheduled departure from Beirut, Lebanon. They wore civilian clothes and carried military assault rifles, ammunition bandoleers, and hand grenades. Appellant took control of the cockpit and forced the pilot to take off immediately. The remaining hijackers tied up Jordanian air marshals assigned to the flight and held the civilian passengers, including two American citizens, captive in their seats. The hijackers explained to the crew and passengers that they wanted the plane to fly to Tunis, where a conference of the Arab League was under way. The hijackers further explained that they wanted a meeting with delegates to the conference and that their ultimate goal was removal of all Palestinians from Lebanon.

After a refueling stop in Cyprus, the airplane headed for Tunis but turned away when authorities blocked the airport runway. Following a refueling stop at Palermo, Sicily, another attempt to land in Tunis, and a second stop in Cyprus, the plane returned to Beirut, where more hijackers came aboard. These reinforcements included an official of Lebanon's Amal Militia, the group at whose direction Yunis claims he acted. The plane then took off for Syria, but was turned away and went back to Beirut. There, the hijackers released the passengers, held a press conference reiterating their demand that Palestinians leave Lebanon, blew up the plane, and fled from the airport.

An American investigation identified Yunis as the probable leader of the hijackers and prompted U.S. civilian and military agencies, led by the Federal Bureau of Investigation (FBI), to plan Yunis' arrest. After obtaining an arrest warrant, the FBI put "Operation Goldenrod" into effect in September 1987. Undercover FBI agents lured Yunis onto a yacht in the eastern Mediterranean Sea with promises of a drug deal, and arrested him once the vessel entered international waters. The agents transferred Yunis to a United States Navy munitions ship and interrogated him for several days as the vessel steamed toward a second rendezvous, this time with a Navy aircraft carrier. Yunis was flown to Andrews Air Force Base from the aircraft carrier, and taken from there to Washington, D.C. In Washington, Yunis was arraigned on an original indictment charging him with conspiracy, hostage taking, and aircraft damage. A grand jury subsequently returned a superseding indictment adding additional aircraft damage counts and a charge of air piracy.

Yunis filed several pretrial motions, among them a motion to suppress statements he made while aboard the munitions ship. In *United States v. Yunis (Yunis I),* 859 F.2d 953 (D.C. Cir. 1988), this court reversed a district court order suppressing the statements, and authorized their introduction at trial. We revisited the case on a second interlocutory appeal relating to discovery of classified information, reversing the district court's disclosure order. *United States v. Yunis (Yunis II),* 276 U.S. App. D.C. 1, 867 F.2d 617 (D.C. Cir. 1989).

Yunis admitted participation in the hijacking at trial but denied parts of the government's account and offered the affirmative defense of obedience to military orders, asserting that he acted on instructions given by his superiors in Lebanon's Amal Militia. The jury convicted Yunis of conspiracy, 18 U.S.C. § 371 (1988), hostage taking, 18 U.S.C. § 1203 (1988), and air piracy, 49 U.S.C. App. § 1472(n) (1988). However, it acquitted him of three other charged offenses that went to trial: violence against people on board an aircraft, 18 U.S.C. § 32(b)(1) (1988), aircraft damage, 18 U.S.C. § 32(b)(2) (1988), and placing a destructive device aboard an aircraft, 18 U.S.C. § 32(b)(3) (1988). The district court imposed concurrent sentences of five years for conspiracy, thirty years for hostage taking, and twenty years for air piracy. Yunis appeals his conviction and seeks dismissal of the indictment.

II. Analysis

Yunis argues that the district court lacked subject matter and personal jurisdiction to try him on the charges of which he was convicted, that the indictment should have been dismissed because the government seized him in violation of the Posse Comitatus Act and withheld classified materials useful to his defense, and that the convictions should be reversed because of errors in the jury instructions. We consider these claims in turn.

A. *Jurisdictional Claims*

Yunis appeals first of all from the district court's denial of his motion to dismiss for lack of subject matter and personal jurisdiction. *See United States v. Yunis,* 681 F. Supp. 896 (D.D.C. 1988). Appellant's principal claim is that, as a matter of domestic law, the federal hostage taking and air piracy statutes do not authorize assertion of federal jurisdiction over him. Yunis also suggests that a contrary construction of these statutes would conflict with established principles of international law, and so should be avoided by this court. Finally, appellant claims that the district court lacked personal jurisdiction because he was seized in violation of American law.

1. Hostage Taking Act

The Hostage Taking Act provides, in relevant part:

(a) Whoever, whether inside or outside the United States, seizes or detains and threatens to kill, to injure, or to continue to detain another person in order to compel a third person or a governmental organization to do or to abstain from any act . . . shall be punished by imprisonment by any term of years or for life.

(b)(1) It is not an offense under this section if the conduct required for the offense occurred outside the United States unless

(A) the offender or the person seized or detained is a national of the United States;

(B) the offender is found in the United States; or

(C) the governmental organization sought to be compelled is the Government of the United States.

18 U.S.C. § 1203. Yunis claims that this statute cannot apply to an individual who is brought to the United States by force, since those convicted under it must be "found in the United States." But this ignores the law's plain language. Subsections (A), (B), and (C) of section 1203(b)(1) offer *independent* bases for jurisdiction where "the offense occurred outside the United States." Since two of the passengers on Flight 402 were U.S. citizens, section 1203(b)(1)(A), authorizing assertion of U.S. jurisdiction where "the offender or the person seized or detained is a national of the United States," is satisfied. The statute's jurisdictional requirement has been met regardless of whether or not Yunis was "found" within the United States under section 1203(b)(1)(B).

Appellant's argument that we should read the Hostage Taking Act differently to avoid tension with international law falls flat. Yunis points to no treaty obligations of the United States that give us pause. Indeed, Congress intended through the Hostage Taking Act to execute the International Convention Against the Taking of Hostages, which authorizes any signatory state to exercise jurisdiction over persons who take its nationals hostage "if that State considers it appropriate." International Convention Against the Taking of Hostages, *opened for signature* Dec. 18, 1979, art. 5, para. 1, 34 UN GAOR Supp. (No. 39), 18 I.L.M. 1456, 1458. *See* H.R. Conf. Rep. No. 1159, 98th Cong., 2d Sess. 418 (1984), *reprinted in* 1984 U.S. Code Cong. & Admin. News 3710, 3714.

[handwritten margin note: Not inconsistent w/ IL.]

Nor is jurisdiction precluded by norms of customary international law. The district court concluded that two jurisdictional theories of international law, the "universal principle" and the "passive personal principle," supported assertion of U.S. jurisdiction to prosecute Yunis on hijacking and hostage-taking charges. Under the universal principle, states may prescribe and prosecute "certain offenses recognized by the community of nations as of universal concern, such as piracy, slave trade, attacks on or hijacking of aircraft, genocide, war crimes, and perhaps certain acts of terrorism," even absent any special connection between the state and the offense. *See* RESTATEMENT (THIRD) OF THE FOREIGN RELATIONS LAW OF THE UNITED STATES §§ 404, 423 (1987) [hereinafter RESTATEMENT]. Under the passive personal principle, a state may punish non-nationals for crimes committed against its nationals outside of its territory, at least where the state has a particularly strong interest in the crime. *See id.* at § 402 comment g; *United States v. Benitez*, 741 F.2d 1312, 1316 (11th Cir. 1984) (passive personal principle invoked to approve prosecution of Colombian citizen convicted of shooting U.S. drug agents in Colombia).

[handwritten margin note: CIL, 2 principles authorize: 1) Universal prin. 2) Passive personal prin.]

Relying primarily on the Restatement, Yunis argues that hostage taking has not been recognized as a universal crime and that the passive personal principle authorizes assertion of jurisdiction over alleged hostage takers only where the victims were seized because they were nationals of the prosecuting state. Whatever merit appellant's claims may have as a matter of international law, they cannot prevail before this court. Yunis seeks to portray international law as a self-executing code that trumps domestic law whenever the two conflict. That effort misconceives the role of judges as appliers of international law and as participants in the federal system. Our duty is to enforce the Constitution, laws, and treaties of the United States, not to conform the law of the land to norms of customary international law. *See* U.S. Const. art. VI. As we said in *Committee of U.S. Citizens Living in Nicaragua v. Reagan*, 859 F.2d 929 (D.C. Cir. 1988): "Statutes inconsistent with principles of customary international law may well lead to international law violations. But within the domestic legal realm, that inconsistent statute simply modifies or supersedes customary international law to the extent of the inconsistency." *Id. at 938. See also Federal Trade Comm'n. v. Compagnie de Saint-Gobain-Pont-a-Mousson*, 205 U.S. App. D.C. 172, 636 F.2d 1300, 1323 (D.C. Cir. 1980) (U.S. courts "obligated to give effect to an unambiguous exercise by Congress of its jurisdiction to prescribe even if such an exercise would exceed the limitations imposed by international law").

To be sure, courts should hesitate to give penal statutes extraterritorial effect absent a clear congressional directive. Similarly, courts will not blind themselves to potential violations of international law where legislative intent is ambiguous. *See Murray v. The Schooner Charming Betsy*, 6 U.S. (2 Cranch) 64, 118, 2 L. Ed. 208 (1804) ("An act of congress ought never to be construed to violate the law of nations, if any other possible construction remains. . . ."). But the statute in question reflects an unmistakable congressional intent, consistent with treaty obligations of the United States, to authorize prosecution of those who take Americans hostage abroad no matter where the offense occurs or where the offender is found. Our inquiry can go no further.

2. Antihijacking Act

The Antihijacking Act provides for criminal punishment of persons who hijack aircraft operating wholly outside the "special aircraft jurisdiction" of the United States, provided that the hijacker is later "found in the United States." 49 U.S.C. App. § 1472(n). Flight 402, a Jordanian aircraft operating outside of the United States, was not within this nation's special aircraft jurisdiction. *See* 49 U.S.C. App. § 1301. Yunis urges this court to interpret the statutory requirement that persons prosecuted for air piracy must be "found" in the United States as precluding prosecution of alleged hijackers who are brought here to stand trial. But the issue before us is more fact-specific, since Yunis was indicted for air piracy while awaiting trial on hostage-taking and other charges; we must determine whether, once arrested and brought to this country on those other charges, Yunis was subject to prosecution under the Antihijacking Act as well.

The Antihijacking Act of 1974 was enacted to fulfill this nation's responsibilities under the Convention for the Suppression of Unlawful Seizure of Aircraft (the "Hague Convention"), which requires signatory nations to extradite or punish hijackers "present in" their territory. Convention for the Suppression of Unlawful Seizure of Aircraft, Dec. 16, 1970, art. 4, para. 2, Dec. 16, 1970. This suggests that Congress intended the statutory term "found in the United States" to parallel the Hague Convention's "present in [a contracting state's] territory," a phrase which does not indicate the voluntariness limitation urged by Yunis. Moreover, Congress interpreted the Hague Convention as requiring the United States to extradite or prosecute "offenders in its custody," evidencing no concern as to how alleged hijackers came within U.S. territory. From this legislative history we conclude that Yunis was properly indicted under section 1472(n) once in the United States and under arrest on other charges.

The district court correctly found that international law does not restrict this statutory jurisdiction to try Yunis on charges of air piracy. Aircraft hijacking may well be one of the few crimes so clearly condemned under the law of nations that states may assert universal jurisdiction to bring offenders to justice, even when the state has no territorial connection to the hijacking and its citizens are not involved. *See . . .* Randall, *Universal Jurisdiction under International Law,* 66 Tex. L. Rev. 785, 815-34 (1988). But in any event we are satisfied that the Antihijacking Act authorizes assertion of federal jurisdiction to try Yunis regardless of hijacking's status vel non as a universal crime. Thus, we affirm the district court on this issue.

Affirm J. [handwritten margin note]

3. Legality of Seizure

Yunis further argues that even if the district court had jurisdiction to try him, it should have declined to exercise that jurisdiction in light of the government's allegedly outrageous conduct in bringing him to the United States. This claim was rejected by the district court before trial.

Principally, Yunis relies on *United States v. Toscanino,* 500 F.2d 267 (2d Cir. 1974), in which the court held that due process requires courts to divest themselves of personal jurisdiction acquired through "the government's deliberate, unnecessary and unreasonable invasion of the accused's constitutional rights." *Id.* at 275. *Toscanino* establishes, at best, only a very limited exception to the general rule (known as the "*Ker-Frisbie* doctrine") that "the power of a court to try a person for crime is not impaired by the fact that he had been brought within the court's jurisdiction by reason of a 'forcible abduction.'" *Frisbie v. Collins,* 342 U.S. 519, 522, 72 S. Ct. 509 (1952) (citing, *inter alia, Ker v. Illinois,* 119 U.S. 436, 7 S. Ct. 225, 30 L. Ed. 421 (1886)). *Toscanino's* rule has, moreover, been limited to cases of "torture, brutality, and similar outrageous conduct," *United States ex rel. Lujan v. Gengler,* 510 F.2d 62, 65 (2d Cir.), and the Supreme Court has since reaffirmed the *Ker-Frisbie* doctrine.

[handwritten margin notes: "△ argues"; "ct's reading of Toscanino exptn → torture/brutality"]

Even assuming, arguendo, that a district court could correctly dismiss a case otherwise properly before it for the reasons given in *Toscanino,* we find no merit in Yunis' claim. In *Yunis I,* we reviewed the facts of Operation Goldenrod in some detail, including the deception used to arrest Yunis, his injuries and hardships while in custody, and the delay between his arrest and arraignment in the United States. The court sought to determine whether or not these circumstances voided Yunis' waiver of Fifth and Sixth Amendment rights; we concluded that while the government's conduct was neither "picture perfect" nor "a model for law enforcement behavior," the "discomfort and surprise" to which appellant was subjected did not render his waiver invalid. *Yunis I,* 859 F.2d at 969. Similarly, we now find nothing in the record suggesting the sort of intentional, outrageous government conduct necessary to sustain appellant's jurisdictional argument. *Cf. Sami v. United States,* 199 U.S. App. D.C. 173, 617

[handwritten margin note: "also, the facts don't support such a claim"]

F.2d 755, 774 (D.C. Cir. 1979) (finding "no shocking behavior characterized by abduction or brutality which would support an actionable constitutional claim").

B. *Posse Comitatus Act*

Next, Yunis appeals from the district court's denial of his motion to dismiss on the basis of the government's alleged violation of the Posse Comitatus Act, 18 U.S.C. § 1385 (1988), which establishes criminal penalties for willful use of "any part of the Army or the Air Force" in law enforcement, unless expressly authorized by law. Despite the Posse Comitatus Act's express limitation to the Army and Air Force, appellant seeks dismissal of the indictment on the grounds that the Navy played a direct role in Operation Goldenrod.

We cannot agree that Congress' words admit of any ambiguity. By its terms, 18 U.S.C. § 1385 places no restrictions on naval participation in law enforcement operations; an earlier version of the measure would have expressly extended the bill to the Navy, but the final legislation was attached to an Army appropriations bill and its language was accordingly limited to that service. Reference to the Air Force was added in 1956, consistent with reassignment of Army aviation responsibilities to that new branch of the military. Nothing in this history suggests that we should defy the express language of the Posse Comitatus Act by extending it to the Navy, and we decline to do so.

Furthermore, some courts have taken the view that the Posse Comitatus Act imposes no restriction on use of American armed forces abroad, noting that Congress intended to preclude military intervention in domestic civil affairs. *See Chandler v. United States,* 171 F.2d 921, 936 (1st Cir. 1948); *D'Aquino v. United States,* 192 F.2d 338, 351 (9th Cir. 1951). And even if these difficulties could be overcome, a remedial problem would remain, as dismissal of all charges against Yunis might well be an inappropriate remedy if violations of the Posse Comitatus Act were found.

Nor is Yunis helped by 10 U.S.C. § 375 (1988), which requires the Secretary of Defense to issue regulations prohibiting "direct participation" by military personnel in a civilian "search, seizure, arrest, or other similar activity" unless expressly authorized by law. Reliance on this provision faces the same remedial hurdle as direct reliance on the Posse Comitatus Act: Under the *Ker-Frisbie* doctrine, outright dismissal of the charges against Yunis would not be an appropriate remedy for legal violations relating to his arrest. Nor would a violation of the regulations at issue amount to a constitutional violation, making application of an exclusionary rule or similar prophylactic measures inappropriate.

In any event, we agree with the district court that no governmental illegality occurred. Regulations issued under 10 U.S.C. § 375 require Navy compliance with the restrictions of the Posse Comitatus Act, but interpret that Act as allowing "indirect assistance" to civilian authorities that does not "subject civilians to the exercise of military power that is regulatory, proscriptive, or compulsory in nature." The regulations are consistent with judicial interpretations of the Posse Comitatus Act; in fact, they incorporate one of three tests employed to identify violations.

The district court found that Navy personnel played only a "passive" role in housing, transporting, and caring for Yunis while he was in the custody of the FBI, and that "none of the Navy's activities constituted the exercise of regulatory, proscriptive, or compulsory military power." Nor did the Navy's participation in Operation Goldenrod violate either of the other judicial tests for violations of the Posse Comitatus Act: The Navy's role did not amount to "direct active involvement in the execution of the laws," and it did not "pervade the activities of civilian authorities." We see no error in this assessment of the record, and accordingly conclude that no violation of military regulations occurred.

C. *Discovery Claim*

Yunis appeals from the district court's denial of his motion to dismiss on the basis that pre-trial discovery provisions of the Classified Information Procedures Act (CIPA), 18 U.S.C. App. (1988), infringe upon procedural protections guaranteed him by the Fifth and Sixth Amendments. In light of our holding in *Yunis II* that CIPA "creates no new rights of or limits on discovery" of classified material, but only requires courts to consider secrecy concerns when applying general discovery rules, we find no merit in this claim. [CIPA is considered in § 5.02 *infra*.]

Yunis also objects to the district court's refusal to order the government to produce records of conversations between Flight 402 and the Beirut control tower. After *ex parte, in camera* review of classified materials relevant to Yunis' various discovery requests, the trial court ordered disclosure of numerous documents, including "all audio or video tapes and/or transcripts of conversations between defendant and all airport authorities covering the period of the alleged hijacking . . . ." Upon the government's motion for reconsideration, however, the court narrowed this disclosure order by excluding materials, including tapes and transcripts of conversations with airport authorities, that "do not help the defendant's cause." Yunis subsequently renewed his request for conversations between Yunis and the Beirut tower, claiming that these transcripts were "vital to understand what outside influence or 'orders' were being transmitted to the hijackers by person(s) not on the plane." Relying on its earlier rulings, the district court denied the request. Yunis now appeals from that denial.

To prevail on a discovery request for classified information, a defendant must make a threshold showing that the requested material is relevant to his case. If this "low hurdle" is successfully jumped, the court must determine whether or not the government has asserted a "colorable" claim to privilege. If the government has asserted such a claim, the defendant must show that the information would be helpful to his defense. We never have had occasion to adopt a rule to guide trial courts when all these showings are made, and we do not do so here; other circuits, however, have endorsed a balancing approach. *See United States v. Sarkissian*, 841 F.2d 959, 965 (9th Cir. 1988); *United States v. Smith*, 780 F.2d 1102, 1110 (4th Cir. 1985).

Having ourselves reviewed *in camera* the government's classified submissions to the district court, we find very little in them that is both responsive to the discovery request at issue and relevant in any way to Yunis' trial. We certainly agree with the court below that they reveal no information within the scope of Yunis' discovery request that would have helped him at trial. Moreover, *Yunis II* establishes that the government has at least a colorable interest in avoiding release of information that might reveal "the time, place, and nature of the government's ability to intercept the conversations at all." Under these circumstances, the district court properly declined to order the government to release classified information responsive to Yunis' discovery request.

D. *Jury Instructions*

Lastly, Yunis challenges the district court's instructions to the jury insofar as they relate to intent requirements of the federal hostage taking, hijacking, and conspiracy statutes and to appellant's affirmative defense of obedience to military orders.

1. Intent Requirements

Yunis claims that the Antihijacking Act, 49 U.S.C. App. § 1472(n), and the Hostage Taking Act, 18 U.S.C. § 1203, make specific intent an element of the offenses they establish, and that the district court erred in failing to adopt jury instructions offered by the defense that would have made this clear. In appellant's view, the trial judge's instruction that Yunis could be convicted on these counts only if he acted "intentionally, deliberately and knowingly" was inadequate.

49 U.S.C. App. § 1472(n) suggests no specific intent requirement on its face, criminalizing any "unlawful" hijacking of an aircraft. Nor do judicial interpretations of related statutes support appellant's position. In fact, courts have interpreted a companion provision criminalizing domestic hijacking, 49 U.S.C. App. § 1472(i), as requiring only general criminal intent, even though (unlike section 1472(n)) it specifies that hijackers must act with "wrongful intent." *See United States v. Castaneda-Reyes,* 703 F.2d 522, 525 (11th Cir.); *United States v. Busic,* 592 F.2d 13, 21 (2d Cir. 1978); *United States v. Bohle,* 445 F.2d 54, 60 (7th Cir. 1971). In light of these decisions, and absent any encouragement from Congress, we decline Yunis' invitation to graft a specific intent requirement onto the Antihijacking Act.

Yunis' claim that the Hostage Taking Act requires specific intent also fails. The statutory language suggests no intent requirement other than that the offender must act with the purpose of influencing some third person or government through the hostage taking, a point on which the jury received proper instructions. Nor are we aware of any legislative history suggesting that Congress meant to impose a specific intent requirement. Thus, we conclude that the trial judge's instructions on this count of the indictment accorded with law.

We find no merit in Yunis' objection (not raised at trial) that the district court failed to instruct the jury that specific intent is a necessary element of the crime of conspiracy. True, "the specific intent required for the crime of conspiracy is in fact the intent to advance or further the unlawful object of the conspiracy." *United States v. Haldeman,* 181 U.S. App. D.C. 254, 559 F.2d 31, 112 (D.C. Cir. 1976) (footnote omitted). But the jury received instructions that the government "must show beyond a reasonable doubt that the conspiracy was knowingly formed and that the defendant willfully participated in the unlawful plan with the intent to advance or further some object or purpose of the conspiracy." We discern no defect in this instruction.

2. Obedience to Military Orders

The final issues before us concern jury instructions relating to Yunis' affirmative defense of obedience to military orders. Yunis and the government agree on the elements of this common law defense, which are established by several civilian court decisions of rather ancient vintage and by military practice. These precedents generally accord with a formulation approved by the Court of Military Appeals in *United States v. Calley,* 22 C.M.A. 534, 48 C.M.R. 19, 22 U.S.C.M.A. 534 (1973):

> The acts of a subordinate done in compliance with an unlawful order given him by his superior are excused and impose no criminal liability upon him unless the superior's order is one which a man of ordinary sense and understanding would, under the circumstances, know to be unlawful, or if the order in question is actually known to the accused to be unlawful.

Id. at 542.

Appellant does not disagree with the district court's jury instructions on the general elements of this affirmative defense. Instead, Yunis claims that the district court erred as a matter of law when it instructed the jury that Yunis could prevail on this defense only if the Amal Militia – to which Yunis belonged and which, he claimed, ordered the hijacking – is a "military organization." The court further instructed the jury that it could find that the Amal Militia is a military organization only if the group has a hierarchical command structure and "conducts its operations in accordance with the laws and customs of war," and if its members have a uniform and carry arms openly.

Yunis disputes the district court's position that members of a legitimate military organization must have a uniform. Since the hijackers wore civilian clothes and there was evidence that members of the Amal Militia often dressed this way, appellant concludes that the instruction was prejudicial to his defense. Yunis argues that the relevance of uniforms to the ultimate factual question of whether or not the Amal Militia is a military organization is itself a factual question for the jury, not a question of law. He notes that U.S. courts have not developed any test for determining whether or not defendants who invoke the obedience defense actually belong to bona fide military organizations. But the government responds that courts have not developed such a test simply because the issue has not arisen in U.S. courts; heretofore, the defense has been raised only by members of the United States armed forces. In the government's view, the district court properly adapted its instructions on the obedience defense when faced with novel factual circumstances.

We agree that the district court did not commit legal error when it looked beyond domestic precedents to give jurors guidance in evaluating the Amal Militia's military credentials. Moreover, we find that the test of a bona fide military organization adopted by the district court reflects international practice, providing assurance that Yunis did not suffer from parochial projection of American norms onto the issue of whether he should be treated as a soldier for purposes of the obedience defense.

Specifically, the district court's uniform instruction finds sufficient support in international agreements that bear on the question. *See* Geneva Convention Relative to the Treatment of Prisoners of War, art. 4(A)(2); Hague Convention No. IV Respecting the Law and Customs of War on Land, art. 1. The Geneva Convention, signed by 167 nations including the United States and Lebanon, establishes "having a fixed and distinctive signal recognizable at a distance" as one of four necessary conditions that qualify the members of a militia for treatment as prisoners of war. The Hague Convention No. IV, to which the United States and forty-two other nations are parties, uses having "a fixed distinctive emblem recognizable at a distance" as a test for whether militiamen and members of volunteer corps have the rights and responsibilities of national armies. At oral argument, counsel for appellant disavowed reliance on the district court's substitution of "uniform" for "signal" or "emblem," and we agree that this free interpretation of the treaty language did not prejudice the defense.

Geneva Convention

Yunis' second objection to the district court's "military organization" test relates to the instruction, tracking language found in article 4 of the Geneva Convention and chapter I of the annex to the Hague Convention No. IV, that militias must "conduct [their] operations in accordance with the laws and customs of war" to qualify as military organizations. Appellant alleges that this instruction must be considered in tandem with the trial judge's statement to the jury that the hijacking of Flight 402 violated international law. Together, he says, these instructions directed the jury to conclude that the defense of obedience to military orders was unavailable to Yunis because no organization could have given the instruction to hijack Flight 402 without violating "the laws and customs of war."

We disagree with appellant's reading of the record, however, and find that when the district court's instructions are considered as a whole, it is highly improbable that a reasonable juror would have understood them to direct a verdict on the affirmative defense. In the first place, appellant ignores the trial judge's charge to the jury that it was responsible for determining, based on the evidence, whether or not the Amal Militia is a military organization. So too, the court told jurors that if they found that Yunis was a soldier in a military organization under the definition given them, they would then have to address the issue of whether or not Yunis knew that his orders were illegal. Both of these instructions contradict appellant's suggested reading, leading us to conclude that the jury would not have understood the question of whether or not the Amal Militia is a military organization to be foreclosed.

Appellant's interpretation becomes even more attenuated in light of the government's closing argument, during which the prosecution told jurors that they would have to determine whether the Amal Militia is "a military organization that *basically* plays by the rules." This statement framed the issue correctly, albeit informally, providing additional assurance that any ambiguity arising from the court's juxtaposition of the illegality instruction and the adherence to international law instruction did not prejudice Yunis' defense. Because the jury instructions, read as a whole and in light of the evidence and arguments at trial, leave us confident that no prejudicial error occurred, we find that the district court acted within the scope of its discretion.

III. Conclusion

For the foregoing reasons, the convictions are
Affirmed.

NOTES AND QUESTIONS

1. The DC Circuit makes two statements about the relationship between U.S. law and international law. Are there potential inconsistencies in these statements?

2. The court discusses two bases of extraterritorial application of U.S. law, the "passive personal principle" (nationality of the victim) and "universal jurisdiction." In *United States v. Layton*, 509 F. Supp. 212 (N.D. Cal. 1981), the court described five different bases of extraterritorial jurisdiction; in addition to the two in *Yunis*, the *Layton* court stated that jurisdiction could be based on the nationality of the offender, effects felt within the prosecuting nation, or "protective jurisdiction" to address harms to interests or possessions of the prosecuting nation.

3. RESTATEMENT (THIRD) OF FOREIGN RELATIONS LAW OF THE UNITED STATES § 402:

> Subject to §403, a state has jurisdiction to prescribe law with respect to:
>
> (1)(a) conduct that, wholly or in substantial part, takes place within its territory;
>
> (b) the status of persons, or interests in things, present within its territory;
>
> (c) conduct outside its territory that has or is intended to have substantial effect within its territory;
>
> (d) the activities, interests, status, or relations of its nationals outside as well as within its territory; and
>
> (e) certain conduct outside its territory by persons not its nationals that is directed against the security of the state or against a limited class of other state interests.

Does the Restatement authorize "universal" jurisdiction? Are the other four headings of extraterritorial jurisdiction framed by the Restatement in the same way that they are by the courts?

4. The RESTATEMENT, and many of the courts, refer to this issue as jurisdiction to prescribe or to apply its law. Are we not really more concerned with jurisdiction to adjudicate or punish? Think back to your Civil Procedure class and the difference between "long-arm jurisdiction" and choice of law.

5. 18 USC § 7 defines "special maritime and territorial jurisdiction of the United States" to include such areas as the high seas, vessels and vehicles registered in the U.S. or owned by U.S. citizens, military installations within the U.S., and diplomatic or consular properties overseas. Of particular note for some of our purposes are subsections 7 & 8:

> (7) Any place outside the jurisdiction of any nation with respect to an offense by or against a national of the United States.

(8) To the extent permitted by international law, any foreign vessel during a voyage having a scheduled departure from or arrival in the United States with respect to an offense committed by or against a national of the United States.

Subsection 8 is the only provision limited by the language "to the extent permitted by international law." Although some of the special statutes related to terrorism refer back to 18 USC § 7, most of them also carry their own jurisdictional statements. The combination can make for very confusing efforts to parse the statutes.

6. Yunis made an argument that he could not be subject to a U.S. prosecution because of the circumstances of his capture abroad. In *Yunis I*, the court described his capture and interrogation this way:

> Investigation of this crime by American law enforcement officials eventually focused on Yunis as the probable leader of the hijackers. Accordingly, the FBI – in concert with other federal agencies – developed "Operation Goldenrod." With the aid of an informant in the Middle East, Operation Goldenrod sought to lure Yunis into international waters to effect his arrest. The plan succeeded on September 13, 1987, when Yunis boarded a yacht manned by FBI agents in the eastern Mediterranean – allegedly drawn there by the promise of a profitable drug transaction. Yunis was promptly arrested by means of a "take down": agents on either side of Yunis grabbed his arms and kicked his feet out from under him, so that he ended up face down on the deck of the boat. He was handcuffed and shackled and then told that he was under arrest and was being taken to America to stand trial for the 1985 hijacking. The yacht proceeded to a prearranged rendezvous with an American munitions ship (the USS Butte) of the United States' Sixth Fleet. Yunis and two agents on the yacht boarded a transfer boat, which was then hoisted up the side of the Butte. In the process, the mechanical hoist failed and the boat's occupants were left swaying in midair as the Butte's crew completed the operation by hand. During this time, Yunis evidently grew seasick and either experienced dry heaves or vomited over the side of the boat.
>
> Once on board the Butte, Yunis was taken to a small room that was to be his living quarters for the next four days, as the Butte made its way westward across the Mediterranean. The room was small – eight by ten feet – and poorly ventilated, as a malfunctioning vent evidently blew hot air into the room; the room's estimated temperature was 85 degrees. Although there were no windows, a hatch door (which at all times remained open) gave out onto a deck area, with some exposure to the ocean. In this room, a naval doctor examined Yunis and found him to be in good health, aside from his seasickness. During the examination, an FBI agent who was fluent in Arabic served as interpreter, since Yunis speaks very little English. The doctor did not notice any problem with Yunis' wrists, and Yunis did not complain about them at this time. However, it was later established by x-rays (after Yunis reached the United States) that both wrists had been

fractured, apparently when the FBI agents first arrested him by means of the "take down."

When the doctor concluded his exam, he prescribed rest and clear liquids to alleviate Yunis' seasickness. The doctor then left Yunis' room, and FBI Special Agent Thomas Hansen, who was in charge of investigating the 1985 hijacking, began to talk to Yunis – communicating through the FBI interpreter. At the outset, Yunis was told that when he reached the United States he "would be appointed an attorney and would be formally charged . . . [and then] would go through a number of legal proceedings which may terminate in a trial." Agent Hansen further informed Yunis that "from this point forward, he would be afforded all the rights of a citizen of the United States and that he didn't have to be concerned with the fact that he wasn't an American, that now those rights would apply to him." The agents then gave Yunis a form, on which the warnings required under *Miranda v. Arizona*, were written in Arabic. Yunis was asked to read these warnings; thereafter, agent Hansen read the warnings aloud in English and the FBI interpreter translated each warning orally into Arabic. Both agents subsequently testified that Yunis was repeatedly asked whether he understood what had just been read to him and that Yunis answered affirmatively.

After thus informing Yunis of the constitutional rights that are afforded American citizens, agent Hansen asked Yunis "whether he was, knowing these rights, was he willing to talk to Agent Droujinsky [the interpreter] and myself about the hijacking. . . . He said yes. And then I requested that he sign the form." Between the time that agent Hansen initiated the conversation and the time that Yunis agreed to answer questions about the hijacking, nine minutes elapsed.

Yunis did sign the form and then, in response to agent Hansen's questions, began to recount the hijacking – how he was assigned to lead the 1985 hijacking by officials of Lebanon's Amal militia (of which he was then a member), how he and his accomplices arrived at Beirut Airport and boarded the Royal Jordanian airliner, and so on. After about half an hour of interrogation, Yunis said he felt sleepy, and agent Hansen proposed that they go out on the deck for some fresh air. Once outside, however, Yunis felt nauseous. Accordingly, agent Hansen told Yunis he could lie down in his room, and the first interrogation session ended.

In the afternoon, Yunis again experienced seasickness and vomited once. The naval doctor returned to examine Yunis in the early evening. During the examination, Yunis experienced dry heaves; the doctor once again prescribed clear liquids and rest. Not long thereafter, agent Hansen and the interpreter asked Yunis if he wished to resume talking, and Yunis consented. Neither at this time nor during any of the seven subsequent interrogation sessions on board the Butte did agent Hansen readminister the Miranda warnings. This second period of questioning was conducted out on the deck, rather than in the room. After talking for about forty minutes, Yunis indicated that he was again feeling seasick, and the session ended.

Before Yunis went to sleep, he was given a scopolamine patch, which gradually releases medication through the skin behind the ear to mitigate nausea.

Early the following morning, Yunis ate a substantial breakfast but again became sick to his stomach and experienced dry heaves. The naval doctor again examined him, and on this occasion Yunis specifically complained that his wrists were bothering him. The doctor found Yunis' wrists "mildly swollen and . . . the right wrist had a bit of a bruise on th[e] inner part of the wrist." The injury was treated with ice packs and by keeping the wrists elevated.

Later that morning, agent Hansen and his interpreter returned, and Yunis agreed to resume the narrative of the hijacking. After half an hour, however, Yunis again complained that he was dizzy, and the session ended. By afternoon, the scopolamine patch had evidently begun to work. For the remainder of his journey on the Butte, Yunis appeared more animated and did not noticeably suffer from motion sickness. Accordingly, the interrogation sessions grew longer.

All told, Yunis answered questions during nine sessions aboard the Butte for a total of twelve hours. He not only described the full saga of the hijacking but also gave details about other events in Lebanon and the Middle East. At the end of the fourth day on the Butte, agent Hansen presented Yunis with a written confession (in Arabic), which distilled the salient details from Yunis' narrative. Yunis asked why he should sign it. As agent Hansen later testified at the suppression hearing:

> "I indicated to him that by signing it, it would be a matter of record indicating exactly what he told us. And that we could not change what he had said to us and conversely he could not change what he had said to us. And again, just like anything else, he did not have to sign it, but if he cared to do so, it was up to him. He said he would sign it, which he did."

The general issue of interrogation techniques is taken up in Chapter 9. For now we are concerned with abduction from other countries, so we will look at an incident that required the use of a little more force than did the capture of Yunis – the invasion of Panama.

UNITED STATES v. NORIEGA
117 F.3d 1206 (11th Cir. 1997)

KRAVITCH, Senior Circuit Judge:

Manuel Antonio Noriega appeals: (1) his multiple convictions stemming from his involvement in cocaine trafficking; and (2) the district court's denial of his motion for a new trial based on newly discovered evidence. In attacking his convictions, Noriega asserts that the district court should have dismissed the indictment against him due to his status as a head of state and the manner in which the United States brought him to justice. Noriega also contends that the district court committed two reversible evidentiary errors. Alternatively, he

N involved in cocaine trafficking from Columbia to U.S. apprehended & tried in US.

seeks a new trial based on his discovery of: (1) the government's suppression of its pact with a non-witness; and/or (2) certain allegations, lodged after his conviction, that a group associated with the undisclosed, cooperating non-witness bribed a prosecution witness. We affirm Noriega's convictions and the district court's order denying his new trial motion.

Affirmed

I.

On February 4, 1988, a federal grand jury for the Southern District of Florida indicted Manuel Antonio Noriega on drug-related charges. At that time, Noriega served as commander of the Panamanian Defense Forces in the Republic of Panama. Shortly thereafter, Panama's president, Eric Arturo Delvalle, formally discharged Noriega from his military post, but Noriega refused to accept the dismissal. Panama's legislature then ousted Delvalle from power. The United States, however, continued to acknowledge Delvalle as the constitutional leader of Panama. Later, after a disputed presidential election in Panama, the United States recognized Guillermo Endara as Panama's legitimate head of state.

head of state of Panama

On December 15, 1989, Noriega publicly declared that a state of war existed between Panama and the United States. Within days of this announcement by Noriega, President George Bush directed United States armed forces into combat in Panama for the stated purposes of "safeguarding American lives, restoring democracy, preserving the Panama Canal treaties, and seizing Noriega to face federal drug charges in the United States." *United States v. Noriega*, 746 F. Supp. 1506, 1511 (S.D. Fla. 1990). The ensuing military conflagration resulted in significant casualties and property loss among Panamanian civilians. Noriega lost his effective control over Panama during this armed conflict, and he surrendered to United States military officials on January 3, 1990. Noriega then was brought to Miami to face the pending federal charges.

military action ↓ apprehension of Noriega

Following extensive pre-trial proceedings and a lengthy trial, a jury found Noriega guilty of eight counts in the indictment and not guilty of the remaining two counts. The district court entered judgments of conviction against Noriega upon the jury's verdict and sentenced him to consecutive imprisonment terms of 20, 15 and five years, respectively. Noriega timely appealed his convictions. During the pendency of that appeal, Noriega filed in district court a motion for a new trial based on newly discovered evidence. This court deferred further consideration of Noriega's initial appeal while the district court heard Noriega's new trial motion. When the district court denied that motion, Noriega took a second, timely appeal. Both matters now are properly before this court.

jury decision

II.

At trial, the government presented the testimony of numerous witnesses as well as documentary evidence to prove Noriega's guilt. Noriega, through both cross-examination and defense witness testimony, fervently contested the veracity of the witnesses and the significance of the documents offered by the government. Under the defense theory of the case, Noriega's subordinates used his name in their drug-trafficking schemes, but Noriega had no personal connection to the alleged offenses. "The facts set out below are those which the jury might reasonably have found from the evidence properly admitted at trial."

From the early 1970s to 1989, Noriega secured progressively greater dominion over state military and civilian institutions in Panama, first as his nation's chief of military intelligence and later as commander of the Panamanian Defense Forces. In the early 1980s, Noriega's position of authority brought him into contact with a group of drug traffickers from the Medellin area of Colombia (the "Medellin Cartel"). Various Medellin Cartel operatives met with Noriega's associates and, later, with Noriega personally, regarding the Medellin Cartel's desire to ship cocaine through Panama to the United States. Eventually, Noriega and the Medellin Cartel reached the first of a series of illicit agreements. Thereafter, from 1982 through 1985, with Noriega's assistance, the Medellin Cartel transported significant quantities of cocaine through Panama to the United States. It also utilized its relationship with Noriega to move ether for cocaine processing and substantial cash proceeds from drug sales from the United States to or through Panama.

Noriega and his associates personally met with Medellin Cartel leaders in Colombia, Panama and Cuba regarding the transhipping arrangement, unofficial asylum for Medellin Cartel members fleeing prosecution and a botched plan to operate a cocaine processing laboratory in the Darien region of Panama. The Medellin Cartel directed large cash payments to Noriega in connection with its drug, ether and cash shipments through Panama. During this period, Noriega opened secret accounts in his name and the names of his family members with the Bank of Credit and Commerce International ("BCCI") in Panama. Noriega's associates made large, unexplained cash deposits into these accounts for him. In 1988, Noriega transferred approximately $20,000,000 of his amassed fortune to banks in Europe. The government ultimately located more than $23,000,000 of funds traceable to Noriega in financial institutions outside of Panama.

III.

Noriega challenges his convictions on five distinct grounds: the first three relate to the district court's decision to exercise jurisdiction over this case and the final two concern evidentiary rulings by the district court. Noriega does not contend that the record contains insufficient evidence to support the jury's verdicts of guilt and the resultant judgments of conviction entered by the district court.

A.

Noriega raised two of his three quasi-jurisdictional appellate claims via a pre-trial motion to dismiss the indictment which the district court denied.

1.

Noriega first argues that the district court should have dismissed the indictment against him based on head-of-state immunity. He insists that he was entitled to such immunity because he served as the de facto, if not the de jure, leader of Panama. The district court rejected Noriega's head-of-state immunity claim because the United States government never recognized Noriega as Panama's legitimate, constitutional ruler.

The Supreme Court long ago held that "the jurisdiction of courts is a branch of that which is possessed by the nation as an independent sovereign power. The jurisdiction of the nation within its own territory is necessarily exclusive and absolute. It is susceptible of no limitation not imposed by itself." *The Schooner Exchange v. M Faddon*, 11 U.S. (7 Cranch) 116, 136, 3 L. Ed. 287 (1812). The Court, however, ruled that nations, including the United States, had agreed implicitly to accept certain limitations on their individual territorial jurisdiction based on the "common interest impelling [sovereign nations] to mutual intercourse, and an interchange of good offices with each other . . . ." Chief among the exceptions to jurisdiction was "the exemption of the person of the sovereign from arrest or detention within a foreign territory."

The principles of international comity outlined by the Court in *The Schooner Exchange* led to the development of a general doctrine of foreign sovereign immunity which courts applied most often to protect foreign nations in their corporate form from civil process in the United States. To enforce this foreign sovereign immunity, nations concerned about their exposure to judicial proceedings in the United States:

> followed the accepted course of procedure [and] by appropriate representations, sought recognition by the State Department of [their] claim of immunity, and asked that the [State] Department advise the Attorney General of the claim of immunity and that the Attorney General instruct the United States Attorney for the [relevant district] to file in the district court the appropriate suggestion of immunity . . . .

Ex Parte Republic of Peru, 318 U.S. 578, 581 (1943) (citations omitted). As this doctrine emerged, the "Court consistently deferred to the decisions of the political branches – in particular, those of the Executive Branch – on whether to take jurisdiction over actions against foreign sovereigns and their instrumentalities."

In 1976, Congress passed the Foreign Sovereign Immunities Act ("FSIA"), 28 U.S.C. §§ 1602-1611. The FSIA . . . codified the State Department's general criteria for making suggestions of immunity, and transferred the responsibility for case-by-case application of these principles from the Executive Branch to the Judicial Branch. Because the FSIA addresses neither head-of-state immunity, nor foreign sovereign immunity in the criminal context, head-of-state immunity could attach in cases, such as this one, only pursuant to the principles and procedures outlined in *The Schooner Exchange* and its progeny. As a result, this court must look to the Executive Branch for direction on the propriety of Noriega's immunity claim. *See Kadic v. Karadzic*, 70 F.3d 232, 248 (2d Cir. 1995) (questioning viability of head-of-state immunity doctrine in light of FSIA, but noting that, even if still operative, doctrine was inapplicable because Executive Branch had not recognized defendant as head of state).

Generally, the Executive Branch's position on head-of-state immunity falls into one of three categories: the Executive Branch (1) explicitly suggests immunity; (2) expressly declines to suggest immunity; or (3) offers no guidance. Some courts have held that absent a formal suggestion of immunity, a putative head of state should receive no immunity. The Executive Branch has not merely refrained from taking a position on this matter; to the contrary, by pursuing Noriega's capture and this prosecution, the Executive Branch has manifested its

Exec has made it not clear via the operation to extend immunity

clear sentiment that Noriega should be denied head-of-state immunity. Noriega has cited no authority that would empower a court to grant head-of-state immunity under these circumstances. Moreover, given that the record indicates that Noriega never served as the constitutional leader of Panama, that Panama has not sought immunity for Noriega and that the charged acts relate to Noriega's private pursuit of personal enrichment, Noriega likely would not prevail even if this court had to make an independent determination regarding the propriety of immunity in this case.

2.

Noriega next contends his conviction should be reversed because he alleges he was brought to the United States in violation of the Treaty Providing for the Extradition of Criminals, May 25, 1904, United States of America-Republic of Panama, 34 Stat. 2851 ("U.S.-Panama Extradition Treaty"). The Supreme Court's decision in *United States v. Alvarez-Machain*, 504 U.S. 655 (1992), forecloses this argument. In *Alvarez-Machain*, the Court considered the issue of "whether a criminal defendant, abducted to the United States from a nation with which it has an extradition treaty, thereby acquires a defense to the jurisdiction of this country's courts." In answer, the Court stated: "We hold that he does not, and that he may be tried in federal district court for violations of the criminal law of the United States."

In reaching this decision, the Court considered whether the treaty at issue expressly barred abductions. It determined that the treaty's provision that "'neither Contracting Party shall be bound to deliver up its own nationals . . .' [fails] to specify the only way in which one country may gain custody of a national of the other country for purposes of prosecution." *Id.* at 663-64 (quoting Extradition Treaty, May 4, 1978, United States of America-United Mexican States, 31 U.S.T. 5059 ("U.S.-Mexico Extradition Treaty"). The Court also rejected the argument that, by entering into an extradition treaty with Mexico, the United States impliedly agreed to seek custody of persons in Mexico only via extradition. ("To infer from this Treaty and its terms that it prohibits all means of gaining the presence of an individual outside of its terms goes beyond established precedent and practice.")

Extradition treaties do not preclude self-help

The article of the U.S.-Panama Extradition Treaty upon which Noriega relies for his extradition treaty claim contains almost the same language as the provision of the U.S.-Mexico Extradition Treaty at issue in *Alvarez-Machain*. Noriega contends that *Alvarez-Machain* is distinguishable despite the near identity of the relevant clauses because, at the time the United States entered into the U.S.-Panama Extradition Treaty, it knew or should have known that Panama's constitution prohibited the extradition of its nationals. This bald assertion, even if accepted, does not save Noriega's claim. A clause in Panama's constitution regarding the extradition of Panamanians, at most, informs the United States of the hurdles it will face when pursuing such extraditions in Panama; such a provision says nothing about the treaty signatories' rights to opt for self-help (i.e., abduction) over legal process (i.e., extradition).

Under *Alvarez-Machain,* to prevail on an extradition treaty claim, a defendant must demonstrate, by reference to the express language of a treaty and/or the established practice thereunder, that the United States affirmatively agreed not to seize foreign nationals from the territory of its treaty partner. Noriega has not carried this burden, and therefore, his claim fails.

3.

In his pre-trial motion, Noriega also sought the dismissal of the indictment against him on the ground that the manner in which he was brought before the district court (i.e., through a military invasion) was so unconscionable as to constitute a violation of substantive due process. Noriega also argued that to the extent the government's actions did not shock the judicial conscience sufficiently to trigger due process sanctions, the district court should exercise its supervisory power to decline jurisdiction. The district court rejected Noriega's due process argument, and it declared Noriega's alternative supervisory power rationale non-justiciable. On appeal, Noriega offers no substantive argument regarding the due process prong of this claim, but rather discusses only his alternative supervisory power theory. Because, however, the due process and supervisory power issues are intertwined, we discuss them both.

Noriega's due process claim "falls squarely within the [Supreme Court's] *Ker-Frisbie* doctrine, which holds that a defendant cannot defeat personal jurisdiction by asserting the illegality of the procurement of his presence." Noriega has not alleged that the government mistreated him personally, and thus, he cannot come within the purview of the caveat to *Ker-Frisbie* recognized by the Second Circuit in *United States v. Toscanino*, 500 F.2d 267 (2d Cir. 1974), were this court inclined to adopt such an exception. Further, whatever harm Panamanian civilians suffered during the armed conflict that preceded Noriega's arrest cannot support a due process claim in this case. *See United States v. Payner*, 447 U.S. 727, 737 n.9 (1980) (holding that even where government's conduct toward third parties "was so outrageous as to offend fundamental canons of decency and fairness, the fact remains that the limitations of the Due Process Clause . . . come into play only when the Government activity in question violates some protected right of the defendant" (internal quotations omitted)).

[handwritten margin note: Ker-Frisbie doctrine]

NOTES AND QUESTIONS

1. *United States v. Alvarez-Machain*, 504 U.S. 655 (1992), discussed in the Noriega case, is one of several incidents that have produced friction between the U.S. and Mexico. The opinions in the case contain stark contrasts in perceptions of the executive and judicial roles in response to international criminal behavior.

The Supreme Court described the abduction of Alvarez-Machain as follows:

Respondent, Humberto Alvarez-Machain, is a citizen and resident of Mexico. He was indicted for participating in the kidnap and murder of United States Drug Enforcement Administration (DEA) special agent Enrique Camarena-Salazar and a Mexican pilot working with Camarena, Alfredo Zavala-Avelar. The DEA believes that respondent, a medical doctor, participated in the murder by prolonging Agent Camarena's life so that others could further torture and interrogate him. On April 2, 1990, respondent was forcibly kidnaped from his medical office in Guadalajara,

Mexico, to be flown by private plane to El Paso, Texas, where he was arrested by DEA officials. The District Court concluded that DEA agents were responsible for respondent's abduction, although they were not personally involved in it.

The torture and murder of Camerena was particularly debilitating to the morale of DEA and other federal agents, so there was a substantial amount of pressure on the executive branch to pursue this prosecution. Mexico officially protested the abduction of Alvarez-Machain as a violation of both international law and the extradition treaty, and simultaneously requested extradition of two individuals from the U.S. whom Mexico wanted to prosecute for kidnapping of Alvarez-Machain. The lower courts dismissed the indictment on the basis of the treaty violation, but the Supreme Court held that the treaty did not specifically bar abductions. In response to arguments that prosecution under these circumstances would damage U.S. interests by being perceived as a violation of international law or treaty expectations, the Court held that these concerns were for the executive branch to deal with in pursuit of its diplomatic functions.

Justice Stevens in dissent pointed out that Mexico had already tried and sentenced several other conspirators in the Camerena incident, and had asserted its interest in prosecuting Alvarez-Machain. Justice Stevens' response to the majority's assertion of executive diplomatic prerogatives emphasized the independent role of the judicial function:

> As the Court observes at the outset of its opinion, there is reason to believe that respondent participated in an especially brutal murder of an American law enforcement agent. That fact, if true, may explain the Executive's intense interest in punishing respondent in our courts. Such an explanation, however, provides no justification for disregarding the Rule of Law that this Court has a duty to uphold. That the Executive may wish to reinterpret the Treaty to allow for an action that the Treaty in no way authorizes should not influence this Court's interpretation. Indeed, the desire for revenge exerts "a kind of hydraulic pressure . . . before which even well settled principles of law will bend," but it is precisely at such moments that we should remember and be guided by our duty "to render judgment evenly and dispassionately according to law, as each is given understanding to ascertain and apply it."

> The significance of this Court's precedents is illustrated by a recent decision of the Court of Appeal of the Republic of South Africa. Based largely on its understanding of the import of this Court's cases – including our decision in *Ker* – that court held that the prosecution of a defendant kidnaped by agents of South Africa in another country must be dismissed. *S v. Ebrahim*, S. Afr. L. Rep. (Apr.-June 1991). The Court of Appeal of South Africa – indeed, I suspect most courts throughout the civilized world – will be deeply disturbed by the "monstrous" decision the Court announces today. For every nation that has an interest in preserving the Rule of Law is affected, directly or indirectly, by a decision of this character. As Thomas Paine warned, an "avidity to punish is always dangerous to liberty" because it leads a nation "to stretch, to misinterpret, and to misapply even the best

of laws." To counter that tendency, he reminds us: "He that would make his own liberty secure must guard even his enemy from oppression; for if he violates this duty he establishes a precedent that will reach to himself."

2. Michael J. Glennon, *International Kidnapping: State-sponsored Abduction: A Comment on* United States v. Alvarez-Machain, 86 A.J.I.L. 746 (1992):

[The] Supreme Court confronted what the Permanent Court of International Justice termed in *The Lotus* to be "the first and foremost restriction imposed by international law upon a State: . . . that – failing the existence of a permissive rule to the contrary – it may not exercise its power in any form in the territory of another State." Contrary to popular criticism, the Court did not challenge that proposition. But it did apply, without adequate analysis, an antiquated doctrine that permits a defendant to be tried regardless of the unlawfulness of the seizure. In so doing, it ignored altogether the issue of presidential constitutional power to conduct such seizures.

3. *United States v. Rezaq*, 134 F.2d 1121 (D.C. Cir. 1998):

Rezaq is Palestinian, and was, at the time of the hijacking, a member of a Palestinian terrorist organization, which planned and ordered the hijacking. On the evening of November 23, 1985, Rezaq boarded Air Egypt Flight 648 in Athens. He was accompanied by two other hijackers; one of his confederates, named Salem, was the leader of the operation, and the name of the other is unknown. Shortly after the plane took off, the three produced weapons, announced that they were seizing the plane, and demanded that the captain fly it to Malta. A gun battle ensued between the hijackers and an Egyptian plainclothes sky marshal stationed on the plane, as a result of which Salem was killed and the sky marshal was wounded.

Rezaq then took charge of the hijacking. After the plane arrived in Malta, he separated the Israeli and American passengers from the others, and moved them to the front of the plane. He released a number of Egyptian and Filipino female passengers, as well as two wounded flight attendants. He then demanded that the aircraft be refueled; when the authorities refused, he announced that he would shoot a passenger every fifteen minutes until his demand was met.

Rezaq carried out his threat. He first shot Israeli national Tamar Artzi. Although he shot her twice, once in the head, she survived. Fifteen minutes later, he shot her companion, Nitzan Mendelson, also an Israeli; Ms. Mendelson died of her injuries nine days later. Rezaq then shot Patrick Baker, an American, but only succeeded in grazing his head. Two or three hours later, Rezaq shot Scarlett Rogenkamp – a United States citizen and an employee of the United States Air Force – in the head, killing her. Some time later, he shot Jackie Pflug, also an American, in the head, injuring her very seriously. Rezaq shot his victims near the front door of the plane, and either threw them or let them fall onto the tarmac; this may explain why three of the five were able to survive, either by escaping (Artzi and Baker), or by feigning death (Pflug).

In the evening of November 24th – about a day after the hijacking began – Egyptian commandos stormed the plane. The operation seems to have been a singularly incompetent one. The commandos fired indiscriminately, and set off an explosive device of some kind, as a result of which the aircraft burst into flames. Fifty-seven passengers were killed, as was the third hijacker. Rezaq was injured, and was taken, with a multitude of injured passengers, to a hospital. There, he was identified as the hijacker by passengers, members of the crew, and several of his victims.

The authorities in Malta charged Rezaq with murder, attempted murder, and hostage taking. He pled guilty, and was sentenced to 25 years' imprisonment. For reasons unclear, Maltese authorities released him some seven years later, in February 1993, and allowed him to board a plane to Ghana. Rezaq's itinerary was to carry him from there to Nigeria, and then to Ethiopia, and finally to Sudan. Ghanaian officials detained Rezaq for several months, but eventually allowed him to proceed to Nigeria. When Rezaq's plane landed in Nigeria, Nigerian authorities placed him in the custody of FBI agents, who transported him on a waiting aircraft to the United States.

Rezaq argued that the Hi-Jacking Act's application to one who is "found in the United States" must mean something other than brought before the court involuntarily because that would make the provision a nullity. The court said that requiring the defendant to be present before the court is not meaningless because "at a minimum, it confirms the rule, issuing from the Confrontation Clause of the Sixth Amendment and from the Due Process Clause, that a defendant ordinarily may not be tried in absentia." Ordinarily? When might a defendant be tried *in absentia*?

3. The *Noriega* court expresses doubts about the *Toscanino* "unconscionable conduct" exception to *Ker-Frisbie*, and the *Yunis* court questions whether an exception should result in dismissal of an indictment. Assume that U.S. agents savagely beat a person in their custody while overseas, either attempting to get information about additional suspects or just because they are angry. What do you think a court should do about this? Are U.S. agents held to the same levels of propriety while acting abroad that they should be while on home soil? Should there be different standards for dealing with suspected terrorists? The "prisoner abuse" scandals of 2003-04 will be considered in Chapter 9.

UNITED STATES v. YOUSEF
927 F. Supp. 673 (S.D.N.Y. 1996)

DUFFY, District Judge:

Defendants, Ramzi Ahmed Yousef, ("Yousef"), Abdul Hakim Murad ("Murad"), and Wali Khan Amin Shah, ("Shah"), are charged with conspiring and attempting to damage, destroy and bomb numerous United States commercial airliners operating in East Asia routes, all but one of which had some United States city as a scheduled stop. Defendants are also alleged to have been responsible for the detonation of a bomb in the Greenbelt Theater in Manila, Philippines, on or about December 1, 1994. Defendant Yousef is charged with the detonation of another bomb on December 11, 1994, aboard Philippine Airlines Flight 434 bound for Tokyo, Japan, which exploded while the airplane was in flight, causing the death of one passenger, Haruki Ikegami, and injuring several others. Both of these explosions are included as overt acts in the conspiracy to blow up the United States airliners, and the explosion aboard the Philippines airliner is charged as a separate count in the indictment.

The specific violations with which these Defendants are charged include: conspiring and attempting to destroy aircraft in foreign air commerce within the special aircraft jurisdiction of the United States, in violation of 18 U.S.C. §§ 32(a)(1), (2), (7) & 371 (Counts Twelve, Thirteen and Fourteen); conspiring to kill a national of the United States with malice aforethought, in violation of 18 U.S.C. § 2332(b) and (d) (Count Fifteen); conspiring to use a weapon of mass destruction in relation to the conspiracy charged in Count Fifteen of the indictment in violation of 18 U.S.C. § 2332a (Count Sixteen); using and carrying an improvised explosive device in relation to the conspiracy charged in Counts Twelve and Fifteen, in violation of 18 U.S.C. § 924(c) and 2 (Counts Seventeen and Eighteen); Defendant Yousef is charged with placing and causing the detonation of a bomb aboard a Philippines airliner, in violation of 18 U.S.C. § 32(b) (Count Nineteen); and finally, Defendant Shah is charged with attempting to escape from the custody of the United States in violation of 18 U.S.C. § 751(a) (Count Twenty).

All three Defendants have made various pretrial motions. Yousef moves for (1) dismissal of the indictment because of the alleged mistreatment he suffered while in the custody of unidentified individuals in Pakistan and Pakistani law enforcement agents; (2) dismissal of Count Nineteen of the Indictment, which charges the unlawful placing of a bomb aboard a Philippines airliner, based on jurisdictional "principles of both domestic and international law."

Defendant Murad also moves for dismissal of the indictment for lack of jurisdiction, arguing that the charged offenses did not occur in the "special aircraft jurisdiction" of the United States and that the indictment does not specify the particular United States citizens or property which were the target of the alleged conspiracy.

Defendant Shah moves for dismissal of the indictment alleging that the prosecution of a non-citizen for these extraterritorial crimes in the United States violates the Fifth and Sixth Amendments of the United States Constitution, federal statutory law, and provisions of international law and extradition treaties to which the United States is a party.

For the following reasons, Defendants' motions are denied.

Yousef's Motion to Dismiss the Indictment

Yousef argues that his abduction in Pakistan and the United States' direction of or acquiescence in his alleged torture and interrogation warrant dismissal of the indictment based on the Second Circuit decision in *United States v. Toscanino,* 500 F.2d 267 (2d Cir. 1974). Yousef argues that under the holding in Toscanino, jurisdiction over him was acquired as a result of a deliberate, unnecessary and unreasonable invasion of his rights. However, contrary to Yousef's arguments, *Toscanino* does not stand for the proposition that such allegations must result in dismissal of an indictment. *See United States ex rel. Lujan v. Gengler*, 510 F.2d 62, 66 (absent a set of incidents like that posited by the Court of Appeals as being present in *Toscanino*, not every violation by prosecution or police is so egregious that it requires nullification of the indictment).

The court in *Toscanino* merely remanded to the District Court for an evidentiary hearing to be held only if the defendant "offers some credible supporting evidence, including specifically evidence that the action was taken by or at the direction of United States officials." *Id.* at 281. On remand, *Toscanino*'s only evidence of his torture and coercive interrogation was his own affidavit, which failed to show participation by United States officials. The trial court, therefore refused to hold an evidentiary hearing and denied the motion to vacate the conviction and dismiss the indictment.

Like the trial court in the original case, subsequent courts have interpreted the Second Circuit decision in *Toscanino* narrowly, and generally have refused to dismiss indictments either because of the defendant's failure to establish abusive activity or the defendant's failure to establish United States involvement in the offensive conduct. *See United States v. Yunis,* 681 F. Supp. 909, 919 (D.D.C. 1988) ("Although most circuits have acknowledged the exception carved out by *Toscanino*, it is highly significant that no court has ever applied it to dismiss an indictment.")

Yousef has failed to meet the requirements of *Toscanino*. Yousef's affidavit does not sufficiently allege that United States agents participated in his alleged abduction and torture in Pakistan. In his affidavit in support of this motion, Yousef alleges that he was subject to months of torture at the hands of unidentified individuals in Pakistan who were somehow under the direction of United States officials. Yousef maintains that he was abducted from his relatives' home in Pakistan sometime at the end of November 1994, and remained in the custody of these original abductors and other Pakistan officials until he was surrendered to United States law enforcement agents on February 8, 1995. It was during these months that Yousef allegedly suffered the torture.

Yousef maintains that a United States official was present during a period of his interrogation when he was taken to a desert jail cell in Pakistan some days after his alleged abduction, but before his arrest and surrender to United States officials in Islamabad on February 8, 1995. According to Yousef, the torture which he suffered while in the desert consisted of forced intake of drugs to keep him awake and the denial of rest except at meal times. Yousef does not claim that he was tortured or otherwise mistreated during his period of custody in Islamabad, from February 7 to February 8, 1995, or after his transfer to United States agents.

Yousef's allegations of a period of over two months of torture appear incredible, given that there is no record of his arrest by anyone until February 7, 1995 in Islamabad. Additionally, a passport issued in the name of "Ali

Muhammad Baloch"[2] with Yousef's picture, was found in Yousef's possession at the time of his arrest and contained date stamps that tend to show that Yousef departed Pakistan on January 31, 1995, entered Bangkok, Thailand on February 1, 1995 and departed Bangkok on February 5, 1995. This passport, therefore, belies his claim that he was in custody in Pakistan between the period of November 1994 and February 7, 1995.

Yousef does not allege a sufficient factual basis for his assertion that a United States official was present during his alleged torture. Yousef alleges that he heard English being spoken during the desert interrogation and that he later recognized the voice as belonging to an FBI agent who questioned him in Islamabad as the same FBI agent who participated in the desert interrogation with unidentified Pakistanis. Yousef has not identified which FBI agent's voice he now claims he recognized as the one present in the desert. Nor has he stated what role this FBI agent played in the alleged torture.

Two FBI agents did in fact question Yousef in Islamabad. However, these agents, Legal Attache Ralph Paul Horton and Special Agent Bradley J. Garret, were not in Pakistan until February 4, 1995 and February 7, 1995 respectively. Moreover, according to Legal Attache Horton, who at the time was responsible for all FBI personnel entering Pakistan, no FBI agent was in Pakistan investigating the Yousef matter during this period prior to his arrival.

In *United States v. Lira,* 515 F.2d 68 (2d Cir.), the Circuit Court affirmed the denial of a motion to dismiss an indictment where the defendant's allegations of United States involvement were based on the defendant's overhearing English being spoken during his interrogation. The District Court held that the defendant's allegations were not sufficient "evidence that American agents were present at or privy to [defendant's] interrogation or that the persons overheard to speak English were Americans, much less Government agents."

Since no FBI agent was in Pakistan during the period of alleged torture, Yousef's allegations of voice recognition appear to be baseless and do not allege sufficient United States involvement under Toscanino and Lira.

[handwritten margin note: No FBI agents were in Pakistan during the period of alleged torture]

Moreover, the United States request for Yousef's extradition is not sufficient United States involvement to warrant a dismissal of the indictment. As stated in Lira, "the DEA can hardly be expected to monitor the conduct of representatives of each foreign government to assure that a request for extradition or expulsion is carried out in accordance with American constitutional standards." This same principle must apply to other United States law enforcement agencies as well. Thus, a request to extradite is not sufficient United States involvement to warrant dismissal of the indictment.

Yousef's motion to dismiss the indictment because of the United States involvement in the alleged torture suffered while in Pakistan is denied.

---

[2] Baloch is an acknowledged alias of Yousef, as evidenced by Yousef's own use of this name in signing a rights waiver form.

Extraterritorial Jurisdiction

Each Defendant has made various arguments as to why this court should not exercise extraterritorial jurisdiction over the crimes charged in the Indictment. All Defendants argue that this court does not have subject matter jurisdiction to try them for the conspiracy or the attempt to blow up United States civil aircraft in the "special aircraft jurisdiction" of the United States in violation of 18 U.S.C. §§ 32(a)(1), (2), (7) & 371 (Counts Twelve, Thirteen and Fourteen). Defendant Yousef challenges jurisdiction for the actual bombing of the Philippine aircraft in violation of 18 U.S.C. § 32(b) (Count Nineteen). All Defendants also attack the propriety of any other count which relies on these counts.

Defendants' various jurisdictional arguments rely on either constitutional due process principles, statutory interpretation and other domestic law, or international law. While the form of each Defendants' argument differs, in substance each Defendant challenges the assertion of extraterritorial jurisdiction by United States courts where the offenses charged did not occur on United States soil, did not involve United States citizens as defendants, or did not result in the death or injury of a United States citizen.

Jurisdiction is based primarily on Section 32 of Title 18, which states in relevant part:

(a) Whoever willfully

(1) sets fire to, damages, destroys, disables, or wrecks any aircraft in the special aircraft jurisdiction of the United States or any civil aircraft used, operated, or employed in interstate, overseas, or foreign air commerce;

(2) places or causes to be placed a destructive device or substance in, upon, or in proximity to, or otherwise makes or causes to be made unworkable or unusable or hazardous to work or use, any such aircraft, or any part or other materials used or intended to be used in connection with the operation of such aircraft, if such placing or causing to be placed or such making or causing to be made is likely to endanger the safety of any such aircraft; ...

(7) attempts to do anything prohibited under paragraphs (1) through (6) of this subsection;

shall be fined under this title or imprisoned not more than twenty years, or both.

(b) Whoever wilfully

(3) places or causes to be placed on a civil aircraft registered in a country other than the United States while such aircraft is in service, a device or substance which is likely to destroy that aircraft, or to cause damage to that aircraft which renders that aircraft incapable of flight or which is likely to endanger that aircraft's safety in flight; . . .

shall, if the offender is later found in the United States, be fined under this title or imprisoned not more than twenty years, or both.

Defendants have been charged under Section 32(a)(1), (2), and (7) in conjunction with the federal conspiracy statute, 18 U.S.C. § 371, with conspiring to bomb eleven United States airliners operating in East Asia. Defendant Yousef has also been charged in a separate count for violation of section 32(b)(3) for the actual bombing of the Philippines airliner. Had the prosecution for the Philippines airliner bombing been brought separately, the argument that "this case has far more nexus to the Philippines than it does to the United States", may have been more persuasive. However, this prosecution alleges that the Philippines airliner bombing was just one step in the overall plot to sabotage United States airliners. As such, the Philippines airliner bombing is alleged to have been part of Defendants' continuous course of conduct in relation to the overall bombing plot. Correctly construed, therefore, it becomes apparent that this court has the authority to assert extraterritorial jurisdiction over the three Defendants for the crimes charged in this indictment consistent with the statutory jurisdictional requirements of Section 32, principles of international law, and the United States Constitution. Not only does this court have the authority to exercise extraterritorial jurisdiction in this case, but, under treaty obligations of the United States, it is required to do so.

Section 32, adopted as part of the Aircraft Sabotage Act, was enacted in 1984 to fulfill this country's responsibilities under the Montreal Convention for the Suppression of Unlawful Acts against the Safety of Civil Aviation, ("the Montreal Convention"), which came into effect on January 26, 1973. A principal purpose of the act was to provide federal jurisdiction over individuals who were accused of committing crimes involving aircraft sabotage and over whom the courts would not otherwise have jurisdiction under domestic law.

Traditional notions of jurisdiction provided that a country's jurisdiction extended internationally over vessels or aircraft flying that country's flag based on a "floating or flying territory" rationale. *See* RESTATEMENT (THIRD) § 402, Reporter's Note 4. This traditional concept was codified in some respects in the Aircraft Sabotage Act.

Section 32(a) proscribes destruction, bombing, and endangering the safety of any aircraft in the "special aircraft jurisdiction of the United States or any civil aircraft used, operated or employed in interstate, overseas or foreign air commerce." There are therefore two possible avenues for establishing jurisdiction under this section. The term "special aircraft jurisdiction" is defined to include "a civil aircraft of the United States" while that aircraft is in flight.

The indictment details a bombing plan by Defendants that targeted United States-flagged commercial airlines, all but one of which were bound for various cities in the United States. As part of the evidence in this case, the government will present a computer printout which it contends contains the specific flight numbers and itineraries for the aircraft involved. All the aircraft involved are from the fleets of well-known United States airline companies, which according to the government, were registered under chapter 441, making them "civil aircraft of the United States." Since the indictment alleges that the bombs were scheduled to explode while these civil aircraft were in flight, the allegations satisfy the "special aircraft jurisdiction" provision.

As part of the overt acts listed in the indictment, the government alleges that Defendants were in possession of a letter that specifically threatened United States civilians. Additionally, all of the aircraft targeted in the alleged plot were

United States carriers, and all but one were scheduled to make stops in the United States. At the very least, some members of the flight crew assigned to the various flights were United States nationals. The indictment therefore sufficiently alleges that United States nationals and other United States interests were targets of the alleged conspiracy.

32b3 charge against Y.

Defendant Yousef challenges jurisdiction over Count Nineteen of the indictment, which concerns the Philippines airliner bombing. Section 32(b)(3), provides for criminal punishment of persons who place aboard a civil aircraft registered in a country other than the United States while that aircraft is in service, any device or substance which is likely to destroy or otherwise damage or endanger the aircraft's safety, provided the saboteur is later "found in the United States." 18 U.S.C. § 32(b)(3). Philippines Airlines Flight 434 was a civil aircraft registered outside the United States, which was en route from the Philippines to Tokyo, Japan when a bomb exploded on board, causing the death of one passenger, Haruki Ikegami, and injuring several others.

Y argues - not "found" in US

Yousef argues that he was not properly "found" within the United States as that term is used in section 32(b). Yousef argues that the sole reason he was present in the United States was because the government brought him to the United States to stand trial for the other charges in the indictment related to the bombing of the World Trade Center. Yousef argues that the government knowingly delayed indicting him on the airliner bombing plot until he was brought to the United States, in order to establish his presence in the United States for purposes of this count of the indictment. Therefore, according to Yousef, he was not present within the United States voluntarily, and jurisdiction cannot be asserted over him pursuant to Section 32(b).

The question of whether a defendant is "found" within the United States for purposes of establishing jurisdiction for aircraft-related crimes, where the defendant was brought to the United States to stand trial on other charges, was considered in *United States v. Yunis*, 288 U.S. App. D.C. 129, 924 F.2d 1086, 1089 (D.C. Cir. 1984). There, the court held that jurisdiction was properly established under the Antihijacking Act, 49 U.S.C. § 1472(n), where the defendant was "found" within the United States as a result of his having been brought within the jurisdiction to stand trial for other charges contained in the same indictment.

Defendant Yousef was surrendered to United States officials by the Pakistani government pursuant to an extradition request made by the United States. Yousef was then returned to the Southern District of New York and subsequently indicted for the airliner bombing plot. These circumstances are at least as compelling as the facts presented in Yunis. The circumstances by which Yousef was "found" within the United States satisfy the statutory jurisdictional requirements.

Int'l argument

Defendants Yousef and Shah argue that this court does not have jurisdiction based on principles of international law. Yousef argues that the only international law principle of jurisdiction applicable in this prosecution is that of universal jurisdiction. Yousef argues that "while courts have discussed universality as a basis of jurisdiction, in practice, it has never been used as the sole basis for the United States to assert jurisdiction over a defendant."

The issue of exercising extraterritorial jurisdiction over a criminal prosecution based on universal jurisdiction was also discussed in *United States v. Yunis, supra.* Yousef attempts to distinguish *Yunis* from this case by arguing that in *Yunis,* the presence of two United States citizens aboard the hijacked plane provided an "independent basis for jurisdiction" over the defendant.

The *Yunis* court did not decide that universal jurisdiction was insufficient as the sole basis for jurisdiction under the Antihijacking Act, but rather that the decision to exercise jurisdiction was bolstered by the fact that two of the passengers were United States citizens. The *Yunis* court held that the defendant had been "found" in the United States and therefore the prosecution satisfied the statutory jurisdictional requirements.

Endorsing the exercise of universal jurisdiction in the prosecution of an aircraft-related crime, the court stated that "aircraft hijacking may well be one of the few crimes so clearly condemned under the law of nations that states may assert universal jurisdiction to bring offenders to justice, even when the state has no territorial connection to the hijacking and its citizens are not involved."

The court in Yunis cited to the Restatement (Third) of the Foreign Relations Law to support exercise of universal jurisdiction in a criminal prosecution related to crimes involving aircraft. Section 404 states, "[a] state has jurisdiction to define and prescribe punishment for certain offenses recognized by the community of nations as of universal concern, such as piracy, slave trade, attacks on or hijacking of aircraft, genocide, war crimes, and perhaps certain acts of terrorism, even where none of the other bases of jurisdiction indicated in § 402 is present." *[handwritten: Universal J.]*

The disregard for human life which would accompany the placing of a bomb aboard an airplane with the intent for that bomb to explode while the airplane is in flight and fully occupied with people, or otherwise sabotaging that plane, is at least as heinous a crime of international concern as hijacking a plane. The same rationale that supports jurisdiction under the Antihijacking Act also supports jurisdiction under the Aircraft Sabotage Act, regardless of where the alleged crimes occurred.

Moreover, contrary to Yousef's arguments, there is an additional basis for jurisdiction in this case. The indictment alleges that the bombing aboard the Philippines airliner was not an isolated incident, but part of a continuing course of conduct related to the alleged conspiracy to blow up United States airliners in East Asia. As discussed above, jurisdiction is properly alleged for those counts related to the conspiracy to blow up United States airliners, and therefore, jurisdiction is proper for acts committed in the continuous course of conduct of that conspiracy.

The exercise of extraterritorial jurisdiction in this case is reasonable, since the crimes charged have a "substantial, direct, and foreseeable effect" in the United States and clearly affect United States interests, as would be required by *[handwritten: Crimes have substantial effect in the US]* principles of international law. The alleged crimes clearly had intended effects on the United States and its citizens, although they were committed abroad. The fact that the planned consequences of the plot did not come to fruition, and thereby did not directly injure any United States citizen, does not wrest jurisdiction over the prosecution from this court.

The fact that the Philippines airliner bombing is a part of the continuous course of conduct charged against the defendants squelches Shah's argument that the prosecution of the defendants in the United States does not have a "territorial nexus or other direct nexus to the U.S.," rendering the prosecution "arbitrary and fundamentally unfair," and in violation of the Fifth and Sixth Amendments. Any constitutionally required nexus to the United States is clearly present.

Yousef, Murad, and Shah also challenge this court's jurisdiction under Counts Twelve, Seventeen, and Eighteen, on the grounds that the statutes upon which these counts rely do not contain specific grants of extraterritorial jurisdiction. Extraterritorial jurisdiction over a conspiracy charge depends on whether extraterritorial jurisdiction exists as to the underlying substantive crime. Since this court has jurisdiction over the substantive Section 32 charges, jurisdiction over the conspiracy charged in Count Twelve is also proper.

The charge contained in Count Fifteen, a violation of Section 2332, which proscribes conspiracy to kill United States citizens abroad, clearly applies extraterritorially. Because the charges regarding the use and carrying of bombs charged in Counts Seventeen and Eighteen arise directly from the conspiracy offenses charged in Counts Twelve and Fifteen, this Court has jurisdiction over Counts Seventeen and Eighteen as well.

Conclusion

I find that exercising extraterritorial jurisdiction over Defendants Yousef, Murad, and Shah for the crimes charged in the indictment is consistent with the statutory requirements, principles of domestic and international law, and the United States Constitution. Defendants' motions to dismiss the indictment and its various counts for lack of jurisdiction are therefore denied.

NOTES AND QUESTIONS

1. Ramzi Ahmed Yousef is the bridge to our consideration of terrorist actions on U.S. soil. His name appears as a key player in the cases stemming from the first bombing of the World Trade Center. *United States v. Salameh*, p. 23. He fled the U.S. after that bombing and was active in a series of bombings of airliners and theaters in the Philippines during 1994.

2. Jurisdiction under the hostage and aircraft statutes, which themselves carry out treaty obligations under various international conventions, does not depend on showing a political motivation for the action. The nations signing these conventions have declared that these particularly dangerous actions are universally condemned regardless of the motivation. The rationales are similar to the reasons underlying the Torture Convention. Given that, could any nation exercise universal jurisdiction over a hostage-taker or an aircraft bomber? If so, then is the jurisdictional requirement of a U.S. victim necessary? Should these acts of violence be considered "terrorism" only if they carry a political motivation? So once again we should explore the questions of how to define a terrorist and whether the terrorist label really matters.

3. Professor Bradley argues that the exercise of extraterritorial jurisdiction, even if based on universal jurisdiction, is still an exercise of judicial power to be delineated by Congress under the "Define and Punish" clause, not an exercise of international law. Thus, it is not particularly problematic for American criminal cases, although it may be a bit more problematic in civil cases. Curtis Bradley, *Universal Jurisdiction and U.S. Law*, 2001 U. CHI. L. REV. 323.

§ 4.03 CIVIL ACTIONS

There are three principal statutes under which injured persons can bring civil actions against state sponsors of terrorism or against private individuals. The Torture Victims Protection Act (TVPA) is codified at 28 U.S.C. § 1350 note. The civil version of the criminal "material support" statutes is generally known as the Anti Terrorism Act (ATA) and is codified at 18 U.S.C. § 2333. The Foreign Sovereign Immunity Act (FSIA) withholds sovereign immunity for acts committed by designated terrorist states and for torts committed within the U.S., 28 U.S.C. § 1605.

Although it is tempting to downplay the role of civil lawsuits in light of the extensive action of the past decade in criminal law enforcement, bear in mind that some of the most severe blows struck at the Ku Klux Klan was a series of lawsuits by which the Klan and its supporters lost most of their assets and thus much of their ability to function. The website of the Southern Poverty Law Center describes the evolution of its "Klanwatch" program into its current "Intelligence Project." http://www.splcenter.org/intel.

Prior to the 1990s, there was a serious question about the ability of an alien to sue another alien in U.S. courts for violations of humanitarian law. In *Filartiga v. Pena-Irala*, 630 F.2d 876 (2d Cir. 1980), the plaintiff citizens of Paraguay sued a Paraguayan official for torturing and killing their son and brother. The Alien Tort Statute, 28 U.S.C. § 1350, provided jurisdiction over suits "by an alien for a tort only, committed in violation of the law of nations or a treaty of the United States." Because Article III does not provide for diversity jurisdiction between two aliens, the statute would not be valid except to the extent that it applies to a suit that "arises under" federal law. Treaty law would be such law but treaties very seldom create private rights of action. Therefore, the question was whether the "law of nations" was federal law that would support subject matter jurisdiction. The Second Circuit held that "an act of torture committed by a state official against one held in detention violates established norms of the international law of human rights, and hence the law of nations."

Tel-Oren v. Libyan Arab Republic, 726 F.2d 774 (D.C. Cir. 1984), produced a badly splintered court in what Judge Edwards called "an area of the law that cries out for clarification by the Supreme Court." The *Tel-Oren* case was brought by survivors and representatives of victims of an attack on a bus in Israel in 1978. Two of the many defendants were Libya and the PLO, who were alleged to have acted in complicity in carrying out the attack. The three judges on the panel could agree on only a terse *per curiam* statement affirming the dismissal of the action by the district court. Each wrote a separate concurring opinion.

Judge Edwards argued that international law could supply the rule of decision for a claim of torture but not for murder. Libya was not alleged to have tortured anyone and would have enjoyed sovereign immunity at the time. The PLO was "not a recognized member of the community of nations" and thus was not subject to the rules and conventions on torture.

Judge Bork insisted international law did not recognize a private right of action for either torture or murder. Thus, unless Congress created a right of action, none would exist as a matter of federal law. Judge Edwards' response to this argument was that international law states the norms but leaves to each nation the methods of protection, whether through civil suit or otherwise.

Judge Robb would have declared the whole dispute to be a political question lacking in judicially manageable standards.

The Supreme Court did not accept Judge Edwards' plea for clarification, but Congress did. The Torture Victims Protection Act, codified as a note to 18 U.S.C. § 1350, in 1991 explicitly created a civil action for official torture or "extrajudicial killing." The civil remedy usually known as the Anti-Terrorism Act, 18 U.S.C. § 2333, was added in 1992. In 1996, Congress adopted amendments to the Foreign Sovereign Immunity Act (FSIA). These are the principal statutes that form the basis for the civil suits in the following cases.

PRICE v. SOCIALIST PEOPLE'S LIBYAN ARAB JAMAHIRIYA
352 U.S. App. D.C. 284, 294 F.3d 82 (D.C. Cir. 2002)

EDWARDS, Circuit Judge:

This case involves a lawsuit brought under the Foreign Sovereign Immunities Act ("FSIA") by two American citizens who sued the Socialist People's Libyan Arab Jamahiriya ("Libya") for torture and hostage taking. Plaintiffs' lawsuit seeks cover under a recent amendment to the FSIA which strips certain foreign states – including Libya of their sovereign immunity in American courts when they engage in such conduct. *See* 28 U.S.C. § 1605(a)(7).

In response to plaintiffs' suit, Libya moved to dismiss, claiming sovereign immunity and a lack of personal jurisdiction. The District Court denied the motion to dismiss and Libya now seeks review in this interlocutory appeal. Two central questions have been raised on appeal: first, whether plaintiffs have alleged facts that are legally sufficient to revoke Libya's immunity under the FSIA; and, second, whether the assertion of personal jurisdiction over Libya in the manner specifically authorized by the FSIA violates the Due Process Clause.

We hold, first, that plaintiffs have failed to state a claim for hostage taking adequate to abrogate sovereign immunity and establish subject matter jurisdiction. The allegations set forth in the complaint do not come close to satisfying the definition of "hostage taking" prescribed by the FSIA. In contrast to the hostage-taking claim, however, plaintiffs have at least intimated that they can allege facts that might state a proper claim for torture under the FSIA.

Accordingly, we will remand the case to allow plaintiffs to attempt to amend their complaint in an effort to satisfy the statute's rigorous definition of torture. As a word of caution, we note that there is a question as to whether the complaint states a claim for relief upon which plaintiffs can recover; although this matter is not properly before us on interlocutory review, we are not foreclosing review of the issue in the District Court.

Finally, we hold that Libya, as a foreign state, is not a "person" within the meaning of the Due Process Clause. We therefore conclude that the Constitution imposes no limitation on the exercise of personal jurisdiction by the federal courts over Libya.

I. BACKGROUND

The facts and procedural history of this case are relatively straightforward. Plaintiffs Michael Price and Roger Frey, Americans who had been living in Libya in the employ of a Libyan company, were arrested in March of 1980 after taking pictures of various places in and around Tripoli. Libyan government officials apparently believed that these photographs constituted anti-revolutionary propaganda, because they would portray unfavorable images of life in Libya.

Price and Frey allege that, following their arrest, they were denied bail and kept in a "political prison" for 105 days pending the outcome of their trial. In their complaint, plaintiffs assert that they endured deplorable conditions while incarcerated, including urine-soaked mattresses, a cramped cell with substandard plumbing that they were forced to share with seven other inmates, a lack of medical care, and inadequate food. The complaint also asserts that the plaintiffs were "kicked, clubbed and beaten" by prison guards, and "interrogated and subjected to physical, mental and verbal abuse." The complaint contends that this incarceration was "for the purpose of demonstrating Defendant's support of the government of Iran which held hostages in the U.S. Embassy in Tehran, Iran."

Ultimately, plaintiffs were tried and acquitted of the crimes with which they had been charged. After the verdict was announced, however, the Libyan government retained their passports for another 60 days while the prosecution pursued an appeal, which is permitted under the Libyan Code of Criminal Procedure. When this appeal was eventually rejected, plaintiffs were permitted to leave Libya.

On May 7, 1997, Price and Frey commenced a civil action against Libya in federal court. Their complaint asserted claims for hostage taking and torture and sought $ 20 million in damages for each man. Following receipt of process, Libya filed a motion to dismiss, arguing that (1) the grant of subject matter jurisdiction over plaintiffs' action was unconstitutional, (2) the court's exercise of personal jurisdiction was unconstitutional, and (3) plaintiffs had failed to state a claim on which relief could be granted. The District Court rejected each of these arguments, thus vitiating Libya's sovereign immunity defense and allowing the court to assert both subject matter jurisdiction over plaintiffs' claims and personal jurisdiction over the defendant. Libya now pursues an interlocutory appeal.

II. DISCUSSION

On appeal, Libya has not renewed its constitutional attack on the court's subject matter jurisdiction. Instead, it claims that the District Court erred in not resolving certain disputed issues of fact, proceeding instead as if plaintiffs' factual allegations had already been established. Libya also argues that, even assuming that these facts were true, the plaintiffs have failed to make out a valid claim either for torture or hostage taking under the FSIA. Finally, Libya asserts that the Due Process Clause does not permit an American court to take jurisdiction over a foreign sovereign based on conduct that has no connection to the United States save for the nationality of the plaintiff.

A. Plaintiffs' Cause of Action

Before we address the issues arising under the FSIA and the Due Process Clause, we first want to make it clear that our decision today does not address or decide whether the plaintiffs have stated a *cause of action* against Libya. The parties appear to assume that a substantive claim against Libya arises under the FSIA, but this is far from clear. The FSIA is undoubtedly a jurisdictional statute which, in specified cases, eliminates foreign sovereign immunity and opens the door to subject matter jurisdiction in the federal courts. There is a question, however, whether the FSIA creates a federal cause of action for torture and hostage taking *against foreign states. See Roeder v. Islamic Republic of Iran,* 195 F. Supp. 2d 140, 171-73 (D.D.C. 2002).

The "Flatow Amendment" to the FSIA confers a right of action for torture and hostage taking against an "official, employee, or agent of a foreign state," *see Flatow v. Islamic Republic of Iran,* 999 F. Supp. 1, 12-13 (D.D.C. 1998), but the amendment does not list "foreign states" among the parties against whom such an action may be brought. While it is possible that such an action could be brought under the "international terrorism" statute, 18 U.S.C. § 2333(a), no such claim has been raised in this case.

The question relating to plaintiffs' cause of action has yet to be raised or addressed in the District Court, and it was neither briefed nor argued by the parties during this appeal. Therefore, although we flag the issue, we will leave its disposition to the District Court in the first instance following remand of this case. We will turn our attention now to the matters before us, *i.e.*, the issues arising under the FSIA and the Due Process Clause.

B. The 1996 Amendments to the Foreign Sovereign Immunities Act

The FSIA provides a basis for asserting jurisdiction over foreign nations in the United States. *Argentine Republic v. Amerada Hess Shipping Corp.,* 488 U.S. 428, 443, 109 S. Ct. 683 (1989). The statute, which was originally enacted in 1976, confers immunity on foreign states in all cases that do not fall into one of its specifically enumerated exceptions. *See McKesson HBOC, Inc. v. Islamic Republic of Iran,* 271 F.3d 1101, 1105 (D.C. Cir. 2001). These exceptions were crafted in order to codify the "restrictive theory" of sovereign immunity, under which immunity is generally limited to a foreign state's public or governmental acts (*jure imperii*) but withheld from its private or commercial acts (*jure gestionis*).

(originally)
when there is
no immunity

The FSIA [provides] a list of specific circumstances in which that immunity is unavailable. These include cases in which the state has waived its immunity, cases based upon various forms of commercial activity, takings of property in violation of international law, and torts committed in the United States. The original FSIA was not intended as human rights legislation. *See* Jennifer A. Gergen, *Human Rights and the Foreign Sovereign Immunities Act,* 36 VA. J. INT'L L. 765, 771 (1996). *Thus, no matter how allegedly egregious a foreign state's conduct, suits that did not fit into one of the statute's discrete and limited exceptions invariably were rejected. See, e.g., Saudi Arabia v. Nelson,* 507 U.S. 349 (1993) (holding that a claim arising from the detention and torture of an American citizen in Saudi Arabia was not "based upon a commercial activity carried on in the United States"); *Smith v. Socialist People's Libyan Arab Jamahiriya,* 101 F.3d 239 (2d Cir. 1996) (holding that Libya retained its sovereign immunity for the bombing of Pam Am 103 over Lockerbie, Scotland); *Princz v. Fed. Republic of Germany*, 307 U.S. App. D.C. 102, 26 F.3d 1166 (D.C. Cir. 1994) (holding that plaintiff could not recover for slave labor performed at Nazi concentration camps, because Germany's conduct was not commercial activity causing a "direct effect in the United States" and did not constitute an implied waiver of sovereign immunity); *Siderman de Blake v. Republic of Argentina,* 965 F.2d 699 (9th Cir. 1992) (holding that Argentina was immune from liability for acts of torture committed by the ruling junta); *Tel-Oren v. Libyan Arab Republic,* 233 U.S. App. D.C. 384, 726 F.2d 774, 775 n.1 (D.C. Cir. 1984) (Edwards J., concurring) (FSIA precludes jurisdiction over Libya for armed attack on civilian bus in Israel); *cf. Amerada Hess,* 488 U.S. at 436 ("Immunity is granted in those cases involving violations of international law that do not come within one of the FSIA's exceptions.").

Under the original FSIA, therefore, terrorism, torture, and hostage taking committed abroad were immunized forms of state activity. Indeed, in *Nelson*, the Supreme Court recognized that conduct of the sort alleged in the present case – "wrongful arrest, imprisonment, and torture" – amounted to abuses of police power, and "however monstrous such abuse undoubtedly may be, a foreign's state's exercise of the power of its police has long been understood for purpose of the restrictive theory as peculiarly sovereign in nature." *See also* Mathias Reimann, *A Human Rights Exception to Sovereign Immunity: Some Thoughts on Princz v. Federal Republic of Germany,* 16 MICH. J. INT'L L. 403, 417-18 (1995) (observing that under the unamended FSIA "efforts to persuade the courts to recognize a human rights exception to sovereign immunity" had failed).

The mounting concern over decisions such as these eventually spurred the political branches into action. *See* John F. Murphy, *Civil Liability for the Commission of International Crimes as an Alternative to Criminal Prosecution,* 12 HARV. HUM. RTS. J. 1, 34 (1999). In 1996, as part of the comprehensive Antiterrorism and Effective Death Penalty Act ("AEDPA"), Congress amended the FSIA to add a new class of claims for which certain foreign states would be precluded from asserting sovereign immunity. Specifically, the amendment vitiates immunity in cases

Amendment 1996

in which money damages are sought against a foreign state for personal injury or death that was caused by an act of torture, extrajudicial killing, aircraft sabotage, hostage taking, or the provision of material support or resources . . . for such an act if such act or provision of material support is engaged in by an official, employee, or agent of such foreign state while acting within the scope of his or her office, employment, or agency[.]

28 U.S.C. § 1605(a)(7). In enacting this provision, Congress sought to create a judicial forum for compensating the victims of terrorism, and in so doing to punish foreign states who have committed or sponsored such acts and deter them from doing so in the future. *See Daliberti v. Republic of Iraq,* 97 F. Supp. 2d 38, 50 (D.D.C. 2000); Molora Vadnais, *The Terrorism Exception to the Foreign Sovereign Immunities Act,* 5 UCLA J. INT'L L. & FOREIGN AFF. 199, 216 (2000).

While such legislation had long been sought by victims 'groups, it had been consistently resisted by the executive branch. See ALAN GERSON & JERRY ADLER, THE PRICE OF TERROR 212-26 (2001). Executive branch officials feared that the proposed amendment to FSIA might cause other nations to respond in kind, thus potentially subjecting the American government to suits in foreign countries for actions taken in the United States. Although these reservations did not prevent the amendment from passing, they nevertheless left their mark in the final version of the bill.

Section 1605(a)(7) has some notable features which reveal the delicate legislative compromise out of which it was born. First, not all foreign states may be sued. Instead, only a defendant that has been specifically designated by the State Department as a "state sponsor of terrorism" is subject to the loss of its sovereign immunity. § 1605(a)(7)(A). Second, even a foreign state listed as a sponsor of terrorism retains its immunity unless (a) it is afforded a reasonable opportunity to arbitrate any claim based on acts that occurred in that state, and (b) either the victim or the claimant was a U.S. national at the time that those acts took place. § 1605(a)(7)(B). In the present case, Libya has been designated as a sponsor of terrorism. *See Rein v. Socialist People's Libyan Arab Jamahiriya,* 162 F.3d 748, 764 (2d Cir. 1998). Moreover, both plaintiffs are American citizens, and Libya does not contend that it has been denied a chance to arbitrate their claims.

If service of process has been made under § 1608, personal jurisdiction over a foreign state exists for every claim over which the court has subject matter jurisdiction. *See* 28 U.S.C. § 1330(b). In turn, the statute automatically confers subject matter jurisdiction whenever the state loses its immunity pursuant to § 1605(a)(7). Personal jurisdiction determinations always have been made in this way under the FSIA. *See* JOSEPH W. DELLAPENNA, SUING FOREIGN GOVERNMENTS AND THEIR CORPORATIONS 9 (1988) (commenting on this "significant compression," whereby both "competence [subject matter jurisdiction] and personal jurisdiction depend upon whether the foreign state is immune under the substantive rules in the act"); *see also Harris v. VAO Intourist, Moscow,* 481 F. Supp. 1056, 1065 (E.D.N.Y. 1979) (Weinstein, J.) (noting the way in which the FSIA collapses subject matter jurisdiction, *in personam* jurisdiction, and sovereign immunity into a single inquiry).

Under the original FSIA, however, it was generally understood that in order for immunity to be lost, there had to be some tangible connection between the conduct of the foreign defendant and the *territory* of the United States. In this way, the original statute's immunity exceptions "prescribed the necessary contacts which must exist before our courts can exercise personal jurisdiction."

When Congress passed the original FSIA, it was assumed that the exercise of personal jurisdiction over foreign states under the statute always would satisfy the demands of the Constitution. *See* Joseph W. Glannon & Jeffery Atik, *Politics and Personal Jurisdiction: Suing State Sponsors of Terrorism under the 1996 Amendments to the Foreign Sovereign Immunities Act*, 87 GEO. L.J. 675, 681-82 (1999). This assumption proved accurate.

The antiterrorism amendments changed this statutory framework. Under § 1605(a)(7), the only required link between the defendant nation and the territory of the United States is the nationality of the claimant. Thus, § 1605(a)(7) now allows personal jurisdiction to be maintained over defendants in circumstances that do not appear to satisfy the "minimum contacts" requirement of the Due Process Clause.

[handwritten margin note: ✗ No territorial link is necessary]

C. Challenges to the Factual Underpinnings of an FSIA Complaint

[W]hen a foreign state defendant raises "a dispute over the factual basis of the court's subject matter jurisdiction under the FSIA," the trial court is required to "go beyond the pleadings and resolve any disputed issues of fact the resolution of which is necessary to a ruling upon the motion to dismiss." Libya still did not challenge the factual basis of plaintiffs' allegations. Instead, it wrote that, "even viewed in the light most favorable to the plaintiffs, the facts alleged in the complaint do not establish 'acts of torture' by Libya."

E. Torture

The FSIA's definition of torture derives from the meaning given that term in section 3 of the Torture Victim Protection Act of 1991 ("TVPA"). Section 3(b)(1) of the TVPA defines "torture" to include

[handwritten margin note: Torture]

> any act, directed against an individual in the offender's custody or physical control, by which *severe* pain or suffering (other than pain or suffering arising only from or inherent in, or incidental to, lawful sanctions), whether physical or mental, is intentionally inflicted on that individual *for such purposes* as obtaining from that individual or a third person information or a confession, punishing that individual for an act that individual or a third person has committed or is suspected of having committed, intimidating or coercing that individual or a third person, or for any reason based on discrimination of any kind.

(Emphases added). This definition, in turn, borrows extensively from the 1984 United Nations Convention Against Torture and Other Cruel, Inhuman or Degrading Treatment or Punishment ("Torture Convention"), which the United States signed in 1988 and ratified two years later. Indeed, the TVPA was passed in part to fulfill the Convention's mandate that ratifying nations take action to ensure that torturers are held legally accountable for their actions.

The drafters of the Convention, as well as the Reagan Administration that signed it, the Bush Administration that submitted it to Congress, and the Senate that ultimately ratified it, therefore all sought to ensure that "only acts of a certain gravity shall be considered to constitute torture." This understanding thus makes clear that torture does not automatically result whenever individuals in official custody are subjected even to direct physical assault. Not *all* police brutality, not *every* instance of excessive force used against prisoners, is torture under the FSIA.

As to the purposes for which abuse must be inflicted, it is clear from the text of the TVPA that the list of purposes provided was not meant to be exhaustive. Instead, this list was included in order to reinforce that torture requires acts both intentional and malicious, and to illustrate the common motivations that cause individuals to engage in torture. Moreover, this requirement ensures that, whatever its specific goal, torture can occur under the FSIA only when the production of pain is purposive, and not merely haphazard. In order to lose its sovereign immunity, a foreign state must impose suffering cruelly and deliberately, rather than as the unforeseen or unavoidable incident of some legitimate end.

[I]n light of the serious and far-reaching implications of the 1996 FSIA amendments, it is especially important for the courts to ensure that foreign states are not stripped of their sovereign immunity unless they have been charged with actual torture, and not mere police brutality.

In this case, plaintiffs' complaint offers no useful details about the nature of the kicking, clubbing, and beatings that plaintiffs allegedly suffered. As a result, there is no way to determine from the present complaint the severity of plaintiffs' alleged beatings – including their frequency, duration, the parts of the body at which they were aimed, and the weapons used to carry them out – in order to ensure that they satisfy the TVPA's rigorous definition of torture. In short, there is no way to discern whether plaintiffs' complaint merely alleges police brutality that falls short of torture. Thus, the facts pleaded do not reasonably support a finding that the physical abuse allegedly inflicted by Libya evinced the degree of cruelty necessary to reach a level of torture.

Furthermore, the present complaint says virtually nothing about the purpose of the alleged torture. Plaintiffs seemingly have left it for the courts to conjure some illicit purpose to fill in this pleading gap. Obviously this will not do.

In sum, plaintiffs' allegations of torture as presently stated are insufficient to survive defendant's motion to dismiss. Plaintiffs must allege more than that they were abused. They must demonstrate in their pleadings that Libya's conduct rose to such a level of depravity and caused them such intense pain and suffering as to be properly classified as torture. Although it is far from certain, their complaint hints that they might be able to state a proper claim for torture under the FSIA. Accordingly, we will remand the case to the District Court to allow plaintiffs to attempt to amend their complaint in an effort to satisfy TVPA's stringent definition of torture.

F. Hostage Taking

As with torture, the FSIA draws its definition of "hostage taking" from an exogenous legal source, here article 1 of the International Convention Against the Taking of Hostages. This provision reads as follows:

Any person who seizes or detains and threatens to kill, to injure or to continue to detain another person *in order to compel a third party*, namely, a State, an international governmental organization, a natural or judicial person or a group of persons, *to do or abstain from doing any act as an explicit or implicit condition for the release of the hostage* commits the offense of taking hostages within the meaning of the Convention.

(Emphases added). Under no reasonable reading of the plaintiffs' complaint does their admittedly unpleasant imprisonment qualify as hostage taking so defined.

The Convention does not proscribe all detentions, but instead focuses on the intended purpose of the detention. In this case, the complaint asserts only that Libya incarcerated Price and Frey "for the purpose of demonstrating Defendant's support of the government of Iran which held hostages in the U.S. Embassy in Tehran, Iran." Such motivation does not satisfy the Convention's intentionality requirement. The definition speaks in terms of conditions of release; the defendant must have detained the victim in order to compel some particular result, specifically to force a third party either to perform an act otherwise unplanned or to abstain from one otherwise contemplated so as to ensure the freedom of the detainee. Accordingly, detention for the goal of expressing support for illegal behavior – even for behavior that would itself qualify as "hostage taking" – does not constitute the taking of hostages within the meaning of the FSIA.

In this case, the plaintiffs have suggested no demand for *quid pro quo* terms between the government of Libya and a third party whereby Price and Frey would have been released upon the performance or non-performance of any action by that third party. Indeed, even when read most favorably to them, their complaint points to no nexus between what happened to them in Libya and any concrete concession that Libya may have hoped to extract from the outside world. The one purpose that plaintiffs have alleged is plainly inadequate, and they have advanced no others. Their allegation thus falls short of the standard for hostage taking under § 1605(a)(7).

For these reasons, Libya cannot be stripped of its sovereign immunity based on plaintiffs' allegation of hostage taking. The District Court thus erred in refusing to dismiss this count. Accordingly, we reverse on this point.

G. Personal Jurisdiction

The last question that we face is whether the Due Process Clause is offended by the District Court's assertion of personal jurisdiction over Libya. If, on remand, plaintiffs can state a claim of torture under § 1605(a)(7) sufficient to survive a motion to dismiss, and if they have properly served process on the defendant, personal jurisdiction will be established under the FSIA.

The Due Process Clause requires that if the defendant "be not present within the territory of the forum, he have certain minimum contacts with it such that the maintenance of the suit does not offend 'traditional notions of fair play and substantial justice.' "

In the present case, it is undisputed that Libya has no connection with the District of Columbia or with the United States, except for the alleged fact that it tortured two American citizens in Libya. This would be insufficient to satisfy the usual "minimum contacts" requirement.

Implicit in Libya's argument is the claim that a foreign state is a "person" within the meaning of the Due Process Clause. In previous cases, we have proceeded *as if* this proposition were true, but we have never so held. Now, however, this assumption has been challenged. And, with the issue directly before us, we hold that foreign states are not "persons" protected by the Fifth Amendment.

H: states are not persons

Our conclusion is based on a number of considerations. [I]t is highly significant that in *South Carolina v. Katzenbach,* 383 U.S. 301, 323-24, 86 S. Ct. 803 (1966), the Court was unequivocal in holding that "the word 'person' in the context of the Due Process Clause of the Fifth Amendment cannot, by any reasonable mode of interpretation, be expanded to encompass the States of the Union." Therefore, absent some compelling reason to treat foreign sovereigns more favorably than "States of the Union," it would make no sense to view foreign states as "persons" under the Due Process Clause.

Indeed, we think it would be highly incongruous to afford greater Fifth Amendment rights to foreign nations, who are entirely alien to our constitutional system, than are afforded to the states, who help make up the very fabric of that system. The States are integral and active participants in the Constitution's infrastructure, and they both derive important benefits and must abide by significant limitations as a consequence of their participation. However, a "foreign State lies outside the structure of the Union." Given this fundamental dichotomy between the constitutional status of foreign states and States within the United States, we cannot perceive why the former should be permitted to avail themselves of the fundamental safeguards of the Due Process Clause if the latter may not.

It is especially significant that the Constitution does not limit foreign states, as it does the States of the Union, in the power they can exert against the United States or its government. Indeed, the federal government cannot invoke the Constitution, save possibly to declare war, to prevent a foreign nation from taking action adverse to the interest of the United States or to compel it to take action favorable to the United States. It would therefore be quite strange to interpret the Due Process Clause as conferring upon Libya rights and protections *against* the power of federal government.

In addition to text and structure, history and tradition support our conclusion. Never has the Supreme Court suggested that foreign nations enjoy rights derived from the Constitution, or that they can use such rights to shield themselves from adverse actions taken by the United States. This is not surprising. Relations between nations in the international community are seldom governed by the domestic law of one state or the other. And legal disputes between the United States and foreign governments are not mediated through the Constitution. *See Nat'l Council of Resistance of Iran v. Dep't of State*, 346 U.S. App. D.C. 131, 251 F.3d 192, 202 (D.C. Cir. 2001) (recognizing that "sovereign states interact with each other through diplomacy and even coercion in ways not affected by constitutional protections such as the Due Process Clause").

Rather, the federal judiciary has relied on principles of comity and international law to protect foreign governments in the American legal system. This approach recognizes the reality that foreign nations are external to the constitutional compact, and it preserves the flexibility and discretion of the political branches in conducting this country's relations with other nations.

An example of this approach is seen with respect to the right of access to the courts. Private individuals have "a constitutional right of access to the courts," that is, the "right to sue and defend in the courts." Foreign states also have been afforded the right to use the courts of the United States to prosecute civil claims "upon the same basis as a domestic corporation or individual might do." But the right of access enjoyed by foreign nations derives from "principles of comity," and it is "neither a matter of absolute obligation, on the one hand, nor of mere courtesy and good will, upon the other." This privilege is not to be denied lightly, because to do so "would manifest a want of comity and friendly feeling." Nonetheless, foreign nations do not have a *constitutional* right of access to the courts of the United States. Indeed, only nations recognized by and at peace with the United States may avail themselves of our courts, and "it is within the exclusive power of the Executive Branch to determine which nations are entitled to sue."

While we recognize that the present case implicates not the right of affirmative access to the courts, but rather its reverse – the right not to be haled into court – this does not change the analysis under the Due Process Clause. The personal jurisdiction requirement is not a structural limitation on the power of courts. Rather, "the personal jurisdiction requirement recognizes and protects an individual liberty interest. It represents a restriction on judicial power not as a matter of sovereignty, but as a matter of individual liberty." This makes sense, because "the requirement that a court have personal jurisdiction flows not from Art. III, but from the Due Process Clause." It is thus quite clear that the constitutional law of personal jurisdiction secures interests quite different from those at stake when a sovereign nation such as Libya seeks to defend itself against the prerogatives of a rival government. It therefore follows that foreign states stand on a fundamentally different footing than do private litigants who are compelled to defend themselves in American courts.

Unlike private entities, foreign nations are the juridical equals of the government that seeks to assert jurisdiction over them. If they believe that they have suffered harm by virtue of being haled into court in the United States, foreign states have available to them a panoply of mechanisms in the international arena through which to seek vindication or redress. These mechanisms, not the Constitution, set the terms by which sovereigns relate to one another.

Finally, it is worth noting that serious practical problems might arise were we to hold that foreign states may cloak themselves in the protections of the Due Process Clause. For example, the power of Congress and the President to freeze the assets of foreign nations, or to impose economic sanctions on them, could be challenged as deprivations of property without due process of law. The courts would be called upon to adjudicate these sensitive questions, which in turn could tie the hands of the other branches as they sought to respond to foreign policy crises. The Constitution does not command this.

In sum, we hold that the Fifth Amendment poses no obstacle to the decision of the United States government to subject Libya to personal jurisdiction in the federal courts. Our decision on this point reaches only an actual foreign government; we express no view as to whether other entities that fall within the FSIA's definition of "foreign state" including corporations in which a foreign state owns a majority interest – could yet be considered persons under the Due Process Clause.

NOTES AND QUESTIONS

1. The "Flatow Amendment" problem arises because of the distinction between subject matter jurisdiction and a cause of action. Although § 1605(a)(7) provides subject matter jurisdiction, the question is whether there is a source of law for a claim. The D.C. Circuit in *Price* left open the question of whether there is a source of law for a claim against a foreign state based on conduct occurring outside the U.S. On remand, the district court explained and resolved the issue in this fashion:

By the 1990s, Congress had grown increasingly frustrated with the federal courts for having dismissed a number of actions, on subject matter jurisdiction grounds, that had been brought by American victims of abuse by foreign nations. In 1996, Congress addressed this problem by including within the Antiterrorism and Effective Death Penalty Act, 110 Stat. 1214 ("AEDPA"), an amendment to the FSIA revoking the foreign sovereign immunity of nations which sponsored terrorist acts. This amendment ("the state-sponsored terrorism exception") created a new exception under the FSIA for any foreign nation designated by the State Department as a sponsor of terrorism, if that nation either commits a terrorist act resulting in the death or personal injury of a U.S. national, or provides material support and resources to an individual or entity that commits such a terrorist act.

Realizing that the new exception did not unambiguously explain the potential causes of action for which sovereign immunity had been waived, Congress acted swiftly to clarify the issue. On September 30, 1996, it passed an amendment to 28 U.S.C. 1605(a)(7), providing, in relevant part:

An official, employee, or agent of a foreign state designated as a state sponsor of terrorism designated under section 6(j) of the Export Administration Act of 1979 while acting within the scope of his or her office, employment, or agency shall be liable to a United States national or the national's legal representative for personal injury or death caused by acts of that official, employee, or agent for which the courts of the United States may maintain jurisdiction under section 1605(a)(7).

(codified at 28 U.S.C. § 1605 note). This provision of law is commonly referred to as the "Flatow Amendment." [T]his Court has consistently interpreted the Flatow Amendment to provide a cause of action against foreign states for any act that would provide a court with jurisdiction under 28 U.S.C. § 1605(a)(7).

Price v. Socialist People's Libyan Arab Jamahiriya, 274 F. Supp. 2d 20 (D.D.C. 2003). The same question also was answered in the affirmative by the district court in *Pugh v. Socialist People's Libyan Arab Jamahiriya*, 290 F. Supp. 2d 54 (D.D.C. 2003) (*see* p. 199 *infra*). That incident involved bombing of a UTA airliner bound from the Congo to Paris in which seven U.S. citizens were killed.

2. Section (a)(7) strips sovereign immunity for torture, hostage taking, extrajudicial death, and aircraft sabotage. Does this exhaust the list of torts for which a state ought to be held accountable? Why not plain police brutality that does not rise to the level of torture? Why not false imprisonment that does not carry the *quid pro quo* nature of hostage taking? Some allegations against Central and South American regimes in the 1960s to 1980s involved people who simply disappeared. Should extended secret detention be a violation?

3. *Rein v. Socialist People's Libyan Arab Jamahiriya,* 162 F.3d 748(2d Cir. 1998), was the second try for representatives of the victims of the Pan Am Lockerbie bombing, which killed 259 persons, many of them U.S. citizens.

In 1994, some of the present plaintiffs brought suit against some of the present defendants, claiming that Libya and its agents were responsible for destroying Pan Am 103. Libya moved to dismiss for lack of jurisdiction under the FSIA or any other applicable law. The FSIA establishes that foreign states are generally immune from suit. But it gives the federal district courts jurisdiction over actions against such states when either §§ 1605-07 of the Act or relevant international agreements permit them to be sued. When the previous litigation was brought in 1994, no provision of the FSIA deprived Libya of sovereign immunity in suits of this sort. Accordingly, the [district court] dismissed the case for lack of subject matter jurisdiction [and the Second Circuit affirmed].

In 1996, the Antiterrorism and Effective Death Penalty Act ("AEDPA") amended the FSIA by adding what is now 28 U.S.C. § 1605(a)(7). Under this new section, foreign states that have been designated as state sponsors of terrorism are denied immunity from damage actions for personal injury or death resulting from aircraft sabotage. Shortly after passage of the AEDPA, the present plaintiffs filed (against the present defendants) substantially the same claims that had been previously dismissed.

Libya argues that § 1605(a)(7) is unconstitutional as a bill of attainder and as an ex post facto law. For a law to be unconstitutional as a bill of attainder, it must impose punishment. [A] finding of civil liability and the attendant imposition of compensatory damages does not suffice to make the retrospective application of a law invalid. Where a retroactive law is civil rather than criminal, it is only the imposition of punitive damages that might, in particular circumstances, raise a constitutional problem. But if it is only the possibility that punitive damages may be assessed that raises the question of the statute's being a bill of attainder or an ex post facto law, then those issues are not properly before us at this stage of the case. There has as yet been no trial on the merits and no finding of liability, let alone a punitive damage award.

The Second Circuit also dealt with an argument by Libya that Congress unconstitutionally delegated power to the Executive through the assignment of liability premised on designation of foreign states as sponsors of terrorism. Because the designation fell within an area of traditional executive discretion in foreign affairs, the delegation was not invalid even though it affected the subject matter jurisdiction of the federal judiciary.

BOIM v. QURANIC LITERACY INSTITUTE
291 F.3d 1000 (7th Cir. 2002)

ROVNER, Circuit Judge.

In this case of first impression, the parents of a young United States citizen murdered in Israel by Hamas terrorists have sued several individuals and organizations for the loss of their son. Two of the organizational defendants moved to dismiss the complaint, and the district court denied the motion. In this interlocutory appeal, we are asked to consider the viability of a claim brought under the never-tested 18 U.S.C. § 2333, which allows U.S. nationals who have been injured "by reason of an act of international terrorism" to sue therefor and recover treble damages. We affirm the district court's denial of the defendants' motion to dismiss.

I.

David Boim was the son of Joyce and Stanley Boim, who are United States citizens. David held dual citizenship in the United States and Israel. In 1996, the Boims were living in Israel, where seventeen-year-old David was studying at a yeshiva. On May 13, 1996, David was murdered as he waited with other students at a bus stop near Beit El in the West Bank. He was struck by bullets fired from a passing car, and was pronounced dead within an hour of the shooting. His two attackers were later identified as Amjad Hinawi and Khalil Tawfiq Al-Sharif. The Palestinian Authority apprehended Hinawi and Al-Sharif, and temporarily imprisoned them in early 1997. They were released shortly thereafter, apparently pending trial. Al-Sharif subsequently killed himself and five civilians and injured 192 other people in a suicide bombing in Jerusalem on September 4, 1997. Two other suicide bombers joined him in this action. Hinawi, who confessed to participating in the shooting of David Boim, was eventually tried for David's murder by a Palestinian Authority court and was sentenced to ten years' imprisonment on February 17, 1998.

Both Hinawi and Al-Sharif were known members of the military wing of Hamas. The Boims describe Hamas as an extremist, Palestinian militant organization that seeks to establish a fundamentalist Palestinian state. The group is divided into two branches, one political and one military. The military branch receives orders and material support from the political branch. Hamas seeks to advance its political objectives through acts of terrorism and works to undermine the Middle East peace process through violent attacks on civilians. Hamas has a global presence, and terrorist operatives in Gaza and the West Bank receive their instructions, funds, weapons and practical support for their missions from Hamas organizers throughout the world. The Boims believe that Hamas has command and control centers in the United States, Britain and several Western European countries. The leaders of these control centers coordinate fund-raising efforts from sympathetic parties in these various countries and then launder and channel the money to Hamas operatives in Gaza and the West Bank. They also arrange for the purchase of weapons and for the recruitment and training of military personnel. They work with local commanders in the West Bank and Gaza to plan terrorist attacks. Hamas was designated a terrorist organization by President Clinton in 1995 by Executive Order [under IEEPA – *see* § 6.01[A] *infra*]. In 1997, Hamas was designated a foreign terrorist organization pursuant to 8 U.S.C. § 1189 [*see* § 6.03 *infra*].

The Boims allege that Hamas' military wing depends on foreign contributions, with approximately one-third of its multi-million dollar annual budget coming from fund-raising in North America and Western Europe. The Boims believe that the Quranic Literacy Institute ("QLI") and the Holy Land Foundation for Relief and Development ("HLF"), along with other defendants not involved in this appeal, are the main fronts for Hamas in the United States. They allege that these organizations' allegedly humanitarian functions mask their core mission of raising and funneling money and other resources to Hamas operatives in support of terrorist activities.

QLI is an Illinois not-for-profit corporation that purports to translate and publish sacred Islamic texts, but the Boims believe it is also engaged in raising and laundering money for Hamas. QLI also employed another defendant, Mohammed Abdul Hamid Khalil Salah, nominally as a computer analyst. The FBI has seized $ 1.4 million in cash and property from Salah, who is the admitted United States based leader of the military branch of Hamas. He has been prosecuted for channeling money to Hamas and for recruiting, organizing and training terrorist operatives in Israel. Salah is named on a list of Specially Designated Terrorists compiled by the United States Treasury Department's Office of Foreign Assets Control.[3]

HLF is also a not-for-profit corporation, whose ostensible mission is to fund humanitarian relief and development efforts. HLF's director has acknowledged providing money to Hamas, and the Boims allege that, although HLF purports to have a charitable purpose, its true function is to raise and channel money to

---

[3] The United States has proceeded against Salah and Mousa Mohammed Abu Marzook in an unrelated action to seize funds used in terrorism. *See United States v. One 1997 Ford Van*, 50 F. Supp. 2d 789 (N.D. Ill. 1999). In that action, the United States has alleged that Salah and Marzook employed a number of charitable organizations in the United States to raise and launder money for Hamas. The FBI presented evidence in that action that Salah actively recruited Hamas terrorists, arranged for and financed their training, served as a financial conduit for Hamas operations directed from the U.S., paid for plane tickets to transport terrorists from the U.S. to the Middle East, and gave approximately $100,000 to another Hamas operative for the express purpose of procuring weapons.

Hamas for terrorist activities. The U.S. base of HLF's operations is in Texas. HLF also has offices in Jerusalem and in Illinois. HLF, QLI and the other organizational defendants are linked by interlocking directorates and by ties to Salah and Mousa Mohammed Abu Marzook, another individual defendant (not involved in this appeal) who has a leadership role in the military branch of Hamas.

According to the Boims, money flows from American contributors to Hamas in a three-step process: first, the front organizations solicit contributions; second, the leaders arrange for the money to be laundered and wired overseas; and third, Hamas operatives in Gaza and the West Bank use the money to finance terrorist activities. Because it is illegal to provide financial support to recognized terrorist groups, the money flows through a series of complicated transactions, changing hands a number of times, and being commingled with funds from the front organizations' legitimate charitable and business dealings. The funds are laundered in a variety of ways, including through real estate deals and through Swiss bank accounts. The Boims allege that money raised by HLF and QLI was transferred to Hamas terrorists using these various methods in order to finance terrorist activities. Hamas used the money raised in this way to purchase weapons to carry out terrorist attacks, including the attack on David Boim. Hamas regularly drew money from a pool of laundered funds in order to finance training, weapons purchases, lodging, false identification, communications equipment, lethal substances, explosives, personnel, transportation and other material support for terrorist operations. The Boims believe that expenditures from this pool of funds paid for the vehicle, machine guns and ammunition used to kill David Boim, and also paid for the training of Hinawi, Al-Sharif and other Hamas operatives involved in the attack on David Boim. The funds were also used to provide a stipend for Al-Sharif's family, as it is a common practice to pay the families of suicide bombers in order to encourage others to volunteer for these activities.

The Boims bring their suit against HLF, QLI and other organizational and individual defendants pursuant to 18 U.S.C. § 2333. They charge that all of the defendants are civilly liable for David's murder. They name Hinawi and Al-Sharif as the persons who actually killed David, but allege that the other defendants aided, abetted and financed Hinawi and Al-Sharif. They assert that the organizational defendants provided material support or resources to Hamas as those terms are defined in 18 U.S.C. § § 2339A and 2339B. The Boims seek compensation for the extreme physical pain David suffered before his death, and for the cost of his funeral and the loss of accretion to his estate due to his death at age seventeen. They also seek damages for their own extreme mental anguish and loss of the society of their son. They ask for $100,000,000 compensatory damages, $100,000,000 punitive damages, plus costs and attorney's fees, and request the trebling of damages pursuant to the statute.

In the district court, QLI and HLF moved to dismiss the complaint for failure to state a claim upon which relief may be granted. In particular, the defendants argued that section 2333 does not support a cause of action for aiding and abetting acts of international terrorism, and that the suit is foreclosed by the Supreme Court's ruling in *Central Bank of Denver, N.A. v. First Interstate Bank of Denver, N.A.*, 511 U.S. 164, 114 S. Ct. 1439 (1994). The district court denied the motion to dismiss.

II.

The district court granted HLF and QLI's motion for a certificate of appealability, and we subsequently granted them leave to file an interlocutory appeal. In this case, the district court correctly certified three issues for appeal:

(1) Does funding, *simpliciter*, of an international terrorist organization constitute an act of terrorism under 18 U.S.C. § 2331?

(2) Does 18 U.S.C. § 2333 incorporate the definitions of international terrorism found in 18 U.S.C. §§ 2339A and 2339B?

(3) Does a civil cause of action lie under 18 U.S.C. § § 2331 and 2333 for aiding and abetting international terrorism?

We turn now to the Boims' three theories of liability under section 2333: (1) that funding Hamas, without more, is an act of international terrorism because it is conduct that involves violent acts or acts dangerous to human life; (2) that funding Hamas constitutes the provision of material support or resources to a terrorist organization in violation of the criminal provisions set forth in sections 2339A and 2339B, and that violations of these criminal provisions give rise to civil liability under section 2333; and (3) that aiding and abetting an act of terrorism gives rise to civil liability under section 2333.

A.

The plaintiffs' first theory is that the simple provision of funds to Hamas by QLI and HLF constitutes an act of international terrorism because it "involves violent acts or acts dangerous to human life." The Boims liken payments to Hamas to murder for hire: the person who pays for the murder does not himself commit a violent act, but the payment "involves" violent acts in the sense that it brings about the violent act and provides an incentive for someone else to commit it. The Boims urge us to adopt a very broad definition of "involves" that would include any activity that touches on and supports a violent act. They argue that David's murder was indisputably a violent act, and we have no quarrel with that premise. But they further argue that the provision of money or in-kind services to persons outside the country who set up the infrastructure used to recruit and train David's murderers, buy their weapons, and compensate their families also "involves" violent acts. The defendants, in turn, urge us to read the statute to hold liable only those who actually commit a violent act.

No court has yet considered the meaning or scope of sections 2331 and 2333, and so we write upon a tabula rasa. The controversy here centers on the definition of international terrorism, and in particular on the definition of the word "involve," which is susceptible to many meanings. The statutory definition of international terrorism in section 2331(1) is drawn verbatim from the Foreign Intelligence Surveillance Act, 50 U.S.C. § 1801(c) ("FISA") [*see* § 5.01 *infra*]. No court has yet expounded on the meaning or scope of "international terrorism" as it is used in FISA either, so we are not aided by that origin. A dictionary definition of "involve" demonstrates the many levels of participation that could constitute involvement. To involve is: to enfold or envelop so as to encumber; to engage as a participant; to oblige to take part; to occupy (as oneself) absorbingly; to commit emotionally; to relate closely; to have within or as part of itself; to require as a necessary accompaniment; to have an effect on. Webster's Ninth New Collegiate Dictionary (1983).

The government, in its very helpful amicus curiae brief, delineates some of the legislative history of sections 2331 and 2333. That history, in combination with the language of the statute itself, evidences an intent by Congress to codify general common law tort principles and to extend civil liability for acts of international terrorism to the full reaches of traditional tort law. In particular, the statute itself contains all of the elements of a traditional tort: breach of a duty (i.e., committing an act of international terrorism); injury to the person, property or business of another; and causation (injured "by reason of"). Although the statute defines the class of plaintiffs who may sue, it does not limit the class of defendants, and we must therefore look to tort law and the legislative history to determine who may be held liable for injuries covered by the statute.

The legislative record is replete with references to the then-recent decision in *Klinghoffer v. S.N.C. Achille Lauro Ed Altri-Gestione Motonave Achille Lauto In Amministrazione*, 739 F. Supp. 854 (S.D.N.Y. 1990), *vacated*, 937 F.2d 44 (2d Cir. 1991). Leon Klinghoffer was a U.S. citizen who was murdered in a terrorist attack on a cruise ship in the Mediterranean Sea. The district court found that his survivors' claims were cognizable in federal court under federal admiralty jurisdiction and the Death on the High Seas Act because the tort occurred in navigable waters. The repeated favorable references to *Klinghoffer* indicate a desire on the part of Congress to extend this liability to land-based terrorism that occurred in a foreign country. H.R. Rep. 102-1040, at 5 (1992) ("Only by virtue of the fact that the [Klinghoffer] attack violated certain Admiralty laws and the organization involved – the Palestinian Liberation Organization – had assets and carried on activities in New York, was the court able to establish jurisdiction over the case. A similar attack occurring on an airplane or in some other locale might not have been subject to civil action in the U.S. In order to facilitate civil actions against such terrorists the Committee [on the Judiciary] recommends [this bill].")

The statute clearly is meant to reach beyond those persons who themselves commit the violent act that directly causes the injury. The Senate report on the bill notes that "the substance of [an action under section 2333] is not defined by the statute, because the fact patterns giving rise to such suits will be as varied and numerous as those found in the law of torts. This bill opens the courthouse door to victims of international terrorism." This same report also remarks that the legislation, with "its provisions for compensatory damages, treble damages, and the imposition of liability at any point along the causal chain of terrorism," would "interrupt, or at least imperil, the flow of money." All of this history indicates an intent by Congress to allow a plaintiff to recover from anyone along the causal chain of terrorism.

But to the extent that the Boims urge a reading of the statute that would lead to liability for merely giving money to Hamas, a group which then sponsored a terrorist act in the manner the Boims have alleged, we agree with the district court, the defendants and the government that those allegations would be inadequate. To say that funding simpliciter constitutes an act of terrorism is to give the statute an almost unlimited reach. Any act which turns out to facilitate terrorism, however remote that act may be from actual violence and regardless of the actor's intent, could be construed to "involve" terrorism. Without also requiring the plaintiffs to show knowledge of and intent to further the payee's violent criminal acts, such a broad definition might also lead to constitutional infirmities by punishing mere association with groups that engage in terrorism, as we shall discuss later in addressing the First Amendment concerns raised here.

Additionally, the statute itself requires that in order to recover, a plaintiff must be injured "by reason of" an act of international terrorism. The Supreme Court has interpreted identical language to require a showing of proximate cause. Foreseeability is the cornerstone of proximate cause, and in tort law, a defendant will be held liable only for those injuries that might have reasonably been anticipated as a natural consequence of the defendant's actions. In the circumstances of this case, the Boims cannot show that David Boim was injured "by reason of" the defendants' payments to Hamas in the traditional tort sense of causation unless they can also show that murder was the reasonably foreseeable result of making the donation. To hold the defendants liable for donating money without knowledge of the donee's intended criminal use of the funds would impose strict liability. Nothing in the language of the statute or its structure or history supports that formulation. The government, in its amicus brief, maintains that funding may be enough to establish liability if the plaintiff can show that the provider of funds was generally aware of the donee's terrorist activity, and if the provision of funds substantially assisted the terrorist act in question. We will consider the government's proposed standard separately in our discussion of aiding and abetting liability. For now we note only that the complaint cannot be sustained on the theory that the defendants themselves committed an act of international terrorism when they donated unspecified amounts of money to Hamas, neither knowing nor suspecting that Hamas would in turn financially support the persons who murdered David Boim. In the very least, the plaintiffs must be able to show that murder was a reasonably foreseeable result of making a donation. Thus, the Boims' first theory of liability under section 2333, funding simpliciter of a terrorist organization, is insufficient because it sets too vague a standard, and because it does not require a showing of proximate cause.

B.

The Boims' second theory of liability is that the defendants' violation of sections 2339A and 2339B, the criminal counterparts to section 2333, gives rise to civil liability under section 2333. The Boims further contend that sections 2339A and 2339B demonstrate Congress' intent to include the provision of material support to terrorist organizations in the definition of international terrorism for the purposes of section 2333. The district court concluded that Congress viewed violations of sections 2339A and 2339B as "activities involving violent acts or acts dangerous to human life," and therefore found that violations of sections 2339A and 2339B gave rise to civil liability under section 2333.

Because much of the conduct the Boims alleged occurred before the passage of sections 2339A and 2339B, however, the district court ruled that the Boims would have to rely primarily on their aiding and abetting theory.

Section 2339A prohibits the provision of material support for an extensive list of violent crimes associated with terrorism – assassination, kidnapping, arson, destruction of aircraft – that make clear what types of conduct Congress had in mind when it defined "international terrorism" in section 2331(1) as not just the violent acts themselves, but also "activities that involve violent acts or acts dangerous to human life." There is no textual, structural or logical justification for construing the civil liability imposed by section 2333 more narrowly than the corresponding criminal provisions. Because Congress intended to impose criminal liability for funding violent terrorism, we find that it also intended through sections 2333 and 2331(1) to impose civil liability for funding at least as broad a class of violent terrorist acts. If the plaintiffs could show that HLF and QLI violated either section 2339A or section 2339B, that conduct would certainly be sufficient to meet the definition of "international terrorism" under sections 2333 and 2331. Such acts would give rise to civil liability under section 2333 so long as knowledge and intent are also shown, as we shall discuss shortly in the context of aiding and abetting.

We hasten to add that, although proof of a criminal violation under sections 2339A or 2339B might satisfy the definition of international terrorism under section 2333, such proof is not necessary to sustain a section 2333 claim. As we discuss in the context of aiding and abetting, we believe Congress intended for civil liability for financing terrorism to sweep more broadly than the conduct described in sections 2339A and 2339B. We also note that the district court seems to have inadvertently redefined the term "material" in the context of sections 2339A and 2339B as meaning substantial or considerable. The statute itself defines "material support or resources" as "currency or other financial securities, financial services, lodging, training, safehouses, false documentation or identification, communications equipment, facilities, weapons, lethal substances, explosives, personnel, transportation, and other physical assets, except medicine or religious materials." 18 U.S.C. § 2339A(b). Thus, the term relates to the type of aid provided rather than whether it is substantial or considerable. For civil liability, section 2333 requires that the plaintiff be injured "by reason of" the act of international terrorism. Because we believe Congress intended to import standard tort law into section 2333, causation may be demonstrated as it would be in traditional tort law. Congress has made clear, though, through the criminal liability imposed in sections 2339A and 2339B, that even small donations made knowingly and intentionally in support of terrorism may meet the standard for civil liability in section 2333. Congress' goal of cutting off funding for terrorism would be seriously compromised if terrorist organizations could avoid liability by simply pooling together small donations to fund a terrorist act.

The district court believed there was a timing problem for the Boims in making their case under these criminal provisions because much of the funding conduct allegedly committed by HLF and QLI occurred prior to the passage of sections 2339A and 2339B. Indeed, Hamas was not designated a terrorist organization under section 1189 until 1997, after David's murder. Certainly HLF and QLI could not be held criminally liable for conduct that occurred before the statutes were enacted, but that argument misses the point. We are using sections 2339A and 2339B not as independent sources of liability under section 2333, but to amplify what Congress meant by "international terrorism." Sections 2339A and 2339B merely lend further support to our finding that Congress considered the provision of material support to terrorists an act of international terrorism. This reading simply amplifies the conclusion we have already reached by examining the language and legislative history of section 2333. Sections 2339A and 2339B provide criminal liability for the provision of material support, and section 2333 provides civil liability. The Boims may thus show that QLI and HLF committed an act of international terrorism subject to civil liability under section 2333 by proving that QLI and HLF provided material support to terrorist organizations. No timing problem arises because sections 2339A and 2339B merely elucidate conduct that was already prohibited by section 2333.

C.

We turn next to the Boims' theory that HLF and QLI may be held civilly liable under section 2333 for aiding and abetting an act of international terrorism. Under this theory, the Boims urge us to find that aiding and abetting a violent act is conduct that "involves" a violent act as that word is used in section 2331(1). HLF and QLI contend that section 2333 does not provide for aiding and abetting liability, and that the Supreme Court in *Central Bank* held that aiding and abetting liability is available only when a statute expressly provides for it. *See Central Bank of Denver N.A. v. First Interstate Bank of Denver, N.A.*, 511 U.S. 164 (1994).

In *Central Bank*, the Supreme Court held that a private plaintiff may not maintain an aiding and abetting suit under section 10(b) of the Securities Exchange Act of 1934. 511 U.S. at 177-78. As the Court has interpreted it, section 10(b) imposes private civil liability on those who commit a manipulative or deceptive act in connection with the purchase or sale of securities. 511 U.S. at 167. Yet, that section contains no express cause of action giving private plaintiffs a right to sue. Nonetheless, through judicial interpretation of the securities laws, an implied right of action was created allowing private parties to sue for damages for violations of section 10(b). Prior to *Central Bank*, some lower courts had interpreted the statute to create a private right of action not only against those who violate section 10(b), but also against those who aid and abet a violation of section 10(b); other courts had found that there was no private right of action for aiding and abetting liability. The Court granted certiorari to resolve the continuing confusion in the circuit courts over the existence and scope of an aiding and abetting action under section 10(b) [and held that there was no private right of action for that behavior].

Here we have an express private right of action, where Congress' intent is clear from the language and structure of the statute itself as well as from the legislative history. [A]lthough the words "aid and abet" do not appear in the statute, Congress purposely drafted the statute to extend liability to all points along the causal chain of terrorism. It is not much of a leap to conclude that

Congress intended to extend section 2333 liability beyond those persons directly perpetrating acts of violence. Indeed, the statute itself defines international terrorism so broadly – to include activities that "involve" violent acts – that we must construe it carefully to meet the constitutional standards regarding vagueness and First Amendment rights of association.

Unlike section 10(b), Congress also expressed an intent in section 2333 to make civil liability at least as extensive as criminal liability. Finally, if we failed to impose liability on aiders and abettors who knowingly and intentionally funded acts of terrorism, we would be thwarting Congress' clearly expressed intent to cut off the flow of money to terrorists at every point along the causal chain of violence. Also, and perhaps more importantly, there would not be a trigger to pull or a bomb to blow up without the resources to acquire such tools of terrorism and to bankroll the persons who actually commit the violence. Moreover, the organizations, businesses and nations that support and encourage terrorist acts are likely to have reachable assets that they wish to protect. The only way to imperil the flow of money and discourage the financing of terrorist acts is to impose liability on those who knowingly and intentionally supply the funds to the persons who commit the violent acts. For all of these distinguishing reasons, we do not think *Central Bank* controls the result here, but that aiding and abetting liability is both appropriate and called for by the language, structure and legislative history of section 2333.

D.

The defendants raise two First Amendment objections to this section 2333 action against them. First, they argue that the Boims seek to hold them liable for their mere association with Hamas. Harking back to a line of cases involving the Communist party, HLF and QLI contend that, when an organization has both legal and illegal aims, a person may not be punished for mere membership in or association with that organization, but may be held civilly liable only if he or she possesses the specific intent to further the organizations' illegal purposes. Second, they contend that, to the extent the Boims' claim is founded on a violation of section 2339B, it cannot withstand First Amendment scrutiny because section 2339B fails to account for the intent and the associational rights of the contributors who donate money for humanitarian purposes.

HLF and QLI begin their argument with the well-established proposition that the Constitution protects against the imposition of liability based solely upon association with a group. *See NAACP v. Claiborne Hardware Co.*, 458 U.S. 886, 920 (1982). We have no quarrel with that general proposition or with its corollary, that in order to impose liability on an individual for association with a group, it is necessary to establish that the group possessed unlawful goals and that the individual held a specific intent to further those illegal aims.

HLF and QLI protest that the Boims have not alleged their specific intent to further the illegal activities of Hamas, and that the claim does not, therefore, survive First Amendment scrutiny. Amici also emphasize that individuals may not be penalized for their association with a political organization that engages in both lawful and unlawful ends, absent a showing of specific intent to further the organization's illegal goals. The arguments of the defendants and amici beg the question, though, because section 2333 does not seek to impose liability for association alone but rather for involvement in acts of international terrorism. The defendants nonetheless object that the definition of acts of international terrorism is so broad that they might be held liable for involvement in terrorist activity when all they intended was to supply money to fund the legitimate, humanitarian mission of Hamas or other organizations. To resolve the tension that arises when a group engages in both protected advocacy and unprotected criminal acts, we look to *Claiborne Hardware* and to earlier cases that arose out of the McCarthy era, when the government sought to impose liability on persons for their association with the Communist Party.

In *Claiborne Hardware*, a group of white merchants and business owners sued the National Association for the Advancement of Colored People ("NAACP") for engaging in a boycott of white-owned businesses. The merchants alleged that, in enforcing the boycott, some of the members of the defendant NAACP had engaged in acts of physical force and violence, and that the NAACP should therefore be held liable for the merchants' losses. The Court concluded that no federal rule of law restricts a state from imposing tort liability for business losses caused by violence or the threat of violence, but that when such conduct occurs in the context of constitutionally protected activity, precision of regulation is required. Citing [Communist-era cases], the Court summarized the rule to be applied:

> Civil liability may not be imposed merely because an individual belonged to a group, some members of which committed acts of violence. For liability to be imposed by reason of association alone, it is necessary to establish that the group itself possessed unlawful goals and that the individual held a specific intent to further those illegal aims.

We have already held that the Boims may prevail on their claim by showing, among other things, that the defendants aided and abetted David's murder. This requires them to prove that the defendants knew of Hamas' illegal activities, that they desired to help those activities succeed, and they engaged in some act of helping the illegal activities. If the Boims are able to prove the defendants aided and abetted terrorist acts, liability would not offend the principles announced in Claiborne Hardware. The Boims have alleged that HLF and QLI supplied money to Hamas to fund terrorist operations, that they are "front" organizations with ostensibly legitimate purposes which are actually engaged in fund-raising and money laundering in support of terrorist activities. They have alleged that HLF and QLI provided the money to purchase the weapons and train the men who killed David Boim. HLF and QLI, of course, deny these allegations and argue that as a factual matter, Hamas is primarily a humanitarian organization, and that any money supplied to Hamas by QLI and HLF was intended to fund humanitarian efforts, not terrorism. This is a classic factual dispute, not suitable for resolution on a motion to dismiss for failure to state a claim. If the Boims are able to prove their allegations, that HLF and QLI provided legitimate-looking fronts for raising money to support the terrorist operation that resulted in David Boim's murder, their claim will not run afoul of the First Amendment. The Boims are not seeking to hold HLF and QLI liable for their mere association with Hamas, nor are they seeking to hold the defendants liable for contributing money for humanitarian efforts. Rather, they are seeking to hold them liable for aiding and abetting murder by supplying the money to buy the weapons, train the shooters, and compensate the families of the murderers. That Hamas may also engage in legitimate advocacy or humanitarian efforts is irrelevant for First Amendment purposes if HLF and QLI knew about Hamas' illegal operations, and intended to help Hamas accomplish those illegal goals when they contributed money to the organization.

III.

In short, we answer the three questions certified by the district court as follows: funding, simpliciter, of a foreign terrorist organization is not sufficient to constitute an act of terrorism under 18 U.S.C. § 2331. However, funding that meets the definition of aiding and abetting an act of terrorism does create liability under sections 2331 and 2333. Conduct that would give rise to criminal liability under section 2339B is conduct that "involves" violent acts or acts dangerous to human life, and therefore may meet the definition of international terrorism as that term is used in section 2333. Finally, as we have set forth the elements of an action under section 2333, civil liability for funding a foreign terrorist organization does not offend the First Amendment so long as the plaintiffs are able to prove that the defendants knew about the organization's illegal activity, desired to help that activity succeed and engaged in some act of helping.

NOTES AND QUESTIONS

1. The court decides that a person cannot be held liable for the actions of another unless "involved" in that conduct. A careful parsing of the statutes is necessary to set the context for this discussion. The source of law for a federal civil action is § 2333, which refers to "international terrorism," which is defined in § 2331 as an act that "involves" violence. The defendants' argument was that provision of money does not "involve" violence, to which the court responds that the statute "reaches beyond those persons who commit the violent act." At the other extreme, mere supplying of money is not enough to "involve" the donor. Are you satisfied that the court has provided a workable test in the middle ground?

2. What is the relevance of the criminal material support statues, § 2339A and § 2339B? Why not simply imply a private right of action from the criminal provisions? What is the point of the discussion about aiding and abetting in light of the previous holding that the defendant must be "involved" in the act?

3. Finally, having satisfied ourselves on the analysis of the statutory scheme, we need to obtain some measure of confidence on the constitutional issue. This will be considered more extensively when we focus on the material support statutes themselves in Chapter 6, but *Claiborne Hardware* is at the center of that issue. What would be wrong with saying that donating money to a designated illegal entity is the same as purchasing an illegal drug regardless of whether the drug would cause harm? Conversely, is limiting liability to those who donate with knowledge of, and a "desire to further," illegal activities by the donee sufficient protection for the First Amendment interests at stake?

4. *Pugh v. Socialist People's Libyan Arab Jamahiriya*, 290 F. Supp. 2d 54 (D.D.C. 2003). This opinion addressed the question of personal jurisdiction over individual defendants in a § 2333 case. Libya was a defendant along with seven individual defendants in wrongful death actions arising from the bombing of a UTA flight over Africa in which seven U.S. citizens were killed. The State was subject to personal jurisdiction under the reasoning of *Price*, but the individual defendants claimed they had not contacts with the U.S. The district court responded:

> While the courts and legislatures have developed numerous approaches to ascertaining whether a defendant meets the "minimum contacts" test, the single most important consideration is whether a defendant's "conduct and connection with the forum State are such that he should reasonably anticipate being haled into court there." Taking the factual allegations of the complaint as true for present purposes, the individual defendants in the instant action conspired to sabotage and succeeded in destroying a civilian commercial aircraft filled to capacity with innocent and unsuspecting passengers while in flight. As the plane they chose to destroy was on an international flight and expected to stop in several nations before reaching its final destination, the individual defendants could and should have reasonably postulated that passengers of many nationalities would be on board, from which they could also expect they might be haled into the courts of those nations whose citizens would die. Given the number of passengers on UTA Flight 772, and the international nature of the flight, it was also altogether foreseeable that some Americans would be aboard the plane, whose lives would be lost, and that the individual defendants would have to answer in some fashion in American courts for the consequences of their actions if their identities were ever discovered.

> The interest of the United States in preventing and punishing international terrorism has been a matter of worldwide common knowledge for years. Congress has not been indifferent to providing judicial sanctions for terrorist acts committed abroad. Beginning at least five years before the UTA Flight 772 bombing, a succession of federal statutes had evinced an intent to assure the criminal prosecution of foreign individuals who committed terrorist acts overseas against U.S. persons or property.

> These criminal statutes all contemplated the assertion by a United States court of jurisdiction over a foreign national for terrorist activities committed abroad, irrespective of the number and nature of that individual's other "contacts" with the United States. It logically follows that if federal courts may constitutionally exercise criminal jurisdiction over such individuals, the Constitution should be no bar to those same federal courts, in a civil action for damages, exercising civil in personam jurisdiction over those same individuals for the same acts.

> Thus, in light of the pre-existing statutory authority providing for the criminal prosecution of those who carry out terrorist acts, and the defendants' intentional targeting of foreign nationals at the risk of killing Americans among them, defendants should have anticipated the possibility

of being "haled into court" in the United States in some capacity. And because they should have anticipated as much, this Court concludes that it may constitutionally exercise personal jurisdiction over the individual defendants in their personal capacities without offending any "traditional notions of fair play and substantial justice."

IN RE TERRORIST ATTACKS ON SEPTEMBER 11, 2001
2005 U.S. Dist. LEXIS 640

RICHARD CONWAY CASEY, District Judge:

Pursuant to 28 U.S.C. § 1407, on December 9, 2003 the Mulitidistrict Litigation Panel centralized six then-pending September 11-related cases before this Court "for coordinated or consolidated pretrial proceedings." Additional actions, that are not the subject of this opinion, have since been filed. Plaintiffs in these consolidated actions are more than three thousand survivors, family members, and representatives of victims, and insurance carriers seeking to hold responsible for the attacks the persons and entities that supported and funded al Qaeda. The complaints allege that over two hundred defendants directly or indirectly provided material support to Osama bin Laden and the al Qaeda terrorists. Generally, these defendants fall into one of several categories: al Qaeda and its members and associates; state sponsors of terrorism; and individuals and entities, including charities, banks, front organizations, terrorist organizations, and financiers who provided financial, logistical, and other support to al Qaeda.

The complaints assert subject matter jurisdiction under the Foreign Sovereign Immunities Act ("FSIA"), 28 U.S.C. § 1602 et seq.; and causes of action under the Torture Victim Protection Act ("TVPA"), 28 U.S.C. § 1350 note; the Antiterrorism Act ("ATA"), 18 U.S.C. § 2331 et seq.; the Alien Tort Claims Act ("ATCA"), 28 U.S.C. § 1350; the Racketeer Influenced and Corrupt Organizations Act ("RICO"), 18 U.S.C. § 1961 et seq.; theories of aiding and abetting, conspiracy, intentional infliction of emotional distress, negligence, survival, wrongful death, trespass, and assault and battery.

[The plaintiffs are labeled by the court as the Ashton and Burnett groups, the Federal Plaintiffs, and Federal Insurance plaintiffs. Neither the circumstances of the plaintiffs nor differences among their claims appear to be critically important in the court's analysis.]

I. Subject Matter Jurisdiction Under the FSIA

Under the FSIA, a foreign state and its instrumentalities are presumed immune from United States courts' jurisdiction. *Saudi Arabia v. Nelson,* 507 U.S. 349, 355 (1993). The FSIA's exceptions to immunity provide the sole basis for obtaining subject matter jurisdiction over a foreign state and its instrumentalities in federal court.

A. Standard of Review

In a Rule 12(b)(1) motion to dismiss challenging subject matter jurisdiction under the FSIA, "the defendant must first 'present a prima facie case that it is a foreign sovereign.'" *Virtual Countries v. Republic of South Africa,* 300 F.3d 230,

241 (2d Cir. 2002). In response, the plaintiff must present evidence that one of the statute's exceptions nullifies the immunity.

Before turning to the allegations against the Defendants claiming immunity, the Court notes it is keenly aware of the "delicate balance 'between permitting discovery to substantiate exceptions to statutory foreign sovereign immunity and protecting a sovereign's or sovereign's agency's legitimate claim to immunity from discovery.'" The Second Circuit has instructed "that generally a plaintiff may be allowed limited discovery with respect to the jurisdictional issue; but until [plaintiff] has shown a reasonable basis for assuming jurisdiction, she is not entitled to any other discovery."

B. Allegations Against Defendants Asserting Foreign Sovereign Immunity

   1. Prince Sultan

Prince Sultan has been Saudi Arabia's Minister of Defense and Aviation and Inspector General of its Armed Forces since 1962. In 1982, his brother King Fahd bin Abdulaziz Al-Saud named him Second Deputy President of Saudi Arabia's Council of Ministers, the Kingdom's governing body. As such, he is the third-highest ranking member of the Saudi government.

Especially relevant here, Prince Sultan is the Chairman of the Supreme Council of Islamic Affairs, which was established in 1995 and is responsible for the Kingdom's Islamic policy abroad. Prince Sultan disagrees with Plaintiffs' claim that the Supreme Council monitors and approves domestic and foreign charitable giving on behalf of the Kingdom. Prince Sultan prefers the characterization that the Supreme Council "carries out the foreign policy of Saudi Arabia as determined by the Council of Ministers." Finally, Prince Sultan, as the head of the Special Committee of the Council of Ministers, which is a foreign policy advisory resource for King Saud, exercises authority over disbursements by the Special Committee. In the past, these disbursements, which are government funded, have included grants to Islamic charities.

The various complaints make substantially similar accusations against Prince Sultan. Prince Sultan is alleged to have met with Osama bin Laden after Iraq invaded Kuwait in the summer of 1990. At that meeting, which Prince Turki also attended, bin Laden purportedly offered his family's support to Saudi military forces. Plaintiffs allege that, at the time of the Gulf War, Prince Sultan "took radical stands against western countries and publicly supported and funded several Islamic charities that were sponsoring Osama bin Laden and al Qaeda operations." After the attacks of September 11, Prince Sultan allegedly advocated against granting the United States use of Saudi military bases to stage attacks against Afghanistan.

Prince Sultan allegedly made personal contributions, totaling $6,000,000 since 1994, to various Islamic charities that Plaintiffs claim sponsor or support al Qaeda. The specific charities that Prince Sultan donated to include Defendants

International Islamic Relief Organization ("IIRO"),[16] Al Haramain,[17] Muslim World League ("MWL"),[18] and the World Assembly of Muslim Youth ("WAMY").[19] According to Plaintiffs, with respect to his alleged donations, "at best, Prince Sultan was grossly negligent in the oversight and administration of charitable funds, knowing they would be used to sponsor international terrorism, but turning a blind eye. At worse, Prince Sultan directly aided and abetted and materially sponsored al Qaeda and international terrorism."

2. Prince Turki

Prince Turki is currently the Kingdom of Saudi Arabia's ambassador to the United Kingdom. From 1977 until August 2001, he was the Director of Saudi Arabia's Department of General Intelligence ("DGI," also known by its Arabic name, Istakhbarat). As such, Plaintiffs allege he was or should have been aware of the terrorist threat posed by Osama bin Laden, al Qaeda, and the Taliban. Prince Turki allegedly met with Osama bin Laden five times in the mid-1980s and mid-1990s. At one of those meetings, which Prince Sultan also attended, bin Laden allegedly offered the Saudis the use of his family's engineering equipment and suggested bolstering Saudi military forces with militants. Prince Turki is alleged to have close ties with an al Qaeda financier, Mr. Zouaydi, and is allegedly implicated in Mr. Zouaydi's financial support of al Qaeda. Further, Plaintiffs claim Prince Turki met with members of the Taliban and, in 1995, gave the Taliban financial and material support. In July 1998, Prince Turki is alleged to have met with members of the Taliban and representatives of bin Laden and agreed to not extradite bin Laden or close terrorist camps in exchange for bin Laden's protection of the Saudi Royal family. Plaintiffs allege Prince Turki facilitated money transfers from wealthy Saudis to the Taliban and al Qaeda. Additionally, the Federal Plaintiffs claim that, while Prince Turki was the head of DGI, Saudi Arabian intelligence officers allegedly trained a member of the al Qaeda Spanish cell in explosives and provided material support to two of the September 11 hijackers. The Federal complaint also alleges that Prince Turki made personal contributions to Saudi-based charities that he knew were sponsors of al Qaeda, including IIRO, MWL, WAMY, BIF, the Saudi High Commission, Saudi Joint Relief Committee for Kosovo and Chechnya ("SJRC"), and Al Haramain.

---

[16] IIRO is allegedly an al Qaeda front that has been tied to the 1993 World Trade Center attack and the 1998 embassy bombings.

[17] Beginning in 2002, certain branches of Al Haramain were designated by the United States as terrorist organizations.

[18] MWL is the parent of IIRO.

[19] WAMY is a suspected al Qaeda front, allegedly "preaching good . . . while plotting evil," connected to charity Defendant Benevolence International Foundation ("BIF"). BIF is now a designated terrorist, but it previously concealed its relationship with Osama bin Laden and al Qaeda.

Prince Turki denies the allegations against him [and] states that [he met] with the Taliban to relay the official Saudi request that Osama bin Laden be extradited to Saudi Arabia for trial. The Taliban denied the Saudi request and Saudi Arabia subsequently suspended diplomatic relations with the Taliban in September 1998. Prince Turki denies facilitating money transfers to Osama bin Laden or al Qaeda, he denies offering material assistance to Osama bin Laden, his representatives, or al Qaeda in return for their not attacking Saudi Arabia, he denies promising or providing oil or financial assistance to the Taliban, and denies ever hearing of the Syrian financier Mr. Zouaydi, with whom he is alleged to have ties.

3. Kingdom of Saudi Arabia

The Federal Plaintiffs claim that "more than any other factor, al Qaida's phenomenal growth and development into a sophisticated global terrorist network were made possible by the massive financial, logistical and other support it received from the Kingdom of Saudi Arabia, members of the Saudi Royal family, and prominent members of Saudi society." Further, the Federal Plaintiffs allege September 11 was "a direct, intended and foreseeable product of the Kingdom of Saudi Arabia's participation in al Qaida's jihadist campaign." Specifically, the Kingdom allegedly maintained and controlled several of the charities within al Qaeda's infrastructure. The Federal Plaintiffs claim Saudi Arabia knew the threat that these charities posed particularly to the United States, and did nothing to stop it. The Kingdom allegedly used its relationship with the Taliban to sustain al Qaeda in the mid-1990s. Finally, Plaintiffs allege that members of the Saudi Royal family provided support to al Qaeda in their official capacities as members of the Supreme Council of Islamic Affairs.

4. National Commercial Bank

NCB was established in 1950 by Salim bin Mahfouz, the father of Defendant Khalid bin Mahfouz, as the first commercial bank of Saudi Arabia. The Ashton Plaintiffs allege that the bin Mahfouz family controlled NCB until 1999 when the Saudi government bought a majority of its shares.

Plaintiffs claim Osama bin Laden and al Qaeda used NCB as "a financial arm, operating as a financial conduit for [their] operations." In 1986, Khalid bin Mahfouz became NCB's President and CEO and remained so until 1999. Also in 1986, Khalid bin Mahfouz became the Chief Operating Officer and a major shareholder of the Bank of Credit and Commerce International ("BCCI"). He was subsequently indicted in New York state in connection with his involvement in BCCI's fraudulent practices, which also implicated NCB.

Plaintiffs claim both NCB and BCCI supported international terrorism. Specifically, a "1999 United States Senate Report on the BCCI scheme detailed the role of [NCB] in hiding assets, money laundering, the cover-up and obstruction of a Senate investigation, and sponsoring international terrorism." Additionally, a 1998 NCB bank audit revealed irregularities involving direct donations to several charities and that $74 million had been funneled by the bank's Zakat Committee to IIRO. NCB also allegedly made loans to charitable organizations without the knowledge of the Zakat Committee. Plaintiffs allege "direct donations were received through NCB facilities to the Red Crescent

Committee, [IIRO], and the Muwaffaq Foundation," all Defendants in these actions. Muwaffaq allegedly provided Osama bin Laden with $3 million in 1998. Plaintiffs claim NCB knew or should have known it was materially supporting al Qaeda, Osama bin Laden, and international terrorism.

C. Defendants' Status as Foreign States for FSIA Purposes

Several courts have recognized that "immunity under the FSIA extends also to agents of a foreign state acting in their official capacities [since] 'it is generally recognized that a suit against an individual acting in his official capacity is the practical equivalent of a suit against the sovereign directly.'" Accordingly, both Prince Sultan and Prince Turki are immune from suit for their official acts unless an exception under the FSIA applies.

NCB submits that it is an instrumentality of the Kingdom of Saudi Arabia and therefore immune from suit. To enjoy immunity from suit under the FSIA, NCB must demonstrate that it is an agency or instrumentality, or a political subdivision of the Kingdom. NCB claims that at the time the suit was filed a majority of its shares were owned by an administrative unit of the Saudi Ministry of Finance, the Public Investment Fund ("PIF"). The Court finds that resolution of the PIF's and thereby NCB's status is not determinable on the current record and, therefore, limited jurisdictional discovery is warranted.

D. Application of FSIA Exceptions to the Princes and Kingdom of Saudi Arabia

Three exceptions to foreign sovereign immunity are implicated in these motions – the commercial activities exception, the state sponsor of terrorism exception, and the torts exception.

Commercial Activities. Section 1605(a)(2) states:

> A foreign state shall not be immune . . . in any case . . . in which the action is based . . . upon an act performed in the United States in connection with a commercial activity of the foreign state elsewhere; or upon an act outside the territory of the United States in connection with a commercial activity of the foreign state elsewhere and that act causes a direct effect in the United States.

The Federal Plaintiffs allege that the Kingdom of Saudi Arabia, Prince Sultan, and Prince Turki financed terrorism by contributing to or supporting charities known to support terrorist activities. In these Plaintiffs' view, this is essentially money laundering and, therefore, a commercial activity. The Second Circuit has made very clear that, for purposes of the FSIA, a commercial activity must be one in which a private person can engage lawfully. Since money laundering is an illegal activity, it cannot be the basis for applicability of the commercial activities exception.

State Sponsor Exception. Subsection (a)(7) lifts immunity in cases:

> in which money damages are sought against a foreign state for personal injury or death that was caused by an act of torture, extrajudicial killing, aircraft sabotage, hostage taking, or the provision of material support or resources . . . for such an act . . . except that the court shall decline to hear a claim under this paragraph

(A) if the foreign state was not designated as a state sponsor of terrorism

28 U.S.C. § 1605(a)(7). The parties agree that the Kingdom of Saudi Arabia has not been designated a state sponsor of terrorism. Thus, this exception does not provide an exception to immunity for any of the Defendants raising the FSIA defense here.

Torts Exception. In relevant part, the torts exception deprives a foreign sovereign of immunity in actions:

> in which money damages are sought against a foreign state for personal injury or death, or damage to or loss of property, occurring in the United States and caused by the tortious act or omission of that foreign state or of any official or employee of that foreign state while acting within the scope of his office or employment; except this [exception] shall not apply to -
>
> > (A) any claim based upon the exercise or performance or the failure to exercise or perform a discretionary function regardless of whether the discretion be abused.

28 U.S.C. § 1605(a)(5). Second Circuit law instructs that district courts must determine whether the defendant's alleged acts were tortious under the laws of New York and, if so, whether the defendant's acts were discretionary.

The FSIA's discretionary function exception replicates the discretionary function exception found in the Federal Tort Claims Act. Generally, acts are discretionary if they are performed at the planning level of government, as opposed to the operational level.

Defendants submit that, since the allegations are precisely those outlined in § 1605 (a)(7) – "personal injury or death that was caused by an act of . . . extrajudicial killing, aircraft sabotage . . . or the provision of material support or resources . . . for such an act" – none of the other exceptions should be read to apply in its place. Defendants argue the Court's adjudication of Plaintiffs' claims would interfere with the executive branch's discretion to designate state sponsors of terror. Finally, Defendants submit the purpose of (a)(5) was "to eliminate a foreign state's immunity for traffic accidents and other torts committed in the United States, for which liability is imposed under domestic tort law."

Plaintiffs note the two exceptions have been interpreted to encompass different situations. Subsection (a)(7) covers acts of terrorism committed abroad by a state sponsor of terrorism, while subsection (a)(5) governs tortious acts, including terrorism, performed in the United States. *See Flatow v. Islamic Republic of Iran,* 999 F. Supp. 1, 15 (D.D.C. 1998) (finding (a)(7) applied to conduct outside the United States and stating "(a)(5) already provides jurisdiction over state-sponsored terrorist acts in the United States, . . . the state sponsored terrorism exception would be redundant if it were held to apply only within the United States"). Again, Plaintiffs argue that Defendants' argument of exclusivity would lead to absurd results, such that if a foreign sovereign not designated a state sponsor of terror was involved in a car accident stemming from negligence it would not be immune; but if it undertook a deliberate act of violence it would enjoy immunity from suit.

While there are certainly obstacles to (a)(5)'s application – and the Court is not convinced the Plaintiffs have or can overcome them – the Court will not rule as a matter of law that subsections (a)(7) and (a)(5) are mutually exclusive. Accordingly, the Court will consider Plaintiffs' evidence demonstrating the torts exception outlined in (a)(5) provides a basis for subject matter jurisdiction here.

To fit within the exception outlined in § 1605(a)(5), the Plaintiffs must come forward with evidence demonstrating the Princes' or Kingdom's tortious acts or omissions caused Plaintiffs' injuries. "Any terrorist act, including the September 11 attacks, might have been the natural and probable consequence of knowingly and intentionally providing financial support to al Qaeda, given [the complaints'] allegations that, prior to September 11, al Qaeda and Osama bin Laden had proclaimed their intentions to commit murderous terrorist activities against the United States and its citizens, . . . and had accompanied these words with actions by implementing, and publicly acknowledging responsibility for, such terrorist schemes as the 1993 bombing of the World Trade Center, the 1998 attack of the U.S. embassies in Kenya and Tanzania, and the 2000 attack of the U.S.S. Cole in Yemen." 274 F. Supp. 2d at 105 [opinion prior to consolidation].

a. Prince Sultan and Prince Turki

Both Princes are alleged to have tortiously aided and abetted terrorism through their contributions to, and support of, Islamic charities that they knew or should have known were supporting terrorist organizations such as al Qaeda. Additionally, Plaintiffs allege Prince Turki aided and abetted the terrorists by attempting to deflect their activities away from Saudi Arabia and by serving as a "facilitator of Osama bin Laden's network of charities." Plaintiffs allege both Princes must have known that the United States would have been al Qaeda's target, making the attacks on September 11 a foreseeable result of the Princes' actions.

i. Causation

Plaintiffs place great reliance on *Halberstam v. Welch*, 227 U.S. App. D.C. 167, 705 F.2d 472 (D.C. Cir. 1983) and *Boim v. Quranic Literacy Institute & Holy Land Foundation for Relief & Development*, 291 F.3d 1000, 1023 (7th Cir. 2002) ("*Boim II*"). Neither of these cases concern the tortious activity exception to the FSIA, but they do explain liability under the ATA and for aiding and abetting and conspiracy. In *Halberstam*, the defendant was found liable as a joint venturer for a killing that occurred during a burglary at which she was not present. The court found that the defendant's intimate relationship with the burglar and her assistance in his other illegal ventures "defied credulity that [she] did not know that something illegal was afoot."

In *Boim*, the Seventh Circuit held that the parents of a yeshiva student killed in 1996 in Israel by members of the military wing of Hamas could prove that the defendants aided and abetted their son's murder under the ATA if they could demonstrate that the charities "knew of Hamas' illegal activities, that they desired to help those activities succeed, and they engaged in some act of helping the illegal activities." Plaintiffs submit the court's decision in *Boim* – that the

ATA was designed "to extend liability to all points along the causal chain of terrorism" – supports the finding that Prince Sultan's and Prince Turki's conduct caused the attacks on September 11, 2001.

Plaintiffs exert much effort outlining the connections between al Qaeda and the Defendant charities that Prince Sultan and Prince Turki supported. Plaintiffs argue that the indirect nature of the Princes' contributions to al Qaeda is not fatal to their claims since they allegedly knew that funds they donated to the Defendant charities were being diverted to al Qaeda. The Court has reviewed the exhibits on which Plaintiffs rely and finds only a handful relate to Plaintiffs' arguments. Even construing these allegations and exhibits in the light most favorable to Plaintiffs, and drawing all inferences in their favor, none of these exhibits amount to admissible evidence that Prince Sultan or Prince Turki knew the charities they supported were fronts for al Qaeda.

Alternatively, Plaintiffs argue that, since Osama bin Laden and al Qaeda made no effort to hide their hatred for the United States, Prince Sultan and Prince Turki had to have been aware that the United States was a target, making the atrocities of September 11, 2001 a foreseeable result of their actions. Unlike Hamas in *Boim*, none of the organizations the Princes are alleged to have supported in an official capacity were designated a sponsor of terrorism at the time of the alleged contributions. In fact, only BIF and certain branches of Al Haramain have since been designated.

Plaintiffs have pleaded al Qaeda's repeated, public targeting of the United States. They have not, however, pleaded facts to support an inference that the Princes were sufficiently close to the terrorists' illegal activities to satisfy *Halberstam* or New York law. Similarly, Plaintiffs have not pleaded facts to suggest the Princes knew they were making contributions to terrorist fronts and provided substantial assistance or encouragement to the terrorists to satisfy *Boim* or New York law. The Court is not ruling as a matter of law that a defendant cannot be liable for contributions to organizations that are not themselves designated terrorists. But in such a case, there must be some facts presented to support the allegation that the defendant knew the receiving organization to be a solicitor, collector, supporter, front or launderer for such an entity. There must be some facts to support an inference that the defendant knowingly provided assistance or encouragement to the wrongdoer. Here, there are no such factual bases presented, there are only conclusions.

ii. Discretionary Function

Plaintiffs argue that there is no discretion to conduct illegal activities and the so-called discretionary function exception to the tortious act exception should not apply to Prince Sultan or Prince Turki. The Court finds the discretionary function exception independently bars Plaintiffs' claims against Prince Sultan and Prince Turki. Both Princes are accused of donating money or recommending government grants to charities that allegedly supported al Qaeda. As the head of DGI, Prince Turki is also alleged to have attempted to protect Saudi Arabia from terrorism and to have implemented the Kingdom's foreign relations with the Taliban and Osama bin Laden. In determining whether these were discretionary functions, the Court must decide whether the actions involved an element of choice or judgment based on considerations of public policy.

There can be little doubt that, as the chairman of the Supreme Council of Islamic Affairs, charged with making recommendations to the Council of Ministers regarding requests for aid from Islamic organizations located abroad, and as the head of the Special Committee of the Council of Ministers, charged with deciding which grants should be made to Islamic charities, Prince Sultan's decisions were made at the planning level of government. Similarly, as the head of DGI, Prince Turki's decisions regarding the treatment of the Taliban and Osama bin Laden were judgments based on considerations of public policy.

b. Kingdom of Saudi Arabia

There is no dispute that the Kingdom of Saudi Arabia is a foreign state within the meaning of the FSIA. The Federal Plaintiffs have the "burden of going forward with evidence that, under exceptions to the FSIA, immunity should not be granted."

The Federal Plaintiffs' allegations arise "predominantly from misconduct of ostensible charities under the Kingdom's control." Thus, the Federal Plaintiffs claim the Kingdom of Saudi Arabia aided and abetted the terrorists through these charities. In attempting to overcome the presumption of the Kingdom's sovereign immunity, the Federal Plaintiffs argue the merits of their claims against the charities. Based on news accounts that the Kingdom has dissolved its international charities and terrorist financing reports that implicate certain charities, the Federal Plaintiffs urge the Court to find that the Kingdom had previously willfully ignored the charities' support for terrorism.

In response, the Kingdom argues that Plaintiffs ignore Osama bin Laden's public targeting of the Kingdom. The 9/11 Commission Report: Final Report of the National Commission on Terrorist Attacks Upon the United States, 48, 373 (July 2004) (hereinafter "9/11 Report"). The Kingdom also submits it has worked with the United States to share information in the fight against terrorism. The U.S. State Department has not designated the Kingdom a state sponsor of terrorism. Additionally, the presidentially-appointed September 11 commission found no evidence of the Kingdom's funding or support for the September 11 terrorists. 9/11 Report, at 171.

The Court finds the Plaintiffs' allegations cannot overcome the discretionary function exception to the tortious acts exception.

II. Personal Jurisdiction

To avoid dismissal for lack of personal jurisdiction under Rule 12(b)(2), Plaintiffs must establish personal jurisdiction over each Defendant. Because these motions are brought before discovery and decided without an evidentiary hearing, Plaintiffs need only make a prima facie showing that personal jurisdiction exists [under either the New York long-arm statute or Rule 4(k)].

Any exercise of personal jurisdiction must comport with the requirements of due process. "The due process analysis is basically the same under both the Fifth and Fourteenth Amendments. The principal difference is that under the Fifth Amendment the court can consider the defendant's contacts throughout the

United States, while under the Fourteenth Amendment only the contacts with the forum state may be considered." Here, personal jurisdiction under the New York long-arm statute requires minimum contacts with New York pursuant to the Fourteenth Amendment. The exercise of personal jurisdiction under Rule 4(k) requires contacts with the United States as a whole pursuant to the Fifth Amendment.

Plaintiffs urge the Court to deny Defendants' motions and order jurisdictional discovery. Courts are not obligated to subject a foreign defendant to discovery, however, where the allegations of jurisdictional facts, construed in plaintiffs' favor, fail to state a basis for the exercise of jurisdiction or where discovery would not uncover sufficient facts to sustain jurisdiction.

1. Prince Sultan

The Court outlined the allegations against Prince Sultan in Part I.B.1. Plaintiffs do not offer any facts to lend support to their allegation that Prince Sultan purposefully directed his activities at this forum by donating to charities that he knew at the time supported international terrorism. Accordingly, Prince Sultan's motions to dismiss for lack of personal jurisdiction over the claims concerning his personal acts are granted. Plaintiffs' request for jurisdictional discovery with respect to Prince Sultan is denied.

2. Prince Turki

The allegations against Prince Turki are outlined in Part I.B.2. The Plaintiffs have not presented any specific facts from which this Court could infer Prince Turki's primary and personal involvement in, or support of, international terrorism and al Qaeda. Conclusory allegations that he donated money to charities, without specific factual allegations that he knew they were funneling money to terrorists, do not suffice. Accordingly, Prince Turki's motion to dismiss for lack of personal jurisdiction is granted. Jurisdictional discovery is not appropriate with respect to Prince Turki because Plaintiffs have not identified any genuine issue of jurisdictional fact.

3. Prince Mohamed

The Ashton and Federal Plaintiffs allege that Prince Mohamed is or was the chairman or chief executive officer of three financial institutions in Saudi Arabia: Dar al Maal al Islami ("DMI"), Islamic Investment Company of the Gulf-Bahrain EC ("IICG"), and Faisal Islamic Bank-Sudan ("FIBS"), which are all shareholders of Defendant Al Shamal Islamic Bank. They claim that Prince Mohamed knew or should have known that each of these financial institutions "acted as an aider and abettor and material sponsor of al Qaeda, Bin Laden, and international terrorism."

Plaintiffs have not alleged that Prince Mohamed had any knowledge or involvement in any al Qaeda accounts at any of the banks he chaired. FIBS' relationship with Al Shamal Islamic Bank, which purportedly knowingly opened accounts for al Qaeda operatives, including Osama bin Laden, is too remote in time and proximity to implicate Prince Mohamed. To make a prima facie case of personal jurisdiction, Plaintiffs must either allege personal acts by Prince Mohamed by which he purposefully directed his activities at the United States by supporting Osama bin Laden, al Qaeda, or their terrorist agenda, or demonstrate that the acts of the banks he chaired can be imputed to him. Plaintiffs have not met their burden.

4. Estate of Mohammad Abdullah Aljomaih

Plaintiffs submit that Mr. Aljomaih is implicated by the "Golden Chain." The "Golden Chain" is a group of documents that was discovered by Bosnian authorities searching the offices of charity Defendant BIF in March 2002. Plaintiffs claim the "Golden Chain" contains a list of early direct donors to al Qaeda. It includes the entry "Al-Jumaih. Jeddah (S.A.)." The Court finds the Plaintiffs have not established a prima facie case of jurisdiction over Mr. Aljomaih to defeat his motion or warrant jurisdictional discovery. Their theory of jurisdiction rests almost entirely on a document with serious foundational flaws. Even assuming, as the Court must, that the "Golden Chain" refers to Mr. Aljomaih, with no indication of who wrote the list, when it was written, or for what purpose, the Court cannot make the logical leap that the document is a list of early al Qaeda supporters. Mr. Aljomaih's motion to dismiss the Burnett complaint for lack of personal jurisdiction is accordingly granted.

5. Sheikh Hamad Al-Husani

The Burnett Plaintiffs claim that Mr. Al-Husani is also implicated by the "Golden Chain," and thus an early supporter of al Qaeda. The Plaintiffs place great weight on the United States' inclusion of the "Golden Chain" in its proffer of evidence in *United States v. Arnaout*, the government's case against an executive of Defendant charity BIF. The court presiding over that case, however, ruled that the document was inadmissable hearsay. *United States v. Arnaout*, 2003 U.S. Dist. LEXIS 1635 (N.D.Ill. Feb. 4, 2003). Nevertheless, by supporting al Qaeda, Plaintiffs assert Mr. Al-Husani purposefully directed his activities toward the United States, making the exercise of personal jurisdiction appropriate. Plaintiffs have not established a prima facie showing of jurisdiction over Mr. Al-Husani to survive his motion to dismiss or warrant jurisdictional discovery. The "Golden Chain" does not say what the Plaintiffs argue it says. It is only a list of names found in a charity's office.

6. NCB

The Court outlined the Ashton and Burnett Plaintiffs' claims against NCB in Part I.B.4. For purposes of the personal jurisdiction analysis, the Court will assume at this point that the FSIA does not provide for subject matter and personal jurisdiction over NCB. Accordingly, the Plaintiffs will have to make a prima facie showing to survive NCB's motion to dismiss. In that vein, Plaintiffs argue that NCB purposefully directed its activities at the United States and participated in a conspiracy that culminated in the attacks of September 11.

NCB claims the rare contacts it does have with the United States do not satisfy the requirements of due process. Although it maintains correspondent banking relationships with U.S. commercial banks, NCB argues such relationships are insufficient to establish personal jurisdiction over NCB. NCB offers its customers the opportunity to open accounts directly with United States-based securities broker-dealers, but NCB does not act as a broker-dealer for securities sold in the United States and is not so licensed.

Taken individually, NCB's contacts with the United States would not satisfy due process requirements. However, when they are examined as a whole – the presence of a branch office until 1992, a subsidiary until 2001, taking advantage of the privilege of its presence in New York by instigating a lawsuit in this forum, advertisements in U.S. publications – the Court finds that they may, with the help of limited jurisdictional discovery, comport with due process. NCB's motion to dismiss is therefore denied without prejudice.

7. Abdulrahman bin Mahfouz

Abdulrahman bin Mahfouz is a Defendant in the Burnett action. He is the son of Defendant Khalid bin Mahfouz and a director of the Defendant charity Blessed Relief Society, also known as Muwaffaq. Blessed Relief is a branch of the Human Concern International Society, which Osama bin Laden identified as a supporter in 1995. He is a shareholder and the CEO of former Defendant Nimir, LLC, also known as Nimir Petroleum Ltd. Finally, Plaintiffs claim that Mr. bin Mahfouz was a member of the board and Vice Chairman of the Executive Management Committee of Defendant National Commercial Bank. The Burnett complaint does not contain any specific actions by Mr. bin Mahfouz from which the Court could infer that he purposefully directed his activities at the United States. His affiliations with entities that are alleged to have U.S. contacts will not sustain jurisdiction.

8. Saudi Binladin Group, Tariq Binladin, Omar Binladin, and Bakr Binladin

The Ashton and Burnett complaints name the Saudi Binladin Group ("SBG") as a Defendant. The Burnett complaint also names Tariq Binladin, Omar Binladin, and Bakr Binladin, Osama's half-brothers, as Defendants. In both actions, these Defendants move to dismiss the complaint or for a more definite statement.

Based in Jeddah, Saudi Arabia, SBG is the successor to a construction company founded by Mohammed Binladin, the father of Osama bin Laden. It is now one of the largest engineering and construction companies in the Arab world and is managed by Osama bin Laden's half brothers, including defendants Bakr Binladin, who runs SBG, and Tariq Binladin, who holds a position on the board. Tariq Binladin allegedly had a prominent role at IIRO in 1990. Osama bin Laden purportedly used SBG to build an infrastructure in Afghanistan. After the Soviets withdrew from Afghanistan in 1989, Osama bin Laden returned to work with SBG in Jeddah. SBG allegedly continued to support Osama bin Laden after he relocated to Sudan in 1991. For example, SBG, through two subsidiaries allegedly supported Osama bin Laden's participation in the construction of the Tahaddi road and Port Sudan Airport. Plaintiffs claim Osama bin Laden's name is still listed on SBG corporate records. Defendants dispute this and argue he was formally removed from SBG's ownership documents in June 1993. Plaintiffs also claim that Osama bin Laden never "broke" with his family after he was exiled to Sudan and that SBG continued to provide him financial assistance and engineering support. Defendants also dispute this statement and argue that Bakr formally ostracized Osama from the family and the company in a February 1994 statement.

SBG "sheltered and directly supported operatives of the al Qaeda terrorist organization." Mohammad Jamal Khalifa, allegedly a key al Qaeda operative, was taken in by a branch of SBG, the Mohammed Bin Laden Organization. The Mohammed Bin Laden Organization is allegedly a wholly-owned subsidiary of SBG and its board members include defendants Bakr, Tariq, and Omar Binladin. Khalifa listed the Mohammed Bin Laden Organization address on his visa application. Additionally, U.S.-designated terrorist Yassin Abdullah al-Kadi was allegedly introduced to the Global Diamond Resource's Chairman by an executive of SBG.

Plaintiffs claim that SBG had an address in Rockville, Maryland until very recently. SBG claims the Rockville address was the headquarters of a separately incorporated company, SBG USA, which was formally dissolved in December 1999.

[T]he Court finds jurisdictional discovery is warranted to determine if SBG purposefully directed its activities at the United States. Specifically, the complaints are not specific about when, at the very least, SBG provided construction support to Osama bin Laden. A branch of SBG allegedly took in an al Qaeda operative who listed the SBG branch address on his visa application. It is alleged to have ties to U.S.-designated terrorist Yassin Abdullah Al-Kadi. At this stage, the Court must accept as true Plaintiffs' contentions that SBG still contains Osama bin Laden's name in its corporate documents. Additionally, although it would not satisfy the due process requisites on its own, SBG's presence in Maryland three years before the complaints were filed, also warrants some discovery. Accordingly, SBG's motion to dismiss the Ashton and Burnett complaints are denied without prejudice.

9. SAAR Network

The Federal Plaintiffs claim the SAAR Network [known by the initials of its alleged founder Suleiman Abdel Aziz al-Raghi] is a network of "interrelated ostensible charities" that was established in the 1980s "to generate and surreptitiously transfer funds to terrorist organizations, including al-Qaeda." Allegedly, many of the entities are related by common management, few of them maintained a physical presence at their purported place of business, and they all "have long acted as fully integrated components of al Qaeda's logistical and financial support infrastructure."

Plaintiffs argue the Court has personal jurisdiction over the SAAR Network because it participated in the conspiracy that resulted in catastrophic effects in this district. After an ongoing investigation in the Eastern District of Virginia, federal authorities raided the offices of several of these Defendants in Herndon, Virginia in March 2002. The investigation has allegedly revealed that SAAR Network funds have been transferred to designated terrorists and al Qaeda operatives Youssef Nada and Ahmed Idris Nasreddin. Additionally, Plaintiffs claim that the investigation has revealed that SAAR Network entities have engaged in transactions with Bait Ul-mal, Inc. (BMI), which has transferred funds to terrorist organizations including al Qaeda, and materially supported the 1998 embassy bombings in Africa.

At this stage, the Court must accept as true Plaintiffs' allegations concerning the relationships of the SAAR Network. Defendants correctly argue, however, that Defendants have provided scant basis for linking these entities under the SAAR Network title. Certain of these groups may be subject to personal jurisdiction in light of Plaintiffs' allegation that they purposefully directing its activities at the United States by transferring money to designated terrorists Youssef Nada and Ahmed Idris Nasreddin, particularly if they intended the money to support terrorism. Additionally, general jurisdiction could be appropriate for the SAAR Network entities having offices in Virginia. Accordingly, the SAAR Network's motion to dismiss is denied without prejudice. The parties are to engage in jurisdictional discovery to determine which of the Network's entities have a presence in Virginia and which entities transferred money to Nada and Nasreddin.

10. Adel A. J. Batterjee

The Burnett Plaintiffs claim that Defendant Adel A. J. Batterjee is an associate of Osama bin Laden. On December 21, 2004, the U.S. Department of Treasury designated Mr. Batterjee as a Specially Designated Global Terrorist. Mr. Batterjee is the chairman of Al Shamal Islamic Bank, "an instrumental bank in Osama bin Laden's financial support network." Mr. Batterjee is also chairman of al-Bir Saudi Organization, whose United States branch, Defendant BIF, is allegedly a "front for al Qaeda sponsorship." BIF is also a designated terrorist organization. The Saudi government closed Al-Bir in 1993 "at the same time it was closing other organizations for ties to terrorism." Mr. Batterjee then allegedly moved the charity's headquarters to Chicago in the name of BIF. Mr. Batterjee is listed as one of BIF's three founders in its articles of incorporation filed in Illinois. Through an alias, Mr. Batterjee allegedly sent money to BIF's branches. Mr. Batterjee allegedly transferred control of BIF to Defendant Enaam M. Arnaout, on September 15, 1997. In October 2001, Arnaout allegedly told Batterjee he was worried about being under scrutiny of the U.S. government and in January 2002, Batterjee requested that Aranout relocate his family to Saudi Arabia.[38] Plaintiffs also claim that Mr. Batterjee's name is on a BIF list of wealthy Saudi Arabian sponsors of al Qaeda and Osama bin Laden.

Plaintiffs also claim that Defendant charity WAMY and BIF are closely connected and that Mr. Batterjee was the Secretary General of WAMY when he founded BIF in the United States. In his capacity as Secretary General of WAMY, Mr. Batterjee allegedly commissioned a biography of Osama bin Laden and the origins of al Qaeda, which was jointly published by WAMY and BIF in 1991.

---

[38] Mr. Arnaout was "criminally indicted for his role in the September 11, 2001 attacks." But in its "written plea agreement, the government agreed to dismiss sensational and highly publicized charges of providing material support to terrorists and terrorist organizations." *United States v. Arnaout*, 282 F. Supp. 2d 838, 843 (N.D.Ill. 2003). The Burnett Plaintiffs allege Mr. Arnaout and Osama bin Laden have ties. For example, law enforcement officials in Bosnia-Herzegovina raided BIF's offices in March 2002 and allegedly recovered documents establishing direct communications between Mr. Arnaout and Osama bin Laden in the late 1980s and early 1990s.

With respect to his contacts with the United States, Plaintiffs claim that the documents filed in 1992 in conjunction with the establishment of BIF in Chicago state that Mr. Batterjee is a founder of BIF and that BIF's founders travel to the United States on a regular basis. In 1993 BIF filed an application to conduct business in Florida and listed Mr. Batterjee as a director with an address in Florida.

Mr. Batterjee disputes the claims against him. He states he was born in Saudi Arabia, attended college in the United States in the 1960s, and returned to Saudi Arabia. He claims he was last in the United States in June 2000 for personal reasons. He denies owning any real property, bank accounts, or investments in the United States. With respect to the allegations contained in the complaint, Mr. Batterjee claims BIF was never a branch of Al Bir or vice versa. He claims he never sent money to BIF in all of its history. He states he transferred away all control of BIF in 1993. He claims he never served as an executive of WAMY, never wrote a biography of Osama bin Laden, and denies having any knowledge of Osama bin Laden's or al Qaeda's activities other than what is widely published in the press.

The Court finds the Burnett Plaintiffs made a prima facie showing of personal jurisdiction over Mr. Batterjee. While perhaps not dispositive on its own, Mr. Batterjee's designation as a terrorist lends substantial weight to Plaintiffs' claims that he purposefully directed his activities at the United States and that the exercise of personal jurisdiction over him comports with due process. Mr. Batterjee purportedly commissioned a book about al Qaeda and Osama bin Laden. He is the chairman of Al Shamal Islamic Bank, a bank with admitted and substantial ties to Osama bin Laden. Additionally, he is involved in the United States operations of designated terrorist, BIF. In the ten years leading up to the commencement of this action, Mr. Batterjee has had contacts with the United States that could be related to the terrorist attacks inasmuch as BIF participated in those attacks. Specifically, Mr. Batterjee traveled to Chicago for BIF and had an address in Florida for BIF. Accordingly, Mr. Batterjee's motion to dismiss the Burnett complaint for lack of personal jurisdiction is denied.

III. Failure to State a Claim

A. Elements of Claims

Plaintiffs' claim that each Defendant provided material support to the al Qaeda terrorists who perpetrated the attacks on September 11, 2001. Under the ATA, material support includes money, financial services, lodging, training, safehouses, and false documentation or identification. 18 U.S.C. §§ 2339A(b), 2339B(g). Assuming such support is alleged, Plaintiffs will have to present a sufficient causal connection between that support and the injuries suffered by Plaintiffs. Proximate cause will support this connection. In light of al Qaeda's public acknowledgments of its war against the United States, the September 11 attacks may be the natural and probable consequence of knowingly and intentionally providing material support to al Qaeda.

Plaintiffs rely on theories of concerted action liability – conspiracy and aiding and abetting – in support of this causal link. "Concerted action liability under New York law is based on the principle that 'all those who, in pursuance of a common plan or design to commit a tortious act, actively take part in it, or further it by cooperation or request, or who lend aid or encouragement to the wrongdoer . . . are equally liable with him.'" To be liable under either conspiracy or aiding and abetting, however, the defendant "must know the wrongful nature of the primary actor's conduct," and the conduct must be tied to a substantive cause of action. In this regard, Plaintiffs rely on the ATCA, RICO, the TVPA, the ATA, and various state laws, including wrongful death, survival, intentional infliction of emotional distress, trespass, assault and battery, negligence, and negligent infliction of emotional distress.

1. ATCA

The Alien Tort Claims Act provides that "the district courts shall have original jurisdiction of any civil action by an alien for a tort only, committed in violation of the law of nations or a treaty of the United States." 28 U.S.C. § 1350. "This statute confers subject matter jurisdiction when the following three conditions are satisfied: (1) an alien sues (2) for a tort (3) committed in violation of the law of nations (i.e., international law)." *Kadic v. Karadzic,* 70 F.3d 232, 238 (2d Cir. 1995); see also *Flores v. Southern Peru Corp.,* 343 F.3d 140, 143 & n.2 (2d Cir. 2003). Certain Plaintiffs in these actions are aliens and the complaints all allege common law torts. The Court finds that "aircraft hijacking is generally recognized as a violation of international law." Further, "courts, including the Second Circuit, have almost unanimously permitted actions premised on a theory of aiding and abetting and conspiracy."

2. RICO

To state a claim under civil RICO, a plaintiff must plead seven elements: '(1) that the defendant (2) through the commission of two or more acts (3) constituting a 'pattern' (4) of 'racketeering activity' (5) directly or indirectly invests in, maintains an interest in, or participates in (6) an 'enterprise' (7) the activities of which affect interstate or foreign commerce.' 18 U.S.C. §1962.

The Federal Plaintiffs' RICO statements against Arab Bank and the SAAR Network assert claims under § 1962(c) and § 1962(d). Subsection (c) states, in part: "It shall be unlawful for any person employed by or associated with any enterprise engaged in, or the activities of which affect, interstate or foreign commerce, to conduct or participate, directly or indirectly, in the conduct of such enterprise's affairs through a pattern of racketeering activity." Assuming for now that the Plaintiffs have pleaded an enterprise, an alleged RICO defendant must have had 'some part in directing' the 'operation or management' of the enterprise itself to be liable." *Dubai Islamic Bank v. Citibank, N.A.,* 256 F. Supp. 2d 158, 164 (S.D.N.Y. 2003). The complaints allege the moving Defendants may have assisted al Qaeda, but they do not allege "anything approaching active 'management or operation.'" Accordingly, the Court finds Plaintiffs have failed to state a RICO claim against the moving Defendants.

3. TVPA

"The TVPA establishes a cause of action in federal court against an individual who, under actual or apparent authority, or color of law, of any foreign nation subjects an individual to torture or extrajudicial killing." *Arndt v. UBS AG,* 342 F. Supp. 2d 132, 141 (E.D.N.Y. 2004); 28 U.S.C. § 1350 note. Only individuals may be sued under the TVPA. Accordingly, to the extent Plaintiffs have not already withdrawn these claims, the TVPA claims are dismissed against Al Rajhi Bank, Saudi American Bank, Arab Bank, Al Baraka Investment & Development Corp., NCB, Saudi Binladin Group, and the SAAR Network. Similarly, there have been no allegations that Saleh Abdullah Kamel or Adel Batterjee acted under color of law and, therefore, the TVPA claims against these individuals are dismissed as well.

4. ATA

The ATA provides a civil remedy for "any national of the United States injured in his or her person, property, or business by reason of an act of international terrorism, or his or her estate, survivors, or heirs." 18 U.S.C. § 2333(a). To adequately plead the provision of material support under this section, a plaintiff would have to allege that the defendant knew about the terrorists' illegal activities, the defendant desired to help those activities succeed, and the defendant engaged in some act of helping those activities. *Boim II,* 291 F.3d at 1023; see also *Boim v. Quranic Literacy Inst.,* 340 F. Supp. 2d 885, 906-913 (N.D. Ill. 2004) (*"Boim III"*) (granting summary judgment against two entity defendants where record evidence demonstrated the charities' concession that Hamas used terrorism in pursuit of its goals, the organizations' repeated desire to help Hamas by recruiting donations to the Holy Land Foundation, a known supporter of Hamas, distributing pro-Hamas literature, and featuring pro-Hamas speakers at their meetings). Under a conspiracy theory, the Plaintiffs have to allege that the Defendants were involved in an agreement to accomplish an unlawful act and that the attacks of September 11 were a reasonably foreseeable consequence of that conspiracy. Plaintiffs do not have to allege that Defendants knew specifically about the September 11 attacks or that they committed any specific act in furtherance of that attack.

5. Wrongful Death and [Other Torts]

[I]f Plaintiffs are personal representatives and their allegations sufficiently allege that Defendants supported, aided and abetted, or conspired with the September 11 terrorists, they will have also stated claims for wrongful death. [Trespass to property would require similar showings. Other tort claims such as assault, negligence, and intentional infliction of emotional distress were dismissed either on the basis of statute of limitations or lack of duty.]

B. Analysis of Claims Against the Moving Defendants

While applying the liberal notice pleading requirements of Rule 8, the Court notes that in light of "the extreme nature of the charge of terrorism, fairness requires extra-careful scrutiny of Plaintiffs' allegations as to any particular defendant, to ensure that he – or it – does indeed have fair notice of [the claims]."

1. Al Rajhi Bank

Al Rajhi Bank was founded in 1987 and now has a network of nearly 400 branch offices throughout Saudi Arabia and seventeen worldwide subsidiaries. All the banking Defendants are alleged to have "provided essential support to the al Qaeda organization and operations. The banking Defendants in this lawsuit have acted as instruments of terror, in raising, facilitating and transferring money to terrorist organizations." Plaintiffs claim that Al Rajhi Bank is "the primary bank for a number of charities that serve as al Qaeda front groups," including Al Haramain, MWL, WAMY, SJRC, and IIRO. "Al Rajhi continues to maintain Al Haramain's accounts despite Al Haramain's designation on March 11, 2002 as terrorist organizations by both the United States and Saudi Arabian authorities."

The Burnett Plaintiffs claim that Saudi Arabia has "ineffective and/or rudimentary bank supervisory, anti-money laundering laws and anti-terrorist financing in place." In 1999, William Weschler of the National Security Council and Richard Newcomb of the Office of Foreign Assets Control traveled to Saudi Arabia to warn Al Rajhi Bank and its regulator, the Saudi Arabian Monetary Agency ("SAMA"), "that their financial systems were being manipulated or utilized to fund terrorist organizations such as Al Qaeda." The United States encouraged SAMA to adopt "know your customer" rules. "Despite these warnings, Al Rajhi failed to adopt even the most minimal standards, [which] resulted in the use of Al Rajhi as an instrument of terror and a material supporter, aider and abettor of al Qaeda and international terrorist activities."

One of the hijackers on board American Airlines Flight 11, Abdulaziz al-Omari, held an account at Al Rajhi Bank. Another hijacker, Mohammed Atta, made a transfer to this account at some time.

The Burnett Plaintiffs also claim that Al Rajhi Bank has relationships with Hamas and other terrorists. Al Rajhi Bank chose Texas-based Infocom to host its website. Infocom has provided funding to Hamas and is owned and operated by Hamas leader and designated terrorist, Mousa Marzook.

Members of the Al Rajhi family, which owns and controls Al Rajhi Bank, are alleged to have ties to Osama bin Laden's personal secretary. The Al Rajhi family is purportedly a major donor to the SAAR Network, a Defendant here, being investigated by federal authorities in Virginia.

Judge Robertson found that the only allegation in the Third Amended Burnett Complaint that stated a claim upon which relief could be granted was that Al Rajhi Bank acted as an instrument "of terror, in raising, facilitating and transferring money to terrorist organizations." Judge Robertson noted that there was no support "for the proposition that a bank is liable for injuries done with money that passes through its hands in the form of deposits, withdrawals, check clearing services, or any other routine banking service."

Al Rajhi Bank argues that Plaintiffs offer no factual allegations in support of their conclusion that Al Rajhi Bank had to know that the charities it supported through Zakat and Hararm[40] payments were really fronts for al Qaeda. Al Rajhi Bank contends it had a legal and religious duty to make its charitable donations and any terrorist activity by the recipient charities was unknown to Al Rajhi Bank. Contrary to Plaintiffs' arguments, Al Rajhi Bank submits it did not have a duty, or a right, to inspect the Defendant charities' financial transactions to ascertain the ultimate destination of its donations. Al Rajhi Bank submits that SAMA did not implement any duty to investigate Zakat payments after its meeting with representatives of the National Security Council and Office of Foreign Assets Control.

Plaintiffs do not allege that Al Rajhi Bank provided direct material support to al Qaeda. Rather, Plaintiffs claim Al Rajhi Bank aided and abetted the September 11 terrorists by donating to certain Defendant charities and acting as the bank for these Defendants. New York law and the courts interpreting the ATA in *Boim* make very clear that concerted action liability requires general knowledge of the primary actor's conduct. Even with the opportunity to clarify their claims against Al Rajhi Bank, the Burnett Plaintiffs do not offer facts to support their conclusions that Al Rajhi Bank had to know that Defendant charities WAMY, MWL, IIRC, and SJRC were supporting terrorism.

This Court, like Judge Robertson before it, has found no basis for a bank's liability for injuries funded by money passing through it on routine banking business. Similarly, allegations concerning the Al Rajhi family cannot support a claim against Al Rajhi Bank because there is no allegation that the family members were acting in furtherance of Al Rajhi Bank business. Finally, Plaintiffs' allegations that Al Rajhi Bank has connections to Hamas supporters fails to state a claim because Plaintiffs have not alleged any relationship between Hamas and al Qaeda or the terrorist attacks of September 11. Even accepting all the allegations against Al Rajhi Bank as true, Plaintiffs have failed to state a claim that would entitle them to relief. Accordingly, Al Rajhi Bank's motion to dismiss the Burnett complaint is granted in its entirety.

2. Saudi American Bank

Saudi American Bank is based in Rihadh, Saudi Arabia and was formed in 1980 pursuant to a royal decree to take over the then-existing branches of Citibank in Riyadh and Jeddah. It is the second largest bank in Saudi Arabia and has offices in the United States, based in New York.

The essence of Plaintiffs' claim is that through its relationships with other banks and support of the Saudi Binladin group's work in Sudan, Saudi American Bank provided material support to al Qaeda. It is not alleged to have done anything to directly support al Qaeda, Osama bin Laden, or their terrorist agenda. As the Court has stated before, there can be no bank liability for injuries caused by money routinely passing through the bank. Saudi American Bank is not alleged to have known that anything relating to terrorism was occurring through the services it provided.

---

[40] Under Islamic banking laws, Hararm is forbidden income that must be given away. The disposal of Hararm cannot be considered charitable giving.

3. Arab Bank

The Federal Plaintiffs claim Arab Bank is a financial institution headquartered in Egypt with branch offices throughout the world, including New York. Arab Bank claims it is actually a Jordanian bank headquartered in Amman, Jordan. Arab Bank allegedly has "long provided financial services and other forms of material support to terrorist organizations, including al Qaeda." Further, these Plaintiffs allege that the September 11 attacks were a "direct, intended and foreseeable product of Arab Bank's participation in al Qaeda's jihadist campaign." These claims are based on the allegation that Arab Bank has "long known that accounts it maintained were being used to solicit and transfer funds to terrorist organizations [and despite this knowledge] Arab Bank has continued to maintain those accounts."

The Federal and Burnett complaints do not include any facts to support the inference that Arab Bank knew or had to know that it was providing material support to terrorists by providing financial services to the charity Defendants or by processing wire transfers in Spain. The paragraphs do not allege any involvement by, knowledge of, or participation in any wrongful conduct by Arab Bank. These Plaintiffs do not claim that Arab Bank ignored any regulations regarding their customer accounts. Providing routine banking services, without having knowledge of the terrorist activities, cannot subject Arab Bank to liability. While claiming Arab Bank has ties with known Hamas fronts, the Federal complaint does not contain any allegation of a connection between Hamas and Osama bin Laden, al Qaeda, or the September 11 attacks.

4. Al Baraka Investment & Development Corporation and Saleh Abdullah Kamel

The Ashton and Burnett complaints detail nearly identical claims against Al Baraka Investment & Development Corp. ("Al Baraka") and Saleh Abdullah Kamel. Saleh Abdullah Kamel was born in Saudi Arabia in 1941 and founded Dallah Albaraka Group LLC in 1969. Dallah Albaraka is a diversified conglomerate based in Jeddah and includes twenty-three banks in Arab and Islamic countries. Dallah Albaraka is a shareholder of Aqsa Islamic Bank, a bank that Israel has refused to approve, "citing its obvious ties with known terrorists." One of Dallah Albaraka's subsidiaries is Dallah Avco Trans-Arabia Co., based in Jeddah. Omar al Bayoumi, a suspect wanted by the FBI in connection with the September 11 attacks, was the Assistant to the Director of Finance for Dallah Avco and paid rent in San Diego for the house occupied by two September 11 hijackers of American Airlines Flight 77. Mr. Kamel is also one of three founders of Defendant Al Shamal Islamic Bank.

The allegation that an employee of a Dallah Albaraka subsidiary financially supported two of the hijackers in San Diego does not translate into an allegation that Mr. Kamel provided material support to terrorism or aided and abetted those that provided material support. An employee's actions cannot be a basis for employer liability unless the employee was acting in furtherance of the employer's business. There is no allegation that Mr. Kamel knew Mr. al Bayoumi or directed anyone at the Della Albaraka subsidiary to support al Qaeda or the hijackers. Similarly, the allegation that Mr. Kamel was one of three founders of Al Shamal Islamic Bank in 1983, without additional allegations, does not state a claim for relief. Thus, the Ashton and Burnett claims against Al Baraka and Mr. Kamel are dismissed in their entirety.

5. NCB

The Ashton and Burnett Plaintiffs' allegations against NCB are outlined in Part I.B.4. The Court finds it would be premature to analyze Plaintiffs' largely conclusory claims against NCB under Rule 12(b)(6) at this time. NCB may be immune from suit and further discovery if it is found to be an instrumentality of the Kingdom of Saudi Arabia and its actions do not fit within the FSIA's exceptions to immunity. Additionally, the Court is not yet convinced that it would be proper to exercise personal jurisdiction over NCB. Accordingly, NCB's motion to dismiss for failure to state a claim is denied without prejudice. NCB may renew its motion upon completion of the limited jurisdictional discovery – first with respect to its instrumentality status – outlined by the Court above.

6. Saudi Binladin Group

The Ashton and Burnett allegations against the SBG are outlined in Part II.C.8. The same allegations that warrant limited jurisdictional discovery to investigate whether SBG purposefully directed its activities at the United States and its contacts with the United States preclude dismissal under 12(b)(6) at this time. SBG provided construction support to Osama bin Laden. A branch of SBG purportedly provided shelter to an al Qaeda operative. SBG has, at some point, had a close relationship with Osama bin Laden, but the complaints do not specify when or whether the relationship continues. While these allegations are certainly not sufficient to reach a jury, if Plaintiffs demonstrate that this Court has personal jurisdiction over SBG they are entitled the opportunity to develop these claims. SBG's motions to dismiss the Ashton and Burnett complaints for failure to state a claim are therefore denied without prejudice.

7. SAAR Network

The Federal Plaintiffs' allegations against the SAAR Network are outlined in Part II.C.9. The Court's analysis of the SAAR Network's arguments in favor of 12(b)(6) dismissal depend on a predicate finding of which entities are subject to this Court's personal jurisdiction and which entities – and under what circumstances – transferred money to terror fronts. Accordingly, the SAAR Network's motion to dismiss is denied without prejudice. It may be renewed upon completion of personal jurisdiction discovery.

8. Adel A. J. Batterjee

The Burnett Plaintiffs' allegations against Mr. Batterjee are outlined in Part II.C.10. For substantially the same reasons the Court found it had personal jurisdiction over Mr. Batterjee, it denies his motion to dismiss for failure to state a claim. The allegations against him and his designation as a terrorist are sufficient to permit the inference that he provided support to al Qaeda directly or through Al Shamal Islamic Bank, BIF, or WAMY.

IV. Conclusion and Order

[All motions were granted except for the following.] NCB's motions to dismiss for lack of subject matter and personal jurisdiction are denied without prejudice.

The negligence claims against NCB are dismissed for failure to state a claim. The Saudi Binladin Group's motions to dismiss for lack of personal jurisdiction and failure to state a claim are denied without prejudice, but the TVPA and negligence claims against SBG are dismissed. The SAAR Network's motion to dismiss for lack of personal jurisdiction and failure to state a claim is denied without prejudice. The RICO, TVPA, assault and battery, intentional infliction of emotional distress, and negligence claims against the SAAR Network are dismissed. Adel Batterjee's motion to dismiss the Burnett complaint is denied.

So ordered.

NOTES AND QUESTIONS

1. Referring back to the history set out at the beginning of this chapter, in light of all the statutory developments, are there still any significant gaps in tort coverage for acts of terrorism?

    a. What about a terrorist killing by an alien in another country of another alien? Is there any reason why the U.S. courts should hear this case? The TVPA applies to actions "under actual or apparent authority, or color of law." What is the source of congressional power to enact federal law creating the right of action?

    b. The court in *Terrorist Attacks* seems to read the note as if it applies only when the tort also fits the body of the ATCA as a violation of the "law of nations." If an act occurs as part of a "widespread and systematic" pattern of violence, then under the holdings of the ICTY and ICTR, it could violate international law without being imputed to the authority of the state.

    c. What about an act that causes serious bodily harm but is neither a killing nor official torture? For example, many of the instances of beatings and rapes involved in Kosovo and Rwanda were violations of international law as crimes against humanity but were neither killings nor torture. Would they be cognizable in a U.S. civil court action?

2. The *Terrorist Attacks* court holds that there is no claim for relief based upon giving money to a terrorist organization absent at least "general knowledge of the primary actor's conduct." As we will see in Chapter 6, the courts interpreting the material support statutes in criminal cases have struggled with whether a mens rea element is constitutionally required and whether it must include an intent to support the illegal behavior of the organization (as opposed, for example, to additional charitable activities of the organization). What would you require the plaintiff to prove in order to establish liability in a tort action? knowledge of some bad motive? knowledge of intent to kill? knowledge of the exact target of an attack?

SELECTED READINGS

▸ Douglas Kash, *Abducting Terrorists Under PDD-39: Much Ado About Nothing New*, 13 AM. U. INT'L L. REV. 139 (1997).

- Jonathan A. Bush, *How Did We Get Here? Foreign Abduction After Alvarez-Machain*, 45 STAN. L. REV. 939 (1993).

- Michael J. Glennon, *International Kidnapping: State-sponsored Abduction: A Comment on United States v. Alvarez-Machain*, 86 A.J.I.L. 746 (1992).

- Curtis Bradley, *Universal Jurisdiction and U.S. Law*, 2001 U. CHI. L. REV. 323

- Kristin Berdan Weissman, *Extraterritorial Abduction: The Endangerment of Future Peace*, 27 U.C. DAVIS L. REV. 460 (1994).

- M. Cherif Bassiouni, *Universal Jurisdiction for International Crimes: Historical Perspectives and Contemporary Practice*, 42 VA. J. INT'L LAW 81 (Fall 2001)

- Mark A. Summers, *The International Court of Justice's Decision in* Congo v. Belgium: *How Has It Affected the Development of a Principle of Universal Jurisdiction That Would Obligate All States to Prosecute War Criminals?* 21 BOSTON U. INT'L L.J. 63 (Spring 2003).

- James D. Fry, *Terrorism As A Crime Against Humanity and Genocide: The Backdoor to Universal Jurisdiction*, 7 UCLA J. INT'L L. & FOR. AFFAIRS 169 (Spring/Summer 2002).

- Henry A. Kissinger, *The Pitfalls of Universal Jurisdiction*, FOREIGN AFFAIRS, July/August 2001 (Vol. 80, No. 4), 86.

- Adam W. Wenger, *Extraterritorial Jurisdiction Under International Law: The* Yunis *Decision as a Model for the Prosecution of Terrorists in U.S. Courts*, 22 LAW AND POLICY IN INT'L BUSINESS 409 (1991).

Chapter 5

INVESTIGATION AND PROSECUTION
OF TERRORIST PLOTS

Ordinary criminal investigations begin after a completed crime has been discovered. The investigator knows what the crime was because the results are visible, and the focus will be on discovering who did it and collecting the evidence to prove that person's guilt. By contrast, an investigation aimed at preventing criminal harm must start from some other premise, perhaps a tip from an informant, or a set of rumors circulating in a given community, or maybe even a suspicion in the mind of an investigator looking at the aftermath of another completed crime.

In this chapter, we explore the operation of two statutes that appear frequently in terrorism investigations and prosecutions: the Foreign Intelligence Surveillance Act (FISA) and the Classified Information Procedures Act (CIPA). This chapter also sets us up for some of the principal controversies of the post-9/11 Bush Administration counter-terrorism strategy because FISA is the statute most affected by the controversial provisions of the USA PATRIOT Act. In addition, CIPA is cited in a number of situations not because of its direct relevance but because it reflects general policy regarding judicial handling of government secrets.

The classic terrorism case, whether involving a completed act or a plot, will involve government surveillance (wiretaps and other electronic surveillance) carried out under FISA, seizure of dangerous material and arrest of the defendants (often without warrant under exigent circumstances), and the defendants' desire to obtain or introduce into evidence information that the government considers secret and subject to CIPA. Our study will begin by setting the context with a prototypical terrorist conspiracy investigation.

Running throughout these cases is a question of how a court itself is supposed to handle secret information, including the access of clerks and clerical personnel to information in the court's possession, but that issue can be left to the end of this chapter because it will be more understandable after we have some knowledge of the types and potential uses of classified information.

§ 5.01 FOREIGN INTELLIGENCE SURVEILLANCE ACT

Following World War II, as the U.S. and USSR faced off across the espionage divide, and as technology began to open new channels of information gathering, the U.S. Executive branch began routinely to claim the power to conduct electronic surveillance "in the interest of national security." Meanwhile, in cases discussed below, the Supreme Court held essentially that "wiretaps" and similar intrusions into zones of privacy were subject to the fourth amendment requirements of warrants based on probable cause, and also held that "domestic security" did not provide an adequate basis for warrantless wiretaps while hinting that the situation might be different with respect to foreign operatives.

Congress responded in 1978 by enacting FISA's procedures and standards to be met in conducting "foreign intelligence surveillance." The heart of the statutory scheme is the special court (FISC) consisting of sitting district judges designated by the Chief Justice to review applications for surveillance of foreign agents.

UNITED STATES v. SARKISSIAN
841 F.2d 959 (9th Cir. 1988)

SKOPIL, Circuit Judge:

Sarkissian, Dadaian, and Hovsepian appeal their convictions for conspiracy to bomb, transportation of explosive materials, and possession of an unregistered firearm. They contend that (1) the government's warrantless search of a suitcase violated the fourth amendment; (2) the government was required to obtain wiretap authorization under Title III of the Omnibus Crime Control and Safe Streets Act of 1968 (Title III), not under the Foreign Intelligence Surveillance Act of 1978 (FISA); and (3) the district court erred in not disclosing the government's ex parte in camera submission of classified information. We affirm.

FACTS AND PROCEEDINGS BELOW

This case involves the Federal Bureau of Investigation's (FBI) attempt to prevent Armenian terrorists from bombing the Honorary Turkish Consulate in Philadelphia. On September 17, 1982, the FBI, as part of an ongoing investigation of Armenian terrorist groups, obtained authorization from the United States Foreign Surveillance Court (USFSC) to place a wiretap on Hovsepian's telephone in Santa Monica, California. The wiretap paid off from the start. Although defendants spoke in Armenian and used simple code words, FBI translators and investigators soon cracked the code. By late September the FBI knew that Hovsepian, Sarkissian, and others planned to take some type of violent action against the Honorary Turkish Consulate in Philadelphia and that they had a contact person in Boston. FBI Agent Maples, who headed the investigation in Los Angeles, believed that Hovsepian and others would act in early October.

Later intercepted phone calls convinced Maples that Hovsepian had postponed his plans. By October 19, Maples realized that Hovsepian's plans were on again; defendants were assembling a bomb. On October 21, the USFSC authorized a continuation of the surveillance. Shortly after 3:00 a.m. eastern daylight time (EDT), Maples discovered that one of Hovsepian's colleagues had missed a flight from Los Angeles but would take the next one, which would arrive at its destination at noon.

Maples and his agents continued the investigation through the early morning hours. He concluded that components of a bomb, if not an assembled bomb, were being transported from Los Angeles on an unidentified flight by an unidentified person or persons in unidentified luggage to an unidentified city. By checking the schedule of flights out of Los Angeles, Maples determined that the bomb's courier or couriers were probably on a Northwest Orient (NWO) flight due to arrive in Boston's Logan International Airport at noon EDT. He warned Boston's FBI office before 9:00 a.m. EDT of the danger.

At 9:10 a.m. EDT Maples discovered that the courier or couriers were "S. Tataian" and/or "V. Lopez." At 9:25 a.m. EDT Maples concluded that defendant Dadaian was probably one of the couriers. At 9:30 a.m. EDT he called Boston FBI agent Hildreth to warn that the suspect or suspects apparently were on a Trans World Airlines or NWO flight that would arrive at about 11:00 a.m. or noon EDT following stopovers in Minneapolis and New Jersey. Maples provided Hildreth with the names of four suspects. Between 9:45 and 10:00 a.m. EDT, Maples told Hildreth to disregard the names provided earlier. He advised Hildreth to focus on Dadaian who was on the NWO flight due to arrive at noon EDT. Maples gave Hildreth a general physical description of Dadaian.

Around 9:30 a.m. EDT the Boston FBI sent an agent to Logan Airport to to set up a command post. By 11:00 a.m. EDT fifty agents had assembled at the airport. The agents manned surveillance positions and established a search procedure that included a dog sniff and x-ray scan. After the NWO flight landed around 12:15 p.m. EDT, a Massachusetts state police officer boarded the plane and posed as a first class passenger. The officer spotted a man matching Dadaian's description and followed him to the baggage claim area.

A trained dog sniffed the fifty-seven pieces of luggage unloaded from the flight, but did not react to any of them. The agents then ran the luggage through the x-ray scanner and detected parts of a bomb in a suitcase labeled "V. Lopez." They opened the suitcase and found an unassembled bomb with five sticks of dynamite. The agents did not remove anything from the suitcase, but returned it to the baggage claim carousel. His suspicions aroused by activity around the airport, Dadaian never picked up the suitcase. The FBI arrested him several hours later.

At trial the defendants sought to suppress evidence from the suitcase search and FISA wiretap. The district court denied their suppression motions. The government also made an ex parte in camera submission of classified information. The court sealed the submission without allowing disclosure to the defendants. Defendants were found guilty of conspiracy to bomb, transportation of explosive materials, and possession of an unregistered firearm. They timely appealed.

DISCUSSION

A. Warrantless Search

A warrantless search of luggage requires exigent circumstances supported by probable cause. Defendants concede probable cause. The issue is whether there were exigent circumstances. Exigent circumstances include "those circumstances that would cause a reasonable person to believe that entry (or other relevant prompt action) was necessary to prevent physical harm to the officers or other persons." We view the exigency from the totality of circumstances known to the officer at the time of the warrantless intrusion.

We conclude there were exigent circumstances in this case. The FBI knew that a bomb or parts of a bomb were being carried in a suitcase or suitcases by a member or members of an Armenian terrorist group on a commercial flight to an international airport. *See United States v. Chadwick,* 433 U.S. 1, 15 n.9 (1977) (recognition of exigency created by placement of "some immediately dangerous instrumentality, such as explosives" in luggage); *United States v. Al-Azzawy,* 784 F.2d 890, 893 (9th Cir. 1985) (explosives in trailer); *United States v. Williams,* 626 F.2d 697, 703 (9th Cir. 1980) (bomb in car).

The FBI believed that defendants belonged to the Justice Commandoes of the Armenian Genocide (JCAG). Members of the JCAG were considered "armed and dangerous." An FBI report noted that "they have accomplished some 21 assassinations worldwide and numerous bombings of Turkish targets. JCAG members are known to carry concealed hanguns [sic], and to prefer 9mm browning hi-powered automatics, or .45 caliber colt combat commandos automatics." The FBI attributed three assassinations earlier in the year to the JCAG. One assassination occurred in Los Angeles on January 28, 1982, another in Boston on May 4, 1982, and a third in Ottawa, Canada on August 27, 1982. The JCAG often used bombing as a warning to be followed by an assassination attempt.

The Philadelphia FBI estimated heavy civilian casualties if the JCAG managed to detonate its bomb. The Honorary Turkish Consulate was located "in a highly populated area which has continuous activity at all hours of the day and night." A bomb composed of six sticks of dynamite would cause at least 100 casualties. A daytime explosion could inflict as many as 2,000 to 3,000 casualties. If a shoot out between the FBI and JCAG occurred, "people in the various residence units bordering on the site of the building would be expected to rush to the windows to see what was happening. If that occurs and the bomb was not able to be deactivated the minimal number of casualties would be substantially higher." We agree with the district court's finding that there was a "grave and imminent danger to persons and property."

Exigent circumstances alone, however, are insufficient. The government also bears the burden of showing that it could not have obtained a telephonic warrant under Fed. R. Crim. P. 41(c)(2). It must "attempt, in good faith, to secure a warrant or . . . present evidence explaining why a telephone warrant was unavailable or impractical."

Here, the government did not attempt to obtain a telephonic warrant. The record, however, contains evidence showing why it would have been impractical to do so. Probable cause to search arose almost three hours before the plane landed. By 9:25 a.m. EDT Maples had concluded that Dadaian was the bomb's courier. The plane was scheduled to land at noon EDT but actually landed around 12:15 p.m. EDT. Although the investigation preoccupied Maples throughout the early morning hours, after 10:00 a.m. EDT he did little but wait to "see what happened." Maples never considered trying to get a telephonic warrant. Though we find that troubling, we affirm.

The impracticality of obtaining a warrant compels that result. "Obtaining a telephonic warrant is not a simple procedure; 'among other things, a "duplicate original warrant" must be prepared in writing and read to the magistrate verbatim.' The only step that is saved is the trip to the magistrate's office."

United States v. Good, 780 F.2d 773, 775 (9th Cir. 1986). Here, the procedure was complicated by the fact that the agents with the information were in Los Angeles. Fed. R. Crim. P. 41(a) requires that the warrant be issued by a judicial officer of the district where the property to be seized is located. Thus, the Los Angeles agents would have needed to locate a judicial officer in Boston, prepare a warrant, and then convince the judicial officer that probable cause existed. The district court found that no written summary of the necessary information was then in existence and that collecting and organizing the information would have been difficult.

The passage of time alone is not dispositive of whether the government had enough time to secure a warrant. In *Alvarez,* government agents had at least ninety minutes in which to get an arrest warrant. The agents made no attempt to secure the hotel where the drug deal was to occur or to monitor the suspect's movements before making a warrantless arrest. We refused to find exigent circumstances. "The agent's actions . . . were . . . fundamentally inconsistent with any true exigency." In *Echegoyen,* police officers waited approximately two and one-half to three hours before making their search. *United States v. Echegoyen,* 799 F.2d 1271, 1279 n.6. "The officers were faced with a potentially serious fire hazard and potentially dangerous drug traffickers in an isolated mountain community with little fire and police protection." We found exigent circumstances.

This case is closer to *Echegoyen* than to *Alvarez.* In extraordinary cases, the peril may be so great that law enforcement officers must be afforded sufficient latitude to direct their full attention to protecting lives and property. *See United States v. Jones,* 635 F.2d 1357, 1362 (8th Cir. 1980) ("The police were busily engaged in solving the problem, which they continued to believe was a dangerous one."); *Picariello,* 568 F.2d at 226 ("The emergency conditions . . . and the reasonable speed with which the agents acted substantiate a finding of exigent circumstances."); *United States v. Melville,* 309 F. Supp. 829, 832 (S.D.N.Y. 1970)(Police action to halt wave of bombings in New York and to secure explosives in apartment "cannot be judged in the calm of later philosophical review of what a phlegmatic analysis shows.").

The Boston FBI had to safeguard the people and property within the airport. The FBI set up a command post, contacted and coordinated efforts with the state police and a bomb expert, briefed the fifty agents assembled at the airport and assigned them to their posts, and set up a procedure to check for explosives. Uncertainty made the FBI's task more difficult. The FBI did not know the identity of the courier or couriers, whether the bomb was assembled or unassembled, whether the bomb was contained in one or more suitcases, and what the suitcase or suitcases looked like. Events rapidly unfolded. Here, the potentially violent consequences to the law enforcement agents and the public combined with the considerable amount of time required for the Los Angeles agents to gather the information and obtain a judicial officer's approval justify the warrantless search. Based on the totality of the circumstances, we conclude the time was insufficient to obtain a warrant.

B. FISA

Congress enacted FISA in 1978 "to establish procedures for the use of electronic surveillance in gathering foreign intelligence information." *Matter of Kevork*, 788 F.2d 566, 569 (9th Cir. 1986). The government generally must obtain judicial approval before it engages in such surveillance. A specially constituted court, the USFSC, hears the government's application. The Chief Justice of the Supreme Court designates seven United States District Court judges to serve on the court.

On Oct. 21, 1982 the USFSC authorized the FBI to continue its wiretap of Hovsepian's telephone. Defendants argue that by then the FBI's primary purpose for the surveillance had shifted from an intelligence investigation to a criminal investigation. They contend that (1) the FBI was required to obtain authorization under Title III, not FISA; and (2) the district court erred in not allowing a hearing on the issue. We disagree.

Defendants rely on the primary purpose test articulated in *United States v. Truong Dinh Hung*, 629 F.2d 908 (4th Cir. 1980). *Truong* held that the foreign intelligence exception to the warrant requirement applies "only when the surveillance is conducted 'primarily' for foreign intelligence reasons." One other court has applied the primary purpose test. *United States v. Duggan*, 743 F.2d 59, 77 (2d Cir. 1984). Another court has rejected it. *United States v. Falvey*, 540 F. Supp. 1306, 1313-14 (E.D.N.Y. 1982) (distinguishing *Truong*). A third court has declined to decide the issue. *Matter of Kevork*, 634 F. Supp. 1002, 1015 (C.D. Cal. 1985), *aff'd*, 788 F.2d 566 (9th Cir. 1986).

We also decline to decide the issue. We have generally stated that the purpose of the surveillance must be to secure foreign intelligence information. *United States v. Ott*, 827 F.2d 473, 475 (9th Cir. 1987); *Cavanagh*, 807 F.2d at 790-91 ("the purpose of the surveillance is not to ferret out criminal activity but rather to gather intelligence"). Regardless of whether the test is one of purpose or primary purpose, our review of the government's FISA materials convinces us that it is met in this case.

We refuse to draw too fine a distinction between criminal and intelligence investigations. "International terrorism," by definition, requires the investigation of activities that constitute crimes. That the government may later choose to prosecute is irrelevant. FISA contemplates prosecution based on evidence gathered through surveillance. "Surveillances . . . need not stop once conclusive evidence of a crime is obtained, but instead may be extended longer where protective measures other than arrest and prosecution are more appropriate." S. Rep. No. 701, 95th Cong., 2d Sess. 11.

FISA is meant to take into account "the differences between ordinary criminal investigations to gather evidence of specific crimes and foreign counterintelligence investigations to uncover and monitor clandestine activities . . ." *Id.* At no point was this case an ordinary criminal investigation. *See Badia*, 827 F.2d at 1461 (conspiracy to manufacture machine guns and silencers for "Omega-7," an anti-Castro group); *Duggan*, 743 F.2d at 78 (IRA attempt to buy parts for bombs and surface-to-air missiles); *Kevork*, 634 F. Supp. at 1015

(Armenian terrorist plot to assassinate Turkish diplomat); *Falvey*, 540 F. Supp. at 1314 (IRA arms smuggling).

C. Ex Parte In Camera Material

Defendants contend that the district court erred in not disclosing material submitted to the district court *ex parte* and *in camera*. They argue that (1) the court impermissibly balanced the parties' interests under the Classified Information Procedures Act (CIPA); (2) the court erred in accepting an *ex parte in camera* submission without requiring the filing of a public claim of privilege; and (3) the government failed to assert a formal claim to a state secret privilege under *United States v. Reynolds*, 345 U.S. 1 (1953). We again disagree.

Congress passed CIPA to prevent the problem of "graymail," where defendants pressed for the release of classified information to force the government to drop the prosecution. CIPA permits "the trial judge to rule on questions of admissibility involving classified information before introduction of the evidence in open court. This procedure . . . permit[s] the government to ascertain the potential damage to national security of proceeding with a given prosecution before trial." CIPA creates a pretrial procedure for ruling upon the admissibility of classified information. *United States v. Smith*, 780 F.2d 1102, 1105 (4th Cir. 1985) (en banc). *See generally United States v. Collins*, 720 F.2d 1195, 1196-97 (11th Cir. 1983).

[handwritten margin note: purpose of CIPA]

Defendants argue that CIPA forbids balancing national security concerns against defendant's need for documents. Their argument is meritless. Congress intended section 4 to clarify the court's powers under Fed. R. Crim. P. 16(d)(1) to deny or restrict discovery in order to protect national security. On issues of discovery, the court can engage in balancing.

Defendants next contend that the government must file a public claim of privilege before making an *ex parte in camera* submission. The clear language of the statute and its legislative history foreclose that contention. Section 4 allows the court to "permit the United States to make a request . . . in the form of a written statement to be inspected by the court alone." The legislative history emphasizes that "since the government is seeking to withhold classified information from the defendant, an adversary hearing with defense knowledge would defeat the very purpose of the discovery rules." Nowhere does CIPA require the government to file a public claim of privilege before making an *in camera ex parte* submission.

Defendants finally argue that the government failed to make a formal claim of state secret privilege under *Reynolds*. *Reynolds* requires "a formal claim of privilege, lodged by the head of the department which has control over the matter after actual personal consideration by that officer." We assume *arguendo* that the enactment of CIPA does not affect the validity of *Reynolds*. We have examined the government's sealed submission and conclude that it satisfies *Reynolds*.

The district court is AFFIRMED.

NOTES AND QUESTIONS

1. *Sarkissian* presents a classic example of the difficulty of knowing when to intervene in a criminal plot. Can government agents create "exigent circumstances" for a warrantless search merely by waiting for the conspiracy to unfold until it reaches a danger point? How do you feel about the FBI's allowing a suitcase full of dynamite to be checked into the luggage hold of a public passenger plane bound from Los Angeles to Boston? On the other hand, would prosecution at an earlier stage have been viable?

2. The Ninth Circuit says it is "troubled" by Agent Maple's waiting for three hours as events unfolded in Boston without attempting to obtain a search warrant. A somewhat optimistic version of investigative practice prior to 9/11 would have had a prosecutor from the U.S. Attorney's Office in Los Angeles involved as soon as the FBI agents learned of an active plot to use explosives. An affidavit could be drafted and amended as new information became available so that it was ready to go by fax from LA to Boston at a moment's notice. The Boston U.S. Attorney's Office could be prepared to take the affidavit to a magistrate, obtain a signature, and telephone or radio the authorization for search to the agents in the field. With this procedure in place, the warrant could have been issued well before the plane touched down in Boston, allowing special handling of all the luggage on the plane, and thus eliminating much of the danger to the public that the court finds to create exigent circumstances. (After 9/11, the Counter-Terrorism Section of Justice would coordinate any terrorist investigation out of Washington, but the rest of the scenario remains the same.)

This scenario would allow for an effective prosecution while decreasing some of the risk to the public. But, obviously, a procedure of this type entails time and expense, not to mention bureaucratic crossing of turf from FBI to Justice Department lawyers. How realistic do you think this scenario is? How much expense is the public willing to bear to maximize effective prosecutions while minimizing risks to public safety?

From a prosecutor's standpoint, this scenario raises two concerns: 1) Will a court accept the justification for a warrantless search. 2) Are agents flirting with danger by delaying intervention?

UNITED STATES v. DUGGAN (*members of PIRA*)
743 F.2d 59 (2d Cir. 1984)

KEARSE, Circuit Judge:

The principal issues raised in this appeal by alleged agents of the Provisional Irish Republican Army ("PIRA") concern the constitutionality and proper application of the Foreign Intelligence Surveillance Act ("FISA" or the "Act"). [Defendants Andrew Duggan, Eamon Meehan, Gabriel Megahey, and Colm Meehan were convicted of[violations of various federal statutes dealing with interstate shipments of firearms and explosive devices. Each of the defendants received sentences ranging from two to seven years.]

On appeal, all of the defendants contend principally (1) that the district court erred in refusing to suppress evidence obtained through a wiretap pursuant to

Δs Appeal

Δs, members of PIRA, sought guns/explosives/SAMs. FBI investigation ensued including warrantless wiretaps of the residences of 2 of the members.
H: FISA is Const; FISA rules were followed. Affirmed

FISA on the grounds that (a) FISA is unconstitutionally broad and violates the probable cause requirement of the Fourth Amendment, and (b) the government failed to comply with FISA's prerequisites for wire surveillance; (2) that the district court erred in excluding their defense that their actions were taken in reasonable good faith reliance on the apparent authority of one Michael Hanratty, a government informant, to act as an agent of the Central Intelligence Agency ("CIA"); and (3) that the conduct of government agents was so outrageous as to deprive them of due process of law. In addition, Eamon and Colm Meehan contend that the district court erred in rejecting their proffered defense of insanity. We reject the defendants' contentions and affirm the convictions.

I. BACKGROUND

Although none of the defendants challenges the sufficiency of the proof to convict him, we summarize here so much of the trial evidence, taken in the light most favorable to the government, as is necessary to place defendants' major contentions in context. In general the evidence, presented largely through the testimony of Hanratty, videotapes of meetings between PIRA members and undercover law enforcement agents, and tape recordings of telephone conversations involving Megahey, showed defendants as part of a network of men working clandestinely on behalf of PIRA to acquire explosives, weapons, ammunition, and remote-controlled detonation devices in the United States to be exported to Northern Ireland for use in terrorist activities. Megahey, an Irish national who sought political asylum in the United States, was the leader and financier of PIRA operations in the United States. Duggan, an American citizen, was Megahey's assistant in contacting sellers of electronic equipment to be used in remote-controlled bombs and other sophisticated weaponry. Eamon Meehan, under the direction of Megahey, gathered and stored firearms and explosives; Eamon and his brother Colm — both aliens living illegally in the United States – secreted these materials in a shipment of goods bound for Northern Ireland.

A. *The Events*

1. *PIRA Meets Hanratty*

The events that culminated in the June 1982 arrests of the defendants began a year earlier, when Duggan, on the recommendation of an acquaintance, sought out Michael Hanratty, a seller of surveillance and countersurveillance equipment and other electronic items. At this first meeting, Duggan and an associate, Brendon Docherty, a/k/a Brendon Sloan ("Sloan"), identified themselves to Hanratty as members of PIRA, and explained that they sought to purchase equipment for use against the British in Northern Ireland. At a meeting that evening, Duggan, Sloan, and a third companion explained to Hanratty their political views and PIRA's equipment needs. Although Duggan and his associates inquired about the availability of a variety of equipment – including bullet proof vests, electronic tracking systems, and devices to detect the presence of electronic surveillance – their principal interest was in acquiring sophisticated remote-controlled explosive detonators, items that Hanratty could not supply.

Hanratty promptly informed the Federal Bureau of Investigation ("FBI") of these conversations and agreed to provide FBI agents with information gained from any future meetings, in particular the types of electronic equipment Duggan and his associates desired to purchase. Although the agents did not instruct Hanratty to initiate any further contact with Duggan's group, they requested that he attempt to introduce an undercover FBI agent into future dealings if the opportunity arose.

Over the next six months, Hanratty was contacted by Duggan and Sloan several times for the purchase of a variety of equipment that could be used as fusing mechanisms for bombs. In addition, Sloan asked Hanratty if he could supply surface-to-air missiles ("SAMs"), with which PIRA could shoot down British helicopters.

During these meetings Duggan and his associates frequently spoke of consulting their "money man" for the PIRA purchases. In January 1982, Hanratty was summoned by Duggan for his first meeting with the "money man" and was presented to Megahey. Megahey introduced himself as the leader of PIRA operations in the United States, and stated that all PIRA activities in the United States were conducted with his knowledge. Megahey said he had chosen to reveal himself to Hanratty because Hanratty had become a valuable asset to their organization, and he, *inter alia*, reminded Hanratty of the importance of acquiring certain previously ordered devices that were needed as safety mechanisms in the construction of remote-controlled bombs.

2. *PIRA Meets the FBI*

After Hanratty was introduced to Megahey, the government obtained from a judge of the United States Foreign Intelligence Surveillance Court ("FISA Court" and, generally, "FISA Judge") an order authorizing the FBI to conduct electronic surveillance of Megahey's home telephone. The surveillance was initiated on February 10, 1982, continued pursuant to a renewal order obtained on May 6, 1982, and terminated on June 21, 1982, the date of Megahey's arrest by the FBI. The wiretap intercepted several conversations between Megahey and Duggan concerning PIRA activities, and information from the wiretap led the FBI to conduct surveillance of the home of Eamon Meehan.

In March 1982, Hanratty obtained the bomb safety devices requested by Megahey and his associates and delivered them to Duggan under surveillance by the FBI. The switches had been microscopically marked by FBI laboratory personnel for future identification. Two months later these switches, along with weapons and explosive devices, were found hidden in a shipment of goods loaded by Eamon and Colm Meehan into a shipping container bound for Northern Ireland. Agents who had observed the Meehans' activities secured the container, and caused it to be searched by United States Customs Service officials just before it was to be shipped to Northern Ireland.

In the meantime, two of Duggan's associates had reopened with Hanratty the question of obtaining SAMs. Hanratty told them he could not personally supply the missiles but said he knew of a possible source, a man he identified as "Luis." Hanratty described Luis as a Miami-based wheeler-dealer who supplied arms to Central American and other countries. Hanratty later gave the same story to Duggan in response to a question that Hanratty thought referred to Duggan's associates' inquiries about obtaining SAMs. Thereafter, Duggan and Megahey repeatedly asked Hanratty if he had been contacted by Luis.

On May 2, 1982, at the direction of the FBI, Hanratty introduced Duggan to "Enrique," supposedly one of Luis's lieutenants, played by FBI Special Agent Enrique Ghimenti. The FBI videotaped Duggan's discussion with Ghimenti, in which Duggan described himself as a "buffer" who located available weapons for others to purchase. Duggan told Ghimenti that although he was interested in purchasing hand grenades and automatic weapons, his top-priority was the purchase of SAMs. The session concluded with an agreement to arrange another meeting, to be attended by PIRA representatives more experienced in weapons and prices. Duggan later reported to Hanratty that the meeting had gone well, that he believed Enrique and Luis had access to the missiles PIRA sought, and that although Hanratty was not to be involved in the upcoming transactions, he would remain the contact for both sides.

The meeting with PIRA's technical specialists took place in New Orleans and was also videotaped. Duggan introduced his associates and then absented himself from the discussions. Duggan's associates told Enrique and two undercover FBI agents, playing the roles of Luis and his technical advisor, that they were the "provisionals . . . the Irish Republican Army," and stated that "what we want is a weapon which will take down . . . [British] helicopters, . . . warships of the sky." Ultimately, an agreement was reached for PIRA to buy five "Redeye" missiles for $50,000.

The transaction was never consummated, however, as Megahey repeatedly sought to assure himself that PIRA was not dealing with law enforcement agents. (Megahey commented to Enrique that "the only thing we can lose in this is if you're a policeman.") Megahey proposed to have the buyers and sellers exchange hostages until the deal was done and the weapons were in place, reasoning that law enforcement agents would not risk either the loss of their hostage's life or the loss of the missiles. The FBI rejected the hostage proposal, and the proposed purchase of the SAMs was cancelled.

Shortly after these negotiations fell through, the four defendants herein were arrested. They and several of their associates were indicted in a seven-count indictment charging the firearms, explosives, munitions, and conspiracy offenses described at the outset of this opinion.

II. FISA

Enacted in 1978, FISA generally allows a federal officer, if authorized by the President of the United States acting through the Attorney General (or the Acting Attorney General or the Deputy Attorney General) of the United States, to obtain from a judge of the specially created FISA Court an order "approving electronic surveillance of a foreign power or an agent of a foreign power for the purpose of obtaining foreign intelligence information." 50 U.S.C. § 1802(b).

FISA contains several definitions of "foreign power" and "agent of a foreign power." Most pertinently to this case, FISA defines "foreign power" to include "a group engaged in international terrorism or activities in preparation therefor." § 1801(a)(4).

what FISA requires

A federal officer making application for a FISA order approving electronic surveillance must include in his application "the identity, if known, or a description of the target of the electronic surveillance," "a statement of the facts and circumstances relied upon by the applicant to justify his belief that . . . the target of the electronic surveillance is a foreign power or an agent of a foreign power," and a certification by an executive branch designee of the President that the certifying official deems the information sought to be foreign intelligence information and that the purpose of the surveillance is to obtain foreign intelligence information, together with a statement of the basis for the certification that the information sought is the type of foreign intelligence information designated. When the target is a United States person [citizen or resident alien], the government is required to minimize the acquisition and retention of nonpublic available information and to prohibit its dissemination, consistent with the need of the United States to obtain, produce, and disseminate foreign intelligence information, and the application must set out what minimization procedures are proposed.

The FISA Judge is authorized to enter an order approving electronic surveillance if he finds, *inter alia*, that "on the basis of the facts submitted by the applicant there is probable cause to believe that—

1st A protection

(A) the target of the electronic surveillance is a foreign power or an agent of a foreign power: *Provided*, That no United States person may be considered a foreign power or an agent of a foreign power solely upon the basis of activities protected by the first amendment to the Constitution of the United States."

§ 1805(a)(3).

Defendants mount two types of challenge with regard to FISA. First, they contend that the Act is unconstitutional on several grounds. In addition, they contend that even if FISA is not unconstitutional, its requirements were not met in this case.

A. *The Constitutionality of FISA*

Defendants contend that FISA is unconstitutional principally on the grounds that (1) it is so broad as to deprive certain persons of due process of law, (2) it violates the probable cause requirement of the Fourth Amendment, and (3) it deprives nonresident aliens of the equal protection of the law. We find no merit in these contentions.

1. *The Scope of the Act*

Defendants argue that FISA is impermissibly broad in several respects. They point out that foreign intelligence information includes "information with respect to a foreign power . . . that relates to . . . (A) the national defense or the security of the United States; or (B) the conduct of the foreign affairs of the United States." They also point to the definition of an agent of a foreign power as a person, other than a United States person, who

acts for or on behalf of a foreign power which engages in clandestine intelligence activities in the United States contrary to the interests of the United States, when the circumstances of such person's presence in the

United States indicate that such person *may* engage in such activities in the United States,

§ 1801(b)(1)(B) (emphasis added), and to the definition of an agent of a foreign power as any person who

knowingly engages in clandestine intelligence gathering activities for or on behalf of a foreign power, which activities involve or *may* involve a violation of the criminal statutes of the United States,

§ 1801(b)(2)(A) (emphasis added). Defendants argue that the breadth of the above definitions gives the Act unlimited scope and permits the electronic surveillance of persons who "may" be engaging in activities that "may" violate United States law.

Interesting though these arguments may be in the abstract, they have no application to the case at hand. The information relayed by Hanratty to the FBI clearly portrayed Megahey as a member of a "group engaged in international terrorism or activities in preparation therefor;" Megahey was therefore an agent of a foreign power under. There is no suggestion in the record that Megahey was targeted because he was or may have been gathering intelligence. The sections of the Act relied upon by the defendants to show that the Act is impermissibly broad are simply irrelevant to this case. The sections and definitions plainly applicable to Megahey are explicit, unequivocal, and clearly defined.

Nor are we impressed by defendants' argument that insofar as § 1801(e)(2) defines foreign intelligence information as information that "relates to . . . (A) the national defense or the security of the United States; or (B) the conduct of the foreign affairs of the United States" it is impermissibly vague. Section 1801(e)(1)(B) defines foreign intelligence information as "information that relates to . . . the ability of the United States to protect against . . . international terrorism by a foreign power or an agent of a foreign power." Given the information provided by Hanratty, the government plainly had a basis under this section for describing the information sought by surveillance of Megahey, self-proclaimed leader of an international terrorist group, as foreign intelligence information. Thus, even if we thought § 1801(e)(2)'s concepts of national defense, national security, or conduct of foreign affairs to be vague, which we do not, we would find therein no basis for reversing the convictions of these defendants, whose circumstances were governed by an entirely different definition.

2. *The Probable Cause Requirement of the Fourth Amendment*

The Fourth Amendment provides that "no warrants shall issue, but upon probable cause. . . ." Defendants argue principally (1) that the Amendment applies to all proposed surveillances, including those in national security cases, and (2) that even if there were an exception for national security matters, it would not apply to terrorism cases where the objects of the terrorism are entirely outside of the United States. We reject these contentions.

Prior to the enactment of FISA, virtually every court that had addressed the issue had concluded that the President had the inherent power to conduct warrantless electronic surveillance to collect foreign intelligence information, and that such surveillances constituted an exception to the warrant requirement of the Fourth Amendment. The Supreme Court specifically declined to address this issue in *United States v. United States District Court [Keith, J.]*, 407 U.S. 297 (1972) (hereinafter referred to as "*Keith*"), but it had made clear that the requirements of the Fourth Amendment may change when differing governmental interests are at stake, and it observed in *Keith* that the governmental interests presented in national security investigations differ substantially from those presented in traditional criminal investigations.

In *Keith*, the government argued that Title III of the Omnibus Crime Control and Safe Streets Act, 18 U.S.C. §§ 2510 *et seq.* ("Title III"), recognized the constitutional authority of the President to conduct domestic security surveillances without a warrant. The Court rejected this argument, noting that the legislative history made clear that Title III was not intended to legislate with respect to national security surveillances. The Court went on to hold that a warrant was required in *Keith* under the Fourth Amendment; but the implication of its discussion was that the warrant requirement is flexible and that different standards may be compatible with the Fourth Amendment in light of the different purposes and practical considerations of domestic national security surveillances. Thus, the Court observed

> that domestic security surveillance may involve different policy and practical considerations from the surveillance of "ordinary crime." The gathering of security intelligence is often long range and involves the interrelation of various sources and types of information. The exact targets of such surveillance may be more difficult to identify than in surveillance operations against many types of crime specified in Title III. Often, too, the emphasis of domestic intelligence gathering is on the prevention of unlawful activity or the enhancement of the Government's preparedness for some possible future crisis or emergency. Thus, the focus of domestic surveillance may be less precise than that directed against more conventional types of crime.
>
> Different standards [for surveillance involving domestic security] may be compatible with the Fourth Amendment if they are reasonable both in relation to the legitimate need of Government for intelligence information and the protected rights of our citizens. For the warrant application may vary according to the governmental interest to be enforced and the nature of citizen rights deserving protection.

Id. at 322-23.

Against this background, Congress passed FISA to settle what it believed to be the unresolved question of the applicability of the Fourth Amendment warrant requirement to electronic surveillance for foreign intelligence purposes, and to "remove any doubt as to the lawfulness of such surveillance." In constructing this framework, Congress gave close scrutiny to departures from those Fourth Amendment doctrines applicable in the criminal-investigation context in order

> to ensure that the procedures established in [FISA] are reasonable in relation to legitimate foreign counterintelligence requirements and the protected rights of individuals. Their reasonableness depends, in part, upon

an assessment of the difficulties of investigating activities planned, directed, and supported from abroad by foreign intelligence services and foreign-based terrorist groups. The differences between ordinary criminal investigations to gather evidence of specific crimes and foreign counterintelligence investigations to uncover and monitor clandestine activities have been taken into account. Other factors include the international responsibilities of the United States, the duties of the Federal Government to the States in matters involving foreign terrorism, and the need to maintain the secrecy of lawful counterintelligence sources and methods.

Senate Report 95-701, at 14-15, *reprinted in* 1978 U.S. Code Cong. & Ad. News 3973, 3983.

We regard the procedures fashioned in FISA as a constitutionally adequate balancing of the individual's Fourth Amendment rights against the nation's need to obtain foreign intelligence information. The governmental concerns are detailed in the passages quoted above from *Keith* and the legislative history of FISA, and those concerns make reasonable the adoption of prerequisites to surveillance that are less stringent than those precedent to the issuance of a warrant for a criminal investigation. Against this background, the Act requires that the FISA Judge find probable cause to believe that the target is a foreign power or an agent of a foreign power, and that the place at which the electronic surveillance is to be directed is being used or is about to be used by a foreign power or an agent of a foreign power; and it requires him to find that the application meets the requirements of the Act. These requirements make it reasonable to dispense with a requirement that the FISA Judge find probable cause to believe that surveillance will in fact lead to the gathering of foreign intelligence information.[5] Further, if the target is a United States person, the Act requires the FISA Judge to determine that the executive branch's certifications pursuant to § 1804(a)(7) are not clearly erroneous in light of the application as a whole, and to find that the application properly proposes to minimize the intrusion upon the target's privacy.

We conclude that these requirements provide an appropriate balance between the individual's interest in privacy and the government's need to obtain foreign intelligence information, and that FISA does not violate the probable cause requirement of the Fourth Amendment.

4. *Equal Protection*

In several respects FISA treats United States persons, who are defined principally to include United States citizens and resident aliens, differently from non-United States persons.

Although both the Fourth Amendment and the Equal Protection Clause afford protection to all aliens, nothing in either provision prevents Congress from

---

[5] A fortiori we reject defendants' argument that a FISA order may not be issued consistent with the requirements of the Fourth Amendment unless there is a showing of probable cause to believe the target has committed a crime.

adopting standards and procedures that are more beneficial to United States citizens and resident aliens than to nonresident aliens, so long as the differences are reasonable. In *[Mathews v.] Diaz*, the Supreme Court unanimously upheld a federal statute denying aliens the right to enroll in the Medicare program unless they had been admitted for permanent residence and had resided in the United States for five years. The Court noted that

> the fact that all persons, aliens and citizens alike, are protected by the Due Process Clause does not lead to the further conclusion that all aliens are entitled to enjoy all the advantages of citizenship. . . . [A] host of constitutional and statutory provisions rest on the premise that a legitimate distinction between citizens and aliens may justify attributes and benefits for one class not accorded to the other.

Thus, the Court recognized, as it had in the past, that it was appropriate that the political branches of government have the responsibility for regulating the relationship between the United States and aliens, since these matters implicate relations with foreign powers, and "a wide variety of classifications must be defined in the light of changing political and economic circumstances." Accordingly, the Court has adopted a stance of minimal scrutiny respecting federal regulations that contain alienage-based classifications.

In enacting FISA, Congress plainly perceived a need to treat nonresident aliens and United States persons differently. In discussing a provision in an earlier draft of the Act, which provided for a less strict probable cause standard for non-United States persons, Senate Report 95-604 observed that

> where there are compelling considerations of national security, alienage distinctions are clearly lawful. This Committee is aware that less intrusive investigative techniques may not be able to obtain sufficient information about persons visiting here only for a limited time; the additional showing required for United States citizens and permanent resident aliens, therefore, may simply not be possible.

We agree with the district court that the different treatment accorded nonresident aliens under FISA is rationally related to the "Act's purposes of attempting to protect the United States against various types of acts of foreign powers and to acquire information necessary to the national defense or the conduct of foreign affairs." In each instance, the distinctions are justified both by the greater likelihood that those engaged in the type of activities against which FISA seeks to protect the United States will be nonresident aliens, and by the need for the government to be able to act more quickly in situations where the target is unlikely to reside permanently in the United States.

B. *Compliance with the Requirements of FISA*

Defendants contend that, even if FISA is constitutional, the evidence derived from the wiretap should have been suppressed because the provisions of FISA were not complied with, in that (1) the surveillance was conducted as part of a criminal investigation, rather than a national security investigation; (2) the district court erred in failing to disclose the information contained in the FISA applications and orders; and (3) Duggan, although allegedly a "target" of the

FISA surveillance, was not so named in the FISA applications. We reject each of these contentions.

1. *The Alleged Use of FISA Surveillance To Conduct a Criminal Investigation*

Defendants contend that the surveillance of Megahey's telephone was not authorized by FISA because the information was sought as part of a criminal investigation. We see no grounds for concluding that the requirements of FISA were not met.

FISA permits federal officials to obtain orders authorizing electronics surveillance "for the purpose of obtaining foreign intelligence information." The requirement that foreign intelligence information be the primary objective of the surveillance is plain not only from the language of § 1802(b) but also from the requirements in § 1804 as to what the application must contain. The application must contain a certification by a designated official of the executive branch that the purpose of the surveillance is to acquire foreign intelligence information, and the certification must set forth the basis for the certifying official's believe that the information sought is the type of foreign intelligence information described.

Once this certification is made, however, it is, under FISA, subjected to only minimal scrutiny by the courts. Congress deemed it a sufficient check in this regard to require the FISA Judge (1) to find probable cause to believe that the target of the requested surveillance is an agent of a foreign power; (2) to find that the application is complete and in proper form; and (3) when the target is a United States person, to find that the certifications are not "clearly erroneous." The FISA Judge, in reviewing the application, is not to second-guess the executive branch official's certification that the objective of the surveillance is foreign intelligence information. Further, Congress intended that, when a person affected by a FISA surveillance challenges the FISA Court's order, a reviewing court is to have no greater authority to second-guess the executive branch's certifications than has the FISA Judge.[6]

We see no basis for any suggestion in the present case that the application to the FISA Court did not meet the statutory requirement for certifying that the information sought was foreign intelligence information. At the time of the FISA application, the executive branch was aware that PIRA was an international terrorist organization and that Megahey played a leadership role in PIRA activities. In such circumstances, the foreign intelligence value of a FISA wiretap on Megahey's telephone would be plain: he would likely be a prime source of information relating to PIRA membership, goals, methods, and operations. The publicly filed government affidavits in this case make clear that the FISA surveillance was instituted as part of an investigation of international terrorism.

---

[6] FISA cannot, of course, give the government carte blanche to obtain a surveillance order in violation of a target's right to due process, and an application in which the requisite representations were fraudulently made would constitute such a violation. To be entitled to a hearing as to the validity of those presentations, the person challenging the FISA surveillance would be required to make "a substantial preliminary showing that a false statement knowingly and intentionally, or with reckless disregard for the truth, was included" in the application and that the allegedly false statement was "necessary" to the FISA Judge's approval of the application. Defendants have made no such showing here.

main purpose was for intel not info.

Moreover, we have reviewed the *in camera* submissions to the FISA Judge, and we agree with the district court's finding that "the purpose of the surveillance in this case, both initially and throughout, was to secure foreign intelligence information and was not, as [the] defendants assert, directed towards criminal investigation or the institution of a criminal prosecution."

Finally, we emphasize that otherwise valid FISA surveillance is not tainted simply because the government can anticipate that the fruits of such surveillance may later be used, as allowed by § 1806(b), as evidence in a criminal trial. Congress recognized that in many cases the concerns of the government with respect to foreign intelligence will overlap those with respect to law enforcement. Thus, one Senate Report noted that

> intelligence and criminal law enforcement tend to merge in [the area of foreign counterintelligence investigations]. . . .

> Surveillances conducted under [FISA] need not stop once conclusive evidence of a crime is obtained, but instead may be extended longer where protective measures other than arrest and prosecution are more appropriate.

In sum, FISA authorizes surveillance for the purpose of obtaining foreign intelligence information; the information possessed about Megahey involved international terrorism; and the fact that domestic law enforcement concerns may also have been implicated did not eliminate the government's ability to obtain a valid FISA order.

2. *The District Court's Refusal to Disclose the Substance of the FISA Applications*

Defendant's contention that the district court erred in refusing to disclose the substance of the affidavits and certifications that accompanied the FISA applications need not detain us long. Section 1806(f) of FISA provides for *in camera, ex parte* review of the documents where the Attorney General has filed an affidavit stating that disclosure of the FISA applications and orders would harm the national security of the United States. The judge has the discretion to disclose portions of the documents, under appropriate protective procedures, only if he decides that such disclosure is "necessary to make an accurate determination of the legality of the surveillance." Such a need might arise if the judge's initial review revealed potential irregularities such as "possible misrepresentation of fact, vague identification of the persons to be surveilled or surveillance records which include . . . a significant amount of nonforeign intelligence information, calling into question compliance with the minimization standards contained in the order."

3. *The Failure to Name Duggan as a Target of the Surveillance*

Defendants contend that the fruits of the FISA surveillance should be suppressed because Duggan was not named as a target of the surveillance. The import of this argument is, apparently, that because Duggan is a United States person, the preconditions to granting an FISA order allowing surveillance of Duggan would have been more stringent than they were for surveillance of Megahey, a nonresident alien.

The identification requirement imposed by FISA is only that an application for surveillance identify the "target of the electronic surveillance." Once the proper preconditions are established with respect to a particular target, there is no requirement in FISA that all those likely to be overheard engaging in foreign intelligence conversations be named. The consequent differences between the prerequisites for surveillance for crime control purposes and those for surveillance for national security purposes under FISA are reflections of Congress's view of the differing governmental interests to be served.

IV. APPELLANTS' OTHER CONTENTIONS

Defendants make a variety of other arguments, chiefly that (1) the district court should have instructed the jury that it should find the defendants not guilty if it found they had relied on the apparent authority of Hanratty as an agent of the CIA; (2) the conduct of the government in conducting the investigation was so outrageous that it deprived them of due process of law; and (3) the court erred in making various evidentiary rulings.[9] We find merit in none of them.

A. *The Mistake of Law Defense*

Defendants contend that the district court erred in refusing to give their proposed jury instruction allowing them a defense for reasonable good faith reliance on apparent authority, based on their alleged mistaken belief that Hanratty had apparent authority to sanction their gun-running activities. We conclude that the court properly refused to give the instruction since defendants had failed to demonstrate a basis warranting submission of this requested charge to the jury.

The only evidence presented by defendants to justify their reliance on Hanratty's apparent authority is their testimony that Hanratty represented himself to be a CIA agent and showed Duggan and Megahey a white laminated card with "Central Intelligence Agency" printed on it, and their testimony that Sloan had "checked Hanratty out." No objective evidence was presented regarding Hanratty's purported CIA claim and there was no corroboration of defendants' claims about Hanratty's alleged assertions. The defendants knew Hanratty for only three weeks before they began dealing with him, they lacked personal knowledge of his claimed status, and they sought no independent verification that he was a CIA agent.

Nor was any reasonable legal basis shown for defendants' professed belief that Hanratty had authority to sanction such plainly unlawful activity as international trafficking in firearms and explosives. Indeed, Megahey acknowledged, on cross-examination, that he was aware that CIA operatives had been sought on criminal charges, despite their CIA background, for engaging in the same conduct the defendants attributed to Hanratty.

---

[9] Among their other arguments, defendants assert that the district court should have suppressed the evidence, obtained through the search by customs officials at Port Newark, New Jersey, of the shipping container loaded with weapons and electronics equipment by Eamon and Colm Meehan. [S]ince the containers were scheduled to be shipped from port imminently, the search was authorized under the border-search exception to the Fourth Amendment.

In sum, we agree with the district court that the defendants failed to establish that they were entitled to a jury instruction on any defense based on an exception to the general principle that a mistake of law is no defense.

B. The "Outrageous Government Behavior" Defense

Defendants argue that the behavior of the government in the investigation of this case was so outrageous and shocking as to deprive them of due process of law. They contend chiefly that Hanratty, the FBI informant, played on their emotional and psychological sensitivities to the situation in Northern Ireland in a successful effort to coerce them into committing unlawful acts. We find these contentions without merit.

The Supreme Court has noted the possibility that a due process violation grounded in outrageous government conduct might be available even if the defendant, because of his predisposition, could not establish an entrapment defense.

We have rarely sustained due process claims concerning government investigative conduct, stressing that the conduct involved must be "most egregious," and "'so repugnant and excessive' as to shock the conscience." Thus, we have upheld against due process challenges drug convictions resulting from transactions initiated by government informants using government-supplied drugs, and convictions in the Abscam cases, where government operatives proposed various unlawful schemes.

[I]n this case Duggan has admitted that it was he who sought out Hanratty. Duggan was not introduced to undercover FBI agents until after he and Megahey repeatedly asked Hanratty about his gun-running acquaintance, "Luis"; and all other initiatives came from the defendants as well. The overwhelming evidence presented through tape, videotape, and the testimony of the government witnesses supports the district court's refusal to grant defendants' motion to dismiss on this due process argument.

We have considered all of defendants' remaining contentions and find them to be without merit.

CONCLUSION

The judgments of conviction are affirmed.

NOTES AND QUESTIONS

1. Several aspects of FISA, which is a complicated statutory scheme at first glance, may make the structure more clear:

   a. Under FISA, agents do not even need a court order to engage in electronic surveillance of communications or premises of foreign powers if the Attorney General certifies that there is "no substantial likelihood that the surveillance will acquire the contents of any communication to which a United States person is a party."

   b. To obtain a court order authorizing electronic surveillance of foreign agents, it is not necessary for the investigator to allege probable cause of a criminal violation; it is enough that there is probable cause to believe that the "target of the surveillance is a foreign power or agent of a foreign power," that "a significant purpose of the surveillance is to obtain" information helpful for protection of national security, and that acceptable "minimization procedures" are in place. Some observers believe that the order could be called a warrant, but the terminology helps distinguish it from a warrant based on probable cause to believe that a crime has been committed by a specified person.

c. If information acquired in a FISA surveillance is subsequently used in a criminal prosecution, the defendant may make a motion to suppress on the basis that the information was not lawfully acquired or that the surveillance did not conform to the court order. In this instance, the government may provide the court *ex parte* and *in camera* with "such materials relating to the surveillance as may be necessary to determine whether the surveillance was lawfully authorized and conducted."

d. Similar procedures and criteria apply with regard to physical searches of premises.

2. Prior to the USA PATRIOT Act, passed in October 2001, the "purpose" language required that "the purpose" of the surveillance be acquisition of foreign intelligence information. In ruling on motions to suppress, trial courts frequently had to assess whether the purpose of the surveillance was truly for intelligence purposes rather than to obtain evidence for a prosecution. Under the minimization guidelines of the Justice Department, a "wall" was erected between intelligence and prosecution so that the transfer of information from an intelligence operation to prosecution required approval of higher officials. As the courts struggled with this issue, they were split on whether "the purpose" meant "sole purpose," "dominant purpose," or "any purpose." The 2001 change to "a significant purpose" was designed to resolve this controversy, but it also could have the effect of reducing the level of judicial review over the application. The FISA Court of Review opinion below addresses these issues.

3. It may be helpful at this stage to revisit the prosecutions in *Salameh* and *Rahman* with the fourth amendment issues in mind. *Sarkissian* and *Duggan* are both examples of how a FISA surveillance can generate evidence for a criminal prosecution.

4. Bearing in mind the "purpose" requirement, a tragic and interesting example is *United States v. Isa*, 923 F.2d 1300 (8th Cir. 1991), in which a FISA surveillance resulted in electronic taping of the target's murdering of his 16-year-old daughter. When the Attorney General decided to turn the tapes over to the state for prosecution of the murder, the U.S. sought a declaratory judgment in federal court of the legality under federal law of using that evidence in the state prosecution. The information on which the FISA order was based was presented to the court *ex parte* and *in camera* to prevent disclosure of the reasons for surveilling the target. The result of the federal court's ruling on the validity of the surveillance would then be to prevent public disclosure of that information in a subsequent state hearing to suppress the evidence.

5. The operations of the FISC are conducted in a highly secure controlled-access room within the building of the Justice Department in Washington, soon

to be replaced by the court's own facility. Given the feeling of being "special" that is attached to appointment to this court, and the "glamor" of being on the inside of important proceedings, isn't there a significant likelihood that the judges will be "co-opted" to the point of view of the government in these proceedings? Most criticisms of the PATRIOT Act amendments to FISA have argued against its search and seizure provisions almost as if there were no judicial review of FBI requests for FISA orders. On the other hand, Article III judges tend to be fiercely proud of the independent status of the U.S. judiciary, and it is very difficult to know how these procedures will intrude into that feeling of independence.

6. *United States v. Cavanagh*, 807 F.2d 787 (9th Cir. 1987), held that the FISA designation of judges is not unconstitutional even though they serve limited terms because they are still Article III judges and serve an Article III purpose.

IN RE SEALED CASE NO. 02-001
310 F.3d 717 (FIS Ct. Review 2002)

On Motions for Review of Orders of the
United States Foreign Intelligence Surveillance Court.

Before: GUY, Senior Circuit Judge, Presiding; SILBERMAN and LEAVY, Senior Circuit Judges.

PER CURIAM:

This is the first appeal from the Foreign Intelligence Surveillance Court to the Court of Review since the passage of the Foreign Intelligence Surveillance Act (FISA) in 1978. This appeal is brought by the United States from a FISA court surveillance order which imposed certain restrictions on the government. Since the government is the only party to FISA proceedings, we have accepted briefs filed by the American Civil Liberties Union (ACLU)[1] and the National Association of Criminal Defense Lawyers (NACDL) as *amici curiae*.

Not surprisingly this case raises important questions of statutory interpretation, and constitutionality. After a careful review of the briefs filed by the government and *amici*, we conclude that FISA, as amended by the Patriot Act, supports the government's position, and that the restrictions imposed by the FISA court are not required by FISA or the Constitution. We therefore remand for further proceedings in accordance with this opinion.

I.

The court's decision from which the government appeals imposed certain requirements and limitations accompanying an order authorizing electronic surveillance of an "agent of a foreign power" as defined in FISA. There is no disagreement between the government and the FISA court as to the propriety of the electronic surveillance; the court found that the government had shown

---

[1] Joining the ACLU on its brief are the Center for Democracy and Technology, Center for National Security Studies, Electronic Privacy Information Center, and Electronic Frontier Foundation.

probable cause to believe that the target is an agent of a foreign power and otherwise met the basic requirements of FISA. The government's application for a surveillance order contains detailed information to support its contention that the target, who is a United States person, is aiding, abetting, or conspiring with others in international terrorism.[3] The FISA court authorized the surveillance, but imposed certain restrictions, which the government contends are neither mandated nor authorized by FISA. Particularly, the court ordered that

> law enforcement officials shall not make recommendations to intelligence officials concerning the initiation, operation, continuation or expansion of FISA searches or surveillances. Additionally, the FBI and the Criminal Division [of the Department of Justice] shall ensure that law enforcement officials do not direct or control the use of the FISA procedures to enhance criminal prosecution, and that advice intended to preserve the option of a criminal prosecution does not inadvertently result in the Criminal Division's directing or controlling the investigation using FISA searches and surveillances toward law enforcement objectives.

To ensure the Justice Department followed these strictures the court also fashioned what the government refers to as a "chaperone requirement"; that a unit of the Justice Department, the Office of Intelligence Policy and Review (OIPR) (composed of 31 lawyers and 25 support staff), "be invited" to all meetings between the FBI and the Criminal Division involving consultations for the purpose of coordinating efforts "to investigate or protect against foreign attack or other grave hostile acts, sabotage, international terrorism, or clandestine intelligence activities by foreign powers or their agents." If representatives of OIPR are unable to attend such meetings, "OIPR shall be apprized of the substance of the meetings forthwith in writing so that the Court may be notified at the earliest opportunity."

The opinion was issued after an oral argument before all of the then-serving FISA district judges and clearly represents the views of all those judges. We think it fair to say, however, that the May 17 opinion of the FISA court does not clearly set forth the basis for its decision. It appears to proceed from the assumption that FISA constructed a barrier between counterintelligence/intelligence officials and law enforcement officers in the Executive Branch — indeed, it uses the word "wall" popularized by certain commentators (and journalists) to describe that supposed barrier. Yet the opinion does not support that assumption with any relevant language from the statute.

The "wall" emerges from the court's implicit interpretation of FISA. The court apparently believes it can approve applications for electronic surveillance only if the government's objective is *not* primarily directed toward criminal prosecution of the foreign agents for their foreign intelligence activity. But the court neither refers to any FISA language supporting that view, nor does it reference the Patriot Act amendments, which the government contends

---

[3] The bracketed information is classified and has been redacted from the public version of the opinion.

specifically altered FISA to make clear that an application could be obtained even if criminal prosecution is the primary counter mechanism.

Instead the court relied for its imposition of the disputed restrictions on its statutory authority to approve "minimization procedures" designed to prevent the acquisition, retention, and dissemination within the government of material gathered in an electronic surveillance that is unnecessary to the government's need for foreign intelligence information.

II.

The government makes two main arguments. The first, it must be noted, was not presented to the FISA court; indeed, insofar as we can determine it has never previously been advanced either before a court or Congress.[6] That argument is that the supposed pre-Patriot Act limitation in FISA that restricts the government's intention to use foreign intelligence information in criminal prosecutions is an illusion; it finds no support in either the language of FISA or its legislative history. The government does recognize that several courts of appeals, while upholding the use of FISA surveillances, have opined that FISA may be used only if the government's primary purpose in pursuing foreign intelligence information is not criminal prosecution, but the government argues that those decisions, which did not carefully analyze the statute, were incorrect in their statements, if not incorrect in their holdings.

Alternatively, the government contends that even if the primary purpose test was a legitimate construction of FISA prior to the passage of the Patriot Act, that Act's amendments to FISA eliminate that concept. And as a corollary, the government insists the FISA court's construction of the minimization procedures is far off the mark both because it is a misconstruction of those provisions *per se*, as well as an end run around the specific amendments in the Patriot Act designed to deal with the real issue underlying this case. The government, moreover, contends that the FISA court's restrictions, which the court described as minimization procedures, are so intrusive into the operation of the Department of Justice as to exceed the constitutional authority of Article III judges.

The government's brief, and its supplementary brief requested by this court, also set forth its view that the primary purpose test is not required by the Fourth Amendment. The ACLU and NACDL argue, *inter alia*, the contrary; that the statutes are unconstitutional unless they are construed as prohibiting the government from obtaining approval of an application under FISA if its "primary purpose" is criminal prosecution.

The 1978 FISA

We turn first to the statute as enacted in 1978. It authorizes a judge on the FISA court to grant an application for an order approving electronic surveillance

---

[6] Since proceedings before the FISA court and the Court of Review are ex parte – not adversary – we can entertain an argument supporting the government's position not presented to the lower court.

FISA language

to "obtain foreign intelligence information" if "there is probable cause to believe that . . . the target of the electronic surveillance is a foreign power or an agent of a foreign power," and that "each of the facilities or places at which the surveillance is directed is being used, or is about to be used, by a foreign power or an agent of a foreign power." 50 U.S.C. § 1805(a)(3).

The definition of an agent of a foreign power, if it pertains to a U.S. person (which is the only category relevant to this case), is closely tied to criminal activity. The term includes any person who "knowingly engages in clandestine intelligence gathering activities . . . which activities involve or may involve a violation of the *criminal statutes* of the United States," or "knowingly engages in sabotage or international terrorism, or activities that are in preparation therefor." §§ 1801(b)(2)(A), (C) (emphasis added). International terrorism refers to activities that "involve violent acts or acts dangerous to human life that are a violation of the *criminal laws* of the United States or of any State, or that would be a *criminal violation* if committed within the jurisdiction of the United States or any State." § 1801(c)(1) (emphasis added). Sabotage means activities that "involve a violation of chapter 105 of [the criminal code], or that would involve such a violation if committed against the United States." § 1801(d). For purposes of clarity in this opinion we will refer to the crimes referred to in section 1801(a)-(e) as foreign intelligence crimes.

In light of these definitions, it is quite puzzling that the Justice Department, at some point during the 1980s, began to read the statute as limiting the Department's ability to obtain FISA orders if it intended to prosecute the targeted agents – even for foreign intelligence crimes. To be sure, section 1804, which sets forth the elements of an application for an order, required a national security official in the Executive Branch – typically the Director of the FBI – to certify that "the purpose" of the surveillance is to obtain foreign intelligence information (amended by the Patriot Act to read "a significant purpose"). But as the government now argues, the definition of foreign intelligence information includes evidence of crimes such as espionage, sabotage or terrorism. Indeed, it is virtually impossible to read the 1978 FISA to exclude from its purpose the prosecution of foreign intelligence crimes, most importantly because, as we have noted, the definition of an agent of a foreign power – if he or she is a U.S. person – is grounded on criminal conduct.

It does not seem that FISA, at least as originally enacted, even contemplated that the FISA court would inquire into the government's purpose in seeking foreign intelligence information. Section 1805, governing the standards a FISA court judge is to use in determining whether to grant a surveillance order, requires the judge to find that

> the application which has been filed contains all statements and certifications required by section 1804 of this title and, if the target is a United States person, the certification or certifications are not clearly erroneous on the basis of the statement made under section 1804(a)(7)(E) of this title and any other information furnished under section 1804(d) of this title.

FISA requires

And section 1804(a)(7)(E) requires that the application include "a statement of the basis of the certification that (i) the information sought is the type of foreign intelligence information designated; and (ii) such information cannot reasonably be obtained by normal investigative techniques." That language certainly suggests that, aside from the probable cause, identification of facilities, and minimization procedures the judge is to determine and approve (also set forth in section 1805), the only other issues are whether electronic surveillance is necessary to obtain the information and whether the information sought is actually foreign intelligence information – not the government's proposed use of that information.

The government argues persuasively that arresting and prosecuting terrorist agents of, or spies for, a foreign power may well be the best technique to prevent them from successfully continuing their terrorist or espionage activity. The government might wish to surveil the agent for some period of time to discover other participants in a conspiracy or to uncover a foreign power's plans, but typically at some point the government would wish to apprehend the agent and it might be that only a prosecution would provide sufficient incentives for the agent to cooperate with the government. Indeed, the threat of prosecution might be sufficient to "turn the agent." It would seem that the Congress actually anticipated the government's argument and explicitly approved it. The House Report said:

The info can be used for crim pros.

> *How this information may be used* "to protect" against clandestine intelligence activities *is not prescribed* by the definition of foreign intelligence information, although, of course, how it is used may be affected by minimization procedures . . . . And no information acquired pursuant to this bill could be used for other than lawful purposes . . . . *Obviously, use of "foreign intelligence information" as evidence in a criminal trial is one way the Government can lawfully protect against clandestine intelligence activities, sabotage, and international terrorism.* The bill, therefore, explicitly recognizes that information which is evidence of crimes involving [these activities] can be sought, retained, and used pursuant to this bill.

The Senate Report is on all fours:

> U.S. persons may be authorized targets, and the surveillance is part of an investigative process often designed to protect against the commission of serious crimes such as espionage, sabotage, assassination, kidnaping, and terrorist acts committed by or on behalf of foreign powers. *Intelligence and criminal law enforcement tend to merge in this area.* . . . Surveillances conducted under [FISA] need not stop once conclusive evidence of a crime is obtained, but instead may be extended longer where protective measures other than arrest and prosecution are more appropriate.

Congress was concerned about the government's use of FISA surveillance to obtain information not truly intertwined with the government's efforts to protect against threats from foreign powers. Accordingly, the certification of purpose under section 1804(a)(7)(B) served to

Certification Req.

> prevent the practice of targeting, for example, a foreign power for electronic surveillance when the true purpose of the surveillance is to gather

information about an individual for other than foreign intelligence purposes. It is also designed to make explicit that the sole purpose of such surveillance is to secure "foreign intelligence information," as defined, and not to obtain some other type of information.

But Congress did not impose any restrictions on the government's use of the foreign intelligence information to prosecute agents of foreign powers for foreign intelligence crimes. Admittedly, the House, at least in one statement, noted that FISA surveillances "are not primarily for the purpose of gathering evidence of a crime. They are to obtain foreign intelligence information, which when it concerns United States persons must be necessary to important national concerns." That, however, was an observation, not a proscription. And the House as well as the Senate made clear that prosecution is one way to combat foreign intelligence crimes.

The origin of what the government refers to as the false dichotomy between foreign intelligence information that is evidence of foreign intelligence crimes and that which is not appears to have been a Fourth Circuit case decided in 1980. *United States v. Truong Dinh Hung,* 629 F.2d 908 (4th Cir. 1980). That case, however, involved an electronic surveillance carried out prior to the passage of FISA and predicated on the President's executive power. In approving the district court's exclusion of evidence obtained through a warrantless surveillance subsequent to the point in time when the government's investigation became "primarily" driven by law enforcement objectives, the court held that the Executive Branch should be excused from securing a warrant only when "the object of the search or the surveillance is a foreign power, its agents or collaborators," and "the surveillance is conducted 'primarily' for foreign intelligence reasons." Targets must "receive the protection of the warrant requirement if the government is primarily attempting to put together a criminal prosecution." Although the *Truong* court acknowledged that "almost all foreign intelligence investigations are in part criminal" ones, it rejected the government's assertion that "if surveillance is to any degree directed at gathering foreign intelligence, the executive may ignore the warrant requirement of the Fourth Amendment."

Several circuits have followed *Truong* in applying similar versions of the "primary purpose" test, despite the fact that *Truong* was not a FISA decision. (It was an interpretation of the Constitution, in the context of measuring the boundaries of the President's inherent executive authority, and we discuss *Truong's* constitutional analysis at length in Section III of this opinion.) In one of the first major challenges to a FISA search, *United States v. Megahey,* 553 F. Supp. 1180 (E.D.N.Y. 1982), *aff'd sub nom. United States v. Duggan,* 743 F.2d 59 (2d Cir. 1984), the district court acknowledged that while Congress clearly viewed arrest and prosecution as one of the possible outcomes of a FISA investigation, surveillance under FISA would nevertheless be "appropriate only if foreign intelligence surveillance is the Government's primary purpose." Six months earlier, another judge in the same district had held that the *Truong* analysis did not govern FISA cases, since a FISA order was a warrant that met Fourth Amendment standards. *United States v. Falvey,* 540 F. Supp. 1306, 1314 (E.D.N.Y. 1982). *Falvey,* however, was apparently not appealed and *Megahey* was. The Second Circuit, without reference to *Falvey*, and importantly in the context of affirming the conviction, approved *Megahey*'s finding that the surveillance was not "directed towards criminal investigation or the institution of a criminal prosecution." Implicitly then, the Second Circuit endorsed the *Megahey* dichotomy. Two other circuits, the Fourth and the Eleventh, have similarly approved district court findings that a surveillance was primarily for foreign intelligence purposes without any discussion [of] the validity of the dichotomy. *See United States v. Pelton*, 835 F.2d 1067, 1075-76 (4th Cir. 1987); *United States v. Badia,* 827 F.2d 1458, 1464 (11th Cir. 1987).

Then, the First Circuit, seeing *Duggan* as following *Truong*, explicitly interpreted FISA's purpose wording in section 1804(a)(7)(B) to mean that "although evidence obtained under FISA subsequently may be used in criminal prosecutions, the investigation of criminal activity cannot be the primary purpose of the surveillance." *United States v. Johnson*, 952 F.2d 565, 572 (1st Cir. 1991). Notably, however, the Ninth Circuit has refused

to draw too fine a distinction between criminal and intelligence investigations. 'International terrorism,' by definition, requires the investigation of activities that constitute crimes. That the government may later choose to prosecute is irrelevant. . . . FISA is meant to take into account 'the differences between ordinary criminal investigations to gather evidence of specific crimes and foreign counterintelligence investigations to uncover and monitor clandestine activities.'

United States v. Sarkissian, 841 F.2d 959, 964 (9th Cir. 1988).

Neither *Duggan* nor *Johnson* tied the "primary purpose" test to *actual* statutory language. It is almost as if *Duggan*, and particularly *Johnson*, assume that the government seeks foreign intelligence information (counterintelligence) for its own sake – to expand its pool of knowledge – because there is no discussion of how the government would use that information outside criminal prosecutions. That is not to say that the government could have no other use for that information. The government's overriding concern is to stop or frustrate the agent's or the foreign power's activity by any means, but if one considers the actual ways in which the government would foil espionage or terrorism it becomes apparent that criminal prosecution analytically cannot be placed easily in a separate response category. It may well be that the government itself, in an effort to conform to district court holdings, accepted the dichotomy it now contends is false. Be that as it may, since the cases that "adopt" the dichotomy do affirm district court opinions permitting the introduction of evidence gathered under a FISA order, there was not much need for the courts to focus on the issue with which we are confronted.

In sum, we think that the FISA as passed by Congress in 1978 clearly did *not* preclude or limit the government's use or proposed use of foreign intelligence information, which included evidence of certain kinds of criminal activity, in a criminal prosecution. In order to understand the FISA court's decision, however, it is necessary to trace developments and understandings within the Justice Department post-*Truong* as well as after the passage of the Patriot Act. As we have noted, some time in the 1980s – the exact moment is shrouded in historical mist – the Department applied the *Truong* analysis to an interpretation of the FISA statute. What is clear is that in 1995 the Attorney General adopted "Procedures for Contacts Between the FBI and the Criminal Division Concerning Foreign Intelligence and Foreign Counterintelligence Investigations."

Apparently to avoid running afoul of the primary purpose test used by some courts, the 1995 Procedures limited contacts between the FBI and the Criminal Division in cases where FISA surveillance or searches were being conducted by the FBI for foreign intelligence (FI) or foreign counterintelligence (FCI) purposes. The procedures state that "the FBI and Criminal Division should ensure that advice intended to preserve the option of a criminal prosecution does not inadvertently result in either the fact or the appearance of the Criminal Division's *directing or controlling* the FI or FCI investigation toward law enforcement objectives." Although these procedures provided for significant information sharing and coordination between criminal and FI or FCI investigations, based at least in part on the "directing or controlling" language, they eventually came to be narrowly interpreted within the Department of Justice, and most particularly by OIPR, as requiring OIPR to act as a "wall" to prevent the FBI intelligence officials from communicating with the Criminal Division regarding ongoing FI or FCI investigations. *See Final Report of the Attorney General's Review Team on the Handling of the Los Alamos National Laboratory Investigation* (AGRT Report), Chapter 20 at 721-34 (May 2000). Thus, the focus became the nature of the underlying investigation, rather than the general purpose of the surveillance. Once prosecution of the target was being considered, the procedures, as interpreted by OIPR in light of the case law, prevented the Criminal Division from providing any meaningful advice to the FBI.

The Department's attitude changed somewhat after the May 2000 report by the Attorney General and a July 2001 Report by the General Accounting Office both concluded that the Department's concern over how the FISA court or other federal courts might interpret the primary purpose test has inhibited necessary coordination between intelligence and law enforcement officials. In August 2001, the Deputy Attorney General issued a memorandum clarifying Department of Justice policy governing intelligence sharing and establishing additional requirements. But it does not appear that the Department thought of these internal procedures as "minimization procedures" required under FISA. Nevertheless, the FISA court was aware that the procedures were being followed by the Department and apparently adopted elements of them in certain cases.

The Patriot Act and the FISA Court's Decision

The passage of the Patriot Act altered and to some degree muddied the landscape. In October 2001, Congress amended FISA to change "the purpose" language in 1804(a)(7)(B) to "a significant purpose." It also added a provision allowing "Federal officers who conduct electronic surveillance to acquire foreign intelligence information" to "consult with Federal law enforcement officers to coordinate efforts to investigate or protect against" attack or other grave hostile acts, sabotage or international terrorism, or clandestine intelligence activities, by foreign powers or their agents. § 1806(k)(1). And such coordination "shall not preclude" the government's certification that a significant purpose of the surveillance is to obtain foreign intelligence information, or the issuance of an order authorizing the surveillance. § 1806(k)(2). Although the Patriot Act amendments to FISA expressly sanctioned consultation and coordination between intelligence and law enforcement officials, in response to the first applications filed by OIPR under those amendments, in November 2001, the FISA court for the first time adopted the 1995 Procedures, as augmented by the January 2000 and August 2001 Procedures, as "minimization procedures" to apply in all cases before the court.

The Attorney General interpreted the Patriot Act quite differently. On March 6, 2002, the Attorney General approved new "Intelligence Sharing Procedures" to implement the Act's amendments to FISA. The 2002 Procedures supersede prior procedures and were designed to permit the complete exchange of information and advice between intelligence and law enforcement officials. They eliminated the "direction and control" test and allowed the exchange of advice between the FBI, OIPR, and the Criminal Division regarding "the initiation, operation, continuation, or expansion of FISA searches or surveillance." On March 7, 2002, the government filed a motion with the FISA court, noting that the Department of Justice had adopted the 2002 Procedures and proposing to follow those procedures in all matters before the court. The government also asked the FISA court to vacate its orders adopting the prior procedures as minimization procedures in all cases and imposing special "wall" procedures in certain cases.

Unpersuaded by the Attorney General's interpretation of the Patriot Act, the court ordered that the 2002 Procedures be adopted, *with modifications*, as minimization procedures to apply in all cases. The court emphasized that the definition of minimization procedures had not been amended by the Patriot Act, and reasoned that the 2002 Procedures "cannot be used by the government to amend the Act in ways Congress has not." The court explained:

> Given our experience in FISA surveillances and searches, we find that these provisions, particularly those which authorize criminal prosecutors to advise FBI intelligence officials on the initiation, operation, continuation or expansion of FISA's intrusive seizures, are designed to enhance the acquisition, retention and dissemination of *evidence for law enforcement purposes*, *instead* of being consistent with the need of the United States to "obtain, produce, and disseminate *foreign intelligence information*" . . . as mandated in § 1801(h) and § 1821(4).

May 17, 2001 Opinion at 22 (emphasis by the FISA court).[18]

---

[18] In describing its experience with FISA searches and surveillance, the FISA court's opinion makes reference to certain applications each of which contained an FBI agent's affidavit that was inaccurate, particularly with respect to assertions regarding the information shared with criminal investigators and prosecutors. Although we do not approve any misrepresentations that may have taken place, our understanding is that those affidavits were submitted during 1997 through early 2001, and therefore any inaccuracies may have been caused in part by the confusion within the Department of Justice over implementation of the 1995 Procedures, as augmented in January 2000. In any event, while the issue of the candor of the FBI agent(s) involved properly remains under

Essentially, the FISA court took portions of the Attorney General's augmented 1995 Procedures – adopted to deal with the primary purpose standard – and imposed them generically as minimization procedures. In doing so, the FISA court erred. It did not provide any constitutional basis for its action – we think there is none – and misconstrued the main statutory provision on which it relied. The court mistakenly categorized the augmented 1995 Procedures as FISA minimization procedures and then compelled the government to utilize a modified version of those procedures in a way that is clearly inconsistent with the statutory purpose.

As is evident from the face of section 1801(h), minimization procedures are designed to protect, as far as reasonable, against the acquisition, retention, and dissemination of non-public information which is not foreign intelligence information. If the data is not foreign intelligence information as defined by the statute, the procedures are to ensure that the government does not use the information to identify the target or third party, unless such identification is necessary to properly understand or assess the foreign intelligence information that is collected. By minimizing *acquisition*, Congress envisioned that, for example, "where a switchboard line is tapped but only one person in the organization is the target, the interception should probably be discontinued where the target is not a party" to the communication. By minimizing *retention*, Congress intended that "information acquired, which is not necessary for obtaining[,] producing, or disseminating foreign intelligence information, be destroyed where feasible." Furthermore, "even with respect to information needed for an approved purpose, *dissemination* should be restricted to those officials with a need for such information."

The minimization procedures allow, however, the retention and dissemination of non-foreign intelligence information which is evidence of *ordinary crimes* for preventative or prosecutorial purposes. Therefore, if through interceptions or searches, evidence of "a serious crime totally unrelated to intelligence matters" is incidentally acquired, the evidence is "not . . . required to be destroyed." As we have explained, under the 1978 Act, "evidence of certain crimes like espionage would itself constitute 'foreign intelligence information,' as defined, because it is necessary to protect against clandestine intelligence activities by foreign powers or their agents." In light of these purposes of the minimization procedures, there is simply no basis for the FISA court's reliance on section 1801(h) to limit criminal prosecutors' ability to advise FBI intelligence officials on the initiation, operation, continuation, or expansion of FISA surveillances to obtain foreign intelligence information, even if such information includes evidence of a foreign intelligence crime.

The FISA court's decision and order not only misinterpreted and misapplied minimization procedures it was entitled to impose, but as the government argues persuasively, the FISA court may well have exceeded the constitutional bounds

---

investigation by the Department of Justice's Office of Professional Responsibility, the issue whether the wall between the FBI and the Criminal Division required by the FISA court has been maintained is moot in light of this court's opinion.

that restrict an Article III court. The FISA court asserted authority to govern the internal organization and investigative procedures of the Department of Justice which are the province of the Executive Branch (Article II) and the Congress (Article I). Subject to statutes dealing with the organization of the Justice Department, however, the Attorney General has the responsibility to determine how to deploy personnel resources.

We also think the refusal by the FISA court to consider the legal significance of the Patriot Act's crucial amendments was error. The government, in order to avoid the requirement of meeting the "primary purpose" test, specifically sought an amendment to section 1804(a)(7)(B) which had required a certification "that the purpose of the surveillance is to obtain foreign intelligence information" so as to delete the article "the" before "purpose" and replace it with "a." The government made perfectly clear to Congress why it sought the legislative change. Congress, although accepting the government's explanation for the need for the amendment, adopted language which it perceived as not giving the government quite the degree of modification it wanted. Accordingly, section 1804(a)(7)(B)'s wording became "that *a significant* purpose of the surveillance is to obtain foreign intelligence information." There is simply no question, however, that Congress was keenly aware that this amendment relaxed a requirement that the government show that its primary purpose was other than criminal prosecution.

No committee reports accompanied the Patriot Act but the floor statements make congressional intent quite apparent. The Senate Judiciary Committee Chairman Senator Leahy acknowledged that "protection against these foreign-based threats by any lawful means is within the scope of the definition of 'foreign intelligence information,' and the use of FISA to gather evidence for the enforcement of these laws was contemplated in the enactment of FISA." To be sure, some Senate Judiciary Committee members including the Chairman were concerned that the amendment might grant too much authority to the Justice Department – and the FISA court. Senator Leahy indicated that the change to significant purpose was "very problematic" since it would "make it easier for the FBI to use a FISA wiretap to obtain information where the Government's most important motivation for the wiretap is for use in a criminal prosecution." Therefore he suggested that "it will be up to the courts to determine how far law enforcement agencies may use FISA for criminal investigation and prosecution *beyond* the scope of the statutory definition of 'foreign intelligence information.'" But the only dissenting vote against the act was cast by Senator Feingold. Senator Feingold recognized that the change to "significant purpose" meant that the government could obtain a FISA warrant "even if the primary purpose is a criminal investigation," and was concerned that this development would not respect the protections of the Fourth Amendment.

In sum, there can be no doubt as to Congress' intent in amending section 1804(a)(7)(B). Indeed, it went further to emphasize its purpose in breaking down barriers between criminal law enforcement and intelligence (or counterintelligence) gathering by adding section 1806(k):

(k) Consultation with Federal law enforcement officer

(1) Federal officers who conduct electronic surveillance to acquire foreign intelligence information under this title may consult with Federal law enforcement officers to coordinate efforts to investigate or protect against

(A) actual or potential attack or other grave hostile acts of a foreign power or an agent of a foreign power; or

(B) sabotage or international terrorism by a foreign power or an agent of a foreign power; or

(C) clandestine intelligence activities by an intelligence service or network of a foreign power or by an agent of a foreign power.

(2) Coordination authorized under paragraph (1) shall not preclude the certification required by section [1804](a)(7)(B) of this title or the entry of an order under section [1805] of this title.

The FISA court noted this amendment but thought that Congress' approval of consultations was not equivalent to authorizing law enforcement officers to give *advice* to officers who were conducting electronic surveillance nor did it sanction law enforcement officers "directing or controlling" surveillances. However, dictionary definitions of "consult" include giving advice.

Accordingly, the Patriot Act amendments clearly disapprove the primary purpose test. And as a matter of straightforward logic, if a FISA application can be granted even if "foreign intelligence" is only a significant – not a primary – purpose, another purpose can be primary. One other legitimate purpose that could exist is to prosecute a target for a foreign intelligence crime. We therefore believe the Patriot Act amply supports the government's alternative argument but, paradoxically, the Patriot Act would seem to conflict with the government's first argument because by using the term "significant purpose," the Act now implies that another purpose is to be distinguished from a foreign intelligence purpose.

In short, even though we agree that the original FISA did not contemplate the "false dichotomy," the Patriot Act actually did – which makes it no longer false. The addition of the word "significant" to section 1804(a)(7)(B) imposed a requirement that the government have a measurable foreign intelligence purpose, other than just criminal prosecution of even foreign intelligence crimes. Although section 1805(a)(5), as we discussed above, may well have been intended to authorize the FISA court to review only the question whether the information sought was a type of foreign intelligence information, in light of the significant purpose amendment of section 1804 it seems section 1805 must be interpreted as giving the FISA court the authority to review the government's purpose in seeking the information.

That leaves us with something of an analytic conundrum. On the one hand, Congress did not amend the definition of foreign intelligence information which, we have explained, includes evidence of foreign intelligence crimes. On the other hand, Congress accepted the dichotomy between foreign intelligence and law enforcement by adopting the significant purpose test. Nevertheless, it is our task to do our best to read the statute to honor congressional intent. The better reading, it seems to us, excludes from the purpose of gaining foreign intelligence information a sole objective of criminal prosecution. We therefore reject the government's argument to the contrary. Yet this may not make much practical difference. Because, as the government points out, when it commences an electronic surveillance of a foreign agent, typically it will not have decided whether to prosecute the agent (whatever may be the subjective intent of the investigators or lawyers who initiate an investigation). So long as the government entertains a realistic option of dealing with the agent other than through criminal prosecution, it satisfies the significant purpose test.

The important point is – and here we agree with the government – the Patriot Act amendment, by using the word "significant," eliminated any justification for the FISA court to balance the relative weight the government places on criminal prosecution as compared to other counterintelligence responses. If the certification of the application's purpose articulates a broader objective than criminal prosecution – such as stopping an ongoing conspiracy – and includes other potential non-prosecutorial responses, the government meets the statutory test. Of course, if the court concluded that the government's sole objective was merely to gain evidence of past criminal conduct – even foreign intelligence crimes – to punish the agent rather than halt ongoing espionage or terrorist activity, the application should be denied.

The government claims that even prosecutions of *non*-foreign intelligence crimes are consistent with a purpose of gaining foreign intelligence information so long as the government's objective is to stop espionage or terrorism by putting an agent of a foreign power in prison. That interpretation transgresses the original FISA. It will be recalled that Congress intended section 1804(a)(7)(B) to prevent the government from targeting a foreign agent when its "true purpose" was to gain non-foreign intelligence information – such as evidence of ordinary crimes or scandals. (If the government inadvertently came upon evidence of ordinary crimes, FISA provided for the transmission of that evidence to the proper authority.) It can be argued, however, that by providing that an application is to be granted if the government has only a "significant purpose" of gaining foreign intelligence information, the Patriot Act allows the government to have a primary objective of prosecuting an agent for a non-foreign intelligence crime. Yet we think that would be an anomalous reading of the amendment. For we see not the slightest indication that Congress meant to give that power to the Executive Branch. Accordingly, the manifestation of such a purpose, it seems to us, would continue to disqualify an application. That is not to deny that ordinary crimes might be inextricably intertwined with foreign intelligence crimes. For example, if a group of international terrorists were to engage in bank robberies in order to finance the manufacture of a bomb, evidence of the bank robbery should be treated just as evidence of the terrorist act itself. But the FISA process cannot be used as a device to investigate wholly unrelated ordinary crimes.

In describing its experience with FISA searches and surveillance, the FISA court's opinion makes reference to certain applications each of which contained an FBI agent's affidavit that was inaccurate, particularly with respect to assertions regarding the information shared with criminal investigators and prosecutors. Although we do not approve any misrepresentations that may have taken place, our understanding is that those affidavits were submitted during 1997 through early 2001, and therefore any inaccuracies may have been caused in part by the confusion within the Department of Justice over implementation of the 1995 Procedures, as augmented in January 2000. In any event, while the issue of the candor of the FBI agent(s) involved properly remains under investigation by the Department of Justice's Office of Professional Responsibility, the issue whether the wall between the FBI and the Criminal Division required by the FISA court has been maintained is moot in light of this court's opinion.

III.

Having determined that FISA, as amended, does not oblige the government to demonstrate to the FISA court that its primary purpose in conducting electronic surveillance is *not* criminal prosecution, we are obliged to consider whether the statute as amended is consistent with the Fourth Amendment. The Fourth Amendment provides:

> The right of the people to be secure in their persons, houses, papers, and effects, against unreasonable searches and seizures, shall not be violated, and no Warrants shall issue, but upon probable cause, supported by Oath or affirmation, and particularly describing the place to be searched, and the persons or things to be seized.

Although the FISA court did not explicitly rely on the Fourth Amendment, it at least suggested that this provision was the animating principle driving its statutory analysis. The FISA court indicated that its disapproval of the Attorney General's 2002 Procedures was based on the need to safeguard the "privacy of Americans in these highly intrusive surveillances and searches," which implies the invocation of the Fourth Amendment. The government, recognizing the Fourth Amendment's shadow effect on the FISA court's opinion, has affirmatively argued that FISA is constitutional.

[I]n asking whether FISA procedures can be regarded as reasonable under the Fourth Amendment, we think it is instructive to compare those procedures and requirements with their Title III counterparts. [Title III of the Omnibus Crime Control and Safe Streets Act of 1968, 18 U.S.C. § 2811 *et seq.* governs wiretap and other electronic intercepts.] Obviously, the closer those FISA procedures are to Title III procedures, the lesser are our constitutional concerns.

Comparison of FISA Procedures with Title III

It is important to note that while many of FISA's requirements for a surveillance order differ from those in Title III, few of those differences have any constitutional relevance. In the context of ordinary crime, beyond requiring searches and seizures to be reasonable, the Supreme Court has interpreted the warrant clause of the Fourth Amendment to require three elements:

> First, warrants must be issued by neutral, disinterested magistrates. Second, those seeking the warrant must demonstrate to the magistrate their probable cause to believe that "the evidence sought will aid in a particular apprehension or conviction" for a particular offense. Finally,

"warrants must particularly describe the 'things to be seized,'" as well as the place to be searched.

Dalia v. United States, 441 U.S. 238, 255 (1979).

With limited exceptions not at issue here, both Title III and FISA require prior judicial scrutiny of an application for an order authorizing electronic surveillance. And there is no dispute that a FISA judge satisfies the Fourth Amendment's requirement of a "neutral and detached magistrate."

The statutes differ to some extent in their probable cause showings. Title III allows a court to enter an *ex parte* order authorizing electronic surveillance if it determines on the basis of the facts submitted in the government's application that "there is probable cause for belief that an individual is committing, has committed, or is about to commit" a specified predicate offense. FISA by contrast requires a showing of probable cause that the target is a foreign power or an agent of a foreign power. We have noted, however, that where a U.S. person is involved, an "agent of a foreign power" is defined in terms of criminal activity. Admittedly, the definition of one category of U.S-person agents of foreign powers – that is, persons engaged in espionage and clandestine intelligence activities for a foreign power – does not necessarily require a showing of an imminent violation of criminal law. *See* 50 U.S.C. § 1801(b)(2)(A) (defining such activities as those which "involve" or "may involve" a violation of criminal statutes of the United States). Congress clearly intended a lesser showing of probable cause for these activities than that applicable to ordinary criminal cases. And with good reason – these activities present the type of threats contemplated by the Supreme Court in *Keith* when it recognized that the focus of security surveillance "may be less precise than that directed against more conventional types of crime" even in the area of *domestic* threats to national security

Congress allowed this lesser showing for clandestine intelligence activities – but not, notably, for other activities, including terrorism – because it was fully aware that such foreign intelligence crimes may be particularly difficult to detect. At the same time, however, it provided another safeguard not present in Title III – that is, the requirement that there be probable cause to believe the target is acting "for or on behalf of a foreign power." Under the definition of "agent of a foreign power" FISA surveillance could not be authorized

> against an American reporter merely because he gathers information for publication in a newspaper, even if the information was classified by the Government. Nor would it be authorized against a Government employee or former employee who reveals secrets to a reporter or in a book for the purpose of informing the American people. This definition would not authorize surveillance of ethnic Americans who lawfully gather political information and perhaps even lawfully share it with the foreign government of their national origin. It obviously would not apply to lawful activities to lobby, influence, or inform Members of Congress or the administration to take certain positions with respect to foreign or domestic concerns. Nor would it apply to lawful gathering of information preparatory to such lawful activities.

Similarly, FISA surveillance would not be authorized against a target engaged in purely domestic terrorism because the government would not be able to show that the target is acting for or on behalf of a foreign power. As should be clear from the foregoing, FISA applies only to certain carefully delineated, and particularly serious, foreign threats to national security.

Turning then to the first of the particularity requirements, while Title III requires probable cause to believe that particular communications concerning the specified crime will be obtained through the interception, FISA instead requires an official to designate the type of foreign intelligence information being sought, and to certify that the information sought is foreign intelligence information. When the target is a U.S. person, the FISA judge reviews the certification for clear error, but this "standard of review is not, of course, comparable to a probable cause finding by the judge." Nevertheless, FISA provides additional protections to ensure that only pertinent information is sought. The certification must be made by a national security officer – typically the FBI Director – and must be approved by the Attorney General or the Attorney General's Deputy. Congress recognized that this certification would "assure[] written accountability within the Executive Branch" and provide "an internal check on Executive Branch arbitrariness." In addition, the court may require the government to submit any further information it deems necessary to determine whether or not the certification is clearly erroneous.

With respect to the second element of particularity, although Title III generally requires probable cause to believe that the facilities subject to surveillance are being used or are about to be used in connection with commission of a crime or are leased to, listed in the name of, or used by the individual committing the crime, FISA requires probable cause to believe that each of the facilities or places at which the surveillance is directed is being used, or is about to be used, by a foreign power or agent. In cases where the targeted facilities are not leased to, listed in the name of, or used by the individual committing the crime, Title III requires the government to show a nexus between the facilities and communications regarding the criminal offense. The government does not have to show, however, anything about the target of the surveillance; it is enough that "an *individual*" – not necessarily the target – is committing a crime. On the other hand, FISA requires probable cause to believe the target is an agent of a foreign power (that is, the individual committing a foreign intelligence crime) who uses or is about to use the targeted facility. Simply put, FISA requires less of a nexus between the facility and the pertinent communications than Title III, but more of a nexus between the target and the pertinent communications.

There are other elements of Title III that at least some circuits have determined are constitutionally significant – that is, necessity, duration of surveillance, and minimization. Both statutes have a "necessity" provision, which requires the court to find that the information sought is not available through normal investigative procedures. Although the court's clearly erroneous review under FISA is more limited than under Title III, this greater deference must be viewed in light of FISA's additional requirement that the certification of necessity come from an upper level Executive Branch official. The statutes also have duration provisions; Title III orders may last up to 30 days, while FISA orders may last up to 90 days for U.S. persons. And where Title III requires minimization of what is acquired, as we have discussed, for U.S. persons, FISA requires minimization of what is acquired, retained, and disseminated. The FISA court notes, however, that in practice FISA surveillance devices are normally left on continuously, and the minimization occurs in the process of indexing and logging the pertinent communications. The reasonableness of this approach depends on the facts and circumstances of each case. Less minimization in the acquisition stage may well be justified to the extent the intercepted communications are "ambiguous in nature or apparently involve guarded or coded language," or "the investigation is focusing on what is thought to be a widespread conspiracy [where] more extensive surveillance may be justified in an attempt to determine the precise scope of the enterprise." Given the targets of FISA surveillance, it will often be the case that intercepted communications will be in code or a foreign language for which there is no contemporaneously available translator, and the activities of foreign agents will involve multiple actors and complex plots.

Amici particularly focus on the differences between the two statutes concerning notice. Title III requires notice to the target (and, within the discretion of the judge, to other persons whose communications were intercepted) once the surveillance order expires. FISA does not require notice to a person whose communications were intercepted unless the government "intends to enter into evidence or otherwise use or disclose" such communications in a trial or other enumerated official proceedings. As the government points out, however, to the extent evidence obtained through a FISA surveillance order is used in a criminal proceeding, notice to the defendant is required. Of course, where such evidence is not ultimately going to be used for law enforcement, Congress observed that "the need to preserve secrecy for sensitive counterintelligence sources and methods justifies elimination of the notice requirement."

Based on the foregoing, it should be evident that while Title III contains some protections that are not in FISA, in many significant respects the two statutes are equivalent, and in some, FISA contains additional protections. Still, to the extent the two statutes diverge in constitutionally relevant areas – in particular, in their probable cause and particularity showings – a FISA order may not be a "warrant" contemplated by the Fourth Amendment. The government itself does not actually claim that it is, instead noting only that there is authority for the proposition that a FISA order is a warrant in the constitutional sense. *See Cavanagh,* 807 F.2d at 790 (concluding that FISA order can be considered a warrant since it is issued by a detached judicial officer and is based on a reasonable showing of probable cause); *see also Pelton,* 835 F.2d at 1075 (joining *Cavanagh* in holding that FISA procedures meet constitutional requirements); *Falvey,* 540 F. Supp. at 1314 (holding that unlike in *Truong,* a congressionally crafted warrant that met Fourth Amendment standards was obtained authorizing the surveillance). We do not decide the issue but note that to the extent a FISA order comes close to meeting Title III, that certainly bears on its reasonableness under the Fourth Amendment.

Did Truong *Articulate the Appropriate Constitutional Standard?*

Ultimately, the question becomes whether FISA, as amended by the Patriot Act, is a reasonable response based on a balance of the legitimate need of the government for foreign intelligence information to protect against national security threats with the protected rights of citizens. To answer that question – whether the Patriot Act's disavowal of the primary purpose test is constitutional – besides comparing the FISA procedures with Title III, it is necessary to consider carefully the underlying rationale of the primary purpose test.

It will be recalled that the case that set forth the primary purpose test *as constitutionally required* was *Truong.* The Fourth Circuit thought that *Keith*'s balancing standard implied the adoption of the primary purpose test. We reiterate that *Truong* dealt with a pre-FISA surveillance based on the President's constitutional responsibility to conduct the foreign affairs of the United States. Although *Truong* suggested the line it drew was a constitutional minimum that would apply to a FISA surveillance, it had no occasion to consider the application of the statute carefully. The *Truong* court, as did all the other courts to have decided the issue, held that the President did have inherent authority to conduct warrantless searches to obtain foreign intelligence information. It was incumbent upon the court, therefore, to determine the boundaries of that constitutional authority in the case before it. We take for granted that the President does have that authority and, assuming that is so, FISA could not encroach on the President's constitutional power. The question before us is the reverse, does FISA amplify the President's power by providing a mechanism that at least approaches a classic warrant and which therefore supports the government's contention that FISA searches are constitutionally reasonable.

The district court in the *Truong* case had excluded evidence obtained from electronic surveillance after the government's investigation – the court found – had converted from one conducted for foreign intelligence reasons to one conducted primarily as a criminal investigation. (The defendants were convicted based in part on surveillance evidence gathered before that point.) The district judge had focused on the date that the Criminal Division had taken a central role in the investigation. The court of appeals endorsed that approach stating:

> We think that the district court adopted the proper test, because once surveillance becomes primarily a criminal investigation, the courts are entirely competent to make the usual probable cause determination, and because, importantly, individual privacy interests come to the fore *and government foreign policy concerns recede* when the government is primarily attempting to form the basis of a criminal prosecution.

That analysis, in our view, rested on a false premise and the line the court sought to draw was inherently unstable, unrealistic, and confusing. The false premise was the assertion that once the government moves to criminal prosecution, its "foreign policy concerns" recede. As we have discussed in the first part of the opinion, that is simply not true as it relates to counterintelligence. In that field the government's primary purpose is to halt the espionage or terrorism efforts, and criminal prosecutions can be, and usually are, interrelated with other techniques used to frustrate a foreign power's efforts. Indeed, the Fourth Circuit itself, rejecting defendant's arguments that it should adopt a "solely foreign intelligence purpose test," acknowledged that "almost all foreign intelligence investigations are in part criminal investigations." (It would have been more accurate to refer to counterintelligence investigations.)

The method the court endorsed for determining when an investigation became primarily criminal was based on the organizational structure of the Justice Department. The court determined an investigation became primarily criminal when the Criminal Division played a lead role. This approach has led, over time, to the quite intrusive organizational and personnel tasking the FISA court adopted. Putting aside the impropriety of an Article III court imposing such organizational strictures (which we have already discussed), the line the *Truong* court adopted – subsequently referred to as a "wall" – was unstable because it generates dangerous confusion and creates perverse organizational incentives. That is so because counterintelligence brings to bear both classic criminal investigation techniques as well as less focused intelligence gathering. Indeed, effective counterintelligence, we have learned, requires the wholehearted cooperation of all the government's personnel who can be brought to the task. A standard which punishes such cooperation could well be thought dangerous to national security. Moreover, by focusing on the subjective motivation of those who initiate investigations, the *Truong* standard, as administered by the FISA court, could be thought to discourage desirable initiatives.

Recent testimony before the Joint Intelligence Committee amply demonstrates that the *Truong* line is a very difficult one to administer. Indeed, it was suggested that the FISA court requirements based on *Truong* may well have contributed, whether correctly understood or not, to the FBI missing opportunities to anticipate the September 11, 2001 attacks.[29] That is not to say that we should be prepared to jettison Fourth Amendment requirements in the interest of national security. Rather, assuming *arguendo* that FISA orders are not Fourth Amendment warrants, the question becomes, are the searches constitutionally reasonable. And in judging reasonableness, the instability of the *Truong* line is a relevant consideration.

The Fourth Circuit recognized that the Supreme Court had never considered the constitutionality of warrantless government searches for foreign intelligence reasons, but concluded the analytic framework the Supreme Court adopted in *Keith* – in the case of domestic intelligence surveillance – pointed the way to the

---

[29] An FBI agent recently testified that efforts to conduct a criminal investigation of two of the alleged hijackers were blocked by senior FBI officials – understandably concerned about prior FISA court criticism – who interpreted that court's decisions as precluding a criminal investigator's role. One agent, frustrated at encountering the "wall," wrote to headquarters: "Someday someone will die – and wall or not – the public will not understand why we were not more effective and throwing every resource we had at certain 'problems.' Let's hope the National Security Law Unit will stand behind their decisions then, especially since the biggest threat to us now, [Usama Bin Laden], is getting the most 'protection.'" The agent was told in response that headquarters was frustrated with the issue, but that those were the rules, and the National Security Law Unit does not make them up. *The Malaysia Hijacking and September 11th: Joint Hearing Before the Senate and House Select Intelligence Committees* (Sept. 20, 2002) (written statement of New York special agent of the FBI).

line the Fourth Circuit drew. The Court in *Keith* had, indeed, balanced the government's interest against individual privacy interests, which is undoubtedly the key to this issue as well; but we think the *Truong* court misconceived the government's interest and, moreover, did not draw a more appropriate distinction that *Keith* at least suggested. That is the line drawn in the original FISA statute itself between ordinary crimes and foreign intelligence crimes.

It will be recalled that *Keith* carefully avoided the issue of a warrantless foreign intelligence search: "We have not addressed, and express no opinion as to, the issues which may be involved with respect to activities of foreign powers or their agents." But in indicating that a somewhat more relaxed warrant could suffice in the domestic intelligence situation, the court drew a distinction between the crime involved in that case, which posed a threat to national security, and "ordinary crime." It pointed out that "the focus of domestic surveillance may be less precise than that directed against more conventional types of crimes."

The main purpose of ordinary criminal law is twofold: to punish the wrongdoer and to deter other persons in society from embarking on the same course. The government's concern with respect to foreign intelligence crimes, on the other hand, is overwhelmingly to stop or frustrate the immediate criminal activity. As we discussed in the first section of this opinion, the criminal process is often used as part of an integrated effort to counter the malign efforts of a foreign power. Punishment of the terrorist or espionage agent is really a secondary objective; indeed, punishment of a terrorist is often a moot point.

Supreme Court's Special Needs Cases

The distinction between ordinary criminal prosecutions and extraordinary situations underlies the Supreme Court's approval of entirely warrantless and even suspicionless searches that are designed to serve the government's "special needs, beyond the normal need for law enforcement." *Vernonia School Dist. 47J v. Acton,* 515 U.S. 646, 653 (1995) (quoting *Griffin v. Wisconsin,* 483 U.S. 868, 873 (1987) (internal quotation marks omitted)) (random drug-testing of student athletes).[32] Apprehending drunk drivers and securing the border constitute such unique interests beyond ordinary, general law enforcement. *Id.* at 654 (citing *Michigan Dep t of State Police v. Sitz,* 496 U.S. 444 (1990), and *United States v. Martinez-Fuerte,* 428 U.S. 543 (1976)).

A recent case, *City of Indianapolis v. Edmond,* 531 U.S. 32 (2000), is relied on by both the government and *amici*. In that case, the Court held that a highway check point designed to catch drug dealers did not fit within its special needs exception because the government's "primary purpose" was merely "to uncover evidence of ordinary criminal wrongdoing." The Court rejected the government's argument that the "severe and intractable nature of the drug problem" was

---

[32] The Court has also allowed searches for certain administrative purposes to be undertaken without particularized suspicion of misconduct. *See, e.g., New York v. Burger,* 482 U.S. 691, 702-04 (1987) (warrantless administrative inspection of premises of closely regulated business); *Camara v. Municipal Court,* 387 U.S. 523, 534-39 (1967) (administrative inspection to ensure compliance with city housing code).

sufficient justification for such a dragnet seizure lacking any individualized suspicion. *Amici* particularly rely on the Court's statement that "the gravity of the threat alone cannot be dispositive of questions concerning what means law enforcement officers may employ to pursue a given purpose."

But by "purpose" the Court makes clear it was referring not to a subjective intent, which is not relevant in ordinary Fourth Amendment probable cause analysis, but rather to a programmatic purpose. The Court distinguished the prior check point cases *Martinez-Fuerte* (involving checkpoints less than 100 miles from the Mexican border) and *Sitz* (checkpoints to detect intoxicated motorists) on the ground that the former involved the government's "long-standing concern for the protection of the integrity of the border," and the latter was "aimed at reducing the immediate hazard posed by the presence of drunk drivers on the highways." The Court emphasized that it was decidedly not drawing a distinction between suspicionless seizures with a "non-law-enforcement primary purpose" and those designed for law enforcement. Rather, the Court distinguished general crime control programs and those that have another particular purpose, such as protection of citizens against special hazards or protection of our borders. The Court specifically acknowledged that an appropriately tailored road block could be used "to thwart an imminent terrorist attack." The nature of the "emergency," which is simply another word for threat, takes the matter out of the realm of ordinary crime control.

Conclusion

FISA's general programmatic purpose, to protect the nation against terrorists and espionage threats directed by foreign powers, has from its outset been distinguishable from "ordinary crime control." After the events of September 11, 2001, though, it is hard to imagine greater emergencies facing Americans than those experienced on that date.

We acknowledge, however, that the constitutional question presented by this case – whether Congress's disapproval of the primary purpose test is consistent with the Fourth Amendment has no definitive jurisprudential answer. The Supreme Court's special needs cases involve random stops (seizures) not electronic searches. In one sense, they can be thought of as a greater encroachment into personal privacy because they are not based on any particular suspicion. On the other hand, wiretapping is a good deal more intrusive than an automobile stop accompanied by questioning.

Although the Court in *City of Indianapolis* cautioned that the threat to society is not dispositive in determining whether a search or seizure is reasonable, it certainly remains a crucial factor. Our case may well involve the most serious threat our country faces. Even without taking into account the President's inherent constitutional authority to conduct warrantless foreign intelligence surveillance, we think the procedures and government showings required under FISA, if they do not meet the minimum Fourth Amendment warrant standards, certainly come close. We, therefore, believe firmly, applying the balancing test drawn from *Keith*, that FISA as amended is constitutional because the surveillances it authorizes are reasonable.

Accordingly, we reverse the FISA court's orders in this case to the extent they imposed conditions on the grant of the government's applications, vacate the FISA court's Rule 11, and remand with instructions to grant the applications as submitted and proceed henceforth in accordance with this opinion.

NOTES AND QUESTIONS

1. There are two aspects of FISA at stake in the *Sealed Case* opinions, the "wall" between intelligence and criminal investigators, and the degree of showing required before obtaining a surveillance or search order. Both elements run throughout discussions of the PATRIOT Act. For particularly searching criticisms, see DAVID COLE & JAMES X. DEMPSEY, TERRORISM AND THE CONSTITUTION (2002); RANETA LAWSON MACK & MICHAEL J. KELLY, EQUAL JUSTICE IN THE BALANCE (2004).

2. The opinion reviewed in *Sealed Case* is reported as *In re All Matters Submitted to the Foreign Intelligence Surveillance Court*, 218 F. Supp. 611 (FISC 2002). The FISA Court was interpreting and approving Minimization Guidelines required by the statute in the light of what it perceived to be misrepresentations in prior cases. Beginning in March 2000 and running through the summer of 2001, the FBI had admitted to at least 75 breaches of the wall and misrepresentations to the court. Does the Court of Review too lightly pass off the "misrepresentations" as having resulted from confusion over the requirements?

3. Is the Court of Review persuasive in arguing that the minimization requirement does not provide authority to insist on a wall of separation between intelligence and criminal investigation? The "wall" erected by FISC may have had more to do with avoiding direction of the investigation toward prosecutorial evidence than with ensuring that private noncriminal information remained private. It is on that ground that the Court of Review insisted that the lower court was delving too deeply into the organization of the Justice Department. These cases illustrate some level of independence of the judges from the executive branch, but is it enough? Is the lower court's involvement with oversight of the internal workings of the Justice Department troubling by intermingling the Judiciary and Executive? or is the Court of Review's deference more troubling?

4. A rare academic approval of expanded investigatory powers argues that PATRIOT appropriately eliminates two barriers to investigative cooperation – the FISA wall and secrecy of grand jury testimony:

Although the Patriot Act plainly expands the powers of those charged with responding to terrorist threats, it would be incorrect to view those powers as wholly unregulated and discretionless. Indeed, the Patriot Act could be viewed as shifting the duties of regulation from the judicial branch to the legislative and executive branches. Given that questions of national security and privacy rights, and their appropriate balance, are among the most important policy issues confronting the nation, it would surely seem appropriate, and even preferable, that such debates take place openly, and in our elected branches.

Craig S. Lerner, *The USA PATRIOT Act: Promoting the Cooperation of Foreign Intelligence Gathering and Law Enforcement*, 11 GEO. MASON L. REV. 493, 495 (2003).

5. One commentator has argued that FISA should be abandoned entirely after the *Sealed Case* opinion:

> The USA PATRIOT Act has virtually eliminated the specialized intelligence-gathering function of FISA orders; they now can be used with the specific purpose of obtaining evidence to be used in criminal prosecutions, as long as this is not the sole purpose of such investigations. Additionally, prosecutors and intelligence officials may now consult over FISA warrant application and execution. A FISA warrant has become little more than a regular Title III warrant issued secretly with no required showing of probable cause of criminal activity. In view of these significant changes, the FISC retains little unique jurisdiction. The FISC's secret, perfunctory procedures no longer provide constitutionally adequate protection for surveillance targets who will be unknowingly investigated and prosecuted as a direct result of its orders, especially now that FISA surveillance may be used specifically for criminal – and not simply intelligence-gathering – investigations.

Nola K. Breglio, *Leaving FISA Behind: The Need To Return to Warrantless Foreign Intelligence Surveillance*, 113 YALE L.J. 179, 180 (2003). The argument continues that judicial review of unregulated warrantless surveillance under a "reasonableness" standard could be more effective than mere FISC review of certification that the target is an agent of a foreign power. Of course, one problem is that in that system, judicial review would occur only when a criminal prosecution occurs or when the target learns of the surveillance through some other means, if then.

6. The FISA Court of Review allows the Attorney General's certification to satisfy the first particularity requirement of the Fourth Amendment – probable cause. If the certification stood alone, then this would seem to negate the neutral judicial requirement. But the court allows review for clear error to satisfy that element. What is it that ameliorates the Fourth Amendment requirements in this area? the severe threat of terrorism? the difficulty of investigation? or that the targets often have links to foreign powers and thus implicate foreign affairs?

7. Another commentary argues that the Court of Review misinterpreted the statutory framework:

> While the Court of Review was correct in allowing criminal and foreign intelligence investigators to collaborate during FISA investigations, the court's opinion goes too far in eroding restrictions on the government's use of FISA searches to the extent that it invites abuse of those searches. Even though the court recognized the Foreign Intelligence Surveillance Court's role in reviewing the government's purpose in seeking information under FISA, it diminished the FISC's ability to perform its oversight duties by applying a "measurable purpose" standard in reviewing applications for FISA searches and surveillances.

John E. Branch III, *Statutory Misinterpretation: The Foreign Intelligence Court of Review's Interpretation of the "Significant Purpose" Requirement of the Foreign Intelligence Surveillance Act*, 81 N.C.L. REV. 2075 (2003).

§ 5.02 CLASSIFIED INFORMATION PROCEDURES ACT

Investigation of terrorist plots will often involve information that the government does not wish disclosed. Among the possibilities are the following:

1. *Informants.* The courts have long recognized an "informer's privilege" so that government may be able to keep secret the identity of an informant who is lodged within a criminal scheme. Some of the best information leading to prosecutions of mafiosi, drug rings, and paramilitary groups has come from insiders. The informer's privilege may be invoked when the defendant challenges probable cause for a search or attempts to discover information that might shed light on the background of the investigation. It does not mean that government may introduce anonymous testimony at trial. The Sixth Amendment right of confrontation means that, if the informer is to remain anonymous, conviction must be based on other admissible information developed from the informer's information.

[handwritten margin note: doesn't trump Confront Cl.]

2. *Hardware specifications.* Terrorists may get their hands on explosives, military equipment, or related hardware that the government does not want described in detail during trial. Can the prosecution introduce evidence that the defendant stole secret stuff without describing the things stolen? [One of the cases below deals with C-4 explosives. I went online to get information about C-4 and was unsuccessful. I wonder what federal databases now contain my attempts to gain information about this material. Ah, the hazards of being a diligent law professor.]

3. *Technology and investigative techniques.* High-tech industries have developed, often with government funding, some rather amazing abilities over the past few decades. The combination of sophisticated software to go with micro electronic devices allows eavesdropping on conversations in ways that most of us can only imagine. Satellites can pick up millions of telephone conversations while software filters those conversations for voice patterns or key words to isolate and record conversations that are of interest to an investigation. Other devices can monitor and record conversations taking place at great distances inside buildings and other structures. Infrared and similar devices can monitor human movements. Computers can break most codes, although concepts such as "one-time pads" and insider jargon may still baffle cryptography programs until behavior confirms what was communicated. Exactly how good all these devices are and what they can accomplish in many instances remain government-protected secrets.

4. *Government planning and foreign relations.* The earliest recognition of government secrets came in the form of the courts' noting that the executive branch should be allowed to keep secrets about other governments and about its own plans. "[The President] has his confidential sources of information. He has his agents in the form of diplomatic, consular, and other officials. Secrecy in

respect of information gathered by them may be highly necessary, and the premature disclosure of it productive of harmful results. Indeed, so clearly is this true that the first President refused to accede to a request to lay before the House of Representatives the instructions, correspondence and documents relating to the negotiation of the Jay Treaty, a refusal the wisdom of which was recognized by the House itself and has never since been doubted." *United States v. Curtiss-Wright Export Corp.*, 299 U.S. 304 (1936).

Government secrets are protected by criminal sanctions under the espionage provisions of the criminal statutes. "The term 'classified information' means information which, at the time of a violation of this section, is, for reasons of national security, specifically designated by a United States Government Agency for limited or restricted dissemination or distribution." 18 U.S.C. § 798. Each agency is responsible for making its own determinations, but the classifications and procedures for handling classified documents are governed by Executive Order 12958. The three classifications provided in the EO are "Top Secret," "Secret," and "Confidential." Because the procedures for handling classified information can be quite elaborate and the persons entitled to handle it carefully controlled, one question that has arisen is how to handle this type of information when it must be disclosed to a judge.

At the outset, it is important to realize that very little will allow the government to rely on secret information in presenting its own evidence in a prosecution. As the next case illustrates, the Sixth Amendment's right to confront witnesses will allow hearsay testimony or summaries of secret information to be used in lieu of cross-examination of the most knowledgeable person only in recognized exceptions to the hearsay rule. Government secrecy may sometimes curtail the production of evidence and result in an acquittal, but that is just the price of protecting against tyranny. In a few rare instances, the right to a public trial may be compromised so that the public could be excluded from a portion of the trial in which secret information is placed before the factfinder. These issues are explored in the cases below.

The Classified Information Procedures Act (CIPA), 18 U.S.C. App. IV, adopted in 1980, stems from the proposition that a defendant is entitled to provide his or her best defense but that the government is also entitled to a national security privilege for classified information. The two competing interests are both of constitutional dimension and CIPA attempts to provide a framework for dealing with the conflict by allowing the trial judge to review the material in secret to attempt reaching an accommodation of both interests. In reading the cases, it may be helpful to compare the CIPA discussions of a national security privilege with assertion of an attorney-client privilege in ordinary civil litigation. The practice of *ex parte in camera* inspection of privilege claims is more routine in that setting, but the constitutional and institutional concerns in a CIPA case add significantly different dimensions.

CIPA § 4 addresses defense requests for discovery of information in classified documents. CIPA § 5 requires the defendant to give advance notice of intent to introduce classified information at trial. Both sections are subject to the procedural provisions of § 6, which allows the government to make an *in camera* disclosure to the judge of secret information seeking a ruling on admissibility and relevance. If the judge agrees that the information would not be helpful to the defense, that is the end of the matter. If the information would be helpful but a substantial equivalent can be obtained by redacting the secrets or providing a summary, then the judge can order disclosure in the appropriate form. Finally, if the information is necessary to the defense and the government refuses to allow its admission, dismissal of the prosecution would be the ultimate remedy.

3 of the possibilities

UNITED STATES v. SMITH
780 F.2d 1102 (4th Cir. 1985) (en banc)

Smith charged w/ espionage. Allegedly sold info to Soviet agent, probably double agent. S. contends that he thought he was working for the CIA; seeks to enter class'd evid. to prove this pt.

WIDENER, Circuit Judge:

Richard Craig Smith has been indicted on five counts of espionage under 18 U.S.C. §§ 793(a), 794(a) and (c). Prior to trial, Smith gave notice to the government and to the court pursuant to 18 U.S.C.App. § 5 that he intended to disclose classified information as part of his defense. Following the procedures set out in the Classified Information Procedures Act (CIPA), the district court conducted a closed hearing to determine the use, relevance, or admissibility of the classified information the defendant proffered. At the conclusion of the hearing, the court ruled that part of the classified information Smith sought to introduce would be admissible at trial. The government invoked CIPA's provision allowing interlocutory appeals and sought a reversal of the district court's ruling allowing introduction of the classified information. A panel of this court upheld the district court's finding that the classified information in question could be introduced at trial. We vacated the panel decision and granted en banc review. We conclude that the district court applied an incorrect legal standard in ruling upon the introduction of the classified information, and accordingly vacate the order of the district court and remand.

Dct said it shall be allowed

vacate & remand

Smith was employed by the Army Intelligence Security Command (INSCOM) between 1973 and 1980. He is here charged with unlawfully selling in 1982 and 1983 certain classified information to Victor I. Okunev, an agent of the Soviet Union. The indictment charges that Smith met with Okunev at the Soviet Commercial Compound in Tokyo, Japan, twice in November 1982 and once in February 1983. Smith allegedly gave Okunev classified information regarding five INSCOM double agent operations, for which he received $11,000 from Okunev.

allegedly sold secrets to a Soviet agent

In his defense, on account of the facts he relates just below, Smith argues that he believed he was working for the Central Intelligence Agency (CIA) when he turned over the information to Okunev. He claims that he was sought out by two men who claimed to be CIA agents, Ken White and Danny Ishida. White and Ishida sought Smith's help in setting up a double agent project directed toward the Russians in Japan. Smith was to gain the confidence of the Soviets by supplying them with the details of eight INSCOM double agent operations. White and Ishida told Smith that this information would be of no real value to the Russians because those eight operations had been discontinued. Smith became convinced that White and Ishida were indeed working for the CIA and agreed to help them by supplying the specified information to the Russians.

S thought he was working for CIA

PH: Dct allowed evid; App Ct panel aff'd; App Ct en banc vacated/remand.
H: Dct's analysis stopped @ determining that the evid was relevant. CIPA also requires the Roviaro balancing; ie public interest in protection through v. individual's right to prepare defense

Smith seeks to introduce at trial several pieces of classified information to support his defense that he thought he was working for the CIA when he sold the information to the Russians. Such proof may negate an essential element of the crimes charged, intent or reason to believe the information sold would be used to injure the United States or to the advantage of a foreign country. After a lengthy hearing, the district court ruled that Smith could introduce part of the classified information he relied upon in his defense. It found that certain classified information was relevant to Smith's defense and therefore was admissible at trial. For example, in a ruling not appealed from, the court found that details of the INSCOM operations White and Ishida allegedly gave to Smith to pass on to the Soviets were admissible because such information made the existence of White and Ishida more probable than otherwise would be the case.

The district court further found that CIPA was not intended to change the existing law of evidence regarding admissibility; and Congress did not intend to allow exclusion of evidence relevant to the defense simply because that evidence was classified. Because the evidence proffered was found to be relevant, it reasoned, it could be introduced at trial.

A panel of this court affirmed the district court's finding that the evidence in question was admissible. It concluded that the district court correctly applied the standards for judging relevance under Fed.R.Evid. 401 and 403. It rejected the government's argument that governmental privilege required that a balancing test similar to the one set out in *Roviaro v. United States*, 353 U.S. 53 (1957), should be applied here. The *Roviaro* standard as we view it is one that calls for balancing the public interest in protecting the information against the individual's right to prepare his defense. Its application results in a more strict rule of admissibility, and we think that standard should have been applied here.

In order to properly understand the troubling issue before us, we should review CIPA and the legislative history surrounding it. CIPA was enacted by Congress in an effort to combat the growing problem of graymail, a practice whereby a criminal defendant threatens to reveal classified information during the course of his trial in the hope of forcing the government to drop the criminal charge against him. Prior to the enactment of CIPA, the government had no method of evaluating such disclosure claims before trial actually began. Oftentimes it would abandon prosecution rather than risk possible disclosure of classified information.

CIPA established a pretrial procedure for ruling upon the admissibility of classified information.[7] A criminal defendant must notify the United States and the court if he reasonably expects to disclose classified information during his trial or during any pretrial proceeding. A defendant is forbidden from disclosing any such information absent the giving of notice. 18 U.S.C.App. § 5. The notice must specifically set out the classified information the defendant believes he will

---

[7] The Act also provides a procedure by which the court can delete portions of classified documents to be discovered by a defendant. Substitutions are also permitted under certain circumstances. 18 U.S.C.App. § 4. No issues are raised here regarding Smith's discovery rights

rely upon in his defense. A general statement of the areas the evidence will cover is insufficient.

Once the defendant gives notice of his intention to introduce classified information, the United States may request a hearing at which the court shall determine the "use, relevance, or admissibility of classified information that would otherwise be made during the trial or pretrial proceeding." 18 U.S.C.App. § 6. Upon a determination by the court that the classified information is admissible, the United States may move to substitute either a statement admitting relevant facts that the classified information would tend to prove or a summary of the classified information instead of the classified information itself. 18 U.S.C.App. § 6(c)(1). The court shall grant the government's motion if the substitution will give the defendant substantially the same ability to make his defense as would the disclosure of the classified information. If the court denies a motion for a substitution, the Attorney General can submit an affidavit objecting to the disclosure of the classified information at issue. 18 U.S.C.App. § 6(e). Once such an affidavit is filed, the defendant is barred from disclosing the classified information. 18 U.S.C.App. § 6(e). The court then can dismiss certain counts of the indictment, find against the United States on issues relating to the classified information, strike testimony, or as a last resort dismiss the indictment. 18 U.S.C.App. § 6(e). The United States can take an interlocutory appeal from an adverse district court decision with respect to the disclosure of classified information. 18 U.S.C.App. § 7.

This appeal concerns the construction and meaning of § 6 of CIPA as it sets out the district court's role in deciding the use, relevance or admissibility of classified information as evidence. The legislative history is clear that Congress did not intend to alter the existing law governing the admissibility of evidence. Thus, the Conference Report provided "the conferees agree that, as noted in the report to accompany S. 1482 and H.R. 4736, nothing in the conference substitute is intended to change the existing standards for determining relevance and admissibility."[8] The circuits that have considered the matter agree with the legislative history cited that ordinary rules of evidence determine admissibility

---

[8] Should it be argued that our decision is contrary to the understanding of the House, we think a reading of the House Report in that light reads into the report a necessary inconsistency within the report itself, for the report provided that "the existing standards of use, relevance, and/or admissibility of information or materials in criminal trials not be affected." We think the "higher standard of admissibility" rejected in the House Report may only mean a higher standard of admissibility than that already required by existing law. Our construction of the legislative history is supported by the Conference Report we have mentioned in the text.

Like reasoning applies to the Senate Report. That report provides, ". . . on the question of a standard for admissibility of evidence at trial, the committee intends to retain current law." The Committee's later recital that the court should not balance the national security interest against the right of the defendant to obtain the information is entirely inconsistent with the committee's intent to retain existing law as to admissibility if it is read to forbid all balancing. Thus, we do not read into the Senate Report a necessary inconsistency, and construe it as we do the House Report to mean any balancing not already required by existing law.

The Conference Report notably leaves out all reference to such matter, and states, as we have noted in the text, that the existing standards for determining relevance and admissibility are unchanged. We follow the Conference Report.

under CIPA. No new substantive law was created by the enactment of CIPA. Neither did the adoption of the Federal Rules of Evidence change the existing law on the subject where not addressed.

The district court correctly concluded that CIPA was merely a procedural tool requiring a pretrial court ruling on the admissibility of classified information. The court then looked at the two groups of classified information at a CIPA hearing and concluded that they were relevant to Smith's defense. Under the standards of Fed.R.Evid. 401, we find no error in the district court's conclusion as to some of the classified information it held should be admitted which would make Smith's account of the events more probable than without that evidence and hence relevant.

The relevance of some of the information is apparent when reviewing Smith's defense. He does not deny that he gave the classified information to the Soviets. He defends the charges against him solely on the grounds that he did not have the necessary intent or reason to believe the information would be used to harm the United States or to give advantage to a foreign nation. Instead, he claims that he thought he was aiding the United States by working for the CIA in setting up a double agent operation.

Not all relevant evidence is admissible at trial, however. Fed.R.Evid. 402. The government argues that even if the evidence in question is relevant it should be excluded under a privilege similar to the informer's privilege recognized by *Roviaro*. We believe that the district court committed an error of law in not applying such a privilege before ruling the relevant classified information admissible. Although evidence may be relevant, it yet may be inadmissible because of common law privileges with respect to the testimony. Fed.R.Evid. 501. Some such common law privileges include the attorney-client privilege, marital privilege, military or state secrets, and the informant's privilege.

Roviaro recognizes the existence of a qualified privilege to withhold the identity of persons who furnish information regarding criminal activity to law enforcement officials. Such a privilege is designed to protect and foster the interests of law enforcement by encouraging citizens to aid criminal justice without fear of public disclosure.

The privilege is a qualified one, however. The privilege ceases once the reasons for it cease, that is, once disclosure occurs to "those who would have cause to resent the communication." The privilege must also give way when the informant or the contents of his communication "is relevant and helpful to the defense of an accused, or is essential to a fair determination of a cause." The trial court is required to balance the public interest in nondisclosure against the defendant's right to prepare a defense. A decision on disclosure of such information must depend on the "particular circumstances of each case, taking into consideration the crime charged, the possible defenses, the possible significance of the informer's testimony, and other relevant factors."

The defendant in *Roviaro* was convicted of selling heroin to one John Doe and illegally transporting that heroin. Roviaro moved to learn the identity of John Doe. The motion was denied. At trial, prosecution witnesses described John Doe's part in the drug transaction but he was never produced or identified. The

Court vacated the conviction after concluding that John Doe was a material witness to the defendant because of his participation in the crime. Because John Doe was the only other participant in the crimes charged, his testimony was "highly relevant and might have been helpful to the defense."

Dual interests arise from nondisclosure of informers and the information they possess. First, the public interest is served by nondisclosure because it encourages persons to come forward with information that can aid effective law enforcement. Second, the safety and security of the person supplying the information is best protected by nondisclosure of his identity to those who may cause him harm. Those interests must be balanced against a defendant's right to present his defense. The privilege must give way to the "fundamental requirements of fairness." The defendant must come forward with something more than speculation as to the usefulness of such disclosure. Disclosure is not required despite the fact that a criminal defendant may have no other means of determining what relevant information the informant possesses. Disclosure is only required after a court has determined that the informer's testimony is highly relevant. One of the most important factors to be considered is the materiality of the evidence to the defendant's particular defense.

The government's privilege does not give way simply because the defendant knows the informant's name or identity. Protection of the informant can justify nondisclosure of his address or location. When the informant's identity is known to the defendant but his location is not, the same balancing of the public interest in nondisclosure against the defendant's need for disclosure must occur. Defendant must still show that disclosure will significantly aid his defense.

The government has a substantial interest in protecting sensitive sources and methods of gathering information. The gathering of such information and the methods used resemble closely the gathering of law enforcement information. The confidentiality of sources and the methods used in both instances are critical. Persons who supply information to the government regarding matters taking place in foreign countries are likely to be located outside the United States. Their safety would immediately be placed in jeopardy if their identity were made public. Revealing such information absent an essential need by a defendant would also result in the drying up of a primary source of information to our intelligence community.[12]

Law enforcement domestic informers generally know who their enemies are; intelligence agents ofttimes do not. To give the domestic informer of the police more protection than the foreign informer of the CIA seems to us to place the security of the nation from foreign danger on a lower plane than the security of the nation from the danger from domestic criminals. In our opinion the national

---

[12] Much of the Bishop, Baldwin information sought to be disclosed here falls within our interpretation of such a government privilege. Smith seeks to introduce evidence relating to the details of the operation of the Bishop, Baldwin agency and the CIA's involvement in that operation. Included in this information are other operations of the CIA in the Far East, for example, which would seem to have no relevancy in this case under any standard. As well, when the balance of the details permitted by the district court to be proved are properly balanced against the public interest in nondisclosure, the admissibility of many of them is suspect as we discuss later in this opinion.

interest is as well served by cooperation with the CIA as with the domestic police.

As the Supreme Court has reasoned, albeit in the context of a civil action,

"The Government has a compelling interest in protecting both the secrecy of information to our national security and the appearance of confidentiality so essential to the effective operation of our foreign intelligence service." If potentially valuable intelligence sources come to think that the Agency will be unable to maintain the confidentiality of its relationship to them, many could well refuse to supply information to the Agency in the first place.

Even a small chance that some court will order disclosure of a source's identity could well impair intelligence gathering and cause sources to "close up like a clam." To induce some sources to cooperate, the Government must tender as absolute an assurance of confidentiality as it possibly can. "The continued availability of [intelligence] sources depends upon the CIA's ability to guarantee the security of information that might compromise them and even danger [their] personal safety."

CIA v. Sims, 471 U.S. 159, 175 (1985).

We find the privilege applicable here even though Smith has had access to the information he seeks to admit at trial. *Roviaro* speaks of protection from "those who would have cause to resent the communication." This is not the typical informant case where the criminal defendant is usually the one that would resent the communications. Here, a significant part of the risk of harm arises from disclosure to the public. The government's interest is still protectable although Smith may have had access to the information. The privilege is not extinguished by previous disclosure to the defendant alone. The government interest to be protected here includes disclosure of the information to the public. We therefore conclude that the privilege did not cease because Smith has had access to the information.

Smith argues that even if the government's *Roviaro* type privilege exists, in the government's exercise of that privilege it must follow the substitution procedure of § 6(c) of CIPA rather than seek exclusion of the evidence altogether. Adoption of Smith's argument would result in a substantive change in the law of evidence, exactly what Congress said CIPA was not designed to do. Had CIPA not been enacted, the government could have raised its privilege at trial. The trial court then should have engaged in the balancing test of *Roviaro.* If it determined that the government's interest was superior, taking all proper factors into account, the evidence would not be disclosed. That is yet the law, but CIPA dictates that such a decision be made prior to trial.

The court decisions construing CIPA are consistent with our holding here. In *United States v. Pringle,* 751 F.2d 419 (1st Cir.1984), the defendants were convicted of possession and conspiracy to possess marijuana with the intent to import after a ship full of marijuana in their charge was seized. The defendants sought to have the government produce information regarding the surveillance, boarding and seizure of their ship. Instead of supplying the information, the government moved for a hearing under CIPA to prevent release of the material. Following an *in camera ex parte* examination of the material, the district court refused to require the release of the information to the defendants. The court of appeals affirmed after applying *Roviaro*. It agreed with the district court that the information "was not relevant to the determination of the guilt or innocence of the defendants, was not helpful to the defense and was not essential to a fair determination of the cause." The significance of *Pringle*, of course, is that it applied *Roviaro* as the standard in its construction of CIPA.

We find no CIPA case that has involved the issue now before us. We reject Smith's argument that several cases hold that relevancy is the only determination to be made by the trial court. In those cases, the trial court determined that the evidence was not relevant so that it did not need to go further and decide if that relevant evidence was admissible. *United States v. Wilson,* 732 F.2d 404, 412 (5th Cir.1984) (affirming the district court's holding that evidence was irrelevant and immaterial).

Our holding is also supported by the language used by Congress in § 6 of CIPA, requiring the district court to rule upon the use, relevance, or admissibility of classified information. Such language is consistent with existing law. Had Congress wished to allow all relevant classified information to be automatically admissible at trial, it would have so provided. The error of the district court here was in doing just that. It did not go further with its analysis than determine that the evidence was relevant. It should still have determined whether any relevant evidence was admissible in light of the applicable government privilege.

Having held that the district court erred by its failure to consider the government's privilege in arriving at its conclusion that the evidence in question was admissible at trial, we think it is not out of order to call to that court's attention some of the principles the cases have established, although we do not lay down at this time any rigid rule, for *Roviaro* requires that "[w]hether a proper balance renders nondisclosure erroneous must depend upon the particular circumstance of each case, taking into consideration the crime charged, the possible defense, the possible significance of the informer's testimony, and other relevant factors." A district court may order disclosure only when the information is at least "essential to the defense," "necessary to his defense," and neither merely cumulative nor corroborative, nor speculative. We do hold, however, that we equate the disclosure of the classified information sought in this case with the disclosure of the various kinds of information sought about informers in the cases construing *Roviaro*. The *Roviaro* standard of *admissibility* is at the least more restrictive than the ordinary rules of *relevancy* would indicate.

The judgment of the district court is vacated and the case is remanded for reconsideration not inconsistent with this opinion.

VACATED AND REMANDED[13]

---

[13] In applying its rule that relevance and admissibility are synonymous, the district court permitted Smith to introduce into evidence broad classes of classified information about Bishop, Baldwin, including evidence that Bishop, Baldwin was used as a CIA cover organization, that subsidiaries of Bishop, Baldwin were established for cover purposes, and that the CIA deposited

BUTZNER, Senior Circuit Judge, dissenting, with whom WINTER, Chief Judge, PHILLIPS, MURNAGHAN, and ERVIN, Circuit Judges join:

For reasons set forth in the opinion of the panel, I believe the district court properly interpreted and applied the Classified Information Procedures Act, 18 U.S.C.App. 3, and its order should be affirmed. Two additional comments are prompted by the opinion of the en banc court.

Congress was aware of the government's desire to impress on pending legislation the standard of admissibility of classified evidence derived from *Roviaro v. United States.* An assistant attorney general testified:

> The "relevant and material" standard we propose for inclusion in S. 1482 is based on the standard adopted by the Supreme Court in *Roviaro v. United States,* for determining whether the defendant is entitled to obtain and disclose the identity of a government informant in a criminal case. Noting the important "public interest in effective law enforcement" served by the protection of the identity of informants, the Court in *Roviaro* ruled that disclosure of such sensitive information is not required unless the information "is relevant and helpful to the defense of an accused or is essential to a fair determination of a cause." Certainly a similar standard would be appropriate in cases involving national security matters, for the interest in protecting the confidentiality of classified information is equally, if not more, compelling than that in protecting the identities of law enforcement informants.

Testimony of Feb. 7, 1980, before Subcommittee on Criminal Justice of the Committee on the Judiciary, S. No. 96-57 at 18.

---

funds into Bishop, Baldwin's account. It also permitted the defense to show the activities of a CIA agent known as Richard Cavanaugh, including double agent programs in the Far East not related to the current charges. Smith was permitted to show that Cavanaugh engaged in covert activities without prior authorization and that his "free lance style" offended his superiors. Smith was further permitted to show that the CIA began to terminate its relationship with Bishop, Baldwin due in part to an IRS investigation.

The broad range of proof the district court would have permitted concerning Bishop, Baldwin is centered around the activities of Cavanaugh. Yet, despite wide discovery permitted the defendant and the defendant's proffer of testimony of numerous witnesses acquainted with the intelligence community and even with Bishop, Baldwin and the United States Far East intelligence operations, Smith has failed to connect Cavanaugh to his double agent operation. In his lengthy proffer of testimony, Smith does not even claim that White and Ishida would testify that they worked for Cavanaugh. Yet he would ask the jury to infer that Cavanaugh directed his double agent operation and that he was left dangling because Cavanaugh was trying to protect himself.

Thus, the inferences Smith would ask the jury to draw are strained and of marginal relevance at best. Certainly they are no better than speculative and hence do not support the admission of the privileged information.

In its brief in this court, the government states that it has no objection if Smith shows that White and Ishida told him to communicate with them through a telephone number which was in fact a number of Bishop, Baldwin and that calls to that number were transmitted to CIA agents. These facts would seem to be admissible under the balancing test we have outlined in the text of the opinion. They would be essential to the defense, not merely cumulative, corroborative nor speculative. All the balance of the classified information held admissible by the district court under the heading "Bishop, Baldwin Information" we think is inadmissible and that the holding of the district court admitting the same was an abuse of discretion.

In testimony before a House Subcommittee, the assistant attorney general explicitly characterized the standard derived from *Roviaro* as an "important" difference between the House and the administration bills. Noting that the House bill did not include the *Roviaro* standard of "relevant and material," he testified at length on the reasons this omission should be rectified. The government's argument in this appeal is essentially a paraphrase of the assistant attorney general's testimony.

The Congress rejected the assistant attorney general's recommendation. Congressional intent not to incorporate the *Roviaro* standard is manifest from legislative history. The Senate Report states:

> It should be emphasized, however, that the court should not balance the national security interests of the Government against the rights of the defendant to obtain the information. The sanctions against the Government are designed to make the defendant whole again.

S. Rep. No. 823, 96th Cong., 2d Sess. at 9, *reprinted in* 1980 U.S.CONG. AND AD.NEWS 4294, 4303. We cannot accept the notion expressed in note 8 of the majority opinion that this unequivocal statement is inconsistent with congressional intent. It is clear from the text of the Act and its legislative history that the Congress intended the Executive, not the courts, to decide whether to expose relevant classified information subject to sanctions the Act provides. The Act does not incorporate the *Rovario* standard. It omitted the requirement that the evidence be "relevant and material," as urged by the Department of Justice's spokesman. Now the majority opinion embraces what the Congress rejected.

[handwritten margin note: Congress did not intend to include the Roviaro std]

Smith is not seeking disclosure by the government of two items of classified evidence that are the subject of this appeal. He has no need to discover it. He possesses this evidence and seeks to introduce it in his defense. The district court has ruled that it is relevant and admissible.

The text of the statute, its legislative history, and cases interpreting it establish that the Act does not alter existing standards for determining relevance and admissibility of evidence. Existing standards apply *Roviaro* to requests for discovery of information known to the government but unknown to the defendant. Under existing standards which the Congress intended to leave intact, *Roviaro* did not exclude the introduction of relevant evidence known to the defendant. Consequently, the majority is unable to cite a case in which the informer's privilege was successfully invoked to bar a defendant from calling an informant as a witness when his identity and whereabouts were known to the defendant and his testimony was relevant.

If under existing standards *Roviaro* governed admissibility of evidence known to the defendant, there would be little need for the Act. A simple pretrial disclosure rule such as those required for alibi, insanity, or rape would suffice if the government was required to disclose to the court the necessary information to balance intelligently the defendant's needs against the interests of national security. The Act, however, was designed to shield the government from the necessity of explaining to the court at the hearing contemplated by § 6(a) the information that is ordinarily furnished by the government when a *Roviaro* request is denied under existing law.

The application of *Roviaro* to exclude relevant evidence known to the defendant, instead of confining its principles to discovery requests, significantly alters the existing standard for determining the admissibility of evidence in contravention of express congressional intent. This novel alteration of the standard is made at the cost of introducing confusion into a well drafted, straightforward procedure that at once protects national security and affords the defendant a fair trial. Contrary to the provisions of the Act, the court, in a hearing required by Section 6(a), will have to require the government to produce information in support of its claim that the interests of national security outweigh the defendant's need to introduce relevant evidence which he already possesses. Alternatively, the court will have to try and balance these interests without the information which *Roviaro* contemplates it should have.

Roviaro, of course, is still applicable to discovery requests. This is clearly explained in *United States v. Pringle,* 751 F.2d 419 (1st Cir.1984), on which the majority relies. There the court pointed out that none of the defendants "possessed classified information which they threatened to disclose. Quite to the contrary, they were seeking classified information which the government sought to protect." Consequently, the court held that the district court did not err in refusing discovery without convening a hearing under Section 6(a). It is apparent that *Pringle* dealt with a situation quite different from the issues raised in this appeal about the Section 6(a) hearing.

The majority opinion, for which there is no precedent, departs both from the procedure set out in the Act and from existing standards for determining the admissibility of evidence that the Congress intended to leave intact. Sadly, the departure is altogether needless. If a district court follows step by step the procedures established by the Act and adheres to the congressional admonition to apply existing standards for determining the admissibility of evidence, the government's interest in national security, which the district judge and all members of this court seek to protect, will be preserved. At the same time, the need of the defendant to present relevant evidence, which Congress recognized, will be addressed in the manner provided by the Act.

Section 6(c)(2) of the Act directs the district court to hold a hearing on a motion by the government for an alternative procedure for disclosure of classified information. Until this appeal is resolved, the district court cannot conduct a hearing pursuant to this section. Nevertheless, without a motion and without a hearing, the majority has decreed that two alternatives suggested by the government in its brief adequately serve the needs of the defendant.

Appellate pre-emption of the district judge's functions specified by Section 6(c)(2) is unauthorized by the Act, and it is prejudicial. It deprives the defendant of the hearing Congress intended him to have. As a predicate to one of its rulings, the majority misapprehends the reasons the defense seeks to introduce certain evidence and the basis for the district court's ruling. A hearing contemplated by Section 6(c)(2) would enable the district court to avoid such an error.

I respectfully dissent.

NOTES AND QUESTIONS

1. *United States v. Wilson*, 732 F.2d 404 (5th Cir. 1984), cited in *Smith*, involved an attempted sale and export to Libya of 20 tons of C-4 explosives. Wilson introduced evidence of his prior relationship with the CIA and testified that, on the basis of continuing contacts with CIA agents, he believed his activities were authorized or at least would not be prosecuted. His professed belief was that he was being encouraged to ingratiate himself with the Qaddafi regime to bring back information to the U.S. The CIA sought to have a high-ranking official testify pseudonymously, and ultimately the judge settled on the compromise of an affidavit from the CIA personnel director stating that Wilson "was not asked or requested, directly or indirectly, to perform or provide any service, directly or indirectly, for [the] CIA."

Twenty years later, in response to Wilson's motion to vacate his sentence, the Government finally turned over information showing that there were "more than 80" contacts between him and CIA agents during the relevant time and that lawyers knew this at the time of trial. The district court judge was not pleased:

> The government discussed among dozens of its officials and lawyers whether to correct the testimony. No correction was made – not after trial, not before sentencing, not on appeal, and not in this review. Confronted with its own internal memoranda, the government now says that, well, it might have misstated the truth, but that it was Wilson's fault, it did not really matter, and it did not know what it was doing. Because the government knowingly used false evidence against him and suppressed favorable evidence, his conviction will be vacated. This opinion refers only to the part of the record that the government has reluctantly agreed may be made public. It does not attempt to recount even that limited range of data in its entirety; the governmental deceit mentioned here is illustrative – not exhaustive.

United States v. Wilson, 289 F. Supp. 2d 801 (S.D. Tex. 2003).

This was not exactly a CIPA case because it involved government submission of a substitute for live testimony in rebuttal of defense testimony. It may be interesting to note that Wilson remains in prison under other convictions for such offenses as attempted murder and retaliation against witnesses. It also bears mention that Justice Department lawyers dispute the District Judge's characterization of the proceedings.

2. *United States v. Fernandez*, 913 F.2d 148 (4th Cir. 1990), was part of the fallout of the Oliver North Iran-Contra scandal of 1984-86. Fernandez was CIA Station Chief in Costa Rica during the time that Congress prohibited use of U.S. funds for supplying the "Contras," paramilitary organizations attempting to overthrow the leftist government of Nicaragua from bases in El Salvador, Honduras, and Costa Rica. As part of the 1980 settlement with Iran of the hostage situation in that country, the U.S. sold Iran military equipment. Colonel North diverted proceeds of those sales to "private benefactors" who would help supply the Contras. When questioned about these activities, Fernandez allegedly lied and misled investigators by obfuscating the purpose of building an airstrip in Costa Rica. Fernandez wanted to introduce as part of his defense particulars of other CIA projects in the region and the U.S. objected under CIPA. The opinion of the Fourth Circuit is instructive for its omissions and difficulty of handling this type of case. In the excerpts below, classified material is identified as ****:

The first category of classified information admitted by the trial judge concerned three intelligence projects undertaken jointly by the United States and Costa Rica: (1) ****, (2) ****, and (3) **** (collectively referred to as the "projects"). The district court agreed with Fernandez that classified information concerning these programs would corroborate his claim that the airstrip project was part of a larger Costa Rican effort to protect itself against a Nicaraguan invasion, which would in turn support the truth of his allegedly false statements about the origin and purpose of, and his involvement in, the airstrip project.

The second category of classified material that the trial judge authorized for disclosure at trial concerned the location of CIA **** (collectively referred to as "locations" ****). At the CIPA hearing, Fernandez's attorney argued, and the district court agreed, that Fernandez needed to present the identity and location of these **** to the jury in order to demonstrate the CIA's extensive involvement in the resupply operation. One of the **** was located **** through their operations, were deeply involved in the private benefactor program. The identity and location of these **** were relevant because they would help paint a picture of massive CIA involvement in and knowledge of the resupply of the Contras. This picture, in turn, would support Fernandez's claim that he never made the allegedly false statements (which were never recorded or transcribed), and thus did not lie, and had no motive or intent to lie, concerning his knowledge of North's role in the Contra resupply operation or his knowledge of the nature of the supplies delivered in 1986.

Following the district court's order authorizing the disclosure of information about the locations and the projects, the United States submitted a series of proposed substitutions under § 6(c) of CIPA. The government's proposed substitutions were introduced on July 12, and revised on July 14, 21, and 24. As explained below, the district court rejected these various substitution proposals over the course of several days as inadequate to "provide the defendant with substantially the same ability to make his defense as would disclosure of the specific classified information."

In lieu of information about the **** projects in Costa Rica, the government offered on July 12 to acknowledge ****. The district court rejected these proposed substitutions because they failed to describe the nature and extent of the programs in operation at the same time as the airstrip. The court explained that the substitutions would undermine Fernandez's ability to show the seriousness with which the Costa Rican government took the Nicaraguan threat, the substantial efforts the Costa Rican government took (in the form of the three projects) to address this threat, and the close relationship between the three projects and the airstrip.

The district court also rejected the substitution proposals concerning the locations of the ****. In place of the information about the location and activities of the CIA **** facilities, the government proposed on July 12 to acknowledge that ****. The court rejected these proposed substitutions as "insufficient" after reiterating its earlier determination that the identities of the **** were critical to Fernandez's defense.

Ultimately, the government refused to allow disclosure of the material, and the district court ordered the indictment dismissed. The Fourth Circuit affirmed on the basis that the classified material was critical to Fernandez's ability to present his case because the other projects would show that he had no reason to lie about the airstrip and that the CIA was fully knowledgeable of his activities.

3. The Fourth Circuit discloses a lot about Fernandez's defense while attempting to keep secret information out of its opinion. By contrast, the Ninth Circuit tells us nothing about the information that Sarkissian wanted, although we can guess that it had something to do with informants or wiretap tapes. If you were going to provide instructions to Courts of Appeals about how to report CIPA cases so that the legal profession could understand development of this area of the law, how would you describe the role of the reviewing court?

4. The DC Circuit in *Yunis* responded as follows to the argument that the defendant is handicapped in arguing materiality of classified material because he does not know what the material says: "Yunis was present during all the relevant conversations. It does not impose upon him any burden of absolute memory, omniscience, or superhuman mental capacity to expect some specificity as to what benefit he expects to gain from the evidence sought here." What if in fact Yunis was not present? How does a defendant who is the subject of a mistaken identity, and has no knowledge of the crime, defend himself? Secondly, is it proper to insist on "materiality" of the desired evidence rather than a mere "helpful to the defense" standard?

5. The Ninth Circuit in *Sarkissian* cited cases from the Fourth Circuit and First Circuit to the effect that CIPA required balancing of the defendant's need for the information with the government's (or public's) harm if the information were disclosed. The DC Circuit in *Yunis* refused to adopt a balancing approach, and the Fourth Circuit in *Fernandez* had this to say about "balancing" interests:

The judge emphasized that he reached this decision after weighing the interests of national security against the need to provide Fernandez with a fair trial. He concluded by emphasizing: "I believe that the identity of these **** is necessary for the defense, and would rule that your substitution would not be adequate." It was clearly within the district court's discretion to conclude that the government's vague, compressed descriptions about the CIA's general presence in the region and about its general familiarity with the resupply operations were no substitute for live testimony from witnesses and the introduction of actual documents detailing the CIA's intimate involvement with the resupply operation.

Is this "balancing" or is it placing a burden on the government to justify imposition on the right to confront witnesses? CIPA provides that the court will accept substitute material "if it finds that the statement or summary will provide the defendant with substantially the same ability to make his defense as would disclosure of the specific classified information." If the government has sole discretion whether to authorize disclosure, then should the court balance rather than simply deciding the question of whether the substituted material is a substantial equivalent of the actual material?

UNITED STATES v. MOUSSAOUI
382 F.3d 453 (4th Cir. 2004)

[As mentioned earlier, Zacarias Moussaoui is the alleged "20th hijacker" who was supposed to have been on one of the planes on 9/11 but was already in jail on visa violations. He is being prosecuted in the Eastern District of Virginia for a variety of claims including conspiracy to murder U.S. nationals. In essence, what has occurred is that Moussaoui demands to depose some members of the Al Qaeda organization who are in U.S. custody at undisclosed locations (presumably outside the U.S.). Probably the key deponent would be Khalid Sheikh Muhammed (KSM), who we mentioned earlier at p. 64 and who is generally regarded as the mastermind of the 9/11 plot. The Government resisted on the ground that the identity of these persons as well as any information that they might possess are classified – that even disclosure of their identity or location would endanger national security.

[The District Judge rejected the Government's proposed substituted redactions and summaries, stating that Moussaoui must have the ability to find out what these persons know before it can then be determined whether that information could be disclosed at trial. The parties assumed that if the Government did not allow the depositions to occur, then the Court would have no further recourse than to dismiss the indictment. The Government stated that if the case were dismissed, Moussaoui could be remitted to military detention as an "enemy combatant," but that option may have been foreclosed by the Supreme Court in the *Hamdi* case, p. 492.

[The Government first sought to appeal the Court's orders requiring the government to allow defense counsel to take depositions of these witnesses. That appeal was premised on the provisions of CIPA that allow interlocutory appeal of orders requiring "disclosure" of classified information. In July 2004, the Fourth Circuit held that the orders were not appealable because they were not really based on CIPA and the taking of the deposition would not by itself "disclose" classified information. The Government still refused to allow access to the witnesses and suggested that the trial judge should dismiss the indictment so that there would be a final appealable order. Instead, the judge imposed other sanctions, eliminating the possibility of the death penalty and excluding any evidence relating to the 9/11 plot.]

Before WILKINS, Chief Judge, and WILLIAMS and GREGORY, Circuit Judges. Affirmed in part, vacated in part, and remanded by published opinion. Chief

Judge WILKINS announced the judgment of the court and wrote an opinion, in which Judge WILLIAMS concurs, and in which Judge GREGORY concurs except as to Part V.C. Judge WILLIAMS wrote a concurring opinion. Judge GREGORY wrote an opinion concurring in part and dissenting in part.

WILKINS, Chief Judge:

The Government appeals a series of rulings by the district court granting Appellee Zacarias Moussaoui access to certain individuals[1] ("the enemy combatant witnesses" or "the witnesses") for the purpose of deposing them pursuant to Federal Rule of Criminal Procedure 15; rejecting the Government's proposed substitutions for the depositions; and imposing sanctions for the Government's refusal to produce the witnesses. We are presented with questions of grave significance – questions that test the commitment of this nation to an independent judiciary, to the constitutional guarantee of a fair trial even to one accused of the most heinous of crimes, and to the protection of our citizens against additional terrorist attacks. These questions do not admit of easy answers.

For the reasons set forth below, we reject the Government's claim that the district court exceeded its authority in granting Moussaoui access to the witnesses. We affirm the conclusion of the district court that the enemy combatant witnesses could provide material, favorable testimony on Moussaoui's behalf, and we agree with the district court that the Government's proposed substitutions for the witnesses' deposition testimony are inadequate. However, we reverse the district court insofar as it held that it is not possible to craft adequate substitutions, and we remand with instructions for the district court and the parties to craft substitutions under certain guidelines. Finally, we vacate the order imposing sanctions on the Government.

I.

A. *Background Information*

Moussaoui was arrested for an immigration violation in mid-August 2001 and, in December of that year, was indicted on several charges of conspiracy related to the September 11 attacks. In July 2002, the Government filed a superceding indictment charging Moussaoui with six offenses: conspiracy to commit acts of terrorism transcending national boundaries, 18 U.S.C. § 2332b(a)(2), (c); conspiracy to commit aircraft piracy, 49 U.S.C. § 46502(a)(1)(A), (a)(2)(B); conspiracy to destroy aircraft, 18 U.S.C. §§ 32(a)(7), 34; conspiracy to use weapons of mass destruction, 18 U.S.C. § 2332a(a); conspiracy to murder United States employees, 18 U.S.C. §§ 1114, 1117; and conspiracy to destroy property, 18 U.S.C. § 844(f), (i), (n). The Government seeks the death penalty on the first four of these charges.

According to the allegations of the indictment, Moussaoui was present at an al Qaeda training camp in April 1998. The indictment further alleges that Moussaoui arrived in the United States in late February 2001 and thereafter

---

[1] The names of these individuals are classified, as is much of the information pertinent to this appeal. We have avoided reference to classified material to the greatest extent possible.

began flight lessons in Norman, Oklahoma. Other allegations in the indictment highlight similarities between Moussaoui's conduct and the conduct of the September 11 hijackers. Each of the four death-eligible counts of the indictment alleges that the actions of Moussaoui and his coconspirators "result[ed] in the deaths of thousands of persons on September 11, 2001."

B. *Events Leading to this Appeal*

Simultaneously with its prosecution of Moussaoui, the Executive Branch has been engaged in ongoing efforts to eradicate al Qaeda and to capture its leader, Usama bin Laden. These efforts have resulted in the capture of numerous members of al Qaeda, including the witnesses at issue here: ___ ("Witness A"), ___ ("Witness B"), ___ and ___ ("Witness C"), ___

Witness A was captured ___. Shortly thereafter, Moussaoui (who at that time was representing himself in the district court) moved for access to Witness A, asserting that the witness would be an important part of his defense. Moussaoui's motion was supported by then-standby counsel, who filed a motion seeking pretrial access to Witness A and a writ of habeas corpus *ad testificandum* to obtain Witness A's trial testimony. The Government opposed this request.

The district court conducted a hearing, after which it issued an oral ruling granting access to Witness A ("the January 30 order"). The district court concluded that Witness A could offer material testimony in Moussaoui's defense; in particular, the court determined that Witness A had extensive knowledge of the September 11 plot and that his testimony would support Moussaoui's claim that he was not involved in the attacks. At a minimum, the court observed, Witness A's testimony could support an argument that Moussaoui should not receive the death penalty if convicted.

The district court acknowledged that Witness A is a national security asset and therefore denied standby counsel's request for unmonitored pretrial access and declined to order his production at trial. The court also determined, however, that the Government's national security interest must yield to Moussaoui's right to a fair trial. Accordingly, the court ordered that Witness A's testimony be preserved by means of a Rule 15 deposition (providing that court may order deposition of witness to preserve testimony for trial "because of exceptional circumstances and in the interest of justice"). In an attempt to minimize the effect of its order on national security, the district court ordered that certain precautions be taken. Specifically, the court directed that the deposition would be taken by remote video, with Witness A in an undisclosed location and Moussaoui, standby counsel, and counsel for the Government in the presence of the district court, ___

[The Government's interlocutory appeal from that order was dismissed.] On July 14, 2003, the Government filed a pleading indicating that it would refuse to provide access to Witness A for the purpose of conducting a deposition. On August 29, the district court entered an order ("the August 29 order") granting access to Witnesses B and C for purposes of conducting Rule 15 depositions of those witnesses. The order imposed the same conditions as those applicable to Witness A. The court also directed the Government to file any proposed substitutions for the witnesses' testimony by September 5, and it directed standby counsel to file any response to the substitutions by September 12.

On September 8, the district court rejected the Government's proposed substitutions without requiring any response from the defense. The court stated that the Government's proposed substitutions for the deposition testimony of Witnesses B and C failed for the same reasons as the Government's proposed substitutions for the deposition testimony of Witness A. Following the rejection of its proposed substitutions, the Government informed the court that it would not comply with the August 29 order.

The district court then directed the parties to submit briefs concerning the appropriate sanction to be imposed for the Government's refusal to comply with the January 30 and August 29 orders. Standby counsel sought dismissal but alternatively asked the district court to dismiss the death notice. The Government filed a responsive pleading stating that "[t]o present the issue most efficiently to the Court of Appeals, and because [CIPA] prescribes dismissal as the presumptive action a district court must take in these circumstances, we do not oppose standby counsel's suggestion that the appropriate action in this case is to dismiss the indictment."

Noting that "[t]he unprecedented investment of both human and material resources in this case mandates the careful consideration of some sanction other than dismissal," the district court rejected the parties' claims that the indictment should be dismissed. Rather, the court dismissed the death notice, reasoning that Moussaoui had adequately demonstrated that the witnesses could provide testimony that, if believed, might preclude a jury from finding Moussaoui eligible for the death penalty. Further, because proof of Moussaoui's involvement in the September 11 attacks was not necessary to a conviction, and because the witnesses' testimony, if believed, could exonerate Moussaoui of involvement in those attacks, the district court prohibited the Government "from making any argument, or offering any evidence, suggesting that the defendant had any involvement in, or knowledge of, the September 11 attacks." In conjunction with this ruling, the district court denied the Government's motions to admit into evidence cockpit voice recordings made on September 11; video footage of the collapse of the World Trade Center towers; and photographs of the victims of the attacks.

The Government appealed, attacking multiple aspects of the rulings of the district court.

C. *Events Leading to Issuance of this Amended Opinion*

We issued our decision on April 22, 2004. *See United States v. Moussaoui*, 365 F.3d 292 (4th Cir.2004). Moussaoui thereafter timely filed a petition for rehearing and suggestion for rehearing en banc (the Petition). On May 12, the Government submitted a letter to the court purporting to "clarify certain factual matters." Letter to Deputy Clerk from United States Attorney at 1 (May 12, 2004) [hereinafter "Letter"]. In particular, the Government referred to pages 50-51 of the classified slip opinion, where the court stated:

    "——"

In response to the emphasized portion of the above quotation, the Government stated that

members of the prosecution team, including FBI Special Agents assigned to the September 11 and other related investigations, ___ have provided ___ information ___ consistent with the ___ desire to maximize their own efforts to obtain actionable information ___.

Based in part on the revelations in the May 12 letter, we directed the Government to file a response to the Petition. In particular, we directed the Government to provide answers to the following questions:

(1) Why was the information in the May 12 Letter not provided to this court or the district court prior to May 12?

(4) ___ provided inculpatory of exculpatory information regarding Moussaoui?

(5) In light of the information contained in the Letter and any other pertinent developments, would it now be appropriate to submit written questions to any of the enemy combatant witnesses?

(9) If circumstances have changed such that submission of written questions is now possible, when did the circumstances change and why was neither this court nor the district court so informed at that time?

Underlying this order were concerns among the panel members that members of the prosecution team may have ___ rendered the witnesses' statements less reliable.

D. *Additional Facts Contained in the Government's Submissions in Response to the Petition*

4. *Intelligence Community Use of Information*

___ the intelligence community is interested only in obtaining information that has foreign intelligence value; the intelligence community is not concerned with obtaining information to aid in the prosecution of Moussaoui. ___ not create special ___ reports for use by the prosecution, rather, the prosecution and the PESTTBOM team receive the same reports that are distributed to the intelligence community at large. Information is included in these reports only if ___ the information to have foreign intelligence value.[14]

II.

Before turning to the merits, we consider the preliminary question of our jurisdiction. [18 U.S.C. § 3731 allows interlocutory appeals by the government from orders dismissing indictments or excluding evidence under certain

---

[14] The Government's submissions indicate that those responsible for ___ the witnesses record and pass on only information ___ to have foreign intelligence value. Consequently, it is at least possible, albeit unlikely, that one of the witnesses has imparted significant exculpatory information related to Moussaoui that has not been included ___. If so, there may be a due process problem under *Brady v. Maryland*, 373 U.S. 83, 83 S.Ct. 1194, 10 L.Ed.2d 215 (1963). *See United States v. Perdomo*, 929 F.2d 967, 971 (3d Cir.1991) (stating that prosecution is obligated under *Brady* to disclose all exculpatory information "in the possession of some arm of the state"). We need not consider this question, however, as there is no evidence before us that the Government possesses exculpatory material that has not been disclosed to the defense.

circumstances.] The district court sanctioned the Government for refusing to produce the enemy combatant witnesses for depositions by dismissing the death notice and excluding specific items of evidence. Both aspects of the sanction are appealable under U.S.C. § 3731 – the latter under the text of the statute itself, and the former by liberal construction of the term "dismissing."

III.

With respect to the merits, the Government first argues that the district court erred in ordering the production of the enemy combatant witnesses for the purpose of deposing them. Within the context of this argument, the Government makes two related claims. First, the Government asserts that because the witnesses are noncitizens outside the territorial boundaries of the United States, there is no means by which the district court can compel their appearance on Moussaoui's behalf. Second, the Government maintains that even if the district court has the power to reach the witnesses, its exercise of that power is curtailed by the reality that the witnesses are in military custody in time of war, and thus requiring them to be produced would violate constitutional principles of separation of powers. We address these arguments seriatim.

A. *Process Power*

The Sixth Amendment guarantees that "[i]n all criminal prosecutions, the accused shall enjoy the right . . . to have compulsory process for obtaining witnesses in his favor." U.S. Const. amend. VI. The compulsory process right is circumscribed, however, by the ability of the district court to obtain the presence of a witness through service of process. The Government maintains that because the enemy combatant witnesses are foreign nationals outside the boundaries of the United States, they are beyond the process power of the district court and, hence, unavailable to Moussaoui.

The Government's argument rests primarily on the well established and undisputed principle that the process power of the district court does not extend to foreign nationals abroad. Were this the governing rule, Moussaoui clearly would have no claim under the Sixth Amendment. This is not the controlling principle, however.

The Government's argument overlooks the critical fact that the enemy combatant witnesses are ___ of the United States Government.[15] Therefore, we are concerned not with the ability of the district court to issue a subpoena to the witnesses, but rather with its power to issue a writ of habeas corpus *ad testificandum* ("testimonial writ") to the witnesses' custodian.

B. *Person to be Served*

Ordinarily, a habeas writ must be served on a prisoner's immediate custodian – "the individual with day-to-day control over" the prisoner. Here, however, the immediate custodian is unknown. Under such circumstances, the writ is properly served on the prisoner's ultimate custodian. It would appear – at least the Government has not disputed – that the witnesses are in military custody.

---

[15] The Government will neither confirm nor deny that the witnesses are ___. However, it concedes, and we agree, that for purposes of this appeal we must assume that the witnesses are ___.

Therefore, Secretary of Defense Donald Rumsfeld is their ultimate custodian. Secretary Rumsfeld – who is indisputably within the process power of the district court – is thus a proper recipient of a testimonial writ directing production of the witnesses. ___

IV.

The Government next argues that even if the district court would otherwise have the power to order the production of the witnesses, the January 30 and August 29 orders are improper because they infringe on the Executive's warmaking authority, in violation of separation of powers principles.[18]

A. *Immunity Cases*

We begin by examining the Government's reliance on cases concerning governmental refusal to grant immunity to potential defense witnesses. The Government argues that these cases stand for the proposition that the district court may be precluded from issuing certain orders that implicate the separation of powers. We reject this characterization of these cases.

The Self-Incrimination Clause of the Fifth Amendment guarantees that no person "shall be compelled in any criminal case to be a witness against himself." The circuit courts, including the Fourth Circuit, have uniformly held that district courts do not have any authority to grant immunity, even when a grant of immunity would allow a defendant to present material, favorable testimony. These holdings have been based on the facts that no power to grant immunity is found in the Constitution and that Congress reserved the statutory immunity power to the Attorney General. Because a district court has no power to grant immunity to compel the testimony of a potential witness who has invoked the privilege against self-incrimination, a defendant has no Sixth Amendment right to such testimony.

The circuits are divided with respect to the question of whether a district court can ever compel the government, on pain of dismissal, to grant immunity to a potential defense witness. The Fourth Circuit, consistent with the majority rule, has held that a district court may compel the government to grant immunity upon a showing of prosecutorial misconduct and materiality.

The Government claims that these "immunity cases" stand for the proposition that, under certain circumstances, legitimate separation of powers concerns effectively insulate the Government from being compelled to produce evidence or witnesses. In fact, the majority rule and the law of this circuit stand for precisely the opposite proposition, namely, that courts *will* compel a grant of immunity, ~~despite the existence of separation of powers concerns, when the~~ defendant demonstrates that the Government's refusal to grant immunity to an

___

[18] Moussaoui asserts that we should not consider this argument because any conflict between the Governments' interests and Moussaoui's is of the Government's making. There is no question that the Government cannot invoke national security concerns as a means of depriving Moussaoui of a fair trial. That is not what the Government is attempting to do, however. The Government's claim is that separation of powers principles place the enemy combatant witnesses beyond the reach of the district court. If that is so (although we ultimately conclude it is not), then Moussaoui would not have an enforceable Sixth Amendment right to the witnesses' testimony.

essential defense witness constitutes an abuse of the discretion granted to the Government by the Immunity Act. A showing of misconduct is necessary because, as explained above, a defendant has no Sixth Amendment right to the testimony of a potential witness who has invoked the Fifth Amendment right against self-incrimination; therefore, the defendant has no Sixth Amendment right that could outweigh the Government's interest in using its immunity power sparingly. Governmental abuse of the immunity power, however, vitiates this interest because when the Government's misconduct threatens to impair the defendant's right to a fair trial, it is proper for the district court to protect that right by compelling the Government to immunize the witness.

For these reasons, the analogy between this case and the immunity cases is inapt. The witnesses at issue here, unlike potential witnesses who have invoked their Fifth Amendment rights, are within the process power of the district court, and Moussaoui therefore has a Sixth Amendment right to their testimony. As discussed below, this right must be balanced against the Government's legitimate interest in preventing disruption ___ of the enemy combatant witnesses.

B. *Governing Principles*

The concept that the various forms of governmental power – legislative, executive, and judicial – should be exercised by different bodies predates the Constitution.

Separation of powers does not mean, however, that each branch is prohibited from *any* activity that might have an impact on another. Stated in its simplest terms, the separation of powers doctrine prohibits each branch of the government from "intrud[ing] upon the central prerogatives of another." Such an intrusion occurs when one branch arrogates to itself powers constitutionally assigned to another branch or when the otherwise legitimate actions of one branch impair the functions of another.

This is not a case involving arrogation of the powers or duties of another branch. The district court orders requiring production of the enemy combatant witnesses involved the resolution of questions properly – indeed, exclusively – reserved to the judiciary. Therefore, if there is a separation of powers problem at all, it arises only from the burden the actions of the district court place on the Executive's performance of its duties.

The Supreme Court has explained on several occasions that determining whether a judicial act places impermissible burdens on another branch of government requires balancing the competing interests.

C. *Balancing*

1. *The Burden on the Government*

The Constitution charges the Congress and the Executive with the making and conduct of war. Thus, "[i]n accordance with [the] constitutional text, the Supreme Court has shown great deference to the political branches when called upon to decide cases implicating sensitive matters of foreign policy, national security, or military affairs." *Hamdi II,* 296 F.3d at 281.

The Government alleges – and we accept as true – that ___ the enemy combatant witnesses is critical to the ongoing effort to combat terrorism by al Qaeda. The witnesses are ___ al Qaeda operatives who have extensive knowledge concerning not just the September 11 attacks, but also other past attacks, future operations, and the structure, personnel, and tactics of al Qaeda. Their value as intelligence sources can hardly be overstated. And, we must defer to the Government's assertion that interruption ___ of these witnesses will have devastating effects on the ability to gather information from them. ___ it is not unreasonable to suppose that interruption ___ could result in the loss of information that might prevent future terrorist attacks.

The Government also asserts that production of the witnesses would burden the Executive's ability to conduct foreign relations. The Government claims that if the Executive's assurances of confidentiality can be abrogated by the judiciary, the vital ability to obtain the cooperation of other governments will be devastated.

In summary, the burdens that would arise from production of the enemy combatant witnesses are substantial.

2. *Moussaoui's Interest*

The importance of the Sixth Amendment right to compulsory process is not subject to question – it is integral to our adversarial criminal justice system. [The judicial system itself, not just the defendant, needs all available evidence to ensure its full functioning and credibility.]

The compulsory process right does not attach to any witness the defendant wishes to call, however. Rather, a defendant must demonstrate that the witness he desires to have produced would testify "in his favor." Thus, in order to assess Moussaoui's interest, we must determine whether the enemy combatant witnesses could provide testimony material to Moussaoui's defense.

In the CIPA context,[20] we have adopted the standard articulated by the Supreme Court in *Roviaro v. United States,* 353 U.S. 53 (1957), for determining whether the government's privilege in classified information must give way. Under that standard, a defendant becomes entitled to disclosure of classified information upon a showing that the information "is relevant and helpful to the defense . . . or is essential to a fair determination of a cause."

Because Moussaoui has not had – and will not receive – direct access to any of the witnesses, he cannot be required to show materiality with the degree of specificity that applies in the ordinary case. Rather, it is sufficient if Moussaoui can make a "plausible showing" of materiality. However, in determining whether

---

[20] We adhere to our prior ruling that CIPA does not apply because the January 30 and August 29 orders of the district court are not covered by either of the potentially relevant provisions of CIPA: § 4 (concerning deletion of classified information from documents to be turned over to the defendant during discovery) or § 6 (concerning the disclosure of classified information by the defense during pretrial or trial proceedings). Like the district court, however, we believe that CIPA provides a useful framework for considering the questions raised by Moussaoui's request for access to the enemy combatant witnesses.

Moussaoui has made a plausible showing, we must bear in mind that Moussaoui *does* have access to the ___ summaries.

[T]he Government argues that even if the witnesses' testimony would tend to exonerate Moussaoui of involvement in the September 11 attacks, such testimony would not be material because the conspiracies with which Moussaoui is charged are broader than September 11. Thus, the Government argues, Moussaoui can be convicted even if he lacked any prior knowledge of September 11. This argument ignores the principle that the scope of an alleged conspiracy is a jury question, and the possibility that Moussaoui may assert that the conspiracy culminating in the September 11 attacks was distinct from any conspiracy in which he was involved. Moreover, even if the jury accepts the Government's claims regarding the scope of the charged conspiracy, testimony regarding Moussaoui's non-involvement in September 11 is critical to the penalty phase. If Moussaoui had no involvement in or knowledge of September 11, it is entirely possible that he would not be found eligible for the death penalty.

We now consider the rulings of the district court regarding the ability of each witness to provide material testimony in Moussaoui's favor.

a. *Witness A*

The district court did not err in concluding that Witness A could offer material evidence on Moussaoui's behalf. ___ Several statements by Witness A tend to exculpate Moussaoui. ___ to undermine the theory (which the Government may or may not intend to advance at trial) that Moussaoui was to pilot a fifth plane into the White House. ___ This statement is significant in light of other evidence ___ This is consistent with Moussaoui's claim that he was to be part of a post-September 11 operation.

all 3 could have provided material evid in support of M.

The Government argues that Witness A's statements are actually incriminatory of Moussaoui. It is true that Witness A has made some statements that arguably implicate Moussaoui in the September 11 attacks. ___ On balance, however, Moussaoui has made a sufficient showing that evidence from Witness A would be more helpful than hurtful, or at least that we cannot have confidence in the outcome of the trial without Witness A's evidence.

b. *Witness B*

There can be no question that Witness B could provide material evidence on behalf of Moussaoui. ___ Witness B ___ has indicated that Moussaoui's operational knowledge was limited, a fact that is clearly of exculpatory value as to both guilt and penalty. ___ Thus, of all three witnesses, Witness B is of the greatest exculpatory value.

c. *Witness C*

The district court determined that Witness C could provide material evidence because he could support Moussaoui's contention that he was not involved in the September 11 attacks. We agree with the district court that a jury might reasonably infer, from Witness C___ that Moussaoui was not involved in September 11. We therefore conclude that Moussaoui has made a plausible showing that Witness C would, if available, be a favorable witness.

3. *Balancing*

Having considered the burden alleged by the Government and the right claimed by Moussaoui, we now turn to the question of whether the district court should have refrained from acting in light of the national security interests asserted by the Government. The question is not unique; the Supreme Court has addressed similar matters on numerous occasions. In all cases of this type – cases falling into "what might loosely be called the area of constitutionally guaranteed access to evidence" – the Supreme Court has held that the defendant's right to a trial that comports with the Fifth and Sixth Amendments prevails over the governmental privilege. Ultimately, as these cases make clear, the appropriate procedure is for the district court to order production of the evidence or witness and leave to the Government the choice of whether to comply with that order. If the government refuses to produce the information at issue – as it may properly do – the result is ordinarily dismissal.

For example, in *Roviaro,* the Supreme Court considered the conflict between the governmental interest in protecting the identity of a confidential informant and a defendant's right to present his case. The Court acknowledged the importance of the so-called informer's privilege but held that this privilege is limited by "the fundamental requirements of fairness. Where the disclosure of an informer's identity, or of the contents of his communication, is relevant and helpful to the defense of an accused, or is essential to a fair determination of a cause, the privilege must give way." The Court emphasized that the choice to comply with an order to disclose the identity of a confidential informant belongs to the Government.

In addition to the pronouncements of the Supreme Court in this area, we are also mindful of Congress' judgment, expressed in CIPA, that the Executive's interest in protecting classified information does not overcome a defendant's right to present his case. Under CIPA, once the district court determines that an item of classified information is relevant and material, that item must be admitted unless the government provides an adequate substitution. If no adequate substitution can be found, the government must decide whether it will prohibit the disclosure of the classified information; if it does so, the district court must impose a sanction, which is presumptively dismissal of the indictment.

In view of these authorities, it is clear that when an evidentiary privilege – even one that involves national security – is asserted by the Government in the context of its prosecution of a criminal offense, the "balancing" we must conduct is primarily, if not solely, an examination of whether the district court correctly determined that the information the Government seeks to withhold is material to the defense. We have determined that the enemy combatant witnesses can offer material testimony that is essential to Moussaoui's defense, and we therefore affirm the January 30 and August 29 orders, Thus, the choice is the Government's whether to comply with those orders or suffer a sanction.

V.

As noted previously, the Government has stated that it will not produce the enemy combatant witnesses for depositions (or, we presume, for any other purpose related to this litigation). We are thus left in the following situation: the district court has the power to order production of the enemy combatant witnesses and has properly determined that they could offer material testimony on Moussaoui's behalf, but the Government has refused to produce the witnesses. Under such circumstances, dismissal of the indictment is the usual course. Like the district court, however, we believe that a more measured approach is required. Additionally, we emphasize that no punitive sanction is warranted here because the Government has rightfully exercised its prerogative to protect national security interests by refusing to produce the witnesses.

Although, as explained above, this is not a CIPA case, that act nevertheless provides useful guidance in determining the nature of the remedies that may be available. Under CIPA, dismissal of an indictment is authorized only if the government has failed to produce an adequate substitute for the classified information, and the interests of justice would not be served by imposition of a lesser sanction. CIPA thus enjoins district courts to seek a solution that neither disadvantages the defendant nor penalizes the government (and the public) for protecting classified information that may be vital to national security.

A similar approach is appropriate here. Under such an approach, the first question is whether there is any appropriate substitution for the witnesses' testimony. Because we conclude, for the reasons set forth below, that appropriate substitutions are available, we need not consider any other remedy.

A. *Standard*

CIPA provides that the government may avoid the disclosure of classified information by proposing a substitute for the information, which the district court must accept if it "will provide the defendant with substantially the same ability to make his defense as would disclosure of the specific classified information." We believe that the standard set forth in CIPA adequately conveys the fundamental purpose of a substitution; to place the defendant, as nearly as possible, in the position he would be in if the classified information (here, the depositions of the witnesses) were available to him. Thus, a substitution is an appropriate remedy when it will not materially disadvantage the defendant.

B. *Substitutions proposed by the Government*

The Government proposed substitutions for the witnesses' deposition testimony in the form of a series of statements derived from the ___ summaries. The district court rejected all proposed substitutions as inadequate. The ruling of the district court was based on its conclusions regarding the inherent inadequacy of the substitutions and its findings regarding the specific failings of the Government's proposals. For the reasons set forth below, we reject the ruling of the district court that any substitution for the witnesses' testimony would be inadequate. We agree, however, with the assessment that the particular proposals submitted by the Government are inadequate in their current form.

First, the district court deemed the substitutions inherently inadequate because the ___ reports, from which the substitutions were ultimately derived, were unreliable.[29] This was so, the court reasoned, because the witnesses' ___. The district court also complained that it cannot be determined whether the ___ reports accurately reflect the witnesses' statements ___. The court further commented that the lack of quotation marks in the ___ reports made it impossible to determine whether a given statement is a verbatim recording or ___.

The conclusion of the district court that the proposed substitutions are inherently inadequate is tantamount to a declaration that there could be no adequate substitution for the witnesses' deposition testimony. We reject this conclusion. The answer to the concerns of the district court regarding the accuracy of the ___ reports is that those who are ___ the witnesses have a profound interest in obtaining accurate information from the witnesses and in reporting that information accurately to those who can use it to prevent acts of terrorism and to capture other al Qaeda operatives. These considerations provide sufficient indicia of reliability to alleviate the concerns of the district court.

Next, the district court noted that the substitutions do not indicate that they are summaries of statements made over the course of several months. We agree with the district court that in order to adequately protect Moussaoui's right to a fair trial, the jury must be made aware of certain information concerning the substitutions. [A]t the very least the jury should be informed that the substitutions are derived from reports ___ of the witnesses. The instructions must account for the fact that members of the prosecution team have provided information and suggested ___. The jury should also be instructed that the statements were obtained under circumstances that support a conclusion that the statements are reliable.[31]

We reject the suggestion of the district court that the Government acted improperly in attempting to organize the information presented in the substitutions. Counsel rarely, if ever, present information to the jury in the order they received it during pretrial investigations. Indeed, organizing and distilling voluminous information for comprehensible presentation to a jury is a hallmark of effective advocacy. In short, while there may be problems with the *manner* in

---

[29] The court also deemed the substitutions inadequate because the use of substitutions would deprive Moussaoui of the ability to question the witnesses regarding matters that do not appear in the ___ reports. In essence, the district court appears to have concluded that the substitutions are inadequate because they are not the same thing as a deposition. However, we have already determined that a proposed substitution need not provide Moussaoui with all the benefits of a deposition in order to be adequate.

[31] Nothing in the Government's submissions in connection with the Petition contradicts our conclusion that those ___ the witnesses have a profound interest in obtaining truthful information. To the contrary, we are even more persuaded that the ___ process is carefully designed to elicit truthful and accurate information from the witnesses.

We emphasize that we have never held, nor do we now hold, that the witnesses' statements are in fact truthful, and the jury should not be so instructed. Instead, the jury should be informed that the circumstances were designed to elicit truthful statements from the witnesses. We offer no opinion regarding whether this instruction may include information regarding ___.

which the Government organized the substitutions, the fact that the Government has attempted such organization is not a mark against it.

The district court identified particular problems with the proposed substitutions for Witness A's testimony. For example, the court noted that the proposed substitutions failed to include exculpatory information provided by Witness A and incorporated at least one incriminatory inference not supplied by Witness A's statements. ___ Our own review of the proposed substitutions for the testimony of Witnesses B and C reveals similar problems ___. These problems, however, may be remedied as described below.

C. Instructions for the District Court

1. Submission of Questions by Moussaoui

The Government's submissions in response to the Petition make clear that members of the prosecution team, ___ have had some input ___ the enemy combatant witnesses. Our review of the circumstances of this access indicates that the input by the prosecution team into the ___ process has worked no unfairness on Moussaoui. Nevertheless, in order to provide Moussaoui with the fullest possible range of information from the witnesses, we direct the district court to provide Moussaoui with an opportunity to ___ for ___ discretionary use ___ of the witnesses.[34]

2. Substitutions

For the reasons set forth above, we conclude that the district court erred in ruling that any substitution for the witnesses' testimony is inherently inadequate to the extent it is derived from the ___ reports. To the contrary, we hold that the ___ summaries (which, as the district court determined, accurately recapitulate the ___ reports) provide an adequate basis for the creation of written statements that may be submitted to the jury in lieu of the witnesses' deposition testimony.

summaries are adequate

The compiling of substitutions is a task best suited to the district court, given its greater familiarity with the facts of the case and its authority to manage the presentation of evidence.[35] Nevertheless, we think it is appropriate to provide some guidance to the court and the parties.

First, the circumstances of this case – most notably, the fact that the substitutions may very well support Moussaoui's defense – dictate that the

---

[34] During the hearing regarding the Petition, defense counsel expressed concern over whether ___ would result in the disclosure of trial strategy to the Government. The Government, in its June 16 filing, informs us that measures can be taken to avoid such disclosures. We leave the particulars of any such process to the discretion of the district court. At an absolute minimum, however, whatever process is adopted must ensure that the prosecution team is not privy to ___ propounded by the defense, just as the defense was unaware or ___ propounded by the prosecution team.

[35] We note that the district court will not be drafting original language for submission to the jury. Instead, as we discuss further in the text, Moussaoui will designate portions of the ___ summaries for submission; the Government will raise objections and cross-designate portions of the summaries it believes are required by the rule of completeness; and the district court will make rulings as necessary to compile an appropriate set of substitutions.

compiling of substitutions be an interactive process among the parties and the district court. Second, we think that accuracy and fairness are best achieved by compiling substitutions that use the exact language of the ___ summaries to the greatest extent possible. We believe that the best means of achieving both of these objectives is for defense counsel to identify particular portions of the ___ summaries that Moussaoui may want to admit into evidence at trial. The Government may then offer any objections and argue that additional portions must be included in the interest of completeness, as discussed below. If the substitutions are to be admitted at all (we leave open the possibility that Moussaoui may decide not to use the substitutions in his defense), they may be admitted only by Moussaoui. Based on defense counsel's submissions and the Government's objections, the district court could then compile an appropriate set of substitutions. We leave to the discretion of the district court the question of whether to rule on the admissibility of a particular substitution (*e.g.*, whether a substitution is relevant) at trial or during pre-trial proceedings.

As previously indicated, the jury must be provided with certain information regarding the substitutions. While we leave the particulars of the instructions to the district court, the jury must be informed, at a minimum, that the substitutions are what the witnesses would say if called to testify; that the substitutions are derived from statements obtained under conditions that provide circumstantial guarantees of reliability; that the substitutions contain statements obtained over the course of weeks or months; that members of the prosecution team have contributed to ___ the witnesses; and, if applicable, that Moussaoui has ___ to the witnesses.[38]

On rehearing, both parties acknowledged our holding that CIPA does not apply here but indicated their belief that once the district court has approved substitutions for the witnesses' testimony, CIPA comes into play, with the result that the Government may object to the disclosure of the classified information in the substitutions and request that the district court adopt an alternative form of evidence. We disagree.

It must be remembered that the substitution process we here order is a *replacement* for the testimony of the enemy combatant witnesses. Because the Government will not allow Moussaoui to have contact with the witnesses, we must provide a remedy adequate to protect Moussaoui's constitutional rights. Here, that remedy is substitutions. Once Moussaoui has selected the portions of the ___ summaries he wishes to submit to the jury and the Government has been given an opportunity to be heard, the district court will compile the substitutions, using such additional language as may be necessary to aid the understanding of the jury. Once this process is complete, the matter is at an end – there are to be no additional or supplementary proceedings under CIPA regarding the substitutions.

---

[38] We are mindful of the fact that no written substitution will enable the jury to consider the witnesses' demeanor in determining their credibility. We believe that the instructions outlined above, plus any other instructions the district court may dean necessary in the exercise of its discretion, adequately address this problem.

VI.

In summary, the judgment of the court is as follows. The January 30 and August 29 orders are affirmed, as is the rejection of the Government's proposed substitutions by the district court. The order imposing sanctions on the Government is vacated, and the case is remanded for the compiling of substitutions for the deposition testimony of the enemy combatant witnesses.

AFFIRMED IN PART, VACATED IN PART, AND REMANDED

GREGORY, Circuit Judge, concurring in part and dissenting in part.

I concur with my colleagues' conclusion that the witnesses at issue in this appeal could provide material, favorable testimony on Moussaoui's behalf. I further concur with their conclusion that the witnesses' overseas location does not preclude a finding that they are within the reach of the Compulsory Process Clause because they are, for purposes of this litigation, deemed to be ___ of the United States. I wholeheartedly agree with my colleagues that the Government has an absolute right to refuse access to the witnesses on national security grounds; we shall not, indeed we must not, question the Government's determination that permitting the witnesses to be deposed would put our nation's security at risk. Further, as noted in the majority opinion, the district court correctly found that the proposed substitutions offered by the Government are not adequate to protect Moussaoui's right to a fair trial. However, as both the district court and the majority have recognized, the Government's refusal to comply with the district court's orders necessarily brings with it some consequences. The remedy proposed by the majority does not begin to vindicate Moussaoui's rights. Thus, it is in formulating the remedy for the Government's refusal to comply with the district court's order that I must part ways with the majority.

The ___ summaries paint a complete, if disjointed, picture of the statements made by the witnesses to date; if the summaries are to be used as a substitution for the witnesses' testimony, they should be used in their entirety, subject to the district court's trial rulings on admissibility of any given passage to which either party objects, whether on hearsay grounds, as cumulative, as unduly prejudicial, or upon any other evidentiary basis.

Additionally, I disagree with the majority's decision to vacate the district court's order striking the Government's death notice at this juncture.[5]

Moussaoui's theory of the case, as we understand it, is that even though he is a member of al Qaeda who has pledged his allegiance to Osame bin Laden, and

---

[5] The majority leaves open the possibility that if the substitutions compiled by the district court are inadequate, or if the jury is not properly instructed as to the circumstances of the substitutions and their reliability, the death notice could be stricken and other sanctions could be imposed. In my view, however, Moussaoui's inability to question the witnesses critically impairs his ability to prepare a defense, particularly (though not solely) as to a potential death sentence. Accordingly, as explained more fully below, if Moussaoui must proceed to trial on the basis of substitutions rather than the witnesses' testimony, as we all agree he must, the death penalty should be removed from the range of possible sentences Moussaoui may face.

even though he was willing to engage in terrorist acts, and was indeed training to participate in terrorist acts, he was not involved in the terrorist acts that occurred on September 11, 2001, nor did he know of the plans before the attack took place. Instead, his participation was to involve later attacks, attacks that may or may not have been planned to occur in the United States or against this country's interests abroad.

Even if Moussaoui is permitted to admit substitutions derived from the ___ summaries, those substitutions cannot be considered a functional equivalent of live (or deposition) testimony, nor are they adequate or sufficient to substitute for testimony. Because the summaries are not responses to the questions that Moussaoui would ask if given the opportunity to depose the witnesses, and because the jury will not be able to see the witnesses and judge their credibility, use of the summaries will necessarily place severe limits on the evidence Moussaoui can present in his defense, particularly during the penalty phase of a capital proceeding. The Government may argue that no one, other than Moussaoui himself, has stated he was not involved. Moussaoui has no access to those who could exonerate him from death eligibility, and the jury will not have any evidence upon which to base a finding in this regard except, possibly, for Moussaoui's own testimony, which he is not obligated to provide. Moussaoui will not be able to offer the most relevant evidence with which he might be able to avoid the death penalty.

After we issued our opinion, the Government filed a letter dated May 12, 2004, purporting to "clarify certain factual matters." In that letter, the Government stated that this court's opinion erroneously relied on a presumption that the Government's attorneys had not been privy to, nor had any input into, the ___ witnesses at issue. Until now, no parallel access to the ___ process has been available to Moussaoui.

The Government's May 12 letter, and its positions taken during the hearing before the panel on June 3, 2004, only serve to reinforce my conclusion that the district court was correct in holding that the death penalty should not be within the range of sentencing options available when, as here, the Defendant's ability to mount a defense is severely impaired. As the Government has made clear, the summaries of witness statements provided to the defense are not a complete account of the witnesses' responses ___ the only ___ responses passed to the prosecution, and subsequently provided to the defense, are those responses deemed ___ to have actionable foreign intelligence value. Thus, as the majority acknowledges, it is certainly possible that the witnesses, ___ may have provided information that, although exculpatory as to Moussaoui, was not passed on to the prosecution, and in turn to the defense team, because ___ the information had no actionable foreign intelligence value.[6] As the majority further recognizes,

---

[6] Although the prosecutorial function is to achieve justice, and as such prosecutors must seek out both inculpatory and exculpatory evidence, the Government makes clear that ___. ___ have no duty ___ exculpatory evidence unless that evidence would have actionable foreign intelligence value. Accordingly, even though ___ "have a profound interest in obtaining truthful information," they do not have an interest in ensuring that justice is achieved in this case.

if ___ have exculpatory evidence that they have not passed on to the prosecution, Moussaoui's due process rights may be implicated. The majority downplays this possibility, calling it unlikely, and states that it need not be further explored because "there is no evidence before us that the Government possesses exculpatory material that has not been disclosed to the defense." This conclusion is, at best, misguided. Because of the highly classified nature of the evidence at issue in this case, there is no way this court or Moussaoui could know whether an arm of the Government possesses exculpatory evidence that does not have foreign intelligence value; indeed, even the prosecution would not have access to any such evidence, ___ distribute only those witness summaries that have foreign intelligence value. How there could ever be any evidence before us from which we could conduct a *Brady* analysis under these circumstances is a mystery.

Further, the reliability (or lack thereof) of the witnesses' statements poses real stumbling blocks to the admission of those statements. The Government admits that the summaries are simply accurate reflections of the witnesses' responses ___. However, we do not have all of the witnesses' statements; instead, we are privy only to those portions of their statements that are deemed to have actionable foreign intelligence value. We do not have ___ we do not have ___ we do not know ___. Although the Government assures us that the statements have some indicia of reliability ___. Without this context, however, we have only the bare statement, which the jury may consider to be true ___. This is a slim reed indeed upon which to base a jury verdict, especially where a man's life hangs in the balance.

I cannot disagree with the majority's statement that "[b]ecause the Government will not allow Moussaoui to have contact with the witnesses, this court must provide a remedy adequate to protect Moussaoui's constitutional rights." However, the majority's effort to craft such a remedy rings hollow. The entire process is cloaked in secrecy, making it difficult, if not impossible, for the courts to ensure the provision of Moussaoui's rights. Although the prosecution is laboring under the same constraints ___ Moussaoui has constitutional rights, not extended to the prosecution, that are implicated by this procedure. Because the majority decrees that this so-called "remedy" will fulfill this court's obligation to protect Moussaoui's constitutional rights, today justice has taken a long stride backward.

Here, the reliability of a death sentence would be significantly impaired by the limitations on the evidence available for Moussaoui's use in proving mitigating factors (if he is found guilty). Although it has been repeated often enough to have the ring of cliche, death is different. It is the ultimate penalty, and once carried out, it is irrevocable. A sentence of death cannot be imposed unless the defendant has been accorded the opportunity to defend himself fully; it cannot be imposed without the utmost certainty, the fundamental belief in the fairness of the result. Because Moussaoui will not have access to the witnesses who could answer the question of his involvement, he should not face the ultimate penalty of death. Accordingly, I would uphold the district court's sanction to the extent that it struck the Government's death notice. On this basis, I must dissent.

NOTES AND QUESTIONS

1. Bear in mind that the Government also took the position prior to the *Hamdi* decision of the Supreme Court that it could, at any time, remand an accused terrorist such as Moussaoui to military custody as an "enemy combatant" with nothing more than a Presidential order. As of February 2005, at least two persons, al Maari and Padilla, remain in custody under these conditions.

2. The redacted version of the Fourth Circuit's opinion makes it extremely difficult to know who knows what about the interrogation of the three witnesses. Your author has edited out a great deal of even more unintelligible language to reduce your frustration in reading. My understanding of the situation is that interrogators were asking the questions in which they are interested, providing summaries of the answers that provide "actionable foreign intelligence information," and passing those summaries to the prosecution team. At some point, however, it appears that the prosecution team had access to the witnesses or at least was able to propound questions for them. Judge Gregory makes a strong argument that this procedure (a) is unfair because it is one-sided, (b) does not allow the defense to propound its own questions, and (c) is wholly inadequate as a substitute for jury observation of the witnesses. But he makes this argument only as applied to the death penalty. Is it not a complete argument against allowing the prosecution to proceed at all under these conditions?

3. The majority asserts that the interrogators of these witnesses have "a profound interest in obtaining accurate information from the witnesses and in reporting that information accurately to those who can use it." But do the interrogators have any interest in obtaining information exculpatory of someone such as Moussaoui? And does their interest substitute for questioning by someone with Moussaoui's own knowledge? In this regard, be alert to the explanation for why the defendant must be present at questioning of government witnesses in *Hamdan v. Rumsfeld*, p. 533.

4. The majority states that "the 'balancing' we must conduct is primarily, if not solely, an examination of whether . . . the information the Government seeks to withhold is material to the defense." Is this balancing? Once this conclusion is reached, then what is the basis for not allowing the defense to have access to the witness?

5. All three judges reiterate that, in Judge Gregory's words, they "must not question the Government's determination that permitting the witnesses to be deposed would put our nation's security at risk." But that is not the question presented. The question is what to do with Moussaoui in light of the Government's refusal to accord him a constitutionally guaranteed right of access to witnesses. What might be lost if Moussaoui were set "free" to go about his business under heavy government surveillance?

6. As mentioned above, Abdelghani Mzoudi, an alleged key member of the "Hamburg cell" that provided support for the 9/11 hijackers, was acquitted in a German court for lack of evidence. The trial judge complained that both sides had sought and been denied evidence from witnesses in U.S. custody. "One of the main problems in this trial was that it was not possible to get files from intelligence services. . . . You are acquitted not because the court is convinced of your innocence, but because the evidence was not enough to convict you."

§ 5.03   PUBLIC TRIALS, THE JUDICIARY, AND CLASSIFIED INFORMATION

[handwritten margin notes: G charged of attempted espionage. I: public trial. H: App Ct revd conviction because much of the trial was closed to the public even tho much of the testimony was not classified.]

UNITED STATES v. GRUNDEN
United States Court of Military Appeals
2 M.J. 116 (1977)

FLETCHER, Chief Judge:

The appellant's court-martial resulted in his conviction of two specifications of failing to report contact with persons believed by him to be agents of governments hostile to the United States and one specification of attempted espionage, in violation of Articles 92 and 134, respectively, Uniform Code of Military Justice, 10 U.S.C. §§ 892 & 934. The appellant challenges the validity of his conviction on several grounds. We find it necessary for the resolution of this case to address only two: first, the failure of the military judge to sua sponte instruct the court members on evidence of uncharged misconduct; and, second, the denial of his right to a public trial. We find on both counts the judge erred.

The facts are not in dispute. The appellant, after a series of discussions with three individuals, each of whom worked covertly for the government, failed to report these conversations and ultimately attempted to communicate information relating to national defense, contrary to Air Force Regulation 205-37 and 18 U.S.C. § 793(d).

Throughout the proceedings the prosecution adduced numerous acts of misconduct, over defense objection, including possible earlier acts of espionage. The military judge, in an Article 39(a) session, subsequent to the presentment of evidence on the merits, accurately noted each act of uncharged misconduct. He correctly stated that he was required to instruct the court members as to the limited purpose of this evidence. Appellant's counsel requested that an uncharged misconduct instruction not be given. The judge considered the request and did not so instruct.

No evidence can so fester in the minds of court members as to the guilt or innocence of the accused as to the crime charged as evidence of uncharged misconduct. Its use must be given the weight of judicial comment, *i.e.,* an instruction as to its limited use.[1]

This Court's statement in *United States v. Graves,* 23 U.S.C.M.A. 434, 437 (1975):

---

[1] The basic legal tenet and the seven exceptions to that rule which permit the introduction of uncharged misconduct are set forth in paragraph 138g of the Manual for Courts-Martial, United States, 1969 (Rev.), as reiterated by this Court in *United States v. Janis,* 1 M.J. 395 (1976). The fact that this evidence was admissible under that test gives rise to the question of the need for an instruction.

Irrespective of the desires of counsel, the military judge must bear the primary responsibility for assuring that the jury properly is instructed on the elements of the offenses raised by the evidence as well as potential defenses and other questions of law. Simply stated, counsel do not frame issues for the jury; that is the duty of the military judge based upon his evaluation of the testimony related by the witnesses during the trial.

encases the judge's obligation to instruct. When evidence of uncharged misconduct is permitted, nothing short of an instruction will suffice.

As to the second error, the military judge during the preliminary Article 39(a) session, stated that because the trial on the espionage charges could delve into classified matters, certain procedures would be instituted. These included ascertaining that all court members and personnel would have the appropriate security clearances, and that the public would be excluded from portions of the trial. Thus, despite the objection of the defense counsel, and the trial judge's own assurances that he would "bend over backwards" to protect the appellant's rights, the public was excluded from virtually the entire trial as to the espionage charges.[2] During this portion of the trial, nine witnesses testified, only one of whom discussed classified matters at any length. Of the remaining eight witnesses one made less than 10 references to classified matters, three made only one reference, and the remaining four made no references. In excising the public from the trial, the trial judge employed an ax in place of the constitutionally required scalpel.

The right of an accused to a public trial is a substantial right secured by the Sixth Amendment to the Constitution of the United States. *In re Oliver,* 333 U.S. 257 (1948). Indeed, this Court has long held that an accused is, at the very least, entitled to have his friends, relatives, and counsel present regardless of the offense charged. *United States v. Brown*, 7 U.S.C.M.A. 251, 22 C.M.R. 41 (1956).[3]

---

[2] The propriety or impropriety of the exclusion of the public from all or part of a trial cannot, as attempted by the government in this case, be reduced to solution by mathematical formulas. The logic and rationale governing the exclusion, not mere percentages of the total pages of the record, must be dispositive.

The dissenting judge has apparently adopted the government position that as over 60 percent of the total record was conducted in open session, there can be little or no question but that the trial judge exercised discretion in his exclusion of the public. Unfortunately what both the dissenting judge and the government have failed to do is to analyze what portions of the record are involved in this question. The "over 60 percent" figure which has been bandied about entails the preliminary procedural matters the entire trial on the merits as to the charge of which the appellant was acquitted, final instructions, and the sentencing phase of the trial. The fact that these portions of the trial were open to the public can have no bearing on the resolution of the propriety of the judge's exclusion of the public from virtually the entire trial as to the espionage matters. Further, simple examination of the record reveals that the "bulk of the closed session" did not contain numerous and repeated references to classified matters; in fact, as noted by the government in its pleadings, only two witnesses of the total of nine would fit into this category.

[3] This Court is in full agreement with the concurrence of then Chief Judge Quinn that the right to a public trial is indeed required in a court-martial. To the extent that *United States v. Brown* implies a "military exception" to the right to a public trial for service personnel in reliance upon *Ex parte Quirin*, 317 U.S. 1 (1942), it is overruled.

The improper exclusion of the public has been treated as error per se in recognition that to do otherwise is to place the defendant in the ironic position of having "to prove what the disregard of his constitutional right has made it impossible for him to learn."

As recognized in *Brown,* the right to a public trial is not absolute, and under exceptional circumstances, limited portions of a criminal trial may be partially closed over defense objection. In each instance the exclusion must be used sparingly with the emphasis always toward a public trial. Historical exceptions have evolved and expanded[4] which need not be discussed, for the stated basis for the exclusion of the public in this case was the fact that classified or security matters might be presented. Exclusion of the public on such a basis is provided for in paragraph 53*e*, Manual for Courts-Martial, United States, 1969 (Rev.) which provides in pertinent part that

> As a general rule, the public shall be permitted to attend open sessions of courts-martial. Unless otherwise limited by directives of the Secretary of a Department, the convening authority, the military judge, or the president of a special court-martial without a military judge may, for security or other good reasons, direct that the public or certain portions thereof be excluded from a trial. However, all spectators may be excluded from an entire trial, over the accused's objection, only to prevent the disclosure of classified information. The authority to exclude should be cautiously exercised, and the right of the accused to a trial completely open to the public must be weighed against the public policy considerations justifying exclusion.

Although the presentation of classified or security matters did not develop as an historical exception to the requirement of a public trial, this Court recognizes that, within carefully limited guidelines, partial exclusion of the public on such a basis can be justified. Military appellate courts have noted the necessity to require that court personnel and members have designated security clearances, and that questions of classified materials could properly be disposed of in closed sessions. Yet, in each instance the exclusion of the public was narrowly and carefully drawn. The blanket exclusion of the spectators from all or most of a trial, such as in the present case, has not been approved by this Court, nor could it be absent a compelling showing that such was necessary to prevent the disclosure of classified information. The simple utilization of the terms "security" or "military necessity" cannot be the talisman in whose presence the protections of the Sixth Amendment and its guarantee to a public trial must vanish.[5] Unless

---

[4] *See, e.g.,* Note, *The Accused's Right to a Public Trial,* 42 Notre Dame Lawyer 499 (1967); Note, *The Right to a Public Trial in Criminal Cases,* 41 N.Y.U.L.R Rev. 1138 (1966); Radin, *The Right to a Public Trial,* 6 Temp. L.Q. 381 (1932). These traditional exceptions have been broadened to include limited exclusions to protect undercover policemen or agents, to ensure full and honest testimony by government witnesses, to protect airline hijacking profiles, and to preserve order.

[5] This Court recognizes that the Supreme Court in *Parker v. Levy,* 417 U.S. 733, 743 (1974), acknowledged the uniqueness of the military society, and that it has reaffirmed that belief in recent decisions. Yet, this Court once again must state that analysis and rationale will be determinative of the propriety of given situations, and that the mere uniqueness of the military society or military

an appropriate balancing test is employed with examination and analysis of the need for, and the scope of any suggested exclusion, the result is, as here, unsupportable.

It is our decision that the balancing test employed by a trial judge in instances involving the possible divulgence of classified material should be as follows. His initial task is to determine whether the perceived need urged as grounds for the exclusion of the public is of sufficient magnitude so as to outweigh "the danger of a miscarriage of justice which may attend judicial proceedings carried out in even partial secrecy." This may be best achieved by conducting a preliminary hearing which is closed to the public at which time the government must demonstrate that it has met the heavy burden of justifying the imposition of restraints on this constitutional right. The prosecution to meet this heavy burden must demonstrate the classified nature, if any, of the materials in question. It must then delineate those portions of its case which will involve these materials.

It is acknowledged that special deference should be accorded matters of national security. Although the actual classification of materials and the policy determinations involved therein are not normal judicial functions, immunization from judicial review cannot be countenanced in situations where strong countervailing constitutional interests exist which merit judicial protection. Before a trial judge can order the exclusion of the public on this basis, he must be satisfied from all the evidence and circumstances that there is a reasonable danger that presentation of these materials before the public will expose military matters which in the interest of national security should not be divulged. The method used by the prosecution to satisfy this burden, as recognized in *United States v. Reynolds,* will vary depending upon the nature of the materials in question and the information offered. It is important to realize that this initial review by the trial judge is not for the purpose of conducting a de novo review of the propriety of a given classification decision. All that must be determined is that the material in question has been classified by the proper authorities in accordance with the appropriate regulations. The ultimate questions of whether these materials "relat[ed] to the national defense" and could be used to the injury of the United States or the advantage of a foreign country must remain for resolution by the jury. The sole purpose of this review is to protect an accused's right to a public trial by preventing circumvention of that right by the mere utterance of a conclusion or blanket acceptance of the government's position without a demonstration of a compelling need.

This Court appreciates full well that such a hearing may involve complex and delicate matters for resolution by the trial judge, yet, as recognized by the Supreme Court, these are matters that judicial officers must and should be equipped to properly determine. Similarly, we feel that objections to this procedure because of the possibility of "leaks" are insufficient to prohibit its use;

---

necessity cannot be urged as the basis for sustaining that which reason and analysis indicate is untenable.

adequate measures exist to insure the necessary confidentiality required when matters of national security are concerned.

The trial judge's determination that the prosecution has met its burden as to the nature of the materials does not complete his review in this preliminary hearing. He must further decide the scope of the exclusion of the public. The prosecution must delineate which witnesses will testify on classified matters, and what portion of each witness' testimony will actually be devoted to this area. Clearly, unlike the instant case, any witness whose testimony does not contain references to classified material will testify in open court. The witness whose testimony is only partially concerned with this area should testify in open court on all other matters. For even assuming a valid underlying basis for the exclusion of the public, it is error of "constitutional magnitude" to exclude the public from all of a given witness' testimony when only a portion is devoted to classified material.[6] The remaining portion of his testimony will be presented to the court members in closed session. This bifurcated presentation of a given witness' testimony is the most satisfactory resolution of the competing needs for secrecy by the government, and for a public trial by the accused. It will be incumbent upon the trial judge to sua sponte instruct the court members both as an introductory matter and in greater detail during his final instructions as to the underlying basis for the use of this bifurcated process. It is imperative that the court members determine whether the documents or information in question are violative of the espionage statute based solely upon the evidence presented. Neither the utilization of a particular document marking, nor the presentation of certain testimony in closed sessions can be, in and of itself, sufficient to sustain a conviction.

Applying the above criteria and procedures to the facts of the instant case it is abundantly clear that the military judge committed error of constitutional magnitude. His blanket exclusion of the public failed to satisfactorily balance the competing interests, and improperly denied the appellant his right to a public trial.

Reversal is required. The findings and sentence as approved by the United States Air Force Court of Military Review are set aside. The record of trial is returned to the Judge Advocate General of the Air Force. A rehearing may be ordered.

COOK, Judge (dissenting):

I disagree with both aspects of the majority opinion. As to the instruction on uncharged misconduct there is a vast difference between the failure of defense counsel to request an appropriate instruction as constituting a waiver of the trial

---

[6] *United States v. Clark,* 475 F.2d 240, 246 (2d Cir. 1973). The Second Circuit sustained the underlying basis for the exclusion in reliance upon its prior decision of *United States v. Bell,* 464 F.2d 667 (2d Cir. 1972) – prevention of the disclosure of airline skyjacking profiles because of a compelling need to protect the air traveling public. However, the court would not permit the total exclusion of the public in a hearing where only a portion of the testimony presented related to this profile, and the remainder, as here, was devoted to a wide range of matters bearing on the defendant's innocence or guilt.

judge's duty to instruct on issues for determination by the court members and an affirmative request by the defense that a particular instruction not be given. In my book, the latter instance represents defense-induced error which, except in the case of a manifest miscarriage of justice, will not be considered by an appellate court as a ground for reversal of an otherwise valid conviction.

As to the public trial issue, the principal opinion acknowledges that the right to a public trial is "not absolute." The fact that the trial judge held a preliminary hearing on the matter demonstrates to me that he was mindful of his responsibility to effect a sensitive accommodation between the accused's right to a public trial and the Government's need to protect classified information affecting national security. His declaration that he would "bend over backwards" to preserve the accused's right demonstrates to me that his criterion for exclusion of the public was at least as stringent as that contemplated by the majority. The question then is whether the judge disregarded his own declaration and, in fact, wielded "an ax in place of the . . . required scalpel," as the majority conclude.

Contrary to the majority's disdain of "mere percentages of the total pages of the record," as indicative of the scope of exclusion, in my opinion, that circumstance is very important to resolution of the issue. The defense brief represents that the trial was conducted "almost entirely in secret." However, Government counsel's analysis of the transcript of the record, with which I agree, indicates that over 60 percent of the proceedings were "open to the public," and that the "bulk of the closed session of the court-martial . . . contained numerous and repeated references to classified matters." In my opinion, therefore, the record does not reflect "blanket exclusion of the public," as the majority describe the trial judge's ruling, but rather it convinces me the trial judge was firmly committed to, and properly applied, the "logic and rationale governing the exclusion" of the public, which the majority posit as an appropriate standard for measuring the validity of the trial judge's ruling. I would affirm the determination by the Court of Military Review that the accused was not improperly denied the right to the presence of the public at portions of his trial.

NOTES AND QUESTIONS

1. When we get to the Presidential Order authorizing military tribunals for alleged terrorists, some people will be interested in the question of whether military courts are "better" or "worse" for defendants than the civilian courts. *Grunden* will be an interesting example to bear in mind. The Court of Military Appeals in this case is so sensitive to the rights of the accused that it even allows what the dissent describes as a "defense-induced error" to result in reversal.

2. The U.S. Court of Military Appeals was renamed in 1994 to be the U.S. Court of Appeals for the Armed Forces, but it remains an Article I court. Its judges are appointed from civilian life for a term of five years.

3. The court discusses a civilian court case in which the public was excluded from a portion of a trial involving classified information. How would a civilian court prevent jurors from disclosing secrets that are received in evidence during a closed proceeding? The members of the "jury" in a military trial can be selected with security classifications in mind and are already under the coverage of Official Secrets Act sanctions. This is one way in which the Presidential Order justifies use of military tribunals. But if the military courts are under the same obligation to provide a public trial, then what difference does this really make?

UNITED STATES v. SMITH
899 F.2d 564 (6th Cir. 1990)

MERRITT, Chief Judge.

The United States appeals the denial of a proposed protective order under a government secrecy statute known as the Classified Information Procedures Act, 18 U.S.C. app. IV (1988), an enabling statute delegating to the Chief Justice authority to issue regulations governing the security clearance of judicial employees in cases in which classified information is admitted. Section 4 of the regulations issued by the Chief Justice provides that "any problem of security involving court personnel or persons acting for the court shall be referred to the court for appropriate action." The issue presented on appeal is whether various police and intelligence agencies of the Executive Branch may, in accordance with their standard security clearance procedures, investigate Judicial Branch employees whom the court has designated to work on a criminal proceeding involving classified information. In light of the provision of section 4 in which the Judicial Branch retains authority to resolve "any problems of security" arising from the administration of the system of security clearances, we hold that such investigations do not violate the principle of separation of powers. We therefore reverse the decision below.

I

According to the indictment, Major Michael L. Smith transported and concealed stolen goods, possessed an unregistered silencer, and possessed a silencer without a serial number. The government alleges that Major Smith illegally obtained $60,000 worth of weapons which Army investigators discovered during a consent search of the major's house. According to the government, when he allegedly stole the weapons, Major Smith was a member of the "Intelligence Support Activity," an Army unit with classified, undisclosed duties. Because the prosecution and defense of this case is said to involve classified information relating to Smith's duties, the United States moved for protection of the information under [CIPA] § 3. The proposed protective order would require court employees, *e.g.*, law clerks and secretaries, to submit to government investigation and clearance before being permitted to handle any classified information.

District Judge Wiseman issued an order protecting the classified information. He did not, however, honor the government's request that the Executive Branch perform background investigations on all courtroom personnel. Instead, Judge Wiseman specified particular individuals, including a secretary and a law clerk, whom he designated as authorized to have access to classified information. Those designated individuals would, according to Judge Wiseman's order, be required to sign a memorandum of understanding, a document indicating that the signer understands the possible dangers to the United States posed by unauthorized release of classified information. When the designated security officer asked Judge Wiseman whether he should arrange for clearances for the personnel, the Judge said it would not be necessary.

The United States moved for reconsideration. It argued that the security regulations that Chief Justice Burger promulgated pursuant to section 9 of the Act[2] (hereinafter "Burger regulations") required Judge Wiseman to permit the Executive Branch to perform background checks on all courtroom personnel before the court received any classified information. Section 4 of the Burger regulations states that

> No person appointed by the court or designated for service therein shall be given access to any classified information in the custody of the court, unless such person has received a security clearance as provided herein and unless access to such information is necessary for the performance of an official function. . . .

> The court shall inform the court security officer or the attorney for the government of the names of court personnel who may require access to classified information. That person shall then notify the Department of Justice Security Officer, who shall promptly make arrangements to obtain any necessary security clearances and shall approve such clearances under standards of the Executive Branch applicable to the level and category of classified information involved. . . .

> Any problem of security involving court personnel or persons acting for the court shall be referred to the court for appropriate action.

In a comprehensive opinion designed to maintain the independence of the Judicial Branch, Judge Wiseman denied the motion. Finding that the "CIPA procedures . . . invite executive officials into a court's chambers and authorize them to dictate to federal judges the manner in which they conduct their business," he held that section 4 of the Burger regulations violated the constitutionally-mandated separation of powers and the independence of the judiciary.

After Judge Wiseman denied the motion for reconsideration, the United States brought an interlocutory appeal to this Court pursuant to § 7(a) of the Act. That section provides that an interlocutory appeal may be taken "from a decision or order of a district court in a criminal case authorizing the disclosure of classified information. . . ." Because Judge Wiseman's order is said to have the effect of permitting the disclosure of classified information to putatively unauthorized persons, we have appellate jurisdiction under § 7(a).

II

Section 9 of the Act directed the Chief Justice of the United States – then Chief Justice Burger – to establish procedures ensuring the security of the

---

[2] The Chief Justice of the United States, in consultation with the Attorney General, the Director of Central Intelligence, and the Secretary of Defense, shall prescribe rules establishing procedures for the protection against unauthorized disclosure of any classified information in the custody of the United States district courts, courts of appeal, or Supreme Court.

classified information while a court is using it. Congress intended these procedures to be basic "housekeeping rules," covering "where safes are to be located, who is to have the combinations, *how many court employees can have access to the documents*, and the like." H.R. Rep. No. 831, 96th Cong., 2d Sess., pt. 2, at 8 (1980) (emphasis added). Congress did not further delineate what procedures the Chief Justice should adopt with regard to background checks of personnel.

The Burger regulations explicitly provide that court personnel must undergo a security examination designed and conducted by Executive Branch personnel. On the question of who shall have the final authority to decide which judicial employees may see the classified information after the background check is performed, section 4 of the regulations states that "any problem of security involving court personnel or persons acting for the court shall be referred to the court for appropriate action." Because Judge Wiseman forbade the Department of Justice from engaging in the first step under the regulations, *i.e.*, performing background checks, the only question ripe for review is whether the Executive Branch may constitutionally investigate the backgrounds of court personnel prior to their participation in a case involving classified information. Only if the Justice Department actually performed a security check on Judge Wiseman's court personnel and denied one or more of them clearance would the final authority issue require judicial resolution.

We analyze the separation of powers issue first by referring to the methods for protecting classified information employed by the special Foreign Intelligence Court and the Legislative Branch – the methods which Congress and Chief Justice Burger seemed to have had in mind in adopting the security provisions at issue here. We will explain those analogous procedures for the light they shed on the separation of powers question presented in the instant case. In the case of the Foreign Intelligence Court and the Legislative Branch, the Court and Congress respectively appear to retain final authority over the security clearance process after background checks are performed.

The legislative history of section 9 is sparse, and states only that Congress based that section on a similar provision under the Foreign Intelligence Surveillance Act. Congressional committees drafted and developed both provisions to delegate rulemaking authority for security procedures to a panel of the Chief Justice and three national security executive officials. The security procedures established by Chief Justice Burger for the special court created under the Surveillance Act "to hear applications for and grant orders approving electronic surveillance anywhere within the United States," provide, in pertinent part, that court personnel

> shall undergo appropriate background investigation by the Federal Bureau of Investigation under the standards established by Director of Central Intelligence Directive No. 1/14 . . . or successor directives as concurred in by the Attorney General. These personnel shall not have access to classified information unless they have received *a security clearance determined appropriate by the court* in consultation with the Attorney General and the Director of Central Intelligence. All court personnel having access to court

records shall sign appropriate security agreements. If a question concerning the security clearance of court personnel is raised subsequent to appointment, *the matter shall be referred to the court* which may consult the Attorney General and the Director of Central Intelligence regarding its security significance before taking such action as it deems appropriate.

The security procedures promulgated pursuant to the Surveillance Act demonstrate that Congress, in analogous circumstances, has subjected the Judiciary, in this case the Surveillance Court, to security measures designed and administered by the Department of Justice.

The Legislative Branch also has delegated responsibility for safeguarding the flow of classified information. The Senate Resolution establishing the Select Committee on Intelligence states that employees of the Committee, or persons performing services for or at the Committee's request, cannot have access to classified information unless they agree to be bound by the Committee's confidentiality requirements. Further, before gaining access to classified materials, they must "receive an appropriate security clearance as determined by such committee in consultation with the Director of Central Intelligence."

It is evident from both Houses' method of protecting classified information that the Legislative Branch has determined that the participation of the Executive Branch in designing and administering security measures is not in itself an intrusion that rises to the level of an unconstitutional interference with its legislative function. In accommodating the interests of the Judicial and Executive Branches in the instant case, we are influenced by the accommodation offered by the legislative committees as well as that offered by the Surveillance Court under the Surveillance Act described above. In making this accommodation, the district courts retain the same level of protection that the Surveillance Court and legislative committees retain against the possibility of overly intrusive inquiries which the Executive might engage in pursuant to its investigation of courtroom personnel.

III

The accommodation of the interests of the three branches mentioned above has its roots in the historical deference paid to the Executive on issues of national security. For example, in *Totten v. United States,* 92 U.S. 105, 106 (1875), the Court recognized the power inherent in the Executive, through the President, to make contracts with secret agents to "enter the rebel lines and obtain information respecting the strength, resources, and movements of the enemy" in times of war. Recognizing the President's power to make such contracts, the Court stated that courts of justice – being open to the public – should not be used for trials

> which would inevitably lead to the disclosure of matters which the law itself regards as confidential, and respecting which it will not allow the confidence to be violated. On this principle, suits cannot be maintained which would require a disclosure of the confidences of the confessional, or those between husband and wife, or of communications by a client to his counsel for professional advice, or of a patient to his physician for a similar purpose. Much greater reason exists for the application of the principle to cases of

contract for secret services with the government, as the existence of a contract of that kind is itself a fact not to be disclosed.

Similarly, by recognizing the need for secrecy in the area of foreign relations, the Court has deferred to the judgment of the Executive to preserve national security and to guard against the unwanted dissemination of political and military secrets:

> Even if courts could require full disclosure, the very nature of executive decisions as to foreign policy is political, not judicial. Such decisions are wholly confided by our Constitution to the political departments of the government, Executive and Legislative. They are delicate, complex, and involve large elements of prophecy. They are and should be undertaken only by those directly responsible to the people whose welfare they advance or imperil. They are decisions of a kind for which the Judiciary has neither aptitude, facilities nor responsibility and which has long been held to belong in the domain of political power not subject to judicial intrusion or inquiry.

Chicago & S. Air Lines v. Waterman Steamship Corp., 333 U.S. 103, 111 (1948); *see also United States v. Curtiss-Wright Export Corp.*, 299 U.S. 304, 320 (1936) ("Secrecy in respect of information gathered by [confidential sources of information] may be highly necessary, and the premature disclosure of it productive of harmful results.").

Clearly the indictment of Major Smith, a member of the "Intelligence Support Activity," for stealing weapons and ammunition from the United States Government, implicates the broad authority of the Executive Branch to exercise its discretion in matters that touch national security and foreign affairs.

IV

District Judge Wiseman's concerns about preserving the judiciary from unwarranted encroachment by co-equal branches are firmly rooted in the Constitution and Supreme Court precedents. Under no circumstances should the Judiciary become the handmaiden of the Executive. The independence of the Judiciary must be jealously guarded at all times against efforts by prosecutors to erode its authority. The Constitution commands that the "'judicial power of the United States' must be reposed in an independent Judiciary," "free from potential domination by other branches of government." However, the Supreme Court also has confirmed the government's "compelling interest in protecting both the secrecy of information important to our national security and the appearance of confidentiality." *Snepp v. United States,* 444 U.S. 507, 509 n.3 (1980). Although permissible measures taken to satisfy this compelling interest would not include those that cause "the encroachment or aggrandizement of one branch at the expense of the other," the requirement of the Burger regulations that courtroom personnel be subject to background checks before gaining access to classified information does not in itself threaten such a result. Such a requirement affecting law clerks, secretaries and bailiffs is not closely related to the deliberative process because these individuals do not and should not decide cases; thus it only mildly intrudes into the manner in which federal judges conduct business. *See In re United States Department of Justice*, No. 87-1205, slip. op. at 4 (4th Cir. Apr. 7, 1988) (unpublished disposition) (in issuing writ of *mandamus* that required security clearances for courtroom staff in civil case, court concluded that contempt or disclosure dilemma justified "minimally intrusive" requirement of routine security clearance). Under section 4 of the Burger regulations, district courts retain sufficient power to preclude the Executive from engaging in procedures that intrude upon both the judicial function and, potentially, the privacy interests of court personnel. Proper administration of the regulations is therefore consistent with the doctrine of separation of powers.

V

We therefore hold that the Executive Branch may conduct reasonable background investigations, subject to district court review, of judicial personnel before such personnel are cleared to work on a case involving classified information. The security clearance procedures established under the Burger regulations do not on their face, or as applied in this case so far, violate principles of separation of powers. Because the District Court precluded the Executive from performing any initial background checks in this case, the propriety of the checks themselves is not at issue.

SELECTED READINGS

[Note: It is difficult to find scholarly writings about FISA that are not criticisms of PATRIOT Act amendments. CIPA itself has been the subject of virtually no scholarly critique.]

- DAVID COLE & JAMES X. DEMPSEY, TERRORISM AND THE CONSTITUTION (2003).

- Nola K. Breglio, *Leaving FISA Behind: The Need To Return to Warrantless Foreign Intelligence Surveillance*, 111 YALE L.J. 179 (2003).

- Kelley Brooke Snyder, *A Clash of Values: Classified Information in Immigration Proceedings*, 88 VA. L. REV. 447 (2002).

- Ronald J. Sievert, *War on Terrorism or Global Law Enforcement Operation?*, 78 NOTRE DAME L. REV. 307 (2003).

Chapter 6

MATERIAL SUPPORT AND THE RIGHT OF ASSOCIATION

The *Salameh* case in Chapter 2 included charges of seditious conspiracy, which sounds much like treason, and Sheikh Rahman raised first amendment defenses that sound much like the concerns of the Framers with regard to treason itself. The Second Circuit pointed out that treason is a crime which applies only to those who have a duty of allegiance to the United States. The court also intimated that there could be a variety of other crimes with similar elements going by different names and questioned whether the constitutional restraints on treason prosecutions (such as two witnesses to the same overt act) would apply to those crimes.

In the Anti-Terrorism and Effective Death Penalty Act of 1996 (AEDPA), Congress created the offenses of "material support" for terrorists or for designated terrorist organizations. These offenses raise similar first amendment concerns to those of treason and conspiracy.

There are subtle differences among material support, conspiracy, and aiding and abetting an attempt. One way to understand the statutes, which also bears on the approach of the courts to the first amendment interests, is to focus on the scienter elements in the statutes. The principal statutory scheme consists of these principal steps:

18 U.S.C. § 2339A (providing material support to terrorists)

18 U.S.C. § 2339B (providing material support to a designated foreign terrorist organization [FTO])

8 U.S.C. § 1189 (designation of FTO by Secretary of State)

The material support statutes are a logical outgrowth of statutes that prohibit "trading with the enemy." In modern times, that concept has been extended to doing business with countries on designated embargo lists. The International Emergency Economic Powers Act, 50 U.S.C. § 1701-07, authorizes the President to exercise broad powers to "deal with any unusual and extraordinary threat, which has its source in whole or substantial part outside the United States, to the national security, foreign policy, or economy of the United States, if the President declares a national emergency with respect to such threat." Specific requirements and prohibitions apply to each nation so designated. Although the statute requires a finding of national emergency, prohibitions on trade may last for extended periods, as is the case with Cuba. Willful violations of regulatory orders under this statute are punishable as crimes.

The material support statutes are closely linked to statutes outlawing money laundering and structuring transactions to evade currency reporting requirements. Money laundering and structuring statutes criminalize apparently benign conduct that could be either a precursor to a know mischief (usually drug trafficking) or a method of covering up a completed offense. In similar fashion, the material support statutes represent an effort to enhance the preventive effectiveness of law enforcement by providing mechanisms to intercede in terrorist planning before an actual attack occurs. Government lawyers describe them as rough corollaries to laws against driving with an open container of alcohol in the car. The progression is something like this: Society wants to minimize automobile fatalities, so we make it a crime to kill someone with an automobile while intoxicated. To make that even more unlikely, we make it a crime to drive while intoxicated whether anyone is injured or not. This gives law enforcement power to prosecute an act before the substantive harm occurs. To extend out even further, most states prohibit driving with an open container of alcohol in the car. That is about the limit to which we can go because driving with a sealed container has sufficient social value that people are unwilling to outlaw that act.

In the "alcohol in the car scenario," recognize that not every drunk driver would kill someone. Further, not everyone with an open container in the car will drive while intoxicated. Yet, in both instances, the precursor conduct is criminalized because the threat of harm outweighs the social utility of the precursor conduct. Another striking example is presented by statutes and ordinances that limit the sale of pseudophedrine and other active ingredients that are precursors for making methamphetamine.

Similarly, prosecution of completed terrorist acts is not deemed sufficient to address the problem. If there were a completed crime, then investigators would (as happened after 9/11) start tracing backwards from that crime to find who supplied the money or other support and thus formed part of the conspiracy. To start that chain of investigation before the completed harm, the material support statutes create a precursor crime so that tracking and reporting requirements can be triggered at an earlier stage. The money laundering and financial reporting statutes move yet one more step out from the completed harm.

A major difference between the material support statutes and the alcohol-in-the-car scenario is that the social utility argument may be encountered much earlier when we are talking about interests of privacy and association. Particularly given the social interest in promoting charitable giving and political activism, there will be constitutional arguments to be made in almost every prosecution of this type.

Examples of proposed legislation that could go too far in reaction to the activities of animal rights groups are collected in STEVEN BEST & ANTHONY NOCELLA II, TERRORIST OR FREEDOM FIGHTERS: REFLECTIONS ON THE LIBERATION OF ANIMALS (2004). One example is a proposed Texas bill that would define an "animal rights or ecological terrorist organization as two or more persons organized for the purpose of supporting any politically motivated activity intended to obstruct or deter any person from participating in any activity involving animals." Another set of proposals would criminalize the photographing or videotaping of animal facilities.

To simplify matters, we will start with a case in which the constitutional arguments did not appear on the surface and move from there into more overt realms of political association.

§ 6.01 TREASON AND RELATED OFFENSES
[A] TRADING WITH THE ENEMY

UNITED STATES v. LINDH
212 F. Supp. 2d 541 (E.D. Va. 2002)

T. S. ELLIS, III, District Judge:

John Phillip Walker Lindh ("Lindh") is an American citizen who, according to the ten-count Indictment filed against him in February 2002, joined certain foreign terrorist organizations in Afghanistan and served these organizations there in combat against Northern Alliance and American forces until his capture in November 2001. In seven threshold motions, Lindh sought dismissal of certain counts of the Indictment on a variety of grounds, including lawful combatant immunity and selective prosecution. All motions were denied following extensive briefing and oral argument. Recorded here are the reasons underlying those rulings.

I.

The Indictment's allegations may be succinctly summarized. In mid-2001, Lindh attended a military training camp in Pakistan run by Harakat ul-Mujahideen ("HUM"), a terrorist group dedicated to an extremist view of Islam.[2] After receiving several weeks of training, Lindh informed HUM officials that "he wished to fight with the Taliban in Afghanistan." Thus, in May or June 2001, he traveled from Pakistan into Afghanistan "for the purpose of taking up arms with the Taliban," eventually arriving at a Taliban recruiting center in Kabul, Afghanistan – the Dar ul-Anan Headquarters of the Mujahideen. On his arrival, Lindh presented a letter of introduction from HUM and advised Taliban personnel "that he was an American and that he wanted to go to the front lines to fight."

While at the Dar ul-Anan Headquarters, Lindh agreed to receive additional and extensive military training at an al Qaeda training camp. He made this decision "knowing that America and its citizens were the enemies of Bin Laden and al-Qaeda and that a principal purpose of al-Qaeda was to fight and kill Americans." In late May or June 2001, Lindh traveled to a bin Laden guest house in Kandahar, Afghanistan, where he stayed for several days, and then traveled to the al Farooq training camp, "an al Qaeda facility located several hours west of Kandahar." He reported to the camp with approximately twenty other trainees, mostly Saudis, and remained there throughout June and July. During this period, he participated fully in the camp's training activities, despite being told early in his stay that "Bin Laden had sent forth some fifty people to carry out twenty suicide terrorist operations against the United States and Israel." As part of his al Qaeda training, Lindh participated in "terrorist training courses in, among other things, weapons, orientating, navigation, explosives and

---

[2] On October 8, 1997, HUM was designated by the Secretary of State as a foreign terrorist organization, pursuant to Section 219 of the Immigration and Nationality Act.

battlefield combat." This training included the use of "shoulder weapons, pistols, and rocket-propelled grenades, and the construction of Molotov cocktails." During his stay at al Farooq, Lindh met personally with bin Laden, "who thanked him and other trainees for taking part in jihad." He also met with a senior al Qaeda official, Abu Mohammad Al-Masri, who inquired whether Lindh was interested in traveling outside Afghanistan to conduct operations against the United States and Israel. Lindh declined Al-Masri's offer in favor of going to the front lines to fight. It is specifically alleged that Lindh swore allegiance to jihad in June or July 2001.

When Lindh completed his training at al Farooq in July or August 2001, he traveled to Kabul, Afghanistan, where he was issued an AKM rifle "with a barrel suitable for long range shooting." Armed with this rifle, Lindh, together with approximately 150 non-Afghani fighters, traveled from Kabul to the front line at Takhar, located in Northeastern Afghanistan, where the entire unit was placed under the command of an Iraqi named Abdul Hady. Lindh's group was eventually divided into smaller groups that fought in shifts against Northern Alliance troops in the Takhar trenches, rotating every one to two weeks. During this period, Lindh "carried various weapons with him, including the AKM rifle, an RPK rifle he was issued after the AKM rifle malfunctioned, and at least two grenades." He remained with his fighting group following the September 11, 2001 terrorist attacks, "despite having been told that Bin Laden had ordered the [September 11] attacks, that additional terrorist attacks were planned, and that additional al Qaeda personnel were being sent from the front lines to protect Bin Laden and defend against an anticipated military response from the United States." Indeed, it is specifically alleged that Lindh remained with his fighting group from October to December 2001, "after learning that United States military forces and United States nationals had become directly engaged in support of the Northern Alliance in its military conflict with Taliban and al Qaeda forces."

In November 2001, Lindh and his fighting group retreated from Takhar to the area of Kunduz, Afghanistan, where they ultimately surrendered to Northern Alliance troops. On November 24, 2001, he and the other captured Taliban fighters were transported to Mazar-e-Sharif, and then to the nearby Qala-i-Janghi (QIJ) prison compound. The following day, November 25, Lindh was interviewed by two Americans – Agent Johnny Micheal Spann from the Central Intelligence Agency (CLA) and another government employee. Later that day, it is alleged that Taliban detainees in the QIJ compound attacked Spann and the other employee, overpowered the guards, and armed themselves. Spann was shot and killed in the course of the uprising and Lindh, after being wounded, retreated with other detainees to a basement area of the QIJ compound. The uprising at QIJ was eventually suppressed on December 1, 2001, at which time Lindh and other Taliban and al Qaeda fighters were taken into custody by Northern Alliance and American forces.

Following his capture, Lindh was interrogated, transported to the United States, and ultimately charged in this district with the following offenses in a ten-count Indictment:

(i) conspiracy to murder nationals of the United States, including American military personnel and other governmental employees serving in Afghanistan following the September 11, 2001 terrorist attacks, in violation of 18 U.S.C. § 2332(b)(2) (Count One);

(ii) conspiracy to provide material support and resources to HUM, a foreign terrorist organization, in violation of 18 U.S.C. § 2339B (Count Two);

(iii) providing material support and resources to HUM, in violation of 18 U.S.C. § 2339B and 2 (Count Three);

(iv) conspiracy to provide material support and resources to al Qaeda, a foreign terrorist organization, in violation of 18 U.S.C. § 2339B (Count Four);

(v) providing material support and resources to al Qaeda, in violation of 18 U.S.C. § 2339B and 2 (Count Five);

(vi) conspiracy to contribute services to al Qaeda, in violation of 50 U.S.C. § 1705(b) (Count Six);

(vii) contributing services to al Qaeda, in violation of 50 U.S.C. § 1705(b) (Count Seven);

(viii) conspiracy to supply services to the Taliban, in violation of 50 U.S.C. § 1705(b) (Count Eight);

(ix) supplying services to the Taliban, in violation of 50 U.S.C. § 1705(b) (Count Nine); and

(x) using and carrying firearms and destructive devices during crimes of violence, in violation of 18 U.S.C. §§ 924(c)(1)(A), 924(c)(1)(B)(ii) and 2 (Count Ten).

At issue are threshold motions to dismiss filed by the defense.

III.

Lindh claims that Count One of the Indictment should be dismissed because, as a Taliban soldier, he was a lawful combatant entitled to the affirmative defense of lawful combatant immunity.[16]

Lawful combatant immunity, a doctrine rooted in the customary international law of war, forbids prosecution of soldiers for their lawful belligerent acts committed during the course of armed conflicts against legitimate military

---

[16] Lindh makes no claim of lawful combatant immunity with respect to the Indictment's allegations that he was a member or soldier of al Qaeda. Instead, Lindh focuses his lawful combatant immunity argument solely on the Indictment's allegations that he was a Taliban member. This focus is understandable as there is no plausible claim of lawful combatant immunity in connection with al Qaeda membership. Thus, it appears that Lindh's goal is to win lawful combatant immunity with respect to the Taliban allegations and then to dispute factually the Indictment's allegations that he was a member of al Qaeda.

Also worth noting is that the government has not argued here that the Taliban's role in providing a home, a headquarters, and support to al Qaeda and its international terrorist activities serve to transform the Taliban from a legitimate state government into a terrorist institution whose soldiers are not entitled to lawful combatant immunity status. Put another way, the government has not argued that al Qaeda controlled the Taliban for its own purposes and that so-called Taliban soldiers were accordingly merely agents of al Qaeda, not lawful combatants.

targets. Belligerent acts committed in armed conflict by enemy members of the armed forces may be punished as crimes under a belligerent's municipal law only to the extent that they violate international humanitarian law or are unrelated to the armed conflict. This doctrine has a long history, which is reflected in part in various early international conventions, statutes and documents. But more pertinent, indeed controlling, here is that the doctrine also finds expression in the Geneva Convention Relative to the Treatment of Prisoners of War ("GPW"), to which the United States is a signatory. Significantly, Article 87 of the GPW admonishes that combatants "may not be sentenced . . . to any penalties except those provided for in respect of members of the armed forces of the said Power who have committed the same acts." Similarly, Article 99 provides that "no prisoner of war may be tried or sentenced for an act which is not forbidden by the law of the Detaining Power or by international law, in force at the time the said act was committed." These Articles, when read together, make clear that a belligerent in a war cannot prosecute the soldiers of its foes for the soldiers' lawful acts of war.

The inclusion of the lawful combatant immunity doctrine as a part of the GPW is particularly important here given that the GPW, insofar as it is pertinent here, is a self-executing treaty to which the United States is a signatory. It follows from this that the GPW provisions in issue here are a part of American law and thus binding in federal courts under the Supremacy Clause. This point, which finds support in the cases, is essentially conceded by the government. Moreover, the government does not dispute that this immunity may, under appropriate circumstances, serve as a defense to criminal prosecution of a lawful combatant.

The GPW sets forth four criteria an organization must meet for its members to qualify for lawful combatant status:

i. the organization must be commanded by a person responsible for his subordinates;

ii. the organization's members must have a fixed distinctive emblem or uniform recognizable at a distance;

iii. the organization's members must carry arms openly; and

iv. the organization's members must conduct their operations in accordance with the laws and customs of war.

[I]t appears that the Taliban lacked the command structure necessary to fulfill the first criterion, as it is manifest that the Taliban had no internal system of military command or discipline. Similarly, it appears the Taliban typically wore no distinctive sign that could be recognized by opposing combatants; they wore no uniforms or insignia and were effectively indistinguishable from the rest of the population. The requirement of such a sign is critical to ensure that combatants may be distinguished from the non-combatant, civilian population. Accordingly, Lindh cannot establish the second criterion. Next, although it appears that Lindh and his cohorts carried arms openly in satisfaction of the third criterion for lawful combatant status, it is equally apparent that members of the Taliban failed to observe the laws and customs of war. Thus, because record evidence supports the conclusion that the Taliban regularly targeted civilian populations in clear contravention of the laws and customs of war, Lindh cannot meet his burden concerning the fourth criterion.

In sum, the President's determination that Lindh is an unlawful combatant and thus ineligible for immunity is controlling here (i) because that determination is entitled to deference as a reasonable interpretation and application of the GPW to Lindh as a Taliban; (ii) because Lindh has failed to carry his burden of demonstrating the contrary; and (iii) because even absent deference, the Taliban falls far short when measured against the four GPW criteria for determining entitlement to lawful combatant immunity.

IV.

Lindh argues that Counts Six through Nine of the Indictment should be dismissed because they charge violations of regulations that were promulgated in excess of the statutory authority provided by the parent legislation, the International Economic Emergency Powers Act ("IEEPA"). Specifically, these four counts charge Lindh with "Contributing Services to al Qaeda," "Supplying Services to the Taliban," and conspiracy to do each of these, all in violation of the "Regulations". Simply put, Lindh contends that IEEPA does not authorize the promulgation of the Regulations to proscribe the conduct alleged in the Indictment. More particularly, Lindh argues that IEEPA cannot be construed to authorize promulgation of any regulations prohibiting his voluntary and noncommercial donation of services to the Taliban and al Qaeda.

The IEEPA is a relatively recent addition to this country's arsenal of sanctions to be used against hostile states and organizations in times of national emergency. For much of the twentieth century, this country's sanctions programs were governed by the Trading with the Enemy Act (hereafter "TWEA"), enacted in 1917. As amended in 1933, TWEA granted the President broad authority "to investigate, regulate, . . . prevent or prohibit . . . transactions" in times of war or declared national emergencies. Congress changed this statutory scheme in 1977 to limit TWEA's application to periods of declared wars, but created IEEPA to provide the President similar authority for use during other times of national emergency. Specifically, the language of IEEPA vests the President with the power to prescribe regulations to

> regulate, direct and compel, nullify, void, prevent or prohibit any acquisition, holding, withholding, use, transfer, withdrawal, transportation, importation or exportation of, or dealing in, or exercising any right, power, or privilege with respect to, or transactions involving, any property in which any foreign country or a national thereof has any interest by any person.

In January 1995, President Clinton, exercising his IEEPA authority, issued Executive Order 12947, declaring a national emergency to deal with the extraordinary threat posed by foreign terrorists who disrupt the Middle East peace process. Thereafter, the Treasury Department, via the Office of Foreign Assets Control ("OFAC"), promulgated, *inter alia,* 31 C.F.R. § 595.204, which, in relevant part, repeated the mandate of Executive Order 12947 regarding the prohibition on "the making or receiving of any contribution of funds, goods, or services" to or for the benefit of terrorists designated in, or pursuant to, the Executive Order.

In July 1999, again drawing upon his IEEPA authority, President Clinton issued Executive Order 13129, declaring a national emergency to deal with the threat posed by the Taliban. Specifically, the President found that the actions of the Taliban in Afghanistan in allowing territory there to be used as a safehaven and base of operations for Usama bin Laden and al Qaeda constituted an unusual and extraordinary threat to the national security and foreign policy of the United States. Presidents Clinton and Bush subsequently determined, in June 2000 and in June 2001, that the national emergency with respect to the Taliban would continue.

Despite the breadth of the Regulations and Executive Orders issued pursuant to IEEPA, Lindh asserts that IEEPA does nothing more than permit the President to freeze the assets of a foreign state or foreign national and prohibit certain international financial transactions during times of a declared national emergency. Lindh argues, moreover, that neither the plain meaning of IEEPA, nor its legislative history, indicate that it provides a basis for the wide-ranging regulations here in issue. Thus, Lindh argues, the Regulations he is charged with violating exceed IEEPA's statutory grant of power.

The straightforward question presented, therefore, is whether the Regulations are within the scope of IEEPA. The IEEPA language in issue is as follows:

the President may, under such regulations as he may prescribe, by means of instructions, licenses, or otherwise

(A) investigate, regulate, or prohibit
(i) any transactions in foreign exchange,
(ii) transfers of credit or payments between, by, through or to any banking institution, to the extent that such transfers or payments involve any interest of any foreign country or a national thereof,
(iii) the importing or exporting of currency or securities; and

(B) investigate, regulate, direct and compel, nullify, void, prevent or prohibit, any acquisition, holding, withholding, use, transfer, withdrawal, transportation, importation or exportation of, or dealing in, or exercising any right, power, or privilege with respect to, or transactions involving, any property in which any foreign country or a national thereof has any interest;

by any person, or with respect to any property, subject to the jurisdiction of the United States.

On the question presented – whether the statute authorizes issuance of the Regulations – the statute's plain language is dispositive. Specifically, the dispositive language authorizes regulation and prohibition of the "use . . . , or dealing in, or exercising any right, power, or privilege with respect to, . . . any property" in which any "foreign country or national" has an interest. This sweeping language provides ample authority for the issuance of the Regulations and also easily reaches Lindh's alleged conduct. This conduct – which includes, for example, attending Taliban and al Qaeda training camps, using and transporting Taliban and al Qaeda weapons and ammunition, and using Taliban and al Qaeda transportation and residence facilities – plainly involves "use" of Taliban and al Qaeda "property." And, given the breadth of the common dictionary meanings of "use," "dealing," "transactions" and "property," there is similarly no doubt that Lindh's provision of combatant services to the Taliban and al Qaeda also falls within the IEEPA and the Regulations.

Lindh seeks to avoid the result reached here by arguing that IEEPA concerns only commercial or economic conduct. In support, he cites the statute's title and the fact that many cases involving IEEPA and TWEA address solely economic or commercial activity. This argument, while not implausible, is again contradicted by the statute's sweeping broad language. As noted, the plain dictionary meanings of statutory terms like "transaction," "dealing," "use," and "property" do not limit their use to commercial transactions; these terms are sufficiently broad to cover the conduct alleged here, including the donations of combatant services.

Lindh also argues unpersuasively that the D.C. Circuit's decision in *American Airways Charters, Inc. v. Regan,* 241 U.S. App. D.C. 132, 746 F.2d 865, 871-74 (D.C. Cir. 1984) precludes the result reached here. There, the court held that under the TWEA the Executive Branch could require a license before execution of a transaction reaching assets of a designated Cuban national, but that it lacked the authority to condition the bare formation of an attorney-client relationship on advance governmental approval. This decision is easily distinguishable from the instant case; it is rooted in constitutional due process concerns arising from the formation of the attorney-client relationship and the ability of a person to choose his or her counsel; it does not address the IEEPA's scope or the question whether that scope is ample authorization for the Regulations in issue.

V.

Lindh next argues that Counts Eight and Nine of the Indictment, which charge Lindh with providing and conspiring to provide prohibited services to the Taliban, should be dismissed because he is the victim of impermissible selective prosecution, in violation of his right to equal protection under the Fifth Amendment. Specifically, Lindh argues (i) he is the first to be prosecuted or criminally investigated under [the Taliban regulations] despite the fact that others appear to have violated these Regulations; and (ii) his selection for prosecution under the Regulations is based on his exercise of First Amendment rights. Should dismissal not be apparent on the existing record, Lindh seeks an evidentiary hearing to demonstrate the validity of his claim.

Significantly, claims of selective prosecution are not easily established. Such a claim "is not a defense on the merits to the criminal charge itself, but an independent assertion that the prosecutor has brought the charge for reasons forbidden by the Constitution."

To be sure, the allegations in the Complaint and the Indictment chronicle Lindh's conversion to Islam, his religious studies in Yemen and Pakistan, his voluntary association with the Taliban, and his oath of allegiance to jihad. Yet, none of this proves, as Lindh suggests, that the government prosecuted him because of his religious association. Instead, these allegations do nothing more than provide a chronology and context to explain how Lindh came to be on the battle front in Afghanistan and to supply services and support to the Taliban and al Qaeda. Discriminatory purpose cannot be inferred from a recitation of historical facts that merely provide context for criminal charges. Here, nothing in the Complaint or the Indictment suggests that Lindh's religious reasons for providing services to the Taliban motivated the government's decision to charge him with the offenses set out in Counts Eight and Nine. To the contrary, the serious offenses with which he is charged, *i.e.,* conspiracy to murder U.S. nationals and aiding foreign terrorist states and organizations, are manifestly the reasons for his prosecution, not his religious affiliation. Given the gravity of the allegations, there is every reason to believe that Lindh would have been prosecuted even had he been, say, a Presbyterian, a Scientologist, or an atheist.

VI.

Lindh also seeks dismissal of Counts Two through Nine of the Indictment on freedom of association, overbreadth, and vagueness grounds.

Lindh's First Amendment argument, distilled to its essence, is that he has a constitutional right to associate with foreign individuals and groups and that Counts Two through Nine impermissibly infringe this right by criminalizing this association. The statutes and regulations on which the Counts rest amount, in his view, to the government's attempt to impose on him guilt by association.

This argument is specious. Lindh is not accused of merely associating with a disfavored or subversive group whose activities are limited to circulating inflammatory political or religious material exhorting opposition to the government. Far from this, Lindh is accused of joining groups that do not merely advocate terror, violence, and murder of innocents; these groups actually carry out what they advocate and those who join them, at whatever level, participate in the groups' acts of terror, violence, and murder. There is, in other words, a clear line between First Amendment protected activity and criminal conduct for which there is no constitutional protection.

The most apposite authority on the issue is *Humanitarian Law Project v. Reno,* 205 F.3d 1130, 1133-34 (9th Cir. 2000), where a Ninth Circuit panel squarely rejected a constitutional challenge to the "material support or resources" prohibition of Section 2339B. There, the court resisted any analogy to cases based on association alone, noting that Section 2339B and related laws do "not prohibit being a member of one of the designated groups or vigorously promoting and supporting the political goals of the group." Rather, "plaintiffs are even free to praise the groups for using terrorism as a means of achieving their ends." What is prohibited by the statute is, in the court's words, "the act of giving material support." For this act, the court went on,

> there is no constitutional right to facilitate terrorism by giving terrorists the weapons and explosives with which to carry out their grisly missions. Nor, of course, is there a right to provide resources with which terrorists can buy weapons and explosives.

Unable to distinguish *Humanitarian Law Project,* Lindh argues instead that he is not a member of al Qaeda's "personnel" as defined by Section 2339B. Lindh maintains that providing "personnel" to HUM and al Qaeda could in certain instances amount to nothing more than the mere act of being physically present among members of a designated organization, obtaining information and training from such members, or simply being a member. Put differently, according to Lindh, allowing a prosecution under Section 2339B for providing "personnel" to a terrorist organization presents a constitutionally unacceptable risk that a mere bystander, sympathizer, or passive member will be convicted on the basis of association alone. This argument founders on the plain meaning of the term "personnel," which means "a body of persons usually employed (as in a factory, office, or organization)," or "a body of persons employed in some service." Thus, in Section 2339B, providing "personnel" to HUM or al Qaeda necessarily means that the persons provided to the foreign terrorist organization work under the direction and control of that organization. One who is merely present with other members of the organization, but is not under the organization's direction and control, is not part of the organization's "personnel." This distinction is sound; one can become a member of a political party without also becoming part of its "personnel;" one can visit an organization's training center, or actively espouse its cause, without thereby becoming "personnel." Simply put, the term "personnel" does not extend to independent actors. Rather, it describes employees or employee-like operatives who serve the designated group and work at its command or, in Lindh's case, who provide themselves to serve the organization.

Lindh also argues that Section 2339B and the IEEPA Regulations are facially unconstitutionally overbroad, as Section 2339B's prohibition of providing "personnel" penalizes mere association and the IEEPA Regulations' ban on the provision of "services" sweeps a substantial amount of protected conduct within its prohibitions. As noted, the term "personnel" entails more than mere presence. Indeed, a person can circulate a pamphlet or give a speech in support of an organization without also working within the organization's body of "personnel." So construed, and when any potential overbreadth is "judged in relation to the statute's plainly legitimate sweep," there is no danger, let alone a substantial one, that Section 2339B will be applied to infringe upon legitimate rights of association.

In support of his vagueness argument, Lindh relies principally on the Ninth Circuit's decision in *Humanitarian Law Project,* 205 F.3d at 1137-38, where the Ninth Circuit concluded that the district court did not abuse its discretion in issuing a limited preliminary injunction on vagueness grounds regarding the term "personnel." The Ninth Circuit stated, "it is easy to see how someone could be unsure about what [Section 2339B] prohibits with the use of the term 'personnel,' as it blurs the line between protected expression and unprotected conduct." The court observed that someone who advocates the cause of a terrorist organization "could be seen as supplying them with personnel," particularly since "having an independent advocate frees up members to engage in terrorist activities instead of advocacy." In response to the government's argument that "personnel" should be construed to extend only to a person's service "under the direction or control" of the terrorist organization, the Ninth Circuit declined to do so on the ground that it was "not authorized to rewrite the law so it will pass constitutional muster," and upheld the preliminary injunction in issue.

As already noted, the plain meaning of "personnel" is such that it requires, in the context of Section 2339B, an employment or employment-like relationship between the persons in question and the terrorist organization. The Ninth Circuit's vagueness holding in *Humanitarian Law Project* is neither persuasive nor controlling. The term is aimed at denying the provision of human resources to proscribed terrorist organizations, and not at the mere *independent* advocacy of an organization's interests or agenda. Thus, the term "personnel" in Section 2339B gives fair notice to the public of what is prohibited and the provision is therefore not unconstitutionally vague.

NOTES AND QUESTIONS

1. Following the district court's decision on the various motions to dismiss, Lindh entered into a plea agreement with the government by which he pleaded guilty to Count 9 (supplying services to the Taliban) and to an additional charge of carrying explosives in the commission of a felony. He accepted a 20-year sentence and agreed to cooperate with the government in its investigations. As part of the plea agreement, the government agreed not to treat him as an enemy combatant subject to military detention.

2. Media coverage of Lindh's transfer to Guantanamo showed him naked, apparently dirty and bruised. The plea agreement waives claims of mistreatment by U.S. agents and specifically states that Lindh does not allege "intentional mistreatment" by U.S. agents. Waiver of civil claims against the police is typical in plea agreements, but a remaining question is whether there really is any substantive "law" constraining the behavior of agents outside the U.S. If an action were brought on behalf of someone captured and interrogated outside the country, what law would apply?

3. If there had been no plea bargain, what elements of "material support" might Lindh have been shown to have provided to Al-Qaeda or the Taliban? If the government had been required to prove these same elements in support of the charge of carrying explosives in the commission of a felony, is there a problem of compounding offenses from the same behavior? Remember back to the discussion of cumulative charging and sentencing by the ICTR in the *Akayesu* case.

4. The court points out that the government did not charge that providing material support to the Taliban was the same as providing material support to al Qaeda. Placing yourself in the position of a prosecutor, if the Taliban were not itself on the list of embargoed regimes, what evidence would you have wanted to show the connection between the Taliban and al Qaeda, and to show Lindh's knowledge of that connection? This question will help set us up for later questions about accumulation of evidence for civilian criminal trials based on behavior in foreign countries, which leads to the issue of using the military justice system for these purposes.

5. A number of defendants were accused of multiple preparations for "violent jihad" in *United States v. Khan*, 309 F. Supp. 2d 789 (E.D. Va. 2004). The defendants used paintball and toy car remote controls in their preparation and training in the hills of Virginia. The defendants were preparing to assist, and some went to train with, the Lashkar-e-Taiba (LET or LT), a group warring against India in the Kashmir. This constituted a conspiracy to violate a slightly arcane federal statute, the Neutrality Act, 18 U.S.C. § 960, even though they never got to engage in action. In addition, some were charged with preparing to assist the Taliban and by inference al Qaeda. The judge disagreed with the inference of assistance to al Qaeda. "Although Khan's fighting on behalf of the Al-Qaeda's protector, the Taliban, would certainly benefit Al-Qaeda, such assistance does not fit the statutory definition of material support or resources."

6. Yaser Hamdi was picked up under similar circumstances, transported to Guantanamo, and then transferred to military custody in South Carolina. Why might Lindh have been treated differently? Why was Lindh not charged with treason? How close did this prosecution come to intruding upon Lindh's right of association?

[B] TREASON AND POLITICAL FREEDOM

Excerpt from *United States v. Rahman*, p. 36 supra:

In the late colonial period, as today, the charge of treason carried a "peculiar intimidation and stigma" with considerable "potentialities . . . as a political epithet." *See* William Hurst, *Treason in the United States (Pt. II)*, 58 HARV. L. REV. 395, 424-25 (1945).

At the time of the drafting of the Constitution, furthermore, treason was punishable not only by death, but by an exceptionally cruel method of execution designed to enhance the suffering of the traitor. *See* 4 WILLIAM BLACKSTONE, COMMENTARIES *92 (observing that the punishment for treason is "terrible" in that the traitor is "hanged by the neck, then cut down alive," that "his entrails [are then] taken out, and burned, while he is yet alive," "that his head [is] cut off," and that his "body [is then] divided into four parts"). In contrast, lesser subversive offenses were penalized by noncapital punishments or less brutal modes of execution. *See id.* at *94-*126. The Framers may have intended to limit the applicability of the most severe penalties – or simply the applicability of capital punishment for alleged subversion – to instances of levying war against, or adhering to enemies of, the United States. Today treason continues to be punishable by death, while seditious conspiracy commands a maximum penalty of twenty years imprisonment.

In recognition of the potential for political manipulation of the treason charge, the Framers may have formulated the Treason Clause as a protection against promiscuous resort to this particularly stigmatizing label, which carries such harsh consequences. It is thus possible to interpret the Treason Clause as applying only to charges denominated as "treason."

The Supreme Court has identified but not resolved the question whether the clause applies to offenses that include all the elements of treason but are not branded as such. *Compare Ex Parte Quirin,* 317 U.S. 1, 38 (1942) (suggesting, in dictum, that citizens could be tried for an offense against the law of war that included all the elements of treason), *with Cramer v. United States,* 325 U.S. 1, 45 (1945) (noting in dictum that the Court did not "intimate that Congress could dispense with [the] two-witness rule merely by giving the same offense another name") The question whether a defendant who engaged in subversive conduct might be tried for a crime involving all the elements of treason, but under a different name and without the constitutional protection of the Treason Clause, therefore remains open. And we need not decide it in this case, because the crime of which Nosair was convicted differs significantly from treason, not only in name and punishment, but also in definition.

The law of treason has not been widely studied in a very long time, but it may offer us some interesting insights. The Framers were so concerned about the potential misuses of treason charges that this is the only "crime" which is given special treatment in the Constitution. Article III, section 3 provides:

> Treason against the United States, shall consist only in levying War against them, or in adhering to their Enemies, giving them Aid and Comfort. No Person shall be convicted of Treason unless on the Testimony of two Witnesses to the same overt Act, or on Confession in open Court.

The Treason Clause builds extremely high barricades against prosecution for this "heinous" crime, so the question becomes whether those barricades can be circumvented by creating other crimes, or by calling the traitor something else such as an "enemy combatant." To be flippant, could we avoid restrictions on prosecution for treason by calling it jaywalking?

Article III's "peculiar phraseology observable in the definition of" treason, and "the equally stringent feature" requiring two eyewitness' testimony of the same overt act, have been said to flow from the Framers' discomfort with "abuses . . under the tyrannical reigns of the Tudors and the Stuarts." *Charge to Grand Jury – Treason*, 30 Fed. Cas. No. 18,271, p. 1035 (S.D.N.Y. 1861). In particular, the Framers were reacting to the concept of "constructive treason" by which anyone who spoke in support of, or was friendly with those who expressed, resistance to policies of the Crown could be accused of treason. Indeed, it is not likely that even the Tudors and Stuarts would have had an easy time of tossing a citizen into jail indefinitely on the mere say-so of a military officer. That they did so on occasion led directly to our constitutional language preventing the possibility.

Is it possible to square this history with the "enemy combatant" concept employed by the Supreme Court in *Quirin* and leading to military incarceration of U.S. citizens? The answer is "not very easily," and the lessons to be learned are not very clear. The Treason Clause creates two categories of treason: levying war against the United States, and providing aid and comfort to the enemy. In the first there must be an armed assemblage and the second requires an enemy.

Chief Justice Marshall gave us our first instruction in the operation of the Treason Clause in *Ex parte Bollman*, 8 U.S. (4 Cranch) 75 (1807), dealing with some of the alleged conspirators in the Burr escapade.

> To constitute that specific crime for which the prisoners now before the court have been committed, war must be actually levied against the United States. However flagitious may be the crime of conspiring to subvert by force the government of our country, such conspiracy is not treason. To conspire to levy war, and actually to levy war, are distinct offences. The first

must be brought into operation by the assemblage of men for a purpose treasonable in itself, or the fact of levying war cannot have been committed. [Even] the actual enlistment of men to serve against the government does not amount to levying war.

It is not the intention of the court to say that no individual can be guilty of this crime who has not appeared in arms against his country. On the contrary, if war be actually levied, that is, if a body of men be actually assembled for the purpose of effecting by force a treasonable purpose, all those who perform any part, however minute, or however remote from the scene of action, and who are actually leagued in the general conspiracy, are to be considered as traitors. But there must be an actual assembling of men for the treasonable purpose, to constitute a levying of war.

Crimes so atrocious as those which have for their object the subversion by violence of those laws and those institutions which have been ordained in order to secure the peace and happiness of society, are not to escape punishment because they have not ripened into treason. The wisdom of the legislature is competent to provide for the case; and the framers of our constitution, . . must have conceived it more safe that punishment in such cases should be ordained by general laws, . . . than that it should be inflicted under the influence of those passions which . . . a flexible definition of the crime, or a construction which would render it flexible, might bring into operation. It is therefore more safe as well as more consonant to the principles of our constitution, . . . that crimes not clearly within the constitutional definition, should receive such punishment as the legislature in its wisdom may provide.

To complete the crime of levying war against the United States, there must be an actual assemblage of men for the purpose of executing a treasonable design. In the case now before the court, a design to overturn the government of the United States in New-Orleans by force, . . . if carried into execution, would have been treason, and the assemblage of a body of men for the purpose of carrying it into execution would amount to levying of war against the United States; but no conspiracy for this object, no enlisting of men to effect it, would be an actual levying of war.

Marshall distinguished strongly between treason and conspiracy: "However flagitious may be the crime of conspiring to subvert by force the government of our country, such conspiracy is not treason." It must be remembered, however, that the Burr escapade did not involve a foreign enemy, so there was no occasion for him to deal with the offense of providing aid and comfort to the enemy.

Marshall went on to deal with our very question. Although "to complete the crime of levying war against the United States, there must be an actual assemblage of men for the purpose of executing a treasonable design," he expressed the view that the legislature could define other offenses to which the strictures of the Treason Clause would not apply. The Framers were concerned about the passions that the thought of treason would engender, but they could have been comfortable with the thought that "crimes not clearly within the constitutional definition, should receive such punishment as the legislature in its wisdom may provide."

In a number of cases stemming from the Civil War, the judges expanded Marshall's view of conspiracy to state that there could be no such concept as an accessory to treason because an act was either treason or not. *United States v. Greathouse*, 26 Fed. Cas. No. 15,254 (C.C. Cal. 1863). They consistently recognized the differences between the two kinds of treason, the first depending on whether the defendant has taken up arms, the second consisting of providing material support to a recognized enemy. It is familiar ground that President Lincoln attempted to use the military courts for prosecution of Southern sympathizers, leading eventually to the opinion in *Ex parte Milligan*, p. 459 *infra*.

After the War, in *Thorington v. Smith*, 75 U.S. (8 Wall.) 1 (1869), the Court dealt with the question of whether debts payable in Confederate currency were still valid as between two individuals (and, thus, payable in U.S. currency after the war ended). Chief Justice Chase distinguished among different levels of *de facto* governments. At one extreme would be a solidly established actual government such that "adherents to it in war against the government *de jure* do not incur the penalties of treason." The government of the Confederacy, he argued, was sufficiently established that it obtained "actual supremacy, however unlawfully gained, in all matters of government within its military lines."

> That supremacy did not justify acts of hostility to the United States. How far it should excuse them must be left to the lawful government upon the re-establishment of its authority. But it made obedience to its authority, in civil and local matters, not only a necessity but a duty. Without such obedience, civil order was impossible.

By this language, Chase was implying that there could be no prosecution for providing aid and comfort to the enemy by a person residing within the military control of the Confederacy. As we know, there were no such prosecutions.

World War I produced the seminal case for all of First Amendment law, *Schenck v. United States*, 249 U.S. 47 (1919). Schenck and his cohorts were convicted of conspiracy to violate the Espionage Act of 1917, which made it unlawful to "cause insubordination . . . in the military and naval forces of the United States, and to obstruct the recruiting and enlistment service of the United States." Justice Holmes' famous opinion for the Court, after using the analogy of "falsely shouting fire in a crowded theater," stated:

> The question in every case is whether the words used are used in such circumstances and are of such a nature as to create a clear and present danger that they will bring about the substantive evils that Congress has a right to prevent. It is a question of proximity and degree. When a nation is at war many things that might be said in time of peace are such a hindrance to its effort that their utterance will not be endured so long as men fight and that no Court could regard them as protected by any constitutional right. It seems to be admitted that if an actual obstruction of the recruiting service were proved, liability for words that produced that effect might be enforced. The statute of 1917 in § 4 punishes conspiracies to

obstruct as well as actual obstruction. If the act, (speaking, or circulating a paper,) its tendency and the intent with which it is done are the same, we perceive no ground for saying that success alone warrants making the act a crime.

Before *Schenck* was decided, Congress had already responded to the emerging level of dissension regarding U.S. entry into the war in Europe by passing the 1918 amendments to the Espionage Act. Under the amendments, it was unlawful to "urge, incite, or advocate" actions that could disrupt the war. In *Abrams v. United States*, 250 U.S. 616 (1919), the majority of the Court found that an intent to disrupt the war effort was sufficient to uphold conviction under the statute. Justice Holmes, joined by Brandeis, dissented with the famous "marketplace of ideas" analysis. The combination of opinions sounds as if the majority were treating the statute as if it were a finding by Congress of "clear and present danger." It seems that in this stage, Congress and the Court had accepted Chief Justice Marshall's invitation to Congress to define non-treason offenses.

The only World War II case in the Supreme Court on the subject of Treason was *Cramer v. United States*, 325 U.S. 1 (1945), a follow-up to *Quirin*. One of the eight German saboteurs, Thiel, had a friend in the U.S. named Cramer, who was German by birth and a naturalized U.S. citizen. Thiel contacted Cramer in New York, met with him twice in public places, and gave Cramer some money to hold for him. Cramer testified that he suspected Thiel was here as a propagandist for the German government, but there was no evidence that Cramer suspected anything of the violent intentions of the saboteurs. Cramer was convicted of treason. The basic question presented to the Supreme Court was whether an overt act in furtherance of treason needed to be done with intent by the defendant of furthering enemy action against the government, or whether an innocent overt act could be treasonous because of its role in the enemy's plan.

Justice Jackson's majority opinion in *Cramer* canvassed the history of treason prosecutions from English law through the colonial era. The Framers built protections against treason prosecutions to guard against two dangers: "(1) perversion by established authority to repress peaceful political opposition; and (2) conviction of the innocent as a result of perjury, passion or inadequate evidence." The critical passage for definition of criminal behavior is this:

> Thus the crime of treason consists of two elements: adherence to the enemy; and rendering him aid and comfort. A citizen intellectually or emotionally may favor the enemy and harbor sympathies or convictions disloyal to this country's policy or interest, but so long as he commits no act of aid and comfort to the enemy, there is no treason. On the other hand, a citizen may take actions which do aid and comfort the enemy – making a speech critical of the government or opposing its measures, profiteering, striking in defense plants or essential work, and the hundred other things which impair our cohesion and diminish our strength – but if there is no adherence to the enemy in this, if there is no intent to betray, there is no treason.

Applying these thoughts to the evidence, Jackson pointed out that the prosecution had "withdrawn" the safekeeping of money as an overt act to be submitted to the jury. That left only the two meetings with Thiel that were corroborated by eyewitness testimony. These could not be said to have shown either furtherance of a scheme sufficient to prove either aid or adherence to the enemy. By contrast, the money transaction, if proved by the requisite testimony, would have made "a quite different case." Finally, Justice Jackson addressed the Government's arguments for relaxing the standards related to treason:

> The Government has urged that our initial interpretation of the treason clause should be less exacting, lest treason be too hard to prove and the Government disabled from adequately combating the techniques of modern warfare. But the treason offense is not the only nor can it well serve as the principal legal weapon to vindicate our national cohesion and security. In debating this provision, Rufus King observed to the Convention that the "controversy relating to Treason might be of less magnitude than was supposed; as the legislature might punish capitally under other names than Treason." His statement holds good today. Of course we do not intimate that Congress could dispense with the two-witness rule merely by giving the same offense another name. But the power of Congress is in no way limited to enact prohibitions of specified acts thought detrimental to our wartime safety.

Congress, with the assistance of many subsequent administrations, has accepted this invitation by enacting many statutes that relate to providing aid and comfort to those who threaten the public safety of the United States. Perhaps the most directly relevant are those that criminalize "providing material support to terrorists" (§ 2339A) and "providing material support or resources to designated terrorist organizations" (§ 2339B). There are also crimes, such as what John Walker Lindh pleaded guilty to, defined as violations of Presidential directives blocking trading with, or providing services to, regimes designated in time of national emergency, most of which are punishable under § 1705. Given the history of the Treason Clause, and particularly Justices Marshall's and Jackson's invitations to Congress, there can be little doubt about the validity of these statutes, except insofar as they might in some situations be subject to first amendment restrictions.

§ 6.02 THE COMMUNIST CONSPIRACY AND THE RIGHT OF ASSOCIATION

Whitney v. California, 274 U.S. 357 (1927). Ms. Whitney was convicted of criminal syndicalism under a state statute that defined the offense "as any doctrine, advocating [or] teaching unlawful methods of terrorism as a means of accomplishing a change in industrial ownership or control, or effecting any political change." Although Whitney was a delegate to the state Communist Labor Party convention, at which most members favored violence as a means of securing political change, she argued that she did not favor violence and in fact had attempted to forestall violence as a method of political change. The Supreme Court said that she was raising issues of fact which had been found against her and which an appellate court could not reconsider. The Court also reiterated the familiar formula that acting in concert was a greater threat to the public order than the expressions or acts of individuals acting separately.

Justices Brandeis and Justice Holmes concurred but added some warning thoughts:

The felony which the statute created is a crime very unlike the old felony of conspiracy or the old misdemeanor of unlawful assembly. The mere act of assisting in forming a society for teaching syndicalism, of becoming a member of it, or assembling with others for that purpose is given the dynamic quality of crime. There is guilt although the society may not contemplate immediate promulgation of the doctrine. Thus the accused is to be punished, not for attempt, incitement or conspiracy, but for a step in preparation, which, if it threatens the public order at all, does so only remotely. The novelty in the prohibition introduced is that the statute aims, not at the practice of criminal syndicalism, nor even directly at the preaching of it, but at association with those who propose to preach it.

The right of free speech, the right to teach and the right of assembly are, of course, fundamental rights. These may not be denied or abridged. But, although the rights of free speech and assembly are fundamental, they are not in their nature absolute. Their exercise is subject to restriction, if the particular restriction proposed is required in order to protect the state from destruction or from serious injury, political, economic or moral. That the necessity which is essential to a valid restriction does not exist unless speech would produce, or is intended to produce, a clear and imminent danger of some substantive evil which the state constitutionally may seek to prevent has been settled.

Those who won our independence believed that the final end of the state was to make men free to develop their faculties, and that in its government the deliberative forces should prevail over the arbitrary. They valued liberty both as an end and as a means. They believed liberty to be the secret of happiness and courage to be the secret of liberty. They believed that freedom to think as you will and to speak as you think are means indispensable to the discovery and spread of political truth; that without free speech and assembly discussion would be futile; that with them, discussion affords ordinarily adequate protection against the dissemination of noxious doctrine; that the greatest menace to freedom is an inert people; that public discussion is a political duty; and that this should be a fundamental principle of the American government. They recognized the risks to which all human institutions are subject. But they knew that order cannot be secured merely through fear of punishment for its infraction; that it is hazardous to discourage thought, hope and imagination; that fear breeds repression; that repression breeds hate; that hate menaces stable government; that the path of safety lies in the opportunity to discuss freely supposed grievances and proposed remedies; and that the fitting remedy for evil counsels is good ones.

Fear of serious injury cannot alone justify suppression of free speech and assembly. Men feared witches and burnt women. It is the function of speech to free men from the bondage of irrational fears. To justify suppression of free speech there must be reasonable ground to fear that serious evil will result if free speech is practiced. There must be reasonable ground to believe that the danger apprehended is imminent. There must be reasonable ground to believe that the evil to be prevented is a serious one. Every denunciation of existing law tends in some measure to increase the probability that there will be violation of it. Condonation of a breach enhances the probability. Expressions of approval add to the probability. Propagation of the criminal state of mind by teaching syndicalism increases it. Advocacy of law-breaking heightens it still further. But even advocacy of violence, however reprehensible morally, is not a justification for denying free speech where the advocacy falls short of incitement and there is nothing to indicate that the advocacy would be immediately acted on. The wide difference between advocacy and incitement, between preparation and attempt, between assembling and conspiracy, must be borne in mind. In order to support a finding of clear and present danger it must be shown either that immediate serious violence was to be expected or was advocated, or that the past conduct furnished reason to believe that such advocacy was then contemplated.

Those who won our independence by revolution were not cowards. They did not fear political change. They did not exalt order at the cost of liberty. To courageous, self-reliant men, with confidence in the power of free and fearless reasoning applied through the processes of proper government, no danger flowing from speech can be deemed clear and present, unless the incidence of the evil apprehended is so imminent that it may befall before there is opportunity for full discussion. If there be time to expose through discussion the falsehood and fallacies, to avert the evil by the processes of education, the remedy to be applied is more speech, not enforced silence. Only an emergency can justify repression. Such must be the rule if authority is to be reconciled with freedom. Such, in my opinion, is the command of the Constitution. It is therefore always open to Americans to challenge a law abridging free speech and assembly by showing that there was no emergency justifying it.

Dennis v. United States, 341 U.S. 494 (1951). Several leaders of the American Communist Party were convicted of violating the federal Smith Act:

Sec. 2. (a) It shall be unlawful for any person

(1) to knowingly or willfully advocate, abet, advise, or teach the duty, necessity, desirability, or propriety of overthrowing or destroying any government in the United States by force or violence, or by the assassination of any officer of any such government;

(3) to organize or help to organize any society, group, or assembly of persons who teach, advocate, or encourage the overthrow or destruction of any government in the United States by force or

violence; or to be or become a member of, or affiliate with, any such society, group, or assembly of persons, knowing the purposes thereof.

Sec. 3. It shall be unlawful for any person to attempt to commit, or to conspire to commit, any of the acts prohibited by the provisions of this title.

The majority opinion for the Supreme Court stated that it accepted the "clear and present danger" test as amplified by Brandeis and Holmes in *Whitney* but found that the circumstances of the U.S. in the 1940s met the test in this fashion:

If Government is aware that a group aiming at its overthrow is attempting to indoctrinate its members and to commit them to a course whereby they will strike when the leaders feel the circumstances permit, action by the Government is required. Certainly an attempt to overthrow the Government by force, even though doomed from the outset because of inadequate numbers or power of the revolutionists, is a sufficient evil for Congress to prevent. The damage which such attempts create both physically and politically to a nation makes it impossible to measure the validity in terms of the probability of success, or the immediacy of a successful attempt. In the instant case the trial judge charged the jury that they could not convict unless they found that petitioners intended to overthrow the Government "as speedily as circumstances would permit." This does not mean, and could not properly mean, that they would not strike until there was certainty of success. What was meant was that the revolutionists would strike when they thought the time was ripe. We must therefore reject the contention that success or probability of success is the criterion.

The mere fact that from the period 1945 to 1948 petitioners' activities did not result in an attempt to overthrow the Government by force and violence is of course no answer to the fact that there was a group that was ready to make the attempt. The formation by petitioners of such a highly organized conspiracy, with rigidly disciplined members subject to call when the leaders, these petitioners, felt that the time had come for action, coupled with the inflammable nature of world conditions, similar uprisings in other countries, and the touch-and-go nature of our relations with countries with whom petitioners were in the very least ideologically attuned, convince us that their convictions were justified on this score. And this analysis disposes of the contention that a conspiracy to advocate, as distinguished from the advocacy itself, cannot be constitutionally restrained, because it comprises only the preparation. It is the existence of the conspiracy which creates the danger. If the ingredients of the reaction are present, we cannot bind the Government to wait until the catalyst is added.

Justice Jackson concurred on this basis:

The authors of the clear and present danger test never applied it to a case like this, nor would I. What really is under review here is a conviction of conspiracy. The Constitution does not make conspiracy a civil right. The basic rationale of the law of conspiracy is that a conspiracy may be an evil in itself, independently of any other evil it seeks to accomplish. Having held that a conspiracy alone is a crime and its consummation is another, it would be weird legal reasoning to hold that Congress could punish the one only if there was "clear and present danger" of the second.

Justices Black and Douglas dissented.

Following *Dennis*, the government attempted a few more prosecutions for violation of the Smith Act and found essentially that the Court was not so receptive as it was initially. In *Yates v. United States*, 354 U.S. 298, 324 (1957), Justice Harlan recast the holding of *Dennis*:

> The essence of the *Dennis* holding was that indoctrination of a group in preparation for future violent action, as well as exhortation to immediate action, by advocacy found to be directed to "action for the accomplishment" of forcible overthrow, to violence "as a rule or principle of action," and employing "language of incitement," is not constitutionally protected when the group is of sufficient size and cohesiveness, is sufficiently oriented towards action, and other circumstances are such as reasonable to justify apprehension that action will occur.

Scales v. United States, 367 U.S. 203, 228 (1961), further limited the Smith Act in ways that will be relevant in the cases below, implying that the limitations were required by the first amendment. The Court held that "active" participation in group with "guilty knowledge and intent" could be punished but not "merely an expression of sympathy with the alleged criminal enterprise, unaccompanied by any significant action in its support or any commitment to undertake such action."

McCarthyism in its extreme form died of the weight of its own intolerance and the misdeeds of its principal proponent. Senator McCarthy was censured by the Senate in 1954 and died in 1957. Nevertheless, the "red scare" continued to occupy a central place in the politics of the United States throughout much of the Cold War era. Prosecutions of communist sympathizers, however, became very rare. The Supreme Court then found that it was a threat from another quarter that would cause it to rethink much of its first amendment lore.

BRANDENBURG v. OHIO
395 U.S. 444, 89 S. Ct. 1827, 23 L. Ed. 2d 430 (1969)

PER CURIAM:

The appellant, a leader of a Ku Klux Klan group, was convicted under the Ohio Criminal Syndicalism statute for "advocat[ing] the duty, necessity, or propriety of crime, sabotage, violence, or unlawful methods of terrorism as a means of accomplishing industrial or political reform" and for "voluntarily assembl[ing] with any society, group, or assemblage of persons formed to teach or advocate the doctrines of criminal syndicalism." Ohio Rev. Code Ann. § 2923.13.

The Ohio Criminal Syndicalism Statute was enacted in 1919. From 1917 to 1920, identical or quite similar laws were adopted by 20 States and two territories. In 1927, this Court sustained the constitutionality of California's Criminal Syndicalism Act, the text of which is quite similar to that of the laws of Ohio. *Whitney v. California.* The Court upheld the statute on the ground that, without more, "advocating" violent means to effect political and economic change involves such danger to the security of the State that the State may outlaw it. But *Whitney* has been throughly discredited by later decisions. *See Dennis v. United States.* These later decisions have fashioned the principle that the constitutional guarantees of free speech and free press do not permit a State to forbid or proscribe advocacy of the use of force or of law violation except where such advocacy is directed to inciting or producing imminent lawless action and is likely to incite or produce such actions. A statute which fails to draw this distinction impermissibly intrudes upon the freedoms guaranteed by the First and Fourteenth Amendments. It sweeps within its condemnation speech which our Constitution has immunized from governmental control.

Measured by this test, Ohio's Criminal Syndicalism Act cannot be sustained. The Act punishes persons who "advocate or teach the duty, necessity, or propriety" of violence "as a means of accomplishing industrial or political reform;" or who publish or circulate or display any book or paper containing such advocacy; or who "justify" the commission of violent acts "with intent to exemplify, spread or advocate the propriety of the doctrines of criminal syndicalism;" or who "voluntarily assemble" with a group formed "to teach or advocate the doctrines of criminal syndicalism." Neither the indictment nor the trial judge's instructions to the jury in any way refined the statute's bald definition of the crime in terms of mere advocacy not distinguished from incitement to imminent lawless action.

Accordingly, we are here confronted with a statute which, by its own words and as applied, purports to punish mere advocacy and to forbid, on pain of criminal punishment, assembly with others merely to advocate the described type of action. Such a statute falls within the condemnation of the First and Fourteenth Amendments. The contrary teaching of *Whitney v. California* cannot be supported, and that decision is therefore overruled.

Justice BLACK, concurring:

I agree with the views expressed by Mr. Justice Douglas in his concurring opinion in this case that the "clear and present danger" doctrine should have no place in the interpretation of the First Amendment. I join the Court's opinion, which, as I understand it, simply cites *Dennis v. United States*, but does not indicate any agreement on the Court's part with the "clear and present danger" doctrine on which *Dennis* purported to rely.

Justice DOUGLAS, concurring:

While I join the opinion of the Court, I desire to enter a caveat. Though I doubt if the "clear and present danger" test is congenial to the First Amendment in time of a declared war, I am certain it is not reconcilable with the First Amendment in days of peace. I see no place in the regime of the First Amendment for any "clear and present danger" test, whether strict and tight as some would make it, or free-wheeling as the Court in *Dennis* rephrased it.

When one reads the opinions closely and sees when and how the "clear and present danger" test has been applied, great misgivings are aroused. First, the threats were often loud but always puny and made serious only by judges so wedded to the status quo that critical analysis made them nervous. Second, the test was so twisted and perverted in *Dennis* as to make the trial of those teachers of Marxism an all-out political trial which was part and parcel of the cold war that has eroded substantial parts of the First Amendment.

Action is often a method of expression and within the protection of the First Amendment. Suppose one tears up his own copy of the Constitution in eloquent protest to a decision of this Court. May he be indicted? Suppose one rips his own Bible to shreds to celebrate his departure from one "faith" and his embrace of atheism. May he be indicted? The line between what is permissible and not subject to control and what may be made impermissible and subject to regulation is the line between ideas and overt acts.

The example usually given by those who would punish speech is the case of one who falsely shouts fire in a crowded theatre. This is, however, a classic case where speech is brigaded with action. They are indeed inseparable and a prosecution can be launched for the overt acts actually caused. Apart from rare instances of that kind, speech is, I think, immune from prosecution. Certainly there is no constitutional line between advocacy of abstract ideas as in *Yates* and advocacy of political action as in *Scales*. The quality of advocacy turns on the depth of the conviction; and government has no power to invade that sanctuary of belief and conscience.

NOTES AND QUESTIONS

1. Prior to *Brandenburg*, the Court had already declared in a number of cases that mere membership in the Communist Party could not be penalized. In the process, there developed a distinct first amendment "right of association." *Scales v. United States*, 367 U.S. 203 (1961), upheld a conviction for membership in the Communist Party only upon a finding of specific intent to engage in illegal action. *Noto v. United States*, 367 U.S. 290 (1961), overturned a similar conviction in which the specific intent was lacking. Both cases read the statute's criminalizing of membership as if it included an element of intent to act.

2. *NAACP v. Alabama ex rel. Patterson*, 357 U.S. 449 (1958), unanimously declared that the state could not seek membership lists because disclosure would negatively impact the now-recognized right of association. Through the 1980s and 1990s, the Court elaborated on the right of association in a number of situations dealing with regulation of political parties and the electoral process. The scope of constitutional protection for election campaign giving, campaign reforms, and the like are all beyond the scope of the discussion here, but it is safe to say that the right of association is now firmly entrenched in the first amendment.

3. *NAACP v. Claiborne Hardware*, 458 U.S. 886 (1982), is cited frequently in the cases below on material support of terrorism. The Court overturned a state court judgment against the NAACP on behalf of merchants who had been damaged by a boycott of their businesses. Although some aspects of the boycott may have been unlawful, neither the organization nor its members could be held liable without a showing of direct participation in the unlawful activity. "Civil liability may not be imposed merely because an individual belonged to a group, some members of which committed acts of violence. For liability to be imposed by reason of association alone, it is necessary to establish that the group itself possessed unlawful goals and that the individual held a specific intent to further those illegal goals." *Id.* at 920.

4. *Buckley v. Valeo*, 424 U.S. 1 (1976), dealt with the validity of the Federal Election Campaign Act of 1971. Among other things, FECA limited individual contributions to federal campaigns and attempted to limit campaign expenditures by individuals or groups, as well as expenditures by candidates themselves. The Supreme Court started with the proposition that all these activities carried first amendment protection as part of the political process and under the right of association. "In a republic where the people are sovereign, the ability of the citizenry to make informed choices among candidates for office is essential." The expenditure limitations were struck down on that basis. With regard to the contribution limitations, the Court found that the claim of freedom of expression was lessened: "A contribution serves as a general expression of support for the candidate and his views, but does not communicate the underlying basis for the support." The Court went on to hold that, although the contribution limits "impinge on protected associational freedoms," they were warranted by a "sufficiently important interest" in "limit[ing] the actuality and appearance of corruption resulting from large individual financial contributions." These basic propositions were revalidated in *McConnell v. FEC*, 124 S. Ct. 619 (2003), while also recognizing that some expenditures could actually be counted as contributions toward a particular campaign when the expenditures were closely coordinated with the campaign itself (recall the controversy in the 2004 campaigns about whether official campaign committees were collaborating with smear tactics of apparently independent groups).

§ 6.03 DESIGNATED FOREIGN TERRORIST ORGANIZATIONS AND THE RIGHT OF ASSOCIATION

What must the government prove to make out a conspiracy case while avoiding impact on the freedom of association? Providing material support "knowing or intending that they are to be used in preparation for, or in carrying out, a violation of" a specified statute differs from providing material support to a "foreign terrorist organization" designated by the Secretary of State. The designation places everyone on notice that mere support of this organization is unlawful, but does that really change the impact of the right of association? In other words, doesn't the Constitution require knowledge of imminent violent or fraudulent behavior before we can punish support of an organization?

Material support prosecutions raise constitutional issues of the right of association, vagueness and overbreadth of the statutes, and due process regarding the methods for designation of foreign terrorist organizations. The following cases address all these issues.

[A] PROHIBITING MATERIAL SUPPORT

HUMANITARIAN LAW PROJECT v. RENO [HLP I]
205 F.3d 1130 (9th Cir. 2000)

KOZINSKI, Circuit Judge:

We consider whether Congress may, consistent with the First Amendment, prohibit contributions of material support to certain foreign terrorist organizations.

I

The Antiterrorism and Effective Death Penalty Act of 1996, known among the cognoscenti as AEDPA, authorizes the Secretary of State to "designate an organization as a foreign terrorist organization . . . if the Secretary finds that (A) the organization is a foreign organization; (B) the organization engages in terrorist activity . . . ; and (C) the terrorist activity of the organization threatens the security of United States nationals or the national security of the United States."

Pursuant to those guidelines, the Secretary had, as of October 1997, designated 30 organizations as foreign terrorist organizations. Two such entities are the Kurdistan Workers' Party ("PKK") and the Liberation Tigers of Tamil Eelam ("LTTE"). Plaintiffs, six organizations and two United States citizens, wish to provide what they fear would be considered material support to the PKK and LTTE. Plaintiffs claim that such support would be directed to aid only the nonviolent humanitarian and political activities of the designated organizations. Being prohibited from giving this support, they argue, infringes their associational rights under the First Amendment. Because the statute criminalizes the giving of material support to an organization regardless of whether the donor intends to further the organization's unlawful ends, plaintiffs claim it runs afoul of the rule set forth in cases such as *NAACP v. Claiborne Hardware Co.*, 458 U.S. 886, 102 S. Ct. 3409 (1982). That rule, as succinctly stated in *Claiborne Hardware*, is "for liability to be imposed by reason of association alone, it is necessary to establish that the group itself possessed unlawful goals and that the individual held a specific intent to further those illegal aims." Plaintiffs further complain that AEDPA grants the Secretary unfettered and unreviewable authority to designate which groups are listed as foreign terrorist organizations, a violation of the First and Fifth Amendments. Lastly, plaintiffs maintain that AEDPA is unconstitutionally vague.

Plaintiffs sought a preliminary injunction barring enforcement of AEDPA against them. The district court denied the injunction, for the most part. However, it agreed with plaintiffs that AEDPA was impermissibly vague, specifically in its prohibition on providing "personnel" and "training." The court therefore enjoined the enforcement of those prohibitions. Each side appeals its losses.

II

A. Plaintiffs try hard to characterize the statute as imposing guilt by association, which would make it unconstitutional under cases such as *Claiborne*

Hardware. But *Claiborne Hardware* and similar cases address situations where people are punished "by reason of association alone" – in other words, merely for membership in a group or for espousing its views. AEDPA authorizes no such thing. The statute does not prohibit being a member of one of the designated groups or vigorously promoting and supporting the political goals of the group. Plaintiffs are even free to praise the groups for using terrorism as a means of achieving their ends. What AEDPA prohibits is the act of giving material support, and there is no constitutional right to facilitate terrorism by giving terrorists the weapons and explosives with which to carry out their grisly missions. Nor, of course, is there a right to provide resources with which terrorists can buy weapons and explosives.

B. Plaintiffs also insist that AEDPA is unconstitutional because it proscribes the giving of material support even if the donor does not have the specific intent to aid in the organization's unlawful purposes. They rely on *American-Arab Anti-Discrimination Comm. v. Reno,* 70 F.3d 1045 (9th Cir. 1995) [deportation allegedly based on membership in subversive groups], where we declared that "the government must establish a 'knowing affiliation' and a 'specific intent to further those illegal aims'" in order to punish advocacy. But advocacy is far different from making donations of material support. Advocacy is always protected under the First Amendment whereas making donations is protected only in certain contexts. Plaintiffs here do not contend they are prohibited from advocating the goals of the foreign terrorist organizations, espousing their views or even being members of such groups. They can do so without fear of penalty right up to the line established by *Brandenburg v. Ohio.*

C. Plaintiffs make a separate First Amendment argument based on the fact that the terrorist organizations in question also engage in political advocacy. Pointing to cases such as *Buckley v. Valeo,* plaintiffs argue that providing money to organizations engaged in political expression is itself both political expression and association.[17] However, the cases equating monetary support with expression involved organizations whose overwhelming function was political advocacy. *Buckley* is the quintessential example where the contributions were made to candidates for political office for the purpose of helping them engage in electioneering. Under those circumstances, money, and the things money can buy, do indeed serve as a proxy for speech and demonstrate one's association with the organization. However, even in *Buckley*, the Court treated limits on donations differently from limits on candidates' expenditures of personal funds. While the First Amendment protects the expressive component of seeking and donating funds, expressive *conduct* receives significantly less protection than pure speech. The government may thus regulate contributions to organizations that engage in lawful – but non-speech related – activities. And it may certainly regulate contributions to organizations performing unlawful or harmful

---

[17] What is at issue here is the right of Americans to express their association with foreign political groups through donations. The political advocacy of the PKK and LTTE directed toward their own governments is not protected by our First Amendment. *Cf. United States v. Verdugo-Urquidez,* 494 U.S. 259 (1990) (refusing to extend constitutional protection to Mexican citizen).

activities, even though such contributions may also express the donor's feelings about the recipient.

Contrary to plaintiffs' argument, the material support restriction here does not warrant strict scrutiny because it is not aimed at interfering with the expressive component of their conduct but at stopping aid to terrorist groups. Intermediate scrutiny applies where, as here, "a regulation . . . serves purposes unrelated to the content of expression."

When we review under the intermediate scrutiny standard, we must ask four questions: Is the regulation within the power of the government? Does it promote an important or substantial government interest? Is that interest unrelated to suppressing free expression? And, finally, is the incidental restriction on First Amendment freedoms no greater than necessary?

Here all four questions are answered in the affirmative. First, the federal government clearly has the power to enact laws restricting the dealings of United States citizens with foreign entities; such regulations have been upheld in the past over a variety of constitutional challenges. *See, e.g., Regan v. Wald,* 468 U.S. 222, 244 (1984) (restrictions on travel to Cuba did not violate Fifth Amendment); *Teague v. Regional Comm'r of Customs,* 404 F.2d 441, 445 (2d Cir. 1968) (upholding regulations "designed to limit the flow of currency to specified hostile nations" despite the fact that regulations "impinged on first amendment freedoms"). Second, the government has a legitimate interest in preventing the spread of international terrorism, and there is no doubt that that interest is substantial. Third, this interest is unrelated to suppressing free expression because it restricts the actions of those who wish to give material support to the groups, not the expression of those who advocate or believe the ideas that the groups supports.

So the heart of the matter is whether AEDPA is well enough tailored to its end of preventing the United States from being used as a base for terrorist fundraising. Because the judgment of how best to achieve that end is strongly bound up with foreign policy considerations, we must allow the political branches wide latitude in selecting the means to bring about the desired goal. Plaintiffs argue that the prior statutory scheme, which allowed the donation of humanitarian assistance to those who were not directly involved in terrorist activity, was properly tailored and the current statutory scheme is therefore overbroad. But the fact that the prior statutory scheme was narrower tells us nothing about whether the current scheme is overbroad, because we don't know how well the prior scheme worked. Presumably Congress thought that it did not work well enough and so decided to broaden it. Moreover, the Supreme Court has held that the government need not select the least restrictive or least intrusive means of accomplishing its purpose.

Congress explicitly incorporated a finding into the statute that "foreign organizations that engage in terrorist activity are so tainted by their criminal conduct that any contribution to such an organization facilitates that conduct." It follows that all material support given to such organizations aids their unlawful goals.[18] Indeed, as the government points out, terrorist organizations do not maintain open books. Therefore, when someone makes a donation to them, there is no way to tell how the donation is used. Further, as amicus Anti-Defamation League notes, even contributions earmarked for peaceful purposes can be used to give aid to the families of those killed while carrying out terrorist acts, thus making the decision to engage in terrorism more attractive. More fundamentally, money is fungible; giving support intended to aid an organization's peaceful activities frees up resources that can be used for terrorist acts. We will not indulge in speculation about whether Congress was right to come to the conclusion that it did. We simply note that Congress has the fact-finding resources to properly come to such a conclusion. Thus, we cannot say that AEDPA is not sufficiently tailored.

D. Plaintiffs also argue that the statute violates their First and Fifth Amendment rights by giving the Secretary "unfettered discretion" to limit their right to associate with certain foreign organizations, and by insulating her decisions from judicial review. AEDPA does not grant the Secretary unfettered discretion in designating the groups to which giving material support is prohibited. The statute authorizes the Secretary to designate only those groups that engage in terrorist activities. This standard is not so vague or indeterminate as to give the Secretary unfettered discretion. For example, the Secretary could not, under this standard, designate the International Red Cross or the International Olympic Committee as terrorist organizations. Rather, the Secretary must have reasonable grounds to believe that an organization has engaged in terrorist acts – assassinations, bombings, hostage-taking and the like – before she can place it on the list. This standard is sufficiently precise to satisfy constitutional concerns. And, because the regulation involves the conduct of foreign affairs, we owe the executive branch even more latitude than in the domestic context.

Plaintiffs argue that any decision the Secretary makes in designating an organization is essentially unreviewable. However, 8 U.S.C. § 1189(b) provides for judicial review of the Secretary's decision in the United States Court of Appeals for the District of Columbia Circuit. Although plaintiffs complain that the review is ineffectual because of the degree of deference accorded to the Secretary's decision, that is a necessary concomitant of the foreign affairs power. In any event, that challenge must be raised in an appeal from a decision to designate a particular organization.

E. Finally, Plaintiffs challenge AEDPA on vagueness grounds. In the district court, they alleged that "foreign terrorist organization" and "material support,"

---

[18] Plaintiffs argue that this finding is undercut by other portions of the statute that allow the donation of unlimited amounts of medicine and religious items. We see things differently. Congress is entitled to conclude that respect for freedom of religion militates in favor of allowing religious items to be donated to foreign organizations, even though doing so may incidentally aid terrorism. Further it could also rationally decide that the humanitarian value of providing medicine to such organizations outweighs the risk that the medicine would be sold to finance terrorist activities. Congress is entitled to strike such delicate balances without giving up its ability to prohibit other types of assistance which would promote terrorism.

as defined in AEDPA, were void for vagueness. The district court agreed in part, finding that two of the components included within the definition of material support, "training" and "personnel," were impermissibly vague. It enjoined the prosecution of any of the plaintiffs' members for activities covered by these terms. The district court did not abuse its discretion in doing so.

When a criminal law implicates First Amendment concerns, the law must be "sufficiently clear so as to allow persons of 'ordinary intelligence a reasonable opportunity to know what is prohibited.'" It is easy to see how someone could be unsure about what AEDPA prohibits with the use of the term "personnel," as it blurs the line between protected expression and unprotected conduct. Someone who advocates the cause of the PKK could be seen as supplying them with personnel; it even fits under the government's rubric of freeing up resources, since having an independent advocate frees up members to engage in terrorist activities instead of advocacy. But advocacy is pure speech protected by the First Amendment.

In order to keep the statute from trenching on such advocacy, the government urges that we read into it a requirement that the activity prohibited be performed "under the direction or control" of the foreign terrorist organization. While we construe a statute in such a way as to avoid constitutional questions, we are not authorized to rewrite the law so it will pass constitutional muster. This is especially true in the case of an interlocutory appeal from a preliminary injunction, because of the deferential standard of review applicable in such situations.

The term "training" fares little better. Again, it is easy to imagine protected expression that falls within the bounds of this term. For example, a plaintiff who wishes to instruct members of a designated group on how to petition the United Nations to give aid to their group could plausibly decide that such protected expression falls within the scope of the term "training." The government insists that the term is best understood to forbid the imparting of skills to foreign terrorist organizations through training. Yet, presumably, this definition would encompass teaching international law to members of designated organizations. The result would be different if the term "training" were qualified to include only military training or training in terrorist activities. Because plaintiffs have demonstrated that they are likely to succeed on the merits of their claim with respect to the terms "training" and "personnel," we conclude that the district court did not abuse its discretion in issuing its limited preliminary injunction.[19]

The judgment of the district court is AFFIRMED.

---

[19] The government invites us to cure any possible vagueness problems with the statute by including the term "knowingly" in it. However, the term "knowingly" modifies the verb "provides," meaning that the only scienter requirement here is that the accused violator have knowledge of the fact that he has provided something, not knowledge of the fact that what is provided in fact constitutes material support.

HUMANITARIAN LAW PROJECT v. UNITED STATES DOJ [HLP II]
352 F.3d 382 (9th Cir. 2003).

[On remand, the district court entered a permanent injunction against enforcement of the "personnel" and "training" provisions. The Government appealed and the Ninth Circuit held that those issues were foreclosed by its prior opinion. In addition to its vagueness arguments, HLP added an argument that due process would not allow conviction of its supporters without a showing of intent to further unlawful purposes.]

We are called upon to analyze a statute that presumes that a person acts with guilty intent whenever that person provides material support to a designated organization. We believe that serious due process concerns would be raised were we to accept the argument that a person who acts without knowledge of critical information about a designated organization presumably acts consistently with the intent and conduct of that designated organization. At oral argument, the government told us that it could convict a person under § 2339B if he or she donates support to a designated organization *even if he or she does not know the organization is so designated.* That is, according to the government, it can convict an individual who gives money to a designated organization that solicits money at their doorstep so long as the organization identifies itself by name. It is no defense, according to the government, that the organization describes to the donor only its humanitarian work to provide basic services to support victims displaced and orphaned by conflict, or to defend the cultural and linguistic rights of ethnic minorities. And, the government further contends, it is no defense that a donor contributes money solely to support the lawful, humanitarian purposes of a designated organization. But we believe that to attribute the intent to commit unlawful acts punishable by life imprisonment to persons who acted with innocent intent – in this context, without critical information about the relevant organization – contravenes the Fifth Amendment's requirement of "personal guilt."

[The court then discusses several of the Communist Party cases for the proposition that punishing mere support of the organization without intent to promote its unlawful purposes would violate due process.].

[W]e are to "construe [a criminal] statute in light of the fundamental principle that a person is not criminally responsible unless 'an evil-meaning mind' accompanies 'an evil-doing hand.'" Because criminal offenses requiring no *mens rea* have a "generally disfavored status," Congressional silence on whether a statute requires *mens rea* does not "justify dispensing with an intent requirement."

It is a question of statutory construction, whether § 2339B requires the government to prove that a person who provides "material support" to a designated organization knew of such designation or knew of the unlawful activities that caused it to be so designated. The language of § 2339B does not in any way suggest that Congress intended to impose strict liability on individuals who donate "material support" to designated organizations. It is significant that Congress used the term "knowingly" to modify "providing material support or resources to a foreign terrorist organization." Indeed, the

Supreme Court and our circuit have construed Congress' inclusion of the word "knowingly" to require proof of knowledge of the law and an intent to further the proscribed act.

In *United States v. X-Citement Video*, [513 U.S. 64 (1999)], the Court read 18 U.S.C. § 2252, which prohibits "knowingly" transporting, shipping, receiving, distributing, or reproducing a visual depiction of a minor engaging in sexually explicit conduct, to require that the defendant also know the minor's age. The Court applied the knowledge requirement to the minor's age even though the "natural grammatical reading [of the statute], adopted by the Ninth Circuit, suggests that the term 'knowingly' modifies only the surrounding verbs[.]" The Court also held that the harsh penalties attached to the statute favored construing the statute to require specific intent. Finally, the Court concluded that an alternative reading of the statute would criminalize otherwise innocent conduct.

Applying these principles, we believe that when Congress included the term "knowingly" in § 2339B, it meant that proof that a defendant knew of the organization's designation as a terrorist organization or proof that a defendant knew of the unlawful activities that caused it to be so designated was required to convict a defendant under the statute.

Like *X-Citement Video* and *Staples*, the maximum fifteen-year penalty under § 2339B is a severe penalty for punishing someone who acted with an innocent intent. Charitable contributions made to organizations are not "inherently dangerous," as are grenades, firearms and corrosive liquids.

The one statement in the Congressional Record that refers to an intent requirement in § 2339B was made by Senator Hatch, who cosponsored AEDPA. In introducing the Senate Conference Report to the Senate, Senator Hatch stated: "this bill also includes provisions making it a crime to *knowingly provide material support to the terrorist functions* of foreign groups designated by a Presidential finding to be engaged in terrorist activities. I am convinced we have crafted a narrow but effective designation provision which meets these obligations while safeguarding the freedom to associate, which none of us would willingly give up." 142 Cong. Rec. S3354 (daily ed. April 16, 1996) (statement of Sen. Hatch) (emphasis added).

Without the knowledge requirement described above, a person who simply sends a check to a school or orphanage in Tamil Eelam run by the LTTE could be convicted under the statute, even if that individual is not aware of the LTTE's designation or of any unlawful activities undertaken by the LTTE. Or, according to the government's interpretation of § 2339B, a woman who buys cookies from a bake sale outside of her grocery store to support displaced Kurdish refugees to find new homes could be held liable so long as the bake sale had a sign that said that the sale was sponsored by the PKK, without regard to her knowledge of the PKK's designation or other activities. Furthermore, the legislative history contains no indication that Congress intended to impose strict liability on persons who provide "material support" to designated organizations.

In light of the text of § 2339B, the Court's longstanding principles interpreting the word "knowingly" to indicate Congress' intent to include a *mens rea* requirement, and the due process concern earlier discussed, we read § 2339B to require proof of knowledge, either of an organization's designation or of the unlawful activities that caused it to be so designated. Thus, to sustain a conviction under § 2339B, the government must prove beyond a reasonable doubt that the donor had knowledge that the organization was designated by the Secretary as a foreign terrorist organization or that the donor had knowledge of the organization's unlawful activities that caused it to be so designated.

NOTES AND QUESTIONS

1. What did John Walker Lindh provide to the Taliban? "personnel" in the form of himself? "training" in the sense that he received training? The Statement of Facts in the *Lindh* case recited that he "willfully and unlawfully supplied and attempted to supply services to the Taliban." Is providing "services" different from supplying "personnel?" In responding to the defendant's motion to dismiss the indictment, the *Lindh* court stated:

> the plain meaning of "personnel" is such that it requires, in the context of Section 2339B, an employment or employment-like relationship between the persons in question and the terrorist organization. The Ninth Circuit's vagueness holding in *Humanitarian Law Project* is neither persuasive nor controlling. The term is aimed at denying the provision of human resources to proscribed terrorist organizations, and not at the mere independent advocacy of an organization's interests or agenda. Thus, the term "personnel" in Section 2339B gives fair notice to the public of what is prohibited and the provision is therefore not unconstitutionally vague.

United States v. Lindh, 212 F. Supp. 2d 541, 574 (E.D. Va. 2002).

2. According to CNN, *http://www.cnn.com/2003/LAW/11/07/virginia.jihad* (November 7, 2003):

> Three members of what government prosecutors called a "Virginia jihad network" were sentenced [to] 11 1/2 years each for travelling to Pakistan and seeking military training at a terrorist training camp. U.S. District Judge Leonie Brinkema rejected a government argument for stiffer sentences for both men. The judge said that she disagreed that their effort to obtain training constituted providing military services, as the prosecution contended. She said they were "absorbing resources, not providing them." She noted they gave no money or other materials to the cause.

If the defendants were "absorbing resources, not providing them," then of what were they guilty? Apparently, they intended to fight with the Taliban against U.S. forces but were captured before they got the chance. Does this constitute "conspiracy" to provide material support? In recently enacted 18 U.S.C. § 2339D, Congress has now specifically criminalized the receipt of training from a designated terrorist organization. Might there be a constitutional problem with this provision?

3. In *United States v. Khan*, 309 F. Supp. 2d 789 (E.D. Va. 2004) (see p. 324 *supra*), Judge Brinkema found that training could be a violation of the material support statute under active circumstances. The charges in *Khan* included provision of material support on the basis of supplying personnel who received training. Noting the *HLP II* holding, the court pointed out that the government had since interpreted the statute to apply only when the training went toward supplying personnel who would act on behalf of the organization in a directed capacity. "The conspiracy alleged in Count 5 was not to provide 'personnel' who would speak on behalf of LET, or provide moral support, or simply receive training, but to provide personnel who, after receiving training, would serve that organization as soldiers, recruiters, and procurers of supplies. Indeed, the evidence shows that the conspirators did much more than just receive training from LET – they returned to the United States, recruited co-conspirators, and purchased technology for LET to use in its attacks on India."

4. Another note regarding Muslim religious practice and tradition is in order before we go further on the financial issues. Shari'ah mandates that Muslims practice the giving of alms, known as "zakat." Zakat is to be calculated not on the basis of income, as is tithing in most Christian denominations, but instead on the basis of accumulated wealth. It is usually calculated at 2.5% per year of cash, jewelry, and similar items over a minimum value. You can find many references on the web to zakat and organizations purporting to collect and distribute it. The giving of money to groups that represent their objectives to be humanitarian aid therefore becomes a hot-button issue in the tracking of Islamist fundamentalist groups.

[B] THE DESIGNATION PROCESS

PEOPLE'S MOJAHEDIN ORGANIZATION OF IRAN v. DEPARTMENT OF STATE
327 F.3d 1238 (D.C. Cir. 2003)

SENTELLE, Circuit Judge:

The People's Mojahedin Organization of Iran ("PMOI" or "Petitioner") seeks review of 1999 and 2001 decisions of the Secretary of State ("Respondent") designating Petitioner as a foreign terrorist organization. After review of Petitioner's various claims that the designation violates constitutional and statutory rights of Petitioner, we conclude that the Secretary acted according to law and in full compliance with the requirements of the Constitution. We therefore deny the petitions for the reasons set forth more fully below.

I. Background

We note at the outset that this is PMOI's third petition to this court to review designations of the PMOI as a foreign terrorist organization. *See People's Mojahedin Org. of Iran v. Dep't. of State,* 337 U.S. App. D.C. 106, 182 F.3d 17 (D.C. Cir. 1999) ("*PMOI*"); *Nat'l Council of Resistance of Iran v. Dep't. of State,* 346 U.S. App. D.C. 131, 251 F.3d 192 (D.C. Cir. 2001) ("*NCOR*").

[The State Department's 2003 "Patterns of Global Terrorism" lists six groups under the umbrella heading of the "MEK":

[Mujahedin-e Khalq Organization (MEK or MKO) a.k.a. The National Liberation Army of Iran (NLA, the militant wing of the MEK), the

People's Mujahedin of Iran (PMOI), National Council of Resistance (NCR), the National Council of Resistance of Iran (NCRI), Muslim Iranian Student's Society (front organization used to garner financial support)

[The MEK philosophy mixes Marxism and Islam. Formed in the 1960s, the organization was expelled from Iran after the Islamic Revolution in 1979, and its primary support came from the former Iraqi regime of Saddam Hussein since the late 1980s. The MEK's history is filled with anti-Western attacks as well as terrorist attacks on the interests of the clerical regime in Iran and abroad. The MEK now advocates the overthrow of the Iranian regime and its replacement with the group's own leadership.

[During the 1970s, the MEK killed U.S. military personnel and U.S. civilians working on defense projects in Tehran and supported the takeover in 1979 of the U.S. Embassy in Tehran. In 1981, the MEK detonated bombs in the head office of the Islamic Republic Party and the Premier's office, killing some 70 high-ranking Iranian officials, including chief Justice Ayatollah Mohammad Beheshti, President Mohammad-Ali Rajaei, and Premier Mohammad-Javad Bahonar. Near the end of the war with Iran during 1980-88, Baghdad armed the MEK with military equipment and sent it into action against Iranian forces. In 1991, it assisted the Government of Iraq in suppressing the Shia and Kurdish uprisings in southern Iraq and the Kurdish uprisings in the north. Coalition aircraft bombed MEK bases during Operation Iraqi Freedom, and the Coalition forced the MEK forces to surrender in May 2003. The future of the MEK forces remains undetermined with Coalition forces.]

[Section 1189] empowers the Secretary of State to designate an entity as a "foreign terrorist organization." Two features distinguish this procedure from other administrative proceedings governed by the Administrative Procedure Act ("APA"). First, the [statute] does not express any right of the aggrieved party to comment on the administrative record or to present evidence for inclusion in that record. Secondly, and most pertinent to the present review, the statute expressly states that the Secretary is to consider the classified information in making a designation and that classified information is not subject to disclosure under the Act except to a reviewing court *ex parte* and *in camera*. A designation under the Act persists for two years, and the Secretary may re-designate a foreign organization as a foreign terrorist organization for succeeding two-year periods.

In order for the Secretary to designate a foreign organization as a foreign terrorist organization, he must make three findings based on the administrative record, that:

A. the organization is a foreign organization;

B. the organization engages in terrorist activity; and

C. the terrorist activity or terrorism of the organization threatens the security of United States nationals or the national security of the United States.

An organization designated as a foreign terrorist organization must seek judicial review of the designation in this court under § 1189(b). That section empowers us only to "hold unlawful and set aside" designations that we find to be

(A) arbitrary, capricious, an abuse of discretion, or otherwise not in accordance with law;

(B) contrary to constitutional right, power, privilege, or immunity;

(C) in excess of statutory jurisdiction, authority, or limitation, or short of statutory right;

(D) lacking substantial support in the administrative record taken as a whole or in classified information submitted to the court [*in camera* and *ex parte*], or

(E) not in accord with the procedures required by law.

The Secretary has made successive designations of Petitioner as a foreign terrorist organization in 1997, 1999, and 2001. Following the 1997 designation, Petitioner sought review in a proceeding that generated our opinion in *PMOI*. In that petition, the PMOI argued that the procedure for designation violated its due process rights to notice and hearing. We easily disposed of any constitutional claim, holding that "[a] foreign entity without property or *presence in* this country has no constitutional rights under the due process clause." We then proceeded to consider the rights of the organization under the statute. This consisted principally of determining the legal sufficiency of the Secretary's administrative record to support the three findings under § 1189(a)(1). As to the first, that the petitioner was a foreign organization, there was no dispute; it was. As to the third, that "the terrorist activity of the organization threatens the security of United States nationals or the national security of the United States" we held that to present a nonjusticiable question. Such questions concerning the foreign policy decisions of the Executive Branch present political judgments, "decisions of a kind for which the Judiciary has neither aptitude, facilities nor responsibilities and have long been held to belong in the domain of political power not subject to judicial intrusion or inquiry."

That left us solely with the question of the sufficiency of the administrative record to support the Secretary's determination that "the organization engages in terrorist activity." We found that record sufficient.

When the Secretary re-designated the PMOI as a foreign terrorist organization in October of 1999, the organization again petitioned this court for review. One item in the 1999 designation differed from the 1997 designation. In 1999 the Secretary's designation included a finding that the National Council of Resistance of Iran, which claimed to be an organization independent of the PMOI, was an alias for the other organization and that the National Council was therefore a foreign terrorist organization as well – indeed, the same foreign terrorist organization. The Secretary's finding that the NCOR and the PMOI were one and the same made a material difference in the result of our review on the constitutional question. Whereas [PMOI] did not have property or presence in the United States and was therefore not entitled to assert due process rights under the Constitution, . . . the National Council did have such presence or property and was therefore entitled to assert that claim. We therefore considered the merits of the due process claim. We held that the statute, as applied by the Secretary, did not provide "the fundamental requirement of due process," that is, "the opportunity to be heard at a meaningful time and in a meaningful manner."

Based on our holding that the designees had not received the process they were due, we remanded the question to the Secretary for reconsideration. We directed that on remand the Secretary should provide the petitioners "the opportunity to file responses to the nonclassified evidence against them, to file evidence in support of their allegations that they are not terrorist organizations," and provide them "an opportunity to be meaningfully heard" on the issues before the Secretary. After the remand, the Secretary provided the PMOI with an opportunity to respond to the unclassified evidence, considered all material submitted by the PMOI along with both the unclassified and classified material in file, and reentered the 1999 designation on September 24, 2001, followed by a new two-year designation on October 5, 2001.

II. Analysis

A. *Due Process and Sufficiency of Evidence*

Petitioner raises several arguments. First, it contends that its redesignation as a terrorist organization is unconstitutional under the Due Process Clause because the statute permitted the Secretary to rely upon secret evidence – the classified information that respondents refused to disclose and against which PMOI could therefore not effectively defend. We reject this contention. As noted above, that statute authorizes designation of a foreign terrorist organization when the Secretary finds three elements. As to the first, that is that the organization is a foreign organization, there is not and cannot be any dispute.

As to the second element, the PMOI advances a colorable argument: that the Secretary was able under § 1189(a)(3)(B) to "consider classified information in making [this designation]" and that the classified information was not "subject to disclosure" except to the court *ex parte* and *in camera* for purposes of this judicial review. Petitioner contends that this violates the due process standard set forth in *Abourezk v. Reagan,* 785 F.2d 1043, 1061 (D.C. Cir. 1986), "that a court may not dispose of the merits of a case on the basis of *ex parte, in camera* submissions." While colorable, this argument will not carry the day.

Granted, petitioners argue that their opportunity to be heard was not meaningful, given that the Secretary relied on secret information to which they were not afforded access. In the context of another statutory scheme involving classified information, we noted the courts are often ill-suited to determine the sensitivity of classified information. *United States v. Yunis* ("Things that did not make sense to [a judge] would make all too much sense to a foreign counter intelligence specialist."). The Due Process Clause requires only that process which is due under the circumstances of the case. We have already established in *NCOR* the process which is due under the circumstances of this sensitive matter of classified intelligence in the effort to combat foreign terrorism. The

Secretary has complied with the standard we set forth therein, and nothing further is due.

However, even if we err in describing the process due, even had the Petitioner been entitled to have its counsel or itself view the classified information, the breach of that entitlement has caused it no harm. This brings us to Petitioner's statutory objection. Petitioner argues that there is not adequate record support for the Secretary's determination that it is a foreign terrorist organization under the statute. However, on this element, even the unclassified record taken alone is quite adequate to support the Secretary's determination. Indeed, as to this element – that is, that the organization engages in terrorist activities – the People's Mojahedin has effectively admitted not only the adequacy of the unclassified record, but the truth of the allegation. By its own admission, the PMOI has

> (1) attacked with mortars the Islamic Revolutionary Prosecutor's Office; (2) assassinated a former Iranian prosecutor and killed his security guards; (3) killed the Deputy Chief of the Iranian Joint Staff Command, who was the personal military adviser to Supreme Leader Khamenei; (4) attacked with mortars the Iranian Central Command Headquarters of the Islamic Revolutionary Guard Corps and the Defense Industries Organization in Tehran; (5) attacked and targeted with mortars the offices of the Iranian Supreme Leader Khamenei, and of the head of the State Exigencies Council; (6) attacked with mortars the central headquarters of the Revolutionary Guards; (7) attacked with mortars two Revolutionary Guards Corps headquarters; and (8) attacked the headquarters of the Iranian State Security Forces in Tehran.

Were there no classified information in the file, we could hardly find that the Secretary's determination that the Petitioner engaged in terrorist activities is "lacking substantial support in the administrative record taken as a whole," even without repairing to the "classified information submitted to the court."

To summarize, the Secretary did not deprive Petitioner of any process to which it was constitutionally entitled. Even if the record supported a finding of violation of due process, such a violation would be harmless as the unaffected portion of the record is ample to support the determination made.

The remaining element under § 1189(a)(1) is that "the terrorist activity or terrorism of the organization threatens the security of United States nationals or the national security of the United States." The thrust of Petitioner's argument is that its allegedly terrorist acts were not acts of terrorism under the statute, because they do not meet the requirement of subsection (C). Petitioner argues that the attempt to overthrow the despotic government of Iran, which itself remains on the State Department's list of state sponsors of terrorism, is not "terrorist activity," or if it is, that it does not threaten the security of the United States or its nationals. We cannot review that claim. In *PMOI* we expressly held that that finding "is nonjusticiable." As we stated in that decision, "it is beyond the judicial function for a court to review foreign policy decisions of the Executive Branch." Even if we differed with the analysis of the prior panel of this court, which we do not, we are bound by its decision. In short, we find neither statutory nor due process errors in the Secretary's designation of petitioner as a foreign terrorist organization.

B. *Petitioner's Other Claims*

Petitioner raises several other arguments to the effect that the designation violates its constitutional rights. Those warranting separate discussion fall under the general heading of First Amendment claims. Petitioner's argument that its First Amendment rights have been violated rests on the consequences of the designation. Petitioner argues that by forbidding all persons within or subject to the jurisdiction of the United States from "knowingly providing material support or resources," 18 U.S.C. § 2339B(a)(1), to it as a designated foreign terrorist organization, the statute violates its rights of free speech and association guaranteed by the First Amendment. We disagree.

[handwritten margin note: Pets argue 1st Amend Rt of speech + assoc.]

As the Ninth Circuit held in *Humanitarian Law Project v. Reno,* the statute "is not aimed at interfering with the expressive component of [the organization's] conduct but at stopping aid to terrorist groups." It is conduct and not communication that the statute controls. We join the Ninth Circuit in observing that "there is no constitutional right to facilitate terrorism by giving terrorists the weapons and explosives with which to carry out their grisly missions.[2] Nor, of course, is there a right to provide resources with which terrorists can buy weapons and explosives."

[handwritten margin note: cf. HLP/Reno]

III. Conclusion

For the reasons set forth above, we conclude that in the designation and redesignation of the People's Mojahedin of Iran as a foreign terrorist organization, the Secretary of State afforded all the process that the organization was due, and that this designation violated neither statutory nor constitutional rights of the Petitioner. We therefore deny the petitions for review.

EDWARDS, Circuit Judge, concurring:

I concur in the judgment denying the petitions for review. I find it unnecessary, however, to reach the constitutional due process challenge to the Secretary's use of classified evidence to designate petitioner.

The public, unclassified administrative record, including petitioner's own submissions to the Secretary, contains more than enough evidence to support the determination that petitioner engages in terrorist activity. The Government followed the procedures that we required in *[NCOR].* Petitioner offered a wealth of submissions to the Secretary, which the public record now includes. Not only is there enough evidence in the public record to support the Secretary's determination that petitioner engaged in the acts alleged, there appears to be no dispute over the facts supporting that determination. Therefore, I find it

[handwritten margin note: there's enough evid that is non class. evid to support the determ.]

---

[2] Although not raised by either party, at the instruction of the court the parties addressed the possibility that the 1999 designation was moot. Both parties agree, as does the court, that a realistic possibility exists of prosecutions under 18 U.S.C. § 2339A-2339C for crimes related to the terrorist designation of the PMOI during the period of that designation so that this controversy escapes mootness under the 'collateral consequences' exception.

unnecessary to reach petitioner's constitutional due process challenge to the Secretary's use of secret, classified material to bolster its determination.

In sum, because there is substantial, unrefuted evidence in the public, unclassified record for the designation of petitioner as a foreign terrorist organization, I agree that the petition for review should be denied.

NOTES AND QUESTIONS

1. *United States v. Rahmani*, 209 F. Supp. 2d 1045 (C.D. Cal. 2002), *rev'd sub nom. United States v. Ashfari*, 2004 U.S. App. LEXIS 26430 (9th Cir. 12/20/2004), p. 377 *infra*. The D.C. Circuit's footnote reference to mootness and the possibility of prosecutions for material support during the hiatus of the 1999 designation was far from idle speculation. Shortly after the D.C. Circuit's second opinion (what it called *NCOR*), a district court in California dismissed an indictment against several fund-raisers for Mujahedin-e Khalq ("MEK"), an alleged alter ego of NCOR and PMOI.

The trial judge stated that the situation presented "this somewhat provocative question:"

If the procedure whereby an organization is designated by the Secretary of State as "terrorist" violates the Due Process Clause of the United States Constitution, may such *designation nevertheless be utilized as a predicate in a criminal prosecution against individuals* for providing material support to that designated terrorist organization?

He then proceeded to hold the statute unconstitutional on its face despite these two arguments of the Government:

First, the government argues that invalidating Section 1189 would have serious negative consequences on this country's counter-terrorism efforts. National security is certainly a matter of grave concern and responsibility. When weighed against a fundamental constitutional right which defines our very existence, the argument for national security should not serve as an excuse for obliterating the Constitution. The moral strength, vitality and commitment proudly enunciated in the Constitution is best tested at a time when forceful, emotionally moving arguments to ignore or trivialize its provisions seek a subordination of time honored constitutional protections. Such protections should not be dispensed with where the Secretary has not shown how the MEK is a national security threat.

The government also cites numerous cases where the Supreme Court found statutes unconstitutional but, nevertheless, upheld actions that occurred under the unconstitutional scheme. The government seems to be saying that the result in *NCRI [NCOR]*, wherein the D.C. Circuit found the MEK's designation unconstitutional but, nevertheless, upheld such designation, is legally supportable. The cases cited by the government are distinguishable from the instant case in one critical respect – they are all civil cases. Where, as here, a criminal defendant is charged with crimes that could result in as much as 15 years imprisonment or more, this court will not abdicate its duty to ensure that the prosecution of such charges comports with due process.

That decision was then reversed by the Ninth Circuit in *United States v. Ashfari* after the D.C. Circuit held that the designation was constitutional on the basis of the publicly disclosed information.

2. In the second round *[NCOR]*, the D.C. Circuit had this to say about the whether the due process violation warranted setting aside the designations:

> We recognize that a strict and immediate application of the principles of law which we have set forth herein could be taken to require a revocation of the designations before us. However, we also recognize the realities of the foreign policy and national security concerns asserted by the Secretary in support of those designations. We further recognize the timeline against which all are operating: the two-year designations before us expire in October of this year. We therefore do not order the vacation of the existing designations, but rather remand the questions to the Secretary with instructions that the petitioners be afforded the opportunity to file responses to the nonclassified evidence against them, to file evidence in support of their allegations that they are not terrorist organizations, and that they be afforded an opportunity to be meaningfully heard by the Secretary upon the relevant findings. While not within our current order, we expect that the Secretary will afford due process rights to these and other similarly situated entities in the course of future designations.

Is national security a sufficient answer to the due process violation? What if the public record did not have sufficient grounds for determining that the organization was engaged in terrorist activity? Would the use of classified information then be a sufficient basis for the imposition of penalties on the organization? And, if the answer to that is yes because the organization is not going to jail, what about the individuals who provide funding? That final question is addressed by the Ninth Circuit in *Ashfari*.

3. The D.C. Circuit seems remarkably cavalier in *PMOI II* about its holding in *Abourezk* regarding the use of secret evidence. We will return to that question after the next case.

4. The Ninth Circuit held, in *HLP I*, that providing resources for humanitarian aid would itself support the violent acts of the organization, so there is no functional difference between the two. In *HLP II*, the court then added a scienter requirement that the defendant must know either that the organization was designated or that support was provided with knowledge that it would be used for terrorist purposes. Can I give money to an apparent charitable organization without being concerned about the possible uses of that money, even if it turns out that the donee is a clandestine front group for a designated organization?

Note on Financial Transactions and Hawala

Tracking of financial transactions to curtail the flow of money to terrorist organizations is complicated in many ways. Charitable giving and the practice of zakat is one aspect of the problem. Hawala or hundi is another. Hawala is the practice of informally transferring value across borders without sending money. It originated in India but is essentially the same as the Chinese "chop" system of prior centuries. In these and other guises, informal value transfer creates a vast international unregulated and untaxed banking system. An excellent description is provided by Interpol at

http://www.interpol.int/Public/FinancialCrime/MoneyLaundering/hawala/default.asp

Suppose that Adam is working in America but has relatives including his father Benny in Balaysia to whom he wishes to send money. Doing so through formal banks would be expensive (as much as a 5% commission rate) and may be impracticable because Adam does not trust the banks in Balaysia or because Benny may have reasons for not wanting to appear in a bank. Adam can go to a storefront business (Store) that sells a variety of merchandise from Balaysia and also provides money transfer services. Adam gives Store hard currency and asks that money be delivered to Benny. Store calls a cooperating counterpart in Balaysia (Business), who delivers equivalent cash (minus a 1% commission) in Balaysian currency to Benny or sets up a line of credit for goods that Benny can obtain from Business.

Store now owes Business money, which will be covered when Business and Store exchange commodities that each wants from the other's country, or when Store decides to risk sending a courier with a satchel of cash. Store will sell goods from Balaysia that are desired in America and vice versa. The net effect is the transfer of value without the use of monitorable banking or other regulated financial institutions. And pertinent to the terrorism investigation is the possibility that some of the profit margin in these transactions (and the tax savings from unreported transactions) will end up in the hands of persons or organizations with terrorist designs.

Immigrant workers are not the only users of the hawala system and hawala is not the only method of transferring money across borders. It is instructive, however, to realize that current estimates are that immigrant workers alone sent $150 billion (yes, billion) out of the U.S. in 2004, some through regulated financial institutions but much not. How much of that ended up in the hands of terrorist organizations would be purest speculation. Other sources of funds for terrorist organizations include the very wealthy who can transfer huge sums in a single transaction by time-honored methods known to embezzlers such as overpayment for goods or services. *Boim* and *In re Terrorist Attacks* involved allegations of a third method, the provision of money to charities which have links to terrorist organizations.

Thus far, we have seen in action units of the Department of Justice, Department of Defense, and the State Department. Money laundering and financial monitoring are areas in which all counter-terrorism agencies of the federal government take an active interest. The Office of Foreign Asset Control (OFAC) within the Department of Treasury issues blockage and asset freezing orders under IEEPA, the statute under which Lindh was prosecuted. The next case deals more explicitly with activity of OFAC, but first we need to take note of another aspect of our current topic, the use of secret information.

Note on Secret Information and the War Analogy

The government claim for secrecy of information in these cases leads eventually to the analogy and terminology of "war" that will be considered later. The cases on use of classified information in criminal trials considered in Chapter 5 proceeded on the assumption that a criminal defendant had an absolute right to know the evidence against him. *Ex parte in camera* submissions were allowed in those cases only to allow the judge to make a decision on what would be disclosed to the defendant or a jury, not for the purpose of forming part of the basis for conviction. If a criminal defendant cannot be convicted on the basis of unknown evidence, then deprivation of property through an administrative designation would seem to be subject to the same due process requirements (even if it were only a temporary deprivation by freezing of assets).

Moreover, if the information is accurate, then it is already known to the organization's representatives and there should be no reason to withhold it from them. Right? Yet the government's asserted interest in withholding secret information from the organization is the same as the claim of need for secrecy of intelligence results during wartime. "If I tell you what I know about you, then you will know how I learned it and can then change your operations to keep future information away from me."

This leads to the perfectly understandable desire on the part of anti- and counter-terrorism specialists to use information acquired through incredibly difficult, and dangerous, methods to shut down terrorist organizations without destroying the intelligence networks by which the information was acquired.

But is proceeding by secret evidence an acceptable practice in a free and open society? That is the heart of several of the civil liberties issues presented in counter-terrorism. In the criminal cases in the previous chapter, the fact-finder would not get the classified information unless the trial were closed to the public and the defendant also received the information. In the designation process, however, neither the organization nor the potential donor knows what the classified information is.

To carry the analogy to wartime further without getting sidetracked at this point, in succeeding chapters we will consider what rules of engagement apply to the known terrorist. Must government agents attempt to capture her and place her on trial? Is it permissible to shoot to kill as in a military engagement? These are questions that will haunt later chapters of our study.

HOLY LAND FOUNDATION v. ASHCROFT
333 F.3d 156 (D.C. Cir. 2003)

SENTELLE, Circuit Judge:

In December 2001, the Office of Foreign Asset Control ("OFAC") designated Holy Land Foundation ("HLF") as a "Specially Designated Global Terrorist" ("SDGT") pursuant to an Executive Order issued under the International Emergency Economic Powers Act, 50 U.S.C. § 1701 et seq. ("IEEPA"). *IEEPA* This designation was accompanied by an order blocking all of the organization's assets. HLF brought an action in the district court challenging this designation

[handwritten: HLF designated a SDGT under IEEPA; all assets blocked. HLF was closely aligned w/ Hamas which had already been designated an SDGT]

and before us now appeals the lower court's decision which affirmed OFAC's actions and dismissed the complaint in substantial part. For the reasons explained below, we hereby affirm the district court's dismissal in part, and order summary judgment for the government.

I. Background

The IEEPA authorizes the President to declare a national emergency when an extraordinary threat to the United States arises that originates in substantial part in a foreign state. Such a declaration clothes the President with extensive authority set out in 50 U.S.C. § 1702. Under that section he may investigate, regulate, or prohibit transactions in foreign exchange, banking transfers, and importation or exportation of currency or securities by persons or with respect to property, subject to the jurisdiction of the United States. Of further special concern to the Holy Land Foundation, he may

> investigate, block during the pendency of an investigation, regulate, direct and compel, nullify, void, prevent or prohibit, any acquisition, holding, withholding, use, transfer, withdrawal, transportation, importation or exportation of, or dealing in, or exercising any right, power, or privilege with respect to, or transactions involving, any property in which any foreign country or a national thereof has any interest by any person, or with respect to any property, subject to the jurisdiction of the United States. . . .

In 1995, the President issued Executive Order 12,947 pursuant to the IEEPA. Exec. Order No. 12,947. That order designated certain terrorist organizations, including the Palestinian organization Hamas, as "Specially Designated Terrorists," or SDTs, and blocked all of their property and interests in property. The order also allowed for additional designations if an organization or person is found to be "owned or controlled by, or to act for or on behalf of" an SDT.

In 2001, as part of his response to the attacks of September 11, the President issued Executive Order 13,224, similar to Order 12,947, pursuant to the IEEPA. Order 13,224 designated specified terrorist organizations, again including Hamas, as "Specially Designated Global Terrorists," or SDGTs, and blocked all of their property and interests in property subject to the jurisdiction of the United States. That order also allowed for additional SDGTs to be designated if organizations or persons are found to "act for or on behalf of" or are "owned or controlled by" designated terrorists, or they "assist in, sponsor, or provide . . . support for," or are "otherwise associated" with them.

HLF was originally established as the Occupied Land Fund and incorporated as a tax-exempt organization in California in 1989. In 1991 it changed its corporate name to the Holy Land Foundation for Relief and Development and moved to Texas. It describes itself as "the largest Muslim charity in the United States." In December 2001, OFAC, a division of the Department of the Treasury, acting pursuant to the IEEPA and the two Executive Orders, designated HLF as both an SDT and an SDGT and blocked all of its assets. The designations were based on information supporting the proposition that HLF was closely linked to Hamas. Soon thereafter, HLF filed a complaint in district court challenging its designations as a terrorist organization and the seizure of its assets, and alleging that its rights under the First, Fourth, and Fifth Amendments, its right to free exercise of religion, and its rights under the Administrative Procedure Act ("APA"), had all been violated. HLF also filed a motion for a preliminary injunction, seeking to enjoin the government from blocking or freezing its assets. In support of the motion, HLF attached exhibits purportedly showing that it was not linked to Hamas and therefore not a terrorist organization. Subsequently, in May 2002, the OFAC redesignated HLF as an SDT and an SDGT, and filed with the district court an administrative record which included HLF's motion for a preliminary injunction with attached exhibits.

II. The District Court's Opinion

The Holy Land Foundation attempted to supplement the record before the district court by the addition of exhibits attached to its opposition to the defendants' motion to dismiss. The government moved *in limine* to strike the supplemental material. The district court granted the government's motion, holding that APA review "must ordinarily be confined to the administrative record." The court then commenced a detailed review of the administrative record and reiterated the evidence on which the Treasury Department relied in making its determination to designate HLF as an SDGT. It found that the record contained "ample evidence that (1) HLF has had financial connections to Hamas since its creation in 1989; (2) HLF leaders have been actively involved in various meetings with Hamas leaders; (3) HLF funds Hamas-controlled charitable organizations; (4) HLF provides financial support to the orphans and families of Hamas martyrs and prisoners; (5) HLF's Jerusalem office acted on behalf of Hamas; and (6) FBI informants reliably reported that HLF funds Hamas." The court concluded, based on the substantial evidence in the record, Treasury's determination that HLF acts for or on behalf of Hamas was not arbitrary and capricious, and therefore, upheld the agency's reasonable determination.

III. Analysis

As a first matter, we reject HLF's claim that its designation exceeded Treasury's authority under the APA, and affirm the district court's dismissal of that claim. The district court correctly reviewed the actions of the Treasury Department under the highly deferential "arbitrary and capricious" standard. The district court noted that this standard does not allow the courts to undertake their own factfinding, but to review the agency record to determine whether the agency's decision was supported by a rational basis.

HLF attacks the reasonableness of this determination by contending that Treasury relied on hearsay evidence to reach its conclusion. This argument is unavailing as it is clear that the government may decide to designate an entity based on a broad range of evidence, including intelligence data and hearsay declarations.

Nor was the designation in any other way so egregiously unfair as to violate any constraints due process may place upon the substance of the agency's decision. Additionally, HLF was accorded all the administrative process it was due when it was redesignated as an SDGT. Even if Treasury's initial designation arguably violated HLF's due process rights, HLF's funds are blocked currently by a redesignation which Treasury applied in accordance with the requirements we outlined in *[NCOR]*.

As we stated in *NCOR*, we do not require an agency to provide procedures which approximate a judicial trial; therefore, HLF has no right to confront and cross-examine witnesses. Additionally, the notice "need not disclose the classified information to be presented *in camera* and *ex parte* to the court under the statute. This is within the privilege and the prerogative of the executive, and we do not intend to compel a breach in the security which that branch is charged to protect." The IEEPA expressly authorizes *ex parte* and *in camera* review of classified information in "any judicial review of a determination made under this section [that] was based on classified information."

HLF argues that the government violated its First Amendment rights of freedom of association and freedom of speech and its right to equal protection under the Fourteenth Amendment. HLF argued below that the government had violated its First Amendment rights by prohibiting it from making any humanitarian contributions by blocking its assets. The district court dismissed these claims, ruling that HLF failed to state a claim because "there is no constitutional right to facilitate terrorism." As set forth in other portions of this opinion, the law is established that there is no constitutional right to fund terrorism. The ample record evidence (particularly taking into account the classified information presented to the court *in camera*) establishing HLF's role in the funding of Hamas and of its terrorist activities is incontrovertible. HLF has had every opportunity to come forward with some showing that that evidence is false or even that its ties to Hamas had been severed. HLF's presentations at the administrative stage did not reach this goal. Even following the district court's judgment, while HLF attempted to supplement the record on appeal, the supplementary material could not have defeated the proposition established by the record evidence that Holy Land was a funder of the terrorist organization Hamas.

In addition to the classified evidence that we have reviewed, all evidence from the government that is unclassified and otherwise discoverable is in the record before us, as is the evidence HLF produced in an effort to create a genuine factual dispute. HLF had every opportunity and incentive to produce the evidence sufficient to rebut the ample evidence supporting the necessary conclusion that it was a funder of Hamas but could not do so. Thus, we review an adequate record and conclude that there is no substantial question as to the material facts necessary to support the district court's judgment.

IV. The [Religion] Claim

Similar reasoning supports a grant of summary judgment for the government on HLF's claim that the designation and blocking order substantially burden its exercise of religion.

Even accepting the dubious proposition that a charitable corporation not otherwise defined can exercise religion as protected in the First Amendment, preventing such a corporation from aiding terrorists does not violate any right contemplated in the Constitution. No one on behalf of Holy Land Foundation has forwarded the proposition that the fomenting and spread of terrorism is mandated by the religion of Islam. At most they argue a right to charitable giving as a pillar of that religion. Acting against the funding of terrorism does not violate the free exercise rights protected by the First Amendment. There is no free exercise right to fund terrorists. The record clearly supports a conclusion that HLF did. [B]ased on the evidence already in the record, summary judgment for the government is warranted.

V. Conclusion

Therefore, we uphold the district court's affirmance of the Treasury Department's decision to designate HLF as an SDGT and to block its assets. We also affirm the district court's dismissal [or summary judgment] of HLF's due process [and first amendment] claims on the basis of the administrative record.

NOTES AND QUESTIONS

1. According to the D.C. Circuit, due process has been satisfied by the administrative record coupled by the organization's ability to submit counter-information. In that view, there is no right of either the organization or criminal defendants to obtain the classified information on which the agency relied. But in *PMOI* the court noted its own holding in *Abourezk* that government cannot take negative action toward a person's rights on the basis of secret evidence. Is it constitutional to "take" (seize or freeze) money that was donated for charitable purposes on the basis of secret evidence? Is this different from the CIPA and related cases considered in Chapter 5? How? Even if this result is constitutional, is it wise?

2. What should be the answer with respect to using classified information to form the basis of a designation resulting in a criminal prosecution? This question still implicates a fundamental policy choice for a free society.

3. *United States v. Sattar*, 272 F. Supp. 2d 348 (S.D.N.Y. 2003). Sheikh Rahman's lawyer, Lynne Stewart, and their interpreter were charged with violating prison regulations and also violating § 2339B by using their consultations with the Sheikh to pass messages to and from the Islamic Group. They moved to dismiss the indictment for many of the same reasons covered by the Ninth Circuit in *HLP* and by Judge Takasugi in *Rahmani*. Specifically, they challenged the portion of the statute that prohibits provision of "communication devices" and the court agreed that their use of telephones could not be the basis of a criminal charge. "[B]y criminalizing the mere use of phones and other means of communication the statute provides neither notice nor standards for its application such that it is unconstitutionally vague as applied." The court agreed with the Ninth Circuit that the "personnel" provision was also unconstitutionally vague.

With regard to the due process issue of designation, the district court preferred the holdings of the D.C. Circuit to that of Judge Takasugi. The heart of the matter was that the defendants were accused of providing support to a designated organization, regardless of whether that designation was proper. "The element of the offense is the designation of IG as an FTO, not the correctness of the determination, and the Government would be required to prove at trial that IG was in fact designated as an FTO."

4. Criminalizing support to an FTO regardless of the propriety of the designation adds a powerful arrow in the quiver of the government investigators and prosecutors. It is, as described above, the equivalent of prohibiting driving with an open container of alcohol in the car. The prosecution is not required to prove that the alcohol is being used improperly nor is the "material support" prosecutor required to prove that the funds are being used in support of terrorism. It is the act itself that is outlawed, not the purpose of the act. This answer is fine with respect to the alcohol because of the limited social utility of the act, but is it satisfactory when the act is involvement with what the defendant believes to be a political or charitable organization?

[C] *MENS REA* OF MATERIAL SUPPORT

UNITED STATES v. AL-ARIAN
308 F. Supp. 2d 1322 (M.D. Fla. 2004)

[Sami Al-Arian has been an Assistant Professor at the University of South Florida since 1986, participating actively in conferences and courses dealing with Arab or Middle Eastern Studies. He was instrumental in formation of a group known as World and Islamic Studies Enterprise (WISE), with which USF co-sponsored several conferences. In November 1994, a PBS documentary alleged that Al-Arian was the "head of the Islamic Jihad terrorist group's domestic support network." From that point on, Al-Arian and USF have been embroiled in political and legal disputes over his employment, including an investigation of academic freedom charges by the American Association of University Professors (AAUP). Finally, the Department of Justice indicted Al-Arian along with a number of others. The opinion here relates to a series of pretrial motions by the defendants.]

MOODY, District Judge:

I. BACKGROUND

A. FACTUAL AND PROCEDURAL BACKGROUND

This is a criminal action against alleged members of the Palestinian Islamic Jihad-Shiqaqi Faction (the "PIJ") who purportedly operated and directed fundraising and other organizational activities in the United States for almost twenty years. The PIJ is a foreign organization that uses violence, principally suicide bombings, and threats of violence to pressure Israel to cede territory to the Palestinian people. On February 19, 2003, the government indicted the Defendants in a 50 count indictment that included counts for: (1) conspiracy to commit racketeering; (2) conspiracy to commit murder, maim, or injure persons outside the United States; (3) conspiracy to provide material support to or for the benefit of foreign terrorists [among others].

Count 1 of the Indictment alleges a wide ranging pattern of racketeering activity beginning in 1984 lasting through February 2003, including murder, extortion, and money laundering. The Indictment details some 256 overt acts, ranging from soliciting and raising funds[5] to providing management, organizational, and logistical support for the PIJ. The overt act section of the Indictment details numerous suicide bombings and attacks by PIJ members causing the deaths of over 100 people, including 2 American citizens, and injuries to over 350 people, including 7 American citizens. These same overt acts (or parts of them) support the remaining counts of the Indictment.

B. STATUTORY BACKGROUND

Center stage in the motions are two statutes: [AEDPA and IEEPA].

On October 8, 1997, the Secretary designated PIJ as a FTO under AEDPA. Neither Congress nor the Secretary revoked the PIJ's designation at any time, and the PIJ has not sought judicial review of its designations as a FTO.

The second statute central to these motions is IEEPA. Under IEEPA, the President is granted the authority "to deal with any unusual and extraordinary threat . . . to the national security, foreign policy, or economy of the United States, if the President declares a national emergency with respect to such threat." 50 U.S.C. § 1701(a). The President's authority includes the power to investigate, regulate, or prohibit financial transactions. Section 1705(b) makes it unlawful to willfully violate or attempt to violate any executive order or regulation issued pursuant to IEEPA and provides for imprisonment of up to 10 years for such a violation.

On January 23, 1995, pursuant to IEEPA, President Clinton issued Executive Order 12947 (the "Executive Order"). The Executive Order declared a national emergency with respect to the Middle East peace process that threatened the United States' national security, foreign policy, and economy. The Executive Order prohibited financial transactions with any specially designated terrorist ("SDT"). The annex to the Executive Order designates the PIJ as a SDT.[14]

The Secretary of the Treasury promulgated regulations that make it unlawful to "deal in property or interests in property of a . . . [SDT], including the making or receiving of any contribution of funds, goods, or services to or for the benefit of a [SDT]." The regulations interpret this prohibition to include charitable contributions or "donation[s] of funds, goods, services, or technology to relieve human suffering, such as food, clothing, or medicine."[16]

Not all transactions with a SDT are banned or are criminal. For example, the regulations make clear that there is no liability for a charitable contribution if the contribution is made "without knowledge or reason to know that the

---

[5] An example of a soliciting or fundraising act is contained in Overt Act 130. In that overt act, the government claims that Defendant Al-Arian wrote a letter to a gentleman in Kuwait requesting additional money so that the PIJ could engage in more bombings and provide financial assistance to the families of recent suicide bombers who belonged to the PIJ.

[14] Fathi Shiqaqi, co-defendant Awda, and co-defendant Shallah were designated SDTs.

[16] Services is also broadly interpreted and includes legal, accounting, public relations, educational, or other services to a SDT. However, [regulations] allow for legal and emergency medical services, including legal services to a SDT regarding its designation.

donation or contribution is destined to or for the benefit of a [SDT]." In addition, the regulations exempt certain transactions from the ban, including transactions that: (a) are licensed or authorized; (b) involve personal communications that do not transfer anything of value; (c) involve some types of information and informational materials; or (d) are incidental to travel.

IEEPA itself does not explicitly or implicitly provide for judicial review of an executive order, but it does provide a procedure for court review of classified information. The regulations provide a process for administrative review of a designation of an organization as an SDT. Courts have held that judicial review of a designation under IEEPA or its regulations exists and that the Administrative Procedures Act governs that review. *See, e.g., Holy Land Foundation for Relief and Development v. Ashcroft,* 333 F.3d 156 (D.C. Cir. 2003). There are no limitations on judicial review like those contained in AEDPA.

II. DISCUSSION

Defendants' motions raise a host of statutory construction and constitutional issues purportedly on which this Court should dismiss or strike Counts 1 through 4 (or parts of Counts 1 through 4).

A. STATUTORY CONSTRUCTION AND CONSTITUTIONAL ISSUES

1. STATUTORY CONSTRUCTION OF AEDPA AND IEEPA

a. First Amendment, Overbreadth, and Vagueness Background

Defendants assert that Counts 1 through 4 are unconstitutional because they do not require either: (a) a specific intent to further the unlawful activities of the PIJ; or (b) an intent to incite and a likelihood of imminent disorder.

As a corollary to their First Amendment argument, Defendants also claim that the doctrines of overbreadth and vagueness invalidate AEDPA or IEEPA in whole or in part. Defendants assert that the statutes sweep so broadly that they include substantial amounts of constitutionally protected advocacy within their prohibitions. Similarly, Defendants argue that the material terms of each statute are so broadly defined that a person is incapable of knowing when otherwise protected activity becomes criminal. In support of Defendants' position, Defendants cite to two Ninth Circuit opinions where that court twice concluded that portions of AEDPA are unconstitutionally vague as applied to the plaintiffs in that case. Defendants argue that the same hypothetical utilized by the Ninth Circuit indicates that other sections of AEDPA and IEEPA are similarly vague and unconstitutional.

The government responds that the Indictment alleges that Defendants engaged in criminal conduct and activities, not protected speech or association. The government asserts that the Indictment alleges that Defendants conspired with the PIJ and assisted the PIJ in the accomplishment of unlawful activities, including, but not limited to, murder, extortion, and money laundering. According to the government, speech is utilized in the Indictment to show Defendants' agreement to participate in the conspiracy, and their role, motive, and intent, all of which is allowable under the First Amendment. The government argues that AEDPA and IEEPA need not contain a specific intent to further unlawful activities or be limited to situations where a defendant intends to incite and a likelihood of imminent disorder, because the statutes and the Indictment are aimed at conduct and not speech or association. The government also cites to the Ninth Circuit's *Humanitarian [HLP I and HLP II]* cases, where the Ninth Circuit twice applied this analysis and concluded that AEDPA did not violate the First Amendment rights of the plaintiffs in those cases.

The government also opposes the Defendants' contentions that AEDPA and IEEPA are overbroad or vague. The government relies on the presence of "knowingly" or "willfully" *mens rea* requirements in the statutes to remove protected speech from the prohibited conduct covered under both statutes. Similarly, the government argues that the statutes in the vast number of applications cover only unprotected conduct and only in remote hypothetical situations do AEDPA and IEEPA even come close to impinging upon protected speech. The government cites to a line of Supreme Court cases, which have held in such circumstances that courts should not use the overbreadth and vagueness doctrines to invalidate statutes.

The broader this Court interprets AEDPA and IEEPA, the more likely that the statutes receive a higher standard of review and are unconstitutional. For example, if this Court interprets AEDPA and IEEPA as requiring a specific intent to further the illegal activities of the FTO or SDT, then no constitutional problems exist. Similarly, if this Court interprets AEDPA's and IEEPA's prohibitions broadly and does not impose a specific intent *mens rea* requirement, it will likely be forced to perform a vagueness analysis and find portions of AEDPA and IEEPA unconstitutional, as did the Ninth Circuit in the *Humanitarian* cases.

b. Standards for interpreting a statute

If an ambiguity exists or an absurd result occurs, this Court is to resort to the canons of statutory construction to determine the meaning of a statutory provision by focusing on the broader, statutory context. *See United States v. X-Citement Video, Inc.*, 513 U.S. 64 (1999). First, courts are to interpret statutes in a manner that avoids constitutional difficulty. Second, courts interpret criminal statutes to include broadly applicable *scienter* requirements.

In *X-Citement Video*, the Supreme Court faced almost the same statutory interpretation issues faced in this case. There, the Supreme Court considered the Protection of Children Against Sexual Exploitation Act, [which] made it unlawful for any person to "knowingly" transport, ship, receive, distribute, or reproduce a visual depiction involving a "minor engaging in sexually explicit conduct." The Ninth Circuit had interpreted "knowingly" to only modify the surrounding verbs, like transport or ship. Under this construction, whether a defendant knew the minority of the performer(s) or even knew whether the material was sexually explicit was inconsequential. The Supreme Court reversed, concluding that, while the Ninth Circuit's construction of Section 2252 complied with the plain meaning rule, the construction caused absurd results. Under the Ninth Circuit's construction, the Court noted that a Federal Express courier who knew that there was film in a package could be convicted even though the courier had no knowledge that the film contained child pornography. To avoid such results, the

Court utilized the canons of statutory construction to imply a "knowing" requirement to each element, including the age of the performers and the sexually explicit nature of the material. The Court stated that in criminal statutes "the presumption in favor of a scienter requirement should apply to each of the statutory elements that criminalize otherwise innocent conduct."

c. Statutory Construction of AEDPA

This Court agrees with the Ninth Circuit in *HLP I* that a purely grammatical reading of the plain language of § 2339B(a)(1) makes it unlawful for any person to knowingly furnish any item contained in the material support categories to an organization that has been designated a FTO. And like *HLP II*, this Court agrees that this construction renders odd results and raises serious constitutional concerns. For example under *HLP I*, a donor could be convicted for giving money to a FTO without knowledge that an organization was a FTO or that it committed unlawful activities, and without an intent that the money be used to commit future unlawful activities. [Similarly, a bank teller who cashes the donor's check for a FTO could also be guilty despite a similar lack of knowledge.]

HLP II attempted to correct this odd result and accompanying constitutional concerns by interpreting "knowingly" to mean that a person knew: (a) an organization was a FTO; or (b) an organization committed unlawful activities, which caused it to be designated a FTO. But, *HLP II*'s construction of § 2339B only cures some of the Fifth Amendment concerns. First, *HLP II* fails to comply with *X-Citement Video*'s holding that a *mens rea* requirement "should apply to each of the statutory elements that criminalize otherwise innocent conduct." *HLP II* implies only a *mens rea* requirement to the FTO element of § 2339B(a)(1) and not to the material support element. Under *HLP II*'s construction, a cab driver could be guilty for giving a ride to a FTO member to the UN, if he knows that the person is a member of a FTO or the member or his organization at sometime conducted an unlawful activity in a foreign country. Similarly, a hotel clerk in New York could be committing a crime by providing lodging to that same FTO member under similar circumstances as the cab driver. Because the *HLP II*'s construction fails to avoid potential Fifth Amendment concerns, this Court rejects its construction of § 2339B.

Second, the *HLP II* construction does not solve the constitutional vagueness concerns of § 2339B(a)(1), which can be avoided by implying a *mens rea* requirement to the "material support or resources" element of § 2339B(a)(1). If this Court accepted the *HLP II* construction, it would likely have to declare many more categories of "material support" (in addition to "training" and "personnel" determined to be unconstitutionally vague in the *HLP* cases) unconstitutionally vague for impinging on advocacy rights, including "financial services," "lodging," "safe houses," "communications equipment," "facilities," "transportation" and "other physical assets." Using the Ninth Circuit's vagueness example on "training," the statute could likewise punish other innocent conduct, such as where a person in New York City (where the United Nations is located) gave a FTO member a ride from the airport to the United Nations before the member petitioned the United Nations. Such conduct could be punished as providing "transportation" to a FTO under § 2339B. The end result of the Ninth Circuit's statutory construction in *HLP II* is to render a substantial portion of § 2339B unconstitutionally vague.[31]

This Court concludes that it is more consistent with Congress's intent, which was to prohibit material support from FTOs to the "fullest possible basis," to imply a *mens rea* requirement to the "material support" element of § 2339B(a)(1). Therefore, this Court concludes that to convict a defendant under § 2339B(a)(1) the government must prove beyond a reasonable doubt that the defendant knew that: (a) the organization was a FTO or had committed unlawful activities that caused it to be so designated; and (b) what he was furnishing was "material support." To avoid Fifth Amendment personal guilt problems, this Court concludes that the government must show more than a defendant knew something was within a category of "material support" in order to meet (b). In order to meet (b), the government must show that the defendant knew (had a specific intent) that the support would further the illegal activities of a FTO.[33]

This Court does not believe this burden is that great in the typical case.[34] Often, such an intent will be easily inferred. For example, a jury could infer a specific intent to further the illegal activities of a FTO when a defendant knowingly provides weapons, explosives, or lethal substances to an organization that he knows is a FTO because of the nature of the support. Likewise, a jury could infer a specific intent when a defendant knows that the organization continues to commit illegal acts and the defendant provides funds to that organization knowing that money is fungible and, once received, the donee can use the funds for any purpose it chooses. That is, by its nature, money carries an inherent danger for furthering the illegal aims of an organization. Congress said as much when it found that FTOs were "so tainted by their criminal conduct that any contribution to such an organization facilitates that conduct."

This opinion in no way creates a safe harbor for terrorists or their supporters to try and avoid prosecution through utilization of shell "charitable

---

[31] Other examples of innocent conduct that could be prohibited include the same person allowing the FTO member to spend the night at his house, cashing a check, loaning the member a cell phone for use during the stay, or allowing the member to use the fax machine or laptop computer in preparing the petition. And, the additional phrase "expert advice or assistance" added by the Patriot Act in 2002 could also fail as unconstitutionally vague.

[33] This Court's conclusion is consistent with the Seventh Circuit's decision in *Boim v. Quranic Literacy Inst.*, 291 F.3d 1000 (7th Cir. 2002). In *Boim*, the Seventh Circuit considered whether a violation of § 2339B could serve as a basis for civil liability under Section 2333. The Seventh Circuit held that to succeed on a Section 2333 claim, plaintiff must prove that the defendant knew about the unlawful activities of the FTO and intended to help in those unlawful activities. This Court's construction of § 2339B avoids the anomaly of civil liability being more narrow than criminal liability based on the same statutory language.

[34] Indeed, Congress recently added 18 U.S.C. § 2339C, which criminalized raising funds with the specific intent that the funds will be or are used to cause the death or serious bodily injury of a civilian with the purpose of intimidating the population or compelling a government to do or abstain from doing any act.

organizations" or by directing money through the memo line of a check towards lawful activities. This Court believes that a jury can quickly peer through such facades when appropriate. This is especially true if other facts indicate a defendant's true intent, like where defendants or conspirators utilize codes or unusual transaction practices to transfer funds. Instead, this Court's holding works to avoid potential constitutional problems and fully accomplish congressional intent.

d. Construction of IEEPA, the Executive Order, and the Regulations

Section 1705(b) makes it unlawful to "willfully" violate or attempt to violate any regulation or order issued pursuant to IEEPA.

While no court has construed the criminal prohibition contained in IEEPA, this Court concludes that a conviction under IEEPA in these circumstances requires similar proof of intent similar to that required under AEDPA. In other words, this Court concludes that to criminally convict a defendant for violating IEEPA the government must prove a defendant: (a) knew either that an organization was a SDT or committed unlawful activities that caused it to be designated as a SDT; and (b) had a specific intent that the contribution be used to further the unlawful activities of the SDT.

This Court's conclusion is based on the plain language of Section 1705(b), which criminalizes only "willfully" committed violations of the Executive Order and the regulations interpreting the Executive Order. The Supreme Court has interpreted "willfully" in criminal statutes to "differentiate between deliberate and unwitting conduct" and means an act "undertaken with a bad purpose. . . [the person need not be aware of the specific law or rule that his conduct may be violating. But he must act to do something that the law forbids.]"

While knowledge of IEEPA, the Executive Order, or the regulations thereunder is not necessary to support a conviction, some "bad purpose" must be demonstrated by the government. This Court concludes that a "bad purpose" cannot be demonstrated by proof of knowledge of past unlawful activity alone. The government must show some additional intent to further future unlawful activity to support criminal liability.

This Court's interpretation of § 1705(b) is not contrary to the intent of the Executive Order or its regulations. First, IEEPA contains a separate civil penalty provision that penalizes violations that are not willful. It makes sense that the regulations punish some unlawful transactions by a civil penalty only, while punishing worse transgressions both civilly and criminally. Second, the regulations themselves contain an exception for charitable contributions, if the contribution is made without knowledge or reason to know that it was made to or for the benefit of a SDT. Such an exception reinforces this Court's interpretation of a requirement of proof of a specific intent because it shows that the administering agency interprets the prohibition to not reach purely innocent or unwitting conduct.

Finally, this Court is concerned that without such a *scienter* requirement the prohibitions in the Executive Order may be unconstitutionally vague or violate the Fifth Amendment's requirement of personal guilt. By requiring a specific intent to further the illegal activities of the SDT, this Court avoids considering whether the regulations are unconstitutionally vague or violate the Fifth Amendment's requirement of personal guilt.

2. FIRST AMENDMENT

Given this Court's construction of the *mens rea* requirements of AEDPA and IEEPA, little remains to be said of Defendants' First Amendment challenges to Counts 3 and 4. This Court will address two points raised by Defendants as to the Indictment in general.

First, this Court agrees with the government that the Indictment does not criminalize "pure speech." Instead, the overt acts section of the Indictment utilizes the speech of Defendants to show the existence of the conspiracies, the Defendants' agreement to participate in them, their level of participation or role in them, and the Defendants' criminal intent. It is well established that the government can use speech to prove elements of crimes such as motive or intent. The fact that Defendants' speech is contained in the overt act section of the Indictment is of little consequence. The reason that an overt act can include even protected speech is that it is the agreement that is punishable in a conspiracy charge and not the overt act itself. Therefore, this Court denies Defendants' motion to dismiss on "pure speech" grounds.

Second, this Court declines Defendants' invitation to heighten the level of First Amendment protection given to seeking and donating funds. The Supreme Court has repeatedly considered the issue and determined that such activities are more like expressive conduct than pure speech. This Court agrees with the Seventh Circuit in *Boim v. Quaranic Literacy* that the *Buckley* standard applies to determine the constitutionality of a regulation prohibiting contributions to foreign organizations.[41] In *Boim*, the plaintiffs claimed defendant was liable to them under 18 U.S.C. § 2333 because the defendant violated § 2339B. Section 2333 provided a civil remedy to U.S. nationals injured by acts of international terrorism. The defendant challenged Section 2333 and 2339B's constitutionality on First Amendment grounds. The Seventh Circuit held that *Buckley*'s contribution analysis applied and concluded that Section 2333 (based on a violation of § 2339B) did not violate the First Amendment. The Seventh Circuit reasoned that *Buckley* applied because both speech and association components are implicated by regulations that restrict or prohibit a person's ability to contribute or fundraise on behalf of an organization.

Under *Buckley* and its progeny, a regulation of fundraising is constitutional if it is closely drawn to further a sufficiently important government interest. This Court concludes that AEDPA, IEEPA, and the other statutes at issue in this case easily meet this analysis.

---

[41] This Court disagrees with the Ninth Circuit that intermediate scrutiny under *United States v. O Brien* applies to whether a prohibition on fundraising and contribution is constitutional under the First Amendment. The Ninth Circuit opinion provides no reason on why *Buckley*'s contribution analysis should not apply to other forms of contributions. This Court sees no basis for a difference in constitutional analysis between political contributions and other forms of contributions. Both have a speech and an associational component. However, as a practical matter, it may be easier for the government to regulate contributions to foreign groups because of the strength of the governmental interests at stake in cases similar to this one.

The Supreme Court has termed the protection of the foreign policy interests of the United States to be of great importance. Likewise, other courts have concluded that the government's interest in stopping the spread of global terrorism is "paramount" or "substantial." This Court agrees and would conclude that stopping the spread of terrorism is not just a sufficiently important governmental interest, but is a compelling governmental interest.

Similarly, a congressional decision to stop the spread of global terrorism by preventing fundraising and prohibiting support is closely drawn to further this interest. This Court's construction of AEDPA and IEEPA (requiring proof of a specific intent to further the unlawful activities of a SDT or FTO) reinforces this Court's conclusion that the prohibitions in AEDPA and IEEPA are closely drawn to further the governmental interest. Therefore, this Court denies Defendants' motion to dismiss on First Amendment grounds.

3. PROCEDURAL DUE PROCESS: PIJ'S FTO DESIGNATION UNDER AEDPA AND SDT DESIGNATION UNDER IEEPA

Defendants argue that Counts 3 and 4 of the Indictment should be dismissed because the PIJ was denied due process under AEDPA and IEEPA when it was designated, respectively, a FTO and a SDT. Defendants rely primarily on the Supreme Court's opinion in *United States v. Mendoza-Lopez*, and a district court decision in *United States v. Rahmani*, in support of their argument. The government argues that *Mendoza-Lopez* is inapplicable to this case because these Defendants lack standing to challenge the PIJ's designation and that *Rahmani* is seriously flawed. This Court concludes for those and additional reasons Defendants may not collaterally attack the designations of the PIJ under AEDPA or IEEPA.

[The Ninth Circuit reversed *Rahmani* in *United States v. Ashfari*, p. 377 below.]

4. EX POST FACTO

Finally, Defendants argue that Counts 1 through 4 attempt to punish the Defendants for conduct that was not criminal when it took place in violation of the *ex post facto* clause of the Constitution. Defendants argue that this Court should strike any overt act or reference to an act that occurred prior to PIJ's designation as a FTO (October 8, 1997) or prior to PIJ's designation as a SDT (January 23, 1995). Alternatively, Defendants argue that this Court should strike any act prior to the respective designation date from Counts 3 and 4. The government responds that the Defendants' conduct in this case has always been unlawful and that the PIJ's designation as a SDT and a FTO provided additional bases for criminal liability. The government also responds that conduct prior to either designation date is relevant to Counts 3 and 4 because Defendants are charged with being in conspiracies that continued after the conduct was criminalized and acts prior to the designation dates go to the existence of a conspiracy, the parties' agreement, and Defendants' purpose, motive, and intent.

Neither of Defendants' arguments are well taken. Defendants are correct only to the extent that the *ex post facto* clause prohibits the enactment by Congress of a statute that punishes an act which was innocent when committed. However, Counts 1 and 2 of the Indictment seek to punish Defendants for violating 18

U.S.C. §§ 1962(d) and 1956(a)(1). Both statutes were enacted (1970 and 1948 respectively) well prior to any act alleged in the Indictment. As to Counts 3 and 4, the Eleventh Circuit has held that the *ex post facto clause* was not violated when a conspiracy continues after the effective date of a statute making that action illegal. The Indictment alleges overt acts in furtherance of the conspiracy after 1995 and 1997. Therefore, this Court denies Defendants' motions to dismiss or strike on *ex post facto* grounds.

UNITED STATES v. HAMMOUD
381 F.3d 316 (4th Cir. 2004) (en banc)

WILKINS, Chief Judge:

Mohammed Hammoud appeals the sentence imposed following his convictions of numerous offenses, all of which are connected to his support of Hizballah, a designated foreign terrorist organization (FTO).

I. Facts

The facts underlying Hammoud's convictions and sentence are largely undisputed. We therefore recount them briefly.

A. Hizballah

Hizballah is an organization founded by Lebanese Shi'a Muslims in response to the 1982 invasion of Lebanon by Israel. Hizballah provides various forms of humanitarian aid to Shi'a Muslims in Lebanon. However, it is also a strong opponent of Western presence in the Middle East, and it advocates the use of terrorism in support of its agenda. Hizballah is particularly opposed to the existence of Israel and to the activities of the American government in the Middle East. Hizballah's general secretary is Hassan Nasserallah, and its spiritual leader is Sheikh Fadlallah.

B. Hammoud

In 1992, Hammoud, a citizen of Lebanon, attempted to enter the United States on fraudulent documents. After being detained by the INS, Hammoud sought asylum. While the asylum application was pending, Hammoud moved to Charlotte, North Carolina, where his brothers and cousins were living. Hammoud ultimately obtained permanent resident status by marrying a United States citizen.

At some point in the mid-1990s, Hammoud, his wife, one of his brothers, and his cousins all became involved in a cigarette smuggling operation. The conspirators purchased large quantities of cigarettes in North Carolina, smuggled them to Michigan, and sold them without paying Michigan taxes. This scheme took advantage of the fact that Michigan imposes a tax of $7.50 per carton of cigarettes, while the North Carolina tax is only 50 [cents]. It is estimated that the conspiracy involved a quantity of cigarettes valued at roughly $7.5 million and that the state of Michigan was deprived of $3 million in tax revenues.

In 1996, Hammoud began leading weekly prayer services for Shi'a Muslims in Charlotte. These services were often conducted at Hammoud's home. At these meetings, Hammoud – who is acquainted with both Nasserallah and Fadlallah, as well as Sheikh Abbas Harake, a senior military commander for Hizballah – urged the attendees to donate money to Hizballah. Hammoud would then forward the money to Harake. The Government's evidence demonstrated that on one occasion, Hammoud donated $3,500 of his own money to Hizballah.

Based on these and other activities, Hammoud was charged with various immigration violations, sale of contraband cigarettes, money laundering, mail fraud, credit card fraud, and racketeering. Additionally, Hammoud was charged with conspiracy to provide material support to a designated FTO and with providing material support to a designated FTO, both in violation of 18 U.S.C.A. § 2339B. The latter § 2339B charge related specifically to Hammoud's personal donation of $3,500 to Hizballah.

At trial, one of the witnesses against Hammoud was Said Harb, who grew up in the same Lebanese neighborhood as Hammoud. Harb testified regarding his own involvement in the cigarette smuggling operation and also provided information regarding the provision of "dual use" equipment (such as global positioning systems, which can be used for both civilian and military activities) to Hizballah. The Government alleged that this conduct was part of the conspiracy to provide material support to Hizballah. Harb testified that Hammoud had declined to become involved in providing equipment because he was helping Hizballah in his own way. Harb also testified that when he traveled to Lebanon in September 1999, Hammoud gave him $3,500 for Hizballah.

C. Conviction and Sentence

The jury convicted Hammoud of 14 offenses: money laundering and conspiracy to commit money laundering (18 U.S.C. § 1956(a)(1), (h)); transportation of contraband cigarettes (18 U.S.C. § 2342); and providing material support to a designated FTO (18 U.S.C. § 2339B).

Applying the 2002 Guidelines Manual, the presentencing report (PSR) recommended that the base offense level correspond to the amount of tax evaded in the cigarette smuggling operation. The PSR recommended several upward adjustments to this base offense level. Most significantly, the PSR recommended a 12-level enhancement for committing a terrorist act, *see id.* § 3A1.4(a). Ultimately, the PSR recommended assignment of an adjusted offense level of 46, which required a sentence of life imprisonment.

Hammoud filed objections to the PSR, in which he challenged the factual basis for several of the upward adjustments. Hammoud also challenged the terrorism enhancement under *Apprendi [v. New Jersey*, 530 U.S. 466 (2000)], maintaining that the enhancement was invalid without a jury finding that he possessed the requisite mental state. Hammoud made similar arguments against the enhancements for his leadership role and obstruction of justice.

The district court conducted a sentencing hearing at which it rejected all of Hammoud's sentencing challenges. The court therefore concluded that the guidelines provided for a sentence of life imprisonment. Because none of the offenses of conviction carried a statutory maximum of life imprisonment, the district court imposed the maximum sentence on each count and ordered all sentences to be served consecutively. This resulted in the imposition of a sentence of 155 years.

We begin by addressing Hammoud's numerous challenges to his convictions for providing (and conspiring to provide) material support to a designated FTO. We then consider Hammoud's claim that *Blakely [v. Washington*, 124 S. Ct. 2531 (2004)], operates to invalidate his sentence.

II. Constitutionality of 18 U.S.C.A. § 2339B

A. Freedom of Association

Hammoud first contends that § 2339B impermissibly restricts the First Amendment right of association. Hammoud concedes (at least for purposes of this argument) that Hizballah engages in terrorist activity. But, he also notes the undisputed fact that Hizballah provides humanitarian aid to citizens of Lebanon. Hammoud argues that because Hizballah engages in both legal and illegal activities, he can be found criminally liable for providing material support to Hizballah only if he had a specific intent to further the organization's illegal aims. Because § 2339B lacks such a specific intent requirement, Hammoud argues that it unconstitutionally restricts the freedom of association. *Cf. United States v. Al-Arian*, 329 F. Supp. 2d 1294 (M.D. Fla. 2004) (construing § 2339B as requiring proof of specific intent to further illegal activity because less stringent interpretation would raise constitutional questions regarding freedom of association and "due process requirements of personal guilt").

It is well established that "the First Amendment . . . restricts the ability of the State to impose liability on an individual solely because of his association with another." Therefore, it is a violation of the First Amendment to punish an individual for mere membership in an organization that has legal and illegal goals. Any statute prohibiting association with such an organization must require a showing that the defendant specifically intended to further the organization's unlawful goals. Hammoud maintains that because § 2339B does not contain such a specific intent requirement, his conviction violates the First Amendment.[42]

Hammoud's argument fails because § 2339B does not prohibit mere association; it prohibits the conduct of providing material support to a designated FTO. Therefore, cases regarding mere association with an organization do not control. Rather, the governing standard is found in *United States v. O Brien*, 391 U.S. 367 (1968), which applies when a facially neutral statute restricts some expressive conduct. Such a statute is valid

> if it is within the constitutional power of the Government; if it furthers an important or substantial governmental interest; if the governmental interest is unrelated to the suppression of free expression; and if the

---

[42] Hammoud relies in part on cases holding that a donation to a political advocacy group is a proxy for speech. *See, e.g., Buckley v. Valeo*, 424 U.S. 1, 16-17 (1976) (per curiam). Hizballah is not a political advocacy group, however. Therefore, while providing monetary support to Hizballah may have an expressive component, it is not the equivalent of pure political speech. *See Humanitarian Law Project v. Reno*, 205 F.3d 1130, 1134-35 (9th Cir. 2000) (rejecting argument that material support prohibition is subject to strict scrutiny review under *Buckley* and similar cases).

incidental restriction on alleged First Amendment freedoms is no greater than is essential to the furtherance of that interest.

[T]he Government's interest in curbing terrorism is unrelated to the suppression of free expression. Hammoud is free to advocate in favor of Hizballah or its political objectives – § 2339B does not target such advocacy. [T]he incidental effect on expression caused by § 2339B is no greater than necessary. In enacting § 2339B and its sister statute, 18 U.S.C. § 2339A, Congress explicitly found that "foreign organizations that engage in terrorist activity are so tainted by their criminal conduct that any contribution to such an organization facilitates that conduct." As the Ninth Circuit reasoned

> it follows that all material support given to [foreign terrorist] organizations aids their unlawful goals. Indeed, . . . terrorist organizations do not maintain open books. Therefore, when someone makes a donation to them, there is no way to tell how the donation is used. Further, . . . even contributions earmarked for peaceful purposes can be used to give aid to the families of those killed while carrying out terrorist acts, thus making the decision to engage in terrorism more attractive. More fundamentally, money is fungible; giving support intended to aid an organization's peaceful activities frees up resources that can be used for terrorist acts.

Humanitarian Law Project, 205 F.3d at 1136. In light of this reasoning, the prohibition on material support is adequately tailored to the interest served and does not suppress more speech than is necessary to further the Government's legitimate goal. We therefore conclude that § 2339B does not infringe on the constitutionally protected right of free association.

B. Overbreadth

Hammoud next argues that § 2339B is overbroad. A statute is overbroad only if it "punishes a substantial amount of protected free speech, judged in relation to the statute's plainly legitimate sweep." The overbreadth must be substantial "not only in an absolute sense, but also relative to the scope of the law's plainly legitimate applications." It is also worth noting that when, as here, a statute is addressed to conduct rather than speech, an overbreadth challenge is less likely to succeed.

Hammoud argues that § 2339B is overbroad because (1) it prohibits mere association with an FTO, and (2) it prohibits such plainly legitimate activities as teaching members of an FTO how to apply for grants to further the organization's humanitarian aims. As discussed above, § 2339B does not prohibit mere association with an FTO and therefore is not overbroad on that basis. Regarding Hammoud's second overbreadth argument, it may be true that the material support prohibition of § 2339B encompasses some forms of expression that are entitled to First Amendment protection.[43] *Cf. Humanitarian Law Project,* 205 F.3d at 1138 (holding that "training" prong of material support

---

[43] A defendant who is prosecuted because his protected speech is incidentally covered by a broader ban on unprotected activity may bring an as-applied challenge. Hammoud is not such a defendant for the reasons previously articulated.

definition is vague because it covers such forms of protected expression as "instructing members of a designated group on how to petition the United Nations to give aid to their group"). Hammoud has utterly failed to demonstrate, however, that any overbreadth is substantial in relation to the legitimate reach of § 2339B.

C. Vagueness

Hammoud next argues that the term "material support" is unconstitutionally vague. As noted above, the term "material support" is specifically defined as a number of enumerated actions. Hammoud relies on *Humanitarian Law Project*, in which the Ninth Circuit ruled that two components of the material support definition – "personnel" and "training" – were vague. The possible vagueness of these prongs of the material support definition does not affect Hammoud's conviction, however, because he was specifically charged with providing material support in the form of currency. *See United States v. Rahman*, 189 F.3d 88, 116 (2d Cir. 1999) (per curiam) (rejecting vagueness challenge because allegedly vague term was not relevant to Appellant's conviction). There is nothing at all vague about the term "currency."

D. Designation of an FTO

Hammoud's final challenge to the constitutionality of § 2339B concerns his inability to challenge the designation of Hizballah as an FTO. Section 2339B(g)(6) defines "terrorist organization" as "an organization designated as a terrorist organization under [8 U.S.C. § 1189]." Section 1189(a)(8) explicitly prohibits a defendant in a criminal action from challenging a designation. Hammoud argues that his inability to challenge the designation of Hizballah as an FTO is a violation of the Constitution.

Here, Congress has provided that the fact of an organization's designation as an FTO is an element of § 2339B, but the validity of the designation is not. Therefore, Hammoud's inability to challenge the designation is not a violation of his constitutional rights. *See United States v. Bozarov*, 974 F.2d 1037, 1045-46 (9th Cir. 1992) (holding that defendant's inability to challenge administrative classification did not violate due process because the validity of the classification was not an element of the offense).

Affirmed.

GREGORY, Circuit Judge, dissenting:

I . . . dissent from the judgment. I believe the majority incorrectly concludes that AEDPA's "material support" provision, 18 U.S.C. § 2339B, is constitutional as applied in this case. As the Ninth Circuit has held, a strict textual reading of § 2339B(a)(1)'s plain language raises serious due process concerns. *See [HLP II]*[1] ("We believe that serious due process concerns would be raised were we to accept

---

[1] The Ninth Circuit and most other courts citing the *Humanitarian Law Project* cases use these Roman numeral designations, referring to the original district court case, *Humanitarian Law Project v. Reno*, 9 F. Supp. 2d 1176 (C.D. Cal. 1998), as "*Humanitarian Law Project I.*" [The casebook will follow the more common practice of designating each of the Court of Appeals opinions as *HLP I* or *HLP II*.]

the argument that a person who acts without knowledge of critical information about a designated organization presumably acts consistently with the intent and conduct of that designated organization.").

Unlike the Ninth Circuit, however, I do not believe that these constitutional infirmities can be cured by reading the statutory term "knowingly" as a scienter requirement meaning only that the defendant had knowledge of the organization's designation as a foreign terrorist organization ("FTO"), or that he or she knew of the organization's unlawful activities that caused it to be so designated.

Instead, I would follow the reasoning of *United States v. Al-Arian,* and conclude that to save the statute, one must apply the mens rea requirement to the entire "material support" provision such that the government must prove that the defendant (1) knew the organization was a FTO or knew of the organization's unlawful activities that caused it to be so designated and (2) knew what he or she was providing was "material support," i.e., the government must show that the defendant had a specific intent that the support would further the FTO's illegal activities. Because Hammoud was convicted of "material support" without the proper scienter requirement, violating his constitutional rights under the First and Fifth Amendments, I would hold that these constitutional violations constitute plain error and thus vacate his material support conviction.

I.

Hammoud and his *Amici Curiae,* the Center for Constitutional Rights, the National Coalition to Protect Political Freedom, the National Association of Criminal Defense Lawyers, and the National Lawyers Guild, raise a bevy of constitutional challenges to Hammoud's conviction under 18 U.S.C. § 2339B, including assertions that the "material support" provision is vague and overbroad in violation of the First Amendment, and that the statute violates the First and Sixth Amendments because the defendant cannot challenge the FTO designation. Moreover, Hammoud and Amici Curiae challenge Hammoud's conviction on the basis that the statute lacks a specific intent requirement, which they contend is essential to avoid "guilt by association" in violation of the First and Fifth Amendments.

II.

Hammoud and *Amici Curiae* argue that the "material support" provision is unconstitutional because it penalizes association, in violation of the First Amendment, and fails to require the requisite specific intent, thus contravening the Fifth Amendment requirement of "personal guilt." They first frame these arguments by relying on the unimpeachable, but basic and preliminary, proposition that the Constitution protects individuals from being punished solely because of their association with a group.

Here, however, Hammoud and *Amici Curiae* also advance a legally independent – though somewhat interrelated to the First Amendment argument – Fifth Amendment Claim, which *HLP II* and the other cases noted above did not reach. Specifically, to pass Fifth Amendment scrutiny and to avoid a "personal guilt" problem, they argue that AEDPA's material support provision must include a scienter requirement, whereby the defendant must be found guilty of a specific intent to further the illegal aims of the association. Br. of Appellant at 25; Br. of *Amici Curiae* at 6 ("This statute is so sweeping that it would apply to a citizen who sent a human rights or constitutional law treatise to Hizballah to urge it to respect human rights and desist from committing terrorist acts."). Hammoud and *Amici Curiae* rely on more Communist Party cases to support their argument that AEDPA's "material support" provision is unconstitutional without such a specific intent requirement.

Hammoud and *Amici Curiae* assert that without a specific intent requirement, AEDPA's material support provision suffers the same fate. In this context, Amici Curiae posit that *HLP I*'s isolated focus on the First Amendment renders the prohibition on guilt by association a meaningless formality because under the Ninth Circuit's reasoning:

> Every anti-Communist law struck down by the Supreme Court for imposing guilt by association could have simply been rewritten to penalize dues payments to the Party. It would also lead to the anomalous result that while leaders of the NAACP could not be held responsible for injuries sustained during an NAACP-led economic boycott absent proof of specific intent, the NAACP's thousands of individual donors could have been held liable without any showing of specific intent.

While the Ninth Circuit's interpretation of "knowingly" is more advanced than the quasi-strict liability standard upon which Hammoud was convicted, I submit that such an interpretation of § 2339B's mental state requirement is still insufficient to withstand constitutional attack.

In *Al-Arian*, the court . . . disagreed with the Ninth Circuit's attempt to salvage the statute based on application of the statutory term "knowingly" in *HLP II*, stating that the Ninth Circuit's construction "only cures some of the Fifth Amendment concerns." The *Al-Arian* court . . . found that under the Ninth Circuit's construction:

> [A] cab driver could be guilty for giving a ride to a FTO member to the UN, if he knows that the person is a member of a FTO . . . . Similarly, a hotel clerk in New York could be committing a crime by providing lodging to that same FTO member under similar circumstances as the cab driver.[12]

I believe that § 2339B's "material support" provisions constitute a violation of the Fifth Amendment when applied without the necessary specific intent requirement. Unlike the situation faced in *Al-Arian*, however, in Hammoud's case it is many days too late to apply a savings instruction – or to preliminarily enjoin the government from applying the "material support" provision as written, as in *HLP II* – therefore, I turn to the application and effect of the constitutional error in this case.

---

[12] Similarly, *Amici Curiae* properly recognize that the jury was not instructed that it had to find Hammoud intended the donation to be used for any violent, terrorist, or otherwise unlawful purpose, thus setting up the anomalous result that under § 2339B "Hammoud would be guilty even if it were stipulated that his support was intended to further only Hizballah's lawful activities . . . [while] an individual who gave a donation to a non-designated group intending that it be used for terrorist activity would not be guilty."

he should get a new trial on M.S.

III.

For the reasons that follow, I would find that Hammoud satisfies [the] plain error standard and he should be granted a new trial on the "material support" charge.

[T]he Ninth Circuit's absurd construction of the statute in *X-Citement Video* is closely related to the absurd results, which necessarily follow from interpreting AEDPA's "material support" provisions without a scienter requirement. For the end result of applying "knowingly" as did the Ninth Circuit in *HLP II* "is to render a substantial portion of Section 2339B unconstitutionally vague."

IV.

For these reasons, I would hold that the jury instruction upon which Hammoud was convicted of providing material support to Hizballah violated his Fifth Amendment rights, and [was] "plain error," thus entitling him to a new trial. In recommending as much, I do not seek to give comfort to terrorist organizations, or to diminish the reality of clear and present threats posed by such groups. To the contrary, I seek to uphold the Constitution in a manner that does not harken back to a bleaker era of American history when characters were impugned, and individuals indicted, convicted and punished based on little more than suspicion, association and fear, without the "personal guilt" which is the hallmark of our criminal justice system. In applying AEDPA's material support provisions with the requisite scienter requirement, we may help insure that juries are not driven to findings of guilt by mere fear of the unknown, but instead arrive at the just result only after interrogation of the government's case to determine whether criminal intent is present.

I respectfully dissent.

NOTES AND QUESTIONS

1. The Ninth Circuit decided to review *HLP* en banc. *Humanitarian Law Project v. United States DOJ*, 382 F.3d 1154 (9th Cir. 2004) (Sept. 8, 2004). Before any decision was reached by the en banc panel, however, Congress amended § 2339B to provide that

> To violate this paragraph, a person must have knowledge that the organization is a designated terrorist organization, that the organization has engaged or engages in terrorist activity, or that the organization has engaged or engages in terrorism.

The Ninth Circuit then determined to "vacate the judgment and injunction regarding the terms 'personnel' and 'training,' and remand to the district court for further proceedings, if any, as appropriate. We decline to reach any other issue urged by the parties." (Dec. 21, 2004).

Does the amended statute satisfy the requirements of the original panel in *HLR II*? Does it satisfy the requirements of Judges Gregory and Moody? If not, then does the statute become unconstitutional or do the courts continue to construe it to add additional elements of mens rea even after revision by Congress?

2. Judges Gregory and Moody both emulate a number of other judges who have engaged in verbal hand-wringing while issuing decisions counter to Government arguments. Why do you suppose they feel the need to engage in this explanation of what they view to be their judicial duty? In a speech to the Federalist Society on November 14, Attorney General Ashcroft criticized some "activist" federal judges. "The danger I see here is that intrusive judicial oversight and second-guessing of presidential determinations in these critical areas can put at risk the very security of our nation in a time of war." He probably was referring most directly to the opinion of Judge Robertson of the District of Columbia in *Hamdan v. Rumsfeld*, p. 533 below, in which the judge did not seem as abashed as some of the others.

3. Judges Gregory and Moody both think it would be "absurd" to punish the cabbie, bank teller, or hotel manager who provided services to a representative of an FTO. Is that truly so absurd? If the services are provided by a sympathizer with full awareness of the FTO objectives, does Judge Moody's statement regarding the inference of intent render these examples less absurd and more just a matter of evidence and inference?

UNITED STATES v. AFSHARI
2004 U.S. App. LEXIS 26430 (9th Cir. 12/20/2004)

KLEINFELD, Circuit Judge:

We review the constitutionality of a statute prohibiting financial support to organizations designated as "terrorist."

The issue here is the constitutionality of the crime charged in the indictment, that from 1997 to 2001, Rahmani and others knowingly and willfully conspired to provide material support to the Mujahedin-e Khalq ("MEK"),[1] a designated terrorist organization, in violation of 18 U.S.C. § 2339B(a)(1).

According to the indictment, the defendants solicited charitable contributions at the Los Angeles International Airport for the "Committee for Human Rights," gave money and credit cards to the MEK, and wired money from the "Committee for Human Rights" to an MEK bank account in Turkey. They did all this after participating in a conference call with an MEK leader, in which they learned that the State Department had designated the MEK as a foreign terrorist organization. The MEK leader told them to continue to provide material support despite the designation. All told, according to the indictment in this case, the money they sent to the MEK amounted to at least several hundred thousand dollars.

solicited + gave thousands of dollars to MEK, even after an MEK leader told them that MEK was on the FTO list

The MEK was founded in the 1960s as an Iranian Marxist group seeking to overthrow the regime then ruling Iran. It participated in various terrorist activities against the Iranian regime and against the United States, including the taking of American embassy personnel as hostages in 1979. After the Iranian regime fell and was replaced by a clerical, rather than a Marxist, regime, MEK

---

[1] The MEK is also known as the People's Mojahedin Organization for Iraq, or PMOI, and has a variety of other aliases. [See introduction to *PMOI II*, p. 346, *supra*.]

members fled to France. They later settled in Iraq, along the Iranian border. There they carried out terrorist activities with the support of Saddam Hussein's regime, as well as, if the indictment is correct, the money that the defendants sent them.

For purposes of reviewing a motion to dismiss an indictment, we assume the truth of what the indictment alleges. Thus, we take it as true that the defendants knew that they were furnishing assistance to a designated "terrorist" organization, having been informed of the designation in a conference call with an MEK leader.

The district court dismissed the indictment on the ground that the terrorist designation statute was unconstitutional. We reverse.

I. Challenging the designation.

[Section] 1189(a)(1) sets out a carefully articulated scheme for designating foreign terrorist organizations. To make the designation, the Secretary has to make specific findings that "the organization is a foreign organization"; that "the organization engages in terrorist activity";[7] and that "the terrorist activity of the organization threatens the security of United States nationals or the national security of the United States."

The designated organization is entitled to judicial review of the Secretary's action in the United States Court of Appeals for the District of Columbia.

The district court found that it was a facially unconstitutional restriction on judicial review of the designation for Congress to assign such review exclusively to the D.C. Circuit. We reject that position.

Many administrative determinations are reviewable only by petition to the correct circuit court, bypassing the district court, and that procedure has generally been accepted. Many are reviewable only in the D.C. Circuit, or the Federal Circuit, and those restrictions have also been generally accepted. The

---

[7] 8 U.S.C. § 1182(a)(3)(B)(ii). As used in this Act, the term "terrorist activity" means any activity which is unlawful under the laws of the place where it is committed . . . and which involves any of the following:

(I) The highjacking or sabotage of any conveyance . . . .

(II) The seizing or detaining, and threatening to kill, injure, or continue to detain, another individual in order to compel a third person . . . to do or abstain from doing any act as an explicit or implicit condition for the release of the individual seized or detained.

(III) A violent attack upon an internationally protected person . . . or upon the liberty of such a person.

(IV) An assassination.

(V) The use of any
　　(a) biological agent, chemical agent, or nuclear weapon or device, or
　　(b) explosive or firearm . . . ,
　　with intent to endanger, directly or indirectly, the safety of one or more individuals or to cause substantial damage to property.

(VI) A threat, attempt, or conspiracy to do any of the foregoing.

22 U.S.C. § 2656f(d)(2): [T]he term "terrorism" means premeditated, politically motivated violence perpetrated against noncombatant targets by subnational groups or clandestine agents.

congressional restriction does not interfere with the opportunity for judicial review, as the MEK's extensive litigation history shows. And this scheme avoids the awkwardness of criminalizing material support for a designated organization in some circuits but not others, as varying decisions in the different regional circuits might.

II. Due Process claim.

The defendants' central argument is that § 2339B denies them their constitutional rights because it prohibits them from collaterally attacking the designation of a foreign terrorist organization. This contention was recently rejected by the Fourth Circuit en banc. *United States v. Hammoud*, 381 F.3d 316 (4th Cir. 2004) (en banc). We, too, reject it.

The defendants are right that § 1189(a)(8) prevents them from contending, in defense of the charges against them under 18 U.S.C. § 2339B, that the designated terrorist organization is not really terrorist at all. No doubt Congress was well aware that some might be of the view that "one man's terrorist is another man's freedom fighter." Congress clearly chose to delegate policymaking authority to the President and Department of State with respect to designation of terrorist organizations, and to keep such policymaking authority out of the hands of United States Attorneys and juries. Under § 2339B, if defendants provide material support for an organization that has been designated a terrorist organization under § 1189, they commit the crime, and it does not matter whether the designation is correct or not.

The question then is whether due process prohibits a prosecution under § 2339B when the predicate designation was obtained in an unconstitutional manner or is otherwise erroneous. In *Lewis v. United States*, 445 U.S. 55 (1980), the Supreme Court held that a prior conviction could properly be used as a predicate for a subsequent conviction for a felon in possession of a firearm, even though it had been obtained in violation of the Sixth Amendment right to counsel. The Court held that it was proper to prohibit a collateral attack on the predicate during the criminal hearing because the felon-in-possession statute made no exception "for a person whose outstanding felony conviction ultimately might turn out to be invalid for any reason." The Court noted that the prohibition on collateral attack was proper because a convicted felon could challenge the validity of the conviction before he purchased his firearm.

The defendants attempt to distinguish *Lewis* from this § 2339B prosecution because the defendant in *Lewis* had the ability to challenge his predicate, whereas here the defendants, themselves, are prohibited from challenging the designation. But this does not change the principle that a criminal proceeding may go forward, even if the predicate was in some way unconstitutional, so long as a sufficient opportunity for judicial review of the predicate exists. Here there was such an opportunity, which the MEK took advantage of each time it was designated a foreign terrorist organization.

The defendants also attempt to distinguish *Lewis* by relying on *United States v. Mendoza-Lopez*, 481 U.S. 828 (1987). In that case, the Supreme Court held that a prosecution under 8 U.S.C. § 1326 for illegal reentry does not comport with due process if there is no judicial review of whether the predicate deportation proceeding violated the alien's rights. It is not at all clear from *Mendoza-Lopez* that the Supreme Court meant that the due process problem is in the *later* proceeding. The Court held that "where a determination made in an administrative proceeding is to play a critical role in the subsequent imposition of a criminal sanction, there must be *some* meaningful review of the administrative proceeding." Nothing in *Mendoza-Lopez* appears to require that this review be had by the defendant in the subsequent criminal proceeding.

Furthermore, it is obvious in *Lewis* and *Mendoza-Lopez* that the opportunity to seek review would be in the hands of the defendants themselves because it was *their* rights at issue in the hearing that created the predicate in the later criminal proceeding. But here, the defendants' rights were not directly violated in the earlier designation proceeding. The predicate designation was against the MEK, not the defendants. Section 1189 provides for the organizations to seek review of the predicate designation, and that review was had in this case. Therefore, due process does not require another review of the predicate by the court adjudicating the instant § 2339B criminal proceeding.

Our holding is further supported by our decision in *United States v. Bozarov*, 974 F.2d 1037 (9th Cir. 1992). In *Bozarov*, we held that a defendant charged with exporting items listed under the Export Administration Act without a license did not have a due process right to collaterally attack the listing in his criminal proceeding. We held, however, that Bozarov had standing to challenge the constitutionality of the Export Act in his criminal proceeding. This was because the Export Act explicitly provided that all actions taken by the Secretary of Commerce under it were "not subject to judicial review," including a denial of the license that was a predicate for a violation of the criminal provision. If a defendant were not allowed to challenge the Export Act in that proceeding, there would be *no* arbiter of the constitutionality of the Export Act. In contrast, Congress has explicitly provided that the D.C. Circuit is the arbiter of the constitutionality of any designation under § 1189. Thus, there is no constitutional need for the defendants to challenge the predicate designation in this proceeding.

As we noted in another case where we rejected a defendant's right to challenge an export listing in a subsequent criminal proceeding, the defendants' argument here "is analogous to one by a defendant in a drug possession case that his conviction cannot stand because no specific showing has been made that the drug is a threat to society. . . . [A] showing that the drug possessed by the individual defendant has a 'detrimental effect on the general welfare' [is not] an element of the offense." Likewise, the element of the crime that the prosecutor must prove in a § 2339B case is the predicate fact that a particular organization *was* designated at the time the material support was given, not whether the government made a correct designation. Our position is consistent with that of the Fourth Circuit, which held that a defendant's inability to challenge the designation was not a violation of his constitutional rights, since the *validity* of the designation is not an element of the crime. Rather, the element is the *fact* of an organization's designation as a "foreign terrorist organization."

III. First Amendment claim.

The defendants argue that (1) they have a First Amendment right to contribute to organizations that are not terrorist; (2) the statutory scheme denies them the opportunity to challenge the "foreign terrorist organization" designation; therefore (3) it deprives them of their First Amendment right to make such contributions. An organization cannot be designated unless it is foreign, so domestic associations are immune from the scheme. Nevertheless, the defendants assert their own First Amendment rights to contribute to the advancement of their own goals that may be served by the designated foreign terrorist organization. The defendants do not claim a First Amendment right to support terrorism, but rather to support an organization that the State Department, in their view, mistakenly designates as terrorist.

Defendants cite to various general propositions about the protection given to association and expression, and the need to give money in order to make expression effective.[36] Those general propositions, however, do not take us far toward reaching a decision. Defendants persuasively argue that haranguing people in a Los Angeles park about the evils of some foreign regime may be less effective than sending money to someone doing something about it. But money is not the same thing as talk,[37] and the something being done may be something other than talking. Even giving money to perfectly legitimate political expression within the United States can be and is restricted by Congress, consistent with the Constitution.[38] A fortiori, contribution of money to organizations that engage in terrorism, as well as expressing a political agenda with speech, can be restricted by Congress. Terrorism is defined by the statute as "politically motivated violence perpetrated against noncombatant targets by subnational groups or clandestine agents."

It would be anomalous indeed if Congress could prohibit the contribution of money for television commercials saying why a candidate would be a good or bad choice for political office, yet could not prohibit contribution of money to a group designated as a terrorist organization. Thus, we hold that § 2339B does not impermissibly restrict the defendants' First Amendment right of association.

The authority upon which the defendants most heavily rely is the Supreme Court's decision in *McKinney v. Alabama*, 424 U.S. 669 (1976). In *McKinney*, an Alabama statute enabled the district attorney to obtain a civil adjudication of

---

[36] *See Citizens Against Rent Control / Coalition for Fair Housing v. City of Berkeley,* 454 U.S. 290 (1981); *Buckley v. Valeo,* 424 U.S. 1 (1976); *Serv. Employees Int l Union v. Fair Political Practices Comm h,* 955 F.2d 1312 (9th Cir.), *cert. denied,* 505 U.S. 1230 (1992).

[37] *Cf. McConnell v. FEC,* 540 U.S. 93, 249, 157 L. Ed. 2d 491, 124 S. Ct. 619, 721-22 (2003) (Scalia, J., concurring and dissenting) ("The right to use one's own money to hire gladiators, and to fund speech by proxy, are property rights not entitled to the same protection as the right to say what one pleases.") (quotation and alterations omitted).

[38] *See McConnell,* 540 U.S. 93; *Buckley,* 424 U.S. 1, 20 ("[A] limitation upon the amount that any one person or group may contribute to a candidate or political committee entails only a marginal restriction upon the contributor's ability to engage in free communication.").

obscenity against a magazine called New Directions. Subsequently the State Attorney General's office delivered a letter to the proprietor of a Birmingham newsstand, telling him that New Directions and three other magazines had been declared obscene. A few days later, the officers from the Attorney General's office went back and bought a copy of New Directions from the newsstand and charged the proprietor with selling obscene printed matter. The constitutional issue arose out of the proprietor's attempt to have the jury in his criminal case decide whether New Directions really was obscene. The trial court determined that the obscenity of the magazine had already been established by the civil proceeding so the jury could decide only whether the proprietor had sold it.

The Supreme Court of Alabama affirmed the trial court's judgment. On review, the United States Supreme Court held that "the procedures utilized by the State of Alabama, insofar as they precluded [the proprietor] from litigating the obscenity vel non of New Directions as a defense to his criminal prosecution, violated the First and Fourteenth Amendments." The Court found that "there [was] nothing in the opinion of the Supreme Court of Alabama indicating that petitioner had available to him any judicial avenue for initiating a challenge to the Mobile declaration as to the obscenity of New Directions."

McKinney holding

There are several reasons why *McKinney* is distinguishable and does not apply. The plainest logical distinction between the statutes is that the Alabama statute prohibited sale of "obscene printed or written matter," making obscenity an element of the crime, whereas § 2339B prohibits material assistance to "designated" organizations. To see the distinction, one must consider the entire statutory scheme, because . . . § 2339B defines "foreign terrorist organization" to mean one that has been "designated" by the elaborate procedure described above. If the material assistance is rendered to a "foreign terrorist organization" in the common sense meaning of the English words, but the organization is not on the list of "designated" organizations, the crime is not committed. This is a meaningful distinction. The list of "designated" organizations in the Federal Register has only 30 organizations on it, even though it is very likely that there are additional organizations that meet the substantive criteria for designation as foreign terrorist organizations. Conversely, if the material assistance is to a "designated" foreign terrorist organization, the crime is committed regardless of whether the designation was erroneous, or whether the organization has changed so that it is no longer terrorist.

The Alabama and federal statutory schemes also differ in a practical way, because the Alabama statute does not create an incentive to litigate whether the material is "obscene" in the equitable action preceding the criminal action, whereas the federal scheme does. The publisher of New Directions might well have ignored the equitable proceeding to declare the magazine obscene because attorneys' fees would exceed the business value of the litigation, and the Court noted that the record did not show much about the participation of any adverse parties. Under the federal scheme, in contrast, the organization has a very substantial incentive to litigate its designation, and the MEK did, vigorously.

After the Secretary of State designated the MEK a "foreign terrorist organization" in 1997, the MEK challenged the designation in the United States

Court of Appeals for the District of Columbia, and lost.[52] When the Secretary renewed the designation in 1999, the MEK litigated it again, this time successfully.[53] The D.C. Circuit remanded to the Secretary for renewed consideration with greater procedural protections for the MEK. When the Secretary again designated the MEK as a foreign terrorist organization on a new administrative record, the MEK brought its third challenge in the D.C. Circuit, which this time upheld the designation.[55] The D.C. Circuit also reconsidered the 1997 designation on the merits and again upheld it, expressly anticipating the possibility of a criminal prosecution based on either designation. Such extensive and serious litigation is a far cry from a magazine publisher disregarding a local designation proceeding against an individual magazine, perhaps because the cost of litigation could not generate commensurate benefits. But in this case, the stakes and incentives are far different, and the MEK protected its interests vigorously.

Conceivably the MEK developed its practices at a time when the United States supported the previous regime in Iran, and maintained its position while harbored by the Saddam Hussein Ba'ath regime in Iraq, but will change, or has already changed, so that its interest in overturning the current regime in Iran coincides with the interests of the United States. The sometimes subtle analysis of a foreign organization's political program to determine whether it is indeed a terrorist threat is peculiarly within the expertise of the State Department and the Executive Branch. Juries could not make reliable determinations without extensive foreign policy education and the disclosure of classified materials. Leaving the determination to the Executive Branch, coupled with the procedural protections and judicial review afforded by the statute, is both a reasonable and a constitutional way to make a determination of whether a group is a "foreign terrorist organization." The Constitution does not forbid Congress from requiring individuals, whether they agree with the Executive Branch determination or not, to refrain from furnishing material assistance to designated organizations during the two year period of designation.

NOTES AND QUESTIONS

1. The Ninth Circuit does not overtly address the dilemma questioned by Judge Takasugi and the D.C. Circuit's mootness footnote. During the interim between the second and third D.C. opinions, all the organizations covered by the umbrella of POMI or MEK were formally carried on the list of designated organizations, but that designation had been declared to be obtained in violation of due process. Given that finding, plus the importance of political association rights, would the individual defendants in *Ashfari* have been justified in

---

[52] *People's Mojahedin Org. of Iran,* 337 U.S. App. D.C. 106, 182 F.3d 17 (D.C. Cir. 1999).

[53] *Nat'l Council of Resistance of Iran,* 346 U.S. App. D.C. 131, 251 F.3d 192 (D.C. Cir. 2001).

[55] *People's Mojahedin Org. of Iran,* 356 U.S. App. D.C. 101, 327 F.3d 1238 (D.C. Cir. 2003)

believing that they could raise money for transmission to the organizations? Or is the designation sufficiently like the designation of a drug in the Ninth Circuit's analogy?

2. The argument could be made that the right of association changes the equation because it is deserving of more consideration than any claim of right to take a drug. The argument would be that there is more social utility to the associational rights, something like the arguments preventing extension of our alcohol-driving analogy to driving with a closed container.

3. Does the *Ashfari* opinion fundamentally disagree with Judges Moody and Gregory? Both of the latter two would require that the Government show both knowledge of the designation *and* an intent to further unlawful purposes. *Ashfari* says that it is not necessary in a drug case to show that the drug is bad, so it is not necessary in a material support case to show that the money is intended to be used for bad purposes. In *HLP I*, the Ninth Circuit had pointed out the commingling and fungible nature of money so that one dollar for humanitarian purposes frees up another dollar for nefarious purposes. Who has the better of this argument? If Judges Moody and Gregory accept the commingling argument for purposes of the designation requirement, is their insistence on the donor's knowledge of bad purpose inconsistent with that?

4. *POMI II* is a sufficient answer to the designation argument only because the publicly available evidence was sufficient to support a finding that the organization was involved in terrorist activity. What happens when that is not the case, when the finding would need support of undisclosed classified information? Does the ordinary citizen have a claim of associational right to contribute to such an organization? The Ninth Circuit says no, because the giving of money is not as strong an interest as stating support through pure speech or expressive activity. Consider the following examples of what someone in Ashfari's position might have done or might still want to do:

a. encourage others in the U.S. to donate money to MEK without collecting the funds himself. Is he guilty of conspiracy or does *Brandenburg* control?

b. encourage people in other countries to donate money to MEK. Does it matter whether those other countries are signatories to the Convention on Terrorist Financing?

c. receive messages from MEK leaders in other countries and passed them on through the internet. Is this a "providing of communication devices" punishable under § 2339B? *See United States v. Sattar*, p. 359.

d. discuss with MEK leaders in other countries methods by which the organization could get itself off the designation list. Is this a providing of services that falls within *Lindh* or is it subject to the associational interests that prompted the holding in *HLP*?

See generally Rodney A. Smolla, *Terrorism and the Bill of Rights*, 10 Wм. & Mary Bill Rts. J. 551 (2002).

SELECTED READINGS

- Randolph A. Jonakait, *A Double Due Process Denial: The Crime of Providing Material Support or Resources to Designated Foreign Terrorist Organizations*, 48 N.Y.L.S. L. REV. 125 (2003).

- Sahar Aziz, *The Laws on Providing Material Support to Terrorist Organizations: The Erosion of Constitutional Rights or a Legitimate Tool for Preventing Terrorism?* 9 TEX. F. ON C.L. & C.R. 45 (2003).

- Robert Chesney, *Civil Liberties and the Terrorism Prevention Paradigm: The Guilt by Association Critique*, 101 MICH. L. REV. 1409 (2003).

- Robert Chesney, *The Sleeper Scenario: Terrorism-Support Laws and the Demands of Prevention*, 42 HARV. J. LEGIS. ___ (2005).

Chapter 7

PREVENTION, PATRIOT, PRIVACY & SECRECY

§ 7.01 INTELLIGENCE & USA PATRIOT ACT

[A] OVERVIEW OF PREVENTION

Prevention means information. Information means loss of privacy. The more information government acquires, the more safe we can feel and the less privacy we will have in our daily lives. So how safe do we want to be? American political and constitutional traditions include a healthy distrust of government, complete with innumerable references from the Framing to the McCarthy era about the need to keep government agents away from private information. The Bill of Rights stems in large part from that basic proposition.

A corollary of this tradition is a distaste for government secrecy. In interesting fashion, the concern for personal privacy links with the concern about government secrecy because we cannot challenge what we do not know. The more secrets government retains, the more likely some of those secrets will involve matters about individuals that we would rather not have residing in government files.

Three preliminary observations may be helpful:

1. Security is different from law enforcement.

   Security planning uses a risk-threat formula to allocate available resources to a given situation. Risk refers to the potential for harm at a particular location (e.g., an event at a stadium, a nuclear reactor), and threat refers to likely attempts to cause harm. Threat analysis requires information about persons, groups, and political interests that are traditionally part of "protected" freedom.

   Law enforcement most often seeks information about past wrongdoing, using sanctions for past wrongs as deterrence of future misconduct. Its connection to "protected" interests should be secondary. Only in rare instances, such as the Unabomber case, should inquiry into political agendas be necessary for solving past crimes. These also may be instances in which capturing a serial criminal directly prevents future crimes.

2. The committed, resourceful terrorist can beat any security system.

   Security includes both interdiction of threats and physical methods of reducing risks, such as locking doors, screening persons at entry points, deploying high-tech devices, and the like. Even with unlimited resources, physical security can never anticipate nor forestall the imaginative miscreant because the miscreant has the advantages of time and anonymity. Security planners must therefore deal with the reality of making a reasonable allocation of resources to security versus other public needs.

3. Prevention necessarily implies invasions of privacy.

Prevention relies on information. Information threatens privacy and freedom of expression much more directly than traditional law enforcement. Post 9/11, the blurring of separation between security and law enforcement means that civil liberties issues will be raised even more frequently by the increased use of intelligence gathering tools.

The typical criminal investigation with which most of us are familiar begins with a civilian's lodging a complaint with a police officer. When your bicycle is stolen, the insurance company wants to know the "case number" assigned when you report it to the police. More serious crimes become the subject of investigation because a child is reported kidnaped, or a body is found under suspicious circumstances, or a white collar crime is suspected because someone has lost money. Once the "case" is initiated, investigating officers search for clues to what happened with regard to that incident by assembling a profile of the victim, searching for motives and opportunities for the crime, marshaling physical evidence at the scene, and the like. All of these aspects of an investigation have the objective of assembling a virtually complete picture of what happened at some point in the past. Only in the situation of an active serial criminal (e.g., Hillside Strangler, Son of Sam, Unabomber, Maryland Sniper), are the investigators likely to be consciously concerned about hastening to prevent a future crime.

The investigation of a reported crime may produce "probable cause" to believe that a certain person committed the crime, so that search warrants can be issued for that person's house or other premises. In some situations, there might even be probable cause to conduct electronic surveillance (such as a wiretap on the suspect's telephone) because evidence of the past crime might be transmitted either as part of evading detection or planning a future similar crime. Probable cause showings in the typical investigation, thus, are focused on information related to past events.

By contrast, the emphasis in most terrorism investigations is on preventing future crimes on the basis of a suspicion that someone (whether identified or unknown) is likely to be contemplating violent action. This suspicion will not be based on evidence gathered in the context of a past crime so much as on the basis of rumors, reports from members of the public about their neighbors or friends, or just something an investigator reads in the newspaper. A search warrant or wiretap warrant would not even be possible until the "conspiracy" has been cemented through some overt act in furtherance of the conspiracy. Think back to our question regarding when it would have been appropriate to intervene in the *Sarkissian* case. We might fault the FBI agents for putting the public at risk by not moving in before the dynamite was placed in a suitcase and checked as luggage onto an airplane, but are we really being realistic? (How did the agents even have knowledge that the conspiracy was under way given that there was no probable cause to believe that a crime had been committed?) It would have been difficult to obtain a search warrant prior to the dynamite's being packed in the suitcase and, by that time, as Sherlock Holmes would have said, "the game was afoot."

Another feature of intelligence gathering is that it most often works by assembling massive amounts of information, each piece of which may be seemingly innocent, until a malevolent pattern emerges. Modern high-tech artwork offers analogies that might be helpful in understanding the process. Think of the pictures, usually in children's books, that ask you to "find the ____" buried in an elaborate drawing. In this instance, all the irrelevant information is masking the one piece of critical information. The converse can be produced by taking hundreds or thousands of utterly innocent pictures, reducing them to miniature scale, and reassembling them into a pattern, something like a mosaic, that produces an image totally unrelated to the component pictures. In this instance, the critical piece of information exists only as a pattern produced by assembling all the innocent images.

Lest you think we are getting carried away with Robert Ludlum or Tom Clancy fiction, the art analogies are not perfect examples, but they reflect the very real difficulty of assembling information about innocent-seeming persons or events to put together a pattern that could alert officials to something nefarious. One FBI agent in Phoenix had been alerted prior to 9/11 to a pattern of "persons of interest" taking courses in "aviation training." He wrote a memo which was slowly wending its way through channels at the time of the incident. Other agents had noticed the presence in the U.S. of persons who were on terrorist "watch lists." Zacarias Moussaoui had been arrested for visa violations but agents had decided they did not have sufficient probable cause even under FISA for an order to search his computer.

The 9/11 Commission was critical of the lack of follow-up on these and other leads, although not nearly as critical as some politicians and public commentators have been. *See* 9/11 COMMISSION REPORT at 266-77. But how were agents to know that these were the critical pieces of information out of the many thousands of bits that were flowing through their offices at the time? How many other odd bits of information had agents noticed which turned out not to fit any pattern or to constitute patterns no more nefarious than their component parts? How many thousands of suspicions can government agents investigate without destroying the essence of a free society and thus doing some of what the terrorists seek?

The Supreme Court noticed this difficulty during the lull between the turbulence of the 1960s and the beginning of the terrorism expansion in the 1970s. *United States v. U.S. Dist. Ct. (Keith, J)*, 407 U.S. 297 (1972):

> National security cases ... often reflect a convergence of First and Fourth Amendment values not present in cases of "ordinary" crime. Though the investigative duty of the executive may be stronger in such cases, so also is there greater jeopardy to constitutionally protected speech. "Historically the struggle for freedom of speech and press in England was bound up with the issue of the scope of the search and seizure power," *Marcus v. Search Warrant*, 367 U.S. 717, 724 (1961). History abundantly documents the tendency of Government – however benevolent and benign its motives – to view with suspicion those who most fervently dispute its policies. Fourth Amendment protections become the more necessary when the targets of

official surveillance may be those suspected of unorthodoxy in their political beliefs. The danger to political dissent is acute where the Government attempts to act under so vague a concept as the power to protect "domestic security."

[S]ecurity surveillance may involve different policy and practical considerations from the surveillance of "ordinary crime." The gathering of security intelligence is often long range and involves the interrelation of various sources and types of information. The exact targets of such surveillance may be more difficult to identify than in surveillance operations against many types of crime specified in Title III. Often, too, the emphasis of domestic intelligence gathering is on the prevention of unlawful activity or the enhancement of the Government's preparedness for some possible future crisis or emergency. Thus, the focus of domestic surveillance may be less precise than that directed against more conventional types of crime.

In addition to the mere difficulty of intervention, there are very real political dynamics at work. The unfulfilled conspiracy will not result in very much of a prison sentence, so the conspirators can be back out and at work in relatively short order. Moreover, the headlines for arrests in an inchoate conspiracy will be smaller and shorter in duration than the headlines announcing arrests in a completed act of violence. Finally, prevention, as we have said before, operates on information. Acquiring information about politically-motivated conspiracies may produce massive amounts of information about "protected" political expression, something that the public and many law enforcement agencies are reluctant to countenance.

These are some of the factors that make prevention a more delicate exercise than enforcement investigation. Nevertheless, the public has demanded that a shift in strategy be made so that greater assurance of efforts toward prevention can be given.

[B] USA PATRIOT

The USA PATRIOT Act (Uniting and Strengthening America by Providing Appropriate Tools Required to Intercept and Obstruct Terrorism) was passed on October 26, 2001, just six weeks after 9/11. It was a compendium of provisions that had been drafted and debated over the prior decade by various units within the federal government. It runs 130 pages in the Statutes at Large. It contains 156 sections, many of which contain several technical and detailed amendments to various other sections of existing law. Thus the Act contains hundreds of individual statutory changes, few of which could be understood without seeing how the amending language fit into pre-existing law.

It can be argued that PATRIOT did not have nearly the significance attached to it initially. Almost all terrorism-related litigation going against the Government in the first three years after its passage involved either statutes that predated PATRIOT, such as the procedures for designation of foreign terrorist organizations, or administrative initiatives such as indefinite detention of "enemy combatants" and secret deportation proceedings (on which the courts are split). In some instances, such as *Doe v. Ashcroft*, p. 413, *infra*, PATRIOT may have fueled and prompted litigation of an argument that had lain dormant prior to its passage. And, finally, it may be that some of the powers granted by PATRIOT have not been challenged because some of their exercise may yet be secret.

1. *Intelligence Investigations*

FISA allows electronic surveillance without court approval if the target is controlled by a foreign power and there is "no substantial likelihood" that communications of a "U.S. person" will be collected. As adopted in 1978, FISA allowed the FISA Court to approve electronic and personal surveillance of specified premises when the purpose was gathering of intelligence on foreign operatives, and created some barriers between intelligence gathering and prosecution. FISA as amended by PATRIOT (1) permits "roving" surveillance of persons rather than site-specific surveillance, (2) allows application for a FISA surveillance or search order when gathering foreign intelligence is *a significant* reason for the application rather than *the* reason, and (3) allows sharing of intelligence information with prosecution teams. The effect could be to allow acquisition of communications by U.S. persons and use of those communications in a prosecution when the only probable-cause showing prior to interception relates to probable cause of foreign connections.

FISA

2. *Gathering Records*

PATRIOT § 215 (50 U.S.C. § 1861) provides that either the FIS Court or a Magistrate Judge shall order third parties (such as internet service providers and libraries) to turn over records upon an FBI certification that the records are sought in connection with a foreign intelligence investigation. The third party is prohibited from disclosing to anyone that the records have been sought.

3. *Communication, Financial, and Credit Records*

As spelled out in *Doe v. Ashcroft* below, three separate statutes authorize FBI issuance of National Security Letters (NSL's) to electronic communication providers, financial institutions, and credit agencies. An NSL directs the recipient to provide specified types of information on certification by the agents that there is "reason to believe" that the target is a foreign agent and that the information is "relevant to" an intelligence investigation.

NSLs

4. *Tracking Communications*

Prior federal law prohibited electronic eavesdropping on telephone conversations, face-to-face conversations, or computer and other forms of electronic communications without a court order, which was available only for investigation of specified crimes, and required notice to the parties to any conversations seized when the order expired. PATRIOT expands the "predicate crimes," allows delay of notice, and removes stored electronic communications from this protection (thus treating them as records susceptible to administrative demand, grand jury subpoena, or court order). Court orders authorizing trap-and-trace devices or pen registers (which record the source or destination of calls made to or from a particular telephone) are available on mere certification, rather than a finding of a court, that use of the device is likely to produce information relevant to the investigation of a crime.

5. *Tracking Money*

   PATRIOT (1) requires many businesses in addition to banks and brokers to file Suspicious Activity Reports, (2) prohibits U.S. financial institutions from maintaining correspondent accounts for foreign shell banks, (3) establishes minimum new customer identification standards, particularly with respect to the identity of foreign customers, (4) prohibits banks from disclosing to a customer that information has been provided to an agency involved in an intelligence investigation or regulatory demand.

6. *Other Provisions*

   PATRIOT authorizes extended detention of aliens pending a determination of whether a person is connected to terrorist activities; expands the Posse Comitatus Act exceptions; provides a standardized duration of "sneak and peek" warrants; permits nationwide and perhaps worldwide execution of warrants in terrorism cases; allows the Attorney General to collect DNA samples from prisoners convicted of any federal crime of violence or terrorism; lengthens the statute of limitations applicable to crimes of terrorism.

The most controversial aspects of PATRIOT were two amendments to FISA and one to electronic communication statutes:

1. changing "the purpose" to "a significant purpose" for FISC orders

2. adding authority for record seizure orders on the basis of a connection to a terrorism investigation (section 215)

3. subjecting e-mail to pen registers and trap-and-trace as well as to record retrieval orders

To understand the significance of PATRIOT's amendments to FISA, we need to revisit *United States v. Duggan*. The Second Circuit held that a FISA order for electronic surveillance (based on an investigation that could prevent a terrorist activity) placed agents lawfully in a position to record communications and that any evidence obtained during that investigation could be used in a criminal prosecution. The court then took a second step in holding that the agents did not need to obtain an "ordinary warrant" when the focus of the investigation became gathering of evidence for a criminal prosecution. In other words, so long as part of the purposes for surveillance were pursuit of foreign intelligence, then the fourth amendment was satisfied by the FISC order. PATRIOT now codifies that holding by allowing a FISA order to be issued if "a significant purpose" of the investigation meets the statute.

Even more important is that PATRIOT eliminated most if not all of the prior information-sharing barriers between intelligence and law enforcement. Law enforcement agents are now encouraged to share investigatory information with intelligence personnel and intelligence agents are assured that sharing information with law enforcement does not itself remove the "intelligence purpose" for future surveillance.

§ 7.02   ALIEN DETENTIONS AND SECRECY

One aspect of PATRIOT that received vociferous critique was section 412, which authorized the Attorney General hold aliens suspected of terrorist connections for up to six months in renewable increments. In response to congressional inquiries about the use of PATRIOT powers, the Justice Department replied in May 2003 that it had not used the section 412 authorization because it had sufficient authority under existing law to hold aliens considered for deportation without bond.

Just prior to 9/11 and PATRIOT, the Supreme Court decided in *Zadvydas v. Davis*, 533 U.S. 678 (2001), that an alien who was subject to a removal order (deportation) but who had nowhere to go could be held in detention, according to the immigration statutes, only pursuant to the attempt to remove. Therefore, a detained alien would be entitled by due process to a hearing to determine whether removal was possible. The Court assumed that release into the U.S. would be required at some point because "an alien may be held in confinement until it has been determined that there is no significant likelihood of removal in the reasonably foreseeable future."

The internal tensions within the *Zadvydas* opinion, the difficulties it leaves for dealing with removable aliens who have nowhere to go, and the implications for detention of those with suspected terrorist connections are discussed in T. Alexander Aleinikoff, *Detaining Plenary Power: The Meaning and Impact of* Zadvydas v. Davis, 16 GEO. IMMIG. L.J. 365 (2002). The issue of indefinite detention of aliens suspected of terrorist connections was taken up by the British House of Lords in *A v. Home Secretary*, p. 601 *infra*. *Zadvydas* in the context of terrorism suspects is also discussed by Judge Keith in *Detroit Free Press v. Ashcroft,* the next case.

In the meantime, decades of institutional concern about the structure of the Immigration and Nationalization Service (INS) coalesced with terrorism-related concerns when the Department of Homeland Security was created and took over the enforcement of immigration laws. Previously, the INS had attempted to perform both service functions (visas, naturalization, etc) and enforcement (deportation, etc). The two functions were often in conflict and made for confusion. With the splitting of these functions, Homeland Security now has an agency known as Immigration and Customs Enforcement (ICE) with a subdivision Office of Detention and Removal. It is not entirely clear what enforcement functions remain with the Attorney General in the Justice Department, so one court initially decreed that a habeas petitioner held in custody pending deportation should name both the AG and DHS. *Armentero v. INS*, 340 F.3d 1058 (9th Cir. 2003). Just over a year later, the panel granted a rehearing and withdrew its original opinion. *Armentero v. INS*, 382 F.3d 1153 (9th Cir. 2004).

The Office of Detention and Removal housed over 22,000 aliens per day during 2004. It has announced that it is so overwhelmed with mandated detentions, fueled by pressure not to release anyone who might be a threat to public safety for any reason, that it is embarking on aggressive alternatives to detention. *http://www.ice.gov/graphics/news/factsheets/061704detFS2.htm.*

[A] SECRET DEPORTATION PROCEEDINGS

Exacerbating the fears that flow from lack of review is that the government has taken the position that information about the use of these techniques, even frequency of their use, is classified and need not be disclosed to the public. The aura of secrecy that has always been part of law enforcement is thus heightened substantially as part of the shift toward prevention of terrorist activity. Two cases dealing with closure of deportation proceedings to the press and public resulted in conflicting holdings.

DETROIT FREE PRESS v. ASHCROFT
303 F.3d 681 (6th Cir. 2002)

DAMON J. KEITH, Circuit Judge.

[Rabbi Haddad, whose situation is highlighted in the Muslim Community Association complaint, was "subject to deportation, having overstayed his tourist visa. The Government further suspects that the Islamic charity Haddad operates supplies funds to terrorist organizations." For these reasons, he was declared a "special interest case" and his deportation hearing was closed to the public. Newspapers and Congressman Conyers joined to challenge the lack of public access.]

The primary issue on appeal in this case, is whether the First Amendment to the United States Constitution confers a public right of access to deportation hearings. If it does, then the Government must make a showing to overcome that right.

No one will ever forget the egregious, deplorable, and despicable terrorist attacks of September 11, 2001. These were cowardly acts. In response, our government launched an extensive investigation into the attacks, future threats, conspiracies, and attempts to come. As part of this effort, immigration laws are prosecuted with increased vigor. The issue before us today involves these efforts.

The political branches of our government enjoy near-unrestrained ability to control our borders. "These are policy questions entrusted exclusively to the political branches of our government." Since the end of the 19th Century, our government has enacted immigration laws banishing, or deporting, non-citizens because of their race and their beliefs. While the Bill of Rights jealously protects citizens from such laws, it has never protected non-citizens facing deportation in the same way. In our democracy, based on checks and balances, neither the Bill of Rights nor the judiciary can second-guess government's choices. The only safeguard on this extraordinary governmental power is the public, deputizing the press as the guardians of their liberty. "An informed public is the most potent of all restraints upon misgovernment." *Grosjean v. Am. Press Co.*, 297 U.S. 233, 250 (1936).

Today, the Executive Branch seeks to take this safeguard away from the public by placing its actions beyond public scrutiny. Against non-citizens, it seeks the power to secretly deport a class if it unilaterally calls them "special interest" cases. The Executive Branch seeks to uproot people's lives, outside the public eye, and behind a closed door. Democracies die behind closed doors. The

First Amendment, through a free press, protects the people's right to know that their government acts fairly, lawfully, and accurately in deportation proceedings. When government begins closing doors, it selectively controls information rightfully belonging to the people. Selective information is misinformation. The Framers of the First Amendment "did not trust any government to separate the true from the false for us." *Kleindienst v. Mandel*, 408 U.S. 753, 773 (1972). They protected the people against secret government.

The Office of the Chief Immigration Judge, under the authorization of Attorney General John Ashcroft, designates certain cases to be special interest cases, conducted in secret, closed off from the public. Arguing that closure of these hearings was unconstitutional, plaintiffs in three separate cases sought an injunction against such action. The Government filed a motion to dismiss, arguing that closing special interest cases was not unconstitutional.

The district court granted the injunction, finding blanket closure of deportation hearings in "special interest" cases unconstitutional. For the reasons that follow, we affirm the district court's order granting Plaintiffs a preliminary injunction.

I. Facts and Procedural History

On September 21, 2001, Chief Immigration Judge Michael Creppy issued a directive (the "Creppy directive") to all United States Immigration Judges requiring closure of special interest cases. The Creppy directive requires that all proceedings in such cases be closed to the press and public, including family members and friends. The Record of the Proceeding is not to be disclosed to anyone except a deportee's attorney or representative, "assuming the file does not contain classified information." "This restriction on information includes confirming or denying whether such a case is on the docket or scheduled for a hearing."

The district court granted the Newspaper Plaintiffs' motion [for preliminary injunction]. Finding that the Newspaper Plaintiffs had a First Amendment right of access to the proceedings under *Richmond Newspapers Inc., v. Virginia*, 448 U.S. 555 (1980), and its progeny, the district court further declined to review the Government's actions under the highly deferential standard articulated in *Kleindienst v. Mandel*, 408 U.S. 753 (1972). The Government timely filed its notice of appeal. In the interim, on April 10, 2002, the Government obtained a temporary stay of the district court's order from this Court. On April 18, 2002, we dissolved the temporary stay and denied the Government's motion for stay pending this appeal.

III. Analysis

A. Likelihood of Success on the Merits

1. The Effect of the Government's Plenary Power Over Immigration

The Government argues that the district court erred in ruling that the government's plenary power over immigration did not warrant deferential review. *See, e.g., Kleindienst v. Mandel*, 408 U.S. 753 (1972) (no First Amendment bar to excluding people because of their beliefs); *Wong Wing*, 163 U.S. at 237 (court cannot limit Congress from expelling "aliens whose race or habits render them undesirable as citizens"). We are unpersuaded by the Government's claim, which would require complete deference in all facets of immigration law, including non-substantive immigration laws that infringe upon the Constitution. We hold that the Constitution meaningfully limits non-substantive immigration laws and does not require special deference to the Government.

The Government's broad authority over immigration was first announced more than one-hundred years ago in *The Chinese Exclusion Case*, 130 U.S. 581 (1889). In that case, the Court recounted the strife following Chinese immigration to California after the gold rush of the mid-1800s. A convention of lawmakers in California had petitioned Congress to alleviate this "problem." The petition charged, among other things, that:

> the presence of Chinese laborers had a baneful effect upon the material interests of the State, and upon public morals; that their immigration was in numbers approaching the character of an Oriental invasion, and was a menace to our civilization.

Noting this plea against "existing and anticipated evils," the Court valued the "the well-founded apprehension – from the experience of years – that limitation to the immigration of certain classes from China was essential to the peace of the community on the Pacific Coast, and possibly the preservation of our civilization there." Adding that "it seemed impossible for them to assimilate with our people or to make any change in their habits or modes of living," the Court found that "if the government . . . considers the presence of foreigners of a different race in this country, who will not assimilate with us, to be dangerous to its peace and security," this "determination is conclusive upon the judiciary." This power was derived not from an express provision of the Constitution, but from powers incident to sovereignty.

Today, the Government seeks to expand upon the rule from this case. The Government argues that it has plenary authority over not only substantive immigration laws and decisions, but also non-substantive ones, like the Creppy directive. Therefore, whether or not there is a First Amendment right of access to deportation proceedings, the Government argues, it can implement any non-substantive policy infringing upon that right if it is "facially legitimate and bona fide."

Even *The Chinese Exclusion Case*, however, acknowledged that Congress's power over immigration matters was limited by "the constitution itself."

a. *The Government Interprets* Kleindienst *Too Broadly*

In *Kleindienst*, Ernest Mandel, a self-proclaimed "revolutionary Marxist" and Belgian citizen, sought entry into the United States to speak at a conference at Stanford University. Mandel applied for and was denied a non-immigrant visa under a blanket provision of the Immigration and Nationality Act, prohibiting the entrance of "anarchists" or "persons advocating the overthrow of the government." In excluding Mandel, the Attorney General declined to exercise his discretionary authority to waive this prohibition.

Several professors brought suit alleging a violation of their First Amendment rights. The Court stated the issue as this: "Whether the First Amendment confers upon the appellee professors, because they wish to hear, speak, and debate with Mandel in person, the ability to determine that Mandel should be permitted to enter the country or, in other words, to compel the Attorney General to allow Mandel's admission." The Court, while acknowledging that the professors' First Amendment rights were implicated, affirmed the decision denying Mandel a visa. The Court stated:

> Plenary congressional power to make policies and rules for exclusion of aliens has long been firmly established. In the case of an alien excludable under § 212(a)(28), Congress has delegated conditional exercise of this power to the Executive. We hold that when the Executive exercises this power negatively on the basis of a facially legitimate and bona fide reason, the courts will neither look behind the exercise of that discretion, *nor test it by balancing its justification against the First Amendment interests* of those who seek personal communication with the applicant.

Kleindienst differs from the present case in two important, and related, ways. First, *Kleindienst* involved a substantive immigration decision. The law and decision at issue determined who entered the United States. Here, the Creppy directive has no effect on the eventual outcome of the deportation hearings. Second, *Kleindienst*, although recognizing a constitutional right, did not give any weight to that right. It specifically declined to balance the First Amendment right against the government's plenary power, because the law was a substantive immigration law. Therefore, if the First Amendment limits non-substantive immigration laws, *Kleindienst* offers no authority that the Government's actions are entitled to deferential review – *Kleindienst* ignored the existence of the professors' First Amendment rights altogether. In a case such as this, where a non-substantive immigration law involving a constitutional right is at issue, the Supreme Court has always recognized the importance of that constitutional right, never deferring to an assertion of plenary authority.

b. *The Constitution, Including the First Amendment, Meaningfully Limits Non-Substantive Immigration Laws*

[T]he Supreme Court has applied non-deferential review to non-substantive immigration law. In *Zadvydas v. Davis,* 533 U.S. 678 (2001), two non-citizens were being held indefinitely beyond the normal statutory-removal period of ninety days, because no country would accept them. A post-removal-period statute authorized such detention. The issue, however, was whether the post-removal statute authorized a detention indefinitely, or for a period reasonably necessary to secure removal. The language of the statute set no such limit. The Court read an implicit reasonableness limit into the statute to avoid "serious constitutional problems." Significantly, the Court dismissed the government's argument that Congress's plenary power to create immigration law required deference to the political branches' decision-making.

The Government correctly notes that the Court in *Zadvydas* twice indicated that it might be deferential in situations involving terrorism. However, nothing in *Zadvydas* indicates that given such a situation, the Court would defer to the political branches' determination of who belongs in that "small segment of particularly dangerous individuals" without judicial review of the individual circumstances of each case, something that the Creppy directive strikingly lacks. The Court repeated the importance of strong procedural protections when constitutional rights were involved: "The Constitution may well preclude granting an administrative body the unreviewable authority to make determinations implicating fundamental rights."

Importantly, the Creppy directive does not apply to "a small segment of particularly dangerous" information, but a broad, indiscriminate range of information, including information likely to be entirely innocuous. Similarly, no definable standards used to determine whether a case is of "special interest" have been articulated. Nothing in the Creppy directive counsels that it is limited to "a small segment of particularly dangerous individuals." In fact, the Government so much as argues that certain non-citizens known to have no links to terrorism will be designated "special interest" cases. Supposedly, closing a more targeted class would allow terrorists to draw inferences from which hearings are open and which are closed.

While we sympathize and share the Government's fear that dangerous information might be disclosed in some of these hearings, we feel that the ordinary process of determining whether closure is warranted on a case-by-case basis sufficiently addresses their concerns. Using this stricter standard does not mean that information helpful to terrorists will be disclosed, only that the Government must be more targeted and precise in its approach. Given the importance of the constitutional rights involved, such safeguards must be vigorously guarded lest the First Amendment turn into another balancing test.

4. Strict Scrutiny

Under the standard articulated in *Globe Newspaper*, government action that curtails a First Amendment right of access "in order to inhibit the disclosure of sensitive information" must be supported by a showing "that denial is necessitated by a compelling governmental interest, and is narrowly tailored to serve that interest." Moreover, "the interest is to be articulated along with findings specific enough that a reviewing court can determine whether the closure order was properly entered." The Government's ongoing anti-terrorism investigation certainly implicates a compelling interest. However, the Creppy directive is neither narrowly tailored, nor does it require particularized findings. Therefore, it impermissibly infringes on the Newspaper Plaintiffs' First Amendment right of access.

a. *The Government Cites Compelling Interests*

We do not agree with the district court that the Government failed to demonstrate that there are compelling interests sufficient to justify closure. The Government contends that "closure of removal proceedings in special interest cases is necessary to protect national security by safeguarding the Government's investigation of the September 11 terrorist attack and other terrorist conspiracies."

Before the district court, the Government provided the affidavit of James S. Reynolds, Chief of the Terrorism and Violent Crimes Section, to explain the

types of information that public access to removal proceedings would disclose. In his affidavit, Mr. Reynolds explained the rationale for prohibiting public access to the proceedings as follows:

1. "Disclosing the names of 'special interest' detainees . . . could lead to public identification of individuals associated with them, other investigative sources, and potential witnesses . . . and terrorist organizations . . . could subject them to intimidation or harm . . . ."

2. "Divulging the detainees' identities may deter them from cooperating [and] . . . terrorist organizations with whom they have connection may refuse to deal further with them, . . ." thereby eliminating valuable sources of information for the Government and impairing its ability to infiltrate terrorist organizations.

3. "Releasing the names of the detainees . . . would reveal the direction and progress of the investigation . . ." and "official verification that a member [of a terrorist organization] has been detained and therefore can no longer carry out the plans of his terrorist organization may enable the organization to find a substitute who can achieve its goals . . . ."

4. "Public release of names, and place and date of arrest . . . could allow terrorist organizations and others to interfere with the pending proceedings by creating false or misleading evidence."

5. "The closure directive is justified by the need to avoid stigmatizing 'special interest' detainees, who may ultimately be found to have no connection to terrorism . . . ."

Although the district court specifically invited the Government to articulate any other basis for closing Haddad's deportation hearing, the Government provided the district court no other reasons for closure.

The Government certainly has a compelling interest in preventing terrorism. In addition to Mr. Reynold's affidavit, other affidavits have been provided that justify the Government's interest in closure. According to the additional affidavits, public access to removal proceedings would disclose the following information that would impede the Government's investigation:

"Bits and pieces of information that may appear innocuous in isolation," but used by terrorist groups to help form a "bigger picture" of the Government's terrorism investigation, would be disclosed. The Government describes this type of intelligence gathering as "akin to the construction of a mosaic," where an individual piece of information is not of obvious importance until pieced together with other pieces of information.

The identifications of the detainees, witnesses, and investigative sources would be disclosed. Terrorist groups could subject these individuals or their families to intimidation or harm and discourage them from cooperating with the Government.

Methods of entry to the country, communicating, or funding could be revealed. This information could allow terrorist organizations to alter their patterns of activity to find the most effective means of evading detection.

"Information that is *not* presented at the hearings also might provide important clues to terrorist, because it could reveal what the investigation has not yet discovered." The Government provides this example: "If the government discloses the evidence it has about a particular member of a terrorist organization, but fails to mention that the detainee is involved in an impending attack, the other members of the organization may be able to infer that the government is not yet aware of the attack."

Inasmuch as these agents' declarations establish that certain information revealed during removal proceedings could impede the ongoing anti-terrorism investigation, we defer to their judgment. These agents are certainly in a better position to understand the contours of the investigation and the intelligence capabilities of terrorist organizations. *Cf. CIA v. Sims,* 471 U.S. 159, 180 (1985) (stating that "it is the responsibility of the Director of Central Intelligence, not that of the judiciary, to weigh the variety of complex and subtle factors in determining whether the disclosure of information may lead to unacceptable risk of compromising the Agency's intelligence-gathering process.").

b. *The Creppy Directive Does Not Require Particularized Findings*

Although the Government is able to demonstrate a compelling interest for closure, the immigration judge, Defendant Hacker, failed to make specific findings before closing Haddad's deportation proceedings. *Press-Enterprise II* instructs that in cases where partial or complete closure is warranted, there must be specific findings on the record so that a reviewing court can determine whether closure was proper and whether less restrictive alternatives exist. Similarly, the Creppy directive fails this requirement.

c. *The Creppy Directive is Not Narrowly Tailored*

Finally, the blanket closure rule mandated by the Creppy directive is not narrowly tailored. The Government offers no persuasive argument as to why the Government's concerns cannot be addressed on a case-by-case basis. The Newspaper Plaintiffs argue, and the district court agreed, that the Creppy directive is ineffective in achieving its purported goals because the detainees and their lawyers are allowed to publicize the proceedings. According to the Newspaper Plaintiffs, to the extent that Haddad had discussed his proceedings (and disclosed documents) with family, friends and the media, the information that the Government seeks to protect is disclosed to the public anyway. We are not persuaded by the Government's argument in response that few detainees will disclose any information and that their disclosure will be less than complete public access. This contention is, at best, speculative and belies the Government's assertion that *any* information disclosed, even bits and pieces that seem innocuous, will be detrimental to the anti-terrorism investigation.

It is clear that certain types of information that the Government seeks to keep confidential could be kept from the public on a case-by-case basis through protective orders or in camera review – for example, the identification of investigative sources and witnesses. The Government, however, argues that it is impossible to keep some sensitive information confidential if any portion of a hearing is open or if the immigration court conducts a hearing to determine if closure is proper. Stated differently, the Government argues that there is

sensitive information that would be disclosed if closure occurred on a case-by-case basis. First, the Government contends that the identities of the detainees would be revealed if closure occurred on a case-by-case basis, and such information would impede the anti-terrorism investigation. This information, however, is already being disclosed to the public through the detainees themselves or their counsel. Even if, as a result of the interim rule, a detainee remains silent, a terrorist group capable of sophisticated intelligence-gathering would certainly be made aware that one of its operatives, or someone connected to a particular terrorist plot, has disappeared into the Government's custody. Moreover, if a deportee does have links to terrorist organizations, there is nothing to stop that deportee from divulging the information learned from these proceedings once deported.

Next, the Government argues that open hearings would reveal the amount of intelligence that the Government does not possess. The Government argues that evidence concerning a particular detainee could be incomplete, and an incomplete presentation of evidence would permit terrorists groups to gauge how much the Government knows and does not know about their operations. The issue in a removal hearing is, however, narrowly focused and the Government has enormous control over what evidence it introduces. "To deport an overstay, the INS must convince the immigration judge by clear and convincing evidence that the alien was admitted as a non-immigrant for a specific period, that the period has elapsed, and that the alien is still in this country."

Here, the Government has detained Haddad and instituted removal proceedings based on his overstay of a tourist visa. Thus, the Government need only establish that Haddad obtained a visa, the visa has expired, and that he is still in the country. Very little information is required. The fact that the Government may have to contest the non-citizen's application for discretionary relief is similarly unavailing. At oral argument, it was brought to our attention that Haddad intends to apply for asylum, a form of discretionary relief available to non-citizens in deportations proceedings. We see no reason why, in making its case against the applicant's request for discretionary relief, the Government could not seek to keep confidential, pertinent information, as the need arises.

Finally, the Government seeks to protect from disclosure the bits and pieces of information that seem innocuous in isolation, but when pieced together with other bits and pieces aid in creating a bigger picture of the Government's anti-terrorism investigation, i.e., the "mosaic intelligence." Mindful of the Government's concerns, we must nevertheless conclude that the Creppy directive is over-inclusive. While the risk of "mosaic intelligence" may exist, we do not believe speculation should form the basis for such a drastic restriction of the public's First Amendment rights. Fittingly, in this case, the Government subsequently admitted that there was no information disclosed in any of Haddad's first three hearings that threatened "national security or the safety of the American people." Yet, all these hearings were closed. The only reason offered for closing the hearings has been that the presiding immigration judge was told do it by the chief immigration judge who in turn was told to do it by the Attorney General.

There is no limit to the gov'ts argument

Furthermore, there seems to be no limit to the Government's argument. The Government could use its "mosaic intelligence" argument as a justification to close any public hearing completely and categorically, including criminal proceedings. The Government could operate in virtual secrecy in all matters dealing, even remotely, with "national security," resulting in a wholesale suspension of First Amendment rights. By the simple assertion of "national security," the Government seeks a process where it may, without review, designate certain classes of cases as "special interest cases" and, behind closed doors, adjudicate the merits of these cases to deprive non-citizens of their fundamental liberty interests.

This, we simply may not countenance. A government operating in the shadow of secrecy stands in complete opposition to the society envisioned by the Framers of our Constitution.

H: the Creppy dir. is overly inclusive

In sum, we find that the Government's attempt to establish a narrowly tailored restriction has failed. The Creppy directive is under-inclusive by permitting the disclosure of sensitive information while at the same time drastically restricting First Amendment rights. The directive is over-inclusive by categorically and completely closing all special interest hearings without demonstrating, beyond speculation, that such a closure is absolutely necessary.

Lastly, the public's interests are best served by open proceedings. A true democracy is one that operates on faith – faith that government officials are forthcoming and honest, and faith that informed citizens will arrive at logical conclusions. This is a vital reciprocity that America should not discard in these troubling times. Without question, the events of September 11, 2001, left an indelible mark on our nation, but we as a people are united in the wake of the destruction to demonstrate to the world that we are a country deeply committed to preserving the rights and freedoms guaranteed by our democracy. Today, we reflect our commitment to those democratic values by ensuring that our government is held accountable to the people and that First Amendment rights are not impermissibly compromised. Open proceedings, with a vigorous and scrutinizing press, serve to ensure the durability of our democracy.

NOTES AND QUESTIONS

1. Judge Keith acknowledges the Supreme Court's statement in *Zadvydas* that "it might be deferential in situations involving terrorism. However, nothing in *Zadvydas* indicates that given such a situation, the Court would defer to the political branches' determination of who belongs in that 'small segment of particularly dangerous individuals' without judicial review of the individual circumstances of each case, something that the Creppy directive strikingly lacks." But the judicial review of individual circumstances is precisely what the Government seeks to avoid in order to avoid the "mosaic" problem described in the Reynolds Affidavit. Is the Sixth Circuit simply unwilling to yield to the mosaic issue?

2. The *Zadvydas* dictum regarding an exception for indefinite detention of terrorism suspects was answered in the negative by the British House of Lords decision in *A v. Home Secretary*, p. 601 *infra*.

3. *North Jersey Media Group, Inc. v. Ashcroft*, 308 F.3d 198 (3d Cir. 2002):

[W]e find ourselves in disagreement with the Sixth Circuit. . . . Deportation procedures have been codified for approximately 100 years but, despite their constant reenactment during that time, Congress has never explicitly guaranteed public access. Indeed, deportation cases involving abused alien children are mandatorily closed by statute, and hearings are often conducted in places generally inaccessible to the public. While INS regulations promulgated in 1964 create a rebuttable presumption of openness for most deportation cases, we conclude that a recently-created regulatory presumption of openness with significant statutory exceptions does not present the type of "unbroken, uncontradicted history" that *Richmond Newspapers* and its progeny require to establish a First Amendment right of access.

4. The Sixth Circuit stated, "The Government could use its 'mosaic intelligence' argument as a justification to close any public hearing completely and categorically, including criminal proceedings." The Third Circuit disagrees on the ground that a criminal proceeding would be subject to different standards than a deportation proceeding for reasons of tradition. What is the relevance of this issue, and which court has the better of the argument?

5. The Sixth Circuit responds point by point to each of the Government claims for secrecy and finds that information is already available to the public through the detainee himself. Does it matter whether the disclosure comes from the detainee or from another source? The next case touches the same arguments.

6. Much of the criticism of detention of aliens from Arab countries has alluded to the PATRIOT Act's increase of the time that an alien could be detained for suspicion of visa violations without going before an immigration judge. The Justice Department, in response to inquiries from congressional committees, pointed out that it did not rely on the PATRIOT provisions because pre-existing law already allowed it to hold an alien for visa violations without bail when authorized by an immigration judge.

[B] SECRECY OF DETENTIONS

CENTER FOR NATIONAL SECURITY STUDIES v. U.S. DEPARTMENT OF JUSTICE

331 F.3d 918 (D.C. Cir. 2003)

SENTELLE, Circuit Judge:

Various "public interest" groups (plaintiffs) brought this Freedom of Information Act (FOIA) action against the Department of Justice (DOJ or government) seeking release of information concerning persons detained in the wake of the September 11 terrorist attacks, including: their names, their attorneys, dates of arrest and release, locations of arrest and detention, and reasons for detention. The government objected to release, and asserted numerous exceptions to FOIA requirements in order to justify withholding the information. The parties filed cross-motions for summary judgment. The district

Individuals detained after 9/11. Public Interest group P's seek release of info related to the detainees & their attorneys. Def allowed access to names but no other info. H: All info comes under FOIA 7A exception. P's all theories of 1st A + Const. Amer. also rejected

court ordered release of the names of the detainees and their attorneys, but held that the government could withhold all other detention information pursuant to FOIA Exemption 7(A), which exempts "records or information compiled for law enforcement purposes . . . to the extent that the production" of them "could reasonably be expected to interfere with enforcement proceedings." 5 U.S.C. § 552(b)(7)(A) (2000).

Upon de novo review, we agree with the district court that the detention information is properly covered by Exemption 7(A); but we further hold that Exemption 7(A) justifies withholding the names of the detainees and their attorneys. We also reject plaintiffs' alternate theories that the First Amendment and the common law mandate disclosure of the contested information. We therefore affirm in part, reverse in part, and remand the case to the district court for the entry of a judgment of dismissal.

I. Background

A. The Investigation

Consistent with the mutual decision of the parties to seek resolution to this controversy on summary judgment, the facts are not in serious dispute. In the course of the post-September 11 investigation, the government interviewed over one thousand individuals about whom concern had arisen. The concerns related to some of these individuals were resolved by the interviews, and no further action was taken with respect to them. Other interviews resulted in the interviewees' being detained. As relevant here, these detainees fall into three general categories.

The first category of detainees consists of individuals who were questioned in the course of the investigation and detained by the INS for violation of the immigration laws (INS detainees). INS detainees were initially questioned because there were "indications that they might have connections with, or possess information pertaining to, terrorist activity against the United States including particularly the September 11 attacks and/or the individuals or organizations who perpetrated them." Based on the initial questioning, each INS detainee was determined to have violated immigration law; some of the INS detainees were also determined to "have links to other facets of the investigation." Over 700 individuals were detained on INS charges. As of June 13, 2002, only seventy-four remained in custody. Many have been deported. INS detainees have had access to counsel, and the INS has provided detainees with lists of attorneys willing to represent them, as required by 8 U.S.C. § 1229(b)(2) (2000). INS detainees have had access to the courts to file *habeas corpus* petitions. They have also been free to disclose their names to the public.

The second category of detainees consists of individuals held on federal criminal charges (criminal detainees). The government asserts that none of these detainees can be eliminated as a source of probative information until after the investigation is completed. According to the most recent information released by the Department of Justice, 134 individuals have been detained on federal criminal charges in the post-September 11 investigation; 99 of these have been found guilty either through pleas or trials. While many of the crimes bear no direct connection to terrorism, several criminal detainees have been charged with terrorism-related crimes, and many others have been charged with visa or passport forgery, perjury, identification fraud, and illegal possession of weapons. Zacarias Moussaoui, presently on trial for participating in the September 11 attacks, is among those who were detained on criminal charges.

The third category consists of persons detained after a judge issued a material witness warrant to secure their testimony before a grand jury, pursuant to the material witness statute, 18 U.S.C. § 3144 (2000) (material witness detainees). Each material witness detainee was believed to have information material to the events of September 11. The district courts before which these material witnesses have appeared have issued sealing orders that prohibit the government from releasing any information about the proceedings. The government has not revealed how many individuals were detained on material witness warrants. At least two individuals initially held as material witnesses are now being held for alleged terrorist activity.

[handwritten margin note: (3) Material witness]

The criminal detainees and material witness detainees are free to retain counsel and have been provided court-appointed counsel if they cannot afford representation, as required by the Sixth Amendment to the Constitution. In sum, each of the detainees has had access to counsel, access to the courts, and freedom to contact the press or the public at large.

B. The Litigation

To support its FOIA request, plaintiffs cited press reports about mistreatment of the detainees, which plaintiffs claimed raised serious questions about "deprivations of fundamental due process, including imprisonment without probable cause, interference with the right to counsel, and threats of serious bodily injury."

[handwritten margin note: Π's assert mistreatment]

In response to plaintiffs' FOIA request, the government released some information, but withheld much of the information requested. As to INS detainees, the government withheld the detainees' names, locations of arrest and detention, the dates of release, and the names of lawyers. As to criminal detainees, the government withheld the dates and locations of arrest and detention, the dates of release, and the citizenship status of each detainee. The government withheld all requested information with respect to material witnesses. Although the government has refused to disclose a comprehensive list of detainees' names and other detention information sought by plaintiffs, the government has from time to time publicly revealed names and information of the type sought by plaintiffs regarding a few individual detainees, particularly those found to have some connection to terrorism.

FOIA Exemptions 7(A), 7(C), and 7(F) permit withholding information "compiled for law enforcement purposes" whenever disclosure:

[handwritten margin note: FOIA exceptions]

(A) could reasonably be expected to interfere with enforcement proceedings, . . . (C) could reasonably be expected to constitute an unwarranted invasion of personal privacy, . . . or (F) could reasonably be expected to endanger the life or physical safety of any individual.

As to Exemption 7(A), the declarations state that release of the requested information could hamper the ongoing investigation by leading to the identification of detainees by terrorist groups, resulting in terrorists either intimidating or cutting off communication with the detainees; by revealing the progress and direction of the ongoing investigation, thus allowing terrorists to impede or evade the investigation; and by enabling terrorists to create false or misleading evidence. As to Exemption 7(C), the declarations assert that the detainees have a substantial privacy interest in their names and detention information because release of this information would associate detainees with the September 11 attacks, thus injuring detainees' reputations and possibly endangering detainees' personal safety. Finally, as to Exemption 7(F), the government's declarations contend that release of the information could endanger the public safety by making terrorist attacks more likely and could endanger the safety of individual detainees by making them more vulnerable to attack from terrorist organizations. For these same reasons, the counterterrorism officials state that the names of the detainees' lawyers should also be withheld.

II. The FOIA Claims

A. Names of Detainees

Exemption 7(A) allows an agency to withhold "records or information compiled for law enforcement purposes, but only to the extent that the production of such law enforcement records or information . . . could reasonably be expected to interfere with enforcement proceedings."

In *CIA v. Sims,* 471 U.S. 159 (1985), the Supreme Court examined the CIA's claims that the names and institutional affiliations of certain researchers in a government-sponsored behavior modification program were exempt from disclosure under FOIA Exemption 3. The agency claimed that the information was protected from disclosure by a statute charging the CIA to prevent unauthorized disclosure of "intelligence sources and methods." In accepting the CIA Director's judgment that disclosure would reveal intelligence sources and methods, the Court explained that "the decisions of the Director, who must of course be familiar with 'the whole picture,' as judges are not, are worthy of great deference given the magnitude of the national security interests and potential risks at stake." The Court further held that "it is the responsibility of the Director of Central Intelligence, not that of the judiciary, to weigh the variety of subtle and complex factors in determining whether disclosure of information may lead to an unacceptable risk of compromising the Agency's intelligence-gathering process."

The same is true of the Justice Department officials in charge of the present investigation. In light of the deference mandated by the separation of powers and Supreme Court precedent, we hold that the government's expectation that disclosure of the detainees' names would enable al Qaeda or other terrorist groups to map the course of the investigation and thus develop the means to impede it is reasonable. A complete list of names informing terrorists of every suspect detained by the government at any point during the September 11 investigation would give terrorist organizations a composite picture of the government investigation, and since these organizations would generally know the activities and locations of its members on or about September 11, disclosure would inform terrorists of both the substantive and geographic focus of the investigation. Moreover, disclosure would inform terrorists which of their members were compromised by the investigation, and which were not. This information could allow terrorists to better evade the ongoing investigation and more easily formulate or revise counter-efforts. In short, the "records could reveal much about the focus and scope of the [agency's] investigation, and are thus precisely the sort of information exemption 7(A) allows an agency to keep secret."

disclosure would give too much info to terrorist orgs

As the district court noted, courts have relied on similar mosaic arguments in the context of national security. In *Sims*, for example, the Supreme Court cautioned that "bits and pieces" of data " 'may aid in piecing together bits of other information even when the individual piece is not of obvious importance in itself. '" Thus, "what may seem trivial to the uninformed, may appear of great moment to one who has a broad view of the scene and may put the questioned item of information in its proper context."

mosaic argument

For several reasons, plaintiffs contend that we should reject the government's predictive judgments of the harms that would result from disclosure. First, they argue that terrorist organizations likely already know which of their members have been detained. We have no way of assessing that likelihood. Moreover, even if terrorist organizations know about some of their members who were detained, a complete list of detainees could still have great value in confirming the status of their members. For example, an organization may be unaware of a member who was detained briefly and then released, but remains subject to continuing government surveillance. After disclosure, this detainee could be irreparably compromised as a source of information.

π's argument

More importantly, some detainees may not be members of terrorist organizations, but may nonetheless have been detained on INS or material witness warrants as having information about terrorists. Terrorist organizations are less likely to be aware of such individuals' status as detainees. Such detainees could be acquaintances of the September 11 terrorists, or members of the same community groups or mosques. These detainees, fearing retribution or stigma, would be less likely to cooperate with the investigation if their names are disclosed. Moreover, tracking down the background and location of these detainees could give terrorists insights into the investigation they would otherwise be unlikely to have. After disclosure, terrorist organizations could attempt to intimidate these detainees or their families, or feed the detainees false or misleading information. It is important to remember that many of these detainees have been released at this time and are thus especially vulnerable to intimidation or coercion. While the detainees have been free to disclose their names to the press or public, it is telling that so few have come forward, perhaps for fear of this very intimidation.

In support of this conclusion, we note that the Third Circuit confronted a similar issue involving the INS detainees when it considered the constitutionality of closed deportation hearings in *North Jersey Media Group, Inc. v. Ashcroft,* 308 F.3d 198 (3d Cir. 2002). The court was faced with the same Watson Declaration in evidence here and the same government prediction that harm would result from the disclosure of information about the INS detainees. That court acknowledged that the "representations of the Watson Declaration are to some degree speculative." The court concluded: "To the extent that the Attorney General's national security concerns seem credible, we will not lightly second-guess them." We think the Third Circuit's approach was correct and we follow it here. Inasmuch as the concerns expressed in the government's declarations seem credible – and inasmuch as the declarations were made by counter-terrorism experts with far greater knowledge than this Court – we hold that the disclosure of the names of the detainees could reasonably be expected to interfere with the ongoing investigation.

In upholding the government's invocation of Exemption 7(A), we observe that we are in accord with several federal courts that have wisely respected the executive's judgment in prosecuting the national response to terrorism. We realize that not all courts are in agreement. We do not find the Sixth Circuit's reasoning compelling, but join the Third, Fourth, and Seventh Circuits in holding that the courts must defer to the executive on decisions of national security. In so deferring, we do not abdicate the role of the judiciary. Rather, in undertaking a deferential review we simply recognize the different roles underlying the constitutional separation of powers. It is within the role of the executive to acquire and exercise the expertise of protecting national security. It is not within the role of the courts to second-guess executive judgments made in furtherance of that branch's proper role. The judgment of the district court ordering the government to disclose the names of the detainees is reversed.

B. Identity of Counsel

The government contends that a list of attorneys for the detainees would facilitate the easy compilation of a list of all detainees, and all of the dangers flowing therefrom. It is more than reasonable to assume that plaintiffs and *amici* press organizations would attempt to contact detainees' attorneys and compile a list of all detainees. As discussed above, if such a list fell into the hands of al Qaeda, the consequences could be disastrous.

C. Other Detention Information

As outlined above, plaintiffs sought the dates and locations of arrest, detention, and release for each of the detainees. Even more than disclosure of the identities of detainees, the information requested here would provide a complete roadmap of the government's investigation. Knowing when and where each individual was arrested would provide a chronological and geographical picture of the government investigation. Terrorists could learn from this information not only where the government focused its investigation but how that investigation progressed step by step. Armed with that knowledge, they could then reach such conclusions as, for example, which cells had been compromised, and which individuals had been cooperative with the United States. They might well be able to derive conclusions as to how more adequately [to] secure their clandestine operations in future terrorist undertakings. Similarly, knowing where each individual is presently held could facilitate communication between terrorist organizations and detainees and the attendant intimidation of witnesses and fabrication of evidence. As explained in detail above, these impediments to an ongoing law enforcement investigation are precisely what Exemption 7(A) was enacted to preclude. Accordingly, we affirm the district court and hold that the government properly withheld information about the dates and locations of arrest, detention, and release for each detainee.

III. Alternative Grounds

We turn now to plaintiffs' alternative grounds for seeking disclosure of the detainees' names and detention information. Although FOIA does not mandate disclosure, plaintiffs contend that disclosure is independently required by both the First Amendment and the common law right of access to government information.

We will not convert the First Amendment right of access to criminal judicial proceedings into a requirement that the government disclose information compiled during the exercise of a quintessential executive power – the investigation and prevention of terrorism. The dangers which we have catalogued above of making such release in this case provide ample evidence of the need to follow this course.

We also reject plaintiffs' final claim that disclosure is required by the common law right of access to public records. The Supreme Court held in *Nixon v. Warner Communications, Inc.*, 435 U.S. 589 (1978), that "the courts of this country recognize a general right to inspect and copy public records and documents, including judicial documents." Plaintiffs, citing several state court cases finding a common law right of access to arrest records, urge us to recognize a federal common law right to receive the information they seek. In response, the government claims that the common law right of access is limited to judicial records. Even if the common law right applies to executive records, the government contends, FOIA has displaced the common law right. While we question the government's first contention, we accept its second.

[handwritten margin note: FOIA trumps C Law]

IV. Conclusion

For the reasons set forth above, we conclude that the government was entitled to withhold under FOIA Exemption 7(A) the names of INS detainees and those detained as material witnesses in the course of the post-September 11 terrorism investigation; the dates and locations of arrest, detention, and release of all detainees, including those charged with federal crimes; and the names of counsel for detainees. Finally, neither the First Amendment nor federal common law requires the government to disclose the information sought by plaintiffs.

Affirmed in part, reversed in part and remanded.

TATEL, Circuit Judge, dissenting:

Disregarding settled principles governing the release of government records under the Freedom of Information Act, this court holds that the government may keep secret the names of hundreds of persons whom it has detained in connection with its investigation of the September 11, 2001 terrorist attacks without distinguishing between information that can, in FOIA's words, "reasonably be expected to interfere" with the investigation and information that cannot. While the government's reasons for withholding *some* of the information

[handwritten margin note: Too much deference. Some of the info (names) could have been disclosed.]

may well be legitimate, the court's uncritical deference to the government's vague, poorly explained arguments for withholding broad categories of information about the detainees, as well as its willingness to fill in the factual and logical gaps in the government's case, eviscerates both FOIA itself and the principles of openness in government that FOIA embodies.

The government claims that the detainees have access to counsel and freedom to contact whomever they wish, but the public has a fundamental interest in being able to examine the veracity of such claims. Just as the government has a compelling interest in ensuring citizens' safety, so do citizens have a compelling interest in ensuring that their government does not, in discharging its duties, abuse one of its most awesome powers, the power to arrest and jail.

Invoking the "heightened deference to the judgments of the political branches with respect to matters of national security," the government refuses to identify the specific categories of information that would actually interfere with its investigation, but rather asks us simply to trust its judgment. This court obeys, declaring that "the judiciary is in an extremely poor position to second-guess the executive's judgment in this area of national security." But requiring agencies to make the detailed showing FOIA requires is not second-guessing their judgment about matters within their expertise. And in any event, this court is also in an extremely poor position to second-guess the legislature's judgment that the judiciary must play a meaningful role in reviewing FOIA exemption requests. Neither FOIA itself nor this circuit's interpretation of the statute authorizes the court to invoke the phrase "national security" to relieve the government of its burden of justifying its refusal to release information under FOIA.

The only argument that could conceivably support withholding innocent detainees' names is the assertion that disclosure of the names "*may* reveal details about the focus and scope of the investigation and thereby allow terrorists to counteract it." That Reynolds believes these harms *may* result from disclosure is hardly surprising – anything is possible. But before accepting the government's argument, this court must insist on knowing whether these harms "*could reasonably be expected to*" result from disclosure – the standard Congress prescribed for exemption under 7(A). Nothing in Reynolds's declaration suggests that these harms are in fact reasonably likely to occur.

Although I think it unreasonable to infer that all of the information plaintiffs seek in their FOIA request qualifies for exemption, the government may be able to point to more narrowly defined categories of information that might justify the inference. For example, while nothing in the record supports the government's contention that releasing the names of innocent detainees would harm the investigation, perhaps the government could justify withholding the places of arrest on the ground that such information might provide terrorist organizations with some insight into the government's investigative methods and strategy. I would therefore remand to allow the government to describe, for each detainee or reasonably defined category of detainees, on what basis it may withhold their names and other information.

NOTES AND QUESTIONS

1. The Sixth Circuit thought that a detainee's ability to communicate with the public was a good reason for opening deportation hearings. The D.C. Circuit thinks that the same ability is an argument for not requiring government disclosure of information to the public. The difference apparently lies in the manner in which information would become available pursuant to a FOIA request: "even if terrorist organizations know about some of their members who were detained, a complete list of detainees could still have great value in confirming the status of their members. For example, an organization may be unaware of a member who was detained briefly and then released, but remains subject to continuing government surveillance."

2. Judge Tatel and the majority disagree about application of "deference" in the context of terrorism investigations. The heart of the difference seems to be Judge Tatel's view that "requiring agencies to make the detailed showing FOIA requires is not second-guessing their judgment about matters within their expertise." But it is a detailed showing that the Government says would be harmful to matters within its expertise. This is very similar to the disagreement between the Sixth and Third Circuits over the question of making individualized decisions on closing deportation hearings. Thus, the dilemma of how to monitor critical aspects of government behavior in a free society while still protecting the public from unknown risks is highlighted again by these differences of opinion.

Note on Material Witness Warrants

Material witness warrants are an important tool of criminal procedure that are mostly beyond the scope of this course, but which along with grand jury subpoenas make some of the more controversial aspects of PATRIOT virtually irrelevant. A material witness warrant is issued by a judge or magistrate under conditions similar to an arrest warrant but the purpose is to secure that person's testimony rather than to hold the person for trial.

The Justice Department stated to Congress in May 2003 that less than 50 persons had been detained on material witness warrants "in the course of the September 11 investigation." Of those, all but about 5 were "detained for 90 days or less."

The D.C. Circuit in the FOIA case says that even material witness warrants allow the detainee to contact the press. That assumes, of course, that their custodians provide the mechanism to do so. The court notes that two former material witnesses were being held at that time "for alleged terrorist activity." Jose Padilla has been held incommunicado for extended periods of time without the filing of any charges against him, initially as a material witness then as an enemy combatant. Ali alMarri was originally charged with perjury, then detained as an enemy combatant. I do not know who is the other person to whom the court refers in this statement. Because the Government has refused to detail the number of persons held on material witness warrants and the length of time held, on the ground that grand jury proceedings are secret for several reasons, there are a number of advocacy groups expressing deep suspicion about abuse of the material witness warrant in this context.

In *United States v. Awadallah*, 349 F.3d 4 (2d Cir. 2003), Osama Awadallah was taken into custody in Los Angeles after his name and phone number were found on a gum wrapper in the car of one of the 9/11 hijackers. He was detained on a material witness warrant and flown to New York where he testified twice before a grand jury over the course of several weeks. He admitted knowing one of the hijackers but first denied knowing a second one whom he later remembered. Charged with perjury for the first statement, he moved to dismiss the indictment for abuse of the material witness statute. The district judge held that "no Congress has granted the government the authority to imprison an innocent person in order to guarantee that he will testify before a grand jury conducting a criminal investigation. Because Awadallah was unlawfully detained, his grand jury testimony must be suppressed. The indictment is therefore dismissed." The Second Circuit reversed, holding that obtaining grand jury testimony would be an appropriate use of the material witness statute:

> The district court noted (and we agree) that it would be improper for the government to use § 3144 for other ends, such as the detention of persons suspected of criminal activity for which probable cause has not yet been established. However, the district court made no finding (and we see no evidence to suggest) that the government arrested Awadallah for any purpose other than to secure information material to a grand jury investigation. Moreover, that grand jury was investigating the September 11 terrorist attacks. The particular governmental interests at stake therefore were the indictment and successful prosecution of terrorists whose attack, if committed by a sovereign, would have been tantamount to war, and the discovery of the conspirators' means, contacts, and operations in order to forestall future attacks.

See Robert Boyle, *The Material Witness Statute Post September 11: What It Should Not Include Grand Jury Witnesses*, 48 N.Y.L.S. L. REV. 13 (2003).

§ 7.03 PATRIOT AND INDIVIDUAL PRIVACY

Some advocacy groups objected vociferously to various provisions of PATRIOT.

- The American Library Association complained particularly about the ability of investigators to acquire business records from public entities. In particular, librarians objected to allowing access to circulation records that would show which patrons have been reading which books and to pen registers that would show the websites accessed from library computers by public patrons. The ALA has worried that this could become a concern of constitutional dimension through the first amendment.
  See http://www.ala.org/ala/oif/ifissues/fbiyourlibrary.htm.

- The American Civil Liberties Union objected to many aspects of PATRIOT under the general statement that "without a warrant and without probable cause, the FBI now has the power to access your most private" records.
  See http://www.aclu.org/safeandfree/SafeandFree.cfm?ID=12126&c=207.

- The Electronic Privacy Information Center has lobbied and litigated against provisions of PATRIOT having to do with interception of electronic communications. *See http://www.epic.org/privacy/terrorism/usapatriot/*

- PATRIOT split some segments of the conservative side of the political spectrum. The American Conservative magazine came out strongly against PATRIOT and what it viewed as the departure of Attorney General Ashcroft from his prior stands in favor of privacy. *See http://www.amconmag.com/05_19_03/cover.html*. The Gun Owners of America argued aggressively against PATRIOT and any extension of it. *See http://gunowners.org/patriotii.htm*

In response to criticisms of these "invasions of privacy," government spokespersons have put forward several versions of this basic argument. "The war on terrorism is difficult and life-threatening, we need to keep our actions and techniques secret so the terrorists can't track our investigations, the citizenry and courts should trust us because we can't explain in public all that we need to do, and many of the records we need (such as internet communications or library circulation records) involve semi-public (or at least non-private) transactions anyway." In various political statements, Justice Department spokespersons touted the advantages of PATRIOT as providing tools for law enforcement "without modifying the substance" of pre-existing statutory restraints on government action.

One of the complaints of the advocacy groups is that it will be difficult to obtain judicial review of these provisions because the information collected through these devices may never be used in a prosecution. Instead, it could sit in government files for potential misuse at a future date or could be the basis for further investigations that ultimately result in prosecutions in which this information is neither incriminating nor exculpatory, so it is never introduced as evidence.

In this section, we will look at government demands for information, the § 215 seizure of records, and secrecy of government operations related to counter-terrorism.

[A] ACCESS TO THIRD-PARTY RECORDS

[handwritten: π/(ACLU + unnamed ISP)]

DOE v. ASHCROFT
334 F. Supp. 2d 471 (S.D.N.Y. 2004)

MARRERO, Dist. Judge:

I. INTRODUCTION

Plaintiffs in this case challenge the constitutionality of 18 U.S.C. § 2709. That statute authorizes the Federal Bureau of Investigation ("FBI") to compel communications firms, such as internet service providers ("ISPs") or telephone companies, to produce certain customer records whenever the FBI certifies that those records are "relevant to an authorized investigation to protect against international terrorism or clandestine intelligence activities." The FBI's demands under § 2709 are issued in the form of national security letters

[handwritten right margin: Issue is constitutionality of using NSLs to obtain customer records from ISP + phone cos]

[handwritten bottom: Held: § 2709 violates the 4th + 1st A. Ct notes the lack of clarity in the statute which would require it to read too much into it (Can recipient consult a lawyer, what are the penalties, can there be Judicial review?). 1st A: few statutes have the provision for complete non-disclosure.]

("NSLs"), which constitute a unique form of administrative subpoena cloaked in secrecy and pertaining to national security issues. The statute bars all NSL recipients from ever disclosing that the FBI has issued an NSL.

The lead plaintiff, called "John Doe" ("Doe")[3] for purposes of this litigation, is described in the complaint as an internet access firm that received an NSL. The other plaintiffs are the American Civil Liberties Union ("ACLU") and the American Civil Liberties Union Foundation, which is also acting as counsel to Doe (collectively with Doe, "Plaintiffs"). Plaintiffs contend that § 2709's broad subpoena power violates the First, Fourth and Fifth Amendments of the United States Constitution, and that the non-disclosure provision violates the First Amendment. The parties have cross-moved for summary judgment on all claims.

For the reasons explained below, the Court grants Plaintiffs' motion. The Court concludes that § 2709 violates the Fourth Amendment because, at least as currently applied, it effectively bars or substantially deters any judicial challenge to the propriety of an NSL request. In the Court's view, ready availability of judicial process to pursue such a challenge is necessary to vindicate important rights guaranteed by the Constitution or by statute. On separate grounds, the Court also concludes that the permanent ban on disclosure contained in § 2709(c), which the Court is unable to sever from the remainder of the statute, operates as an unconstitutional prior restraint on speech in violation of the First Amendment.

Considering the implications of its ruling and the importance of the issues involved, the Court will stay enforcement of its judgment for 90 days, pending appeal or measures by the Government otherwise to address the flaws in the structure and implementation of § 2709 described here.

II. BACKGROUND

National security is a paramount value, unquestionably one of the highest purposes for which any sovereign government is ordained. Equally scaled among human endeavors is personal security, an interest especially prized in our system of justice in the form of the guarantee bestowed upon the individual to be free from imposition by government of unwarranted restraints on protected fundamental rights. Efficiency, too, counts as a basic value, though it essentially serves as a tool in the service of other interests. To perform its national security functions properly, government must be empowered to respond promptly and effectively to public exigencies as they arise, and in pursuit of those necessary actions to maintain a reasonable measure of secrecy surrounding its operations and methods.

On this point, the United States Supreme Court has imparted consistent guidance, drawn on each occasion from adjudications of the some of the most intense crises in the nation's history. Recently, for example, in addressing the reach of the President's authority to combat terrorism, the Supreme Court

---

[3] By Order dated May 12, 2004, the Court granted the Government's motion to seal the record of this proceeding so as to preclude the disclosure of Doe's identity and other facts relating to Doe's role in this controversy that might identify Doe or otherwise interfere with the underlying FBI activities giving rise to this case.

declared: "We have long . . . made clear that a state of war is not a blank check for the President when it comes to the rights of the nation's citizens." [*Hamdi*]

A. DOE'S RECEIPT OF AN NSL

After receiving a call from an FBI agent informing him that he would be served with an NSL, Doe received a document, printed on FBI letterhead, which stated that, "pursuant to Title 18, United States Code (U.S.C.), Section 2709" Doe was "directed" to provide certain information to the Government. As required by the terms of § 2709, in the NSL the FBI "certified that the information sought [was] relevant to an authorized investigation to protect against international terrorism or clandestine intelligence activities." Doe was "further advised" that § 2709(c) prohibited him, or his officers, agents, or employees, "from disclosing to any person that the FBI has sought or obtained access to information or records under these provisions." Doe was "requested to provide records responsive to [the] request personally" to a designated individual, and to not transmit the records by mail or even mention the NSL in any telephone conversation.

After a subsequent conversation with the same FBI agent, Doe decided to consult ACLU lawyers. The parties dispute the nature of Doe's exchange with the FBI agent, though it is ultimately immaterial to this motion. Doe contends that the agent gave him permission to speak with an attorney; the agent claims that Doe merely informed the agent that he (Doe) would be consulting an attorney. Doe has not complied with the NSL request, and has instead engaged counsel to bring the present lawsuit.

B. § 2709 IN GENERAL

As stated above, § 2709 authorizes the FBI to issue NSLs to compel communications firms to produce certain customer records whenever the FBI certifies, that those records are relevant to an authorized international terrorism or counterintelligence investigation, and the statute also categorically bars NSL recipients from disclosing the inquiry. In relevant part, it states:

(a) Duty to provide. A wire or electronic communication service provider shall comply with a request for subscriber information and toll billing records information, or electronic communication transactional records in its custody or possession made by the Director of the Federal Bureau of Investigation under subsection (b) of this section.

(b) Required certification. The Director of the Federal Bureau of Investigation, or his designee in a position not lower than Deputy Assistant Director at Bureau headquarters or a Special Agent in Charge in a Bureau field office designated by the Director, may

(1) request the name, address, length of service, and local and long distance toll billing records of a person or entity if the Director (or his designee) certifies in writing to the wire or electronic communication service provider to which the request is made that the name, address, length of service, and toll billing records sought are relevant to an authorized investigation to protect against international terrorism or clandestine intelligence activities, provided that such an investigation of

a United States person is not conducted solely on the basis of activities protected by the first amendment to the Constitution of the United States; and

(2) request the name, address, and length of service of a person or entity if the Director (or his designee) certifies in writing to the wire or electronic communication service provider to which the request is made that the information sought is relevant to an authorized investigation to protect against international terrorism or clandestine intelligence activities, provided that such an investigation of a United States person is not conducted solely upon the basis of activities protected by the first amendment to the Constitution of the United States.

(c) Prohibition of certain disclosure. No wire or electronic communication service provider, or officer, employee, or agent thereof, shall disclose to any person that the Federal Bureau of Investigation has sought or obtained access to information or records under this section.

Subsection (d) limits the FBI's ability to disseminate information collected from an NSL, and subsection (e) requires the FBI to periodically report to Congress about its use of NSLs.

Section 2709 is one of only a handful of statutes authorizing the Government to issue NSLs. The other NSL statutes authorize the Government to compel disclosure of certain financial and credit records which it certifies are relevant to international terrorism or counterintelligence investigations, and to compel disclosure of certain records of current or former government employees who have (or have had) access to classified information.[17]

C. LEGISLATIVE HISTORY

Section 2709 was enacted as part of Title II of the Electronic Communications Privacy Act of 1986 ("ECPA"), which sought to "protect privacy interests" in "stored wire and electronic communications" while also "protecting the Government's legitimate law enforcement needs." Congress modeled Title II of the ECPA upon the Right to Financial Privacy Act ("RFPA") of 1978, which espoused similar privacy goals for financial records. The RFPA was an explicit "response to the Supreme Court decision in *United States v. Miller* which held that a customer of a financial institution has no standing under the [Fourth Amendment] to contest government access to financial records."

Generally speaking, Title II (as amended) allows the Government to obtain stored electronic communications information without the subscriber's permission only through compulsory process, such as a subpoena, warrant, or court order. Section 2709 is a notable exception to these privacy protections because it permits the FBI to request records upon a mere self-certification – issued to the ISP or telephone company, not to the subscriber or to any court – that its request complies with the statutory requirements. As first enacted, § 2709 required electronic communication service providers to produce "subscriber

---

[17] *See* 12 U.S.C. § 3414 (financial records); 15 U.S.C. § § 1681u, 1681v (credit records); 50 U.S.C. § 436 (government employee records).

information," "toll billing records information," or "electronic communication transactional records," upon the FBI's internal certification that (1) the information was "relevant to an authorized foreign counterintelligence investigation" and that (2) there were "specific and articulable facts giving reason to believe that the person or entity to whom the information sought pertains [was] a foreign power or an agent of a foreign power."

what FBI had to certify originally

Before the ECPA, the FBI had been issuing non-mandatory NSLs to communications providers, who, in most cases, complied voluntarily. However, because carriers in states with strict privacy laws had recently been resisting those requests, the FBI sought to have mandatory, preemptive federal legislation supporting its issuance of NSLs.

In 1993, Congress broadened § 2709 by relaxing the required nexus to a foreign power. The amended statute allowed the FBI to obtain records "where: (1) there is a contact with a suspected intelligence officer or a suspected terrorist, or (2) the circumstances of the conversation indicate . . . that it may involve spying or an offer of information."

The next and most recent major revision to § 2709 occurred in October 2001, as part of the USA PATRIOT Act of 2001 ("Patriot Act"). In short, the Patriot Act removed the previous requirement that § 2709 inquiries have a nexus to a foreign power, replacing that prerequisite with a broad standard of relevance to investigations of terrorism or clandestine intelligence activities.

Patriot Act amendment

D. NSLs AND OTHER INFORMATION-GATHERING AUTHORITY

It is instructive to place the Government's NSL authority in the context of other means by which the Government gathers information of the type covered by § 2709 because Congress (in passing and amending the NSL statutes) and the parties here (in contesting § 2709's constitutionality) have drawn analogies to those other authorities as grounds for or against its validity.

1. Administrative Subpoenas

The most important set of statutes relevant to this case are those authorizing federal agencies to issue administrative subpoenas for the purpose of executing the particular agency's function. Ordinary administrative subpoenas, which are far more common than NSLs, may be issued by most federal agencies, as authorized by the hundreds of applicable statutes in federal law. For example, the Internal Revenue Service (IRS) may issue subpoenas to investigate possible violations of the tax code, and the Securities Exchange Commission (SEC) may issue subpoenas to investigate possible violations of the securities laws.

There is a wide body of law which pertains to administrative subpoenas generally. According to the Government's central theory in this case, those standing rules would presumably also apply to NSLs, even if not so explicitly stated in the text of the statute. Where an agency seeks a court order to enforce a subpoena against a resisting subpoena recipient, courts will enforce the subpoena as long as: (1) the agency's investigation is being conducted pursuant to a legitimate purpose, (2) the inquiry is relevant to that purpose, (3) the information is not already within the agency's possession, and (4) the proper procedures have been followed. The Second Circuit has described these

Subpoenas standing up to a challenge

standards as "minimal." Even if an administrative subpoena meets these initial criteria to be enforceable, its recipient may nevertheless affirmatively challenge the subpoena on other grounds, such as an allegation that it was issued with an improper purpose or that the information sought is privileged.

Even absent a particular secrecy statute, someone who, with the intent to obstruct an investigation, alerts the target of an investigation that a subpoena has been issued could theoretically face criminal obstruction of justice charges under a federal statute that imposes criminal sanctions upon any person who, among other things, "corruptly endeavors to influence, obstruct, or impede the due and proper administration of the law under which any pending proceeding is being had before any department or agency of the United States."

2. Subpoena Authority in the Criminal Context

In its role as a party to a federal criminal proceeding (including a grand jury proceeding), the Government has broad authority to issue a subpoena to obtain witness testimony or "any books, papers, documents, data, or other objects the subpoena designates." Although such subpoenas "are issued in the name of the district court over the signature of the clerk, they are issued pro forma and in blank to anyone requesting them," and the "court exercises no prior control whatsoever upon their use."

The court becomes involved in the subpoena process only if the subpoenaed party moves to quash the request as "unreasonable or oppressive," or if the Government seeks to compel compliance with the subpoena. The reasonableness of a subpoena depends on the context. For example, to survive a motion to quash, a subpoena issued in connection with a criminal trial "must make a reasonably specific request for information that would be both relevant and admissible at trial." By contrast, a grand jury subpoena is generally enforced as long as there is a "reasonable possibility that the category of materials the Government seeks will produce information relevant to the general subject of the grand jury's investigation." Considering the grand jury's broad investigatory power and minimal court supervision, it is accurate to observe, as the Second Circuit did long ago, that "basically the grand jury is a law enforcement agency."

While materials presented in a criminal trial setting are generally public, the federal rules impose stringent secrecy requirements on certain grand jury participants, including the attorneys, court reporters, and grand jurors. Those secrecy rules make no mention of a subpoena recipient or a witness, both of whom are ordinarily free to disclose to anyone the fact that a subpoena was issued or the contents of any information supplied. Some courts have nevertheless permitted the Government to impose a secrecy obligation upon witnesses in cases of compelling need. The Eleventh Circuit, for example, has held that a district court's authority to protect the integrity of grand jury process gave it power to prevent witnesses from disclosing materials prepared for or testimony given in grand jury proceedings. As an exception to this rule, officers of financial institutions and insurance companies face criminal penalties for disclosing, with the intent to obstruct a judicial proceeding, either the fact that a grand jury subpoena has been issued or its contents. More generally, a subpoena recipient who, with the intent to obstruct a criminal investigation, alerts the target of an investigation that a subpoena had 'been issued could theoretically face criminal obstruction of justice charges.

In certain contexts, the Government may issue subpoenas related to criminal investigations even without initiating a formal criminal proceeding. For example, the United States Attorney General is authorized to issue administrative subpoenas, without convening a grand jury, to investigate federal narcotics crimes, racketeering crimes, health care related crimes, and crimes involving the exploitation of children. In each of these instances, the administrative process is governed by the general rules described above, providing safeguards of judicial review.

3. Background Rules Governing Disclosure of Stored Electronic Communications

Title II of the ECPA, in which § 2709 was enacted, sets forth an intricate framework by which electronic communications providers, such as ISPs and phone companies, may be compelled to disclose stored electronic information to the Government. The framework described below operates independently of the rules governing NSLs issued pursuant to § 2709, but may aid with interpretation of § 2709.

The Government may obtain basic subscriber information[69] merely by issuing an authorized administrative subpoena, trial subpoena, or grand jury subpoena, and the Government need not notify the subscriber of the request.

If the Government gives prior notice to the subscriber, or otherwise complies with certain delayed notice procedures, the Government may also subpoena the contents of electronic communications which are either (1) retained on a system for storage purposes (e.g., opened email which remains on an ISP's server), or (2) retained, for more than 180 days, in intermediate or temporary storage (e.g., unopened email on an ISP's server). For the Government to obtain the contents of electronic communications kept for 180 days or less in intermediate or temporary storage (e.g., unopened email on an ISP's server), it must obtain a search warrant under Federal Rule of Criminal Procedure 41, or the state equivalent. In other words, the Government would have to appear before a neutral magistrate and make a showing of probable cause. The Government may also obtain a court order requiring an electronic communications service provider to turn over transactional and content information by setting forth "specific and articulable facts showing that there are reasonable grounds to believe that" the information sought is "relevant and material to an ongoing criminal investigation."

The ECPA permits the Government to seek a court order prohibiting the communications provider from revealing the Government's inquiry "for such

---

[69] Basic subscriber information includes: (1) a subscriber's name and (2) address; (3) the subscriber's local and long distance telephone connection records, or records of session times and durations; (4) the subscriber's length of service and types of service he has utilized; (5) any telephone or instrument number or other subscriber number or identity, including any temporarily assigned network address; and (6) the subscriber's means and source of payment for the service. *See* 18 U.S.C. § 2703(c)(2).

period as the court deems appropriate" if the court determines that such disclosure, among other things, would result in "destruction of or tampering with evidence" or "seriously jeopardizing an investigation or unduly delaying a trial."

4. Mail

Government law enforcement agencies are authorized to request the Postal Inspector to initiate a so-called "mail cover" to obtain any information appearing on the outside of a particular piece of mail. Among other grounds, the law enforcement agency can obtain a mail cover by "specify[ing] the reasonable grounds to demonstrate the mail cover is necessary" to "protect the national security" or to "obtain information regarding the commission or attempted commission of a crime." There is no requirement that the mail sender or recipient be notified of the mail cover.

The Government must obtain a warrant based upon probable cause to open and inspect sealed mail because the contents of mail are protected by the Fourth Amendment. As the Supreme Court established long ago: "Whilst in the mail, [a person's papers] can only be opened and examined under like warrant, issued upon similar oath or affirmation, particularly describing the thing to be seized, as is required when papers are subjected to search in one's own household."

5. Pen Registers and Trap and Trace Devices

Pen registers and trap and trace devices record certain electronic communications data indicating the origins and destinations of various "dialing, routing, addressing, or signaling information," e.g., the phone numbers dialed to and from a telephone. [18 U.S.C. § 3127(3)-(4)] In criminal investigations, the Government must apply for a court order, renewable in 60-day increments, to install or collect data from such devices, though the standard for issuing such an order is relatively low. [*See id.* § 3123(d)] The Government need only show that "the information likely to be obtained by such installation and use is relevant to an ongoing criminal investigation." [*Id.* § 3123(a)]

The person owning the communications device is prohibited, unless otherwise directed by court order, from disclosing the fact that a pen register or trap and trace device is in effect.

6. Wiretaps and Electronic Eavesdropping

The Fourth Amendment protects against warrantless Government wiretapping. Federal legislation specifies the procedures by which law enforcement officials may obtain a court order to conduct wiretaps and other forms of electronic eavesdropping. [18 U.S.C. §§ 2516-18] The requirements are rigorous. Among other things, the Government must show that: (1) "there is probable cause for belief that an individual is committing, has committed, or is about to commit" one of a list of enumerated crimes; (2) "there is probable cause for belief that particular communications concerning that offense will be obtained through such interception"; and (3) "normal investigative procedures have been tried and have failed or reasonably appear to be unlikely to succeed if tried or to be too dangerous." Such orders are not available "for any period longer than is necessary to achieve the objective of the authorization," subject to a renewable maximum of 30 days. The communications provider is prohibited from disclosing that a wiretap or electronic surveillance is in place, "except as may otherwise be required by legal process and then only after prior notification" to the appropriate law enforcement authorities.

7. Foreign Intelligence Surveillance Act

The Foreign Intelligence Surveillance Act of 1978 ("FISA") establishes standards for the Government's domestic electronic surveillance of foreign governments and their agents. The Government may conduct such surveillance, even without a court order, as long as the Attorney General certifies, among other things, that: (1) the communications at issue would be "exclusively between or among foreign powers" or involve "the acquisition of technical intelligence, other than the spoken communications of individuals, from property or premises under the open and exclusive control of a foreign power"; (2) "there is no substantial likelihood that the surveillance will acquire the contents of any communication to which a United States person is a party"; and (3) the Government will apply certain so-called "minimization procedures" to limit the possibility of impermissible collateral surveillance. In such circumstances, the Attorney General may direct the communications provider to cooperate "in such a manner as will protect [the] secrecy" of the surveillance.

To conduct any broader types of surveillance, the Government must obtain a formal order from a special FISA-created court. The application must specify, among other things, the type of surveillance proposed, the facts supporting the Government's belief that the surveillance pertains to a foreign power, and the minimization procedures which would be taken. The Government must also certify "that a significant purpose of the surveillance is to obtain foreign intelligence information" and that the "information cannot reasonably be obtained by normal investigative techniques." Before issuing the surveillance order, the FISA court must find, among other things, that there is "probable cause to believe" that the surveillance target is a foreign power or a foreign agent, that the proposed minimization procedures meet the statutory requirements, and, if the target is a United States person, that the facts in the Government's certification are not clearly erroneous.

FISA surveillance orders are issued only "for the period necessary to achieve [the] purpose" of the application, with an extendable maximum of either 90 days, 120 days, or one year, depending on the nature of the surveillance target. The court's order may direct a communications provider to cooperate "in such a manner as will protect [the] secrecy" of the surveillance.

The FISA also authorizes the Government to apply to the FISA court "for an order requiring the production of any tangible things (including books, records, papers, documents, and other items) for an investigation to obtain foreign intelligence information not concerning a United States person or to protect against international terrorism or clandestine intelligence activities . . . ." Such an application need only specify that the inquiry is part of an authorized investigation and in accordance with the appropriate guidelines. Recipients of such an order are prohibited from disclosing to anyone (except those whose assistance is necessary to comply with the subpoena) that the inquiry was made.

Finally, FISA authorizes the Government to apply to the FISA court for a an order, renewable in 90-day increments, to install a pen register or trap and trace device as part of "any investigation to obtain foreign intelligence information not concerning a United States person or to protect against international terrorism or clandestine intelligence activities." The Government need only certify to the court that it will likely obtain information relevant to a proper inquiry. Just as in the criminal context, the person owning the communications device is prohibited, unless otherwise directed by court order, from disclosing the fact that a pen register or trap and trace device is in effect.

IV. DISCUSSION

A. SECTION 2709, AS DRAFTED, RAISES SERIOUS CONSTITUTIONAL QUESTIONS

The NSL statutes, particularly § 2709, present interpretive challenges in at least three respects, the first two of which have a direct bearing on the motions now before the Court. First, while two of the NSL statutes explicitly state that an NSL recipient may disclose the Government's inquiry to persons whose assistance is necessary to comply with the demands of the NSL, the other statutes, including § 2709, appear by their telltale silence on that point, to preclude any disclosures. None of the statutes explain whether consulting an attorney constitutes disclosure, even where an attorney's assistance may be necessary for a recipient to comply with an NSL, and none of the statutes states whether the ban on disclosure may ever be lifted by a court. Second, the statutes contain no explicit provision for the Government to seek judicial enforcement of an NSL against a recipient who refuses to comply, nor is there any provision expressly authorizing an NSL recipient to affirmatively challenge, administratively or judicially, the propriety of an NSL request. Third, there is no explicit provision in the statutes imposing penalties against a person who fails to comply with an NSL.

Several bills pending in Congress demonstrate Congress's and the Government's recognition that the NSL statutes could have been drafted with greater particularity and uniformity. [One] would address two of the issues listed above by explicitly providing for judicial enforcement of NSLs and by imposing criminal penalties of up to five years' imprisonment for persons who unlawfully disclose that they have received an NSL.

As explained below, even if the Court were to agree with the Government that § 2709 should be read to allow: (1) an NSL recipient to consult with an attorney and others necessary to enable compliance with the letter; and (2) an NSL recipient to challenge, or the Government to enforce, an NSL in court, the Court would still hold that the statute, as currently applied by the FBI, exerts an undue coercive effect on NSL recipients. The form language of the NSL served upon Doe, preceded by an FBI phone call, directed him to personally provide the information to the FBI, prohibited him, his officers, agents or employees, from disclosing the existence of the NSL to anyone, and made no mention of the availability of judicial review to quash or otherwise modify the NSL or the secrecy mandated by the letter. Nor did the FBI inform Doe personally that any such judicial review of the issuance of the NSL or the secrecy attaching to it was available. The Court concludes that, when combined, these provisions and practices essentially force the reasonable NSL recipient to immediately comply with the request.

unduly
coercive

B. AS APPLIED HERE, SECTION 2709 LACKS PROCEDURAL PROTECTIONS NECESSARY TO VINDICATE CONSTITUTIONAL RIGHTS

1. Section 2709 And The Fourth Amendment[118]

The Fourth Amendment prohibits the Government from conducting "unreasonable searches and seizures," which generally means that any search or seizure must be performed pursuant to a valid warrant based upon probable cause.

While the Fourth Amendment reasonableness standard is permissive in the context of administrative subpoenas, the constitutionality of the administrative subpoena is predicated on the availability of a neutral tribunal to determine, after a subpoena is issued, whether the subpoena actually complies with the Fourth Amendment's demands. In contrast to an actual physical search, which must be justified by the warrant and probable cause requirements occurring before the search, an administrative subpoena "is regulated by, and its justification derives from, [judicial] process" available after the subpoena is issued.

Accordingly, the Supreme Court has held that an administrative subpoena "may not be made and enforced" by the administrative agency; rather, the subpoenaed party must be able to "obtain judicial review of the reasonableness of the demand prior to suffering penalties for refusing to comply."

Rather than dispute the Plaintiffs' interpretation of the relevant constitutional doctrine, the Government's response to these arguments endeavors to heavily repair the statute, essentially by splicing together a string of judicially-sanctioned implications, glosses, or outright patchwork of the various gaps Congress left in the statute, whether inadvertently or purposefully. First, as discussed above, the Government claims that the statute implicitly affords an NSL recipient the opportunity to challenge an NSL on the same terms

---

[118] To be clear, the Fourth Amendment rights at issue here belong to the person or entity receiving the NSL, not to the person or entity to whom the subpoenaed records pertain. Individuals possess a limited Fourth Amendment interest in records which they voluntarily convey to a third party. *See Smith*, 442 U.S. at 742-46; *Miller*, 425 U.S. at 440-43. Nevertheless, as discussed below, many potential NSL recipients may have particular interests in resisting an NSL, *e.g.*, because they have contractually obligated themselves to protect the anonymity of their subscribers or because their own rights are uniquely implicated by what they regard as an intrusive and secretive NSL regime. For example, since the definition of "wire or electronic communication service provider," 18 § 2709(a), is so vague, the statute could (and may currently) be used to seek subscriber lists or other information from an association that also provides electronic communication services (e.g., email addresses) to its members, or to seek records from libraries that many, including the amici appearing in this proceeding, fear will chill speech and use of these invaluable public institutions. Fear that § 2709 may be used as a tool to gain sensitive information from libraries, has led both houses of Congress to introduce bills intended to exclude libraries from the ambit of § 2709. *See* S. 1709, Security and Freedom Assured ("SAFE") Act of 2003, 108th Cong. § 5 (2003) (proposing to amend § 2709(a) to state that a "library shall not be treated as a wire or electronic communication service provider for purposes of this section"); H.R. 3352, 108th Cong. § 5 (2003) (same).

as would be available to any other subpoena recipient, i.e., to either resist the Government's enforcement action, or to affirmatively file a motion to quash. Second, the Government reads the statute to implicitly permit disclosure to an attorney in connection with such a challenge. Third, the government would recognize an additional exception for disclosure to other officers, employees, or agents whose assistance may be reasonably necessary for the recipient to comply with the NSL request.

[T]o fully reach and give effect to the Government's proposal entails inserting into the law not just one, but several distinct terms the Government seeks to incorporate by implication: that the statute permits disclosure by the recipient for the purposes of seeking the assistance of counsel; that disclosure is also permitted to other officers, employees and agents; and that judicial process is available either to challenge or to enforce an NSL.

The Court notes that, conceivably, the Government could endeavor to remedy the defects in § 2709 by alerting all NSL recipients as to what the Government now claims is implicit in § 2709 – that they are entitled to consult an attorney and other persons necessary to facilitate compliance, and to move to quash the NSL. However, accepting as implicit in the statute the protections the Government contends may be inferred does not remedy another deficiency that serves as independent grounds for the statute's facial invalidation: the categorical, indefinite non-disclosure provision § 2709(c), which is not amenable to a "fairly possible" construction that would save it from invalidation.

2. NSLs May Violate ISP Subscribers' Rights.

Plaintiffs have focused on the possibility that § 2709 could be used to infringe subscribers' First Amendment rights of anonymous speech and association. Though it is not necessary to precisely define the scope of ISP subscribers' First Amendment rights, the Court concludes that § 2709 may, in a given case, violate a subscriber's First Amendment privacy rights, as well as other legal rights, if judicial review is not readily available to an ISP that receives an NSL. This conclusion buttresses the Court's holding that, at least as applied, § 2709 does not permit sufficient judicial review to preserve individual subscribers' rights, where impairment of such rights may be implicated by a given NSL.

The Supreme Court has recognized the First Amendment right to anonymous speech at least since *Talley v. California*, which invalidated a California law requiring that handbills distributed to the public contain certain identifying information about the source of the handbills. The Court stated that the "identification requirement would tend to restrict freedom to distribute information and thereby freedom of expression." The Supreme Court has also invalidated identification requirements pertaining to persons distributing campaign literature, persons circulating petitions for state ballot initiatives, and persons engaging in door-to-door religious advocacy.

In a related doctrine, the Supreme Court has held that "compelled disclosure, of affiliation with groups engaged in advocacy" amounts to a "restraint on freedom of association" where disclosure could expose the members to "public hostility." Laws mandating such disclosures will be upheld only where the Government interest is compelling.

The Government asserts that disclosure of the information sought under § 2709 could not violate a subscriber's rights (and thus demands no judicial process) because the information which a § 2709 NSL seeks has been voluntarily conveyed to the ISP who receives the NSL. According to the Government, an internet speaker relinquishes any interest in any anonymity, and any protected claim to that information, as soon as he releases his identity and other information to his ISP. In support of its position, the Government cites the Supreme Court's holding that, at least in the Fourth Amendment context involving the Government installing a pen register or obtaining bank records, when a person voluntarily conveys information to third parties, he assumes the risk that the information will be turned over to the Government.

The Court rejects the Government's reasoning. Every court that has addressed the issue has held that individual internet subscribers have a right to engage in anonymous internet speech, though anonymity may be trumped in a given case by other concerns. No court has adopted the Government's argument here that anonymous internet speech or associational activity ceases to be protected because a third-party ISP is in possession of the identifying information.

Katz v. United States held that the Fourth Amendment's privacy protections applied where the Government wiretapped a telephone call placed from a public phone booth. Especially noteworthy and pertinent to this case is the Supreme Court's remark that: "The Government's activities in electronically listening to and recording the petitioner's words violated the privacy upon which he justifiably relied while using the telephone booth and thus constituted a 'search and seizure' within the meaning of the Fourth Amendment." The Supreme Court also stated that a person entering a phone booth who "shuts the door behind him" is "surely entitled to assume that the words he utters into the mouthpiece will not be broadcast to the world," and held that, "to read the Constitution more narrowly is to ignore the vital role that the public telephone has come to play in private communication."

Applying that reasoning to anonymous internet speech and associational activity is relatively straightforward. A person who signs onto an anonymous forum under a pseudonym, for example, is essentially "shut[ting] the door behind him," and is surely entitled to a reasonable expectation that his speech, whatever form the expression assumes, will not be accessible to the Government to be broadcast to the world absent appropriate legal process. To hold otherwise would ignore the role of the internet as a remarkably powerful forum for private communication and association. Even the Government concedes here that the internet is an "important vehicle for the free exchange of ideas and facilitates associations."

To be sure, the Court is keenly mindful of the Government's reminder that the internet may also serve as a vehicle for crime. The Court equally recognizes that circumstances exist in which the First Amendment rights of association and anonymity must yield to a more compelling Government interest in obtaining records from internet firms. To this end, the Court re-emphasizes that it does not here purport to set forth the scope of these First Amendment rights in general, or define them in this or any other case. The Court holds only that such fundamental rights are certainly implicated in some cases in which the Government may employ § 2709 broadly to gather information, thus requiring that the process incorporate the safeguards of some judicial review to ensure that if an infringement of those rights is asserted, they are adequately protected through fair process in an independent neutral tribunal. Because the necessary procedural protections are wholly absent here, the Court finds on this ground additional cause for invalidating § 2709 as applied.

C. CONSTITUTIONALITY OF THE NON-DISCLOSURE PROVISION

Finally, the Court turns to the issue of whether the Government may properly enforce § 2709(c), the non-disclosure provision, against Doe or any other person who has previously received an NSL. Section 2709(c) states: "No wire or electronic communication service provider, or officer, employee, or agent thereof, shall disclose to any person that the Federal Bureau of Investigation has sought or obtained access to information or records under this section."

[A] blanket permanent prohibition on future disclosures [can be valid only if justified by a compelling governmental interest].

The Court has been able to locate only three statutory provisions even arguably analogous to the automatic, categorical and permanent scope of the NSL statutes' non-disclosure rules. First, communications firms are categorically barred, unless otherwise ordered by a court, from ever disclosing that a pen register or trap and trace device is in effect. Second, communications firms are categorically barred, subject to a similar exception "as may otherwise be required by legal process," from ever disclosing that a wiretap or electronic surveillance is in place. Third, recipients of a subpoena under FISA are categorically prohibited from ever disclosing to any person, "other than those persons necessary to produce" the records sought, that the subpoena was issued.

Furthermore, these provisions are not quite as severe as those contained in the NSL statutes because, with one narrow exception for certain FISA surveillance orders,[208] they apply in contexts in which a court authorizes the investigative method in the first place. Thus, even in these statutes, the silenced party, at least theoretically, would almost always have a forum in which to contest the continuing validity of the non-disclosure obligation or to seek a modified secrecy order. The FISA limits the potential for abuse in yet another way by requiring a clear connection to a foreign power and by sharply limiting the degree to which any United States citizen may be subject to surveillance under a secret FISA order; such protections are not present in § 2709, particularly after the significant broadening of the statute's scope effectuated by

---

[208] Certain FISA electronic surveillance orders may be obtained where the Attorney General merely certifies that the proposed surveillance meets the statutory requirements. *See* 50 U.S.C. § 1802(a)(1). In such cases, the blanket secrecy rule would be triggered without any court involvement, much like § 2709(c). By way of some perhaps justifying distinction, the FISA orders are specifically limited to electronic surveillance of foreign governments and their agents, thus arguably not raising the heightened constitutional concerns and protections implicated when investigations involve the activities of United States nationals.

the Patriot Act. The NSL statutes, including § 2709(c), thus stand virtually alone in providing for blanket secrecy entirely outside the context of judicial process.

The Government's claim to perpetual secrecy surrounding the FBI's issuance of NSLs presupposes a category of information, and thus a class of speech, that, for reasons not satisfactorily explained, must forever be kept from public view, cloaked by an official seal that will always overshadow the public's right to know. In general, as our sunshine laws and judicial doctrine attest, democracy abhors undue secrecy, in recognition that public knowledge secures freedom. Hence, an unlimited government warrant to conceal, effectively a form of secrecy per se, has no place in our open society. Such a claim is especially inimical to democratic values for reasons borne out by painful experience. Under the mantle of secrecy, the self-preservation that ordinarily impels our government to censorship and secrecy may potentially be turned on ourselves as a weapon of self-destruction. When withholding information from disclosure is no longer justified, when it ceases to foster the proper aims that initially may have supported confidentiality, a categorical and uncritical extension of non-disclosure may become the cover for spurious ends that government may then deem too inconvenient, inexpedient, merely embarrassing, or even illicit to ever expose to the light of day. At that point, secrecy's protective shield may serve not as much to secure a safe country as simply to save face.

In response to this standard, the Government's main contention, quite understandably, is that international terrorism and counterintelligence investigations justify more secrecy than other types of investigations. The Court agrees with that basic point so far as it goes. However, under the exacting demands of the First Amendment, the argument does not carry far enough.

The Government correctly states that international terrorism and counterintelligence investigations are generally different from investigations of past crimes in that the latter proceedings usually contemplate a logical endpoint (i.e., trial or hearing) where the Government publicly presents the evidence it has gathered related to allegations of a discrete, past wrongdoing. By contrast, international terrorism and counterintelligence investigations seek to uncover and disrupt future activities of typically large, long-term and expansive conspiracies.

The Court also agrees, insofar as relevant, with the Government's contention that it is sometimes very difficult to determine whether an isolated disclosure implicates national security. International terrorism and counterintelligence investigations may involve continuously expanding or ever-changing players. Hence, determining whether something is sensitive in such a fluid and necessarily broad and indeterminate context may not be simple.

Consequently, particular institutional limitations come into play when the judiciary is asked to make such determinations. Ordinarily, judges do not have national security expertise. Nor is the institution of the judiciary well-equipped to understand the sensitivity of an isolated piece of information in the context of the entire intelligence apparatus.[254] As one Circuit Court remarked in addressing this point: "Things that do not make sense to the District Judge would make all too much sense to a foreign counter-intelligence specialist who could learn much about this nation's intelligence-gathering capabilities from what these documents revealed about sources and methods."[255] These institutional concerns explain the well-settled doctrine that courts grant substantial deference to the political branches in national security matters. The Supreme Court has recognized that in cases of "terrorism or other special circumstances" courts might afford "heightened deference to the judgments of the political branches with respect to matters of national security."[256]

In this Court's judgment, these authorities persuasively confirm that the Government should be accorded a due measure of deference when it asserts that secrecy is necessary for national security purposes in a particular situation involving particular persons at a particular time. Here, however, the Government cites no authority supporting the open-ended proposition that it may universally apply these general principles to impose perpetual secrecy upon an entire category of future cases whose details are unknown and whose particular twists and turns may not justify, for all time and all places, demanding unremitting concealment and imposing a disproportionate burden on free speech.

In fact, all the cases cited above involved some judicial process pertaining to contemporary circumstances, and, for obvious reasons, the general propositions articulated in those opinions cannot always be tailored to every forthcoming or unforeseen set of facts. Thus, the central flaw in the Government's argument is that it invites the Court to "assume that [§ 2709] will always advance the asserted [Government] interests sufficiently to justify its abridgment of expressive activity." The Court cannot uncritically embrace that proposition because there are undoubtedly circumstances in which the need for secrecy either has expired or simply no longer exists with the same compelling force that

---

[254] *See North Jersey Media Group, Inc. v. Ashcroft*, 308 F.3d 198, 219 (3d Cir. 2002) (agreeing with Government's contention that, "given judges' relative lack of expertise regarding national security and their inability to see the mosaic, [judges] should not entrust to themselves the decision whether an isolated fact is sensitive enough to warrant closure").

[255] *United States v. Yunis*, 276 U.S. App. D.C. 1, 867 F.2d 617, 623 (D.C. Cir. 1989).

[256] *Zadvydas v. Davis*, 533 U.S. 678 (2001); *Egan*, 484 U.S. at 530 ("Courts traditionally have been reluctant to intrude upon the authority of the Executive in military and national security affairs."). Of course, a court should not embrace these principles to the point of abdicating its constitutional duties. As the Sixth Circuit accurately observed, the Government's invocation of executive deference may have profound implications if adopted without reservation:

> The Government could use its 'mosaic intelligence' argument as a justification to close any public hearing completely and categorically, including criminal proceedings. The Government could operate in virtual secrecy in all matters dealing, even remotely with 'national security,' resulting in a wholesale suspension of First Amendment rights.

Detroit Free Press v. Ashcroft, 303 F.3d 681, 709 (6th Cir. 2002).

once warranted its imposition. Section 2709(c) provides no mechanism to account for, or exclude any unjustifiable denial of speech in these cases.

The Court cannot, consistent with its constitutional powers, fix the shortcomings of this provision of the statute to make it more "targeted and precise." That is a legislative function. Accordingly, § 2709(c) must be invalidated on its face on this ground.

V. STAY OF JUDGMENT

Considering the implications of its ruling and the importance of the issues involved, the Court will stay enforcement of its judgment pending appeal, or for the Government otherwise to pursue any alternate course of action, for 90 days. The Court is aware that several material issues in this case involve uncharted legal terrain. The stay will give the Government the opportunity to move this Court, or the Court of Appeals, for whatever appropriate relief it may seek to maintain the confidentiality of any information implicated by the Court's ruling. To this end, the Court is aware that invalidating § 2709(c) on its face may carry the potential to compromise legitimately confidential information. The Court declares unequivocally that it is not its intention to cause any such information to fall into the wrong hands.

VI. CONCLUSION

To summarize, the Court concludes that the compulsory, secret, and unreviewable production of information required by the FBI's application of 18 U.S.C. § 2709 violates the Fourth Amendment, and that the non-disclosure provision of 18 U.S.C. § 2709(c) violates the First Amendment. The Government is therefore enjoined from issuing NSLs under § 2709 or from enforcing the non-disclosure provision in this or any other case, but enforcement of the Court's judgment will be stayed pending appeal, or if no appeal is filed, for 90 days.

NOTES AND QUESTIONS

1. In this extremely long and heavily documented opinion, the court covers a number of potential problem areas with government acquisition of information. What is the heart of the matter from your point of view? the lack of judicial involvement before issuance of the demand? lack of notice about the ability to obtain judicial review after receipt? lack of notice to the generator of the information?

2. This opinion could reflect a fundamental bias shared by much of the populace in favor of trusting courts more than investigators. Is that value one that should be or is enshrined in constitutional doctrine? What components would go into that value choice?

3. What weight should be attached to the realization that NSL's are not legally enforceable? If the document itself disclosed this, would it then become just a request for voluntary cooperation? In the absence of that disclosure, does the NSL seem somehow misleading or duplicitous? From the point of view of the recipient who might have contractual obligations of confidentiality with subscribers, what is the significance of knowing that the request is not an order that must be obeyed under threat of penalty or sanction?

4. The "mosaic" argument recurs frequently in government attempts to prevent disclosure of its investigations, not only from public disclosure but even from disclosure to the individuals involved. The argument is noted in this case that even a perceptive federal judge might not grasp the significance of a single bit of information that would fit a central piece of a puzzle to a knowledgeable terrorist. This argument seems to resonate in the terrorism context in a little different way than it might with other organized crime elements. Should we assume or believe that terrorist organizations are more sophisticated or smarter than organizations such as, for example, the Medellin Cartel of the 1980s?

5. How much weight should we give to the claimed right of anonymity by a speaker in public discourse? The court here refers several times to the *Katz* analogy of "closing the door behind" yourself and expecting privacy of communication. But there are different types of doors on the internet. It may be easier to understand the claim of privacy when thinking about e-mail from one person directed specifically to another than to see the same claim for anonymity when posting material for public consumption on a website. In between these examples, there are chat rooms where the technology provides an appearance of anonymity but an ISP or the manager of the chat room may have full awareness of each speaker's identity. In truth, how reliable are our beliefs in privacy when using electronic communication? The technology that allows instant communication also allows identification of the speaker.

Technology aside, isn't the claim for anonymity in a public setting a little disingenuous? If I want to make a public statement, shouldn't I be willing to face the consequences of public disapproval? If not, then shouldn't I keep that communication private?

Note on *Muslim Community Association of Ann Arbor v. Ashcroft*

This case was filed in the Eastern District of Michigan in July 2003 to challenge the constitutionality of Section 215 of PATRIOT. The plaintiffs summarize their claims this way:

> To obtain a Section 215 order, the FBI need only assert that the records or personal belongings are 'sought for' an ongoing foreign intelligence, counterintelligence, or international terrorism investigation. The FBI is not required to show probable cause – or any reason – to believe that the target of the order is a criminal suspect or foreign agent. . . . The targets of Section 215 orders are never notified that their privacy has been compromised – even years later, and even if they are innocent. The law includes a gag provision that prohibits persons or entities served with Section 215 orders from ever disclosing, even in the most general terms, that the FBI has sought information from them.

The complaint goes on to claim that the organizations "have a well-founded belief" that third parties have been ordered to divulge records regarding the organizations and their members. For example, some of the organizations have been associated with expressing support for Sami al-Arian and Rabih Haddad. As a result of that association and the known investigations into the activities of those two persons, "section 215 has caused some of plaintiffs' members and clients to be inhibited from publicly expressing their political views."

Section 215 basically uses the same procedure for acquisition of records in the hands of a third party that the courts have upheld with respect to FISA orders for searches and surveillance. Is there something different about records? Is the lack of notice to the subject of the records a constitutional concern?

In October 2003, the government filed motions to dismiss on the basis of standing, ripeness, and failure to state a claim. As part of its submission to the court, the government filed an affidavit stating that no applications had been presented to the FISA Court under section 215 through September 18, 2003. In May 2004, the government submitted a letter clarifying that any filings after September 2003 would remain classified but would be irrelevant to the ACLU litigation in any event. The ACLU then responded in June that it had obtained information through a FOIA request indicating that at least one section 215 order had been sought as early as October 15, 2003. The government then responded with a letter to the court including an affidavit submitted in two forms, one with classified portions redacted for the public record and a complete version that was submitted to the court security officer to be available to the judge upon request. The ACLU responded with a motion to exclude the *ex parte* communication.

See *http://www.aclu.org/SafeandFree/SafeandFree.cfm?ID=13255&c=207*

[B] INTERCEPTION OF ELECTRONIC COMMUNICATIONS

The Electronic Privacy Information Center (EPIC) has vigorously criticized many aspects of PATRIOT. Among its unique concerns are these:

The implications for online privacy are considerable. For example, the Act increases the ability of law enforcement agencies to authorize installation of pen registers and trap and trace devices (a pen register collects the outgoing phone numbers placed from a specific telephone line; a trap and trace device captures the incoming numbers placed to a specific phone line – a caller-id box is a trap and trace device), and to authorize the installation of such devices to record all computer routing, addressing, and signaling information. . . . Although the use of such devices requires a court order, it does not require a showing of probable cause. There is, in effect, no judicial discretion, as the court is required to authorize monitoring upon the mere certification by a government attorney that the "information likely to be obtained by such installation and use is relevant to an ongoing criminal investigation."

By expanding the nature of the information that can be captured, the new law clearly expanded pen register capacities to the Internet, covering electronic mail, Web surfing, and all other forms of electronic communications. The fact that the provision prohibits the capture of "content" does not adequately take into account the unique nature of information captured electronically, which contains data far more revealing than phone numbers, such as URLs generated while using the Web (which often contain a great deal of information that cannot in any way be analogized to a telephone number). . . . Because Carnivore provides the FBI with access to the communications of all subscribers of a monitored Internet Service Provider (and not just those of the court-designated target), it raises substantial privacy issues for millions of law-abiding American citizens.

Section 214 removes the pre-existing statutory requirement that the government prove the surveillance target is "an agent of a foreign power" before obtaining a pen register/trap and trace order under the FISA. Therefore, the government could obtain a pen register/trap and trace device "for any investigation to gather foreign intelligence information," without a showing that the device has, is or will be used by a foreign agent or by an individual engaged in international terrorism or clandestine intelligence activities. The amendment significantly eviscerates the constitutional rationale for the relatively lax requirements that apply to foreign intelligence surveillance. That laxity is premised on the assumption that the Executive Branch, in pursuit of its national security responsibilities to monitor the activities of foreign powers and their agents, should not be unduly restrained by Congress and the courts. The removal of the "foreign power" predicate for pen register/trap and trace surveillance upsets that delicate balance.

http://www.epic.org/privacy/terrorism/usapatriot

NOTES AND QUESTIONS

1. Why is EPIC so concerned about "pen registers" and "trap and trace" devices? Historically, these devices have merely recorded the numbers called from a particular telephone or the number calling that telephone. They do not record the content of a conversation. By using these devices on computer websites, does government acquire information about the user who accesses the website? Does it matter that government agents know I went online looking for information about C-4 explosives? We probably need to know much more about "cookies" and how the technology works before we can assess all the privacy implications of internet communications, but the central point is whether there is a privacy interest in what we read. Government lawyers have argued in response to the AALL concerns over library circulation records that there is no privacy interest in what a patron reads because the material is acquired in public view just as your grocery purchases are in public view at the checkout counter. What do you think of this line of argument?

In some sense, the internet is a publicly accessible bank of information similar to the open shelves of a library, but it is not a physical space that is normally observable by others. To pursue the library analogy, if government agents were posted near the shelves of a public library and observed who was looking at certain books, would this be a problem? If your answer is "yes," is it a problem of constitutional dimension or a problem of good practice?

2. The owner of a computer that is linked to the web can now ask for "intercept" of communications by "computer trespassers" (hackers). EPIC complains that this "permits wiretapping of the intruder's communications without any judicial oversight, in contrast to most federal communication-intercept laws that require objective oversight from someone outside the investigative chain." So what? Why should we be worried about the privacy of hackers?

3. Some of the concerns about PATRIOT have to do with what have been statutory limits on normal law enforcement investigative tools, specifically the new nationwide service of search warrants and the use of "sneak and peek" warrants. Again, why should we be concerned about removing some limits on the ability of investigators to protect the public safety? What aspects of privacy were protected by the prior limitations?

4. One recommendation of the 9/11 Commission contemplates a unified "network-based information system." This arose from the realization that the FBI and CIA did not easily share information, a barrier that once was built into law but eased by the PATRIOT Act. Is sharing of all intelligence data in one big database a good idea? How realistic is it to expect sharing? and what human could possibly assimilate and evaluate the billions of pieces of information that flow through the IC agencies in any given month?

§ 7.04 DETENTIONS AND ETHNIC PROFILING

Two early responses to 9/11 by the Justice Department had ethnic overtones. One was to interview many U.S. citizens or resident aliens who came from countries with terrorist ties in an effort to obtain information that could be assembled and analyzed to discern patterns related either to 9/11 itself or to future plots. The second initiative was to detain many aliens from those same countries who had overstayed their visas or otherwise violated immigration laws, some of whom eventually might be deportable. As a number of advocacy groups observed, most of the countries considered to be linked to terrorist planning were Arab nations and most of those detained were young Arab males. While not explicitly based on ethnicity, the practice resulted in a clearly disparate impact on Arab aliens.

In that setting, public opinion swung suddenly and visibly to acceptance of racial or ethnic profiling. One survey conducted in Detroit reported that 61% of Arab Americans believed that "extra scrutiny of people with Middle Eastern features or accents by law enforcement officials" was justified. *Arab Americans Expect Scrutiny, Feel Sting of Bias*, DETROIT FREE PRESS (Oct. 1, 2001), *http://www.freep.com/news/nw/terror2001/poll1_20011001.htm*

Ethnic profiling has been a target of some scrutiny in legal academic writing for the past couple of decades. Academic commentary immediately after 9/11 showed a similar swing in emphasis. Noting that as of September 10, 2001, a strong consensus against racial profiling had been accepted by everyone from Jesse Jackson to John Ashcroft, Professors Gross and Livingston argued that harsh realities prompted a rethinking of the issues:

> The September 11 attacks and the threat of future terrorism clearly require an intensive investigation. Given the extremity of the threat and

identity of the known terrorists, the government is justified in focusing that investigation on Middle Eastern men despite the fact that the public decision to do so has caused understandable pain and anxiety for many Arab Americans. But that should be only the beginning of our inquiry. In the end, what the Department of Justice does to those it seeks to interview, for what reasons and on what basis, are more important than the fact that they may have been initially selected for interviews in part because of their ethnicity or national origin.

Samuel R. Gross & Debra Livingston, *Racial Profiling Under Attack*, 102 COLUM. L. REV. 1413, 1437 (2002). Professor Harris now thinks that the earlier unacceptability of racial profiling should be reinstated, although he believes that a sophisticated form of "behavioral profiling" could be more effective without the stigma. David A. Harris, *New Risks, New Tactics: An Assessment of the Re-Assessment of Racial Profiling in the Wake of September 11, 2001*, 2004 UTAH L. REV. ___ (forthcoming 2005).

In only rare instances have courts been asked to address allegations of police discrimination in "stop and frisk" situations. Only when a very strong pattern of unjustified racial or ethnic discrimination has been shown have the courts been willing to step in and set out guidelines for control of police discretion. In one sense, the issues have involved questions of cause and effect – is a disparate stop pattern indicative of racial bias in the police or is it the result of higher likelihood of suspicious behavior among minority groups? In another sense, the cases reflect a reluctance to push the causation issue very aggressively out of fear that a police response would be to decrease law enforcement efforts in low-income, high-crime, predominantly minority neighborhoods. *See generally* RANDALL KENNEDY, RACE, CRIME AND THE LAW (1997).

The classic example of permissible racial segregation is that of separating prison inmates by race during a race riot. When the Supreme Court has cited this example, it has never had reason to speculate about the degree of evidence that would be required to support the conclusion of an emergency for this purpose. Perhaps it is safe to assume that in the context of a prison riot, we would know an emergency when we see it, but more troubling is whether we know a national emergency when we see it. The reason for the difficulty is that the greater the intrusion onto personal liberties, the greater the showing of emergency that should be expected. And, as Justice Jackson intimated, and as we all feel instinctively, at the extremes the courts may be powerless to curtail governmental abuse.

[A] JAPANESE "EXCLUSION" AND NATIONAL EMERGENCY

A consideration of race in the context of declared national emergency must begin with the Japanese cases of World War II. While the most notorious of the three Supreme Court cases is *Korematsu v. United States*, 323 U.S. 214 (1944), *Hirabayashi v. United States*, 320 U.S. 81 (1943), may be a closer precedent to what could happen again. Justice Jackson's dissent in *Korematsu* forecast the concern (while perhaps foreshadowing his role as chief prosecutor at Nuremberg) when he bemoaned the Court's war-time review of military judgments:

[T]he Court for all time has validated the principle of racial discrimination in criminal procedure and of transplanting American citizens. The principle then lies about like a loaded weapon ready for the hand of any authority that can bring forward a plausible claim of an urgent need. (*Id.* at 246)

If the people ever let command of the war power fall into irresponsible and unscrupulous hands, the courts wield no power equal to its restraint. The chief restraint upon those who command the physical forces of the country, in the future as in the past, must be their responsibility to the political judgments of their contemporaries and to the moral judgements of history. (*Id.* at 248)

Japanese exclusion came in three steps. First, there was a Presidential directive broadly authorizing military commanders to exclude persons from certain areas, primarily Hawaii and the Pacific Coast. The second step was an Act of Congress criminalizing violation of military orders issued under the President's authorization. Then the military commanders issued orders setting curfews, authorizing detention, and establishing relocation camps.

Hirabayashi upheld a curfew by which all persons of Japanese ancestry in certain areas were required to be in their residences from 8 p.m. to 6 a.m.. The order was challenged on the grounds that it was beyond the war powers as well as racial discrimination, to which the Court responded that

we cannot reject as unfounded the judgment of the military authorities and of Congress that there were disloyal members of that population, whose number and strength could not be precisely and quickly ascertained. We cannot say that the war-making branches of the Government did not have ground for believing that in a critical hour such persons could not readily be isolated and separately dealt with, and constituted a menace to the national defense and safety, which demanded that prompt and adequate measures be taken to guard against it.

Moving from curfew to detention, the Court upheld "temporary" relocation of thousands of persons of Japanese ancestry while recognizing that relocation carried a much greater impact than curfew:

Compulsory exclusion of large groups of citizens from their homes, except under circumstances of direst emergency and peril, is inconsistent with our basic governmental institutions. But when under conditions of modern warfare our shores are threatened by hostile forces, the power to protect must be commensurate with the threatened danger.

Justice Black's opinion insisted that the Court was addressing only exclusion from the West Coast and was not concerned with "relocation centers" because the curfew was all that Korematsu was charged with violating. Then, when the validity of continued detention was considered in *Ex parte Endo*, 323 U.S. 283 (1944), the Court construed the EO and statute narrowly to find that detention would be authorized only by the exigencies of separating the loyal from the disloyal or as a voluntary measure of humanitarian aid to those excluded from coastal areas:

The authority to detain a citizen or to grant him a conditional release as protection against espionage or sabotage is exhausted at least when his loyalty is conceded. If we held that the authority to detain continued thereafter, we would transform an espionage or sabotage measure into something else. That was not done by Executive Order No. 9066 or by the Act of March 21, 1942, which ratified it. What they did not do we cannot do. Detention which furthered the campaign against espionage and sabotage would be one thing. But detention which has no relationship to that campaign is of a distinct character.

Although the combination of *Korematsu* and *Endo* technically was to authorize exclusion while invalidating detention, as a practical matter one carried implication of the other. First, the burden was on the applicant to prove loyalty and, moreover, it was not clear where this person was to go when excluded from the home and community in which he or she had been born and raised. Even long after the military justification had ceased, inertia delayed the end of detention. The effect was that over 100,000 presumably loyal citizens spent the war years behind barbed wire in mostly desert encampments.

The aftermath of the program eventually led to a congressionally mandated Commission on Wartime Relocation and Internment of Civilians. The CWRIC described the subsequent remorse of many of the participants in the program (including Justices Douglas, Clark, and Warren) and summarized its own findings this way:

The promulgation of Executive Order 9066 was not justified by military necessity, and the decisions which followed from it – detention, ending detention, and ending exclusion – were not driven by analysis of military conditions. The broad historical causes which shaped these decisions were race prejudice, war hysteria and a failure of political leadership. Widespread ignorance of Japanese Americans contributed to a policy conceived in haste and executed in an atmosphere of fear and anger at Japan. A grave injustice was done to American citizens and resident aliens of Japanese ancestry who, without individual review or any probative evidence against them, were excluded, removed and detained by the United States during World War II.

To what extent does *Korematsu* stand as precedent today? As thoroughly regretted and discredited as the Japanese exclusion program itself may be, the opinion has never been overruled and indeed is cited as the beginning of reviewing racial discrimination by government with strict scrutiny.

[B] ETHNIC PROFILING IN LAW ENFORCEMENT

MARSHALL v. COLUMBIA LEA REGIONAL HOSPITAL
345 F.3d 1157 (10th Cir. 2003)

McCONNELL, Circuit Judge.

This case involves troubling allegations regarding possible police misconduct by an officer in Hobbs, New Mexico. We are not in a position to judge the truth of those allegations at this early stage in the litigation, but we conclude that the district court acted prematurely in granting summary judgment on all claims.

In December, 1996, police officer Rodney Porter stopped Plaintiff-Appellant Jimmie Marshall, an African-American part-time resident of Hobbs, New Mexico, for an alleged traffic violation. Officer Porter arrested Marshall, administered field sobriety tests, and took him to the Columbia Lea Regional Hospital for a blood test. Among other legal claims, Mr. Marshall alleges that the traffic stop and arrest were made on account of his race and without probable cause, in violation of the Fourth Amendment and the Equal Protection Clause, and that the coerced blood test violated his rights under the Fourth Amendment and state tort law. The defendants are Officer Porter, who conducted the traffic stop and arrest, and Sergeant Walter Roye, who ordered the blood test. Plaintiff seeks damages and other appropriate relief under 42 U.S.C. § 1983.

In a pair of orders dated June 18, 2002, the district court granted summary judgment for the defendants as to all claims. For the reasons set forth below, we reverse the judgment of the district court insofar as it granted summary judgment in favor of the Hobbs Defendants on the Equal Protection claim and the Fourth Amendment blood-test claim, and remand for further proceedings on these and the related state law claims. With respect to the remaining claims against the Hobbs Defendants, as well as all claims asserted against the Medical Defendants, we affirm the district court's grant of summary judgment.

I. Background

A. *Mr. Marshall's Arrest and Blood Test*

On December 26, 1996, Jimmie Marshall, an African-American self-employed electrician, was driving his gold Toyota pickup in Hobbs, New Mexico, when he noticed a police car parked by the side of the road with its lights off. According to Mr. Marshall, the police officer – later identified as Officer Rodney Porter – followed his pickup for several blocks. While Mr. Marshall was stopped at an intersection with his left-turn signal blinking, Officer Porter pulled up alongside the pickup and "gazed intently at [Marshall's] face," which Marshall infers was for the purpose of ascertaining his race. Officer Porter contends that Mr. Marshall failed to stop at the stop sign, which Mr. Marshall denies. Officer Porter then activated his emergency lights, but Mr. Marshall continued to drive for more than two miles before coming to a stop at his residence. Mr. Marshall claims that he evaded the officer for several miles because he was fearful to stop his vehicle outside of the presence of witnesses, on account of the reputation of the Hobbs Police Department for racist practices. At that time, Mr. Marshall did not know Officer Porter and did not have any information about him. In the criminal complaint filed as a result of the incident, Officer Porter stated that Mr. Marshall accelerated to 100 miles per hour, drove through a four-way stop, and weaved from lane to lane, which Marshall denies. However, Officer Porter made no mention of these allegations in the affidavit he filed in this case describing the events of December 26, 1996, nor were they mentioned in Defendants' later pleadings.

On the street in front of Mr. Marshall's residence, the two men emerged from their vehicles. Officer Porter had drawn his pistol. His first words were to accuse

Mr. Marshall of being on crack, which Marshall has consistently denied. Defendants have proffered no evidence in support of this accusation. Officer Porter states that Mr. Marshall had the odor of alcohol on his breath, which Marshall does not deny, stating that he had imbibed one drink with his brother Alfred. Officer Porter arrested Mr. Marshall on various charges, including the traffic violation, driving under the influence, and resisting arrest. On the written citation form, in the space for indicating the gender of the person receiving the citation, Officer Porter wrote "B/M," presumably meaning black male.

After arresting Mr. Marshall, Officer Porter proceeded to search Marshall's truck. The search revealed a .40 caliber pistol under the driver's seat (apparently lawful), and Officer Porter claimed also to have found a small amount of a "green leafy substance," a contention Marshall denies. Mr. Marshall was taken to the city jail, where several sobriety tests were performed on him. Mr. Marshall passed two breathalyzer tests, but had difficulty completing the recitation of the alphabet (the "ABC test"). [He was eventually taken to the hospital for a blood test, which produced evidence of THC in his bloodstream.]

Later, he was charged in a criminal complaint with (i) possession of a controlled substance (marijuana), (ii) resisting, evading or obstructing a police officer, (iii) negligent use of a firearm (possession while intoxicated), (iv) reckless driving, (v) running a stop sign, and (vi) driving under the influence. In May of 1997, the Assistant District Attorney for Lea County entered a *nolle prosequi* because the evidence in Marshall's case was suppressed. The record does not contain any further information about that proceeding, or the legal basis for the suppression of the evidence.

B. *Officer Porter's Alleged Pattern of Misconduct*

Slightly more than a year before the events in question here, Officer Porter was forced to resign from the Midland, Texas, police force after an internal investigation uncovered evidence of serious misconduct. In response to Mr. Marshall's subpoena, Midland Police Chief John Urby provided documents from his department's internal investigation showing an extensive pattern of misconduct and violation of citizens' constitutional rights by Officer Porter when he was on the Midland force.

If admissible, the Midland documents provide evidence that in more than thirty cases, Officer Porter falsely charged arrestees with possession of narcotics, seriously mishandled narcotics evidence, or both. Further, in other cases, Officer Porter was accused of planting evidence on arrestees, as well as using evidence to barter for sexual favors. According to the documents, Officer Porter denied the charges until after failing a polygraph test, when he admitted mishandling evidence.

According to Mr. Marshall, a review of Officer Porter's arrest reports on cases where he had not logged in drug evidence

> shows that an overwhelming number of the suspects were black. Most of the rest were Hispanic surnamed. Virtually all were stopped for minor traffic violations such as seat belts, failing to signal a turn, failing to stop at a stop sign, or making a wide turn so as to touch the stripe of the other lane. Also,

in many [cases] Porter either claimed to have secured consent or went ahead and conducted searches anyway.

He claims that this pattern closely resembles the facts of his own case, and establishes a *modus operandi* under which Officer Porter targets individuals on the basis of their race and subjects them to traffic stops, arrests, and searches for pretextual drug violations not based on any evidence.

In further support of his equal protection claim, Mr. Marshall presented evidence regarding several lawsuits alleging civil rights violations against African-American citizens of Hobbs pending at the time his complaint was filed. Mr. Marshall also provided newspaper articles dealing with the racial tensions between the Hobbs Police Department and its African-American citizens, including an incident involving Officer Porter in which an allegedly racially motivated arrest at a high school football game resulted in a riot

II. Analysis

A. *Fourth Amendment Challenges to the Traffic Stop and Arrest*

The first issue raised in Mr. Marshall's appellate brief is the validity of the traffic stop and arrest under the Fourth Amendment. Mr. Marshall concedes that the "perceived" traffic violation "may have provided sufficient grounds for the initial stop," but maintains that "Officer Porter did not have justifiable reasons to arrest and seize the plaintiff/appellant."

Whether or not Mr. Marshall failed to obey the stop sign, which is disputed, the actual "stop" did not occur until after Mr. Marshall had driven for two miles without responding to the police officer's emergency lights. This behavior violated N.M. Stat. Ann. § 30-22-1 and constituted probable cause to support the stop, the citation, and the arrest.

B. *Equal Protection Claims*

That Mr. Marshall's stop and arrest were based on probable cause does not resolve his more troubling claim that he was targeted by Officer Porter on account of his race. In *Whren v. United States,* 517 U.S. 806, 813 (1996), the Supreme Court held that claims asserting selective enforcement of a law on the basis of race are properly brought under the Equal Protection Clause, and that the right to equal protection may be violated even if the actions of the police are acceptable under the Fourth Amendment. As the court noted in *United States v. Avery,* 137 F.3d 343, 352 (6th Cir. 1997), "the Equal Protection Clause of the Fourteenth Amendment provides citizens a degree of protection independent of the Fourth Amendment protection against unreasonable searches and seizures."

Racially selective law enforcement violates this nation's constitutional values at the most fundamental level; indeed, unequal application of criminal law to white and black persons was one of the central evils addressed by the framers of the Fourteenth Amendment. *See generally* WILLIAM NELSON, THE FOURTEENTH AMENDMENT: FROM POLITICAL PRINCIPLE TO JUDICIAL DOCTRINE 43-48 (1988); John Frank & Robert Munro, *The Original Understanding of "Equal Protection of the Laws,"* 1972 WASH. U.L.Q. 421, 445-46. In its modern form, however, racially selective law enforcement has only recently come to public attention, and state and federal law enforcement authorities are struggling to develop practical means for distinguishing between legitimate and illegitimate uses of race in the investigation and prevention of crime. *See generally* Samuel R. Gross & Debra Livingston, *Racial Profiling Under Attack,* 102 COLUM. L. REV. 1413 (2002); Albert W. Alschuler, *Racial Profiling and the Constitution*, 2002 U. CHI. LEGAL F. 163 (2002). Recently at the behest of President Bush, the Department of Justice promulgated guidelines designed to end racial profiling in federal law enforcement.

It is one thing for law enforcement administrators to identify the problem and to undertake administrative steps to eliminate the improper use of racial and ethnic stereotypes in law enforcement. It is more difficult to craft judicially manageable standards for determining liability under § 1983. Broad discretion has been vested in executive branch officials to determine when to prosecute, *United States v. Armstrong,* 517 U.S. 456, 464 (1996), and by analogy, when to conduct a traffic stop or initiate an arrest. Police officers and departments should not lightly be put to the expense and risk of trial on charges of racial discrimination that may be easy to make and difficult to disprove. Not only does litigation divert prosecutorial resources and threaten an excessive judicial interference with executive discretion, but it could induce police officers to protect themselves against false accusations in ways that are counterproductive to fair and effective enforcement of the laws. For example, police may be induced to direct their law enforcement efforts in race-conscious ways by focusing law enforcement on neighborhoods with relatively few low-income, minority persons. Perhaps for these reasons, the Supreme Court has held that "to dispel the presumption that a prosecutor has not violated equal protection, a criminal defendant must present 'clear evidence to the contrary.'" Claims of racially discriminatory traffic stops and arrests should be held to a similarly high standard.

Neither this Court nor the Supreme Court has set forth the standards of proof needed for a plaintiff to withstand a motion for summary judgment in a case of an alleged racially discriminatory stop and arrest by a single officer. In analogous contexts, however, the Court has "taken great pains to explain that the standard is a demanding one." *Armstrong.* In *Wade v. United States,* 504 U.S. 181, 186 (1992), the Court held that a defendant is not entitled to an evidentiary hearing on a claim of a prosecutor's racially discriminatory refusal to request a downward departure on the basis of "generalized allegations of improper motive." He must "make . . . a substantial threshold showing." In *Armstrong*, the Court held that a defendant is not entitled to discovery on a claim that the prosecuting attorney singled him out for prosecution on the basis of his race unless he can show "that similarly situated individuals of a different race were not prosecuted."

The plaintiff must demonstrate that the defendant's actions had a discriminatory effect and were motivated by a discriminatory purpose. These standards have been applied to traffic stops challenged on equal protection grounds. *Chavez v. Ill. State Police,* 251 F.3d 612, 635-36 (7th Cir. 2001); *Farm Labor Org. Comm. v. Ohio State Highway Patrol,* 308 F.3d 523, 533-36 (6th Cir. 2002). The discriminatory purpose need not be the only purpose, but it must be a motivating factor in the decision.

In general, the absence of an overtly discriminatory policy or of direct evidence of police motivation results in most claims being based on statistical comparisons between the number of black or other minority Americans stopped or arrested and their percentage in some measure of the relevant population. This requires a reliable measure of the demographics of the relevant population, a means of telling whether the data represent similarly situated individuals, and a point of comparison to the actual incidence of crime among different racial or ethnic segments of the population. This case, however, is different, and perhaps more susceptible to traditional modes of proof before a jury. Here, Mr. Marshall seeks to prove the racially selective nature of his stop and arrest not by means of statistical inference but by direct evidence of Officer Porter's behavior during the events in question, Officer Porter's own statements and testimony (the credibility of which can be evaluated by a jury), and Officer Porter's alleged record of racially selective stops and arrests in drug cases under similar circumstances in Midland, Texas.

Viewing the evidence in the light most favorable to the nonmoving party, Mr. Marshall, and drawing reasonable inferences in his favor, we conclude that the court below erred in granting summary judgment on Mr. Marshall's equal protection claim. We will analyze each fact Marshall invokes in support of his claim, starting with the events surrounding the traffic stop itself.

Mr. Marshall testified that he did not fail to stop at the stop sign or commit any other traffic violation in Officer Porter's presence. This testimony was not sufficient to establish lack of probable cause for the ultimate stop and arrest two miles down the road, but if accepted as true by the trier of fact, would be evidence that the officer's initial decision to pull Mr. Marshall over was pretextual. Moreover, Mr Marshall testified – and Officer Porter did not dispute – that he was aware of the police car following him for several blocks before he came to the intersection where the alleged traffic violation occurred. Since drivers aware of being observed by the police tend to be particularly cautious about traffic regulations, this lends credence to his account of the events.

Second, Mr. Marshall testified, and Officer Porter did not deny, that the officer made eye contact with him while stopped at the intersection prior to activating his emergency lights. From these facts it might reasonably be inferred that Officer Porter was ascertaining Mr. Marshall's race.

The first words out of Officer Porter's mouth when he confronted Mr. Marshall after the stop were a cryptic accusation that Mr. Marshall was on crack. ("Is a few rocks worth all that?") Officer Porter reiterated this accusation during interrogation at the station house, and again at the hospital. [I]n the context of this case as a whole, a jury might reasonably infer from these exchanges that Officer Porter was acting on the basis of stereotype or prejudice rather than evidence.

The record also reflects that on the citation form, in the box designated for the gender of the cited driver, Officer Porter wrote "B/M," making a racial designation where none was called for. Possibly, this reflects unwritten police policy or has some other nondiscriminatory explanation, but the Hobbs Defendants have not suggested one. A jury might also think it significant – at least as it bears on Officer Porter's credibility – that the officer wrote on the original criminal complaint that Mr. Marshall accelerated to 100 miles per hour, drove through a four-way stop, and weaved from lane to lane, but later made no mention of these remarkable corroborating facts in his sworn affidavit in this case about what happened that day.

The record thus contains evidence – disputed, to be sure – that Mr. Marshall did not commit the traffic violation for which he was initially stopped, that Officer Porter ascertained Mr. Marshall's race before initiating the stop, that he made repeated accusations that Mr. Marshall was on crack with no apparent basis, that he made an apparently unnecessary note of Marshall's race, and that his account of the events changed dramatically between the date of the incident and the date of his affidavit. Other than to insist that Mr. Marshall committed the traffic violation and thus that there was probable cause for the stop and the arrest, the Defendants offer no nondiscriminatory explanation for these aspects of Officer Porter's conduct in this case.

It is a close question whether this is sufficient to require the Hobbs Defendants to go to trial on the allegations of racial discrimination. But there is more.

Mr. Marshall presented evidence regarding extensive alleged misconduct by Officer Porter during his prior employment as a police officer in Midland, Texas. In a memo terminating Officer Porter's employment, the Midland police chief stated that Porter had failed "to treat people fairly and equally under the law." If admissible, these documents, together with the other facts of record pertaining to the events of December 26, 1996, may be sufficient to create a triable issue on Mr. Marshall's claim of racially selective law enforcement.

Once the documents have been analyzed, the district court will be able to determine whether they establish a "pattern" of traffic stops and arrests that raises an inference of racial discrimination, or provide evidence that similarly situated individuals of a different race received differential treatment.

In their Reply in Support of Hobbs Defendants' Motion for Summary Judgment, the Hobbs Defendants raised certain objections to the admissibility of the Midland documents. As far as the record reveals, the district court never ruled on those objections. We therefore reverse the grant of summary judgment in favor of the Hobbs Defendants on the equal protection claims, and remand to the district court to determine the admissibility of the Midland documents and to reconsider the Hobbs Defendants' motion for summary judgment in light of this opinion.

NOTES AND QUESTIONS

1. In addition to the *Whren* and *Armstrong* cases, the Supreme Court dealt cautiously with alleged racial disparities in the criminal justice system in *O Shea v. Littleton*, 414 U.S. 488 (1974). Plaintiffs alleged a long-standing pattern of harsher bail and sentences for black defendants than for whites in the town of Cairo, Illinois, a pattern and practice that would be difficult to show on the record of any single case. They sought to enjoin disparate bail and sentencing by the judge and magistrate. Rather than going to the merits, which would have involved highly discretionary roles of the judiciary, the Court dismissed the action on the basis of standing because the plaintiffs could not show that they were likely to be arrested or convicted in the future.

2. Another instance of circumspect handling of racial claims in the criminal justice system was *McCleskey v. Kemp*, 481 U.S. 279 (1987), in which an elaborate statistical study tended to show that imposition of the death penalty in Georgia was imposed disproportionately on the basis of the race of the victim even more than on the basis of the race of the defendant. The Court emphasized the individual decisions of all the prosecutors and jurors in the system and refused to find that the death penalty was imposed through unconstitutional discriminatory intent or purpose.

3. By contrast, the Court has been much more willing to focus on claims of racial discrimination in the selection of a jury, a setting in which the record of a single case can be parsed to determine whether a pattern of racial disparity can be sufficient to infer intent on the part of the prosecutor. *Batson v. Kentucky*, 476 U.S. 79 (1986).

4. Although traffic stops may seem far removed from terrorism investigations, most of the claims of racial profiling have arisen in that setting. The basic Fourth Amendment standard for a reasonable stop that then results in a consensual search is whether the original stop was "pretextual." The Tenth Circuit opinion in *Marshall* discusses the original stop on the basis of whether the officer actually observed a traffic violation. In *United States v. Guzman*, 864 F.2d 1512 (10th Cir. 1988), the court adopted a test that focused on whether the presence of an invalid purpose, such as suspicion that the driver could be a drug courier, prevented a stop from being lawful: "whether under the same circumstances a reasonable officer would have made the stop in the absence of the invalid purpose." The same court later abandoned that test for a more simple test that leaves out the invalid purpose: "a traffic stop is valid under the Fourth Amendment if the stop is based on an observed traffic violation or if the police officer has reasonable articulable suspicion that a traffic or equipment violation has occurred or is occurring." *United States v. Botero-Ospina*, 71 F.3d 783 (10th Cir. 1995) (en banc holding over three dissents). Attempting to carry those thoughts to the context of terrorism investigations, we can ask whether it is valid to detain and question Arab visa violators with greater frequency than visa violators of other ethnic groups. Is the violation a sufficient basis even in the presence of what might be thought to be an "invalid purpose?"

[C] FEDERAL ETHNIC PROFILING

1. The Post-9/11 Investigation

In the wake of 9/11, the FBI questioned many recent immigrants and nonresident aliens. Some were detained on probable visa violations. Information about these detainees was kept from the public, and in many instances even from their families.

The Department of Justice's Office of Inspector General undertook a review of these detentions and the conditions of confinement.

In the aftermath of the September 11 terrorist attacks, the Department of Justice used the federal immigration laws to detain aliens who were suspected of having ties to the attacks or terrorism in general. More than 750 aliens who had violated immigration laws were arrested and detained in connection with the FBI's investigation into the attacks, called PENTTBOM. While recognizing the difficult circumstances confronting the Department in responding to the terrorist attacks, we found significant problems in the way the September 11 detainees were treated.

The report concluded that delays in processing detainees couple with a blanket "no bond" policy based on ethnicity deprived many detainees of the ability to communicate with counsel or family members. The report also found "a pattern of physical and verbal abuse by some correctional officers . . . against some September 11 detainees, particularly during the first months after the attacks."

Attorney General Ashcroft responded to the OIG Report with this statement:

The Justice Department believes that the Inspector General report is fully consistent with what courts have ruled over and over – that our actions are fully within the law and necessary to protect the American people. Our policy is to use all legal tools available to protect innocent Americans from terrorist attacks. We make no apologies for finding every legal way possible to protect the American public from further terrorist attacks.

Detention of illegal aliens is lawful. We detained illegal aliens encountered during the 9/11 terrorist investigation until it was determined they were not involved in terrorist activity, did not have relevant knowledge of terrorist activity, or it was determined that their removal was appropriate.

After reviewing the responses of the AG and INS, the DoJ Inspector General provided a follow-up analysis, which reported progress in improving the agencies' handling of the situation.

NOTES AND QUESTIONS

1. The DoJ Inspector General Report criticized a failure to distinguish between suspected terrorists and mere immigration violators. Why is this significant? Ted Bundy was stopped three times for traffic violations which led to his arrests for serial rape and murder. Other serial killers have been apprehended for similar violations. Criminal conspirators often commit minor violations in the course of their bigger conspiracies. If police are searching for a bank robber, shouldn't they be particularly alert to anyone driving recklessly, waving a pistol around, or wearing a mask on the street? What is wrong with picking up immigration violators to see if there is a terrorist lurking in their midst?

2. The Report also criticizes delays in processing and the conditions of confinement for many of the detainees. This general subject took on heightened importance with the disclosures of serious prisoner abuse at Guatanamo and Abu Ghraib, which we will consider in Chapter 9.

3. The Report also criticizes failure to provide access to lawyers or relatives. AG Ashcroft's statement and the government's position before the DC Circuit claim that secrecy was necessary to prevent terrorists from passing information to each other. How do we evaluate this fear?

2. The Federal Guidelines

The Department of Justice issued guidelines on racial profiling on June 17, 2003. "Guidance Regarding the Use of Race by Federal Law Enforcement Agencies" *http://www.usdoj.gov/crt/split/documents/guidance_on_race.htm*. The Guidelines generally prohibit any federal law enforcement agency from using racial characteristics in routine investigations.

The DoJ Guidelines and similar state statutes allow racial or ethnic descriptions as part of the description of a known suspect. If a description of a suspect characterizes him as a "Hispanic male," the police are likely to stop and question a disproportionate number of Hispanic males as compared to Asian or White males in the same vicinity. Is this ethnic profiling? If not, what is the difference?

The Guidelines distinguish between "traditional law enforcement activities" and "national security and border integrity." For "traditional" activities, the Guidelines state:

- In conducting activities in connection with a specific investigation, federal law enforcement officers may consider race and ethnicity only to the extent that there is trustworthy information, relevant to the locality or time frame, that links persons of a particular race or ethnicity to an identified criminal incident, scheme, or organization.

By contrast, for national security and border control, the Guidelines merely incorporate constitutional standards:

- In investigating or preventing threats to national security or other catastrophic events (including the performance of duties related to air transportation security), or in enforcing laws protecting the integrity of the nation's borders, federal law enforcement officers may not consider race or ethnicity except to the extent permitted by the Constitution and laws of the United States.

The Constitution prohibits consideration of race or ethnicity in law enforcement decisions in all but the most exceptional instances. Given the incalculably high stakes involved in such investigations, however, Federal law enforcement officers who are protecting national security or preventing catastrophic events (as well as airport security screeners) may consider race, ethnicity and other relevant factors to the extent permitted by our laws and the Constitution.

Example: U.S. intelligence sources report that Middle Eastern terrorists are planning to use commercial jetliners as weapons by hijacking them at an airport in California during the next week. Before allowing men appearing to be of Middle Eastern origin to board commercial airplanes in California airports during the next week, Transportation Security

Administration personnel, and other federal and state authorities, may subject them to heightened scrutiny.

These are very difficult "rules" to follow. At first glance, the example would seem to mean that ethnic identifiers can be considered only when there is a very specific threat at a specific place by a specific ethnically identifiable group. But the general statements indicate that ethnicity may be used to the extent of the Constitution. Because there are virtually no cases holding that preliminary screening and investigations are controlled by constitutional restraints, it is difficult to know the limits of using ethnicity in these contexts.

If there were any sanctions attached to the Guidelines, a person attempting to comply with them might complain that they were either vague or ambiguous. The Guidelines, however, are just that – guidelines – and do not seem to have any coercive force behind them.

It has been argued that ethnic profiling is inefficient because "an overwhelming number of 'suspects' will prove to be innocent, no matter what combination of factors is used to focus in on them." Although it could "turn out that in the case of terrorism, a particular segment of the population is in fact disproportionately represented among offenders," she nevertheless worries that "future generations may judge us as harshly as we now judge the supporters of internment during World War II." Sherry F. Colb, "Racial Profiling and Terrorism," *http://writ.news.findlaw.com/colb/20011010.html* (Oct. 10, 2001).

Some people would argue that focused questioning of Arab and Muslim males in the current environment could actually increase the incidence of terrorism. "Whether the targets are Muslim and Arab Americans or Blacks and Latinos, all victims of racial and ethnic profiling are left feeling humiliated, angry and distrustful of law enforcement. These feelings of anger and distrust add to tensions that often exist between ethnic minorities and law enforcement." Dan Salvin, Urban Voices, "Racial/Ethnic Profiling Is Still Wrong," *http://www.urbanvoicesonline.com/Racial%20and%20ethnic%20profiling.htm).*

There was a fear expressed even by such insiders as some former CIA employees in the lead-up to Gulf War II, that invading Iraq would actually produce more terrorists for the anti-American cause.

This area leaves us with any number of difficult policy issues to consider:

1. Are there constitutional or legal limitations on the use of ethnicity in a preliminary screening or investigation?

2. How specific must an ethnic-cultural threat be to trigger the permissible use of ethnicity as a screening device?

3. As a sheer pragmatic matter, setting morality or justice aside if one can do so, is there more to fear from passing up a chance to interdict a given threat or from alienating a segment of the population?

For critical discussions of these issues, see David A. Harris, *New Risks, New Tactics: An Assessment of the Re-Assessment of Racial Profiling in the Wake of September 11, 2001*, 2004 UTAH L. REV. 913; Liam Braber, *Korematsu's Ghost: A Post-September 11th Analysis of Race and National Security*, 47 VILL. L. REV. 451 (2002).

§ 7.05   PREVENTION AND FREE EXPRESSION

A related aspect of the intersection between preventive safety measures and constitutional liberties is the degree to which demonstrations and protests can be curtailed at public or semi-public events. There is not room here to go into all the ramifications of public forum doctrine, but there are some good recent cases dealing primarily with rights of ingress and egress at government facilities and political gatherings. Security planners at a major public event will need to balance concerns over ingress and egress with the first amendment interests of those with dissident positions, while also considering available intelligence that may indicate the potential for disruption or even violence at the event.

UNITED STATES v. BAUGH

187 F.3d 1037 (9th Cir. 1999)

SCHROEDER, Circuit Judge:

Pamela Baugh and other members of a group called Religious Witness with Homeless People ("RWHP") appeal their convictions for demonstrating without a permit on National Park property, in violation of 36 C.F.R. § 2.51(a). At the time of their arrest, the defendants were protesting the Park Service's plan to demolish the Wherry housing in the Presidio in San Francisco instead of using the units to house the homeless.

The defendants challenge the constitutional validity of the permit regulation and its implementing rules both facially and as applied to their protest. We do not reach the facial challenge, for we hold that the Park Service's application of the regulation to the defendants violated the defendants' First Amendment rights.

Facts and Procedural History

The demonstration for which the government arrested the defendants occurred on March 9, 1997. This was not the first time RWHP had protested the planned destruction of the housing that it wanted used to house the homeless. In past protests by the organization at the Presidio, after marching through the Wherry housing area, some RWHP members had trespassed into the housing and had refused to leave until they were arrested. On these occasions, the trespassing demonstrators were arrested both for demonstrating without a permit and for trespass, but were only prosecuted for trespass.

Park Police Lieutenant Kevin Hay learned of the March 9th demonstration a few days before. He telephoned Sister Bernie Galvin, executive director of RWHP, and asked her if the group wanted a permit. Lt. Hay told Sister Bernie that RWHP would receive a permit only if Sister Bernie promised that no trespassing into the units would occur at the march. Sister Bernie indicated that RWHP desired a permit but refused to promise that no trespassing would occur.

Although the earlier protests had taken place solely at the housing area, RWHP intended to convene on March 9th at the Visitor Center, in a different part of the Presidio, before going to the Wherry housing area to march. On March 9th, about 150 to 175 RWHP members gathered before the Visitor Center. Sister Bernie spoke to Lt. Hay two or three times at that location. He again made it clear that the permit would issue only if Sister Bernie would promise that none of the RWHP members would trespass into the housing units. Sister Bernie again refused to make this pledge.

Lt. Hay told Sister Bernie that the group would have to move to an area reserved for protestors known as the "First Amendment area" located 150 to 175 yards from the Visitor Center. Sister Bernie declined this option as well. She and other RWHP members believed that the designated area was located too far away from the Visitor Center to convey RWHP's message to Park Service officials and the public. Because of the Park Service's stance, the group gave up their march and decided instead to hold a prayer service where they stood: on the Visitor Center's lawn. Shortly after the inception of the prayer service, Lt. Hay made several announcements that the group would be arrested if it did not move to the First Amendment area. Although some RWHP demonstrators went to the First Amendment area or crossed the street, those who remained in front of the Visitor Center were promptly arrested.

The record contains some indication that the protestors may have caused some disruption of Visitor Center activities, but the Park Service did not arrest defendants for this reason. It arrested defendants solely for not having a permit to engage in their expressive activities. According to Lt. Hay's testimony, the Park Service might have permitted the demonstration to go forward at a location much closer to the Visitor Center than the so-called First Amendment area had Sister Bernie been willing to negotiate further. Sister Bernie, for her part, testified that she did not believe she possessed this option.

The defendants moved to quash their arrests on the grounds that the arrests violated the First Amendment and the district court denied the motion. The court held that 36 C.F.R. § 2.51 and the Park Service's implementing regulations were constitutional on their face and as applied to the defendants. On April 13, 1998, after a one-day bench trial, defendants were convicted of demonstrating without a permit in violation of § 2.51(a). The district court held that the no-trespassing condition imposed by the Park Service constituted a reasonable condition for the permit. The district court sentenced the defendants to ninety days of unsupervised probation and twelve hours of community service.

The Regulation and Its Implementing Rules

The permit regulation presumptively allows expressive activities, provided the Park superintendent has issued a permit in advance. The regulation further specifies that the superintendent shall, without unreasonable delay, issue a permit upon a proper application unless certain conditions apply. One such condition is "it reasonably appears that the event will present a clear and present danger to the public health or safety." Another condition is the inability to accommodate the event in the applied-for location due to the nature of the event and considering such factors as damage to park resources or facilities, damage to a protected area's atmosphere of peace and tranquility, or disturbance of program activities or public use facilities.

The regulation also provides that the superintendent should designate on a map the locations available for public assemblies. These areas must be available for assemblies unless, *inter alia*, the activities would cause injury or damage to park resources; unreasonably interfere with interpretive, visitor service, or other program activities, or with the administrative activities of the National Park Service; substantially interfere with the operation of public use facilities; or present a clear and present danger to the public health and safety.

The compendium of implementing regulations designates three locations within the Presidio for which the Park Service will issue permits for First Amendment activities. If a group wishes to stage a special event, it may apply to the superintendent for the designation of an additional First Amendment area. If the criteria in the regulations are complied with, the superintendent will designate another specific location for the exercise of First Amendment activities. At trial, a Park Service official testified that he had the authority to issue floating permits to groups who applied and who wished to hold First Amendment activities that warranted such a permit.

The Constitutionality of the Regulation as Applied

A march and other protest activities clearly constitute protected speech. *See Shuttlesworth v. City of Birmingham*, 394 U.S. 147, 152 (1969) (describing the privilege of citizens to assemble, parade, and discuss public questions in streets and parks). We have stressed that a public park, such as the Presidio, represents a "quintessential public forum." "Parks . . . have immemorially been held in trust for the use of the public and, time out of mind, have been used for purposes of assembly, communicating thoughts between citizens, and discussing public questions." (quoting *Hague v. CIO,* 307 U.S. 496, 515 (1939)).

The refusal of the Park Service to authorize any expressive activity in the Presidio absent the defendants' promise to keep out of certain areas constitutes a "prior restraint" that prevented expressive activity from occurring. Prior restraints on speech bear a heavy presumption of unconstitutionality because they "are the most serious and the least tolerable infringements on First Amendment rights." However, even prior restraints may be imposed if they amount to reasonable time, place, and manner restrictions on speech. To qualify as a permissible restriction, the regulation must be content neutral, narrowly tailored to serve a significant governmental interest, and leave open ample alternative channels for communication of the message.

We are not the first court to consider this regulatory scheme. The few decisions have not been uniform.

In *United States v. Kistner,* 68 F.3d 218 (8th Cir. 1995), the Eighth Circuit examined § 2.52, the companion regulation to § 2.51 that pertains to pamphleting and that contains similar language. The court held that the regulation did not violate the First Amendment on its face nor as applied to the defendant. The defendant in *Kistner* had been arrested for distributing religious pamphlets without a permit in Jefferson National Expansion Memorial, in St. Louis. The pro se defendant broadly argued that the latitude given to park officials by the regulation created a risk that the discretion would be exercised based on the content of speech *Kistner* rejected this argument, finding that the regulation contained guidelines for the issuance of the permit and that the record belied the defendant's contention that the park granted and denied permits based on content.

Two district courts, however, have found similar permit schemes to the one that confronts us unconstitutional on their face. *See Naturist Soc y v. Fillyaw,* 858 F. Supp. 1559 (S.D. Fla. 1994); *United States v. Rainbow Family,* 695 F. Supp. 294 (E.D. Tex. 1988). Both courts held that the regulations were unduly vague and thus bestowed too much discretion upon park officials because, *inter alia*, the provisions in the regulations allowed park officials to deny permits if they perceived that the demonstration presented "a clear and present danger."

The regulation before us also authorizes denial of a permit on grounds of "clear and present danger." The government in part relies on this subsection to justify its refusal to issue RWHP a permit absent a promise not to trespass. We need not reach the issue of the facial constitutionality of § 2.51, however, because we hold that even if the regulation on its face created reasonable time, place, and manner constraints, the Park Service unconstitutionally applied the requirement when it refused to issue a permit for any expressive activity in this case.

The first criteria for a reasonable restriction on speech is that the restriction be content neutral, or "justified without reference to the content of the regulated speech." This requirement appears to have been met. Lt. Hay testified that the Park Service insisted on the promise of no trespassing out of a concern for preventing property damage and protecting the safety of protesters who might injure themselves by trespassing into the uninhabited Wherry houses. These concerns did not stem from the underlying content of RWHP's message. The government had a significant interest in protecting the Presidio's facilities and its users, including the protesters.

The critical question is whether the requirement that Sister Bernie promise that no trespassing would occur before the Park Service would issue RWHP a permit was sufficiently narrowly tailored to constitute a valid First Amendment restriction. A narrowly tailored requirement need not be the least restrictive means of furthering the Park Service's interests, but the restriction may not burden substantially more speech than necessary to further the interests. To do otherwise would be to burden substantially those seeking to express their political views. Organizers of protests ordinarily cannot warrant in good faith that all the participants in a demonstration will comply with the law. Demonstrations are often robust. No one can guarantee how demonstrators will behave throughout the course of the entire protest. Thus, the promise the Park Service sought would be illusory and meaningless at best.

We have held that a complete ban on First Amendment activity cannot be justified simply because past similar activity led to violence. *See Collins v. Jordan,* 110 F.3d 1363, 1371-72 (9th Cir. 1997). In *Collins,* this court disapproved of a San Francisco policy instituted in the days following the Rodney King verdict, to disperse demonstrations before the demonstrators acted illegally or posed any threat to other people or activities. We stated that "the generally accepted way of dealing with unlawful conduct that may be intertwined with First Amendment activity is to punish it after it occurs rather than to prevent the First Amendment activity from occurring in order to obviate the possible unlawful conduct." The Park Service, in lieu of restraining the expressive activity by refusing to issue the permit, should have issued the permit for the lawful expressive activity and then arrested the demonstrators if and when they trespassed.

The Supreme Court's decision in *Clark [v. Community for Creative Non-Violence*, 468 U.S. 288 (1984)], illustrates the point. In that case, a group wished to draw attention to the plight of homelessness by holding a day and night wintertime demonstration in Lafayette Park and on the Mall in Washington, D.C. The Park Service granted the group a permit to erect two symbolic tent cities. However, the Park Service refused to grant the group's request for a permit allowing the demonstrators to sleep in the tents. The Supreme Court held that the limitation the Park Service placed on the permit constituted a valid restriction on the manner of the demonstration. The Park Service in *Clark* issued the permit to allow a lawful demonstration to go forward. It did not withhold the right to any demonstration.

In this case, by failing to tailor the no-trespass condition narrowly to allow for lawful demonstrations, the Park Service also failed to leave open sufficient alternative means for the protestors to communicate their views. Lt. Hay ordered the demonstrators to a First Amendment area 150 to 175 yards away from the Visitor Center. The Park Service officials and the public to whom RWHP wished to communicate its message were at the Visitor Center. Such distancing of the demonstrators from the intended audience does not provide a reasonable alternative means for communication of RWHP's views. In *Bay Area Peace Navy*, we held that requiring a 75-yard security zone between demonstrators and the persons to whom they directed their message did not leave open ample alternative means of communicating the protesters' message. 914 F.2d at 1229. We stated that "an alternative is not ample if the speaker is not permitted to reach the 'intended audience.'" *Id.* (citation omitted); *see also Heffron v. International Soc y for Krishna Consciousness, Inc.*, 452 U.S. 640, 655 (1981) ("The First Amendment protects the right of every citizen to 'reach the minds of willing listeners and to do so there must be opportunity to win their attention.'" (citation omitted)); *cf. Schenck v. Pro-Choice Network of W.N.Y.*, 519 U.S. 357, 377 (1997) (floating buffer zones prevent abortion protesters from communicating their message). Because RWHP was left with no alternative that allowed it to reach its intended audience, the Park Service's application of the permit regulations also failed to satisfy the final requirement for valid First Amendment restrictions.

The judgment is REVERSED with instructions to VACATE defendants' convictions and sentences.

SILVERMAN, Circuit Judge, concurring:

On March 9, 1997, the defendants set out to get arrested at the Presidio to generate publicity for their cause. They admit that. They could have obtained the requisite permit if they would have agreed to comply with the permit. They admit that, too. They could have demonstrated in the First Amendment area of the Presidio without any permit whatsoever. That, also, is admitted. The problem is that if the defendants had agreed to comply with the permit or to hold their demonstration in the First Amendment area, they wouldn't have gotten themselves arrested, which is what they wanted to accomplish to begin with. It is in the context of this contrived, intentionally provoked controversy that the defendants attack both the facial constitutionality of 36 C.F.R. § 2.51(a) and the constitutionality of that section as applied.

Although I agree with the result reached by the majority, I write separately to express some sympathy for the situation faced by the officers of the Park Service in this case. Contrary to the main opinion's dramatic overstatement, the Park Service officers did not prohibit the defendants from engaging in "any expressive activity in the Presidio" on the day in question. They could have expressed themselves to their hearts' content in the First Amendment area. The First Amendment area was not Siberia. It was located only 150 yards or so away, and in view of, the Visitors Center.

Likewise, the Park Service officers were ready, willing and able to issue a floating permit so that the defendants could conduct their demonstration elsewhere in the Presidio if they would have agreed to comply with it. And as the main opinion acknowledges, the denial of the permit was content-neutral, i.e., "did not stem from the underlying content of [the defendants'] message."

The Park Service certainly had plenty of reason to believe that the organizers of the demonstration *intended* to violate the very permit for which they were applying. As Sister Bernie testified, at the time Lt. Hays asked for an assurance that the permit would be complied with, "He had a copy of our press release that had gone out earlier which also indicated that we were going to do civil disobedience. * * * We couldn't agree to the condition of no civil disobedience and we found being relegated to a remote area where we indeed could not witness was simply unacceptable."

In retrospect, what the Park Service should have done is issue the permit, await its advertised violation, and then make the arrest. The Park Service should not have denied the permit just because it anticipated a violation. However, one certainly can understand why conscientious officers, concerned with the public safety and the protection of park property, would want to try to head off a 150-person trespass, if possible. Although it is difficult to articulate when threatened First Amendment activity might create such a clear and present danger to public safety that it can be prevented in advance, Sunday in the park with Sister Bernie was not such a case.

NOTES AND QUESTIONS

1. In *Rowley v. McMillan*, 502 F.2d 1326 (4th Cir. 1974), the Fourth Circuit held unconstitutional a Secret Service attempt to prevent dissident members of the public from entering a gathering at which President Nixon was due to appear. The district court had granted a preliminary injunction for future appearances of the President to prevent the defendants from

discriminatorily arresting or detaining, or keeping from the general public presence of the President, plaintiffs and others similarly situated, on account of their mode of dress or hair style, life style, peaceable expression of political (including dissenting) views, exercise of constitutional rights of free speech, petition for redress of grievances or right of association, without prior judicial authorization or without probable cause, or for any other cause not rationally necessary for the personal safety of the President.

The Government did not contest that the injunction accurately reflected constitutional standards but argued only that the case was moot, that the facts did not reflect Secret Service involvement in the decision to exclude plaintiffs, and that the officers involved should have immunity from damages.

Butler v. United States, 365 F. Supp. 1035 (D. Hawaii 1973), was a similar action arising from a visit by President Nixon to an Air Force base in Hawaii.

2. *Service Employees Local 660 v. City of Los Angeles*, 114 F. Supp. 2d 966 (C.D. Cal. 2000). When the Democratic National Convention of 2000 was scheduled at the Staples Center in Los Angeles, the LAPD and Secret Service planned out a "secure zone" of about 12 square blocks around the facility. Entry into that zone was limited by pass, while "some 260 yards from the entrance to the Staples Center, a small 'protest' or 'demonstration' site has been designated for use during the convention." Plaintiffs included groups that wanted to picket closer to the event. The court found that the secure zone was not narrowly tailored, that the protest zone was too far removed to allow access to the speakers' intended audiences, and that the secure zone had to be reconfigured to allow reasonable access by the plaintiffs to those attending the event. Most pertinent to our concerns was this statement: "The government cannot infringe on First Amendment rights on the mere speculation that violence may occur."

3. The Supreme Court's most notable foray into this arena was *Madsen v. Women's Health Center*, 512 U.S. 753 (1994), the principal abortion demonstration case. The Court upheld restrictions imposed by a state court on noise levels outside the clinic and a 36-foot buffer zone to allow unimpeded ingress, and egress to the clinic but struck down other provisions of the state court's order such as restrictions on personal contact with patrons and prohibition of "observable images."

4. What can you as the lawyer advising security personnel do with information about the plans of a dissident group to disrupt an event? Does it matter how the information was gathered? For example, consider the differences among these modes of gathering intelligence in advance of an event:

    a. by undercover officers attending a meeting of a dissident group

        i. without misidentifying themselves in any way

        ii. pretending to be members of the group

    b. by surveillance pursuant to a FISA order

Following some public criticism of FBI practices that included agents' attending mosques and taking notes on conversations or behavior, the Attorney General issued new "Guidelines on . . . Terrorism Enterprise Investigations" in May 2002. With regard to attending public events, the Guidelines stated:

> For the purpose of detecting or preventing terrorist activities, the FBI is authorized to visit any place and attend any event that is open to the public, on the same terms and conditions as members of the public generally. No

information obtained from such visits shall be retained unless it relates to potential criminal or terrorist activity.

SELECTED READINGS

▸ DAVID COLE & JAMES X. DEMPSEY, TERRORISM AND THE CONSTITUTION (2002).

▸ PHILLIP H. MELANSON, SECRECY WARS: NATIONAL SECURITY, PRIVACY, AND THE PUBLIC'S RIGHT TO KNOW (2001).

▸ SAMUEL DASH, THE INTRUDERS: UNREASONABLE SEARCHES AND SEIZURES FROM KING JOHN TO JOHN ASHCROFT (2004).

▸ JEFFREY ROSEN, THE NAKED CROWD: RECLAIMING SECURITY AND FREEDOM IN AN ANXIOUS AGE (2004).

▸ RONALD DANIELS, PATRICK MACKLEM & KENT ROACH, THE SECURITY OF FREEDOM: ESSAYS ON CANADA'S ANTI-TERRORISM BILL (2001).

USA PATRIOT Act:

▸ Nathan C. Henderson, *Note: The Patriot Act's Impact on the Government's Ability to Conduct Electronic Surveillance of Ongoing Domestic Communications*, 52 DUKE L.J. 179 (2002).

▸ Steven A. Osher, *Privacy, Computers and the Patriot Act: The Fourth Amendment Isn't Dead, But No One Will Insure It*, 54 FLA. L. REV. 521 (2002).

▸ Craig S. Lerner, *The USA PATRIOT Act: Promoting the Cooperation of Foreign Intelligence Gathering and Law Enforcement*, 11 GEO. MASON L. REV. 493 (2003).

▸ Symposium, *Internet Surveillance, Privacy & the USA PATRIOT Act*, 72 GEO. WASH. L. REV. 1145 (2004).

▸ David Hard, *Note: The Fuss over Two Small Words: The Unconstitutionality of the USA PATRIOT Act Amendments to FISA Under the Fourth Amendment*, 71 GEO. WASH. L. REV. 291 (2003).

Immigration and Ethnic Profiling:

▸ DAVID COLE, ENEMY ALIENS: DOUBLE STANDARDS AND CONSTITUTIONAL FREEDOMS IN THE WAR ON TERRORISM (2003).

▸ DAVID A. HARRIS, PROFILES IN INJUSTICE: WHY RACIAL PROFILING CANNOT WORK (2002).

▸ Gerald L. Neuman, *Terrorism, Selective Deportation and the First Amendment After* Reno v. AADC, 14 GEO. IMMIGR. L.J. 313 (2000).

▸ Robert M. Chesney, *Civil Liberties and the Terrorism Prevention Paradigm: The Guilt by Association Critique*, 101 MICH. L. REV. 1408 (2003).

▸ Natsu Taylor Smith, *For "Our" Security: Who Is an "American" and What Is Protected by Enhanced Law Enforcement and Intelligence Powers?"* 2 SEATTLE J. SOC. JUSTICE 24 (2003).

Chapter 8

THE MILITARY OPTION

The most powerful physical institution of humanity is the military. At an earlier point in this course, we looked at the international norms of warfare as part of the background for why and how terrorism could be controlled by international institutions. This chapter returns to the mechanisms for deploying and controlling the power of military force, which will take us back to international law because the law to be applied by military commissions and tribunals would be the "law of war," which is international law.

For discussions of the wisdom of using military force in the struggle to contain terrorism, see the readings listed at the end of the chapter.

President Bush's order authorizing military commissions for the trial of suspected terrorists and collaborators was promulgated on November 13, 2001. It is patterned on the orders issued during World War II to deal with suspected spies in *Ex parte Quirin*, 317 U.S. 1 (1942). Similar orders were issued following WWII for war-crimes trials of both German and Japanese officials.

The order allows the Secretary of Defense to establish a military commission for trial of "all offenses" alleged to be committed by any person who the President finds "is or was a member of the organization known as al Qaida" or "has engaged in, aided or abetted, or conspired to commit, acts of international terrorism, or acts in preparation therefor, that have caused, threaten to cause, or have as their aim to cause, injury to or adverse effects on the United States, its citizens, national security, foreign policy, or economy." The order does not appear to attempt creation of any new crimes but refers instead to "offenses triable by military commission" and "penalties under applicable law."

[handwritten margin note: E.O. authorizing use of Mil. Trbs.]

The order was first met with some skepticism but very little open criticism. Professor Paust (a former faculty member at the JAG School) has been the most vigorously outspoken academic critic of the order. Jordan J. Paust, *Antiterrorism Military Commissions: Courting Illegality*, 23 MICH. J. INT'L L. 1 (Fall 2001). An early response to the criticisms was provided by Curtis A. Bradley and Jack L. Goldsmith, *The Constitutional Validity of Military Commissions*, 5 GREEN BAG 2d 249 (2002). Other scholarly exchanges are collected at the end of this chapter.

No prosecutions were begun under the order until after the Supreme Court decided in *Rasul v. Bush*, p. 521 *infra*, that alien military detainees were entitled to some determination of their status by a neutral decision maker. The first prosecution then was derailed by the D.C. District Court in *Hamdan v. Rumsfeld*, p. 535 *infra*.

Meanwhile, the military intelligence community has been incorporated into the hunt for terrorists through mandates to cooperate with the CIA and domestic intelligence agencies. All of this activity causes us to question the wisdom of involving the military in domestic security. We will first look at the "posse comitatus" provisions that impede military involvement in domestic law enforcement, along with the concept of martial law, and then look at the history of military commissions in the United States. In the next section, we will look at the potential for use of military tribunals and military detentions in the terrorism context.

§ 8.01 DOMESTIC ROLE OF THE MILITARY

The "posse comitatus" statute prohibits employment of the military in civil law enforcement. The phrase (roughly translated as "power of the county") refers to the inherent discretion of civil authorities to call on the entire population to assist in maintaining order or apprehending criminals. The thrust of the statute is to exclude the military from that usage.

18 U.S.C. §1385 (2003):

Whoever, except in cases and under circumstances expressly authorized by the Constitution or Act of Congress, willfully uses any part of the Army or the Air Force as a posse comitatus or otherwise to execute the laws shall be fined under this title or imprisoned not more than two years, or both.

These provisions were extended to the Navy and Marines by 10 U.S.C. §375, which also provides for the Secretary of Defense to promulgate regulations "to ensure that any [assistance to state and local authorities] does not include or permit direct participation . . . in a search, seizure, arrest, or other similar activity."

The statute was first adopted in 1875 as part of the end of Reconstruction, the immediate impetus being the presence of military troops as election monitors when civil authority had been restored. Although the sweep of the statute could be read as building a wall between military and civilian authorities, it has not been given that effect by subsequent Congresses. Indeed, Congress has authorized a wide array of military assistance to federal, state, or local authorities in pursuit of maintaining order or law enforcement, so long as military personnel are not directly engaged in searches or arrests. Courts have routinely upheld "passive" engagement of military personnel in support of civilian criminal investigations and have upheld "active" participation of military personnel in criminal enforcement when the offense concerns a military facility or activity.

The effect of the posse comitatus statute on the question of declaring martial law essentially is to preserve the power to make such a declaration in Congress. The military can be used to assist directly in civil law enforcement only when authorized by statute. This approach codifies, with some clarification, the results reached following the Civil War and Reconstruction. Prior to that time, the Judiciary Act of 1789 had authorized federal marshals to call on the military to serve as a posse whenever it was useful for execution of the law. WILLIAM WINTHROP, MILITARY LAW AND PRECEDENTS 866-67 (reprint 1920).

In *Texas v. White*, 74 U.S. 700 (1868), the Supreme Court validated the occupation of Southern states by federal military force following the Civil War. In *Ex parte Milligan*, 71 U.S. 2 (1866), the Court invalidated the trial of civilians by military tribunals in areas in which the civilian courts were open and operating. The combination of these cases could be read as permitting martial law in areas that are in a state of war but not allowing it elsewhere. As Colonel Winthrop points out, however, this would be an oversimplification. WINTHROP at 799.

To go further, we need to distinguish between military government and martial law. The former is the result of occupation of hostile territory, whether foreign or rebellious. The latter is a condition that provides a military complement to the civil authorities on home soil because of an emergency. Military government completely supplants civil government while martial law provides a type of self-defensive use of force commensurate with the necessity. The Supreme Court adopted this view in *Duncan v. Kahanamoku*, 327 U.S. 304 (1946), when it overturned a conviction by military tribunal in Hawaii during a time of declared martial law because the civilian courts were open and operating.

Duncan does not deny the possibility of using military presence to supplement or even replace some functions of civilian government in time of actual emergency. The examples cited in *Duncan* of martial law to quell civil disturbances stemming principally from labor disputes do not seem to have taken into account the *posse comitatus* statute. Given the tacit approval of the use of troops in those cases, so long as crimes were tried in the civilian courts, it is not clear how the Court would deal with this statutory argument. Some further insight might be gleaned from *Youngstown Sheet & Tube v. Sawyer*, 343 U.S. 579 (1952), in which the Court struck down President Truman's attempt to seize the steel mills to avert labor strife during the Korean War. Only the three dissenting Justices were impressed by the argument that there was any level of national emergency justifying unilateral seizure without congressional authorization.

In his classic concurrence analyzing separation of powers, Justice Jackson pointed out that the President is on strongest ground when he acts with congressional authorization, may or may not have constitutional powers when acting in congressional silence, and must have strong independent constitutional grounds when going against the will of Congress. To justify military force to perform civil law enforcement after passage of the posse comitatus legislation, the President would have to persuade a majority of the court that a genuine emergency existed sufficient to justify departure from specific congressional direction. After the experience of *Korematsu*, *Duncan*, and *Youngstown*, it is possible that little short of imminent invasion would justify unilateral action. As a practical matter, however, it would take some time before a court could intervene, by which time the presence of a genuine emergency would likely be known or dispelled.

Other than martial law as an emergency measure, some use of the military to assist civilian authorities in times of civil disturbance is also possible and its limits are found only in the statutes that prevent use of the military in direct search and arrest of offenders.

Although the posse comitatus statute seems to imply that the military can have no involvement in civilian law enforcement, another federal statute offers assistance to state governments in time of "insurrection." 10 U.S.C. § 331:

Whenever there is an insurrection in any State against its government, the President may, upon the request of its legislature or of its governor if the legislature cannot be convened, call into Federal service such of the militia of the other States, in the number requested by that State, and use such of the armed forces, as he considers necessary to suppress the insurrection.

The "insurrection" statute amounts to a standing delegation from Congress of the power to make an exception to the posse comitatus statute when a state government requests assistance and the President finds that there is a need for military force to "suppress the insurrection." It does not, however, appear to be a standing delegation of the power to declare martial law. That power remains implicitly within Congress unless it cannot meet.

The authority of the President under the insurrection statute has come before the Supreme Court on only two occasions, and one of those did not involve insurrection. (One other insurrection case did not involve validity of a military call-out. With regard to Shea's Rebellion, the Court held that it had no power to determine which of the contending parties was the legitimate government of a state, that this is a question for the political branches. *Luther v. Borden*, 48 U.S. 1 (1849).) In *Martin v. Mott*, 25 U.S. (12 Wheat.) 19 (1827), a member of the New York militia had refused to answer the President's call to arms during the War of 1812. He was fined, his belongings were seized, and he brought a replevin action claiming that the President was without authority to order him into service prior to an actual invasion of the territory of the U.S. His first argument was that the fact of a military emergency should have been shown to the court, to which the Supreme Court seemed to respond that the President's determination was conclusive on the courts as well as on military personnel. The only reason to hedge with the phrase "seemed to respond" is that all the arguments put forth by the Court were addressed to the need for immediate unquestioning obedience by military personnel.

[T]he authority to decide whether the exigency has arisen, belongs exclusively to the President, and that his decision is conclusive upon all other persons. We think that this construction necessarily results from the nature of the power itself, and from the manifest object contemplated by the act of Congress. The power itself is to be exercised upon sudden emergencies, upon great occasions of state, and under circumstances which may be vital to the existence of the Union.

The argument is, that the power confided to the President is a limited power, and can be exercised only in the cases pointed out in the statute, and therefore it is necessary to aver the fact which bring the exercise within the purview of the statute. . . . When the President exercises an authority confided to him by law, the presumption that it is exercised in pursuance of law. Every public officer is presumed to act in obedience to his duty, until the contrary is shown; and, a fortiori, this presumption ought to be favourably applied to the chief magistrate of the Union. It is not necessary to aver, that the act which he may rightfully do, was so done. If the fact of the existence of the exigency were averred, it would be traversable, and of course might be passed upon by a jury; and thus the legality of the orders of the President would depend, not on his own judgment of the facts, but upon the finding of those facts upon the proofs submitted to a jury.

Whether those same arguments would hold when a court was faced with a more doubtful situation, one in which the presence of a military threat was less clear, could be a slightly different matter as we will see with *Youngstown Sheet & Tube*.

The *Prize Cases*, 67 U.S. 635 (1863), contained similar language seeming to grant the President unreviewable discretion to engage in acts of war. Several ships owned by foreign nationals and flagged by neutral countries had been seized while running a blockade against the Confederate states. The owners argued that the President lacked authority to enforce a blockade against neutrals, and the Court responded:

> Whether the President in fulfilling his duties, as Commander-in-chief, in suppressing an insurrection, has met with such armed hostile resistance, and a civil war of such alarming proportions as will compel him to accord to them the character of belligerents, is a question to be decided by him, and this Court must be governed by the decisions and acts of the political department of the Government to which this power was entrusted. "He must determine what degree of force the crisis demands." The proclamation of blockade is itself official and conclusive evidence to the Court that a state of war existed which demanded and authorized a recourse to such a measure, under the circumstances peculiar to the case.

Again the word "seeming" is used in describing the Court's deference to the President to emphasize that there was no question about the state of armed conflict between the Union and Confederacy, and that the only significant arguments in the case had to do with the status of the contending sides under international law. Whether the President needed deference regarding the fact of armed conflict was hardly in issue.

The only twentieth century case citing the assistance statute is a federal court case dealing with property damage in DC during the riots following the 1968 assassination of Dr. Martin Luther King. Insurers who had paid out damage claims brought suit against the U.S. alleging that the government had been negligent in failing to call out the militia or use military force to suppress the riots. The district court simply pointed out that "the decision whether to use troops or the militia (National Guard) in quelling a civil disorder is exclusively within the province of the President. The Courts also have made it clear that presidential discretion in exercising those powers granted in the Constitution and in the implementing statutes is not subject to judicial review." *Monarch Ins. Co. v. District of Columbia*, 353 F. Supp. 1249 (D.D.C. 1973).

It is one thing to say that there is no constitutional duty on the part of the President to call out military force, but it would be quite another to say that the President lacked authority to call out military force unless an insurrection justified it to the satisfaction of a court. Common sense would indicate that a judge would be loathe to intervene in the face of any genuine threat of imminent violence, a position that needs little elaboration of a claim of deference to executive judgment.

The most extensive analysis of the posse comitatus and assistance statutes came in a series of cases arising out of the three-week occupation of Wounded Knee by members of the American Indian Movement in 1973. Various defendants were prosecuted for offenses such as trespass, assault, and interference with federal officers in the discharge of their duties. The defendants pointed to the involvement of military units in what could have been viewed as an ordinary law enforcement operation and asserted that this involvement violated the posse comitatus statute. This defense was relevant at least to the question of whether the federal officers were "lawfully engaged in the discharge of their duties."

The FBI and Bureau of Indian Affairs had closed off the town to prevent additional sympathizers from joining those dissidents already on the scene. As part of the control operation, military units assisted with advice, aerial reconnaissance and the loan of equipment. The district judges dealing with the defense of posse comitatus violation reached different conclusions with different standards for testing the validity of military involvement. To Judge Urbom, the statute would be violated if military personnel influenced the decisions of the civilian officers or actively maintained and operated the equipment provided. *United States v. Jaramillo*, 380 F. Supp. 1375 (D. Neb. 1974). Judge Nichol went "one step further" than Judge Ubrom and held that there was no evidence justifying submission of issues to the jury regarding the nature of the military involvement. *United States v. Banks*, 383 F. Supp. 368 (D.S.D. 1974). Judge Bogue provided a more nuanced analysis by concentrating on whether military personnel were "actively engaged in law enforcement." *United States v. Red Feather*, 392 F. Supp. 916 (D.S.D. 1975):

> Based upon the clear intent of Congress, this Court holds that the clause "to execute the laws", contained in 18 U.S.C. § 1385, makes unlawful the use of federal military troops in an active role of direct law enforcement by civil law enforcement officers. Activities which constitute an active role in direct law enforcement are: arrest; seizure of evidence; search of a person; search of a building; investigation of crime; interviewing witnesses; pursuit of an escaped civilian prisoner; search of an area for a suspect and other like activities. Such use of federal military troops to "execute the laws", or as the Court has defined the clause, in "an active role of direct law enforcement", is unlawful under 18 U.S.C. § 1385.
>
> Activities which constitute a passive role which might indirectly aid law enforcement are: mere presence of military personnel under orders to report on the necessity for military intervention; preparation of contingency plans to be used if military intervention is ordered; advice or recommendations given to civilian law enforcement officers by military personnel on tactics or logistics; presence of military personnel to deliver military materiel, equipment or supplies, to train local law enforcement officials on the proper use and care of such material or equipment, and to maintain such materiel or equipment; aerial photographic reconnaissance flights and other like activities.

"a ctive" role

"passive" role

In this sequence of cases, the judges took varying approaches to interpreting the phrase "use [military] forces . . . to execute the laws." Although there were constitutional concerns lurking in the background of the analyses, the focus was on whether Congress had authorized or prohibited the use of military force in domestic disturbances.

§ 8.02 MILITARY TRIBUNALS IN U.S. HISTORY

The Bush Military Tribunal Order was premised on *Ex parte Quirin*, which upheld military commissions to deal with alleged saboteurs on U.S. soil during World War II. *Quirin*, however, was sandwiched between two cases striking down use of military tribunals for civilians.

Ex Parte MILLIGAN

71 U.S. 2 (4 Wall.) (1866)

Mr. Justice DAVIS delivered the opinion of the court.

On the 10th day of May, 1865, Lambdin P. Milligan presented a petition to the Circuit Court of the United States for the District of Indiana, to be discharged from an alleged unlawful imprisonment. The case made by the petition is this: Milligan is a citizen of the United States; has lived for twenty years in Indiana; and, at the time of the grievances complained of, was not, and never had been in the military or naval service of the United States. On the 5th day of October, 1864, while at home, he was arrested by order of General Alvin P. Hovey, commanding the military district of Indiana; and has ever since been kept in close confinement.

On the 21st day of October, 1864, he was brought before a military commission, convened at Indianapolis, by order of General Hovey, tried on certain charges and specifications; found guilty, and sentenced to be hanged; and the sentence ordered to be executed on Friday, the 19th day of May, 1865.

On the 2d day of January, 1865, after the proceedings of the military commission were at an end, the Circuit Court of the United States for Indiana met at Indianapolis and empanelled a grand jury, who were charged to inquire whether the laws of the United States had been violated; and, if so, to make presentments. The court adjourned on the 27th day of January, having, prior thereto, discharged from further service the grand jury, who did not find any bill of indictment or make any presentment against Milligan for any offence whatever; and, in fact, since his imprisonment, no bill of indictment has been found or presentment made against him by any grand jury of the United States.

Milligan insists that said military commission had no jurisdiction to try him upon the charges preferred, or upon any charges whatever; because he was a citizen of the United States and the State of Indians, and had not been, since the commencement of the late Rebellion, a resident of any of the States whose citizens were arrayed against the government, and that the right of trial by jury was guaranteed to him by the Constitution of the United States.

The prayer of the petition was, that under the act of Congress, approved March 3d, 1863, entitled, "An act relating to habeas corpus and regulating judicial proceedings in certain cases,"[2] he may be brought before the court, and either turned over to the proper civil tribunal to be proceeded against according to the law of the land or discharged from custody altogether.

The importance of the main question presented by this record cannot be overstated; for it involves the very framework of the government and the fundamental principles of American liberty.

During the late wicked Rebellion, the temper of the times did not allow that calmness in deliberation and discussion so necessary to a correct conclusion of a purely judicial question. Then, considerations of safety were mingled with the exercise of power; and feelings and interests prevailed which are happily terminated. Now that the public safety is assured, this question, as well as all others, can be discussed and decided without passion or the admixture of any element not required to form a legal judgment. We approach the investigation of this case, fully sensible of the magnitude of the inquiry and the necessity of full and cautious deliberation.

---

[2] [Footnote 2 from the statement of the case by the official reporter]

The first section authorizes the suspension, during the Rebellion, of the writ of habeas corpus, throughout the United States, by the President.

Two following sections limited the authority in certain respects.

The second section required that lists of all persons, being citizens of States in which the administration of the laws had continued unimpaired in the Federal courts, who were then held, or might thereafter be held, as prisoners of the United States, under the authority of the President, otherwise than as prisoners of war, should be furnished by the Secretary of State and Secretary of War to the judges of the Circuit and District Courts. These lists were to contain the names of all persons, residing within their respective jurisdictions, charged with violation of national law. And it was required, in cases where the grand jury in attendance upon any of these courts should terminate its session without proceeding by indictment or otherwise against any prisoner named in the list, that the judge of the court should forthwith make an order that such prisoner, desiring a discharge, should be brought before him or the court to be discharged, on entering into recognizance, if required, to keep the peace and for good behavior, or to appear, as the court might direct, to be further dealt with according to law. Every officer of the United States having custody of such prisoners was required to obey and execute the judge's order, under penalty, for refusal or delay, of fine and imprisonment.

The third section enacts, in case lists of persons other than prisoners of war then held in confinement, or thereafter arrested, should not be furnished within twenty days after the passage of the act, or, in cases of subsequent arrest, within twenty days after the time of arrest, that any citizen, after the termination of a session of the grand jury without indictment or presentment, might, by petition alleging the facts and verified by oath, obtain the judge's order of discharge in favor of any person so imprisoned, on the terms and conditions prescribed in the second section.

This act made it the duty of the District Attorney of the United States to attend examinations on petitions for discharge.

By proclamation, dated the 15th September following the President reciting this statute suspended the privilege of the writ in the cases where, by his authority, military, naval, and civil officers of the United States "hold persons in their custody either as prisoners of war, spies, or aiders and abettors of the enemy, . . . or belonging to the land or naval forces of the United States, or otherwise amenable to military law, or the rules and articles of war, or the rules or regulations prescribed for the military or naval services, by authority of the President, or for resisting a draft, or for any other offence against the military or naval service."

But it is said that this case is ended, as the presumption is, that Milligan was hanged in pursuance of the order of the President.

Although we have no judicial information on the subject, yet the inference is that he is alive; for otherwise learned counsel would not appear for him and urge this court to decide his case. It can never be in this country of written constitution and laws, with a judicial department to interpret them, that any chief magistrate would be so far forgetful of his duty, as to order the execution of a man who denied the jurisdiction that tried and convicted him; after his case was before Federal judges with power to decide it, who, being unable to agree on the grave questions involved, had, according to known law, sent it to the Supreme Court of the United States for decision. But even the suggestion is injurious to the Executive, and we dismiss it from further consideration. There is, therefore, nothing to hinder this court from an investigation of the merits of this controversy.

The controlling question in the case is this: Upon the facts stated in Milligan's petition, and the exhibits filed, had the military commission mentioned in it jurisdiction, legally, to try and sentence him? Milligan, not a resident of one of the rebellious states, or a prisoner of war, but a citizen of Indiana for twenty years past, and never in the military or naval service, is, while at his home, arrested by the military power of the United States, imprisoned, and, on certain criminal charges preferred against him, tried, convicted, and sentenced to be hanged by a military commission, organized under the direction of the military commander of the military district of Indiana. Had this tribunal the legal power and authority to try and punish this man? _Issue_

No graver question was ever considered by this court, nor one which more nearly concerns the rights of the whole people; for it is the birthright of every American citizen when charged with crime, to be tried and punished according to law. The power of punishment is, alone through the means which the laws have provided for that purpose, and if they are ineffectual, there is an immunity from punishment, no matter how great an offender the individual may be, or how much his crimes may have shocked the sense of justice of the country, or endangered its safety. By the protection of the law human rights are secured; withdraw that protection, and they are at the mercy of wicked rulers, or the clamor of an excited people. If there was law to justify this military trial, it is not our province to interfere; if there was not, it is our duty to declare the nullity of the whole proceedings.

The decision of this question does not depend on argument or judicial precedents, numerous and highly illustrative as they are. These precedents inform us of the extent of the struggle to preserve liberty and to relieve those in civil life from military trials. The founders of our government were familiar with the history of that struggle; and secured in a written constitution every right which the people had wrested from power during a contest of ages. By that Constitution and the laws authorized by it this question must be determined.

The provisions of that instrument on the administration of criminal justice are too plain and direct, to leave room for misconstruction or doubt of their true meaning. Those applicable to this case are found in that clause of the original

Constitution which says, "That the trial of all crimes, except in case of impeachment, shall be by jury;" and in the fourth, fifth, and sixth articles of the amendments. The fourth proclaims the right to be secure in person and effects against unreasonable search and seizure; and directs that a judicial warrant shall not issue "without proof of probable cause supported by oath or affirmation." The fifth declares "that no person shall be held to answer for a capital or otherwise infamous crime unless on presentment by a grand jury, except in cases arising in the land or naval forces, or in the militia, when in actual service in time of war or public danger, nor be deprived of life, liberty, or property, without due process of law." And the sixth guarantees the right of trial by jury, in such manner and with such regulations that with upright judges, impartial juries, and an able bar, the innocent will be saved and the guilty punished.

Time has proven the discernment of our ancestors; for even these provisions, expressed in such plain English words, that it would seem the ingenuity of man could not evade them, are now, after the lapse of more than seventy years, sought to be avoided. Those great and good men foresaw that troublous times would arise, when rules and people would become restive under restraint, and seek by sharp and decisive measures to accomplish ends deemed just and proper; and that the principles of constitutional liberty would be in peril, unless established by irrepealable law. The history of the world had taught them that what was done in the past might be attempted in the future. The Constitution of the United States is a law for rulers and people, equally in war and in peace, and covers with the shield of its protection all classes of men, at all times, and under all circumstances. No doctrine, involving more pernicious consequences, was ever invented by the wit of man than that any of its provisions can be suspended during any of the great exigencies of government. Such a doctrine leads directly to anarchy or despotism, but the theory of necessity on which it is based is false; for the government, within the Constitution, has all the powers granted to it, which are necessary to preserve its existence; as has been happily proved by the result of the great effort to throw off its just authority.

Have any of the rights guaranteed by the Constitution been violated in the case of Milligan? and if so, what are they?

Every trial involves the exercise of judicial power; and from what source did the military commission that tried him derive their authority? Certainly no part of the judicial power of the country was conferred on them; because the Constitution expressly vests it "in one supreme court and such inferior courts as the Congress may from time to time ordain and establish," and it is not pretended that the commission was a court ordained and established by Congress. They cannot justify on the mandate of the President; because he is controlled by law, and has his appropriate sphere of duty, which is to execute, not to make, the laws; and there is "no unwritten criminal code to which resort can be had as a source of jurisdiction."

But it is said that the jurisdiction is complete under the "laws and usages of war."

It can serve no useful purpose to inquire what those laws and usages are, whence they originated, where found, and on whom they operate; they can never be applied to citizens in states which have upheld the authority of the government, and where the courts are open and their process unobstructed. This court has judicial knowledge that in Indiana the Federal authority was always unopposed, and its courts always open to hear criminal accusations and redress grievances; and no usage of war could sanction a military trial there for any offence whatever of a citizen in civil life, in nowise connected with the military service. Congress could grant no such power; and to the honor of our national legislature be it said, it has never been provoked by the state of the country even to attempt its exercise. One of the plainest constitutional provisions was, therefore, infringed when Milligan was tried by a court not ordained and established by Congress, and not composed of judges appointed during good behavior.

Why was he not delivered to the Circuit Court of Indiana to be proceeded against according to law? No reason of necessity could be urged against it; because Congress had declared penalties against the offences charged, provided for their punishment, and directed that court to hear and determine them. And soon after this military tribunal was ended, the Circuit Court met, peacefully transacted its business, and adjourned. It needed no bayonets to protect it, and required no military aid to execute its judgments. It was held in a state, eminently distinguished for patriotism, by judges commissioned during the Rebellion, who were provided with juries, upright, intelligent, and selected by a marshal appointed by the President. The government had no right to conclude that Milligan, if guilty, would not receive in that court merited punishment; for its records disclose that it was constantly engaged in the trial of similar offences, and was never interrupted in its administration of criminal justice. If it was dangerous, in the distracted condition of affairs, to leave Milligan unrestrained of his liberty, because he "conspired against the government, afforded aid and comfort to rebels, and incited the people to insurrection," the law said arrest him, confine him closely, render him powerless to do further mischief; and then present his case to the grand jury of the district, with proofs of his guilt, and, if indicted, try him according to the course of the common law. If this had been done, the Constitution would have been vindicated, the law of 1863 enforced, and the securities for personal liberty preserved and defended.

Another guarantee of freedom was broken when Milligan was denied a trial by jury.

The discipline necessary to the efficiency of the army and navy, required other and swifter modes of trial than are furnished by the common law courts; and, in pursuance of the power conferred by the Constitution, Congress has declared the kinds of trial, and the manner in which they shall be conducted, for offences committed while the party is in the military or naval service. Every one connected with these branches of the public service is amenable to the jurisdiction which Congress has created for their government, and, while thus serving, surrenders his right to be tried by the civil courts. All other persons, citizens of states where the courts are open, if charged with crime, are guaranteed the inestimable privilege of trial by jury.

Effect of martial law

It is claimed that martial law covers with its broad mantle the proceedings of this military commission. The statement of this proposition shows its importance; for, if true, republican government is a failure, and there is an end of liberty regulated by law. Martial law, established on such a basis, destroys every guarantee of the Constitution, and effectually renders the "military independent of and superior to the civil power."

It will be borne in mind that this is not a question of the power to proclaim martial law, when war exists in a community and the courts and civil authorities are overthrown. Nor is it a question what rule a military commander, at the head of his army, can impose on states in rebellion to cripple their resources and quell the insurrection. The jurisdiction claimed is much more extensive. The necessities of the service, during the late Rebellion, required that the loyal states should be placed within the limits of certain military districts and commanders appointed in them; and, it is urged, that this, in a military sense, constituted them the theatre of military operations; and, as in this case, Indiana had been and was again threatened with invasion by the enemy, the occasion was furnished to establish martial law. The conclusion does not follow from the premises. If armies were collected in Indiana, they were to be employed in another locality, where the laws were obstructed and the national authority disputed. On her soil there was no hostile foot; if once invaded, that invasion was at an end, and with it all pretext for martial law. Martial law cannot arise from a threatened invasion. The necessity must be actual and present; the invasion real, such ad effectually closes the courts and deposes the civil administration.

No occasion for martial law in this case

It is difficult to see how the safety of the country required martial law in Indiana. If any of her citizens were plotting treason, the power of arrest could secure them, until the government was prepared for their trial, when the courts were open and ready to try them. It was as easy to protect witnesses before a civil as a military tribunal; and as there could be no wish to convict, except on sufficient legal evidence, surely an ordained and established court was better able to judge of this than a military tribunal composed of gentlemen not trained to the profession of the law.

It follows, from what has been said on this subject, that there are occasions when martial rule can be properly applied. If, in foreign invasion or civil war, the courts are actually closed, and it is impossible to administer criminal justice according to law, then, on the theatre of active military operations, where war really prevails, there is a necessity to furnish a substituted for the civil authority, thus overthrown, to preserve the safety of the army and society; and as no power is left but the military, it is allowed to govern by martial rule until the laws can have their free course. As necessity creates the nule, so it limits its duration; for, if this government is continued after the courts are reinstated, it is a gross usurpation of power. Martial rule can never exist where the courts are open, and in the proper and unobstructed exercise of their jurisdiction. It is also confined to the locality of actual war. Because, during the late Rebellion it could have been enforced in Virginia, where the national authority was overturned and the courts driven out, it does not follow that it should obtain in Indiana, where that authority was never disputed, and justice was always administered. And so in the case of a foreign invasion, martial rule may become a necessity in one state, when, in another, it would be "mere lawless violence."

If the military trial of Milligan was contrary to law, then he was entitled, on the facts stated in his petition, to be discharged from custody by the terms of the act of Congress of March 3d, 1863.

But it is insisted that Milligan was a prisoner of war, and, therefore, excluded *M was not a POW* from the privileges of the statute. It is not easy to see how he can be treated as a prisoner of war, when he lived in Indiana for the past twenty years, was arrested there, and had not been, during the late troubles, a resident of any of the states in rebellion. If in Indiana he conspired with bad men to assist the enemy, he is punishable for it in the courts of Indiana; but, when tried for the offence, he cannot plead the rights of war; for he was not engaged in legal acts of hostility against the government, and only such persons, when captured, are prisoners of war. If he cannot enjoy the immunities attaching to the character of a prisoner of war, how can he be subject to their pains and penalties?

Chief Justice CHASE, dissenting:

Four members of the court, concurring with their brethren in the order heretofore made in this cause, but unable to concur in some important particulars with the opinion which has just been read, think it their duty to make a separate statement of their views of the whole case.

We agree that [Milligan is entitled to be discharged from military custody by writ of habeas corpus]. We do not doubt that the positive provisions of the act of Congress require such answers. We do not think it necessary to look beyond these provisions. In them we find sufficient and controlling reasons for our conclusions.

But the opinion which has just been read goes further; and as we understand it, asserts not only that the military commission held in Indiana was not authorized by Congress, but that it was not in the power of Congress to authorize it; from which it may be thought to follow, that Congress has no power to indemnify the officers who composed the commission against liability in civil courts for acting as members of it.

We cannot agree to this.

We agree in the proposition that no department of the government of the United States – neither President, nor Congress, nor the Courts – possesses any power not given by the Constitution.

We assent, fully, to all that is said, in the opinion, of the inestimable value of the trial by jury, and of the other constitutional safeguards of civil liberty. And we concur, also, in what is said of the writ of habeas corpus, and of its suspension, with two reservations: (1.) That, in our judgment, when the writ is suspended, the Executive is authorized to arrest as well as to detain; and (2.) that there are cases in which, the privilege of the writ being suspended, trial and punishment by military commission, in states where civil courts are open, may be authorized by Congress, as well as arrest and detention. *2 reservations*

We think that Congress had power, though not exercised, to authorize the military commission which was held in Indiana.

The Constitution itself provides for military government as well as for civil government. And we do not understand it to be claimed that the civil safeguards of the Constitution have application in cases within the proper sphere of the former.

We by no means assert that Congress can establish and apply the laws of war where no war had been declared or exists.

Where peace exists the laws of peace must prevail. What we do maintain is, that when the nation is involved in war, and some portions of the country are invaded, and all are exposed to invasion, it is within the power of Congress to determine in what states or districts such great and imminent public danger exists as justifies the authorization of military tribunals for the trial of crimes and offences against the discipline or security of the army or against the public safety.

In Indiana, for example, at the time of the arrest of Milligan and his co-conspirators, it is established by the papers in the record, that the state was a military district, was the theatre of military operations, had been actually invaded, and was constantly threatened with invasion. It appears, also, that a powerful secret association, composed of citizens and others, existed within the state, under military organization, conspiring against the draft, and plotting insurrection, the liberation of the prisoners of war at various depots, the seizure of the state and national arsenals, armed cooperation with the enemy, and war against the national government.

We cannot doubt that, in such a time of public danger, Congress had power, under the Constitution, to provide for the organization of a military commission, and for trial by that commission of persons engaged in this conspiracy. The fact that the Federal courts were open was regarded by Congress as a sufficient reason for not exercising the power; but that fact could not deprive Congress of the right to exercise it. Those courts might be open and undisturbed in the execution of their functions, and yet wholly incompetent to avert threatened danger, or to punish, with adequate promptitude and certainty, the guilty conspirators.

In Indiana, the judges and officers of the courts were loyal to the government. But it might have been otherwise. In times of rebellion and civil war it may often happen, indeed, that judges and marshals will be in active sympathy with the rebels, and courts their most efficient allies.

We have confined ourselves to the question of power. It was for Congress to determine the question of expediency. And Congress did determine it. That body did not see fit to authorize trials by military commission in Indiana, but by the strongest implication prohibited them. With that prohibition we are satisfied, and should have remained silent if the answers to the questions certified had been put on that ground, without denial of the existence of a power which we believe to be constitutional and important to the public safety, – a denial which, as we have already suggested, seems to draw in question the power of Congress to protect from prosecution the members of military commissions who acted in obedience to their superior officers, and whose action, whether warranted by law or not, was approved by that up-right and patriotic President under whose administration the Republic was rescued from threatened destruction.

We have thus far said little of martial law, nor do we propose to say much. What we have already said sufficiently indicates our opinion that there is no law for the government of the citizens, the armies or the navy of the United States, within American jurisdiction, which is not contained in or derived from the Constitution. And wherever our army or navy may go beyond our territorial limits, neither can go beyond the authority of the President or the legislation of Congress.

There are under the Constitution three kinds of military jurisdiction: one to be exercised both in peace and war; another to be exercised in time of foreign war without the boundaries of the United States, or in time of rebellion and civil war within states or districts occupied by rebels treated as belligerents; and a third to be exercised in time of invasion or insurrection within the limits of the United States, or during rebellion within the limits of states maintaining adhesion to the National Government, when the public danger requires its exercise. The first of these may be called jurisdiction under MILITARY LAW, and is found in acts of Congress prescribing rules and articles of war, or otherwise providing for the government of the national forces; the second may be distinguished as MILITARY GOVERNMENT, superseding, as far as may be deemed expedient, the local law, and exercised by the military commander under the direction of the President, with the express or implied sanction of Congress; while the third may be denominated MARTIAL LAW PROPER, and is called into action by Congress, or temporarily, when the action of Congress cannot be invited, and in the case of justifying or excusing peril, by the President, in times of insurrection or invasion, or of civil or foreign war, within districts or localities where ordinary law no longer adequately secures public safety and private rights.

We think that the power of Congress, in such times and in such localities, to authorize trials for crimes against the security and safety of the national forces, may be derived from its constitutional authority to raise and support armies and to declare war, if not from its constitutional authority to provide for governing the national forces.

We have no apprehension that this power, under our American system of government, in which all official authority is derived from the people, and exercised under direct responsibility to the people, is more likely to be abused than the power to regulate commerce, or the power to borrow money. And we are unwilling to give our assent by silence to expressions of opinion which seem to us calculated, though not intended, to cripple the constitutional powers of the government, and to augment the public dangers in times of invasion and rebellion.

Mr. Justice WAYNE, Mr. Justice SWAYNE, and Mr. Justice MILLER concur with me in these views.

NOTES AND QUESTIONS

1. The opinion in *Milligan* was presaged by *Ex parte Merryman*, 17 F. Cas. 144 (C.C.D. Md. 1861). Merryman was arrested early in the Civil War as an alleged conspirator to sabotage rail lines and bridges in Maryland. He was placed in military custody under the same Lincoln orders later considered in Milligan. Chief Justice Taney, sitting in Circuit Court, issued an order to the military commander at Fort Baltimore requiring that Merryman be brought forward for the purpose of justifying his detention. The military commander refused and Taney declared that his "power has been resisted by a force too strong for me to overcome." At the time, there was active fighting in Baltimore, Merryman was almost certainly involved in sabotage with others who were still at large, the seat of government in DC was virtually cut off from its loyal states, and there was no hope of enforcing an order to release Merryman. Did the law change after the war was over. Is it too cynical to say that the Court merely waited until it became safe to issue its opinion in *Milligan*? For an excellent treatment of the Lincoln-Taney interaction, see WILLIAM H. REHNQUIST, ALL THE LAWS BUT ONE (1998).

2. If the government had made a return to the habeas petition in *Merryman* stating its evidence of his involvement in blowing up railroad bridges, and asserting an intent to conduct a trial (even a military trial in an active theater of combat might have been acceptable), then there would have been no violation. Perhaps the suspension of the writ by the President was really overkill. Could it be argued that there was no need for it because the judges and the people would have willingly accepted military law enforcement in the face of a genuine emergency, and the government could easily have made satisfactory returns to habeas corpus petitions until the emergency passed? One counter-argument gets into personal political issues because Lincoln knew that Taney was at least somewhat sympathetic to the Southern cause. Merryman was never tried by a military tribunal. He was held for much of the war and eventually released.

3. What level of courage on the part of the judges is required by these situations? As with Taney's order in *Merryman*, there is always the possibility that the President will disregard a court order, particularly one issued in the grey area between genuine emergency and lasting peace. In that instance, Justice Jackson's civics lecture has real bite. Once the court has ruled, if the President does not obey, the political will of the people must have the final say. In the midst of armed conflict, the public would most likely be inclined to go along with the President's wishes.

The opposite side of the courage coin is that the President will obey and disaster befall the community as a result of some person's wrongdoing made possible, or at least contributed to, by the court's ruling. This is probably the more frightening aspect, particularly because the judges will often have the feeling that they are acting without full awareness of the background risks involved. These themes are hinted, and sometimes laid out explicitly in the cases that follow.

Ex Parte QUIRIN
317 U.S. 1 (1942)

Mr. Chief Justice STONE delivered the opinion of the Court.

[Petitioners were eight alleged German saboteurs who arrived by submarine in two groups, one group landing in New Jersey on the night of June 13, 1942, and the other in Florida on June 17. One defendant (Dasch) went to the FBI, apparently at the urging of another (Burger). By June 27, all eight were in custody. Trial before a military commission began on July 8 and evidence was concluded by July 27. Defense counsel sought extraordinary habeas corpus relief first from the District Court and then from the Supreme Court, which heard arguments on July 29 and rendered a brief *per curiam* decision on July 31. The commission then announced its judgment of conviction and recommendation of the death penalty for all the defendants, six of whom were executed on August 8. The Court then issued a full opinion on October 29.]

All the petitioners were born in Germany; all have lived in the United States. All returned to Germany between 1933 and 1941. All except petitioner Haupt are admittedly citizens of the German Reich, with which the United States is at war. Haupt came to this country with his parents when he was five years old; it is contended that he became a citizen of the United States by virtue of the naturalization of his parents during his minority and that he has not since lost his citizenship. The Government, however, takes the position that on attaining his majority he elected to maintain German allegiance and citizenship, or in any case that he has by his conduct renounced or abandoned his United States citizenship. For reasons presently to be stated we do not find it necessary to resolve these contentions.

After the declaration of war between the United States and the German Reich, petitioners received training at a sabotage school near Berlin, Germany, where they were instructed in the use of explosives and in methods of secret writing. While landing [on U.S. shores] they wore German Marine Infantry uniforms or parts of uniforms. Immediately after landing they buried their uniforms. All had received instructions in Germany from an officer of the German High Command to destroy war industries and war facilities in the United States, for which they or their relatives in Germany were to receive salary payments from the German Government. They also had been paid by the German Government during their course of training at the sabotage school and had received substantial sums in United States currency, which were in their possession when arrested.

[handwritten margin note: Paid by German gov't]

The President appointed a Military Commission and directed it to try petitioners for offenses against the law of war, [stating] that "all persons who are subjects, citizens or residents of any nation at war with the United States or who give obedience to or act under the direction of any such nation, and who during time of war enter or attempt to enter the United States . . . through coastal or boundary defenses, and are charged with committing or attempting or preparing to commit sabotage, espionage, hostile or warlike acts, or violations of the law of war, shall be subject to the law of war and to the jurisdiction of military tribunals."

[handwritten margin note: Pres appointed Mil Com]

The Proclamation also stated in terms that all such persons were denied access to the courts.

Petitioners' main contention is that the President is without any statutory or constitutional authority to order the petitioners to be tried by military tribunal for offenses with which they are charged; that in consequence they are entitled to be tried in the civil courts with the safeguards, including trial by jury, which the Fifth and Sixth Amendments guarantee to all persons charged in such courts with criminal offenses. In any case it is urged that the President's Order, in prescribing the procedure of the Commission and the method for review of its findings and sentence, and the proceedings of the Commission under the Order, conflict with Articles of War adopted by Congress, and are illegal and void.

The Government challenges each of these propositions. But regardless of their merits, it also insists that petitioners must be denied access to the courts, both because they are enemy aliens or have entered our territory as enemy belligerents, and because the President's Proclamation undertakes in terms to deny such access to the class of persons defined by the Proclamation, which aptly describes the character and conduct of petitioners. It is urged that if they are enemy aliens or if the Proclamation has force, no court may afford the petitioners a hearing. But there is certainly nothing in the Proclamation to preclude access to the courts for determining its applicability to the particular case. And neither the Proclamation nor the fact that they are enemy aliens forecloses consideration by the courts of petitioners' contentions that the Constitution and laws of the United States constitutionally enacted forbid their trial by military commission.

We are not here concerned with any question of the guilt or innocence of petitioners. Constitutional safeguards for the protection of all who are charged with offenses are not to be disregarded in order to inflict merited punishment on some who are guilty. But the detention and trial of petitioners – ordered by the President in the declared exercise of his powers as Commander in Chief of the Army in time of war and of grave public danger – are not to be set aside by the courts without the clear conviction that they are in conflict with the Constitution or laws of Congress constitutionally enacted.

Congress and the President, like the courts, possess no power not derived from the Constitution. But one of the objects of the Constitution, as declared by its preamble, is to "provide for the common defence."

The Constitution thus invests the President, as Commander in Chief, with the power to wage war which Congress has declared, and to carry into effect all laws passed by Congress for the conduct of war and for the government and regulation of the Armed Forces, and all laws defining and punishing offenses against the law of nations, including those which pertain to the conduct of war.

By the Articles of War, 10 U.S.C. §§ [801 et seq.], Congress has provided rules for the government of the Army. It has provided for the trial and punishment, by courts martial, of violations of the Articles by members of the armed forces and by specified classes of persons associated or serving with the Army. Arts. 1, 2. But the Articles also recognize the "military commission" appointed by military command as an appropriate tribunal for the trial and punishment of offenses against the law of war not ordinarily tried by court martial. And Article

15 [now Art. 21, 10 U.S.C. § 821] declares that "the provisions of these articles conferring jurisdiction upon courts martial shall not be construed as depriving military commissions . . . or other military tribunals of concurrent jurisdiction in respect of offenders or offenses that by statute or by the law of war may be triable by such military commissions . . . or other military tribunals." Article 2 includes among those persons subject to military law the personnel of our own military establishment. But this, as Article 12 provides, does not exclude from that class "any other person who by the law of war is subject to trial by military tribunals" and who under Article 12 may be tried by court martial or under Article 15 by military commission.

[handwritten margin note: Mil Trbl has J. over any person subj to trial by M.P. Trbls pursuant to Law of War]

Similarly the Espionage Act of 1917, which authorizes trial in the district courts of certain offenses that tend to interfere with the prosecution of war, provides that nothing contained in the act "shall be deemed to limit the jurisdiction of the general courts-martial, military commissions, or naval courts-martial."

From the very beginning of its history this Court has recognized and applied the law of war as including that part of the law of nations which prescribes, for the conduct of war, the status, rights and duties of enemy nations as well as of enemy individuals. By the Articles of War, and especially Article 15, Congress has explicitly provided, so far as it may constitutionally do so, that military tribunals shall have jurisdiction to try offenders or offenses against the law of war in appropriate cases.

An important incident to the conduct of war is the adoption of measures by the military command not only to repel and defeat the enemy, but to seize and subject to disciplinary measures those enemies who in their attempt to thwart or impede our military effort have violated the law of war. It is unnecessary for present purposes to determine to what extent the President as Commander in Chief has constitutional power to create military commissions without the support of Congressional legislation. For here Congress has authorized trial of offenses against the law of war before such commissions. We are concerned only with the question whether it is within the constitutional power of the National Government to place petitioners upon trial before a military commission for the offenses with which they are charged. We must therefore first inquire whether any of the acts charged is an offense against the law of war cognizable before a military tribunal, and if so whether the Constitution prohibits the trial. We may assume that there are acts regarded in other countries, or by some writers on international law, as offenses against the law of war which would not be triable by military tribunal here, either because they are not recognized by our courts as violations of the law of war or because they are of that class of offenses constitutionally triable only by a jury. It was upon such grounds that the Court denied the right to proceed by military tribunal in *Ex parte Milligan*. But as we shall show, these petitioners were charged with an offense against the law of war which the Constitution does not require to be tried by jury.

[handwritten margin note: disciplining the enemy]

[handwritten margin note: Congress has authorized M.L. Trbls]

[handwritten margin note: Issue]

[handwritten margin note: distinguishing Milligan]

[handwritten margin note: H]

It is no objection that Congress in providing for the trial of such offenses has not itself undertaken to codify that branch of international law or to mark its precise boundaries, or to enumerate or define by statute all the acts which that law condemns. An Act of Congress punishing "the crime of piracy, as defined by the law of nations" is an appropriate exercise of its constitutional authority, Art. I, § 8, cl. 10, "to define and punish" the offense, since it has adopted by reference the sufficiently precise definition of international law.[6] Similarly, by the reference in the 15th Article of War to "offenders or offenses that . . . by the law of war may be triable by such military commissions," Congress has incorporated by reference, as within the jurisdiction of military commissions, all offenses which are defined as such by the law of war and which may constitutionally be included within that jurisdiction. Congress had the choice of crystallizing in permanent form and in minute detail every offense against the law of war, or of adopting the system of common law applied by military tribunals so far as it should be recognized and deemed applicable by the courts. It chose the latter course.

Such was the practice of our own military authorities before the adoption of the Constitution,[9] and during the Mexican and Civil Wars.[10]

Rules of Land Warfare promulgated by the War Department for the guidance of the Army provides that "All war crimes are subject to the death penalty, although a lesser penalty may be imposed." Paragraph 8 (1940) divides the enemy population into "armed forces" and "peaceful population," and Paragraph 9 names as distinguishing characteristics of lawful belligerents that they "carry arms openly" and "have a fixed distinctive emblem." The definition of lawful belligerents by Paragraph 9 is that adopted by Article 1, Annex to Hague Convention No. IV of October 18, 1907. The preamble to the Convention declares:

> Until a more complete code of the laws of war has been issued, the High Contracting Parties deem it expedient to declare that, in cases not included in the Regulations adopted by them, the inhabitants and the belligerents

---

[6] By universal agreement and practice, the law of war draws a distinction between the armed forces and the peaceful populations of belligerent nations and also between those who are lawful and unlawful combatants. Lawful combatants are subject to capture and detention as prisoners of war by opposing military forces. Unlawful combatants are likewise subject to capture and detention, but in addition they are subject to trial and punishment by military tribunals for acts which render their belligerency unlawful. The spy who secretly and without uniform passes the military lines of a belligerent in time of war, seeking to gather military information and communicate it to the enemy, or an enemy combatant who without uniform comes secretly through the lines for the purpose of waging war by destruction of life or property, are familiar examples of belligerents who are generally deemed not to be entitled to the status of prisoners of war, but to be offenders against the law of war subject to trial and punishment by military tribunals. *See* WINTHROP, MILITARY LAW, 2d ed., pp. 1196-97, 1219-21.

[9] On September 29, 1780, Major John Andre, Adjutant-General to the British Army, was tried by a "Board of General Officers" appointed by General Washington, on a charge that he had come within the lines for an interview with General Benedict Arnold and had been captured while in disguise and travelling under an assumed name. Major Andre was hanged on October 2, 1780.

[10] During the Mexican War military commissions were created in a large number of instances for the trial of various offenses. During the Civil War the military commission was extensively used for the trial of offenses against the law of war. 2 WINTHROP, MILITARY LAWS AND PRECEDENTS (2d ed. 1896).

remain under the protection and the rule of the principles of the law of nations, as they result from the usages established among civilized peoples, from the laws of humanity, and the dictates of the public conscience.

Our Government, by thus defining lawful belligerents entitled to be treated as prisoners of war, has recognized that there is a class of unlawful belligerents not entitled to that privilege, including those who, though combatants, do not wear "fixed and distinctive emblems." And by Article 15 of the Articles of War Congress has made provision for their trial and punishment by military commission, according to "the law of war."

By a long course of practical administrative construction by its military authorities, our Government has likewise recognized that those who during time of war pass surreptitiously from enemy territory into our own, discarding their uniforms upon entry, for the commission of hostile acts involving destruction of life or property, have the status of unlawful combatants punishable as such by military commission. This precept of the law of war has been so recognized in practice both here and abroad, and has so generally been accepted as valid by authorities on international law[12] that we think it must be regarded as a rule or principle of the law of war recognized by this Government by its enactment of the Fifteenth Article of War.

Specification 1 of the first charge is sufficient to charge all the petitioners with the offense of unlawful belligerency, trial of which is within the jurisdiction of the Commission, and the admitted facts affirmatively show that the charge is not merely colorable or without foundation.

As we have seen, entry upon our territory in time of war by enemy belligerents, including those acting under the direction of the armed forces of the enemy, for the purpose of destroying property used or useful in prosecuting the war, is a hostile and warlike act. It subjects those who participate in it without uniform to the punishment prescribed by the law of war for unlawful belligerents. It is without significance that petitioners were not alleged to have borne conventional weapons or that their proposed hostile acts did not necessarily contemplate collision with the Armed Forces of the United States. By passing our boundaries for such purposes without uniform or other emblem signifying their belligerent status, or by discarding that means of identification after entry, such enemies become unlawful belligerents subject to trial and punishment.

Citizenship in the United States of an enemy belligerent does not relieve him from the consequences of a belligerency which is unlawful because in violation of the law of war. Citizens who associate themselves with the military arm of the enemy government, and with its aid, guidance and direction enter this country

---

[12] Authorities on International Law have regarded as war criminals such persons who pass through the lines for the purpose of (a) destroying bridges, war materials, communication facilities, etc.; (b) carrying messages secretly; (c) any hostile act. 2 WINTHROP, MILITARY LAW AND PRECEDENTS (2nd ed. 1896) 1224. These authorities are unanimous in stating that a soldier in uniform who commits the acts mentioned would be entitled to treatment as a prisoner of war; it is the absence of uniform that renders the offender liable to trial for violation of the laws of war.

bent on hostile acts, are enemy belligerents within the meaning of the Hague Convention and the law of war. It is as an enemy belligerent that petitioner Haupt is charged with entering the United States, and unlawful belligerency is the gravamen of the offense of which he is accused.

Nor are petitioners any the less belligerents if, as they argue, they have not actually committed or attempted to commit any act of depredation or entered the theatre or zone of active military operations. The . . . nature of the offense . . . is that each petitioner, in circumstances which gave him the status of an enemy belligerent, passed our military and naval lines and defenses or went behind those lines, in civilian dress and with hostile purpose. The offense was complete when with that purpose they entered – or, having so entered, they remained upon – our territory in time of war without uniform or other appropriate means of identification. For that reason, even when committed by a citizen, the offense is distinct from the crime of treason defined in Article III, § 3 of the Constitution, since the absence of uniform essential to one is irrelevant to the other.

Presentment by a grand jury and trial by a jury of the vicinage where the crime was committed were at the time of the adoption of the Constitution familiar parts of the machinery for criminal trials in the civil courts. But they were procedures unknown to military tribunals, which are not courts in the sense of the Judiciary Article, and which in the natural course of events are usually called upon to function under conditions precluding resort to such procedures. As this Court has often recognized, it was not the purpose or effect of § 2 of Article III, read in the light of the common law, to enlarge the then existing right to a jury trial. The object was to preserve unimpaired trial by jury in all those cases in which it had been recognized by the common law and in all cases of a like nature as they might arise in the future, but not to bring within the sweep of the guaranty those cases in which it was then well understood that a jury trial could not be demanded as of right.

[Petty offenses and criminal contempts] are instances of offenses committed against the United States, for which a penalty is imposed, but they are not deemed to be within Article III, § 2, or the provisions of the Fifth and Sixth Amendments relating to "crimes" and "criminal prosecutions." In the light of this long-continued and consistent interpretation we must conclude that § 2 of Article III and the Fifth and Sixth Amendments cannot be taken to have extended the right to demand a jury to trials by military commission, or to have required that offenses against the law of war not triable by jury at common law be tried only in the civil courts.

The fact that "cases arising in the land or naval forces" are excepted from the operation of the Amendments does not militate against this conclusion. Such cases are expressly excepted from the Fifth Amendment, and are deemed excepted by implication from the Sixth. *Ex parte Milligan*. It is argued that the exception, which excludes from the Amendment cases arising in the armed forces, has also by implication extended its guaranty to all other cases; that since petitioners, not being members of the Armed Forces of the United States, are not within the exception, the Amendment operates to give to them the right to a jury trial. But we think this argument misconceives both the scope of the Amendment and the purpose of the exception.

No exception is necessary to exclude from the operation of these provisions cases never deemed to be within their terms. An express exception from Article III, § 2, and from the Fifth and Sixth Amendments, of trials of petty offenses and of criminal contempts has not been found necessary in order to preserve the traditional practice of trying those offenses without a jury. It is no more so in order to continue the practice of trying, before military tribunals without a jury, offenses committed by enemy belligerents against the law of war.

[An 1806 statute] imposed the death penalty on alien spies "according to the law and usage of nations, by sentence of a general court martial." This enactment must be regarded as a contemporary construction of both Article III, § 2, and the Amendments as not foreclosing trial by military tribunals, without a jury, of offenses against the law of war committed by enemies not in or associated with our Armed Forces. It is a construction of the Constitution which has been followed since the founding of our Government. Such a construction is entitled to the greatest respect. It has not hitherto been challenged, and, so far as we are advised, it has never been suggested in the very extensive literature of the subject that an alien spy, in time of war, could not be tried by military tribunal without a jury. [The Court recites 26 examples from the Revolutionary War, War of 1812, and Civil War of persons executed after being found by military tribunals to be guilty of spying. One was released by President Madison apparently on the ground that he was a U.S. citizen.]

Petitioners, and especially petitioner Haupt, stress the pronouncement of this Court in the *Milligan* case, that the law of war "can never be applied to citizens in states which have upheld the authority of the government, and where the courts are open and their process unobstructed." Elsewhere in its opinion, the Court was at pains to point out that Milligan, a citizen twenty years resident in Indiana, who had never been a resident of any of the states in rebellion, was not an enemy belligerent either entitled to the status of a prisoner of war or subject to the penalties imposed upon unlawful belligerents. We construe the Court's statement as to the inapplicability of the law of war to Milligan's case as having particular reference to the facts before it. From them the Court concluded that Milligan, not being a part of or associated with the armed forces of the enemy, was a non-belligerent, not subject to the law of war save as – in circumstances found not there to be present, and not involved here – martial law might be constitutionally established.

The Court's opinion is inapplicable to the case presented by the present record. We have no occasion now to define with meticulous care the ultimate boundaries of the jurisdiction of military tribunals to try persons according to the law of war. It is enough that petitioners here, upon the conceded facts, were plainly within those boundaries, and were held in good faith for trial by military commission, charged with being enemies who, with the purpose of destroying war materials and utilities, entered, or after entry remained in, our territory without uniform – an offense against the law of war. We hold only that those particular acts constitute an offense against the law of war which the Constitution authorizes to be tried by military commission.

MR. JUSTICE MURPHY took no part in the consideration or decision of these cases.

NOTES AND QUESTIONS

1. The eight defendants in *Quirin* had all lived in the United States before returning to Germany between 1933 and 1941. They claimed that they had no intention of following the orders they were given in Germany but went along with the German plan out of fear of retribution to their families if they failed to make at least a token gesture of compliance. Burger and Dasch's sentences were commuted from death to life imprisonment in 1948. Each served six years in prison and was deported to Germany in 1948. They reportedly lived out their lives as pariahs in Germany.

2. Haupt's father, who lived in Chicago, was convicted of treason and sentenced to life in prison for aiding his son with knowledge of the scheme. *Haupt v. United States*, 330 U.S. 631 (1947). Thiel's friend Cramer was first convicted of treason but his conviction was overturned for lack of evidence that he had knowledge of the conspiracy. *Cramer v. United States*, 325 U.S. 1 (1945).

3. Before attempting to apply *Quirin* to current settings, we should try to isolate what made *Quirin* different from *Milligan*.

a. wartime?

b. foreign power or "enemy government"?

c. foreign citizenry?

d. military theater of operations?

4. For further analysis of *Quirin* in the post-9/11 context, see A. Christopher Bryant & Carl Tobias, *Quirin Revisited*, 2003 WIS. L. REV. 309; Carl Tobias, *Detentions, Military Commissions, Terrorism, and Domestic Case Precedent*, 76 SO. CAL. L. REV. 1371 (2003).

DUNCAN v. KAHANAMOKU

327 U.S. 304, 66 S. Ct. 606, 90 L. Ed. 688 (1946)

MR. JUSTICE BLACK delivered the opinion of the Court.

The petitioners in these cases were sentenced to prison by military tribunals in Hawaii. Both are civilians. The question before us is whether the military tribunals had power to do this. The United States district court for Hawaii in habeas corpus proceedings held that the military tribunals had no such power and ordered that they be set free. The circuit court of appeals reversed, and ordered that the petitioners be returned to prison. Both cases thus involve the rights of individuals charged with crime and not connected with the armed forces to have their guilt or innocence determined in courts of law which provide established procedural safeguards, rather than by military tribunals which fail to afford many of these safeguards. Since these judicial safeguards are prized privileges of our system of government we granted certiorari.

The following events led to the military tribunals' exercise of jurisdiction over the petitioners. On December 7, 1941, immediately following the surprise air attack by the Japanese on Pearl Harbor, the Governor of Hawaii by proclamation undertook to suspend the privilege of the writ of habeas corpus and to place the Territory under "martial law." Section 67 of the Hawaiian Organic Act,[14] authorizes the Territorial Governor to take this action "in case of rebellion or invasion, or imminent danger thereof, when the public safety requires it . . . ." His action was to remain in effect only "until communication can be had with the President and his decision thereon made known." The President approved the Governor's action on December 9th. The Governor's proclamation also authorized and requested the Commanding General, "during the . . . emergency and until danger of invasion is removed, to exercise all the powers normally exercised" by the Governor and by the "judicial officers and employees of this territory."

[handwritten margin note: Mil law +/o habeas after Pearl Harbor]

Pursuant to this authorization the commanding general immediately proclaimed himself Military Governor and undertook the defense of the Territory and the maintenance of order. On December 8th, both civil and criminal courts were forbidden to summon jurors and witnesses and to try cases. The Commanding General established military tribunals to take the place of the courts. These were to try civilians charged with violating the laws of the United States and of the Territory, and rules, regulations, orders or policies of the Military Government. Rules of evidence and procedure of courts of law were not to control the military trials. In imposing penalties the military tribunals were to be "guided by, but not limited to the penalties authorized by the courts martial manual, the laws of the United States, the Territory of Hawaii, the District of Columbia, and the customs of war in like cases." The rule announced was simply that punishment was to be "commensurate with the offense committed" and that the death penalty might be imposed "in appropriate cases." Thus the military authorities took over the government of Hawaii. They could and did, by simply promulgating orders, govern the day to day activities of civilians who lived, worked, or were merely passing through there. The military tribunals interpreted the very orders promulgated by the military authorities and proceeded to punish violators. The sentences imposed were not subject to direct appellate court review, since it had long been established that military tribunals are not part of our judicial system. *Ex parte Vallandigham,* 1 Wall. 243. The military undoubtedly assumed that its rule was not subject to any judicial control whatever, for by orders issued on August 25, 1943, it prohibited even accepting of a petition for writ of habeas corpus by a judge or judicial employee

[handwritten margin note: No appellate Review]

---

[14] That the governor shall be responsible for the faithful execution of the laws of the United States and of the Territory of Hawaii within the said Territory, and whenever it becomes necessary he may call upon the commanders of the military and naval forces of the United States in the Territory of Hawaii, or summon the posse comitatus, or call out the militia of the Territory to prevent or suppress lawless violence, invasion, insurrection, or rebellion in said Territory, and he may, in case of rebellion or invasion, or imminent danger thereof, when the public safety requires it, suspend the privilege of the writ of habeas corpus, or place the Territory, or any part thereof, under martial law until communication can be had with the President and his decision thereon made known.

or the filing of such a petition by a prisoner or his attorney. Military tribunals could punish violators of these orders by fine, imprisonment or death.

White, the petitioner in No. 15, was a stockbroker in Honolulu. Neither he nor his business was connected with the armed forces. On August 20, 1942, more than eight months after the Pearl Harbor attack, the military police arrested him. The charge against him was embezzling stock belonging to another civilian in violation of Chapter 183 of the Revised Laws of Hawaii. Though by the time of White's arrest the courts were permitted "as agents of the Military Governor" to dispose of some non-jury civil cases, they were still forbidden to summon jurors and to exercise criminal jurisdiction. On August 22nd, White was brought before a military tribunal designated as a "Provost Court." The "Court" orally informed him of the charge. He objected to the tribunal's jurisdiction but the objection was overruled. He demanded to be tried by a jury. This request was denied. His attorney asked for additional time to prepare the case. This was refused. On August 25th he was tried and convicted. The tribunal sentenced him to five years imprisonment. Later the sentence was reduced to four years.

Duncan, the petitioner in No. 14, was a civilian shipfitter employed in the Navy Yard at Honolulu. On February 24, 1944, more than two years and two months after the Pearl Harbor attack, he engaged in a brawl with two armed Marine sentries at the yard. He was arrested by the military authorities. By the time of his arrest the military had to some extent eased the stringency of military rule. Schools, bars and motion picture theatres had been reopened. Courts had been authorized to "exercise their normal jurisdiction." They were once more summoning jurors and witnesses and conducting criminal trials. There were important exceptions, however. One of these was that only military tribunals were to try "Criminal prosecutions for violations of military orders." As the record shows, these military orders still covered a wide range of day to day civilian conduct. Duncan was charged with violating one of these orders, which prohibited assault on military or naval personnel with intent to resist or hinder them in the discharge of their duty. He was, therefore, tried by a military tribunal rather than the territorial court, although the general laws of Hawaii made assault a crime. A conviction followed and Duncan was sentenced to six months imprisonment.

The petitioners contend that "martial law" as provided for by § 67 did not authorize the military to try and punish civilians such as petitioners and urge further that if such authority should be inferred from the Organic Act, it would be unconstitutional. We need decide the constitutional question only if we agree with the Government that Congress did authorize what was done here.

We note first that at the time the alleged offenses were committed the dangers apprehended by the military were not sufficiently imminent to cause them to require civilians to evacuate the area or even to evacuate any of the buildings necessary to carry on the business of the courts. In fact, the buildings had long been open and actually in use for certain kinds of trials. Our question does not involve the well-established power of the military to exercise jurisdiction over members of the armed forces, those directly connected with such forces, or enemy belligerents, prisoners of war, or others charged with violating the laws of war.

Ex parte Quirin. We are not concerned with the recognized power of the military to try civilians in tribunals established as a part of a temporary military government over occupied enemy territory or territory regained from an enemy where civilian government cannot and does not function. For Hawaii since annexation has been held by and loyal to the United States. Nor need we here consider the power of the military simply to arrest and detain civilians interfering with a necessary military function at a time of turbulence and danger from insurrection or war. And finally, there was no specialized effort of the military, here, to enforce orders which related only to military functions, such as, for illustration, curfew rules or blackouts. For these petitioners were tried before tribunals set up under a military program which took over all government and superseded all civil laws and courts. If the Organic Act, properly interpreted, did not give the armed forces this awesome power, both petitioners are entitled to their freedom.

Since both the language of the Organic Act and its legislative history fail to indicate that the scope of "martial law" in Hawaii includes the supplanting of courts by military tribunals, we must look to other sources in order to interpret that term. We think the answer may be found in the birth, development and growth of our governmental institutions up to the time Congress passed the Organic Act.

People of many ages and countries have feared and unflinchingly opposed the kind of subordination of executive, legislative and judicial authorities to complete military rule which, according to the Government, Congress has authorized here. In this country that fear has become part of our cultural and political institutions. The story of that development is well known and we see no need to retell it all. But we might mention a few pertinent incidents. As early as the 17th Century our British ancestors took political action against aggressive military rule. When James I and Charles I authorized martial law for purposes of speedily punishing all types of crimes committed by civilians the protest led to the historic Petition of Right which in uncompromising terms objected to this arbitrary procedure and prayed that it be stopped and never repeated. When later the American colonies declared their independence one of the grievances listed by Jefferson was that the King had endeavored to render the military superior to the civil power.

In 1787, the year in which the Constitution was formulated, the Governor of Massachusetts Colony used the militia to cope with Shay's Rebellion. In his instructions to the Commander of the troops the Governor listed the "great objects" of the mission. The troops were to "protect the judicial courts . . . ," "to assist the civil magistrates in executing the laws . . . ," and to "aid them in apprehending the disturbers of the public peace . . . ." The Commander was to consider himself "constantly as under the direction of the civil officer, saving where any armed force shall appear and oppose . . . [his] marching to execute these orders." President Washington's instructions to the Commander of the troops sent into Pennsylvania to suppress the Whiskey Rebellion of 1794 were to the same effect. The troops were to see to it that the laws were enforced and were to deliver the leaders of armed insurgents to the regular courts for trial. The President admonished the Commanding General "that the judge can not be controlled in his functions . . . ." In the many instances of the use of troops to control the activities of civilians that followed, the troops were generally again employed merely to aid and not to supplant the civilian authorities.[18] The last noteworthy incident before the enactment of the Organic Act was the rioting that occurred in the spring of 1899 at the Coeur d'Alene mines of Shoshone County, Idaho. The President ordered the regular troops to report to the Governor for instructions and to support the civil authorities in preserving the peace. Later the State Auditor as agent of the Governor, and not the Commanding General, ordered the troops to detain citizens without trial and to aid the Auditor in doing all he thought necessary to stop the riot. Once more, the military authorities did not undertake to supplant the courts and to establish military tribunals to try and punish ordinary civilian offenders.

Courts and their procedural safeguards are indispensable to our system of government. They were set up by our founders to protect the liberties they valued. *Ex parte Quirin.* Our system of government clearly is the antithesis of total military rule and the founders of this country are not likely to have contemplated complete military dominance within the limits of a territory made part of this country and not recently taken from an enemy. They were opposed to governments that placed in the hands of one man the power to make, interpret and enforce the laws. Their philosophy has been the people's throughout our history. For that reason we have maintained legislatures chosen by citizens or their representatives and courts and juries to try those who violate legislative enactments. We have always been especially concerned about the potential evils of summary criminal trials and have guarded against them by provisions embodied in the Constitution itself. *See Ex parte Milligan; Chambers v. Florida,* 309 U.S. 227. Legislatures and courts are not merely cherished American institutions; they are indispensable to our Government.

Military tribunals have no such standing. For as this Court has said before: ". . . the military should always be kept in subjection to the laws of the country to which it belongs, and that he is no friend to the Republic who advocates the contrary. The established principle of every free people is, that the law shall alone govern; and to it the military must always yield." Congress prior to the time of the enactment of the Organic Act had only once authorized the supplanting of the courts by military tribunals. Legislation to that effect was enacted immediately after the South's unsuccessful attempt to secede from the Union. Insofar as that legislation applied to the Southern States after the war was at an end it was challenged by a series of Presidential vetoes as vigorous as

---

[18] After the passing of the Organic Act disturbances in the coal fields of West Virginia, a longshoremen's strike in Galveston and a packers' strike in Nebraska City, all led to criminal trials of civilians by military tribunals which were upheld by decisions of state and lower federal courts. All these cases rested on the ground that the Governor's determination of the existence of insurrection conclusively established that all the Governor had done was legal. The basis of these decisions was definitely held erroneous in *Sterling v. Constantin*, 287 U.S. 378, 401, where this Court said: "What are the allowable limits of military discretion, and whether or not they have been overstepped in a particular case, are judicial questions." As one commentator puts it, this Court "has knocked out the prop" on which these aforementioned cases Rested. WIENER, A PRACTICAL MANUAL OF MARTIAL LAW, 1940, p. 116.

any in the country's history. And in order to prevent this Court from passing on the constitutionality of this legislation Congress found it necessary to curtail our appellate jurisdiction.[22] Indeed, prior to the Organic Act, the only time this Court had ever discussed the supplanting of courts by military tribunals in a situation other than that involving the establishment of a military government over recently occupied enemy territory, it had emphatically declared that "civil liberty and this kind of martial law cannot endure together; the antagonism is irreconcilable; and, in the conflict, one or the other must perish." *Ex parte Milligan.*

We believe that when Congress passed the Hawaiian Organic Act and authorized the establishment of "martial law" it had in mind and did not wish to exceed the boundaries between military and civilian power, in which our people have always believed, which responsible military and executive officers had heeded, and which had become part of our political philosophy and institutions prior to the time Congress passed the Organic Act. The phrase "martial law" as employed in that Act, therefore, while intended to authorize the military to act vigorously for the maintenance of an orderly civil government and for the defense of the Islands against actual or threatened rebellion or invasion, was not intended to authorize the supplanting of courts by military tribunals. Yet the Government seeks to justify the punishment of both White and Duncan on the ground of such supposed congressional authorization. We hold that both petitioners are now entitled to be released from custody.

Reversed.

MR. JUSTICE JACKSON took no part in the consideration or decision of these cases.

MR. JUSTICE MURPHY, concurring.

The Court's opinion, in which I join, makes clear that the military trials in these cases were unjustified by the martial law provisions of the Hawaiian Organic Act. Equally obvious, as I see it, is the fact that these trials were forbidden by the Bill of Rights of the Constitution of the United States, which applies in both spirit and letter to Hawaii. Indeed, the unconstitutionality of the usurpation of civil power by the military is so great in this instance as to warrant this Court's complete and outright repudiation of the action.

Abhorrence of military rule is ingrained in our form of government. This supremacy of the civil over the military is one of our great heritages. It has made possible the attainment of a high degree of liberty regulated by law rather than by caprice. Our duty is to give effect to that heritage at all times, that it may be handed down untarnished to future generations.

The so-called "open court" rule of the *Milligan* case, to be sure, has been the subject of severe criticism, especially by military commentators. That criticism is repeated by the Government in these cases. It is said that the fact that courts

---

[22] *Ex parte McCardle,* 6 Wall. 318. *See also* WARREN, THE SUPREME COURT IN UNITED STATES HISTORY, Vol. 2, 464, 484.

are open is but one of many factors relevant to determining the necessity and hence the constitutionality of military trials of civilians. The argument is made that however adequate the "open court" rule may have been in 1628 or 1864 it is distinctly unsuited to modern warfare conditions where all of the territories of a warring nation may be in combat zones or imminently threatened with long-range attack even while civil courts are operating. Hence if a military commander, on the basis of his conception of military necessity, requires all civilians accused of crime to be tried summarily before martial law tribunals, the Bill of Rights must bow humbly to his judgment despite the unquestioned ability of the civil courts to exercise their criminal jurisdiction.

The argument thus advanced is as untenable today as it was when cast in the language of the Plantagenets, the Tudors and the Stuarts. It is a rank appeal to abandon the fate of all our liberties to the reasonableness of the judgment of those who are trained primarily for war. It seeks to justify military usurpation of civilian authority to punish crime without regard to the potency of the Bill of Rights. It deserves repudiation.

First. We may assume that the threat to Hawaii was a real one; we may also take it for granted that the general declaration of martial law was justified. But it does not follow from these assumptions that the military was free under the Constitution to close the civil courts or to strip them of their criminal jurisdiction, especially after the initial shock of the sudden Japanese attack had been dissipated.

Second. Delays in the civil courts and slowness in their procedure are also cited as an excuse for shearing away their criminal jurisdiction. It is said that the military "cannot brook a delay" and that "the punishment must be swift; there is an element of time in it, and we cannot afford to let the trial linger and be protracted." This military attitude toward constitutional processes is not novel. Civil liberties and military expediency are often irreconcilable. It does take time to . . . judge guilt or innocence according to accepted rules of law. But experience has demonstrated that such time is well spent. It is the only method we have of insuring the protection of constitutional rights and of guarding against oppression. The swift trial and punishment which the military desires is precisely what the Bill of Rights outlaws.

Third. It is further said that the issuance of military orders relating to civilians required that the military have at its disposal some sort of tribunal to enforce those regulations. [T]he mere fact that it may be more expedient and convenient for the military to try violators of its own orders before its own tribunals does not and should not furnish a constitutional basis for the jurisdiction of such tribunals when civil courts are in fact functioning or are capable of functioning. Constitutional rights are rooted deeper than the wishes and desires of the military.

Fourth. Much is made of the assertion that the civil courts in Hawaii had no jurisdiction over violations of military orders by civilians and that military courts were therefore necessary. Aside from the fact that the civil courts were ordered not to attempt to exercise such jurisdiction, it is sufficient to note that Congress on March 21, 1942, vested in the federal courts jurisdiction to enforce military orders with criminal penalties. It is undisputed that the federal court in Hawaii was open at all times in issue and was capable of exercising criminal jurisdiction.

Fifth. Objection is made to the enforcement in civil courts of military orders on the ground that it would subject the military to "all sorts of influences, political and otherwise, as happened in the cases on the east coast in both Philadelphia and Boston" and that "it is inconceivable that the Military Commander should be subjected for the enforcement of his orders to the control of other agents." This is merely a military criticism of the proposition that in this nation the military is subordinate to the civil authority. It does not qualify as a recognizable reason for closing the civil courts to criminal cases.

Sixth. Further objection is made that the holding of civil trials might interrupt vital work through the attendance as jurors of war workers. This also is too unmeritorious to warrant serious or lengthy discussion. War workers could easily have been excused from jury duty by military order if necessary.

Seventh. The final reason advanced relates to the testimony of military leaders that Hawaii is said to have a "heterogeneous population with all sorts of affinities and loyalties which are alien in many cases to the philosophy of life of the American Government," one-third of the civilian population being of Japanese descent. The court below observed that "Governmental and military problems alike were complicated by the presence in the Territory of tens of thousands of citizens of Japanese ancestry besides large numbers of aliens of the same race." The Government adds that many of the military personnel stationed in Hawaii were unaccustomed to living in such a community and that "potential problems" created in Hawaii by racially mixed juries in criminal cases have heretofore been recognized "although, on the whole, it has been found that members of such mixed juries have not acted on a racial basis."

Especially deplorable is this use of the iniquitous doctrine of racism to justify the imposition of military trials. Racism has no place whatever in our civilization. The Constitution as well as the conscience of mankind disclaims its use for any purpose, military or otherwise. It can only result, as it does in this instance, in striking down individual rights and in aggravating rather than solving the problems toward which it is directed. It renders impotent the ideal of the dignity of the human personality, destroying something of what is noble in our way of life. We must therefore reject it completely whenever it arises in the course of a legal proceeding.

The reasons here advanced for abandoning the "open court" rule of the *Milligan* case are without substance. To retreat from that rule is to open the door to rampant militarism and the glorification of war, which have destroyed so many nations in history. There is a very necessary part in our national life for the military; it has defended this country well in its darkest hours of trial. But militarism is not our way of life. It is to be used only in the most extreme circumstances. Moreover, we must be on constant guard against an excessive use of any power, military or otherwise, that results in the needless destruction of our rights and liberties. There must be a careful balancing of interests. And we must ever keep in mind that "The Constitution of the United States is a law for rulers and people, equally in war and in peace, and covers with the shield of its protection all classes of men, at all times, and under all circumstances." *Ex parte Milligan* 120-121.

MR. CHIEF JUSTICE STONE, concurring.

I take it that the Japanese attack on Hawaii on December 7, 1941, was an "invasion" within the meaning of § 67. But it began and ended long before these petitioners were tried by military tribunals in August 1942 and February 1944. I assume that there was danger of further invasion of Hawaii at the times of those trials. I assume also that there could be circumstances in which the public safety requires, and the Constitution permits, substitution of trials by military tribunals for trials in the civil courts. But the record here discloses no such conditions in Hawaii, at least during the period after February, 1942, and the trial court so found.

MR. JUSTICE BURTON, with whom MR. JUSTICE FRANKFURTER concurs, dissenting.

With the rest of this Court I subscribe unreservedly to the Bill of Rights. I recognize the importance of the civil courts in protecting individual rights guaranteed by the Constitution. I prefer civil to military control of civilian life and I agree that in war our Constitution contemplates the preservation of the individual rights of all of our people in accordance with a plan of constitutional procedure fitted to the needs of a self-governing republic at war.

Our Constitution expressly provides for waging war, and it is with the constitutional instruments for the successful conduct of war that I am concerned. I recognize here, as elsewhere, the constitutional direction that our respective branches of the Government do not exceed their allotted shares of authority. The courts, as well as our other agencies of the Government, accordingly owe a constitutional obligation not to invade the fields reserved either to the people, the States, or the other coordinate branches of the Government.

On December 7 and in the period immediately following, every inch of the Territory of Hawaii was like a frontier stockade under savage attack with notice that such attack would not be restrained by the laws of civilized nations. Measures of defense had to be taken on the basis that anything could happen. The relation of the Constitution of the United States to such a situation is important. Of course, the Constitution is not put aside. It was written by a generation fresh from war. The people established a more perfect union, in part, so that they might the better defend themselves from military attack. In doing so they centralized far more military power and responsibility in the Chief Executive than previously had been done. The Constitution was built for rough as well as smooth roads. In time of war the nation simply changes gears and takes the harder going under the same power.

The conduct of war under the Constitution is largely an executive function. Within the field of military action in time of war, the executive is allowed wide discretion. While, even in the conduct of war, there are many lines of jurisdiction to draw between the proper spheres of legislative, executive and judicial action, it seems clear that at least on an active battle field, the executive discretion to determine policy is there intended by the Constitution to be supreme. The question then arises: What is a battle field and how long does it remain one after the first barrage?

It is well that the outer limits of the jurisdiction of our military authorities is subject to review by our courts even under such extreme circumstances as those of the battle field. This, however, requires the courts to put themselves as nearly as possible in the place of those who had the constitutional responsibility for immediate executive action.

For this Court to intrude its judgment into spheres of constitutional discretion that are reserved either to the Congress or to the Chief Executive, is to invite disregard of that judgment by the Congress or by executive agencies under a claim of constitutional right to do so. On the other hand, this Court can contribute much to the orderly conduct of government, if it will outline reasonable boundaries for the discretion of the respective departments of the Government, with full regard for the limitations and also for the responsibilities imposed upon them by the Constitution.

It is important to approach the present cases with a full appreciation of the responsibility of the executive branch of the Government in Hawaii under the invasion which occurred on December 7, 1941. The question is not shall the Constitution apply under such circumstances? The question is with what authority has the Constitution and laws of this country vested the official representatives of the people upon whom are placed the responsibilities of leadership under those extraordinary circumstances?

The vital distinction is between conditions in "the theatre of actual military operations" and outside of that theatre. In this case Hawaii was not only in the theatre of operations, it was under fire. The actual presence of battle in a community creates a substantially different condition from that which exists in other parts of a nation at war.

Now that the war has been won and the safety of the Islands has been again assured, there is opportunity, in the calm light of peace, for the readjustment of sentences imposed upon civilians and military personnel during the emergency of war and which have not yet expired. It is important, however, that in reviewing the constitutionality of the conduct of our agencies of government in time of war, invasion and threatened invasion, we do not now make precedents which in other emergencies may handicap the executive branch of the Government in the performance of duties allotted to it by the Constitution and by the exercise of which it successfully defended the nation against the greatest attack ever made upon it.

One way to test the soundness of a decision today that the trial of petitioner White on August 25, 1942, and the trial of petitioner Duncan on March 2, 1944, were unconstitutional procedures, is to ask ourselves whether or not on those dates, with the war against Japan in full swing, this Court would have, or should have, granted a writ of habeas corpus, an injunction or a writ of prohibition to release the petitioners or otherwise to oust the provost courts of their claimed jurisdiction. Such a test emphasizes the issue. I believe that this Court would not have been justified in granting the relief suggested at such times. Also I believe that this Court might well have found itself embarrassed had it ordered such relief and then had attempted to enforce its order in the theatre of military operations, at a time when the area was under martial law and the writ of habeas corpus was still suspended, all in accordance with the orders of the President of the United States.

NOTES AND QUESTIONS

1. After *Duncan*, should we read *Milligan* as a constitutional holding or a statutory holding? Justice Black may have been a bit overly enthusiastic about what "our people have always believed" or about what "responsible military and executive officers had heeded," but his message is clearly stated that martial law does not itself close the civilian courts nor authorize diversion of civilian defendants to military tribunals. Is this essentially a statement about constitutional norms in the course of statutory interpretation?

2. How was it determined that Congress had authorized military tribunals for the saboteurs in *Quirin* but not for crimes, even committed on a military base, in *Duncan*? This is perhaps the most clearly visible reason for understanding the nature of the "law of war" with which we started this course.

3. Chief Justice Stone points out that there were no active hostilities in or around Hawaii in 1942, while Justice says that Hawaii was "under fire." How can there be such a difference in perception of the existence of "armed conflict" or "active hostilities?" Are courts really incapable of making the factual determinations necessary for this decision? If so, how does a military tribunal or an international tribunal determine when a state of armed conflict exist?

Johnson v. Eisentrager, **339 U.S. 763 (1950).** This was a habeas corpus petition brought in the D.C. district court on behalf of 21 German citizens who had been captured in China following Germany's surrender and before Japan's surrender. They were tried by U.S. military commission in China and convicted of spying on behalf of Japan in violation of the law of war. They were then transferred to a U.S. military prison in Germany. Justice Jackson for the Supreme Court first engaged in a lengthy discussion of the differences among citizens, resident aliens, resident enemy aliens, and nonresident aliens.

We are here confronted with a decision whose basic premise is that these prisoners are entitled, as a constitutional right, to sue in some court of the United States for a writ of habeas corpus. To support that assumption we must hold that a prisoner of our military authorities is constitutionally entitled to the writ, even though he (a) is an enemy alien; (b) has never been or resided in the United States; (c) was captured outside of our territory and there held in military custody as a prisoner of war; (d) was tried and convicted by a Military Commission sitting outside the United States; (e) for offenses against laws of war committed outside the United States; (f) and is at all times imprisoned outside the United States.

We have pointed out that the privilege of litigation has been extended to aliens, whether friendly or enemy, only because permitting their presence in the country implied protection. No such basis can be invoked here, for these prisoners at no relevant time were within any territory over which the United States is sovereign, and the scenes of their offense, their capture, their trial and their punishment were all beyond the territorial jurisdiction of any court of the United States.

Justice Jackson then went on to an apparent review of the merits of the petitions:

It is not for us to say whether these prisoners were or were not guilty of a war crime, or whether if we were to retry the case we would agree to the findings of fact or the application of the laws of war made by the Military Commission. The petition shows that these prisoners were formally accused of violating the laws of war and fully informed of particulars of these charges. As we observed in the *Yamashit*a case, "If the military tribunals have lawful authority to hear, decide and condemn, their action is not subject to judicial review merely because they have made a wrong decision on disputed facts. Correction of their errors of decision is not for the courts but for the military authorities which are alone authorized to review their decisions. . . . We consider here only the lawful power of the commission to try the petitioner for the offense charged."

That there is a basis in conventional and long-established law by which conduct ascribed to them might amount to a violation seems beyond question. Breach of the terms of an act of surrender is no novelty among war crimes. "That capitulations must be scrupulously adhered to is an old customary rule, since enacted by Article 35 of the Hague Regulations. Any act contrary to a capitulation would constitute an international delinquency if ordered by a belligerent Government, and a war crime if committed without such order. Such violation may be met by reprisals or punishment of the offenders as war criminals." II OPPENHEIM, INTERNATIONAL LAW 433 (6th ed. rev., Lauterpacht, 1944). It being within the jurisdiction of a Military Commission to try the prisoners, it was for it to determine whether the laws of war applied and whether an offense against them had been committed.

The meaning and significance of *Eisentrager* is extensively debated in the military detention cases of 2004 considered in the next section.

§ 8.03 MILITARY DETENTIONS

The clearest example of departure from peacetime norms in the "war on terrorism" is the military detention without trial of a U.S. citizen arrested by the FBI on U.S. soil and accused of planning to engage in a terrorist act on U.S. soil. His name is Jose Padilla, and he has been held in the Navy brig at Charleston, South Carolina, while habeas corpus proceedings test the validity of his detention. Another U.S. citizen held under slightly different circumstances was Yaser Hamdi, who was in military custody since he was picked up in

Afghanistan in early 2002. And then there are the almost 700 persons of various nationalities held at Guantanamo Bay, most of whom were captured in Afghanistan but some of whom may have been captured in other places under different circumstances.

In all three instances, the Government claimed that it could detain these persons as "enemy combatants" pursuant to the war powers of the President. In June 2004, the Supreme Court decided all three cases, rejecting the Government's underlying premise of near-unreviewable executive power. But the opinions need to be read carefully to determine precisely what was held in each instance.

The concepts involved in the "law of war" were introduced in Chapter 3. In short, the "law of war" applies at least during periods of "armed conflict" such that would trigger the Geneva Conventions. Under the law of war, a combatant in an international armed conflict possesses combat immunity for acts that do not violate the law of war, while a civilian would have no combat immunity unless he or she can fall within the definitions of eligibility for POW status under article 4 of Geneva III (GPW). And the law of war generally would not require recognition of combat immunity for violent acts during a period of insurrection or internal armed conflict. These concepts form part of the background for the question of how to deal with violent actors who are not connected with any entity claiming the status of a nation or state.

H, US citizen, apprehended in Afghanistan.

HAMDI v. RUMSFELD
124 S. Ct. 2633 (2004)

O'CONNOR, J., announced the judgment of the Court and delivered an opinion, in which REHNQUIST, C.J., and KENNEDY and BREYER, JJ., joined. SOUTER, J., filed an opinion concurring in part, dissenting in part, and concurring in the judgment, in which GINSBURG, J., joined. SCALIA, J., filed a dissenting opinion, in which STEVENS, J., joined. THOMAS, J., filed a dissenting opinion.

JUSTICE O'CONNOR announced the judgment of the Court and delivered an opinion, in which THE CHIEF JUSTICE, JUSTICE KENNEDY, and JUSTICE BREYER join.

4th Cir

At this difficult time in our Nation's history, we are called upon to consider the legality of the Government's detention of a United States citizen on United States soil as an "enemy combatant" and to address the process that is constitutionally owed to one who seeks to challenge his classification as such. The United States Court of Appeals for the Fourth Circuit held that petitioner's detention was legally authorized and that he was entitled to no further opportunity to challenge his enemy-combatant label. We now vacate and remand. We hold that although Congress authorized the detention of combatants in the narrow circumstances alleged here, due process demands that a citizen held in the United States as an enemy combatant be given a meaningful opportunity to contest the factual basis for that detention before a neutral decisionmaker.

H

I

On September 11, 2001, the al Qaeda terrorist network used hijacked commercial airliners to attack prominent targets in the United States. Approximately 3,000 people were killed in those attacks. One week later, in response to these "acts of treacherous violence," Congress passed a resolution authorizing the President to "use all necessary and appropriate force against those nations, organizations, or persons he determines planned, authorized, committed, or aided the terrorist attacks" or "harbored such organizations or persons, in order to prevent any future acts of international terrorism against the United States by such nations, organizations or persons." Authorization for Use of Military Force ("the AUMF"). Soon thereafter, the President ordered United States Armed Forces to Afghanistan, with a mission to subdue al Qaeda and quell the Taliban regime that was known to support it.

AUMF

This case arises out of the detention of a man whom the Government alleges took up arms with the Taliban during this conflict. His name is Yaser Esam Hamdi. Born an American citizen in Louisiana in 1980, Hamdi moved with his family to Saudi Arabia as a child. By 2001, the parties agree, he resided in Afghanistan. At some point that year, he was seized by members of the Northern Alliance, a coalition of military groups opposed to the Taliban government, and eventually was turned over to the United States military. The Government asserts that it initially detained and interrogated Hamdi in Afghanistan before transferring him to the United States Naval Base in Guantanamo Bay in January 2002. In April 2002, upon learning that Hamdi is an American citizen, authorities transferred him to a naval brig in Norfolk, Virginia, where he remained until a recent transfer to a brig in Charleston, South Carolina. The Government contends that Hamdi is an "enemy combatant," and that this status justifies holding him in the United States indefinitely – without formal charges or proceedings – unless and until it makes the determination that access to counsel or further process is warranted.

G says H is an enemy combatant

In June 2002, Hamdi's father, Esam Fouad Hamdi, filed the present petition for a writ of habeas corpus under 28 U.S.C. § 2241 in the Eastern District of Virginia, naming as petitioners his son and himself as next friend. The elder Hamdi alleges in the petition that he has had no contact with his son since the Government took custody of him in 2001, and that the Government has held his son "without access to legal counsel or notice of any charges pending against him." Although his habeas petition provides no details with regard to the factual circumstances surrounding his son's capture and detention, Hamdi's father has asserted in documents found elsewhere in the record that his son went to Afghanistan to do "relief work," and that he had been in that country less than two months before September 11, 2001, and could not have received military training. The 20-year-old was traveling on his own for the first time, his father says, and "because of his lack of experience, he was trapped in Afghanistan once that military campaign began."

H says it was "relief work"

[T]he Government filed a response and a motion to dismiss the petition. It attached to its response a declaration from one Michael Mobbs (hereinafter "Mobbs Declaration"), who identified himself as Special Advisor to the Under

Secretary of Defense for Policy. Mobbs . . . set forth what remains the sole evidentiary support that the Government has provided to the courts for Hamdi's detention. The declaration states that Hamdi "traveled to Afghanistan" in July or August 2001, and that he thereafter "affiliated with a Taliban military unit and received weapons training." It asserts that Hamdi "remained with his Taliban unit following the attacks of September 11" and that, during the time when Northern Alliance forces were "engaged in battle with the Taliban, . . . Hamdi's Taliban unit surrendered" to those forces, after which he "surrendered his Kalishnikov assault rifle" to them. The Mobbs Declaration also states that, because al Qaeda and the Taliban "were and are hostile forces engaged in armed conflict with the armed forces of the United States," "individuals associated with" those groups "were and continue to be enemy combatants." Mobbs states that Hamdi was labeled an enemy combatant "based upon his interviews and in light of his association with the Taliban." According to the declaration, a series of "U.S. military screening teams" determined that Hamdi met "the criteria for enemy combatants," and "a subsequent interview of Hamdi has confirmed that he surrendered and gave his firearm to Northern Alliance forces, which supports his classification as an enemy combatant."

Mobbs did not [handwritten note in margin]

The District Court found that the Mobbs Declaration fell "far short" of supporting Hamdi's detention. It criticized the generic and hearsay nature of the affidavit, calling it "little more than the government's 'say-so.'" It ordered the Government to turn over numerous materials for *in camera* review. The Fourth Circuit reversed, . . . [and] stressed that, because it was "undisputed that Hamdi was captured in a zone of active combat in a foreign theater of conflict," no factual inquiry or evidentiary hearing allowing Hamdi to be heard or to rebut the Government's assertions was necessary or proper. Concluding that the factual averments in the Mobbs Declaration, "if accurate," provided a sufficient basis upon which to conclude that the President had constitutionally detained Hamdi pursuant to the President's war powers, it ordered the habeas petition dismissed. Relying on *Ex parte Quirin,* 317 U.S. 1 (1942), the court emphasized that "one who takes up arms against the United States in a foreign theater of war, regardless of his citizenship, may properly be designated an enemy combatant and treated as such."

4th Cir. relying on Quirin [handwritten note in margin]

We now vacate the judgment below and remand.

II

The threshold question before us is whether the Executive has the authority to detain citizens who qualify as "enemy combatants." There is some debate as to the proper scope of this term, and the Government has never provided any court with the full criteria that it uses in classifying individuals as such. It has made clear, however, that, for purposes of this case, the "enemy combatant" that it is seeking to detain is an individual who, it alleges, was "'part of or supporting forces hostile to the United States or coalition partners'" in Afghanistan and who "'engaged in an armed conflict against the United States'" there. We therefore answer only the narrow question before us: whether the detention of citizens falling within that definition is authorized.

The Government maintains that no explicit congressional authorization is required, because the Executive possesses plenary authority to detain pursuant to Article II of the Constitution. We do not reach the question whether Article II provides such authority, however, because we agree with the Government's alternative position, that Congress has in fact authorized Hamdi's detention, through the AUMF.

Our analysis on that point, set forth below, substantially overlaps with our analysis of Hamdi's principal argument for the illegality of his detention. He posits that his detention is forbidden by 18 U.S.C. § 4001(a). Section 4001(a) states that "no citizen shall be imprisoned or otherwise detained by the United States except pursuant to an Act of Congress." Congress passed § 4001(a) in 1971 as part of a bill to repeal the Emergency Detention Act of 1950, which provided procedures for executive detention, during times of emergency, of individuals deemed likely to engage in espionage or sabotage. Congress was particularly concerned about the possibility that the Act could be used to reprise the Japanese internment camps of World War II. The Government again presses two alternative positions. First, it argues that § 4001(a), in light of its legislative history and its location in Title 18, applies only to "the control of civilian prisons and related detentions," not to military detentions. Second, it maintains that § 4001(a) is satisfied, because Hamdi is being detained "pursuant to an Act of Congress" – the AUMF. Again, because we conclude that the Government's second assertion is correct, we do not address the first. In other words, for the reasons that follow, we conclude that the AUMF is explicit congressional authorization for the detention of individuals in the narrow category we describe (assuming, without deciding, that such authorization is required), and that the AUMF satisfied § 4001(a)'s requirement that a detention be "pursuant to an Act of Congress" (assuming, without deciding, that § 4001(a) applies to military detentions).

The AUMF authorizes the President to use "all necessary and appropriate force" against "nations, organizations, or persons" associated with the September 11, 2001, terrorist attacks. There can be no doubt that individuals who fought against the United States in Afghanistan as part of the Taliban, an organization known to have supported the al Qaeda terrorist network responsible for those attacks, are individuals Congress sought to target in passing the AUMF. We conclude that detention of individuals falling into the limited category we are considering, for the duration of the particular conflict in which they were captured, is so fundamental and accepted an incident to war as to be an exercise of the "necessary and appropriate force" Congress has authorized the President to use.

The capture and detention of lawful combatants and the capture, detention, and trial of unlawful combatants, by "universal agreement and practice," are "important incidents of war." The purpose of detention is to prevent captured individuals from returning to the field of battle and taking up arms once again.

There is no bar to this Nation's holding one of its own citizens as an enemy combatant. In *Quirin*, one of the detainees, Haupt, alleged that he was a naturalized United States citizen. We held that "citizens who associate themselves with the military arm of the enemy government, and with its aid, guidance and direction enter this country bent on hostile acts, are enemy belligerents within the meaning of . . . the law of war." While Haupt was tried for violations of the law of war, nothing in *Quirin* suggests that his citizenship would have precluded his mere detention for the duration of the relevant hostilities. Nor can we see any reason for drawing such a line here. A citizen, no less than an alien, can be "part of or supporting forces hostile to the United States or coalition partners" and "engaged in an armed conflict against the United States;" such a citizen, if released, would pose the same threat of returning to the front during the ongoing conflict.

In light of these principles, it is of no moment that the AUMF does not use specific language of detention. Because detention to prevent a combatant's return to the battlefield is a fundamental incident of waging war, in permitting the use of "necessary and appropriate force," Congress has clearly and unmistakably authorized detention in the narrow circumstances considered here.

Hamdi objects, nevertheless, that Congress has not authorized the *indefinite* detention to which he is now subject. The Government responds that "the detention of enemy combatants during World War II was just as 'indefinite' while that war was being fought." We take Hamdi's objection to be not to the lack of certainty regarding the date on which the conflict will end, but to the substantial prospect of perpetual detention. We recognize that the national security underpinnings of the "war on terror," although crucially important, are broad and malleable. As the Government concedes, "given its unconventional nature, the current conflict is unlikely to end with a formal cease-fire agreement." The prospect Hamdi raises is therefore not far-fetched. If the Government does not consider this unconventional war won for two generations, and if it maintains during that time that Hamdi might, if released, rejoin forces fighting against the United States, then the position it has taken throughout the litigation of this case suggests that Hamdi's detention could last for the rest of his life.

It is a clearly established principle of the law of war that detention may last no longer than active hostilities. *See* Article 118 of the Geneva Convention (III) Relative to the Treatment of Prisoners of War ("Prisoners of war shall be released and repatriated without delay after the cessation of active hostilities").

Hamdi contends that the AUMF does not authorize indefinite or perpetual detention. Certainly, we agree that indefinite detention for the purpose of interrogation is not authorized. Further, we understand Congress' grant of authority for the use of "necessary and appropriate force" to include the authority to detain for the duration of the relevant conflict, and our understanding is based on longstanding law-of-war principles. If the practical circumstances of a given conflict are entirely unlike those of the conflicts that informed the development of the law of war, that understanding may unravel. But that is not the situation we face as of this date. Active combat operations against Taliban fighters apparently are ongoing in Afghanistan. The United States may detain, for the duration of these hostilities, individuals legitimately determined to be Taliban combatants who "engaged in an armed conflict against the United States." If the record establishes that United States troops are still involved in active combat in Afghanistan, those detentions are part of the exercise of "necessary and appropriate force," and therefore are authorized by the AUMF.

Ex parte Milligan, 4 Wall. 2, 125 (1866), does not undermine our holding about the Government's authority to seize enemy combatants, as we define that term today. In that case, the Court made repeated reference to the fact that its inquiry into whether the military tribunal had jurisdiction to try and punish Milligan turned in large part on the fact that Milligan was not a prisoner of war, but a resident of Indiana arrested while at home there. That fact was central to its conclusion. Had Milligan been captured while he was assisting Confederate soldiers by carrying a rifle against Union troops on a Confederate battlefield, the holding of the Court might well have been different. The Court's repeated explanations that Milligan was not a prisoner of war suggest that had these different circumstances been present he could have been detained under military authority for the duration of the conflict, whether or not he was a citizen.

Quirin was a unanimous opinion. It both postdates and clarifies *Milligan*, providing us with the most apposite precedent that we have on the question of whether citizens may be detained in such circumstances. Brushing aside such precedent – particularly when doing so gives rise to a host of new questions never dealt with by this Court – is unjustified and unwise.

To the extent that Justice Scalia accepts the precedential value of *Quirin*, he argues that it cannot guide our inquiry here because "in *Quirin* it was uncontested that the petitioners were members of enemy forces," while Hamdi challenges his classification as an enemy combatant. But it is unclear why, in the paradigm outlined by Justice Scalia, such a concession should have any relevance. Justice Scalia envisions a system in which the only options are congressional suspension of the writ of habeas corpus or prosecution for treason or some other crime. He does not explain how his historical analysis supports the addition of a third option – detention under some other process after concession of enemy-combatant status – or why a concession should carry any different effect than proof of enemy-combatant status in a proceeding that comports with due process. To be clear, our opinion only finds legislative authority to detain under the AUMF once it is sufficiently clear that the individual is, in fact, an enemy combatant; whether that is established by concession or by some other process that verifies this fact with sufficient certainty seems beside the point.

Further, Justice Scalia largely ignores the context of this case: a United States citizen captured in a *foreign* combat zone. Because Justice Scalia finds the fact of battlefield capture irrelevant, his distinction based on the fact that the petitioner "conceded" enemy combatant status is beside the point. Justice Scalia can point to no case or other authority for the proposition that those captured on a foreign battlefield (whether detained there or in U.S. territory) cannot be detained outside the criminal process.

Moreover, Justice Scalia presumably would come to a different result if Hamdi had been kept in Afghanistan or even Guantanamo Bay. This creates a perverse incentive. Military authorities faced with the stark choice of submitting to the full-blown criminal process or releasing a suspected enemy combatant captured on the battlefield will simply keep citizen-detainees abroad. Indeed, the Government transferred Hamdi from Guantanamo Bay to the United States naval brig only after it learned that he might be an American citizen. It is not at all clear why that should make a determinative constitutional difference.

III

Even in cases in which the detention of enemy combatants is legally authorized, there remains the question of what process is constitutionally due to a citizen who disputes his enemy-combatant status. Hamdi argues that he is owed a meaningful and timely hearing and that "extra-judicial detention [that] begins and ends with the submission of an affidavit based on third-hand hearsay" does not comport with the Fifth and Fourteenth Amendments. The Government counters that any more process than was provided below would be both unworkable and "constitutionally intolerable." Our resolution of this dispute requires a careful examination both of the writ of habeas corpus, which Hamdi now seeks to employ as a mechanism of judicial review, and of the Due Process Clause, which informs the procedural contours of that mechanism in this instance.

A

Though they reach radically different conclusions on the process that ought to attend the present proceeding, the parties begin on common ground. All agree that, absent suspension, the writ of habeas corpus remains available to every individual detained within the United States. All agree suspension of the writ has not occurred here. Thus, it is undisputed that Hamdi was properly before an Article III court to challenge his detention under 28 U.S.C. § 2241. Further, all agree that § 2241 and its companion provisions provide at least a skeletal outline of the procedures to be afforded a petitioner in federal habeas review. Most notably, § 2243 provides that "the person detained may, under oath, deny any of the facts set forth in the return or allege any other material facts," and § 2246 allows the taking of evidence in habeas proceedings by deposition, affidavit, or interrogatories.

The simple outline of § 2241 makes clear both that Congress envisioned that habeas petitioners would have some opportunity to present and rebut facts and that courts in cases like this retain some ability to vary the ways in which they do so as mandated by due process. The Government recognizes the basic procedural protections required by the habeas statute, but asks us to hold that, given both the flexibility of the habeas mechanism and the circumstances presented in this case, the presentation of the Mobbs Declaration to the habeas court completed the required factual development. It suggests two separate reasons for its position that no further process is due.

B

First, the Government urges the adoption of the Fourth Circuit's holding below — that because it is "undisputed" that Hamdi's seizure took place in a combat zone, the habeas determination can be made purely as a matter of law, with no further hearing or factfinding necessary. This argument is easily rejected. [T]he circumstances surrounding Hamdi's seizure cannot in any way be characterized as "undisputed," as "those circumstances are neither conceded in fact, nor susceptible to concession in law, because Hamdi has not been permitted to speak for himself or even through counsel as to those circumstances." Further, the "facts" that constitute the alleged concession are insufficient to support Hamdi's detention. Under the definition of enemy combatant that we accept today as falling within the scope of Congress' authorization, Hamdi would need to be "part of or supporting forces hostile to the United States or coalition partners" and "engaged in an armed conflict against the United States" to justify his detention in the United States for the duration of the relevant conflict. The habeas petition states only that "when seized by the United States Government, Mr. Hamdi resided in Afghanistan." An assertion that one *resided* in a country in which combat operations are taking place is not a concession that one was "*captured* in a zone of active combat operations in a foreign theater of war," and certainly is not a concession that one was "part of or supporting forces hostile to the United States or coalition partners" and "engaged in an armed conflict against the United States." Accordingly, we reject any argument that Hamdi has made concessions that eliminate any right to further process.

C

The Government's second argument requires closer consideration. This is the argument that further factual exploration is unwarranted and inappropriate in light of the extraordinary constitutional interests at stake. Under the Government's most extreme rendition of this argument, "respect for separation of powers and the limited institutional capabilities of courts in matters of military decision-making in connection with an ongoing conflict" ought to eliminate entirely any individual process, restricting the courts to investigating only whether legal authorization exists for the broader detention scheme. At most, the Government argues, courts should review its determination that a citizen is an enemy combatant under a very deferential "some evidence" standard. Under this review, a court would assume the accuracy of the Government's articulated basis for Hamdi's detention, as set forth in the Mobbs Declaration, and assess only whether that articulated basis was a legitimate one.

In response, Hamdi emphasizes that this Court consistently has recognized that an individual challenging his detention may not be held at the will of the Executive without recourse to some proceeding before a neutral tribunal to determine whether the Executive's asserted justifications for that detention have basis in fact and warrant in law. He argues that the Fourth Circuit inappropriately "ceded power to the Executive during wartime to define the conduct for which a citizen may be detained, judge whether that citizen has engaged in the proscribed conduct, and imprison that citizen indefinitely," and that due process demands that he receive a hearing in which he may challenge the Mobbs Declaration and adduce his own counter evidence. The District Court, agreeing with Hamdi, apparently believed that the appropriate process would approach the process that accompanies a criminal trial. It therefore disapproved of the hearsay nature of the Mobbs Declaration and anticipated quite extensive discovery of various military affairs. Anything less, it concluded, would not be "meaningful judicial review."

Both of these positions highlight legitimate concerns. And both emphasize the tension that often exists between the autonomy that the Government asserts is necessary in order to pursue effectively a particular goal and the process that a citizen contends he is due before he is deprived of a constitutional right. The ordinary mechanism that we use for balancing such serious competing interests, and for determining the procedures that are necessary to ensure that a citizen is not "deprived of life, liberty, or property, without due process of law," is the test that we articulated in *Mathews v. Eldridge,* 424 U.S. 319 (1976). *Mathews* dictates that the process due in any given instance is determined by weighing "the private interest that will be affected by the official action" against the Government's asserted interest, "including the function involved" and the burdens the Government would face in providing greater process. The *Mathews* calculus then contemplates a judicious balancing of these concerns, through an analysis of "the risk of an erroneous deprivation" of the private interest if the process were reduced and the "probable value, if any, of additional or substitute safeguards." We take each of these steps in turn.

1

It is beyond question that substantial interests lie on both sides of the scale in this case. Hamdi's "private interest . . . affected by the official action," is the most elemental of liberty interests – the interest in being free from physical detention by one's own government. We have always been careful not to 'minimize the importance and fundamental nature' of the individual's right to liberty, and we will not do so today.

Nor is the weight on this side of the *Mathews* scale offset by the circumstances of war or the accusation of treasonous behavior, for "it is clear that commitment for *any* purpose constitutes a significant deprivation of liberty that requires due process protection," and at this stage in the *Mathews* calculus, we consider the interest of the *erroneously* detained individual. Indeed, as *amicus* briefs from media and relief organizations emphasize, the risk of erroneous deprivation of a citizen's liberty in the absence of sufficient process here is very real (noting ways in which "the nature of humanitarian relief work and journalism present a significant risk of mistaken military detentions"). Moreover, as critical as the Government's interest may be in detaining those who actually pose an immediate threat to the national security of the United States during ongoing international conflict, history and common sense teach us that an unchecked system of detention carries the potential to become a means for oppression and abuse of others who do not present that sort of threat. Because we live in a society in which "mere public intolerance or animosity cannot constitutionally justify the deprivation of a person's physical liberty," our starting point for the *Mathews* v. *Eldridge* analysis is unaltered by the allegations surrounding the particular detainee or the organizations with which he is alleged to have associated. We reaffirm today the fundamental nature of a citizen's right to be free from involuntary confinement by his own government without due process of law, and we weigh the opposing governmental interests against the curtailment of liberty that such confinement entails.

2

On the other side of the scale are the weighty and sensitive governmental interests in ensuring that those who have in fact fought with the enemy during a war do not return to battle against the United States. As discussed above, the law of war and the realities of combat may render such detentions both necessary and appropriate, and our due process analysis need not blink at those realities. Without doubt, our Constitution recognizes that core strategic matters of warmaking belong in the hands of those who are best positioned and most politically accountable for making them. *Youngstown Sheet & Tube Co. v. Sawyer* (acknowledging "broad powers in military commanders engaged in day-to-day fighting in a theater of war").

The Government also argues at some length that its interests in reducing the process available to alleged enemy combatants are heightened by the practical difficulties that would accompany a system of trial-like process. In its view, military officers who are engaged in the serious work of waging battle would be unnecessarily and dangerously distracted by litigation half a world away, and discovery into military operations would both intrude on the sensitive secrets of national defense and result in a futile search for evidence buried under the rubble of war. To the extent that these burdens are triggered by heightened procedures, they are properly taken into account in our due process analysis.

3

Striking the proper constitutional balance here is of great importance to the Nation during this period of ongoing combat. But it is equally vital that our calculus not give short shrift to the values that this country holds dear or to the privilege that is American citizenship. It is during our most challenging and uncertain moments that our Nation's commitment to due process is most severely tested; and it is in those times that we must preserve our commitment at home to the principles for which we fight abroad. See *United States v. Robel,* 389 U.S. 258, 264 (1967) ("It would indeed be ironic if, in the name of national defense, we would sanction the subversion of one of those liberties . . . which makes the defense of the Nation worthwhile").

With due recognition of these competing concerns, we believe that neither the process proposed by the Government nor the process apparently envisioned by the District Court below strikes the proper constitutional balance when a United States citizen is detained in the United States as an enemy combatant. That is, "the risk of erroneous deprivation" of a detainee's liberty interest is unacceptably high under the Government's proposed rule, while some of the "additional or substitute procedural safeguards" suggested by the District Court are unwarranted in light of their limited "probable value" and the burdens they may impose on the military in such cases.

We therefore hold that a citizen-detainee seeking to challenge his classification as an enemy combatant must receive notice of the factual basis for his classification, and a fair opportunity to rebut the Government's factual assertions before a neutral decisionmaker.

At the same time, the exigencies of the circumstances may demand that, aside from these core elements, enemy combatant proceedings may be tailored to *related criminal protection*

alleviate their uncommon potential to burden the Executive at a time of ongoing military conflict. Hearsay, for example, may need to be accepted as the most reliable available evidence from the Government in such a proceeding. Likewise, the Constitution would not be offended by a presumption in favor of the Government's evidence, so long as that presumption remained a rebuttable one and fair opportunity for rebuttal were provided. Thus, once the Government puts forth credible evidence that the habeas petitioner meets the enemy-combatant criteria, the onus could shift to the petitioner to rebut that evidence with more persuasive evidence that he falls outside the criteria. A burden-shifting scheme of this sort would meet the goal of ensuring that the errant tourist, embedded journalist, or local aid worker has a chance to prove military error while giving due regard to the Executive once it has put forth meaningful support for its conclusion that the detainee is in fact an enemy combatant. In the words of *Mathews*, process of this sort would sufficiently address the "risk of erroneous deprivation" of a detainee's liberty interest while eliminating certain procedures that have questionable additional value in light of the burden on the *Government*.

this D.P. only applies for continued detention

We think it unlikely that this basic process will have the dire impact on the central functions of warmaking that the Government forecasts. The parties agree that initial captures on the battlefield need not receive the process we have discussed here; that process is due only when the determination is made to *continue* to hold those who have been seized. The Government has made clear in its briefing that documentation regarding battlefield detainees already is kept in the ordinary course of military affairs. Any factfinding imposition created by requiring a knowledgeable affiant to summarize these records to an independent tribunal is a minimal one. Likewise, arguments that military officers ought not have to wage war under the threat of litigation lose much of their steam when factual disputes at enemy-combatant hearings are limited to the alleged combatant's acts. This focus meddles little, if at all, in the strategy or conduct of war, inquiring only into the appropriateness of continuing to detain an individual claimed to have taken up arms against the United States. While we accord the greatest respect and consideration to the judgments of military authorities in matters relating to the actual prosecution of a war, and recognize that the scope of that discretion necessarily is wide, it does not infringe on the core role of the military for the courts to exercise their own time-honored and constitutionally mandated roles of reviewing and resolving claims like those presented here.

In sum, while the full protections that accompany challenges to detentions in other settings may prove unworkable and inappropriate in the enemy-combatant setting, the threats to military operations posed by a basic system of independent review are not so weighty as to trump a citizen's core rights to challenge meaningfully the Government's case and to be heard by an impartial adjudicator.

D

In so holding, we necessarily reject the Government's assertion that separation of powers principles mandate a heavily circumscribed role for the courts in such circumstances. Indeed, the position that the courts must forgo any examination of the individual case and focus exclusively on the legality of the broader detention scheme cannot be mandated by any reasonable view of separation of powers, as this approach serves only to *condense* power into a single branch of government. We have long since made clear that a state of war is not a blank check for the President when it comes to the rights of the Nation's citizens. *Youngstown Sheet & Tube.* Whatever power the United States Constitution envisions for the Executive in its exchanges with other nations or with enemy organizations in times of conflict, it most assuredly envisions a role for all three branches when individual liberties are at stake. Likewise, we have made clear that, unless Congress acts to suspend it, the Great Writ of habeas corpus allows the Judicial Branch to play a necessary role in maintaining this delicate balance of governance, serving as an important judicial check on the Executive's discretion in the realm of detentions. Thus, while we do not question that our due process assessment must pay keen attention to the particular burdens faced by the Executive in the context of military action, it would turn our system of checks and balances on its head to suggest that a citizen could not make his way to court with a challenge to the factual basis for his detention by his government, simply because the Executive opposes making available such a challenge. Absent suspension of the writ by Congress, a citizen detained as an enemy combatant is entitled to this process.

Because we conclude that due process demands some system for a citizen detainee to refute his classification, the proposed "some evidence" standard is inadequate. Any process in which the Executive's factual assertions go wholly unchallenged or are simply presumed correct without any opportunity for the alleged combatant to demonstrate otherwise falls constitutionally short. Aside from unspecified "screening" processes, and military interrogations in which the Government suggests Hamdi could have contested his classification, Hamdi has received no process. An interrogation by one's captor, however effective an intelligence-gathering tool, hardly constitutes a constitutionally adequate factfinding before a neutral decisionmaker. Plainly, the "process" Hamdi has received is not that to which he is entitled under the Due Process Clause.

There remains the possibility that the standards we have articulated could be met by an appropriately authorized and properly constituted military tribunal. Indeed, it is notable that military regulations already provide for such process in related instances, dictating that tribunals be made available to determine the status of enemy detainees who assert prisoner-of-war status under the Geneva Convention. In the absence of such process, however, a court that receives a petition for a writ of habeas corpus from an alleged enemy combatant must itself ensure that the minimum requirements of due process are achieved. Both courts below recognized as much, focusing their energies on the question of whether Hamdi was due an opportunity to rebut the Government's case against him. The Government, too, proceeded on this assumption, presenting its affidavit and then seeking that it be evaluated under a deferential standard of review based on burdens that it alleged would accompany any greater process.

IV

Hamdi asks us to hold that the Fourth Circuit also erred by denying him immediate access to counsel upon his detention and by disposing of the case without permitting him to meet with an attorney. Since our grant of certiorari in this case, Hamdi has been appointed counsel, with whom he has met for consultation purposes on several occasions, and with whom he is now being granted unmonitored meetings. He unquestionably has the right to access to counsel in connection with the proceedings on remand. No further consideration of this issue is necessary at this stage of the case.

The judgment of the United States Court of Appeals for the Fourth Circuit is vacated, and the case is remanded for further proceedings.

JUSTICE SOUTER, with whom JUSTICE GINSBURG joins, concurring in part, dissenting in part, and concurring in the judgment.

The plurality . . . accept[s] the Government's position that if Hamdi's designation as an enemy combatant is correct, his detention (at least as to some period) is authorized by an Act of Congress as required by § 4001(a), that is, by the Authorization for Use of Military Force. Here, I disagree and respectfully dissent. The Government has failed to demonstrate that the Force Resolution authorizes the detention complained of here even on the facts the Government claims. If the Government raises nothing further than the record now shows, the Non-Detention Act entitles Hamdi to be released.

The threshold issue is how broadly or narrowly to read the Non-Detention Act, the tone of which is severe: "No citizen shall be imprisoned or otherwise detained by the United States except pursuant to an Act of Congress." Should the severity of the Act be relieved when the Government's stated factual justification for incommunicado detention is a war on terrorism, so that the Government may be said to act "pursuant" to congressional terms that fall short of explicit authority to imprison individuals? With one possible though important qualification, the answer has to be no. For a number of reasons, the prohibition within § 4001(a) has to be read broadly to accord the statute a long reach and to impose a burden of justification on the Government.

[E]ven if history had spared us the cautionary example of the internments in World War II, even if there had been no *Korematsu*, and *Endo* had set no principle of statutory interpretation, there would be a compelling reason to read § 4001(a) to demand manifest authority to detain before detention is authorized. The defining character of American constitutional government is its constant tension between security and liberty, serving both by partial helpings of each. In a government of separated powers, deciding finally on what is a reasonable degree of guaranteed liberty whether in peace or war (or some condition in between) is not well entrusted to the Executive Branch of Government, whose particular responsibility is to maintain security. For reasons of inescapable human nature, the branch of the Government asked to counter a serious threat is not the branch on which to rest the Nation's entire reliance in striking the balance between the will to win and the cost in liberty on the way to victory; the responsibility for security will naturally amplify the claim that security legitimately raises. A reasonable balance is more likely to be reached on the judgment of a different branch, just as Madison said in remarking that "the constant aim is to divide and arrange the several offices in such a manner as that each may be a check on the other – that the private interest of every individual may be a sentinel over the public rights." THE FEDERALIST No. 51. Hence the need for an assessment by Congress before citizens are subject to lockup, and likewise the need for a clearly expressed congressional resolution of the competing claims.

Next, there is the Government's claim, accepted by the Court, that the terms of the Force Resolution are adequate to authorize detention of an enemy combatant under the circumstances described, a claim the Government fails to support sufficiently to satisfy § 4001(a) as read to require a clear statement of authority to detain. Since the Force Resolution was adopted one week after the attacks of September 11, 2001, it naturally speaks with some generality, but its focus is clear, and that is on the use of military power. It is fairly read to authorize the use of armies and weapons, whether against other armies or individual terrorists. But, like the statute discussed in *Endo*, it never so much as uses the word detention, and there is no reason to think Congress might have perceived any need to augment Executive power to deal with dangerous citizens within the United States, given the well-stocked statutory arsenal of defined criminal offenses covering the gamut of actions that a citizen sympathetic to terrorists might commit.

Even so, there is one argument for treating the Force Resolution as sufficiently clear to authorize detention of a citizen consistently with § 4001(a). Assuming the argument to be sound, however, the Government is in no position to claim its advantage.

Because the Force Resolution authorizes the use of military force in acts of war by the United States, the argument goes, it is reasonably clear that the military and its Commander in Chief are authorized to deal with enemy belligerents according to the treaties and customs known collectively as the laws of war. Accordingly, the United States may detain captured enemies, and *Ex parte Quirin* may perhaps be claimed for the proposition that the American citizenship of such a captive does not as such limit the Government's power to deal with him under the usages of war. Thus, the Government here repeatedly argues that Hamdi's detention amounts to nothing more than customary detention of a captive taken on the field of battle: if the usages of war are fairly authorized by the Force Resolution, Hamdi's detention is authorized for purposes of § 4001(a).

There is no need, however, to address the merits of such an argument in all possible circumstances. For now it is enough to recognize that the Government's stated legal position in its campaign against the Taliban (among whom Hamdi was allegedly captured) is apparently at odds with its claim here to be acting in accordance with customary law of war and hence to be within the terms of the Force Resolution in its detention of Hamdi. In a statement of its legal position cited in its brief, the Government says that "the Geneva Convention applies to the Taliban detainees." Hamdi presumably is such a detainee, since according to the Government's own account, he was taken bearing arms on the Taliban side of a field of battle in Afghanistan. He would therefore seem to qualify for treatment as a prisoner of war under the Third Geneva Convention, to which the United States is a party.

By holding him incommunicado, however, the Government obviously has not been treating him as a prisoner of war, and in fact the Government claims that no Taliban detainee is entitled to prisoner of war status. This treatment appears to be a violation of the Geneva Convention provision that even in cases of doubt, captives are entitled to be treated as prisoners of war "until such time as their status has been determined by a competent tribunal." The Government answers that the President's determination that Taliban detainees do not qualify as prisoners of war is conclusive as to Hamdi's status and removes any doubt that would trigger application of the Convention's tribunal requirement. But reliance on this categorical pronouncement to settle doubt is apparently at odds with the military regulation, adopted to implement the Geneva Convention, and setting out a detailed procedure for a military tribunal to determine an individual's status. One of the types of doubt these tribunals are meant to settle is whether a given individual may be, as Hamdi says he is, an "innocent civilian who should be immediately returned to his home or released." The regulation, jointly promulgated by the Headquarters of the Departments of the Army, Navy, Air Force, and Marine Corps, provides that "persons who have been determined by a competent tribunal not to be entitled to prisoner of war status may not be executed, imprisoned, or otherwise penalized without further proceedings to determine what acts they have committed and what penalty should be imposed." The regulation also incorporates the Geneva Convention's presumption that in cases of doubt, "persons shall enjoy the protection of the . . . Convention until such time as their status has been determined by a competent tribunal." Thus, there is reason to question whether the United States is acting in accordance with the laws of war it claims as authority.

Whether, or to what degree, the Government is in fact violating the Geneva Convention and is thus acting outside the customary usages of war are not matters I can resolve at this point. What I can say, though, is that the Government has not made out its claim that in detaining Hamdi in the manner described, it is acting in accord with the laws of war authorized to be applied against citizens by the Force Resolution. I conclude accordingly that the Government has failed to support the position that the Force Resolution authorizes the described detention of Hamdi for purposes of § 4001(a).

It is worth adding a further reason for requiring the Government to bear the burden of clearly justifying its claim to be exercising recognized war powers before declaring § 4001(a) satisfied. Thirty-eight days after adopting the Force Resolution, Congress passed the statute entitled Uniting and Strengthening America by Providing Appropriate Tools Required to Intercept and Obstruct Terrorism Act of 2001 (USA PATRIOT Act); that Act authorized the detention of alien terrorists for no more than seven days in the absence of criminal charges or deportation proceedings. It is very difficult to believe that the same Congress that carefully circumscribed Executive power over alien terrorists on home soil would not have meant to require the Government to justify clearly its detention of an American citizen held on home soil incommunicado.

Since the Government has given no reason either to deflect the application of § 4001(a) or to hold it to be satisfied, I need to go no further; the Government hints of a constitutional challenge to the statute, but it presents none here. I will, however, stray across the line between statutory and constitutional territory just far enough to note the weakness of the Government's mixed claim of inherent, extrastatutory authority under a combination of Article II of the Constitution and the usages of war. It is in fact in this connection that the Government developed its argument that the exercise of war powers justifies the detention, and what I have just said about its inadequacy applies here as well. Beyond that, it is instructive to recall Justice Jackson's observation that the President is not Commander in Chief of the country, only of the military.

There may be room for one qualification to Justice Jackson's statement, however: in a moment of genuine emergency, when the Government must act with no time for deliberation, the Executive may be able to detain a citizen if there is reason to fear he is an imminent threat to the safety of the Nation and its people (though I doubt there is any want of statutory authority). This case, however, does not present that question, because an emergency power of necessity must at least be limited by the emergency; Hamdi has been locked up for over two years.

Whether insisting on the careful scrutiny of emergency claims or on a vigorous reading of § 4001(a), we are heirs to a tradition given voice 800 years ago by Magna Carta, which, on the barons' insistence, confined executive power by "the law of the land."

Because I find Hamdi's detention forbidden by § 4001(a) and unauthorized by the Force Resolution, I would not reach any questions of what process he may be due in litigating disputed issues in a proceeding under the habeas statute or prior to the habeas enquiry itself. For me, it suffices that the Government has failed to justify holding him in the absence of a further Act of Congress, criminal charges, a showing that the detention conforms to the laws of war, or a demonstration that § 4001(a) is unconstitutional. I would therefore vacate the judgment of the Court of Appeals and remand for proceedings consistent with this view.

Since this disposition does not command a majority of the Court, however, the need to give practical effect to the conclusions of eight members of the Court rejecting the Government's position calls for me to join with the plurality in ordering remand on terms closest to those I would impose. Although I think litigation of Hamdi's status as an enemy combatant is unnecessary, the terms of the plurality's remand will allow Hamdi to offer evidence that he is not an enemy combatant, and he should at the least have the benefit of that opportunity.

It should go without saying that in joining with the plurality to produce a judgment, I do not adopt the plurality's resolution of constitutional issues that I would not reach. It is not that I could disagree with the plurality's determinations (given the plurality's view of the Force Resolution) that someone in Hamdi's position is entitled at a minimum to notice of the Government's claimed factual basis for holding him, and to a fair chance to rebut it before a neutral decision maker; nor, of course, could I disagree with the plurality's affirmation of Hamdi's right to counsel. On the other hand, I do not mean to imply agreement that the Government could claim an evidentiary presumption casting the burden of rebuttal on Hamdi, or that an opportunity to litigate before a military tribunal might obviate or truncate enquiry by a court on habeas.

Subject to these qualifications, I join with the plurality in a judgment of the Court vacating the Fourth Circuit's judgment and remanding the case.

JUSTICE SCALIA, with whom JUSTICE STEVENS joins, dissenting.

Petitioner, a presumed American citizen, has been imprisoned without charge or hearing in the Norfolk and Charleston Naval Brigs for more than two years, on the allegation that he is an enemy combatant who bore arms against his country for the Taliban. His father claims to the contrary, that he is an inexperienced aid worker caught in the wrong place at the wrong time. This case brings into conflict the competing demands of national security and our citizens' constitutional right to personal liberty. Although I share the Court's evident unease as it seeks to reconcile the two, I do not agree with its resolution.

Where the Government accuses a citizen of waging war against it, our constitutional tradition has been to prosecute him in federal court for treason or some other crime. Where the exigencies of war prevent that, the Constitution's Suspension Clause, allows Congress to relax the usual protections temporarily. Absent suspension, however, the Executive's assertion of military exigency has not been thought sufficient to permit detention without charge. No one contends that the congressional Authorization for Use of Military Force, on which the Government relies to justify its actions here, is an implementation of the Suspension Clause. Accordingly, I would reverse the decision below.

I

The very core of liberty secured by our Anglo-Saxon system of separated powers has been freedom from indefinite imprisonment at the will of the Executive. Blackstone stated this principle clearly:

> "Of great importance to the public is the preservation of this personal liberty: for if once it were left in the power of any, the highest, magistrate to imprison arbitrarily whomever he or his officers thought proper . . . there would soon be an end of all other rights and immunities. . . . To bereave a man of life, or by violence to confiscate his estate, without accusation or trial, would be so gross and notorious an act of despotism, as must at once convey the alarm of tyranny throughout the whole kingdom. But confinement of the person, by secretly hurrying him to gaol, where his sufferings are unknown or forgotten; is a less public, a less striking, and therefore a more dangerous engine of arbitrary government. . . .

> "To make imprisonment lawful, it must either be, by process from the courts of judicature, or by warrant from some legal officer, having authority to commit to prison; which warrant must be in writing, under the hand and

seal of the magistrate, and express the causes of the commitment, in order to be examined into (if necessary) upon a *habeas corpus*. If there be no cause expressed, the gaoler is not bound to detain the prisoner. For the law judges in this respect, . . . that it is unreasonable to send a prisoner, and not to signify withal the crimes alleged against him."

1 W. BLACKSTONE, COMMENTARIES ON THE LAWS OF ENGLAND 132-133 (1765) (hereinafter Blackstone).

These words were well known to the Founders. Hamilton quoted from this very passage in THE FEDERALIST No. 84. The two ideas central to Blackstone's understanding – due process as the right secured, and habeas corpus as the instrument by which due process could be insisted upon by a citizen illegally imprisoned – found expression in the Constitution's Due Process and Suspension Clauses.

The gist of the Due Process Clause, as understood at the founding and since, was to force the Government to follow those common-law procedures traditionally deemed necessary before depriving a person of life, liberty, or property.

To be sure, certain types of permissible *non*criminal detention – that is, those not dependent upon the contention that the citizen had committed a criminal act – did not require the protections of criminal procedure. However, these fell into a limited number of well-recognized exceptions – civil commitment of the mentally ill, for example, and temporary detention in quarantine of the infectious. It is unthinkable that the Executive could render otherwise criminal grounds for detention noncriminal merely by disclaiming an intent to prosecute, or by asserting that it was incapacitating dangerous offenders rather than punishing wrongdoing.

These due process rights have historically been vindicated by the writ of habeas corpus. In England before the founding, the writ developed into a tool for challenging executive confinement. It was not always effective. [As a result, the Habeas Corpus Act of 1679 added additional protections.]

The writ of habeas corpus was preserved in the Constitution – the only common-law writ to be explicitly mentioned. Hamilton lauded "the establishment of the writ of *habeas corpus*" in his FEDERALIST defense as a means to protect against "the practice of arbitrary imprisonments . . . in all ages, [one of] the favourite and most formidable instruments of tyranny." THE FEDERALIST No. 84. Indeed, availability of the writ under the new Constitution (along with the requirement of trial by jury in criminal cases) was his basis for arguing that additional, explicit procedural protections were unnecessary.

II

The allegations here, of course, are no ordinary accusations of criminal activity. Yaser Esam Hamdi has been imprisoned because the Government believes he participated in the waging of war against the United States. The relevant question, then, is whether there is a different, special procedure for imprisonment of a citizen accused of wrongdoing *by aiding the enemy in wartime*.

A

Justice O'Connor, writing for a plurality of this Court, asserts that captured enemy combatants (other than those suspected of war crimes) have traditionally been detained until the cessation of hostilities and then released. That is probably an accurate description of wartime practice with respect to enemy *aliens*. The tradition with respect to American citizens, however, has been quite different. Citizens aiding the enemy have been treated as traitors subject to the criminal process.

The modern treason statute is 18 U.S.C. § 2381; it basically tracks the language of the constitutional provision. Other provisions of Title 18 criminalize various acts of warmaking and adherence to the enemy. The only citizen other than Hamdi known to be imprisoned in connection with military hostilities in Afghanistan against the United States *was* subjected to criminal process and convicted upon a guilty plea. *See United States v. Lindh,* 212 F. Supp. 2d 541 (E.D. Va. 2002).

B

There are times when military exigency renders resort to the traditional criminal process impracticable. English law accommodated such exigencies by allowing legislative suspension of the writ of habeas corpus for brief periods.

Our Federal Constitution contains a provision explicitly permitting suspension, but limiting the situations in which it may be invoked: "The privilege of the Writ of Habeas Corpus shall not be suspended, unless when in Cases of Rebellion or Invasion the public Safety may require it." Although this provision does not state that suspension must be effected by, or authorized by, a legislative act, it has been so understood, consistent with English practice and the Clause's placement in Article I.

The Suspension Clause was by design a safety valve, the Constitution's only "express provision for exercise of extraordinary authority because of a crisis," *Youngstown Sheet & Tube Co. v. Sawyer* (Jackson, J., concurring). Very early in the Nation's history, President Jefferson unsuccessfully sought a suspension of habeas corpus to deal with Aaron Burr's conspiracy to overthrow the Government. During the Civil War, Congress passed its first Act authorizing Executive suspension of the writ of habeas corpus, to the relief of those many who thought President Lincoln's unauthorized proclamations of suspension unconstitutional. Later Presidential proclamations of suspension relied upon the congressional authorization. During Reconstruction, Congress passed the Ku Klux Klan Act, which included a provision authorizing suspension of the writ, invoked by President Grant in quelling a rebellion in nine South Carolina counties.

III

Of course the extensive historical evidence of criminal convictions and habeas suspensions does not *necessarily* refute the Government's position in this case. When the writ is suspended, the Government is entirely free from judicial oversight. It does not claim such total liberation here, but argues that it need only produce what it calls "some evidence" to satisfy a habeas court that a detained individual is an enemy combatant. Even if suspension of the writ on the one hand, and committal for criminal charges on the other hand, have been the only *traditional* means of dealing with citizens who levied war against their own country, it is theoretically possible that the Constitution does not *require* a choice between these alternatives.

I believe, however, that substantial evidence does refute that possibility. First, the text of the 1679 Habeas Corpus Act makes clear that indefinite imprisonment on reasonable suspicion is not an available option of treatment for those accused of aiding the enemy, absent a suspension of the writ. In the United States, this Act was read as "enforcing the common law," and shaped the early understanding of the scope of the writ.

Writings from the founding generation also suggest that, without exception, the only constitutional alternatives are to charge the crime or suspend the writ. President Lincoln, when he purported to suspend habeas corpus without congressional authorization during the Civil War, apparently did not doubt that suspension was required if the prisoner was to be held without criminal trial. In his famous message to Congress on July 4, 1861, he argued only that he could suspend the writ, not that even without suspension, his imprisonment of citizens without criminal trial was permitted.

Further evidence comes from this Court's decision in *Ex parte Milligan*. There, the Court issued the writ to an American citizen who had been tried by military commission for offenses that included conspiring to overthrow the Government, seize munitions, and liberate prisoners of war. The Court rejected in no uncertain terms the Government's assertion that military jurisdiction was proper "under the laws and usages of war:"

> It can serve no useful purpose to inquire what those laws and usages are, whence they originated, where found, and on whom they operate; they can never be applied to citizens in states which have upheld the authority of the government, and where the courts are open and their process unobstructed.

Milligan is not exactly this case, of course, since the petitioner was threatened with death, not merely imprisonment. But the reasoning and conclusion of *Milligan* logically cover the present case. The Government justifies imprisonment of Hamdi on principles of the law of war and admits that, absent the war, it would have no such authority. But if the law of war cannot be applied to citizens where courts are open, then Hamdi's imprisonment without criminal trial is no less unlawful than Milligan's trial by military tribunal.

IV

The Government argues that our more recent jurisprudence ratifies its indefinite imprisonment of a citizen within the territorial jurisdiction of federal courts. It places primary reliance upon *Ex parte Quirin,* a World War II case upholding the trial by military commission of eight German saboteurs, one of whom, Hans Haupt, was a U.S. citizen. The case was not this Court's finest hour. The Court upheld the commission and denied relief in a brief *per curiam* issued the day after oral argument concluded; a week later the Government carried out the commission's death sentence upon six saboteurs, including

Haupt. The Court eventually explained its reasoning in a written opinion issued several months later.

Only three paragraphs of the Court's lengthy opinion dealt with the particular circumstances of Haupt's case. The Government argued that Haupt, like the other petitioners, could be tried by military commission under the laws of war. In agreeing with that contention, *Quirin* purported to interpret the language of *Milligan* quoted above (the law of war "can never be applied to citizens in states which have upheld the authority of the government, and where the courts are open and their process unobstructed") in the following manner:

> Elsewhere in its opinion . . . the Court was at pains to point out that Milligan, a citizen twenty years resident in Indiana, who had never been a resident of any of the states in rebellion, was not an enemy belligerent either entitled to the status of a prisoner of war or subject to the penalties imposed upon unlawful belligerents. We construe the Court's statement as to the inapplicability of the law of war to Milligan's case as having particular reference to the facts before it. From them the Court concluded that Milligan, not being a part of or associated with the armed forces of the enemy, was a non-belligerent, not subject to the law of war.

[E]ven if *Quirin* gave a correct description of *Milligan*, or made an irrevocable revision of it, *Quirin* would still not justify denial of the writ here. In *Quirin* it was uncontested that the petitioners were members of enemy forces. They were "*admitted* enemy invaders," and it was "undisputed" that they had landed in the United States in service of German forces. The specific holding of the Court was only that, "upon the *conceded* facts," the petitioners were "plainly within [the] boundaries" of military jurisdiction. But where those jurisdictional facts are *not* conceded – where the petitioner insists that he is *not* a belligerent – *Quirin* left the pre-existing law in place: Absent suspension of the writ, a citizen held where the courts are open is entitled either to criminal trial or to a judicial decree requiring his release

V

It follows from what I have said that Hamdi is entitled to a habeas decree requiring his release unless (1) criminal proceedings are promptly brought, or (2) Congress has suspended the writ of habeas corpus. A suspension of the writ could, of course, lay down conditions for continued detention, similar to those that today's opinion prescribes under the Due Process Clause. But there is a world of difference between the people's representatives' determining the need for that suspension (and prescribing the conditions for it), and this Court's doing so.

The plurality finds justification for Hamdi's imprisonment in the Authorization for Use of Military Force. [The AUMF] is not remotely a congressional suspension of the writ, and no one claims that it is. Contrary to the plurality's view, I do not think this statute even authorizes detention of a citizen with the clarity necessary to satisfy the interpretive canon that statutes should be construed so as to avoid grave constitutional concerns; with the clarity necessary to comport with cases such as *Ex parte Endo* and *Duncan v. Kahanamoku* or with the clarity necessary to overcome the statutory prescription [of] § 4001(a). But even if it did, I would not permit it to overcome Hamdi's entitlement to habeas corpus relief. The Suspension Clause of the Constitution, which carefully circumscribes the conditions under which the writ can be withheld, would be a sham if it could be evaded by congressional prescription of requirements *other than the common-law requirement of committal for criminal prosecution* that render the writ, though available, unavailing.

Having found a congressional authorization for detention of citizens where none clearly exists; and having discarded the categorical procedural protection of the Suspension Clause; the plurality then proceeds, under the guise of the Due Process Clause, to prescribe what procedural protections *it* thinks appropriate.

Having distorted the Suspension Clause, the plurality finishes up by transmogrifying the Great Writ – disposing of the present habeas petition by remanding for the District Court to "engage in a factfinding process that is both prudent and incremental." This judicial remediation of executive default is unheard of. The role of habeas corpus is to determine the legality of executive detention, not to supply the omitted process necessary to make it legal. It is not the habeas court's function to make illegal detention legal by supplying a process that the Government could have provided, but chose not to. If Hamdi is being imprisoned in violation of the Constitution (because without due process of law), then his habeas petition should be granted; the Executive may then hand him over to the criminal authorities, whose detention for the purpose of prosecution will be lawful, or else must release him.

There is a certain harmony of approach in the plurality's making up for Congress's failure to invoke the Suspension Clause and its making up for the Executive's failure to apply what it says are needed procedures – an approach that reflects what might be called a Mr. Fix-it Mentality. The plurality seems to view it as its mission to Make Everything Come Out Right, rather than merely to decree the consequences, as far as individual rights are concerned, of the other two branches' actions and omissions. Has the Legislature failed to suspend the writ in the current dire emergency? Well, we will remedy that failure by prescribing the reasonable conditions that a suspension should have included. And has the Executive failed to live up to those reasonable conditions? Well, we will ourselves make that failure good, so that this dangerous fellow (if he is dangerous) need not be set free. The problem with this approach is not only that it steps out of the courts' modest and limited role in a democratic society; but that by repeatedly doing what it thinks the political branches ought to do it encourages their lassitude and saps the vitality of government by the people.

VI

Several limitations give my views in this matter a relatively narrow compass. They apply only to citizens, accused of being enemy combatants, who are detained within the territorial jurisdiction of a federal court. This is not likely to be a numerous group; currently we know of only two, Hamdi and Jose Padilla. Where the citizen is captured outside and held outside the United States, the constitutional requirements may be different. Moreover, even within the United States, the accused citizen-enemy combatant may lawfully be detained once prosecution is in progress or in contemplation. The Government has been notably successful in securing conviction, and hence long-term custody or execution, of those who have waged war against the state.

I frankly do not know whether these tools are sufficient to meet the Government's security needs, including the need to obtain intelligence through interrogation. It is far beyond my competence, or the Court's competence, to determine that. But it is not beyond Congress's. If the situation demands it, the Executive can ask Congress to authorize suspension of the writ – which can be made subject to whatever conditions Congress deems appropriate, including even the procedural novelties invented by the plurality today. To be sure, suspension is limited by the Constitution to cases of rebellion or invasion. But whether the attacks of September 11, 2001, constitute an "invasion," and whether those attacks still justify suspension several years later, are questions for Congress rather than this Court. If civil rights are to be curtailed during wartime, it must be done openly and democratically, as the Constitution requires, rather than by silent erosion through an opinion of this Court

Many think it not only inevitable but entirely proper that liberty give way to security in times of national crisis – that, at the extremes of military exigency, *inter arma silent leges*. Whatever the general merits of the view that war silences law or modulates its voice, that view has no place in the interpretation and application of a Constitution designed precisely to confront war and, in a manner that accords with democratic principles, to accommodate it. Because the Court has proceeded to meet the current emergency in a manner the Constitution does not envision. I respectfully dissent.

JUSTICE THOMAS, dissenting.

The Executive Branch, acting pursuant to the powers vested in the President by the Constitution and with explicit congressional approval, has determined that Yaser Hamdi is an enemy combatant and should be detained. This detention falls squarely within the Federal Government's war powers, and we lack the expertise and capacity to second-guess that decision. As such, petitioners' habeas challenge should fail, and there is no reason to remand the case. The plurality reaches a contrary conclusion by failing adequately to consider basic principles of the constitutional structure as it relates to national security and foreign affairs and by using the balancing scheme of *Mathews v. Eldridge*. I do not think that the Federal Government's war powers can be balanced away by this Court. Arguably, Congress could provide for additional procedural protections, but until it does, we have no right to insist upon them. But even if I were to agree with the general approach the plurality takes, I could not accept the particulars. The plurality utterly fails to account for the Government's compelling interests and for our own institutional inability to weigh competing concerns correctly. I respectfully dissent.

I

"It is 'obvious and unarguable' that no governmental interest is more compelling than the security of the Nation." The national security, after all, is the primary responsibility and purpose of the Federal Government. But because the Founders understood that they could not foresee the myriad potential threats to national security that might later arise, they chose to create a Federal Government that necessarily possesses sufficient power to handle any threat to the security of the Nation.

The Founders intended that the President have primary responsibility – along with the necessary power – to protect the national security and to conduct the Nation's foreign relations. They did so principally because the structural advantages of a unitary Executive are essential in these domains. This is because "decision, activity, secrecy, and dispatch will generally characterise the proceedings of one man, in a much more eminent degree, than the proceedings of any greater number."

These structural advantages are most important in the national-security and foreign-affairs contexts. "Of all the cares or concerns of government, the direction of war most peculiarly demands those qualities which distinguish the exercise of power by a single hand." THE FEDERALIST No. 74 (A. Hamilton). Also for these reasons, John Marshall explained that "the President is the sole organ of the nation in its external relations, and its sole representative with foreign nations." To this end, the Constitution vests in the President "the executive Power," provides that he "shall be Commander in Chief of the" armed forces, and places in him the power to recognize foreign governments.

This Court has long recognized these features and has accordingly held that the President has *constitutional* authority to protect the national security and that this authority carries with it broad discretion.

Congress, to be sure, has a substantial and essential role in both foreign affairs and national security. But it is crucial to recognize that *judicial* interference in these domains destroys the purpose of vesting primary responsibility in a unitary Executive. Several points, made forcefully by Justice Jackson, are worth emphasizing. First, with respect to certain decisions relating to national security and foreign affairs, the courts simply lack the relevant information and expertise to second-guess determinations made by the President based on information properly withheld. Second, even if the courts could compel the Executive to produce the necessary information, such decisions are simply not amenable to judicial determination because "they are delicate, complex, and involve large elements of prophecy." Third, the Court has correctly recognized the primacy of the political branches in the foreign-affairs and national-security contexts.

To be sure, the Court has at times held, in specific circumstances, that the military acted beyond its warmaking authority. But these cases are distinguishable in important ways. In *Ex parte Endo,* the Court held unlawful the detention of an admittedly law-abiding and loyal American of Japanese ancestry. It did so because the Government's asserted reason for the detention had nothing to do with the congressional and executive authorities upon which the Government relied. Those authorities permitted detention for the purpose of preventing espionage and sabotage and thus could not be pressed into service for detaining a loyal citizen. And in *Youngstown,* Justice Jackson emphasized that "Congress had not left seizure of private property an open field but had covered it by three statutory policies inconsistent with the seizure."

I acknowledge that the question whether Hamdi's executive detention is lawful is a question properly resolved by the Judicial Branch, though the question comes to the Court with the strongest presumptions in favor of the Government. The plurality agrees that Hamdi's detention is lawful if he is an enemy combatant. But the question whether Hamdi is actually an enemy combatant is "of a kind for which the Judiciary has neither aptitude, facilities nor responsibility and which has long been held to belong in the domain of political power not subject to judicial intrusion or inquiry." That is, although it is appropriate for the Court to determine the judicial question whether the President has the asserted authority, we lack the information and expertise to question whether Hamdi is actually an enemy combatant, a question the resolution of which is committed to other branches.

II

Although the President very well may have inherent authority to detain those arrayed against our troops, I agree with the plurality that we need not decide that question because Congress has authorized the President to do so. The Authorization for Use of Military Force (AUMF), authorizes the President to "use all necessary and appropriate force against those nations, organizations, or persons he determines planned, authorized, committed, or aided the terrorist attacks" of September 11, 2001.

The plurality, however, qualifies its recognition of the President's authority to detain enemy combatants in the war on terrorism in ways that are at odds with our precedent. Thus, the plurality relies primarily on Article 118 of the Geneva Convention (III) Relative to the Treatment of Prisoners of War, for the proposition that "it is a clearly established principle of the law of war that detention may last no longer than active hostilities." It then appears to limit the President's authority to detain by requiring that the record establish that United States troops are still involved in active combat in Afghanistan because, in that case, detention would be "part of the exercise of 'necessary and appropriate force.'" But I do not believe that we may diminish the Federal Government's war powers by reference to a treaty and certainly not to a treaty that does not apply. Further, we are bound by the political branches' determination that the United States is at war. And, in any case, the power to detain does not end with the cessation of formal hostilities.

Accordingly, the President's action here is "supported by the strongest of presumptions and the widest latitude of judicial interpretation." The question becomes whether the Federal Government (rather than the President acting alone) has power to detain Hamdi as an enemy combatant. More precisely, we must determine whether the Government may detain Hamdi given the procedures that were used.

III

I agree with the plurality that the Federal Government has power to detain those that the Executive Branch determines to be enemy combatants. But I do not think that the plurality has adequately explained the breadth of the

President's authority to detain enemy combatants, an authority that includes making virtually conclusive factual findings. In my view, the structural considerations discussed above, as recognized in our precedent, demonstrate that we lack the capacity and responsibility to second-guess this determination.

In a case strikingly similar to this one, the Court addressed a Governor's authority to detain for an extended period a person the executive believed to be responsible, in part, for a local insurrection. [*Moyer v. Peabody*, 212 U.S. 78 (1909).] In *Luther v. Borden*, 48 U.S. 1, 7 How. 1, 12 L. Ed. 581 (1849), the Court discussed the President's constitutional and statutory authority, in response to a request from a state legislature or executive, "'to call forth such number of the militia of any other State or States, as may be applied for, as he may judge sufficient to suppress [an] insurrection.'"

In this context, due process requires nothing more than a good-faith executive determination. To be clear: The Court has held that an executive, acting pursuant to statutory and constitutional authority may, consistent with the Due Process Clause, unilaterally decide to detain an individual if the executive deems this necessary for the public safety *even if he is mistaken*.

The Government's asserted authority to detain an individual that the President has determined to be an enemy combatant, at least while hostilities continue, comports with the Due Process Clause. As these cases also show, the Executive's decision that a detention is necessary to protect the public need not and should not be subjected to judicial second-guessing. Indeed, at least in the context of enemy-combatant determinations, this would defeat the unity, secrecy, and dispatch that the Founders believed to be so important to the warmaking function.

Justice Scalia relies heavily upon *Ex parte Milligan*. I admit that *Milligan* supports his position. But because the Executive Branch there, unlike here, did not follow a specific statutory mechanism provided by Congress, the Court did not need to reach the broader question of Congress' power, and its discussion on this point was arguably dicta. More importantly, the Court referred frequently and pervasively to the criminal nature of the proceedings instituted against Milligan. In fact, this feature serves to distinguish the state cases as well.

Although I do acknowledge that the reasoning of these cases might apply beyond criminal punishment, the punishment-nonpunishment distinction harmonizes all of the precedent. And, subsequent cases have at least implicitly distinguished *Milligan* in just this way. Because the Government does not detain Hamdi in order to punish him, as the plurality acknowledges, *Milligan* and the New York cases do not control.

Accordingly, I conclude that the Government's detention of Hamdi as an enemy combatant does not violate the Constitution. By detaining Hamdi, the President, in the prosecution of a war and authorized by Congress, has acted well within his authority. Hamdi thereby received all the process to which he was due under the circumstances. I therefore believe that this is no occasion to balance the competing interests, as the plurality unconvincingly attempts to do.

NOTES AND QUESTIONS

1. Hamdi was released from U.S. custody pursuant to an agreement with Saudi Arabian authorities to accept him into that country. Hamdi agreed to renounce U.S. citizenship, to reside in Saudi Arabia for at least 5 years, and to report any contacts from persons who he has reason to believe could be involved in hostile or terrorist actions. The agreement can be found at *http://news.findlaw.com/hdocs/docs/hamdi/91704stlagrmnt.html.*

2. The O'Connor plurality opinion is quite explicit that "individuals legitimately determined to be Taliban combatants" could be held without trial for the remainder of their lives if "active hostilities" continue so long. With four votes for that position coupled with Justice Thomas' position, there seems to be a majority of the Court willing to countenance indefinite detention without trial under some circumstances. The plurality just requires a determination by a competent tribunal of – what? combatant status? by what level of evidence? by what procedures? All of these questions are raised in the *Hamdan* case below with regard to noncitizens.

3. Perhaps some slightly tongue-in-cheek examples would clarify the problem of judicial review over executive findings related to national security. If the government's arguments for deference to the President were accepted, would there be anything to prevent the President from classifying a skinhead militant as an enemy combatant? If that worked, how about classifying a politically volatile dissident as an EC? If that worked, how about the President's next election campaign opponent? Obviously, there must be a stopping point but it could be argued that the stopping point should be a matter for citizen or political action rather than judicial action. Which position carries the best message for the democratic process?

4. The central point of disagreement between Justices O'Connor and Scalia concerns the interplay between Due Process and the Suspension Clause.

    a. Justice Scalia asserts that, although there may be more latitude for executive detention of aliens, with regard to citizens the government's choice is criminal trial or suspension of habeas corpus. How does he read the Court's treatment of Haupt in the *Quirin* case? How would it be that Due Process means something different for citizens than for aliens? Although aliens may be treated differently for a number of government entitlements, doesn't the concept of fair procedures apply to both equally?

    b. Justice O'Connor argues that the Suspension Clause is satisfied by the AUMF because the AUMF is a congressional determination triggering the traditional power of military detention of combatants, but that Due Process then requires that the detainee be found by some appropriate process to fit within the category of "enemy combatant."

    c. Justice O'Connor argues that Justice Scalia is making up a third option (other than trial or suspension) in which "concession of enemy combatant status" satisfies the habeas corpus requirement. Justice Scalia in return argues that Justice O'Connor is aggrandizing the role of the courts to make a determination of status that should be made by someone else. Justice O'Connor is willing to allow the determination to be made by any "neutral decisionmaker" whether court or other. Who has the better of this argument?

5. What is the definition of "enemy combatant" in the O'Connor scheme? If the Haupt example means that a U.S. citizen arrested in the U.S. can be an enemy combatant, then can the executive declare any alleged terrorist to be an enemy combatant? What would be the standards for reviewing that determination? Justice O'Connor's explanation of battlefield conditions says that the question is "the appropriateness of continuing to detain an individual claimed to have taken up arms against the United States." In what sense had Haupt "taken up arms" against the U.S.? Has any member of a terrorist organization "taken up arms" by engaging in a conspiracy to bomb either a military installation or a civilian target?

6. Perhaps the enemy combatant posture can be clarified by thinking of a range of persons and actions. At one extreme would be an Iraqi soldier in uniform wounded while firing a weapon at U.S. forces and then taken into custody. At the other extreme would be Jose Padilla, who was arrested by civilian authorities on U.S. soil while unarmed and having no more access to weapons than any other resident of the U.S. Where in this range of actions does a person become an enemy combatant?

a. uniformed soldier on field of battle

b. insurgent in civilian clothing firing weapon against uniformed invading force

c. insurgent attacking either military or civilian units allied with invading force

d. civilian attacking military installation on domestic soil of another country (the 9/11 plane flown into the Pentagon? does the target matter in this instance?)

e. civilian attacking civilian targets on soil of another country (the 9/11 planes flown into the WTC or almost any act of international terrorism)

f. civilian arrested on home soil allegedly intending to attack civilian targets (how distinguish Padilla from McVeigh?)

7. For an interesting and unfamiliar historical perspective, see Ingrid Brunk Wuerth, *The President's Power To Detain "Enemy Combatants:" Modern Lessons from Mr. Madison's Forgotten War*, 98 Nw. U.L. Rev. 1567 (2004).

RASUL v. BUSH
124 S. Ct. 2686 (2004)

JUSTICE STEVENS delivered the opinion of the Court.

These two cases present the narrow but important question whether United States courts lack jurisdiction to consider challenges to the legality of the detention of foreign nationals captured abroad in connection with hostilities and incarcerated at the Guantanamo Bay Naval Base, Cuba.

Since early 2002, the U.S. military has held [petitioners' relatives, Kuwaitis and Australians] – along with, according to the Government's estimate, approximately 640 other non-Americans captured abroad – at the Naval Base at Guantanamo Bay. The United States occupies the Base, which comprises 45 square miles of land and water along the southeast coast of Cuba, pursuant to a 1903 Lease Agreement executed with the newly independent Republic of Cuba in the aftermath of the Spanish-American War. Under the Agreement, "the United States recognizes the continuance of the ultimate sovereignty of the Republic of Cuba over the [leased areas]," while "the Republic of Cuba consents that during the period of the occupation by the United States . . . the United States shall exercise complete jurisdiction and control over and within said areas." In 1934, the parties entered into a treaty providing that, absent an agreement to modify or abrogate the lease, the lease would remain in effect "so long as the United States of America shall not abandon the . . . naval station of Guantanamo."

In 2002, petitioners, through relatives acting as their next friends, filed various actions in the U.S. District Court for the District of Columbia challenging the legality of their detention at the Base. All alleged that none of the petitioners has ever been a combatant against the United States or has ever engaged in any terrorist acts. They also alleged that none has been charged with any wrongdoing, permitted to consult with counsel, or provided access to the courts or any other tribunal.

[T]he District Court dismissed for want of jurisdiction. The court held, in reliance on our opinion in *Johnson v. Eisentrager,* 339 U.S. 763 (1950), that "aliens detained outside the sovereign territory of the United States [may not] invoke a petition for a writ of habeas corpus." The Court of Appeals affirmed. We granted certiorari and now reverse.

Congress has granted federal district courts, "within their respective jurisdictions," the authority to hear applications for habeas corpus by any person who claims to be held "in custody in violation of the Constitution or laws or treaties of the United States." 28 U.S.C. §§ 2241(a), (c)(3). Habeas corpus is, however, "a writ antecedent to statute, . . . throwing its root deep into the genius of our common law." The writ appeared in English law several centuries ago, became "an integral part of our common-law heritage" by the time the Colonies achieved independence, and received explicit recognition in the Constitution, which forbids suspension of "the Privilege of the Writ of Habeas Corpus . . . unless when in Cases of Rebellion or Invasion the public Safety may require it."

As it has evolved over the past two centuries, the habeas statute clearly has expanded habeas corpus "beyond the limits that obtained during the 17th and 18th centuries." But "at its historical core, the writ of habeas corpus has served as a means of reviewing the legality of Executive detention, and it is in that context that its protections have been strongest." As Justice Jackson wrote in an opinion respecting the availability of habeas corpus to aliens held in U.S. custody: "Executive imprisonment has been considered oppressive and lawless since John, at Runnymede, pledged that no free man should be imprisoned, dispossessed, outlawed, or exiled save by the judgment of his peers or by the law of the land. The judges of England developed the writ of habeas corpus largely to preserve these immunities from executive restraint."

Consistent with the historic purpose of the writ, this Court has recognized the federal courts' power to review applications for habeas relief in a wide variety of cases involving Executive detention, in wartime as well as in times of peace. The Court has, for example, entertained the habeas petitions of an American citizen who plotted an attack on military installations during the Civil War, *Ex parte Milligan,* and of admitted enemy aliens convicted of war crimes during a declared war and held in the United States, *Ex parte Quirin,* and its insular possessions, *In re Yamashita.*

The question now before us is whether the habeas statute confers a right to judicial review of the legality of Executive detention of aliens in a territory over which the United States exercises plenary and exclusive jurisdiction, but not "ultimate sovereignty."

Respondents' primary submission is that the answer to the jurisdictional question is controlled by our decision in *Eisentrager.* In that case, we held that a Federal District Court lacked authority to issue a writ of habeas corpus to 21 German citizens who had been captured by U.S. forces in China, tried and convicted of war crimes by an American military commission headquartered in Nanking, and incarcerated in the Landsberg Prison in occupied Germany. The Court of Appeals in *Eisentrager* had found jurisdiction, reasoning that "any person who is deprived of his liberty by officials of the United States, acting under purported authority of that Government, and who can show that his confinement is in violation of a prohibition of the Constitution, has a right to the writ." In reversing that determination, this Court summarized the six critical facts in the case:

> We are here confronted with a decision whose basic premise is that these prisoners are entitled, as a constitutional right, to sue in some court of the United States for a writ of *habeas corpus.* To support that assumption we must hold that a prisoner of our military authorities is constitutionally entitled to the writ, even though he (a) is an enemy alien; (b) has never been or resided in the United States; (c) was captured outside of our territory and there held in military custody as a prisoner of war; (d) was tried and convicted by a Military Commission sitting outside the United States; (e) for offenses against laws of war committed outside the United States; (f) and is at all times imprisoned outside the United States.

On this set of facts, the Court concluded, "no right to the writ of *habeas corpus* appears."

Petitioners in these cases differ from the *Eisentrager* detainees in important respects: They are not nationals of countries at war with the United States, and they deny that they have engaged in or plotted acts of aggression against the United States; they have never been afforded access to any tribunal, much less charged with and convicted of wrongdoing; and for more than two years they have been imprisoned in territory over which the United States exercises exclusive jurisdiction and control.

Because subsequent decisions of this Court have filled the statutory gap that had occasioned *Eisentrager*'s resort to "fundamentals," persons detained outside the territorial jurisdiction of any federal district court no longer need rely on the

Constitution as the source of their right to federal habeas review. In *Braden v. 30th Judicial Circuit Court of Ky.*, 410 U.S. 484, 495 (1973), this Court held that the prisoner's presence within the territorial jurisdiction of the district court is not "an invariable prerequisite" to the exercise of district court jurisdiction under the federal habeas statute. Rather, because "the writ of habeas corpus does not act upon the prisoner who seeks relief, but upon the person who holds him in what is alleged to be unlawful custody," a district court acts "within [its] respective jurisdiction" within the meaning of § 2241 as long as "the custodian can be reached by service of process."

[*Braden* was preceded by] decisions of this Court in cases involving habeas petitioners "confined overseas (and thus outside the territory of any district court)," in which the Court "held, if only implicitly, that the petitioners' absence from the district does not present a jurisdictional obstacle to the consideration of the claim." [citing cases involving U.S. servicemen and civilians tried by courts-martial in other countries] Because *Braden* overruled the statutory predicate to *Eisentrager*'s holding, *Eisentrager* plainly does not preclude the exercise of § 2241 jurisdiction over petitioners' claims.

Application of the habeas statute to persons detained at the base is consistent with the historical reach of the writ of habeas corpus. At common law, courts exercised habeas jurisdiction over the claims of aliens detained within sovereign territory of the realm, as well as the claims of persons detained in the so-called "exempt jurisdictions," where ordinary writs did not run, and all other dominions under the sovereign's control. As Lord Mansfield wrote in 1759, even if a territory was "no part of the realm," there was "no doubt" as to the court's power to issue writs of habeas corpus if the territory was "under the subjection of the Crown."

In the end, the answer to the question presented is clear. Petitioners contend that they are being held in federal custody in violation of the laws of the United States. No party questions the District Court's jurisdiction over petitioners' custodians. Section 2241, by its terms, requires nothing more. We therefore hold that § 2241 confers on the District Court jurisdiction to hear petitioners' habeas corpus challenges to the legality of their detention at the Guantanamo Bay Naval Base.

In addition to invoking the District Court's jurisdiction under § 2241, [some of the petitioners] invoked the court's jurisdiction under 28 U.S.C. § 1331, the federal question statute, as well as § 1350, the Alien Tort Statute. The Court of Appeals, again relying on *Eisentrager*, held that the District Court correctly dismissed the claims founded on § 1331 and § 1350 for lack of jurisdiction, even to the extent that these claims "deal only with conditions of confinement and do not sound in habeas," because petitioners lack the "privilege of litigation" in U.S. courts.

As explained above, *Eisentrager* itself erects no bar to the exercise of federal court jurisdiction over the petitioners' habeas corpus claims. The courts of the United States have traditionally been open to nonresident aliens. And indeed, 28 U.S.C. § 1350 explicitly confers the privilege of suing for an actionable "tort . . . committed in violation of the law of nations or a treaty of the United States" on aliens alone. The fact that petitioners in these cases are being held in military custody is immaterial to the question of the District Court's jurisdiction over their nonhabeas statutory claims.

In the end, the answer to the question presented is clear. Petitioners contend that they are being held in federal custody in violation of the laws of the United States.[15] No party questions the District Court's jurisdiction over petitioners' custodians. Section 2241, by its terms, requires nothing more. We therefore hold that § 2241 confers on the District Court jurisdiction to hear petitioners' habeas corpus challenges to the legality of their detention at the Guantanamo Bay Naval Base.

VI

Whether and what further proceedings may become necessary after respondents make their response to the merits of petitioners' claims are matters that we need not address now. What is presently at stake is only whether the federal courts have jurisdiction to determine the legality of the Executive's potentially indefinite detention of individuals who claim to be wholly innocent of wrongdoing. Answering that question in the affirmative, we reverse the judgment of the Court of Appeals and remand for the District Court to consider in the first instance the merits of petitioners' claims.

It is so ordered.

JUSTICE KENNEDY, concurring in the judgment.

The Court is correct, in my view, to conclude that federal courts have jurisdiction to consider challenges to the legality of the detention of foreign nationals held at the Guantanamo Bay Naval Base in Cuba. While I reach the same conclusion, my analysis follows a different course. In my view, the correct course is to follow the framework of *Eisentrager*.

The decision in *Eisentrager* indicates that there is a realm of political authority over military affairs where the judicial power may not enter. The existence of this realm acknowledges the power of the President as Commander in Chief, and the joint role of the President and the Congress, in the conduct of military affairs. A faithful application of *Eisentrager*, then, requires an initial inquiry into the general circumstances of the detention to determine whether the Court has the authority to entertain the petition and to grant relief after considering all of the facts presented. A necessary corollary of *Eisentrager* is that there are circumstances in which the courts maintain the power and the responsibility to protect persons from unlawful detention even where military affairs are implicated.

---

[15] Petitioners' allegations – that, although they have engaged neither in combat nor in acts of terrorism against the United States, they have been held in Executive detention for more than two years in territory subject to the long-term, exclusive jurisdiction and control of the United States, without access to counsel and without being charged with any wrongdoing – unquestionably describe "custody in violation of the Constitution or laws or treaties of the United States."

Dist[inguish]ly Facts in Eisentrager

① US cntrl over G.tmo

The facts here are distinguishable from those in *Eisentrager* in two critical ways, leading to the conclusion that a federal court may entertain the petitions. First, Guantanamo Bay is in every practical respect a United States territory, and it is one far removed from any hostilities. What matters is the unchallenged and indefinite control that the United States has long exercised over Guantanamo Bay. From a practical perspective, the indefinite lease of Guantanamo Bay has produced a place that belongs to the United States, extending the "implied protection" of the United States to it.

② Indef[inite] dete[ntion] w/o benef[it] of legal proceedings

The second critical set of facts is that the detainees at Guantanamo Bay are being held indefinitely, and without benefit of any legal proceeding to determine their status. In *Eisentrager*, the prisoners were tried and convicted by a military commission of violating the laws of war and were sentenced to prison terms. Having already been subject to procedures establishing their status, they could not justify "a limited opening of our courts" to show that they were "of friendly personal disposition" and not enemy aliens. Indefinite detention without trial or other proceeding presents altogether different considerations. It allows friends and foes alike to remain in detention. It suggests a weaker case of military necessity and much greater alignment with the traditional function of habeas corpus. Perhaps, where detainees are taken from a zone of hostilities, detention without proceedings or trial would be justified by military necessity for a matter of weeks; but as the period of detention stretches from months to years, the case for continued detention to meet military exigencies becomes weaker.

In light of the status of Guantanamo Bay and the indefinite pretrial detention of the detainees, I would hold that federal-court jurisdiction is permitted in these cases. This approach would avoid creating automatic statutory authority to adjudicate the claims of persons located outside the United States, and remains true to the reasoning of *Eisentrager*. For these reasons, I concur in the judgment of the Court.

JUSTICE SCALIA, with whom THE CHIEF JUSTICE and JUSTICE THOMAS join, dissenting.

The Court today holds that the habeas statute, 28 U.S.C. § 2241, extends to aliens detained by the United States military overseas, outside the sovereign borders of the United States and beyond the territorial jurisdictions of all its courts. This is not only a novel holding; it contradicts a half-century-old precedent on which the military undoubtedly relied, *Johnson v. Eisentrager*. This is an irresponsible overturning of settled law in a matter of extreme importance to our forces currently in the field. I would leave it to Congress to change § 2241, and dissent from the Court's unprecedented holding.

In abandoning the venerable statutory line drawn in *Eisentrager*, the Court boldly extends the scope of the habeas statute to the four corners of the earth. Part III of its opinion asserts that "a district court acts 'within [its] respective jurisdiction' within the meaning of § 2241 as long as 'the custodian can be reached by service of process.'"

The consequence of this holding, as applied to aliens outside the country, is breathtaking. It permits an alien captured in a foreign theater of active combat to bring a § 2241 petition against the Secretary of Defense. Over the course of the last century, the United States has held millions of alien prisoners abroad. A great many of these prisoners would no doubt have complained about the circumstances of their capture and the terms of their confinement. The military is currently detaining over 600 prisoners at Guantanamo Bay alone; each detainee undoubtedly has complaints – real or contrived – about those terms and circumstances. The Court's unheralded expansion of federal-court jurisdiction is not even mitigated by a comforting assurance that the legion of ensuing claims will be easily resolved on the merits. To the contrary, the Court says that the "petitioners' allegations . . . unquestionably describe 'custody in violation of the Constitution or laws or treaties of the United States.'" From this point forward, federal courts will entertain petitions from these prisoners, and others like them around the world, challenging actions and events far away, and forcing the courts to oversee one aspect of the Executive's conduct of a foreign war.

Today's carefree Court disregards, without a word of acknowledgment, the dire warning of a more circumspect Court in *Eisentrager*:

> "To grant the writ to these prisoners might mean that our army must transport them across the seas for hearing. This would require allocation for shipping space, guarding personnel, billeting and rations. It might also require transportation for whatever witnesses the prisoners desired to call as well as transportation for those necessary to defend legality of the sentence. The writ, since it is held to be a matter of right, would be equally available to enemies during active hostilities as in the present twilight between war and peace. Such trials would hamper the war effort and bring aid and comfort to the enemy. They would diminish the prestige of our commanders, not only with enemies but with wavering neutrals. It would be difficult to devise more effective fettering of a field commander than to allow the very enemies he is ordered to reduce to submission to call him to account in his own civil courts and divert his efforts and attention from the military offensive abroad to the legal defensive at home. Nor is it unlikely that the result of such enemy litigiousness would be conflict between judicial and military opinion highly comforting to enemies of the United States."

The Court gives only two reasons why the presumption against extraterritorial effect does not apply to Guantanamo Bay. First, the Court says (without any further elaboration) that "the United States exercises 'complete jurisdiction and control' over the Guantanamo Bay Naval Base [under the terms of a 1903 lease agreement], and may continue to exercise such control permanently if it so chooses [under the terms of a 1934 Treaty]." The Court does not explain how "complete jurisdiction and control" without sovereignty causes an enclave to be part of the United States for purposes of its domestic laws. Since "jurisdiction and control" obtained through a lease is no different in effect from "jurisdiction and control" acquired by lawful force of arms, parts of Afghanistan and Iraq should logically be regarded as subject to our domestic laws. Indeed, if "jurisdiction and control" rather than sovereignty were the test, so should the Landsberg Prison in Germany, where the United States held the *Eisentrager* detainees.

The second and last reason the Court gives for the proposition that domestic law applies to Guantanamo Bay is the Solicitor General's concession that there would be habeas jurisdiction over a United States citizen in Guantanamo Bay. "Considering that the statute draws no distinction between Americans and aliens held in federal custody, there is little reason to think that Congress intended the geographical coverage of the statute to vary depending on the detainee's citizenship." But the reason the Solicitor General conceded there would be jurisdiction over a detainee who was a United States citizen had *nothing to do* with the special status of Guantanamo Bay: "Our answer to that question, Justice Souter, is that citizens of the United States, because of their constitutional circumstances, may have greater rights with respect to the scope and reach of the Habeas Statute as the Court has or would interpret it." And *that* position – the position that United States citizens throughout the world may be entitled to habeas corpus rights – is precisely the position that this Court adopted in *Eisentrager,* even while holding that aliens abroad *did not have* habeas corpus rights.

To the extent the writ's "extraordinary territorial ambit" did extend to exempt jurisdictions, outlying dominions, and the like, that extension applied only to British *subjects*. Blackstone explained that the writ "runs into all parts of the king's dominions" because "the king is at all times entitled to have an account why the liberty of any of his *subjects* is restrained."

Departure from our rule of *stare decisis* in statutory cases is always extraordinary; it ought to be unthinkable when the departure has a potentially harmful effect upon the Nation's conduct of a war. The Commander in Chief and his subordinates had every reason to expect that the internment of combatants at Guantanamo Bay would not have the consequence of bringing the cumbersome machinery of our domestic courts into military affairs. Congress is in session. If it wished to change federal judges' habeas jurisdiction from what this Court had previously held that to be, it could have done so. And it could have done so by intelligent revision of the statute, instead of by today's clumsy, countertextual reinterpretation that confers upon wartime prisoners greater habeas rights than domestic detainees. The latter must challenge their present physical confinement in the district of their confinement, *see Rumsfeld v. Padilla*, whereas under today's strange holding Guantanamo Bay detainees can petition in any of the 94 federal judicial districts. The fact that extraterritorially located detainees lack the district of detention that the statute requires has been converted from a factor that precludes their ability to bring a petition at all into a factor that frees them to petition wherever they wish – and, as a result, to forum shop. For this Court to create such a monstrous scheme in time of war, and in frustration of our military commanders' reliance upon clearly stated prior law, is judicial adventurism of the worst sort. I dissent.

NOTES AND QUESTIONS

1. Justice Stevens does not explore the "merits" of the Guantanamo detentions. "In the end, the answer to the question presented is clear. Petitioners contend that they are being held in federal custody in violation of the laws of the

United States." Justice Scalia, however, says essentially that there is no law that protects these persons, making a distinction between citizens and noncitizens, much as he did in *Hamdi*. On remand in these cases, or in ruling on any future habeas corpus petitions, what law will apply to determine whether a detainee in U.S. military custody is being held "in violation of the Constitution or laws" of the U.S.? Consider these possibilities:

a. constitutional rights – It is not clear that an alien held in federal custody outside the U.S. would have constitutional rights other than perhaps some rights regarding conditions of confinement, or perhaps the due process right to a determination of status similar to that accorded to *Hamdi*. In one of the cases reviewed in *Rasul*, the D.C. Circuit stated: "We cannot see why, or how, the writ may be made available to aliens abroad when basic constitutional protections are not. This much is at the heart of *Eisentrager*. If the Constitution does not entitle the detainees to due process, and it does not, they cannot invoke the jurisdiction of our courts to test the constitutionality or the legality of restraints on their liberty." *Al Odah v. United States*, 355 U.S. App. D.C. 189 (D.C. Cir. 2003).

b. statutory rights – An alien seeking admission to the U.S. may have claims to statutory rights under the immigration laws. Are there any statutes protecting the interests of the Guantanamo detainees?

c. treaty rights – Are the Geneva Conventions self-executing or do they create rights on behalf of individuals? The Government argued in the lower courts that the Conventions created diplomatic remedies and not individual remedies, an argument repeated and addressed in *In re Guantanamo Detainees*, *Khalid v. Bush* and *Hamdan v. Rumsfeld* below.

d. customary international law – Professor Paust argues that both treaties and customary international law entitle a person to freedom from "arbitrary" detention, which implies some level of judicial review over the propriety of detention. Jordan J. Paust, *Judicial Power to Determine the Status and Rights of Persons Detained Without Trial*, 44 HARV. INT'L L.J. 503 (2003).

2. After the Supreme Court's decision, proceedings with respect to the Guantanamo detainees split into three tracks:

a. Petitions for habeas corpus filed in various courts were transferred to the District of Columbia. Most were consolidated for initial motions.

b. The military established "Combatant Status Review Tribunals" (CSRT) Guantanamo Bay to make determinations on the status of each detainee. The Department of Defense has established a website with information about the military commissions conducting those hearings. *http://www.defenselink.mil/news/commissions.html*

Human Rights First has been allowed to monitor the commission hearings at Guantanamo Bay. It asserts that the hearings fail to comply with the Supreme Court's directions in several ways. The detainees are not allowed outside counsel but are instead appointed a "personal representative" who is not a lawyer and may have no professional duty to the client. The hearings are being conducted by military officers who HRF claims do not qualify as a "neutral" decisionmaker in the meaning of the *Hamdi* plurality.

http://www.humanrightsfirst.org/us_law/detainees/status_review_08 0204.htm

    c. Some detainees were brought before military commissions to answer charges of violations of the law of war. *See Hamdan v. Rumsfeld*, p. 535 *infra*.

[handwritten: P arrested in Chicago, is US citizen]

RUMSFELD v. PADILLA
124 S. Ct. 2711 (2004).

CHIEF JUSTICE REHNQUIST delivered the opinion of the Court.

Respondent Jose Padilla is a United States citizen detained by the Department of Defense pursuant to the President's determination that he is an "enemy combatant" who conspired with al Qaeda to carry out terrorist attacks in the United States. We confront two questions: First, did Padilla properly file his habeas petition in the Southern District of New York; and second, did the President possess authority to detain Padilla militarily. We answer the threshold question in the negative and thus do not reach the second question presented.

[handwritten: improper habeas Petition]

Because we do not decide the merits, we only briefly recount the relevant facts. On May 8, 2002, Padilla flew from Pakistan to Chicago's O'Hare International Airport. As he stepped off the plane, Padilla was apprehended by federal agents executing a material witness warrant issued by the United States District Court for the Southern District of New York (Southern District) in connection with its grand jury investigation into the September 11th terrorist attacks. Padilla was then transported to New York, where he was held in federal criminal custody. On May 22, acting through appointed counsel, Padilla moved to vacate the material witness warrant.

Padilla's motion was still pending when, on June 9, the President issued an order to Secretary of Defense Donald H. Rumsfeld designating Padilla an "enemy combatant" and directing the Secretary to detain him in military custody. In support of this action, the President invoked his authority as "Commander in Chief of the U.S. armed forces" and the Authorization for Use of Military Force Joint Resolution, enacted by Congress on September 18, 2001.

[handwritten: Named enemy combatant]

That same day, Padilla was taken into custody by Department of Defense officials and transported to the Consolidated Naval Brig in Charleston, South Carolina. He has been held there ever since.

On June 11, Padilla's counsel, claiming to act as his next friend, filed in the Southern District a habeas corpus petition under 28 U.S.C. § 2241. The amended petition named as respondents President Bush, Secretary Rumsfeld, and Melanie A. Marr, Commander of the Consolidated Naval Brig.

The Government moved to dismiss, arguing that Commander Marr, as Padilla's immediate custodian, is the only proper respondent to his habeas petition, and that the District Court lacks jurisdiction over Commander Marr because she is located outside the Southern District.

[handwritten: Gov't motion to dismiss]

The District Court issued its decision in December 2002. The court held that the Secretary's "personal involvement" in Padilla's military custody renders him a proper respondent to Padilla's habeas petition, and that it can assert jurisdiction over the Secretary under New York's long-arm statute, notwithstanding his absence from the Southern District. On the merits, however, the court accepted the Government's contention that the President has authority to detain as enemy combatants citizens captured on American soil during a time of war.

The Court of Appeals for the Second Circuit reversed. The court agreed with the District Court that Secretary Rumsfeld is a proper respondent, reasoning that in cases where the habeas petitioner is detained for "other than federal criminal violations, the Supreme Court has recognized exceptions to the general practice of naming the immediate physical custodian as respondent." Reaching the merits, the Court of Appeals held that the President lacks authority to detain Padilla militarily. The court concluded that neither the President's Commander-in-Chief power nor the AUMF authorizes military detentions of American citizens captured on American soil.

We granted the Government's petition for certiorari to review the Court of Appeals' rulings with respect to the jurisdictional and the merits issues, both of which raise important questions of federal law. The question whether the Southern District has jurisdiction over Padilla's habeas petition breaks down into two related subquestions. First, who is the proper respondent to that petition? And second, does the Southern District have jurisdiction over him or her? We address these questions in turn.

The federal habeas statute straightforwardly provides that the proper respondent to a habeas petition is "the person who has custody over [the petitioner]." The consistent use of the definite article in reference to the custodian indicates that there is generally only one proper respondent to a given prisoner's habeas petition. This custodian, moreover, is "the person" with the ability to produce the prisoner's body before the habeas court. We summed up the plain language of the habeas statute over 100 years ago in this way: "These provisions contemplate a proceeding against some person who has the *immediate custody* of the party detained, with the power to produce the body of such party before the court or judge, that he may be liberated if no sufficient reason is shown to the contrary."

In accord with the statutory language, longstanding practice confirms that in habeas challenges to present physical confinement – "core challenges" – the default rule is that the proper respondent is the warden of the facility where the prisoner is being held, not the Attorney General or some other remote supervisory official. No exceptions to this rule, either recognized or proposed, apply here.[8]

---

[8] We have long implicitly recognized an exception to the immediate custodian rule in the military context where an American citizen is detained outside the territorial jurisdiction of any district court. *Braden v. 30th Judicial Circuit Court of Ky.*, 410 U.S. 484 (1973) (discussing the exception); *United States ex rel. Toth v. Quarles*, 350 U.S. 11 (1955) (court-martial convict detained

We turn now to the second subquestion. District courts are limited to granting habeas relief "within their respective jurisdictions." 28 U.S.C. § 2241(a). We have interpreted this language to require "nothing more than that the court issuing the writ have jurisdiction over the custodian." Thus, jurisdiction over Padilla's habeas petition lies in the Southern District only if it has jurisdiction over Commander Marr. We conclude it does not.

The proviso that district courts may issue the writ only "within their respective jurisdictions" forms an important corollary to the immediate custodian rule in challenges to present physical custody under § 2241. Together they compose a simple rule that has been consistently applied in the lower courts, including in the context of military detentions: Whenever a § 2241 habeas petitioner seeks to challenge his present physical custody within the United States, he should name his warden as respondent and file the petition in the district of confinement.[16]

The dissent contends that the Court has made "numerous exceptions" to the immediate custodian and district of confinement rules, rendering our bright-line rule "far from bright." Yet the dissent cannot cite a single case in which we have deviated from the longstanding rule we reaffirm today – that is, a case in which we allowed a habeas petitioner challenging his present physical custody within the United States to name as respondent someone other than the immediate custodian and to file somewhere other than the district of confinement.[18]

The District of South Carolina, not the Southern District of New York, was the district court in which Padilla should have brought his habeas petition. We therefore reverse the judgment of the Court of Appeals and remand the case for entry of an order of dismissal without prejudice.

JUSTICE KENNEDY, with whom JUSTICE O'CONNOR joins, concurring.

Both Padilla's change in location and his change of custodian reflected a change in the Government's rationale for detaining him. He ceased to be held under the authority of the criminal justice system, and began to be held under

---

in Korea named Secretary of the Air Force as respondent); *Burns v. Wilson*, 346 U.S. 137 (1953) (court-martial convicts detained in Guam named Secretary of Defense as respondent).

[16] As a corollary to the previously referenced exception to the immediate custodian rule, we have similarly relaxed the district of confinement rule when "Americans citizens confined overseas (and thus outside the territory of any district court) have sought relief in habeas corpus." In such cases, we have allowed the petitioner to name as respondent a supervisory official and file the petition in the district where the respondent resides. *Burns v. Wilson,* 346 U.S. 137 (1953) (court-martial convicts held in Guam sued Secretary of Defense in the District of Columbia); *United States ex rel. Toth v. Quarles,* 350 U.S. 11 (1955) (court-martial convict held in Korea sued Secretary of the Air Force in the District of Columbia).

[18] *Demjanjuk v. Meese*, 251 U.S. App. D.C. 310, 784 F.2d 1114 (CADC 1986), on which the dissent relies, is similarly unhelpful: When, as in that case, a prisoner is held in an undisclosed location by an unknown custodian, it is impossible to apply the immediate custodian and district of confinement rules. That is not the case here, where the identity of the immediate custodian and the location of the appropriate district court are clear.

that of the military detention system. Rather than being designed to play games with forums, the Government's removal of Padilla reflected the change in the theory on which it was holding him. Whether that theory is a permissible one, of course, is a question the Court does not reach today.

JUSTICE STEVENS, with whom JUSTICE SOUTER, JUSTICE GINSBURG, and JUSTICE BREYER join, dissenting.

The petition for a writ of habeas corpus filed in this case raises questions of profound importance to the Nation. The arguments set forth by the Court do not justify avoidance of our duty to answer those questions. It is quite wrong to characterize the proceeding as a "simple challenge to physical custody," that should be resolved by slavish application of a "bright-line rule" designed to prevent "rampant forum shopping" by litigious prison inmates. As the Court's opinion itself demonstrates, that rule is riddled with exceptions fashioned to protect the high office of the Great Writ. This is an exceptional case that we clearly have jurisdiction to decide.

All Members of this Court agree that the immediate custodian rule should control in the ordinary case and that habeas petitioners should not be permitted to engage in forum shopping. More narrowly, we agree that if jurisdiction was proper when the petition was filed, it cannot be defeated by a later transfer of the prisoner to another district.

It is reasonable to assume that if the Government had given Newman, who was then representing respondent in an adversary proceeding, notice of its intent to ask the District Court to vacate the outstanding material witness warrant and transfer custody to the Department of Defense, Newman would have filed the habeas petition then and there, rather than waiting two days. Under that scenario, respondent's immediate custodian would then have been physically present in the Southern District of New York carrying out orders of the Secretary of Defense. Surely at that time Secretary Rumsfeld, rather than the lesser official who placed the handcuffs on petitioner, would have been the proper person to name as a respondent to that petition.

The difference between that scenario and the secret transfer that actually occurred should not affect our decision, for we should not permit the Government to obtain a tactical advantage as a consequence of an *ex parte* proceeding. The departure from the time-honored practice of giving one's adversary fair notice of an intent to present an important motion to the court justifies treating the habeas application as the functional equivalent of one filed two days earlier.

At stake in this case is nothing less than the essence of a free society. Even more important than the method of selecting the people's rulers and their successors is the character of the constraints imposed on the Executive by the rule of law. Unconstrained Executive detention for the purpose of investigating and preventing subversive activity is the hallmark of the Star Chamber. Access to counsel for the purpose of protecting the citizen from official mistakes and mistreatment is the hallmark of due process.

Executive detention of subversive citizens, like detention of enemy soldiers to keep them off the battlefield, may sometimes be justified to prevent persons from launching or becoming missiles of destruction. It may not, however, be justified by the naked interest in using unlawful procedures to extract information. Incommunicado detention for months on end is such a procedure. Whether the information so procured is more or less reliable than that acquired by more extreme forms of torture is of no consequence. For if this Nation is to remain true to the ideals symbolized by its flag, it must not wield the tools of tyrants even to resist an assault by the forces of tyranny.

I respectfully dissent.

NOTES AND QUESTIONS

1. The majority in *Padilla* cites with approval the case of Ali al-Marri, who was indicted and preparing for trial in federal court in Illinois for credit fraud and making false statements to government agents, when he was suddenly made the subject of a Presidential finding of enemy combatant status and shipped off to a military jail in South Carolina. The Seventh Circuit held that the proper place for filing a writ of habeas corpus would be South Carolina, not the place of original criminal proceedings. *al-Marri v. Rumsfeld*, 360 F.3d 707 (7th Cir. 2004).

2. On March 1, 2005, the federal court in South Carolina, calling the situation a "law enforcement matter, not a military matter," ordered that Padilla be released in 45 days unless the Government decided to charge him with a crime. Government lawyers had already indicated in several settings that it would be impossible to assemble admissible evidence for a civilian prosecution.

3. If there were sufficient evidence, are there other reasons not to charge Padilla with a criminal offense in an ordinary civilian court proceeding? After all, John Walker Lindh was charged and pleaded guilty, as have a number of other alleged cell members and sympathizers. Hamdi could be prosecuted similarly to Lindh or he could be treated as a prisoner of war. What do you think of each of the following reasons for military detention?

    a. *Indeterminate Duration of Hostilities.* If Hamdi were treated as a prisoner of war, when would he be repatriated and to what country? As a citizen of the U.S. engaged in warfare against the U.S., he might also be tried for treason but the Government's information presented to the district court created the strong impression that there were not two witnesses to the same overt act. If either Hamdi or Padilla were prosecuted for a criminal violation and sentenced to a few years in prison, how safe would you feel with them on the streets at the end of their sentence? Should this be a reason for avoiding the civilian justice system?

    b. *Detention as Incentive To Talk.* The information presented by the Government in all three cases emphasized that government agents wanted to pump the detainees for further information about al Qaeda and other operatives who may still be at large. If they were treated as recalcitrant witnesses before a grand jury, for example, they could be imprisoned until they agreed to disclose. But the government argues that the mere fact of isolation creates a sense of dependency on the interrogator which is conducive to disclosure. Is this a reasonable constitutional argument? To what extent might the Supreme Court have been influenced by the disclosures of prisoner abuse made public while these cases were pending?

c. *Detention to Prevent Violent Acts.* Administrative detention to prevent violence has been discussed loosely in the past, particularly with respect to child molesters and the criminally insane. The Supreme Court has flatly rejected detention without at least a judicial finding of propensity to harm.

d. *Problems With the Civilian Criminal System.* The principal rights that Hamdi and Padilla would be able to claim if charged in the civilian criminal system are notice of charges, right to counsel, confrontation of witnesses, public trial by jury. How would these same rights fare in the military justice system if charges were brought? *See United States v. Grunden, supra.*

e. *The Mosaic Concern.* If Padilla were brought to trial, then the methods by which federal agents discovered his alleged plot would be much more likely to come out into public scrutiny.

§ 8.04 MILITARY TRIBUNALS IN OPERATION

Following the June 2004 Supreme Court cases, the treatment of military detainees split into three tracks. The military established "Combatant Status Review Tribunals" to make determinations on the status of each of the Guantanamo detainees. Meanwhile, some of those detainees continued to pursue their habeas corpus petitions. The third track was that some detainees were brought before military commissions for trial on charges.

The trial before a military commission of a person for alleged "war crimes" raises the question of what law applies to a "non-state actor." Referring back to the concepts in Chapter 3, the "law of war" applies in time of "armed conflict." The Geneva Conventions deal with "combatants" who under Geneva III (GPW) and civilians under Geneva IV (GC). A person who meets the criteria for POW status under GPW article 4 should also have combat immunity for actions that did not violate the law of war. A civilian may be entitled to "protected status" under Geneva IV but may nevertheless be placed on trial for violent crimes committed in the absence of combat immunity. Both conventions depend on a state of armed conflict, but the assertion of criminal jurisdiction over an offender may exist completely apart from the law of war (as, for example, in occupied territory at the conclusion of hostilities). In that instance, one question would be what tribunal would have jurisdiction over the criminal charges.

HAMDAN v. RUMSFELD
2004 U.S. Dist. LEXIS 22724 (D.D.C. Nov. 8, 2004)

JAMES ROBERTSON, District Judge:

Salim Ahmed Hamdan petitions for a writ of habeas corpus, challenging the lawfulness of the Secretary of Defense's plan to try him for alleged war crimes before a military commission convened under special orders issued by the President of the United States, rather than before a court-martial convened under the Uniform Code of Military Justice. The government moves to dismiss. Because Hamdan has not been determined by a competent tribunal to be an offender triable under the law of war, 10 U.S.C. § 821, and because in any event the procedures established for the Military Commission by the President's order are "contrary to or inconsistent" with those applicable to courts-martial, 10 U.S.C. § 836, Hamdan's petition will be granted in part. The government's motion will be denied. The reasons for these rulings are set forth below.

BACKGROUND

Hamdan was captured in Afghanistan in late 2001, during a time of hostilities in that country. He was detained by American military forces and transferred sometime in 2002 to the detention facility set up by the Defense Department at Guantanamo Bay Naval Base, Cuba. On July 3, 2003, acting pursuant to the Military Order he had issued on November 13, 2001, and finding "that there is reason to believe that [Hamdan] was a member of al Qaida or was otherwise involved in terrorism directed against the United States," the President designated Hamdan for trial by military commission. In December 2003, Hamdan was placed in a part of the Guantanamo Bay facility known as Camp Echo, where he was held in isolation. On December 18, 2003, military counsel was appointed for him. On February 12, 2004, Hamdan's counsel filed a demand for charges and speedy trial under Article 10 of the Uniform Code of Military Justice. On February 23, 2004, the legal advisor to the Appointing Authority[19] ruled that the UCMJ did not apply to Hamdan's detention. On July 9, 2004, Hamdan was formally charged with conspiracy to commit the following offenses: "attacking civilians; attacking civilian objects; murder by an unprivileged belligerent; destruction of property by an unprivileged belligerent; and terrorism."

ANALYSIS

1. . . .

2. No proper determination has been made that Hamdan is an offender triable by military tribunal under the law of war.

a. The President may establish military commissions only for offenders or offenses triable by military tribunal under the law of war.

The major premise of the government's argument that the President has untrammeled power to establish military tribunals is that his authority emanates from Article II of the Constitution and is inherent in his role as commander-in-chief. None of the principal cases on which the government relies, *Ex parte Quirin*, [and] *Application of Yamashita*, has so held. In *Quirin* the

---

[19] The Department of Defense has implemented the President's Military Order with a series of Military Commission Orders, Instructions, and other documents. *See generally* *http://www.defenselink.mil/news/commissions.html*. The Secretary of Defense may designate an "Appointing Authority" to issue orders establishing and regulating military commissions. Secretary Rumsfeld designated John D. Altenburg, Jr. as Appointing Authority.

Supreme Court located the power in Article I, § 8. *Quirin* stands for the *Quirin* proposition that the authority to appoint military commissions is found, not in the inherent power of the presidency, but in the Articles of War (a predecessor of the Uniform Code of Military Justice) by which Congress provided rules for the government of the army.

The *Quirin* Court sustained the President's order creating a military commission, because "[b]y his Order creating the . . . Commission [the President] has undertaken to exercise the authority conferred upon him by Congress." This sentence continues with the words ". . . and also such authority as the Constitution itself gives the Commander in Chief, to direct the performance of those functions which may constitutionally be performed by the military arm of the nation in time of war." That dangling idea is not explained – in *Quirin* or in later cases. The Court expressly found it unnecessary in *Quirin* "to determine to what extent the President as Commander in Chief has constitutional power to create military commissions without the support of Congressional legislation. For here Congress has authorized trial of offenses against the law of war before such commissions."

Quirin and *Yamashita* make it clear that Article 21 represents Congressional approval of the historical, traditional, non-statutory military commission. The language of that approval, however, does not extend past "offenders or offenses that by statute or by the law of war may be tried by military commissions . . . ."

> b. *The law of war includes the Third Geneva Convention, which requires trial by court-martial as long as Hamdan's POW status is in doubt.*

"From the very beginning of its history this Court has recognized and applied the law of war as including that part of the law of nations which prescribes, for the conduct of war, the status, rights and duties of enemy nations as well as of enemy individuals." This language is from *Quirin*. The United States has ratified the Geneva Convention Relative to the Treatment of Prisoners of War (the Third Geneva Convention). Afghanistan is a party to the Geneva Conventions. The Third Geneva Convention is acknowledged to be part of the law of war. It is applicable by its terms in "all cases of declared war or of any other armed conflict which may arise between two or more of the High Contracting Parties, even if the state of war is not recognized by one of them." That language covers the hostilities in Afghanistan that were ongoing in late 2001, when Hamdan was captured there.

If Hamdan is entitled to the protections accorded prisoners of war under the Third Geneva Convention, one need look no farther than Article 102 for the rule that requires his habeas petition to be granted:

> A prisoner of war can be validly sentenced only if the sentence has been pronounced by the same courts according to the same procedure as in the case of members of the armed forces of the Detaining Power, and if, furthermore, the provisions of the present Chapter have been observed.

The Military Commission is not such a court. Its procedures are not such procedures.

The government does not dispute the proposition that prisoners of war may not be tried by military tribunal. Its position is that Hamdan is not entitled to the protections of the Third Geneva Convention at all, and certainly not to prisoner-of-war status, and that in any event the protections of the Third Geneva Convention are not enforceable by way of habeas corpus.

(1) The government's first argument that the Third Geneva Convention does not protect Hamdan asserts that Hamdan was captured, not in the course of a conflict between the United States and Afghanistan, but in the course of a "separate" conflict with al Qaeda. That argument is rejected. The government apparently bases the argument on a Presidential "finding" that it claims is "not reviewable." The finding is set forth in Memorandum from the President, stating that the Third Geneva Convention applies to the Taliban detainees, but not to the al Qaeda detainees captured in Afghanistan, because al Qaeda is not a state party to the Geneva Conventions. Notwithstanding the President's view that the United States was engaged in two separate conflicts in Afghanistan, the government's attempt to separate the Taliban from al Qaeda for Geneva Convention purposes finds no support in the structure of the Conventions themselves, which are triggered by the place of the conflict, and not by what particular faction a fighter is associated with. Thus at some level – whether as a prisoner-of-war entitled to the full panoply of Convention protections or only under the more limited protections afforded by Common Article 3 – the Third Geneva Convention applies to all persons detained in Afghanistan during the hostilities there.

(2) The government next argues that, even if the Third Geneva Convention might theoretically apply to anyone captured in the Afghanistan theater, members of al Qaeda such as Hamdan are not entitled to POW status because they do not satisfy the test established by Article 4(2) of the Third Geneva Convention – they do not carry arms openly and operate under the laws and customs of war. We know this, the government argues, because the President himself has determined that Hamdan was a member of al Qaeda or otherwise involved in terrorism against the United States. Presidential determinations in this area, the government argues, are due "extraordinary deference." Moreover (as the court was advised for the first time at oral argument on October 25, 2004) a Combatant Status Review Tribunal (CSRT) found, after a hearing on October 3, 2004, that Hamdan has the status of an enemy combatant "as either a member of or affiliated with Al Qaeda." Article 5 of the Third Geneva Convention provides:

> Should any doubt arise as to whether persons, having committed a belligerent act and having fallen into the hands of the enemy, belong to any of the categories enumerated in Article 4 such persons shall enjoy the protection of the present Convention until such time as their status has been determined by a competent tribunal.

There is nothing in this record to suggest that a competent tribunal has determined that Hamdan is not a prisoner-of-war under the Geneva Conventions. Hamdan has appeared before the Combatant Status Review Tribunal, but the CSRT was not established to address detainees' status under the Geneva Conventions. It was established to comply with the Supreme Court's mandate in *Hamdi*, to decide "whether the detainee is properly detained as an enemy combatant" for purposes of continued detention.

The government's legal position is that the CSRT determination that Hamdan was a member of or affiliated with al Qaeda is also determinative of Hamdan's prisoner-of-war status, since the President has already determined that detained al Qaeda members are not prisoners-of-war under the Geneva Conventions. The President is not a "tribunal," however. The government must convene a competent tribunal (or address a competent tribunal already convened) and seek a specific determination as to Hamdan's status under the Geneva Conventions. Until or unless such a tribunal decides otherwise, Hamdan has, and must be accorded, the full protections of a prisoner-of-war.

H: H.3 a POW until a competent Trib decides otherwise

(3) The government's next argument, that Common Article 3 does not apply because it was meant to cover local and not international conflicts, is also rejected. It is universally agreed, and is demonstrable in the Convention language itself, in the context in which it was adopted, and by the generally accepted law of nations, that Common Article 3 embodies "international human norms," and that it sets forth the "most fundamental requirements of the law of war." The government has asserted a position starkly different from the positions and behavior of the United States in previous conflicts, one that can only weaken the United States' own ability to demand application of the Geneva Conventions to Americans captured during armed conflicts abroad. Amici remind us of the capture of U.S. Warrant Officer Michael Durant in 1993 by forces loyal to a Somali warlord. The United States demanded assurances that Durant would be treated consistently with protections afforded by the Convention, even though, if the Convention were applied as narrowly as the government now seeks to apply it to Hamdan, "Durant's captors would not be bound to follow the convention because they were not a 'state.'"

(4) The government's putative trump card is that Hamdan's rights under the Geneva Conventions, if any, and whatever they are, are not enforceable by this Court – that, in effect, Hamdan has failed to state a claim upon which relief can be granted – because the Third Geneva Convention is not "self-executing" and does not give rise to a private cause of action.

As an initial matter, it should be noted Hamdan has not asserted a "private right of action" under the Third Geneva Convention. The Convention is implicated in this case by operation of the statute that limits trials by military tribunal to "offenders . . . triable under the law of war." The government's argument thus amounts to the assertion that no federal court has the authority to determine whether the Third Geneva Convention has been violated, or, if it has, to grant relief from the violation.

Treaties made under the authority of the United States are the supreme law of the land. U.S. Const. art. VI, cl. 2. United States courts are bound to give effect to international law and to international agreements of the United States unless such agreements are "non-self-executing." A treaty is "non-self-executing" if it manifests an intention that it not become effective as domestic law without enactment of implementing legislation; or if the Senate in consenting to the treaty requires implementing legislation; or if implementing legislation is constitutionally required.

[I]t is quite clear from the legislative history of the ratification of the Geneva Conventions that Congress carefully considered what further legislation, if any, was deemed "required to give effect to the provisions contained in the four conventions," and found that only four provisions required implementing legislation. Articles 5 and 102, which are dispositive of Hamdan's case, were not among them. What did require implementing legislation were Articles 129 and 130, providing for additional criminal penalties to be imposed upon those who engaged in "grave" violations of the Conventions, such as torture, medical experiments, or "wilful" denial of Convention protections, none of which is involved here. Because the Geneva Conventions were written to protect individuals, because the Executive Branch of our government has implemented the Geneva Conventions for fifty years without questioning the absence of implementing legislation, because Congress clearly understood that the Conventions did not require implementing legislation except in a few specific areas, and because nothing in the Third Geneva Convention itself manifests the contracting parties' intention that it not become effective as domestic law without the enactment of implementing legislation, I conclude that, insofar as it is pertinent here, the Third Geneva Convention is a self-executing treaty.

I further conclude that it is at least a matter of some doubt as to whether or not Hamdan is entitled to the protections of the Third Geneva Convention as a prisoner of war and that accordingly he must be given those protections unless and until the "competent tribunal" referred to in Article 5 concludes otherwise. It follows from those conclusions that Hamdan may not be tried for the war crimes he is charged with except by a court-martial duly convened under the Uniform Code of Military Justice.

> *c. Abstention is appropriate with respect to Hamdan's rights under Common Article 3.*

There is an argument that, even if Hamdan does not have prisoner-of-war status, Common Article 3 would be violated by trying him for his alleged war crimes in this Military Commission. Abstention is appropriate, and perhaps required, on that question, because, unlike Article 102, which unmistakably mandates trial of POW's only by general court-martial and thus implicates the jurisdiction of the Military Commission, the Common Article 3 requirement of trial before a "regularly constituted court affording all the judicial guarantees which are recognized as indispensable by civilized peoples" has no fixed, term-of-art meaning. A substantial number of rights and procedures conferred by the UCMJ are missing from the Military Commission's rules. Only Hamdan's right to be present at every phase of his trial and to see all the evidence admitted against him is of immediate pretrial concern. That right is addressed in the next section of this opinion.

> 3. In at least one critical respect, the procedures of the Military Commission are fatally contrary to or inconsistent with those of the Uniform Code of Military Justice.

In most respects, the procedures established for the Military Commission at Guantanamo under the President's order define a trial forum that looks appropriate and even reassuring when seen through the lens of American jurisprudence. The Military Commission is remarkably different from a court-martial, however, in two important respects. The first has to do with the structure of the reviewing authority after trial; the second, with the power of the appointing authority or the presiding officer to exclude the accused from hearings and deny him access to evidence presented against him.

Petitioner's challenge to the first difference is unsuccessful. It is true that the President has made himself, or the Secretary of Defense acting at his direction, the final reviewing authority, whereas under the Uniform Code of Military Justice there would be two levels of independent review by members of the Third Branch of government – an appeal to the Court of Appeals for the Armed Forces, whose active bench consists of five civilian judges, and possible review by the Supreme Court on writ of certiorari. The President has, however, established a Review Panel that will review the trial record and make a recommendation to the Secretary of Defense, or, if the panel finds an error of law, return the case for further proceedings. And, as for the President's naming himself or the Secretary of Defense as the final reviewing authority, that, after all, is what a military commission is. If Hamdan is triable by any military tribunal, the fact that final review of a finding of guilt would reside in the President or his designee is not "contrary to or inconsistent with" the UCMJ.

The second difference between the procedures adopted for the Miliary Commission and those applicable in a court-martial convened under the Uniform Code of Military Justice is far more troubling. That difference lies in the treatment of information that is classified; information that is otherwise "protected;" or information that might implicate the physical safety of participants, including witnesses, or the integrity of intelligence and law enforcement sources and methods, or "other national security interests." Under the Secretary of Defense's regulations, the Military Commission must "[h]old open proceedings except where otherwise decided by the Appointing Authority or the Presiding Officer." Detailed military defense counsel may not be excluded from proceedings, nor may evidence be received that has not been presented to detailed defense counsel. The accused himself may be excluded from proceedings, however, and evidence may be adduced that he will never see (because his lawyer will be forbidden to disclose it to him). Thus, for example, testimony may be received from a confidential informant, and Hamdan will not be permitted to hear the testimony, see the witness's face, or learn his name. If the government has information developed by interrogation of witnesses in Afghanistan or elsewhere, it can offer such evidence in transcript form, or even as summaries of transcripts.

The Presiding Officer or the Appointing Authority may receive it in evidence if it meets the "reasonably probative" standard but forbid it to be shown to Hamdan. As counsel for Hamdan put it at oral argument, portions of Mr. Hamdan's trial can be conducted "outside his presence. He can be excluded, not for his conduct, [but] because the government doesn't want him to know what's in it. They make a great big deal out of I can be there, but anybody who's practiced trial law, especially criminal law, knows that where you get your cross examination questions from is turning to your client and saying, 'Did that really happen? Is that what happened?' I'm not permitted to do that." It is obvious beyond the need for citation that such a dramatic deviation from the confrontation clause could not be countenanced in any American court, particularly after Justice Scalia's extensive opinion in his decision this year in *Crawford v. Washington*, 124 S.Ct. 1354 (2004). It is also apparent that the right to trial "in one's presence" is established as a matter of international humanitarian and human rights law.

But it is unnecessary to consider whether Hamdan can rely on any American constitutional notions of fairness, or whether the nature of these proceedings really is, as counsel asserts, akin to the Star Chamber (and violative of Common Article 3), because – at least in this critical respect – the rules of the Military Commission are fatally "contrary to or inconsistent with" the statutory requirements for courts-martial convened under the Uniform Code of Military Justice, and thus unlawful.

In a general court-martial conducted under the UCMJ, the accused has the right to be present during sessions of the court: "When the members of a court-martial deliberate or vote, only the members may be present. All other proceedings, including any other consultation of the members of the court with counsel or the military judge, shall be made a part of the record and shall be in the presence of the accused, the defense counsel, the trial counsel, and, in cases in which a military judge has been detailed to the court, the military judge." UCMJ Article 39(b), 10 U.S.C. § 839(b).

Article 36 of the Uniform Code of Military Justice, 10 U.S.C. § 836(a), provides [that procedures in commissions] "may not be contrary to or inconsistent with this chapter." The government argues for procedural "flexibility" in military commission proceedings, asserting that "construing Article 36 rigidly to mean that there can be no deviation from the UCMJ . . . would have resulted in having virtually all of the UCMJ provisions apply to the military commissions, which would clearly be in conflict with historical practice, as recognized by the Supreme Court, in . . . *Yamashita*." But the language of Article 36 does not require rigid adherence to all of the UCMJ's rules for courts-martial. It proscribes only procedures and modes of proof that are "contrary to or inconsistent with" the UCMJ.

The government's best argument, drawing on language found in *Yamashita*, is that a "common-law war court" has been "adapted in each instance to the need that called it forth." Neither the President in his findings and determinations nor the government in its briefs has explained what "need" calls forth the abandonment of the right Hamdan would have under the UCMJ to be present at every stage of his trial and to confront and cross-examine all witnesses and challenge all evidence brought against him. Presumably the problems of dealing with classified or "protected" information underlie the President's blanket finding that using the regular rules is "not practicable." The military has not found it impracticable to deal with classified material in courts-martial, however. An extensive and elaborate process for dealing with classified material has evolved in the Military Rules of Evidence. Mil. R. Evid. 505. Alternatives to full disclosure are provided, Mil. R. Evid. 505(i)(4)(D).

Ultimately, to be sure, the government has a choice to make, if the presiding military judge determines that alternatives may not be used and the government objects to disclosure of information. At that point, the conflict between the government's need to protect classified information and the defendant's right to be present becomes irreconcilable, and the only available options are to strike or preclude the testimony of a witness, or declare a mistrial, or find against the government on any issue as to which the evidence is relevant and material to the defense, or dismiss the charges (with or without prejudice), Mil. R. Evid. 505(i)(4)(E). The point is that the rules of the Military Commission resolve that conflict, not in favor of the defendant, but in favor of the government. Unlike the other procedural problems with the Commission's rules that are discussed elsewhere in this opinion, this one is neither remote nor speculative: Counsel made the unrefuted assertion at oral argument that Hamdan has already been excluded from the voir dire process and that "the government's already indicated that for two days of his trial, he won't be there. And they'll put on the evidence at that point." Counsel's appropriate concern is not only for the established right of his client to be present at his trial, but also for the adequacy of the defense he can provide to his client. The relationship between the right to be present and the adequacy of defense is recognized by military courts, which have interpreted Article 39 of the UCMJ in the light of Confrontation Clause jurisprudence.

A tribunal set up to try, possibly convict, and punish a person accused of crime that is configured in advance to permit the introduction of evidence and the testimony of witnesses out of the presence of the accused is indeed substantively different from a regularly convened court-martial. If such a tribunal is not a "regularly constituted court affording all the judicial guarantees which are recognized as indispensable by civilized peoples," it is violative of Common Article 3. That is a question on which I have determined to abstain. In the meantime, however, I cannot stretch the meaning of the Military Commission's rule enough to find it consistent with the UCMJ's right to be present. A provision that permits the exclusion of the accused from his trial for reasons other than his disruptive behavior or his voluntary absence is indeed directly contrary to the UCMJ's right to be present. I must accordingly find on the basis of the statute that, so long as it operates under such a rule, the Military Commission cannot try Hamdan.

4. Hamdan's detention claim appears to be moot, and his speedy trial and equal protection claims need not be ruled upon at this time.

Until a few days before the oral argument on Hamdan's petition, his most urgent and striking claim was that he had been unlawfully and inhumanely held in isolation since December 2003 and that such treatment was affecting his mental and psychological health as well as his ability to assist in the preparation of his defense. Late on the Friday afternoon before the oral argument held on Monday, October 25, 2004, the government filed its "notice of a change in circumstances," advising the court that Hamdan had been moved back to Camp Delta – a separate wing of Camp Delta, to be sure, but nevertheless an open-air part of Camp Delta where pre-commission detainees can communicate with each other, exercise, and practice their religion. That change in status may not exactly moot Hamdan's claim about his confinement in isolation, which the government is capable of repeating and which has evaded review.

The treatment Hamdan may or may not be afforded in the future, however, is not susceptible to review on a writ of habeas corpus. The second most urgent and most important claim in Hamdan's original petition was his claim of entitlement to the protection of the Uniform Code of Military Justice's speedy trial rule and his assertion that he had been detained more than the maximum 90 days permitted by Article 103 of the Third Geneva Convention. These concerns were more urgent before Hamdan was transferred out of Camp Echo and back to Camp Delta and before the Supreme Court made it clear, in *Hamdi*, that, whether or not Hamdan has been charged with a crime, he may be detained for the duration of the hostilities in Afghanistan if he has been appropriately determined to be an enemy combatant.

CONCLUSION

It is now clear, by virtue of the Supreme Court's decision in *Hamdi*, that the detentions of enemy combatants at Guantanamo Bay are not unlawful per se. The granting (in part) of Hamdan's petition for habeas corpus accordingly brings only limited relief. The order that accompanies this opinion provides: (1) that, unless and until a competent tribunal determines that Hamdan is not entitled to POW status, he may be tried for the offenses with which he is charged only by court-martial under the Uniform Code of Military Justice; (2) that, unless and until the Military Commission's rule permitting Hamdan's exclusion from commission sessions and the withholding of evidence from him is amended so that it is consistent with and not contrary to UCMJ Article 39, Hamdan's trial before the Military Commission would be unlawful; and (3) that Hamdan must be released from the pre-Commission detention wing of Camp Delta and returned to the general population of detainees, unless some reason other than the pending charges against him requires different treatment. Hamdan's remaining claims are in abeyance.

NOTES AND QUESTIONS

1. The Government filed an immediate appeal with the D.C. Circuit, to which Hamdan's counsel responded with a request that the Supreme Court grant certiorari prior to judgment in the Court of Appeals. The Supreme Court denied that petition. *Hamdan v. Rumsfeld*, 2004 U.S. LEXIS 7984 (Dec. 6, 2004).

2. What does the court mean by the statement that "the CSRT was not established to address detainees' status under the Geneva Conventions. It was established to comply with the Supreme Court's mandate in Hamdi, to decide 'whether the detainee is properly detained as an enemy combatant' for purposes of continued detention." What is the difference between deciding on the propriety of continued detention and deciding on the status of the detainee as a POW?

3. Perhaps now the connections with the international law considered in Chapter 3 will be more clear. First, we can refer back now to the excerpts of the very extended treatment of Common Article 3 in the opinions of the International Criminal Tribunals for Yugoslavia and Rwanda. Judge Robertson relies on Common Article 3 to insist that Hamdan is entitled at least to some protection, including an Article 5 determination of his status by a "competent tribunal." He "abstains," however, from determining whether a military commission would satisfy Common Article 3's requirement of trial before "a regularly constituted court affording all the judicial guarantees which are recognizable as indispensable by civilized peoples." *See* Jordan J. Paust, *Antiterrorism Military Commissions: The Ad Hoc DoD Rules of Procedure*, 23 MICH. J. INT'L L. 677 (2002).

4. Another overt application of the international law is in determining whether a military commission is authorized by Congress to try alleged terrorists. Judge Robertson alludes to this problem by pointing out that the commission can try only offenses against the "law of war." But what part of the law of war would a civilian unconnected to a national government or a belligerent group violate? A core problem for the law of counter-terrorism is the question of what law applies.

IN RE GUANTANAMO DETAINEE CASES
2005 U.S. Dist. LEXIS 1236 (D.D.C. January 31, 2005)

JOYCE HENS GREEN, United States District Judge.

These eleven coordinated habeas cases were filed by detainees held as "enemy combatants" at the United States Naval Base at Guantanamo Bay, Cuba. Presently pending is the government's motion to dismiss or for judgment as a matter of law regarding all claims filed by all petitioners, including claims based on the United States Constitution, treaties, statutes, regulations, the common law, and customary international law. [F]or the reasons stated below, tie Court concludes that the petitioners have stated valid claims under the Fifth Amendment to the United States Constitution and that the procedures implemented by the government to confirm that the petitioners are "enemy combatants" subject to indefinite detention violate the petitioners' rights to due process of law. The Court also holds that at least some of the petitioners have stated valid claims under the Third Geneva Convention. Finally, the Court holds that the government is entitled to the dismissal of the petitioners' remaining claims.

Because this Memorandum Opinion references classified material, it is being issued in two versions. The official version is unredacted and is being filed with the Court Security Officer at the U.S. Department of Justice responsible for the management of classified information in these cases.

I. BACKGROUND

In addition to belligerents captured during the heat of war in Afghanistan, the U.S. authorities are also detaining at Guantanamo Bay pursuant to the AUMF numerous individuals who were captured hundreds or thousands of miles from a battle zone in the traditional sense of that term. For example, detainees at Guantanamo Bay who are presently seeking habeas relief in the United States District Court for the District of Columbia include men who were taken into custody as far away from Afghanistan as Gambia, Zambia, Bosnia, and Thailand.

Some have already been detained as long as three years while others have been captured as recently as September 2004. Although many of these individuals may never have been close to an actual battlefield and may never have raised conventional arms against the United States or its allies, the military nonetheless has deemed them detainable as "enemy combatants" based on conclusions that they have ties to al Qaeda or other terrorist organizations.

All of the individuals who have been detained at Guantanamo Bay have been categorized to fall within a general class of people the administration calls "enemy combatants." It is the government's position that once someone has been properly designated as such, that person can be held indefinitely until title end of America's war on terrorism or until the military determines on a case by case basis that the particular detainee no longer poses a threat to the United States or its allies. Within the general set of "enemy combatants" is a subset of individuals whom the administration decided to prosecute for war crimes before a military commission established pursuant to a Military Order issued by President Bush on November 13, 2001. Should individuals be prosecuted and convicted in accordance with the Military Order, they would be subject to sentences with fixed terms of incarceration or other specific penalties.

Since the beginning of the military's detention operations at Guantanamo Bay in early 2002, detainees subject to criminal prosecution have been bestowed with more rights than detainees whom the military did not intend to prosecute formally for war crimes. For example, the military regulations governing the prosecutions of detainees required a formal notice of charges, a presumption of innocence of any crime until proven guilty, a right to counsel, pretrial disclosure to the defense team of exculpatory evidence and of evidence the prosecution intends to use at trial, the right to call reasonably available witnesses, the right to have defense counsel cross-examine prosecution witnesses, the right to have defense counsel attend every portion of the trial proceedings even where classified information is presented, and the right to an open tribal with the press present, at least for those portions not involving classified information.[20]

The first of these coordinated cases challenging the legality of the detention of alleged "enemy combatants" at Guantanamo Bay and the terms and conditions of that detention commenced nearly three years ago on February 19, 2002. *Rasul v. Bush*. The action, brought by relatives on behalf of one Australian and two British nationals as their "next friends," was styled as a petition for writ of habeas corpus pursuant to 28 U.S.C. §§ 2241 and 2242. Less than three months after the commencement of *Rasul*, the second of these coordinated cases was filed. *Al Odah v. Bush*. The individuals filing suit on behalf of the twelve Kuwaiti detainees in that case did not expressly request release from custody but rather sought judicial enforcement of the detainees' asserted rights to meet with family members, be informed of any charges against them, and have access to the

---

[20] In a decision issued on November 8, 2004, Judge James Robertson ruled that the procedures for trying Guantanamo detainees for alleged war crimes by military commission were unlawful for failing to comply with the requirements for courts martial set forth in the Uniform Code of Military Justice. *Hamdan v. Rumsfeld*, 344 F. Supp. 2d 152 (D.D.C. 2004).

courts or some other impartial tribunal to exonerate themselves of any wrongdoing.

The Supreme Court held that the District Court did have jurisdiction to hear the detainees' habeas claims. *Rasul v. Bush*, 124 S. Ct. 2686 (2004). The majority opinion, issued June 28, 2004, noted several facts that distinguished the Guantanamo detainees from the petitioners in Eisentrager more than fifty years earlier:

> [The Guantanamo petitioners] are not nationals of countries at war with the United States, and they deny that they have engaged in or plotted acts of aggression against the United States; they have never been afforded access to any tribunal, much less charged with and convicted of wrongdoing; and for more than two years they have been imprisoned in territory over which the United States exercises exclusive jurisdiction and control.

The Supreme Court expressly acknowledged that the allegations contained in the petitions for writs of habeas corpus "unquestionably describe custody in violation of the Constitution or laws or treaties of the United States'" as required by the habeas statute, 124 S. Ct. at 2698 n.15.

On July 7, 2004, nine days after the issuance of the *Rasul* decision, Deputy Secretary of Defense Paul Wolfowitz issued an Order creating a military tribunal called the Combatant Status Review Tribunal (hereinafter "CSRT") to review the status of each detainee at Guantanamo Bay as an "enemy combatant." It appears that this is the first formal document to officially define the term "enemy combatant" as used by the respondents. That definition is as follows:

> The term "enemy combatant" shall mean an individual who was part of or supporting Taliban or al Qaeda forces, or associated forces that are engaged in hostilities against the United States or its coalition partners. This includes any person who has committed a belligerent act or has directly supported hostilities in aid of enemy armed forces.

The Deputy Secretary's Order notes that all Guantanamo detainees were previously determined to be "enemy combatants" through what the Order describes without additional specificity as "multiple levels of review by officers of the Department of Defense." The Order sets forth procedures by which detainees can contest this status before a panel of three commissioned military officers.

The CSRT procedures [provide that] detainees for the first time have the right to hear the factual bases for their detention, at least to the extent that those facts do not involve information deemed classified by the administration. Detainees also have the right to testify why they contend they should not be considered "enemy combatants" and may present additional evidence they believe might exculpate them, at least to the extent the tribunal finds such evidence relevant and "reasonably available." The detainees do not have a right to counsel in the proceedings, although each is assigned a military officer who serves as a "Personal Representative" to assist the detainee in understanding the process and presenting his case. Formal rules of evidence do not apply, and there is a presumption in favor of the government's conclusion that a detainee is in fact an "enemy combatant." Although the tribunal is free to consider classified evidence supporting a contention that an individual is an "enemy combatant," that individual is not entitled to have access to or know the details of that classified evidence.

It is the government's position that in the event a conclusion by the tribunal that a detainee is an "enemy combatant" is affirmed, it is legal to hold the detainee in custody until the war on terrorism has been declared by the President to have concluded or until the President or his designees have determined that the detainee is no longer a threat to national security. If the tribunal finally determines that a detainee should no longer be deemed an "enemy combatant," a written report of the decision is forwarded to the Secretary of Defense or his designee, who is then obligated to contact the Secretary of State for coordination of the transfer of the detainee either to his country of citizenship or elsewhere in accordance with law and U.S. foreign policy.

In the wake of the Supreme Court's decision in *Rasul*, several new habeas cases were filed on behalf of Guantanamo detainees in addition to those cases that were remanded by the Court as part of *Rasul*. As of the end of July 2004, thirteen cases involving more than sixty detainees were pending before eight Judges in this District Court. On July 23, 2004, the respondents filed a motion to consolidate all of the cases pending at that time. The motion was denied without prejudice three days later. On August 4, 2004, the respondents filed a motion seeking coordination of legal issues common to all cases. By order dated August 17, 2004, Judge Gladys Kessler on behalf of the Calendar and Case Management Committee granted the motion in part, designating this Judge to coordinate and manage all proceedings in the pending matters and, to the extent necessary, rule on procedural and substantive issues common to the cases. An Executive Session Resolution dated September 15, 2004 further clarified that this Judge would identify and delineate both procedural and substantive issues common to all or some of these cases and, as consented to by the transferring judge in each case, rule on common procedural issues. The Resolution also provided that to the extent additional consent was given by the transferring Judges, this Judge would address specified common substantive issues. The Resolution concluded by staring that any Judge who did not agree with any substantive decision made by this Judge could resolve the issue in his or her own case as he or she deemed appropriate. Although issues and motions were transferred to this Judge, the cases themselves have remained before the assigned Judges.[14]

After two informal status conferences discussing, among other issues, the factual bases for the government's detention of the petitioners, this Judge issued a scheduling order requiring the respondents to file responsive pleadings showing cause why writs of habeas corpus and the relief sought by petitioners should not be granted. The order also incorporated the respondents' proposed schedule for the filing of factual returns identifying the specific bases upon which

---

[14] As was his prerogative, Judge Richard Leon did not transfer the motions to dismiss in his two Guantanamo cases, *Khalid v. Bush*, and this Memorandum Opinion therefore does not apply to those two cases.

they claim the government is entitled to detain each petitioner at Guantanamo Bay as an "enemy combatant." Although most of the detainees had already been held as "enemy combatants" for more than two years and had been subjected to unspecified "multiple levels of review," the respondents chose to submit as factual support for their detention of the petitioners the records from the CSRT proceedings, which had only commenced in late August or early September 2004. Those factual returns were filed with the Court on a rolling basis as the CSRT proceedings were completed, with the earliest submitted on September 17, 2004 and the latest on December 30, 2004. Because every complete CSRT record contained classified information, respondents filed redacted, unclassified versions on the public record, submitted the full, classified versions for the Court's in camera review, and served on counsel for the petitioners with appropriate security clearances versions containing most of the classified information disclosed in the Court's copies but redacting some classified information that respondents alleged would not exculpate the detainees from their "enemy combatant" status.

II. ANALYSIS

The petitioners in these eleven cases allege that the detention at Guantanamo Bay and the conditions thereof violate a variety of laws. All petitions assert violations of the Fifth Amendment, and a majority claim violations of the Alien Tort Claims Act, the Administrative Procedure Act, and the Geneva Conventions. *Claims*

A. EXTRATERRITORIAL APPLICATION OF THE CONSTITUTION TO ALIENS

Notwithstanding the Supreme Court's decision in *Rasul* that the District Court's dismissal of the petitioners' claims was incorrect as a matter of law, the respondents argue that the *Rasul* decision resolved only whether individuals detained at Guantanamo Bay had the right merely to allege in a United States District Court under the habeas statute that they are being detained in violation of the Constitution and other laws. Respondents argue that the decision was silent on the issue of whether the detainees actually possess any underlying substantive rights, and they further contend that earlier Supreme Court precedent and the law of this Circuit make clear that the detainees do not hold any such substantive rights. Accordingly, it is the respondents' position that although *Rasul* clarified that a detainee has every right to file papers in the Clerk's Office alleging violations of the Constitution, statutes, treaties and other laws, and although the Court has jurisdiction to accept the filing and to consider those papers, the Court must not permit the case to proceed beyond a declaration that no underlying substantive rights exist. While the Court would have welcomed a clearer declaration in the *Rasul* opinion regarding the specific constitutional and other substantive rights of the petitioners, it does not interpret the Supreme Court's decision as narrowly as the respondents suggest it should. To the contrary, the Court interprets *Rasul* in conjunction with other precedent, to require the recognition that the detainees at Guantanamo Bay possess enforceable constitutional rights.

The significance and scope of the *Rasul* decision is best understood after a review of earlier case law addressing the applicability of the Constitution outside of the United States and to individuals who are not American citizens. At the end of the nineteenth century, the Supreme Court interpreted the Constitution to have no applicability outside of the United States, even to activities undertaken by the United States government with respect to American citizens, In *Ross v. McIntyre (In re Ross)*, 140 U.S. 453, 464 (1891), a habeas case involving a U.S. citizen convicted of murder by an American consular tribunal in Japan, the Court declared, "By the constitution a government is ordained and established for the United States of America, and not for countries outside of their limits. The guaranties it affords . . . apply only to citizens and others within the United States, or who are brought there for trial for alleged offenses committed elsewhere, and not to residents or temporary sojourners abroad. The constitution can have no operation in another country."

The Supreme Court reexamined this broad declaration beginning a decade later and recognized the potential for a more liberal view of the Constitution's applicability outside of the United States in a line of precedent known as the "*Insular Cases*." One of the earliest of those cases, *Downes v. Bidwell*, 182 U.S. 244 (1901), addressed whether the imposition of duties on products from Puerto Rico after it became a U.S. territory was a violation of the Constitution's Uniformity Clause, which requires that "all duties, imposts, and excises shall be uniform throughout the United States." As part of its analysis, the Court held that the "unincorporated" territory of Puerto Rico – meaning a territory not destined for statehood – was not part of the "United States" and that, as a result, the imposition of duties on Puerto Rican goods did not violate the Constitution. Significant to the resolution of the cases brought by the Guantanamo detainees, the Court went on to minimize . . . concern by suggesting that the Constitution prevented Congress from denying inhabitants of unincorporated U.S. territories certain "fundamental" rights, including "the right to personal liberty . . .; to free access to courts of justice, [and] to due process of law."

Three years later, the Court faced more directly the applicability of the Constitution outside of the United States when it resolved whether the defendant in a criminal libel action in a Philippines court was entitled to a trial by jury under Article III and the Sixth Amendment of the U.S. Constitution. *Dorr v. United States*, 195 U.S. 138 (1904). At the time of the litigation, the United States had control of the Philippines as an unincorporated territory after the conclusion of the Spanish-American War. Congress, however, had enacted legislation expressly exempting application of the U.S. Constitution to the area. The defendant in that case was prosecuted for libel under the previously existing Spanish system and was not permitted a trial by jury. On appeal, the defendant argued that the right to trial by jury was a "fundamental" right guaranteed by the U.S. Constitution and that Congress did not have the power to deny that right by statute. Although the Court ultimately ruled that the Constitution did not require a right to jury trial in the Philippines, it did so only after examining the legal traditions employed in the Philippines prior to annexation as a U.S. territory, the significance of the constitutional right asserted, and the ability of the existing system to accept the burdens of applying new constitutional constraints. In reaching its conclusion that a right to trial by jury was not a "fundamental" right guaranteed outside of the United States, the Court emphasized that the legal system pursuant to which the defendant was prosecuted already provided numerous procedural safeguards, including fact finding by judges, a right of appeal, a right to testify, a right to retain counsel, a right to confront witnesses, a right against self-incrimination, and a right to due process. After suggesting that a large majority of the population would be unfit to serve as jurors, the Court further noted that recognizing a fundamental constitutional right to a jury trial might, in fact, "work injustice and provoke disturbance rather than . . . aid the orderly administration of justice."[25]

A plurality opinion issued by the Supreme Court in *Reid v. Covert*, 354 U.S. 1 (1957), argued for the further liberalization of the application of the Constitution outside of the United States. *Reid* involved two wives charged with the capital murders of their husbands. Both men were soldiers in the United States military and were killed at overseas posts, one in England and the other in Japan, The wives, who were American citizens, were tried and convicted abroad by courts martial under the Uniform Code of Military Justice and subsequently sought habeas relief, arguing that as civilians they were entitled under the Constitution to civilian trials. Initially, a majority of the Court ruled in the Japanese case during the previous term that the guarantees of an indictment by grand jury and subsequent jury trial under the Fifth and Sixth Amendments in a prosecution by the United States government did not apply in foreign lands for acts committed outside the United States. *Kinsella v. Krueger*, 351 U.S. 470 (1956). Upon further argument and reconsideration the following term, however, the Court overruled its earlier decision, with four Justices subscribing to a plurality opinion and two Justices issuing separate opinions concurring in the result.

The plurality began its analysis of the issues with the following pronouncement, a marked contrast from the language used a half century earlier in *Ross*:

> At the beginning we reject the idea that when the United States acts against citizens abroad it can do so free of the Bill of Rights. The United States is entirely a creature of the Constitution. Its power and authority have no other source. It can only act in accordance with all the limitations imposed by the Constitution. When the Government reaches out to punish a citizen who is abroad, the shield which the Bill of Rights and other parts of the Constitution provide to protect his life and liberty should not be stripped away just because he happens to be in another land. This is not a novel concept. To the contrary, it is as old as government

The plurality went on to clarify that the "fundamental" rights approach limiting the full application of the Constitution to territories under U.S. control had been intended to avoid disruption of long established practices and to

---

[25] At a time critics might call less enlightened, the *Dorr* opinion expressed a fear that further expansion of the application of the Constitution might result in requiring "savages" to serve as jurors.

expedite the carrying out of justice in the insular possessions. Accordingly, the plurality suggested that any further abridgement of constitutional rights under a "fundamental" rights approach should not be countenanced. They reasoned, "If our foreign commitments become of such nature that the Government can no longer satisfactorily operate within the bounds laid down by the Constitution, that instrument can be amended by the method which it prescribes."

Because of the lack of a five Justice majority in *Reid*, *Balzac* continues to be interpreted as binding authority. Indeed, although *Reid* far from settled the issue of the Constitution's application abroad, it certainly did not weaken the long held doctrine that fundamental constitutional rights cannot be denied in territories under the control of the American government, even where the United States technically is not considered "sovereign" and where the claimant is not a United States citizen.

The District of Columbia Circuit so recognized in a case this Court finds to be particularly relevant to the litigation presently under consideration. *Ralpho v. Bell*, 186 U.S. App. D.C. 368, 569 F.2d 607 (D.C. Cir. 1977), required the application of the Fifth Amendment to U.S. government activities in Micronesia, a "Trust Territory" pursuant to a United Nations designation under which the United States acted as administrator. More specifically, the case involved a constitutional challenge to the procedures undertaken by a commission created by Congress to compensate residents who suffered property damage as a result of American military activities against Japan during World War II. [T]he court concluded that at a minimum, due process was a "fundamental" right even with respect to property and that "it is settled that there cannot exist under the American flag any governmental authority untrammeled by the requirements of due process of law."

The Supreme Court again tried to bring some clarity to the issue of extraterritorial application of the Constitution when it reviewed the legality of the search and seizure by American government officials of items in the Mexican residence of a Mexican citizen charged with various narcotics-related offenses under U.S. law. *United States v. Verdugo-Urquidez*, 494 U.S. 259 (1990). Citing language from *Reid* that "the Constitution imposes substantive constraints on the Federal Government, even when it operates abroad," the Court of Appeals for the Ninth Circuit had ruled that the Fourth Amendment required the suppression of the evidence gained through the search, notwithstanding its conclusion that a search warrant obtained in the United States would have had no legal validity in Mexico. The Supreme Court reversed and began its analysis with a comparison of the language in the Fourth Amendment with the terminology in the Fifth and Sixth Amendments, noting that the Fourth Amendment is written to apply to "the people" while the Fifth and Sixth Amendments protect "person[s]" and the "accused." The Court interpreted the linguistic differences as evidence that the drafters of the Fourth Amendment intended it to protect the people of the United States rather than to impose restrictions on the government against nonresident aliens.

Perhaps more significant for purposes of these Guantanamo detainee cases, the majority opinion then addressed the Insular Cases and reaffirmed that in

U.S. territories, only "fundamental" constitutional rights are guaranteed. Accordingly, the Court concluded that the ability of noncitizens in foreign countries to invoke Fourth Amendment rights must be even weaker. Citing *Johnson v. Eisentrager*, the Court then declared, "Indeed, we have rejected the claim that aliens are entitled to Fifth Amendment rights outside the sovereign territory of the United States." The Court described its rejection in *Eisentrager* of the extraterritorial application of the Fifth Amendment as "emphatic," and concluded that if the Fifth Amendment, with the universal term "person," did not apply to aliens extraterritorially, then neither should the Fourth Amendment, which applies only to "the people."

[In] *Rasul v. Bush*, 124 S. Ct. 2686 (2004), the majority opinion addressed two grounds upon which a detainee traditionally could assert a right to habeas relief: statutory and constitutional. The *Rasul* majority interpreted *Eisentrager* to have focused primarily on the German detainees' lack of a constitutional right to habeas review, and distinguished the material facts upon which that portion of the *Eisentrager* decision relied from the circumstances concerning the Guantanamo Bay detainees. Among other distinguishing facts, the *Rasul* opinion emphasized that the Guantanamo Bay detainees were not citizens of countries formally at war with the United States, denied committing any war crimes or other violent acts, were never charged or convicted of wrongdoing, and – most significant to the present motion to dismiss – are imprisoned in "territory over which the United States exercises exclusive jurisdiction and control." Next, *Rasul* turned to the issue of statutory habeas jurisdiction and ruled that post-*Eisentrager* precedent required the recognition of statutory jurisdiction even over cases brought by petitioners held outside the territorial jurisdiction of any federal district court.

[P]erhaps the strongest basis for recognizing that the detainees have fundamental rights to due process rests at the conclusion of the *Rasul* majority opinion. In summarizing the nature of these actions, the Court recognized:

> Petitioners' allegations – that, although they have engaged neither in combat nor in acts of terrorism against the United States, they have been held in Executive detention for more than two years in territory subject to the long-term, exclusive jurisdiction and control of the United States, without access to counsel and without being charged with any wrongdoing – unquestionably describe "custody in violation of the Constitution or laws or treaties of the United States."

Given the *Rasul* majority's careful scrutiny of *Eisentrager*, it is difficult to imagine mat the Justices would have remarked that the petitions "unquestionably describe custody in violation of the Constitution or laws or treaties of the United States'" unless they considered the petitioners to be within a territory in which constitutional rights are guaranteed. Indeed, had the Supreme Court intended to uphold the D.C. Circuit's rejection in Al Odah of underlying constitutional rights, it is reasonable to assume that the majority would have included in its opinion at least a brief statement to that effect, rather than delay the ultimate resolution of this litigation and require the expenditure of additional judicial resources in the lower courts.

*US has
Full cntrl*

There would be nothing impracticable and anomalous in recognizing that the detainees at Guantanamo Bay have the fundamental right to due process of law under the Fifth Amendment. Recognizing the existence of that right at the Naval Base would not cause the United States government any more hardship than would recognizing the existence of constitutional rights of the detainees had they been held within the continental United States. American authorities are in full control at Guantanamo Bay, their activities are immune from Cuban law, and there are few or no significant remnants of native Cuban culture or tradition remaining that can interfere with the implementation of an American system of justice. [T]he imposition of constitutional rights would be less difficult at Guantanamo Bay than it was in any of the *Insular Cases*, where the courts were required to determine whether imposition of American rights such as the right to trial by jury and indictment by grand jury were even possible in places such as the Philippines and Puerto Rico with native legal systems and populations previously unexposed to American jurisprudence.

Of course, it would be far easier for the government to prosecute the war on terrorism if it could imprison all suspected "enemy combatants" at Guantanamo Bay without having to acknowledge and respect any constitutional rights of detainees. That, however, is not the relevant legal test. By definition, constitutional limitations often, if not always, burden the abilities of government officials to serve their constituencies. Although this nation unquestionably must take strong action under the leadership of the Commander in Chief to protect itself against enormous and unprecedented threats, that necessity cannot negate the existence of the most basic fundamental rights for which the people of this country have fought and died for well over two hundred years. As articulated by the Supreme Court after the conclusion of the Civil War:

> The Constitution of the United States is a law for rulers and people, equally in war and in peace, and covers with the shield of its protection all classes of men, at all times, and under all circumstances. No doctrine, involving more pernicious consequences, was ever invented by the wit of man than that any of its provisions can be suspended during any of the great exigencies of government. Such a doctrine leads directly to anarchy or despotism, but the theory of necessity on which it is based is false; for the government, within the Constitution, has all the powers granted to it, which are necessary to preserve its existence; as has been happily proved by the result of the great effort to throw off its just authority.

Ex Parte Milligan, 71 U.S. 2, 120-21 (1866). *See also United States v. Robel*, 389 U.S, 258, 264 (1967) ("It would indeed be ironic if, in the name of national defense, we would sanction the subversion of one of those liberties . . . which makes the defense of the Nation worthwhile.").

In sum, there can be no question that the Fifth Amendment right asserted by the Guantanamo detainees in this litigation – the right not to be deprived of liberty without due process of law – is one of the most fundamental rights recognized by the U.S. Constitution. In light of the Supreme Court's decision in *Rasul*, it is clear that Guantanamo Bay must be considered the equivalent of a U.S. territory in which fundamental constitutional rights apply. Accordingly, and under the precedent set forth in *Verdugo-Urquidez*, *Ralpho*, and the earlier *Insular Cases*, the respondents' contention that the Guantanamo detainees have no constitutional rights is rejected, and the Court recognizes the detainees' rights under the Due Process Clause of the Fifth Amendment.

B. SPECIFIC REQUIREMENTS OF THE FIFTH AMENDMENT'S DUE PROCESS CLAUSE

Having found that the Guantanamo detainees are entitled to due process under the Fifth Amendment to the United States Constitution, the Court must now address the exact contours of that right as it applies to the government's determinations that they are "enemy combatants." Due process is an inherently flexible concept, and the specific process due in a particular circumstance depends upon the context in which the right is asserted. Resolution of a due process challenge requires the consideration and weighing of three factors: the private interest of the person asserting the lack of due process; the risk of erroneous deprivation of that interest through use of existing procedures and the probable value of additional or substitute procedural safeguards; and the competing interests of the government, including the financial, administrative, and other burdens that would be incurred were additional safeguards to be provided.

The Supreme Court applied a *Mathews v. Eldridge* analysis in *Hamdi*, a decision issued the same day as *Rasul* which considered an American citizen's due process challenge to the U.S. military's designation of him as an "enemy combatant." Although none of the detainees in the cases before this Court is an American citizen, the facts under *Hamdi* are otherwise identical in all material respects to those in *Rasul*, Accordingly, *Hamdi* forms both the starting point and core of this Court's consideration of what process is due to the Guantanamo detainees in these cases.

In addressing the detainee's private interest in *Hamdi*, the plurality opinion called it "the most elemental of liberty interests – the interest in being free from physical detention by one's own government." Although the detainees in the cases before this Court are aliens and are therefore not being detained by their own governments, that fact does not lessen the significance of their interests in freedom from incarceration and from being held virtually incommunicado from the outside world. There is no practical difference between incarceration at the hands of one's own government and incarceration at the hands of a foreign government; significant liberty is deprived in both situations regardless of the jailer's nationality.

As was the case in *Hamdi*, the potential length of incarceration is highly relevant to the weighing of the individual interests at stake here. The government asserts the right to detain an "enemy combatant" until the war on terrorism has concluded or until the Executive, in its sole discretion, has determined that the individual no longest poses a threat to national security. The government, however, has been unable to inform the Court how long it believes the war on terrorism will last. Indeed, the government cannot even articulate at this moment how it will determine when the war on terrorism has ended. At a minimum, the government has conceded that the war could last several generations, thereby making it possible, if not likely, that "enemy combatants" will be subject to terras of life imprisonment at Guantanamo Bay. Short of the death penalty, life imprisonment is the ultimate deprivation of liberty, and the uncertainty of whether the war on terror – and thus the period of incarceration – will last a lifetime may be even worse than if the detainees had been tried, convicted, and definitively sentenced to a fixed term.

It must be added that the liberty interests of the detainees cannot be minimized for purposes of applying the balancing test by the government's allegations that they are in fact terrorists or are affiliated with terrorist organizations. The purpose of imposing a due process requirement is to prevent mistaken characterizations and erroneous detentions, and the government is not entitled to short circuit this inquiry by claiming ab initio that the individuals are alleged to have committed bad acts. Moreover, all petitioners in these cases have asserted that they are not terrorists and have not been involved in terrorist activities, and under the standards provided by the applicable rules of procedure, those allegations must be accepted as true for purposes of resolving the government's motion to dismiss.

On the other side of the *Mathews v. Eldridge* analysis is the government's significant interest in safeguarding national security. Having served as the Chief Judge of the United States Foreign Intelligence Surveillance Court (also known as "the FISA Court"), the focus of which involves national security and international terrorism, this Judge is keenly aware of the determined efforts of terrorist groups and others to attack this country and to harm American citizens both at home and abroad. Utmost vigilance is crucial for the protection of the United States of America. Of course, one of the government's most important obligations is to safeguard this country and its citizens by ensuring that those who have brought harm upon U.S. interests are not permitted to do so again. Congress itself expressly recognized this when it enacted the AUMF authorizing the President to use all necessary and appropriate force against those responsible for the September 11 attacks. The Supreme Court also gave significant weight to this governmental concern and responsibility in *Hamdi* when it addressed the "interests in ensuring that those who have in fact fought with the enemy during a war do not return to battle against the United States." The plurality warned against naivete regarding the dangers posed to the United States by terrorists and noted that the legislative and executive branches were in the best positions to deal with those dangers. As articulated by the plurality, "The law of war and the realities of combat may render . . . detentions both necessary and appropriate, and our due process analysis need not blink at those realities. Without doubt, our Constitution recognizes that core strategic matters of warmaking belong in the hands of those who are best positioned and most politically accountable for making them." Indeed, a majority of the Court affirmed the Executive's authority to seize and detain Taliban fighters as long as the conflict in Afghanistan continues, regardless of how indefinite the length of that war may be.

Given the existence of competing, highly significant interests on both sides of the equation – the liberty of individuals asserting complete innocence of any terrorist activity versus the obligation of the government to protect this country against terrorist attacks – the question becomes what procedures will help ensure that innocents are not indefinitely held as "enemy combatants" without imposing undue burdens on the military to ensure the security of this nation and its citizens.

According to the plurality in *Hamdi*, an individual detained by the government on the ground that he is an "enemy combatant" "must receive notice of the factual basis for his classification, and a fair opportunity to rebut the Government's factual assertions before a neutral decisionmaker." Noting the potential burden these requirements might cause the government at a time of ongoing military conflict, the plurality stated that it would not violate due process for the decision maker to consider hearsay as the most reliable available evidence. In addition, the plurality declared it permissible to adopt a presumption in favor of "enemy combatant" status, "so long as that presumption remained a rebuttable one and fair opportunity for rebuttal were provided." For that presumption to apply and for the onus to shift to the detainee, however, the plurality clarified that the government first would have to "put[] forth credible evidence that the [detainee] meets the enemy-combatant criteria."

After setting forth these standards, the plurality suggested the "possibility" that constitutional requirements of due process could be met by an "appropriately authorized and properly constituted military tribunal" and referenced the military tribunals used to determine whether an individual is entitled to prisoner of war status under the Geneva Convention. In the absence of a tribunal following constitutionally mandated procedures, however, the plurality declared that it was the District Court's obligation to provide those procedural rights to the detainee in a habeas action.

Hamdi was decided before the creation of the Combatant Status Review Tribunal, and the respondents contend in their motion to dismiss that were this Court to conclude that the detainees are entitled to due process under the Fifth Amendment, the CSRT proceedings would fully comply with all constitutional requirements. More specifically, the respondents claim that the CSRT regulations were modeled after Army Regulation 190-8 governing the determination of prisoner of war status, referenced in *Hamdi*, and actually exceed the requirements set forth by the *Hamdi* plurality. For example, respondents cite the facts that under CSRT rules, tribunal members must certify that they have not been involved in the "apprehension, detention, interrogation, or previous determination of status of the detainee[s]," that detainees are provided a "Personal Representative" to assist in the preparation of their cases, that the "Recorder" – that is, the person who presents evidence in support of "enemy combatant" status – must search for exculpatory evidence, that the detainee is entitled to an unclassified summary of the evidence against him, and that the tribunal's decisions are reviewed by a higher authority. Notwithstanding the procedures cited by the respondents, the Court finds that the procedures provided in the CSRT regulations fail to satisfy constitutional due process requirements in several respects.

C. SPECIFIC CONSTITUTIONAL DEFECTS IN THE CSRT PROCESS AS WRITTEN IN THE REGULATIONS AND AS APPLIED TO THE DETAINEES

The constitutional defects in the CSRT procedures can be separated into two categories. The first category consists of defects which apply across the board to all detainees in the cases before this Judge. Specifically, those deficiencies are the CSRT's failure to provide the detainees with access to material evidence upon which the tribunal affirmed their "enemy combatant" status and the failure to permit the assistance of counsel to compensate for the government's refusal to disclose classified information directly to the detainees. The second category of defects involves those which are detainee specific and may or may not apply to every petitioner in this litigation. Those defects include the manner in which the CSRT handled accusations of torture and the vague and potentially overbroad definition of "enemy combatant" in the CSRT regulations. While additional specific defects may or may not exist, further inquiry is unnecessary at this stage of the litigation given the fundamental deficiencies detailed below.

1. General Defects Existing in All Cases Before the Court: Failure to Provide Detainees Access to Material Evidence Upon Which the CSRT Affirmed "Enemy Combatant" Status and Failure to Permit the Assistance of Counsel

The CSRT reviewed classified information when considering whether each detainee presently before this Court should be considered an "enemy combatant," and it appears that all of the CSRT's decisions substantially relied upon classified evidence. No detainee, however, was ever permitted access to any classified information nor was any detainee permitted to have an advocate review and challenge the classified evidence on his behalf. Accordingly, the CSRT failed to provide any detainee with sufficient notice of the factual basis for which he is being detained and with a fair opportunity to rebut the government's evidence supporting the determination that he is an "enemy combatant."

The inherent lack of fairness of the CSRT's consideration of classified information not disclosed to the detainees is perhaps most vividly illustrated in the following unclassified colloquy, which, though taken from a case not presently before this Judge, exemplifies the practical and severe disadvantages faced by all Guantanamo prisoners. In reading a list of allegations forming the basis for the detention of Mustafa Ait Idr, the Recorder of the CSRT asserted, "While living in Bosnia, the Detainee associated with a known Al Qaida operative." In response, the following exchange occurred:

Detainee: Give me his name.

Tribunal President: I do not know.

Detainee: How can I respond to this?

Tribunal President: Did you know of anybody that was a member of Al Qaida?

Detainee: No, no.

Tribunal President: I'm sorry, what was your response?

Detainee: No.

Tribunal President: No?

Detainee: No. This is something the interrogators told me a long while ago. I asked the interrogators to tell me who this person was. Then I could tell you if I might have known this person, but not if this person is a terrorist. Maybe I knew this person as a friend. Maybe it was a person that worked with me. Maybe it was a person that was on my team. But I do not know if this person is Bosnian, Indian or whatever. If you tell me the name, then I can respond and defend myself against this accusation.

Tribunal President: We are asking you the questions and we need you to respond to what is on the unclassified summary.

Subsequently, after the Recorder read the allegation that the detainee was arrested because of his alleged involvement in a plan to attack the U.S. Embassy in Sarajevo, the detainee expressly asked in the following colloquy to see the evidence upon which the government's assertion relied:

Detainee: The only thing I can tell you is I did not plan or even think of [attacking the Embassy]. Did you find any explosives with me? Any weapons? Did you find me in front of the embassy? Did you find me in contact with the Americans? Did I threaten anyone? I am prepared now to tell you, if you have anything or any evidence, even if it is just very little, that proves I went to the embassy and looked like that [Detainee made a gesture with his head and neck as if he were looking into a building or a window] at the embassy, then I am ready to be punished. I can just tell you that I did not plan anything. Point by point, when we get to the point that I am associated with Al Qaida, but we already did that one.

Recorder: It was [the] statement that preceded the first point.

Detainee: If it is the same point, but I do not want to repeat myself. These accusations, my answer to all of them is I did not do these things. But I do not have anything to prove this. The only thing is the citizenship. I can tell you where I was and I had the papers to prove so. But to tell me I planned to bomb, I can only tell you that I did not plan.

Tribunal President: Mustafa, does that conclude your statement?

Detainee: That is it, but I was hoping you had evidence that you can give me. If I was in your place – and I apologize in advance for these words – but if a supervisor came to me and showed me accusations like these, I would take these accusations and I would hit him in the face with them. Sorry about that.

[Everyone in the Tribunal room laughs.]

Tribunal President: We had to laugh, but it is okay.

Detainee: Why? Because these are accusations that I can't even answer. I am not able to answer them. You tell me I am from Al Qaida, but I am not an Al Qaida. I don't have any proof to give you except to ask you to catch Bin Laden and ask him if I am a part of Al Qaida. To tell me that I thought, I'll just tell you that I did not. I don't have proof regarding this. What should be done is you should give me evidence regarding these accusations because I am not able to give you any evidence. I can just tell you no, and that is it.

The laughter reflected in the transcript is understandable, and this exchange might have been truly humorous had the consequences of the detainee's "enemy combatant" status not been so terribly serious and had the detainee's criticism of the process not been so piercingly accurate.

The Court fully appreciates the strong governmental interest in not disclosing classified evidence to individuals believed to be terrorists intent on causing great harm to the United States. Indeed, this Court's protective order prohibits the disclosure of any classified information to any of the petitioners in these habeas cases. To compensate for the resulting hardship to the petitioners and to ensure due process in the litigation of these cases, however, the protective order requires the disclosure of all relevant classified information to the petitioners' counsel who have the appropriate security clearances. Although counsel are not permitted to share any classified information with their clients, they at least have the opportunity to examine all evidence relied upon by the government in making an "enemy combatant" status determination and to investigate and ensure the accuracy, reliability and relevance of that evidence. Thus, the governmental and private interests have been fairly balanced in a manner satisfying constitutional due process requirements. In a similar fashion, the rules regulating the military commission proceedings for aliens – rules which the government so vigorously defended in *Hamdan v. Rumsfeld* – expressly provide that although classified evidence may be withheld from the defendant, it may not be withheld from defense counsel. In contrast, the CSRT regulations do not properly balance the detainees' need for access to material evidence considered by the tribunal against the government's interest in protecting classified information.

The CSRT regulations do acknowledge to some extent the detainees' need for assistance during the tribunal process, but they fall far short of the procedural protections that would have existed had counsel been permitted to participate. The implementing regulations create the position of "Personal Representative" for the purpose of "assisting the detainee in reviewing all relevant unclassified information, in preparing and presenting information, and in questioning witnesses at the CSRT." But notwithstanding the fact that the Personal Representative may review classified information considered by the tribunal, that person is neither a lawyer nor an advocate and thus cannot be considered an effective surrogate to compensate for a detainee's inability to personally review and contest classified evidence against him. Additionally, there is no confidential relationship between the detainee and the Personal Representative, and the Personal Representative is obligated to disclose to the tribunal any relevant inculpatory information he obtains from the detainee. Consequently, there is inherent risk and little corresponding benefit should the detainee decide to use the services of the Personal Representative.

In sum, the CSRT's extensive reliance on classified information in its resolution of "enemy combatant" status, the detainees' inability to review that information, and the prohibition of assistance by counsel jointly deprive the detainees of sufficient notice of the factual bases for their detention and deny them a fair opportunity to challenge their incarceration. These grounds alone are sufficient to find a violation of due process rights and to require the denial of the respondents' motion to dismiss these cases.

2. Specific Defects That May Exist in Individual Cases: Reliance on Statements Possibly Obtained Through Torture or Other Coercion and a Vague and Overly Broad Definition of "Enemy Combatant"

Additional defects in the CSRT procedures support the denial of the respondents' motion to dismiss at least some of the petitions, though these grounds may or may not exist in every case before the Court and though the respondents might ultimately prevail on these issues once the petitioners have been given an opportunity to litigate them fully in the habeas proceedings.

a. Reliance on Statements Possibly Obtained Through Torture or Other Coercion

The first of these specific grounds involves the CSRT's reliance on statements allegedly obtained through torture or otherwise alleged to have been provided by some detainees involuntarily. The Supreme Court has long held that due process prohibits the government's use of involuntary statements obtained through torture or other mistreatment, In the landmark case of *Jackson v. Denno*, 378 U.S. 368 (1964), the Court gave two rationales for this rule: first, "because of the probable unreliability of confessions that are obtained in a manner deemed coercive," and second because of the strongly felt attitude of our society that important human values are sacrificed where an agency of the government, in the course of securing a conviction, wrings a confession out of an accused against his will." Arguably, the second rationale may not be as relevant to these habeas cases as it is to criminal prosecutions in U.S. courts, given that the judiciary clearly does not have the supervisory powers over the U.S. military as it does over prosecutors, who are officers of the court. At a minimum, however, due process requires a thorough inquiry into the accuracy and reliability of statements alleged to have been obtained through torture.

Interpreting the evidence in a light most favorable to the petitioners as the Court must when considering the respondents' motion to dismiss, it can be reasonably inferred that the CSRT did not sufficiently consider whether the evidence upon, which the tribunal relied in making its "enemy" combatant" determinations was coerced from the detainees. The allegations and factual return of Mamdouh Habib are illustrative in this regard. Mr. Habib has alleged that after his capture by allied forces in Pakistan, he was sent to Egypt for interrogation and was subjected to torture there, including routine beatings to the point of unconsciousness. Additionally, the petitioner contends that he was locked in a room that would gradually be filled with water to a level just below his chin as he stood for hours on the tips of his toes. He further claims that he was suspended from a wall with his feet resting on the side of a large electrified cylindrical drum, which forced him either to suffer pain from hanging from his arms or pain from electric shocks to his feet. The petitioner asserts that as a result of this treatment, he made numerous "confessions" that can be proven false. According to the classified factual return for Mr. Habib, [redactions] and the CSRT found the allegations of torture serious enough to refer the matter to the Criminal Investigation Task Force. Examined in the light most favorable to the petitioner, this reliance cannot be viewed to have satisfied the requirements of due process.

Mr. Habib is not the only detainee before this Court to have alleged making confessions to interrogators as a result of torture. Notwithstanding the inability of counsel for petitioners to take formal discovery beyond interviewing their clients at Guantanamo Bay, they have introduced evidence into the public record indicating that abuse of detainees occurred during interrogations not only in foreign countries but at Guantanamo Bay itself. One illustration of alleged mistreatment during interrogation by U.S. authorities is [a document filed by petitioners]. In that document, dated August 2, 2004, the author, apparently affiliated with the Federal Bureau of Investigation but whose identity has been redacted, summarized his or her observations of interrogation activities at Guantanamo Bay as follows:

> On a couple of occassions [sic], I entered interview rooms to find a detainee chained hand and foot in a fetal position to the floor, with no chair, food, or water. Most times they had urinated or defacated [sic] on themselves, and had been left there for 18-24 hours or more. On one occassion [sic], the air conditioning had been turned down so far and the temperature was so cold in the room, that the barefooted detainee was shaking with cold. When I asked the MP's what was going on, I was told that interrogators from the day prior had ordered this treatment, and the detainee was not to be moved. On another occassion [sic], the A/C had been turned off, making the temperature in the unventilated room probably well over 100 degrees. The detainee was almost unconcious [sic] on the floor, with a pile of hair next to him. He had apparently been literally pulling his own hair out throughout the night. On another occassion [sic], not only was the temperature unbearably hot, but extremely loud rap music was being played in the room, and had been since the day before, with the detainee chained hand and foot in the fetal position on the tile floor.

The identities of the detainees referenced in this document are unknown to the Court and therefore, it is not certain whether they are even petitioners in any of these cases and, if so, whether the results of the above-described interrogations were used against them in CSRT proceedings. Of course, the veracity of Exhibit D itself must be investigated before it can be definitively relied upon. Indeed, at this stage of the litigation it is premature to make any final determination as to whether any information acquired during interrogations of any petitioner in these cases and relied upon by the CSRT was in fact the result of torture or other mistreatment. What this Court needs to resolve at this juncture, however, is whether the petitioners have made sufficient allegations to allow their claims to survive the respondents' motion to dismiss. On that count, the Court concludes that the petitioners have done so.

   b. Vague and Overly Broad Definition of "Enemy Combatant"

Although the government has been detaining individuals as "enemy combatants" since the issuance of the AUMF in 2001, it apparently did not formally define the term until the July 7, 2004 Order creating the CSRT. The lack of a formal definition seemed to have troubled at least the plurality of the Supreme Court in *Hamdi*, but for purposes of resolving the issues in that case, the plurality considered the government's definition to be an individual who was "part of or supporting forces hostile to the United States or coalition partners in Afghanistan and who engaged in an armed conflict against the United States there." The Court agreed with the government that the AUMF authorizes the Executive to detain individuals falling within that limited definition, with the plurality explaining that "because detention to prevent a combatant's return to the battlefield is a fundamental incident of waging war, in permitting the use of necessary and appropriate force, Congress has clearly and unmistakably authorized detention in the narrow circumstances considered here." The plurality cautioned, however, "that indefinite detention for the purpose of interrogation is not authorized" by the AUMF, and added that a congressional grant of authority to the President to use "necessary and appropriate force" might not be properly interpreted to include the authority to detain individuals for the duration of a particular conflict if that conflict does not take a form that is based on "longstanding law-of-war principles."

The definition of "enemy combatant" contained in the Order creating the CSRT is significantly broader than the definition considered in *Hamdi*. According to the definition currently applied by the government, an "enemy combatant" "shall mean an individual who was part of or supporting Taliban or al Qaeda forces, or associated forces that are engaged in hostilities against the United States or its coalition partners. This includes any person who has committed a belligerent act or has directly supported hostilities in aid of enemy armed forces." Use of the word "includes" indicates that the government interprets the AUMF to permit the indefinite detention of individuals who never committed a belligerent act or who never directly supported hostilities against the U.S. or its allies. This Court explored the government's position on the matter by posing a series of hypothetical questions to counsel at the December 1, 2004 hearing on the motion to dismiss. In response to the hypotheticals, counsel for the respondents argued that the Executive has the authority to detain the following individuals until the conclusion of the war on terrorism: "[a] little old lady in Switzerland who writes checks to what she thinks is a charity that helps orphans in Afghanistan but [what] really is a front to finance al-Qaeda activities," a person who teaches English to the son of an al Qaeda member, and a journalist who knows the location of Osama Bin Laden but refuses to disclose it to protect her source.

The Court can unequivocally report that no factual return submitted by the government in this litigation reveals the detention of a Swiss philanthropist, an English teacher, or a journalist. The Court can also acknowledge the existence of specific factual returns containing evidence indicating that certain detainees fit the narrower definition of "enemy combatant" approved by the Supreme Court in *Hamdi*. The petitioners have argued in opposition to the respondents' motion to dismiss, however, that at least with respect to some detainees, the expansive definition of "enemy combatant" currently in use in the CSRT proceedings violates long standing principles of due process by permitting the detention of individuals based solely on their membership in anti-American organizations rather than on actual activities supporting the use of violence or harm against the United States.

Whether the detention of each individual petitioner is authorized by the AUMF and satisfies the mandates of due process must ultimately be determined on a detainee by detainee basis. At this stage of the litigation, however, sufficient allegations have been made by at least some of the petitioners and certain evidence exists in some CSRT factual returns to warrant the denial of the respondents' motion to dismiss on the ground that the respondents have employed an overly broad definition of "enemy combatant."

[T]he unclassified evidence upon which the CSRT relied in determining Murat Kurnaz's "enemy combatant" status consisted of findings that he was "associated" with an Islamic missionary group named Jama'at-Al-Tabliq, that he was an "associate" of and planned to travel to Pakistan with an individual who later engaged in a suicide bombing, and that he accepted free food, lodging, and schooling in Pakistan from an organization known to support terrorist acts. While these facts may be probative and could be used to bolster the credibility of other evidence, if any, establishing actual activities undertaken to harm American interests, by themselves they fall short of establishing that the detainee took any action or provided any direct support for terrorist actions against the U.S. or its allies. Nowhere does any unclassified evidence reveal that the detainee even had knowledge of his associate's planned suicide bombing, let alone establish that the detainee assisted in the bombing in any way. In fact, the detainee expressly denied knowledge of a bombing plan when he was informed of it by the American authorities. Absent other evidence, it would appear that the government is indefinitely holding the detainee – possibly for life – solely because of his contacts with individuals or organizations tied to terrorism and not because of any terrorist activities that the detainee aided, abetted, or undertook himself. Such detention, even if found to be authorized by the AUMF, would be a violation of due process. Accordingly, the detainee is entitled to fully litigate the factual basis for his detention in these habeas proceedings and to have a fair opportunity to prove that he is being detained on improper grounds.

Similar defects might also exist with respect to the detention of Jamil El-Banna. At the CSRT proceedings, the tribunal concluded that the detainee was an "enemy combatant" on the ground that he was "part of or supporting Al Qaida forces." The CSRT reached this conclusion notwithstanding the Personal Representative's position that it was unsupported by the record before the tribunal. During the CSRT proceedings, the tribunal rejected two grounds cited by the Recorder in support of the detainee's "enemy combatant" status. First, although the detainee was alleged to have been indicted by a Spanish National High Court Judge for membership in a terrorist organization, the tribunal did not find any evidence relating to that indictment "helpful in establishing the detainee's association with Al Qaida." Second, although the detainee was alleged to have attempted "to board an airplane with equipment that resembled a homemade electronic device" [redacted].

Even accepting these factual conclusions as true, a serious legal question exists as to whether such activities would be sufficient to detain the petitioner at Guantanamo Bay indefinitely without formally charging him with a crime. *See Hamdi* ("The purpose of detention is to prevent captured individuals from returning to the field of battle and taking up arms once again.") and ("If the practical circumstances of a given conflict are entirely unlike those of the conflicts that informed the development of the law of war, that understanding [that the AUMF allows indefinite detention] may unravel."). In any event, however, final resolution of that question must be left for another day because at this stage of the proceedings, the Court must interpret the facts in the light most favorable to the party opposing a motion to dismiss. Under that approach, evidence in the record can be fairly interpreted to conclude that the petitioner is being detained indefinitely not because [redacted].

It may well turn out that after the detainee is given a fair opportunity to challenge his detention in a habeas proceeding, the legality of his detention as an "enemy combatant" will be upheld and he will continue to be held at Guantanamo Bay until the end of the war on terrorism or until the government determines he no longer poses a threat to U.S. security. It is also possible, however, that once given a fair opportunity to litigate his case, the detainee will establish that he is being indefinitely detained not because of anything he has done and not to prevent his return to any "battlefield," metaphorical or otherwise, but simply because and the respondents' motion to dismiss must therefore be denied.

This concludes the Court's analysis of the due process issues arising from the respondents' motion to dismiss. Nothing written above should be interpreted to require the immediate release of any detainee, nor should the conclusions reached be considered to have fully resolved whether or not sufficient evidence exists to support the continued detention of any petitioner. The respondents' motion to dismiss asserted that no evidence exists and that the petitioners could make no factual allegations which, if taken as true, would permit the litigation of these habeas cases to proceed further. For the reasons stated above, the Court has concluded otherwise. The Court, however, has not addressed all arguments made by the petitioners in opposition to the respondents' motion to dismiss, and it may be that the CSRT procedures violate due process requirements for additional reasons not addressed in this Memorandum Opinion. In any event, and as *Hamdi* acknowledged, in the absence of military tribunal proceedings that comport with constitutional due process requirements, it is the obligation of the court receiving a habeas petition to provide the petitioner with a fair opportunity to challenge the government's factual basis for his detention. Accordingly, the accompanying Order requests input from counsel regarding how these cases should proceed in light of this Memorandum Opinion.

D. CLAIMS BASED ON THE GENEVA CONVENTIONS

The petitioners have also asserted claims based on the Geneva Conventions, which regulate the treatment of certain prisoners of war and civilians. The respondents contend that all Geneva Convention claims filed by the petitioners must be dismissed because Congress has not enacted any separate legislation specifically granting individuals the right to file private lawsuits based on the Conventions and because the Conventions are not "self-executing," meaning they do not by themselves create such a private right of action. In the alternative, the respondents argue that even if the Geneva Conventions are self-executing, they do not apply to members of al Qaeda because that international terrorist organization is not a state party to the Conventions. Finally, although respondents concede that Afghanistan is a state party to the Conventions and admit that the Geneva Conventions apply to Taliban detainees, they emphasize that President Bush has determined that Taliban fighters are not entitled to prisoner of war status under the Third Geneva Convention and contend that this decision is the final word on the matter.

The Third and Fourth Geneva Conventions do not expressly grant private rights of action, and whether they impliedly create such rights has never been definitively resolved by the D.C. Circuit. The Court of Appeals is currently reviewing the matter in the appeal of *Hamdan v. Rumsfeld*, but until that court issues a definitive ruling, this Court must make its own determination. After reviewing *Hamdan* and the briefs filed by petitioners and respondents in the instant cases, the Court concludes that the Conventions are self-executing and adopts the following reasoning provided by Judge Robertson:

> Because the Geneva Conventions were written to protect individuals, because the Executive Branch of our government has implemented the Geneva Conventions for fifty years without questioning the absence of implementing legislation, because Congress clearly understood that the Conventions did not require implementing legislation except in a few specific areas, and because nothing in the Third Geneva Convention itself manifests the contracting parties' intention that it not become effective as domestic law without the enactment of implementing legislation, I conclude that, insofar as it is pertinent here, the Third Geneva Convention is a self-executing treaty.

Although the Court rejects the primary basis argued by the respondents for dismissal of claims based on the Geneva Conventions, it does accept one of the alternative grounds put forth in their motion, namely that the Geneva Conventions do not apply to al Qaeda. Clearly, al Qaeda is not a "High Contracting Party" to the Conventions, and thus individuals detained on the ground that they are members of that terrorist organization are not entitled to the protections of the treaties.

This does not end the analysis for purposes of resolving the respondents' motion to dismiss, however, because some of the petitioners in the above-captioned cases are being detained either solely because they were Taliban fighters or because they were associated with both the Taliban and al Qaeda. Significantly, the respondents concede that the Geneva Conventions apply to the Taliban detainees in light of the fact that Afghanistan is a High Contracting Party to the Conventions. They argue in their motion to dismiss, however, that notwithstanding the application of the Third Geneva Convention to Taliban detainees, the treaty does not protect Taliban detainees because the President has declared that no Taliban fighter is a "prisoner of war" as defined by the

Convention. The respondents' argument in this regard must be rejected, however, for the Third Geneva Convention does not permit the determination of prisoner of war status in such a conclusory fashion.

Article 4 of the Third Geneva Convention defines who is considered a "prisoner of war" under the treaty. If there is any doubt as to whether individuals satisfy the Article 4 prerequisites, Article 5 entitles them to be treated as prisoners of war "until such time as their status has been determined by a competent tribunal." Army Regulation 190-8 created the rules for the "competent tribunal" referenced in Article 5 of the Third Geneva Convention, and the CSRT was established in accordance with that provision.

def of POW (handwritten)

Nothing in the Convention itself or in Army Regulation 190-8 authorizes the President of the United States to rule by fiat that an entire group of fighters covered by the Third Geneva Convention falls outside of the Article 4 definitions of "prisoners of war." To the contrary, and as Judge Robertson ruled in *Hamdan*, the President's broad characterization of how the Taliban generally fought the war in Afghanistan cannot substitute for an Article 5 tribunal's determination on an individualized basis of whether a particular fighter complied with the laws of war or otherwise falls within an exception denying him prisoner of war status. Clearly, had an appropriate determination been properly made by an Article 5 tribunal that a petitioner was not a prisoner of war, that petitioner's claims based on the Third Geneva Convention could not survive the respondents' motion to dismiss. But although numerous petitioners in the above-captioned cases were found by the CSRT to have been Taliban fighters, nowhere do the CSRT records for many of those petitioners reveal specific findings that they committed some particular act or failed to satisfy some defined prerequisite entitling the respondents to deprive them of prisoner of war status. Accordingly, the Court denies that portion of the respondents' motion to dismiss addressing the Geneva Convention claims of those petitioners who were found to be Taliban fighters but who were not specifically determined to be excluded from prisoner of war status by a competent Article 5 tribunal.

Pres not authorized to decide (handwritten)

E. DISMISSAL OF REMAINING CLAIMS

Upon review of the remaining causes of action asserted by the various petitioners in these cases, the Court concludes that the respondents are entitled to dismissal of the claims not addressed in the preceding sections of this Memorandum Opinion. The Court agrees with the respondents that claims based on the Sixth, Eighth, and Fourteenth Amendments to the Constitution are not sustainable because the Sixth Amendment applies only to criminal proceedings, because the Eighth Amendment applies only after an individual is convicted of a crime, and because the Fourteenth Amendment applies only to the states and not to the federal government. Finally, having found that all detainees possess Fifth Amendment due process rights and that some detainees possibly possess rights under the Geneva Conventions, it is unnecessary to look to customary international law to resolve the petitioners' claims.

III. CONCLUSION

For the reasons provided above, the Court holds that the petitioners have stated valid claims under the Fifth Amendment and that the CSRT procedures are unconstitutional for foiling to comport with the requirements of due process. Additionally, the Court holds that Taliban fighters who have not been specifically determined to be excluded from prisoner of war status by a competent Article 5 tribunal have also stated valid claims under the Third Geneva Convention. Finally, the Court concludes that the remaining claims of the petitioners must be denied. Accordingly, this Memorandum Opinion is accompanied by a separate Order denying in part and granting in part the respondents' Motion to Dismiss or for Judgment as a Matter of Law.

This Judge began her participation as the coordinator of these cases on August 17, 2004, and her involvement will soon be ending. These cases have always remained before the original Judges assigned to them and only particular issues or motions were referred to this Judge for resolution. Therefore, there will be no need to transfer the cases back to those Judges. In the interest of the effective management of this litigation, however, the accompanying Order requests briefing from counsel on an expedited basis regarding their views as to how these cases should proceed in light of this Memorandum Opinion and this Judge's imminent departure.

NOTES AND QUESTIONS

1. *Khalid v. Bush*, 2005 U.S. Dist. LEXIS 749 (D.D.C. 2005) was one of the cases retained by the original judge as mentioned by Judge Green. Judge Leon issued his decision 12 days before Judge Green released hers. Judge Leon concluded that due process did not apply to aliens detained outside the United States (relying on *Eisentrager*), that the Geneva Convention was not self-executing, and that international law provided no cognizable rights to the detainees.

2. The *Khalid* opinion dealt with the question of constitutional rights and habeas jurisdiction by separating the two, holding that *Rasul* did not impliedly overrule *Eisentrager*. By contrast, the *In re* opinion engages in an extensive review of cases before and after *Eisentrager* to determine that at least due process applies to aliens detained on soil under the exclusive control of the U.S. For the Supreme Court to hold in *Rasul* that the courts have power to entertain the petition, did it necessarily hold that there must be some rights that pertain to the petitioners? How can there be jurisdiction in the absence of a claim of right? This is the conundrum presented by Justice Stevens' footnote 15. If *Khalid* is correct, then what is the point of *Rasul*? On the other hand, isn't it odd that the Court would make such an important decision without stating it?

3. Judge Leon held that detention was authorized by Congress but then found that the petitioners could not identify any rights protecting them under federal law. With regard to treaty law, they "conceded at oral argument that [the Geneva] Convention does not apply because these petitioners were not captured in the 'zone of hostilities . . . in and around Afghanistan.'" The combination of these two holdings seems to place the alleged terrorist within authorization to use executive force but outside the protection of any law other than international law. Of course, the Geneva Conventions are not the only source of international law but the petitioners seem to have made no arguments under international other than with respect to their conditions of confinement.

    a. Is the court correct to view allegations regarding conditions of confinement as failing to state a claim regarding the basis of confinement?

    b. What about Professor Paust's argument that customary international law requires some level of judicial review to prevent "arbitrary" confinement? Do you think that other countries have no interest in our imprisoning their citizens? Can the U.S. run around the world apprehending and detaining anyone we want with no controls?

    4. *Khalid* raises what may be the ultimate question to which this course is addressed: what law applies in dealing with terrorists around the world. Is it permissible for U.S. agents to apprehend suspects wherever they may be found? without probable cause? to imprison them without due process? to shoot them?

Note on the Emergence of "Private Military Firms"

A number of the persons alleged to have been involved in prisoner abuse, both in Iraq and Afghanistan, have been employed by private contractors. To the extent that the contractor is a company working directly for the U.S. Government, application of basic federal criminal law might be enhanced by special provisions applying to federal contracts. But the Uniform Code of Military Justice would be of doubtful applicability to anyone not in the uniformed services. The UCMJ applies to "in time of war, persons serving with or accompanying an armed force in the field." A critical question, regardless of whether the UCMJ applies, is simply whether the private military operative is subject to the command structure of the U.S. military.

By some estimates, "private military firms" (PMF's) make up a $100 billion industry. In centuries past, many nations relied on mercenaries to fight their battles. With the Treaty of Westphalia in 1769 and the rise of the "nation-state," nations began to assemble armies from their own citizenry, wars were fought by soldiers who bore allegiance to the sovereign by virtue of their nationality and not just by oath, and military force became the exclusive province of the sovereign. As a corollary, it became possible to enforce distinctions between combatants and noncombatants more rigorously than had been the case, producing the 20th Century treaties such as the Geneva Conventions. In the emerging privatization of military force, these distinctions may once again become more blurred.

The Atlantic Monthly provided a list of the largest private military contracts as of August 2004, which included a number in Iraq such as:

    ▸ Creating a new Iraqi police force, $50 million for the first year (2003): DynCorp.

    ▸ Training a new Iraqi army, $48 million (2003): Vinnell Corp. The contract called for Vinnell to train nine battalions; more than half of the first completed battalion later abandoned the army.

    ▸ Protecting Iraq's oil pipeline, $39.2 million (2003-present): Erinys International. The job requires 14,500 guards.

▸ Providing interrogation services in Iraq, $19.9 million (2003-present): CACI Systems. At least two contractors, one from CACI and one from Titan Corp., have been implicated in the Abu Ghraib scandal.

Matthew Quirk, *Private Military Contractors: A buyer's Guide*, Atlantic Monthly Online, Sept 2004 (*http://www.theatlantic.com/doc/prem/200409/quirk*)

While many of these firms initially found work in the disintegrating states of Africa, it is in Iraq that the private military industry has truly come into its own. The raid on the home of Ahmed Chalabi was overseen by armed civilians who work for DynCorp; two Americans suspected of committing abuses in Abu Ghraib prison were civilian contractors employed to assist interrogations; the four armed Americans murdered in Falluja in March worked for Blackwater USA; Paul Bremer, the chief American administrator in Iraq, was guarded during his tenure not by military personnel but by a team of heavily armed commandos in civilian clothes, who also happened to work for Blackwater. Headline by headline, a picture has begun to take shape over the last year: our military is being privatized before our eyes.

Patrick Radden Keefe, *Iraq: America's Private Armies*, NEW YORK REVIEW OF BOOKS (8/12/04).

One particularly compelling story is that of the Sierra Leone government which was threatened with imminent overthrow by a rebel force and called on a private military company from South Africa. The PMF arrived replete with military aircraft and tanks, ran the rebels back into the hills, and destroyed their bases. P.W. SINGER, CORPORATE WARRIORS: THE RISE OF THE PRIVATIZED MILITARY INDUSTRY (2004). Quirk reports that the private firm then engineered a coup and a new government even more sympathetic to their interests.

Among the factors often cited for the rise of privatized military forces are the need for experts to maintain and control highly sophisticated weapons systems, the scaling back of the uniformed services in the wake of the Cold War, and the resulting "stretched thin" configuration of the American military around the world. Given that this phenomenon is likely to increase unless specific action is taken to curtail it, we should consider some of the possible legal ramifications.

1. How close a connection to the U.S. Government will be required to make a "civilian" subject to federal laws on use of excessive force or abuse of power? For example, if A, a private construction company, has a contract from the U.S. to build a power plant in another country and employs B, a PMF, to guard its facilities and employees, are the agents of B to be considered federal agents for purposes of federal law?

2. It seems clear that employees of a PMF are not in the uniformed services for purposes of the Uniform Code of Military Justice. But should the uniformed officers who enter into these agreements be responsible for exercising discipline over these agents? In this regard, recall the *Yamashita* case. How can the military exert control and discipline over the PMF's?

3. The same questions need to be asked regarding the application of international conventions. The answer may be different for the Geneva Convention that it would be for the Convention on Torture.

Protocol I to the Geneva Convention of 1949 (1977) (to which the United States is not a Party) contains this language:

Art 47. Mercenaries

1. A mercenary shall not have the right to be a combatant or a prisoner of war.

2. A mercenary is any person who:
(a) is specially recruited locally or abroad in order to fight in an armed conflict;
(b) does, in fact, take a direct part in the hostilities;
(c) is motivated to take part in the hostilities essentially by the desire for private gain and, in fact, is promised, by or on behalf of a Party to the conflict, material compensation substantially in excess of that promised or paid to combatants of similar ranks and functions in the armed forces of that Party;
(d) is neither a national of a Party to the conflict nor a resident of territory controlled by a Party to the conflict;
(e) is not a member of the armed forces of a Party to the conflict; and
(f) has not been sent by a State which is not a Party to the conflict on official duty as a member of its armed forces.

SELECTED READINGS

General Treatments of Military Action in Terrorism Context:

- PHILLIP B. HEYMANN, TERRORISM AND AMERICA (1998).
- PHILLIP B. HEYMANN, TERRORISM, FREEDOM, AND SECURITY (2004).
- ALEXANDER T.J. LENNON (ED.), THE BATTLE FOR HEARTS AND MINDS (2004).
- *Symposium on Terrorism, War, and Justice*, 114 ETHICS 647 (2004).
- SEYMOUR M. HERSH, CHAIN OF COMMAND (2004).
- Ronald J. Sievert, *War on Terrorism or Global Law Enforcement Operation?*, 78 NOTRE DAME L. REV. 307 (2003)

Critiques of the Military Commissions Order:

- Jack Goldsmith & Cass R. Sunstein, *Military Tribunals and Legal Culture: What a Difference Sixty Years Makes*, 19 CONST. COMM. 261 (2002) (commenting on the difference in reaction between 1942 and 2002).
- A. Christopher Bryant & Carl Tobias, Quirin *Revisited*, 2003 WIS. L. REV. 309.
- Carl Tobias, *Detentions, Military Commissions, Terrorism, and Domestic Case Precedent*, 76 SO. CAL. L. REV. 1371 (2003).
- Phillip B. Heymann, *Civil Liberties and Human Rights in the Aftermath of September 11*, 25 HARV. J.L. & PUB. POL'Y 441 (2002) ("foolhardy disdain for American pride in, and foreign admiration of, the fairness of our courts").

- Neal K. Katyal & Laurence H. Tribe, *Waging War, Deciding Guilt: Trying the Military Tribunals*, 111 YALE L.J. 1259 (2002) ("flatly unconstitutional").

- Ruth Wedgwood, *Al Qaeda, Terrorism, and Military Commissions*, 96 AM. J. INT'L L. 328 (2002) (valid under both international and constitutional standards).

- Joan Fitzpatrick, *Jurisdiction of Military Commissions and the Ambiguous War on Terrorism*, 96 AM. J. INT'L L. 345 (2002) ("legally insupportable").

- Christopher M. Evans, *Terrorism on Trial: The President's Constitutional Authority To Order the Prosecution of Suspected Terrorists by Military Commissions*, 51 DUKE L.J. 1831 (2002) (valid by constitution but against international law).

Detention Without Trial:

- Wayne McCormack, *Military Detention and the Judiciary: Al Qaeda, the KKK, and Supra-State Law*, 5 S. DIEGO INT'L L.J. 7 (2004).

Chapter 9

INTERROGATION & EMERGENCY POWERS

In the spring of 2004, two separate issues emerged as potential difficulties for the U.S. military. There is not a necessary logical connection between the two phenomena, but they are related in some degree and both certainly have implications for the future of the American military. First came the disclosures of widespread prisoner abuse at the Abu Ghraib Prison in Iraq, followed by disclosures of similar occurrences at Guantanamo Bay and releases of high-level memoranda attempting to justify harsh interrogation of prisoners. The second revelation occurred when three "American civilians" were arrested by Afghan authorities allegedly in the act of torturing Afghan rebels. When put on trial, the three claimed to be working for the U.S. Government in some capacity or at least to be seeking information by which they could claim the multi-million dollar reward offered for the capture of bin Laden. Shortly thereafter, a book appeared on the market detailing the extent to which "civilian contractors" have begun to make up what is coming to be called the Private Military Industry.

These "problems" should be viewed together with the 9/11 Commission's recommendation for revamping the nation's intelligence apparatus. The general theme of this chapter is acquisition of information in foreign countries.

§ 9.01 INTERROGATION & TORTURE REVISITED

The "prisoner abuse" scandal that first broke with the public disclosure of photos from Abu Ghraib prison has challenged the credibility and moral position of the U.S. in the world community. Caleb Carr, urging an approach of "limited progressive war," reminded us before the Iraqi invasion of Vattel's admonition that

> the rights founded on the state of war, . . . do not, externally and between mankind, depend on the justice of the cause, but on the legality of the means in themselves. . . . If you once open the door for continual accusation of outrageous excess in hostilities, you will only augment the number of complaints, and influence the minds of the contending parties with increasing animosity: fresh injuries will be perpetually springing up; and the sword will never be sheathed till one of the parties be utterly destroyed.

EMMERICH DE VATTEL, THE LAW OF NATIONS (1758), *as quoted by* CALEB CARR, THE LESSONS OF TERROR 106-07 (2002).

The current "prisoner abuse" scandal is a matter of current events that have not settled sufficiently to allow in-depth treatment in this volume. We will refer only to a handful of the official reports after a more detailed look at international law on torture and interrogation techniques.

As the Israeli Supreme Court points out in the opinion below, interrogation is inherently coercive and effective interrogation requires understanding of, if not active empathy with, the situation of the detainee. "As the Abu Ghraib scandal reveals, some guards and interrogators can be sadistic ghouls; but many other interrogators could qualify as the most liberal people in the armed services since, for one thing, they have spent years studying the language and the history of their captives. As one Special Forces officer told me in Afghanistan, 'In order to defeat the enemy you first have to love him, and his culture.'" Robert D. Kaplan, *The Interrogators ' and Torture ᷄ Hard Questions*, N.Y. TIMES (January 23, 2005). Kaplan and the Israeli Court also agree that setting specific rules for interrogation in advance is not a productive exercise because the interrogator must constantly revise strategy in light of both how the detainee is feeling and what information is available from whatever source.

[A] THE INTERNATIONAL SCENE

You will recall that the *Pinochet* case discussed the ways in which prohibitions on official torture become part of the domestic law of an Anglo-American legal system. The U.S. has ratified the Convention on Torture and has implemented it through 18 U.S.C. § 2340. One interesting feature of the statute is that its scope is limited by § 2340A to actions "outside the United States." In theory, this should not be of any great significance because § 2340B points out that nothing "shall be construed as precluding the application of State or local laws on the same subject," and all federal laws prohibiting the use of excessive force by federal agents would also be applicable to actions taken within the U.S.

As background to discussion of aggressive interrogation and prisoner abuse, bear in mind the controversy over the "ticking bomb scenario" made famous by Professor Alan Dershowitz, in WHY TERRORISM SUCCEEDS (2000). The scenario posits that no sane person would refuse to torture a terrorist who knows the location of a bomb that is set to go off in a crowded location before protracted interrogation could be expected to produce results. Dershowitz contends that courts should provide oversight of torture by issuing a torture warrant rather than leaving the matter to be resolved either by prosecutorial discretion or the defense of necessity.

Further elaboration of interrogation techniques in the context of terrorism investigations is contained in Mark Bowden, *The Dark Art of Interrogation*, ATLANTIC MONTHLY (Oct. 2003), which describes some of the "aggressive interrogation" techniques of investigators around the world. So far as Bowden discovered, no country at that time sanctioned the use of these techniques, although many investigators admitted that they might be used on occasion in clandestine fashion. Bowden specifically stated that the Bush Administration took the view that these techniques would not be permitted. The principal techniques highlighted in the article were nakedness in cold conditions, sleep deprivation, playing on fears (such as personal fear of dogs or threats to family members), maintaining painful positions for extended periods of time, alternating terrible food with treats.

REPUBLIC OF IRELAND v. UNITED KINGDOM
European Court of Human Rights
(Series A, No 25) (1979-80) 2 EHRR 25

HEADNOTE:

The British Government, faced with serious acts of terrorism perpretrated by members of the Irish Republican Army (IRA) and Loyalist groups in Northern Ireland, introduced special powers of arrest and detention without trial, which were widely used, chiefly against the IRA. Notices of derogation under Article 15(1) were lodged with the Secretary-General of the Council of Europe in view of the 'public emergency threatening the life of the nation'. The Government of the Republic of Ireland brought an application before the Commission alleging, inter alia, (i) that the extrajudicial detention infringed Article 5 (right to liberty) and was not saved by Article 15; (ii) that various interrogation practices – in particular the so-called 'five techniques', which included wall-standing, hooding and deprivation of sleep and food – and other practices to which suspects were subjected amounted to torture and inhuman or degrading treatment contrary to Article 3; and (iii) that the use of the special powers primarily against IRA members constituted discrimination in violation of Article 14. The Commission unanimously found that the five techniques did constitute a practice of torture and that other practices amounted to inhuman and degrading treatment; but that there was no infringement of Article 14, and the derogations from Article 5 were justified under Article 15. The applicant Government referred the case to the Court (although the offending practices had been discontinued and the respondent Government did not contest the allegations or the findings in connection with the five techniques), renewing its original submissions and asking the Court in addition to address a consequential order to the British Government requiring it to institute criminal and disciplinary proceedings against the particular persons responsible for the breaches of Article 3. The case was heard by the plenary Court.

FACTS:

11. The tragic and lasting crisis in Northern Ireland lies at the root of the present case. In order to combat what the respondent Government describes as 'the longest and most violent terrorist campaign witnessed in either part of the island of Ireland', the authorities in Northern Ireland exercised from August 1971 until December 1975 a series of extrajudicial powers of arrest, detention and internment. The proceedings in this case concern the scope and the operation in practice of those measures as well as the alleged ill-treatment of persons thereby deprived of their liberty.

12. Up to March 1975, over 1,100 people had been killed, over 11,500 injured and more than £140,000,000 worth of property destroyed during the recent troubles in Northern Ireland. This violence found its expression in part in civil disorders, in part in terrorism, that is, organised violence for political ends.

34. It was against the background outlined above that on 9 August 1971 the Northern Ireland Government brought into operation extrajudicial measures of detention and internment of suspected terrorists. From then until 7 November

1972, when certain of the Special Powers Regulations were replaced, the authorities in Northern Ireland in fact exercised four such extrajudicial powers: (i) arrest for interrogation purposes during 48 hours; (ii) arrest and remand in custody; (iii) detention of an arrested person; and (iv) internment.

96. Twelve persons arrested on 9 August 1971 and two persons arrested in October 1971 were singled out and taken to one or more unidentified centres. There, between 11 and 17 August and 11 to 18 October respectively, they were submitted to a form of 'interrogation in depth' which involved the combined application of five particular techniques. These methods, sometimes termed 'disorientation' or 'sensory deprivation' techniques, were not used in any cases other than the 14 so indicated above. The techniques consisted of the following:

(a) wall-standing: forcing the detainees to remain for periods of some hours in a 'stress position', described by those who underwent it as being 'spreadeagled against the wall, with their fingers put high above the head against the wall, the legs spread apart and the feet back, causing them to stand on their toes with the weight of the body mainly on the fingers';

(b) hooding: putting a black or navy coloured bag over the detainees' heads and, at least initially, keeping it there all the time except during interrogation;

(c) subjection to noise: pending their interrogations, holding the detainees in a room where there was a continuous loud and hissing noise;

(d) deprivation of sleep: pending their interrogations, depriving the detainees of sleep;

(e) deprivation of food and drink: subjecting the detainees to a reduced diet during their stay at the centre and pending interrogations.

97. From the start, it has been conceded by the respondent Government that the use of the five techniques was authorised at 'high level'. Although never committed to writing or authorised in any official document, the techniques had been orally taught to members of the RUC by the English Intelligence Centre as at seminar held in April 1971.

98. The two operations of interrogation in depth by means of the five techniques led to the obtaining of a considerable quantity of intelligence information, including the identification of 700 members of both IRA factions and the discovery of individual responsibility for about 85 previously unexplained criminal incidents.

99. Reports alleging physical brutality and ill-treatment by the security forces were made public within a few days. A committee of enquiry under the chairmanship of Sir Edmund Compton was appointed by the United Kingdom Government on 31 August 1971 to investigate such allegations. Among the 40 cases this Committee examined were 11 cases of persons subjected to the five techniques in August 1971; its findings were that interrogation in depth by means of the techniques constituted physical ill-treatment but not physical brutality as it understood that term.

100. The Compton reports came under considerable criticism in the United Kingdom. On 16 November 1971, the British Home Secretary announced that a further Committee had been set up under the chairmanship of Lord Parker of

Waddington to consider 'whether, and if so in what respects, the procedures currently authorised for interrogation of persons suspected of terrorism and for their custody while subject to interrogation require amendment'. The Parker report, adopted on 31 January 1972, contained a majority and a minority opinion. The majority report concluded that the application of the techniques, subject to recommended safeguards against excessive use, need not be ruled out on moral grounds. On the other hand, the minority report by Lord Gardiner disagreed that such interrogation procedures were morally justifiable, even in emergency terrorist conditions. Both the majority and the minority considered the methods to be illegal under domestic law, although the majority confined their view to English law and to 'some if not all the techniques'.

101. The Parker report was published on 2 March 1972. On the same day, the United Kingdom Prime Minister stated in Parliament that the techniques would not be used in future as an aid to interrogation. As foreshadowed in the Prime Minister's statement, directives expressly prohibiting the use of the techniques, whether singly or in combination, were then issued to the security forces by the Government.

102. At the hearing before the Court on 8 February 1977, the United Kingdom Attorney-General declared that the 'five techniques' would not in any circumstances be reintroduced as an aid to interrogation.

The Commission found no physical injury to have resulted from the application of the five techniques as such, but loss of weight by the two case-witnesses and acute psychiatric symptoms developed by them during interrogation were recorded in the medical and other evidence. The Commission was unable to establish the exact degree of any psychiatric after-effects produced on T6 and T13, but on the general level it was satisfied that some psychiatric after-effects in certain of the 14 persons subjected to the techniques could not be excluded.

150. Article 3 provides that 'no one shall be subjected to torture or to inhuman or degrading treatment or punishment'.

THE MERITS

162. As was emphasised by the Commission, ill-treatment must attain a minimum level of severity if it is to fall within the scope of Article 3. The assessment of this minimum is, in the nature of things, relative; it depends on all the circumstances of the case, such as the duration of the treatment, its physical or mental effects and, in some cases, the sex, age and state of health of the victim, etc.

163. The Convention prohibits in absolute terms torture and inhuman or degrading treatment or punishment, irrespective of the victim's conduct. Unlike most of the substantive clauses of the Convention and of Protocols 1 and 4, Article 3 makes no provision for exceptions and, under Article 15(2), there can be no derogation therefrom even in the event of a public emergency threatening the life of the nation.

164. In the instant case, the only relevant concepts are 'torture' and 'inhuman or degrading treatment', to the exclusion of 'inhuman or degrading punishment'.

(a) The 'five techniques'

165. The facts concerning the five techniques are summarised at paragraphs 96-104 and 106-107 above. In the Commission's estimation, those facts constituted a practice not only of inhuman and degrading treatment but also of torture. The applicant Government ask for confirmation of this opinion which is not contested before the Court by the respondent Government.

167. The five techniques were applied in combination, with premeditation and for hours at a stretch; they caused, if not actual bodily injury, at least intense physical and mental suffering to the persons subjected thereto and also led to acute psychiatric disturbances during interrogation. They accordingly fell into the category of inhuman treatment within the meaning of Article 3. The techniques were also degrading since they were such as to arouse in their victims feelings of fear, anguish and inferiority capable of humiliating and debasing them and possibly breaking their physical or moral resistance.

On these two points, the Court is of the same view as the Commission.

In order to determine whether the five techniques should also be qualified as torture, the Court must have regard to the distinction, embodied in Article 3, between this notion and that of inhuman or degrading treatment.

In the Court's view, this distinction derives principally from a difference in the intensity of the suffering inflicted.

The Court considers in fact that, whilst there exists on the one hand violence which is to be condemned both on moral grounds and also in most cases under the domestic law of the Contracting States but which does not fall within Article 3 of the Convention, it appears on the other hand that it was the intention that the Convention, with its distinction between 'torture' and 'inhuman or degrading treatment', should by the first of these terms attach a special stigma to deliberate inhuman treatment causing very serious and cruel suffering.

Moreover, this seems to be the thinking lying behind Article 1 . . . of Resolution 3452 (XXX) adopted by the General Assembly of the United Nations on 9 December, 1975, which declares: 'Torture constitutes an aggravated and deliberate form of cruel, inhuman or degrading treatment or punishment'.

Although the five techniques, as applied in combination, undoubtedly amounted to inhuman and degrading treatment, although their object was the extraction of confessions, the naming of others and/or information and although they were used systematically, they did not occasion suffering of the particular intensity and cruelty implied by the word torture as so understood.

168. The Court concludes that recourse to the five techniques amounted to a practice of inhuman and degrading treatment, which practice was in breach of Article 3.

According to the applicant Government (Ireland), the violence in question should also be classified, in some cases, as torture.

On the basis of the data before it, the Court does not share this view. Admittedly, the acts complained of often occurred during interrogation and, to this extent, were aimed at extracting confessions, the naming of others and/or information, but the severity of the suffering that they were capable of causing did not attain the particular level inherent in the notion of torture as understood by the Court.

NOTES AND QUESTIONS

1. The ECHR draws a distinction between torture and inhumane treatment that will become important in the American prisoner abuse cases. Is there any significance to the distinction, however, in terms of the European Covenant?

2. The distinction is perhaps more important in applying the International Convention on Torture and Other Cruel, Inhuman or Degrading Treatment or Punishment, which carries this definition:

> Article 1. For purposes of this Convention, the term "torture" means any act by which severe pain or suffering, whether physical or mental, is intentionally inflicted on a person for such purposes as obtaining from him or a third person information or a confession, punishing him for an act he or a third person has committed or is suspected of having committed, or intimidating or coercing him or a third person, or for any reason based on discrimination of any kind, when such pain or suffering is inflicted by or at the instigation of or with the consent or acquiescence of a public official or other person acting in an official capacity.

In addition, in Article 16, signatory nations

> undertake to prevent in any territory under its jurisdiction other acts of cruel, inhuman or degrading treatment or punishment which do not amount to torture as defined in article 1.

Under the Convention, signatory nations commit to make torture a criminal offense, whereas they merely "undertake to prevent" inhumane treatment. Does that mean that practices short of torture are still "legal" in a signatory nation? under international law?

3. U.S. cases dealing with torture have been brought under either the Torture Victims Protection Act, codified as a note to the Alien Tort Claims Act, 28 U.S.C. § 1350. *See Filartiga v. Pena-Irala*, 630 F.2d 876 (2d Cir. 1980) (holding that international law can be the basis of federal question jurisdiction under Article III); *Tel-Oren v. Libyan Arab Republic*, 726 F.2d 774 (D.C. Cir. 1984) (adopting similar conclusion over the objection of Judge Bork that general incorporation of international law exceeds Congress' jurisdictional grants). Professor Bradley argues that federal jurisdiction for civil actions by aliens for torture committed by other aliens outside the U.S. is difficult to justify because there is no extraterritorial federal law for the courts to apply. By contrast, criminal actions can be brought within federal court jurisdiction because Congress can act to enforce international law under its power to "define and punish offenses against the law of nations." Curtis Bradley, *Universal Jurisdiction and U.S. Law*, 2001 U. CHI. LEGAL FORUM 323.

Note on the Israeli Interrogation Experience

As a result of some highly publicized incidents involving Israeli interrogation of Palestinian suspects, in 1987 a Commission of Inquiry appointed by then-Justice Moshe Landau issued a report usually called the Landau Commission Report. The report recognized that some degree of coercion is inherent in any interrogation, even if it is nothing other than the presence and appearance of the interrogator. The Commission went on to decide that in the face of threats to public safety, a "moderate degree of pressure, including physical pressure, in order to obtain crucial information, is unavoidable under certain circumstances. Such circumstances include situations in which information sought from a detainee believed to be personally involved in serious terrorist activities can prevent imminent murder, or where the detainee possesses vital information on a terrorist organization which could not be uncovered by any other source (for example, location of arms or caches of explosives for planned acts of terrorism)."

The Landau Commission then attempted to outline guidelines for the use of force in interrogations.

(i) Disproportionate exertion of pressure on the suspect is not permissible – pressure must never reach the level of physical torture or maltreatment of the suspect, or grievous harm to his honour which deprives him of his human dignity.

(ii) The use of less serious measures must be weighed against the degree of anticipated danger, according to the information in the possession of the interrogator.

(iii) The physical and psychological means of pressure permitted for use by an interrogator must be defined and limited in advance, by issuing binding directives.

(iv) There must be strict supervision of the implementation in practice of the directives given to GSS interrogators.

(v) The interrogators' supervisors must react firmly and without hesitation to every deviation from the permissible, imposing disciplinary punishment, and in serious cases, causing criminal proceedings to be instituted against the offending interrogator.

In addition to the general guidelines, the Commission provided a detailed set of limits that were to be kept secret so that terrorists would not be able to train and prepare for interrogation knowing the limits to which they might be subjected.

The recommendations of the Commission were accepted by the Government and put into place as guidance for the General Security Service. Following the report, the Supreme Court received occasional petitions from counsel for prisoners seeking injunctions against the use of any physical pressure in their interrogation. In one controversial case, *Hamdan v. GSS* (HCJ 8049/96), the court first granted an injunction and then cancelled it on a showing by GSS that Hamdan likely had information that would be critical to disrupting a dangerous plot.

PUBLIC COMMITTEE AGAINST TORTURE v.
GENERAL SECURITY SERVICE
Israel Supreme Court HCJ No. 5100/94 (1999)

President A. BARAK:

The General Security Service [hereinafter the "GSS"] investigates individuals suspected of committing crimes against Israel's security. Authorization for these interrogations is granted by directives that regulate interrogation methods. These directives authorize investigators to apply physical means against those undergoing interrogation, including shaking the suspect and placing him in the "Shabach" position. These methods are permitted since they are seen as immediately necessary to save human lives. Are these interrogation practices legal? These are the issues before us.

Background

1. Ever since it was established, the State of Israel has been engaged in an unceasing struggle for its security – indeed, its very existence. Terrorist organizations have set Israel's annihilation as their goal. Terrorist acts and the general disruption of order are their means of choice. In employing such methods, these groups do not distinguish between civilian and military targets. They carry out terrorist attacks in which scores are murdered in public areas – in areas of public transportation, city squares and centers, theaters and coffee shops. They do not distinguish between men, women and children. They act out of cruelty and without mercy. (For an in depth description of this phenomenon see the Report of the Commission of Inquiry Regarding the Interrogation Practices of the GSS with Respect to Hostile Terrorist Activities headed by Justice (ret.) M. Landau, 1987 [hereinafter the Report of the Commission of Inquiry]. *See* 1 THE LANDAU BOOK 269, 276 (1995).

The facts before this Court reveal that 121 people died in terrorist attacks between January 1, 1996 and May 14, 1998. Seven hundred and seven people were injured. A large number of those killed and injured were victims of harrowing suicide bombings in the heart of Israel's cities. Many attacks – including suicide bombings, attempts to detonate car bombs, kidnappings of citizens and soldiers, attempts to highjack buses, murders, and the placing of explosives – were prevented due to daily measures taken by authorities responsible for fighting terrorist activities. The GSS is the main body responsible for fighting terrorism.

In order to fulfill this function, the GSS also investigates those suspected of hostile terrorist activities. The purpose of these interrogations includes the gathering of information regarding terrorists in order to prevent them from carrying out terrorist attacks. In the context of these interrogations, GSS investigators also make use of physical means.

The Petitions

2. These petitions are concerned with the interrogation methods of the GSS. They outline several of these methods in detail. Two of the petitions are of a public nature. One of these is brought by the Public Committee against Torture in Israel. It submits that GSS investigators are not authorized to investigate

those suspected of hostile terrorist activities. Moreover, they claim that the GSS is not entitled to employ those methods approved by the Report of the Commission of Inquiry, such as "the application of non-violent psychological pressure" and of "a moderate degree of physical pressure." The second petition is brought by the Association for Civil Rights in Israel. It argues that the GSS should be ordered to cease shaking suspects during interrogations.

The five remaining petitions involve individual petitioners. They each petitioned the Court to hold that the methods used against them by the GSS are illegal.

3. [Two arrested persons] petitioned the Court for an order nisi prohibiting the use of physical force against them during their interrogation. The Court granted the order. The two petitioners were released from custody prior to the hearing. As per their request, we have elected to continue hearing their case, in light of the importance of the issues they raise.

4. Petitioner Hat'm Abu Zayda . . . complained of the interrogation methods allegedly used against him, including sleep deprivation, shaking, beatings, and use of the "Shabach" position. We immediately ordered the petition be heard. The Court was then informed that petitioner's interrogation had ended. Petitioner was subsequently convicted of activities in the military branch of the Hamas terrorist organization. He was sentenced to 74 months in prison. During oral arguments, it was asserted that the information provided by petitioner during his interrogation led to the thwarting of a plan to carry out serious terrorist attacks, including the kidnapping of soldiers.

5. [Petitioner] Ganimat . . . claimed to have been tortured by his investigators, through use of the "Shabach" position, excessively tight handcuffs, and sleep deprivation. His interrogation revealed that he was involved in numerous terrorist activities, which resulted in the deaths of many Israeli citizens. He was instrumental in the kidnapping and murder of Sharon Edry, an IDF soldier. Additionally, he was involved in the bombing of Cafe "Appropo" in Tel Aviv, in which three women were murdered and thirty people were injured. He was charged with all these crimes and convicted at trial. He was sentenced to five consecutive life sentences plus an additional twenty years in prison.

Subsequent to the dismantling and interrogation of the terrorist cell to which petitioner belonged, a powerful explosive device, identical to the one detonated at Cafe "Appropo" in Tel Aviv, was found in Tzurif, petitioner's village. Uncovering this explosive device thwarted an attack like the one at Cafe "Appropo." According to GSS investigators, the petitioner possessed additional crucial information which he revealed only as a result of the interrogation. Revealing this information immediately was essential to safeguarding national and regional security and preventing danger to human life.

Physical Means

8. The GSS did not describe the physical means employed by GSS investigators. The State Attorney was prepared to present this information in camera. Petitioners opposed this proposal. As such, the information before the Court was provided by the petitioners and was not examined in each individual petition. This having been said, the state did not deny the use of these

interrogation methods, and even offered justifications for these methods. This provided the Court with a picture of the interrogation practices of the GSS.

The decision to utilize physical means in a particular instance is based on internal regulations, which requires obtaining permission from the higher ranks of the GSS. The regulations themselves were approved by a special Ministerial Committee on GSS interrogations. Among other guidelines, the committee set forth directives regarding the rank required of an officer who was to authorize such interrogation practices. These directives were not examined by this Court. Different interrogation methods are employed in each situation, depending what is necessary in that situation and the likelihood of obtaining authorization. The GSS does not resort to every interrogation method at its disposal in each case.

Shaking

9. A number of petitioners claimed that they were subject to shaking. Among the investigation methods outlined in the GSS interrogation regulations, shaking is considered the harshest. The method is defined as the forceful and repeated shaking of the suspect's upper torso, in a manner which causes the neck and head to swing rapidly. According to an expert opinion, the shaking method is likely to cause serious brain damage, harm the spinal cord, cause the suspect to lose consciousness, vomit and urinate uncontrollably and suffer serious headaches.

The state entered several opposing expert opinions into evidence. It admits the use of this method by the GSS. It contends, however, that shaking does not present an inherent danger to the life of the suspect, that the risk to life as a result of shaking is rare, that there is no evidence that shaking causes fatal damage, and that medical literature has not, to date, reported a case in which a person died as a direct result of having been shaken. In any event, they argue, doctors are present at all interrogation areas, and the possibility of medical injury is always investigated.

All agree that, in one particular case, the suspect expired after being shaken. According to the state, that case was a rare exception. Death was caused by an extremely rare complication which resulted in pulmonary edema. In addition, the state argues that the shaking method is only resorted to in very specific cases, and only as a last resort. The directives define the appropriate circumstances for its use, and the rank responsible for authorizing its use. The investigators were instructed that, in every case where they consider the use of shaking, they must examine the severity of the danger that the interrogation is intending to prevent, consider the urgency of uncovering the information presumably possessed by the suspect in question, and seek an alternative means of preventing the danger. Finally, the directives state that, in cases where this method is to be used, the investigator must first provide an evaluation of the suspect's health and ensure that no harm comes to him. According to the respondent, shaking is indispensable to fighting and winning the war on terrorism. It is not possible to prohibit its use without seriously harming the ability of the GSS to effectively thwart deadly terrorist attacks. Its use in the past has lead to the prevention of murderous attacks.

Waiting in the "Shabach" Position

10. This interrogation method arose in several petitions. As per petitioners' submission, a suspect investigated under the "Shabach" position has his hands tied behind his back. He is seated on a small and low chair, whose seat is tilted forward, towards the ground. One hand is tied behind the suspect, and placed inside the gap between the chair's seat and back support. His second hand is tied behind the chair, against its back support. The suspect's head is covered by a sack that falls down to his shoulders. Loud music is played in the room. According to the briefs submitted, suspects are detained in this position for a long period of time, awaiting interrogation.

Petitioners claim that prolonged sitting in this position causes serious muscle pain in the arms, the neck and headaches. The state did not deny the use of this method. It submits that both crucial security considerations and the safety of the investigators require the tying of the suspect's hands as he is being interrogated. The head covering is intended to prevent contact with other suspects. Loud music is played for the same reason.

The "Frog Crouch"

11. This interrogation method appeared in one of the petitions. According to the petition, the suspect was interrogated in a "frog crouch" position. This refers to consecutive, periodical crouches on the tips of one's toes, each lasting for five minute intervals. The state did not deny the use of this method, and the Court issued an order nisi in the petition. Prior to hearing the petition, however, this interrogation practice ceased.

Excessively Tight Handcuffs

12. In a number of petitions, several petitioners complained of excessively tight hand or leg cuffs. They contended that this practice results in serious injuries to the suspect's hands, arms and feet, due to the length of the interrogations. The petitioners contend that particularly small cuffs were used. The state, for its part, denies the use of unusually small cuffs, arguing that those used were of standard issue and were properly applied. Even so, the state is prepared to admit that prolonged hand or foot cuffing is likely to cause injuries to the suspect's hands and feet. The state contends, however, that injuries of this nature are inherent to any lengthy interrogation.

Sleep Deprivation

13. In a number of petitions, petitioners complained of being deprived of sleep as a result of being tied in the "Shabach" position, while subject to the playing of loud music, or of being subjected to intense non-stop interrogations without sufficient rest breaks. They claim that the purpose of depriving them of sleep is to cause them to break from exhaustion. While the state agrees that suspects are at times deprived of regular sleep hours, it argues that this does not constitute an interrogation method aimed at causing exhaustion, but rather results from the long amount of time necessary for conducting the interrogation.

Petitioners' Arguments

14. All the petitions . . . argue that the physical means employed by GSS investigators not only infringe the human dignity of the suspect undergoing

interrogation, but also constitute criminal offences. These methods, argue the petitioners, are in violation of international law as they constitute "torture." Furthermore, the "necessity defense" at most constitutes an exceptional post factum defense, exclusively confined to criminal proceedings against investigators.

We asked petitioners whether the "ticking bomb" rationale was sufficiently persuasive to justify the use of physical means. This rationale would apply in a situation where a bomb is known to have been placed in a public area and will cause human tragedy if its location is not revealed. This question elicited different responses from the petitioners. There are those convinced that physical means are not to be used under any circumstances; the prohibition on such methods, to their mind, is absolute, whatever the consequences may be. On the other hand, there are others who argue that, even if it is acceptable to employ physical means in the exceptional circumstances of the "ticking bomb," these methods are used even in absence of "ticking bomb" conditions. The very fact that the use of such means is illegal in most cases warrants banning their use altogether, even if doing so would include those rare cases in which physical coercion may have been justified. Whatever their individual views, all petitioners unanimously highlight the distinction between the post factum possibility of escaping criminal liability and the advance granting of permission to use physical means for interrogation purposes.

The State's Arguments

15. With respect to the physical means employed by the GSS, the state argues that these methods do not violate international law. Indeed, it is submitted that these methods cannot be described as "torture," as "cruel and inhuman treatment," or as "degrading treatment," which are all strictly prohibited under international law. The state further contends that the practices of the GSS do not cause pain and suffering.

Moreover, the state argues that these means are legal under domestic Israeli law. This is due to the "necessity defense" of article 34(11) of the Penal Law-1977. In the specific cases where the "necessity defense" would apply, GSS investigators are entitled to use "moderate physical pressure" as a last resort in order to prevent real injury to human life and well-being. Such "moderate physical pressure" may include shaking. Resort to such means is legal, and does not constitute a criminal offence. In any case, if a specific method is not deemed to be a criminal offence, there is no reason not to employ it, even for interrogation purposes. According to the state, there is no reason to prohibit a particular act if, in specific circumstances, it does not constitute a crime.

The Report of the Commission of Inquiry

16. The authority of the GSS to employ particular interrogation methods was examined by the Commission of Inquiry. The Commission, appointed by the government . . . concluded that, in cases where the saving of human lives requires obtaining certain information, the investigator is entitled to apply both psychological pressure and "a moderate degree of physical pressure." As such, an investigator who, in the face of such danger, applies a degree of physical pressure, which does not constitute abuse or torture of the suspect, but is

proportionate to the danger to human life can, in the face of criminal liability, avail himself of the "necessity defense." The Commission was convinced that its conclusions were not in conflict with international law, but were rather consistent with both the rule of law and the need to effectively protect the security of Israel and its citizens.

The commission approved the use of "moderate degree of physical pressure." Such "moderate physical pressure" could be applied under stringent conditions. Directives to this effect were set out in the second, secret part of the report, and subject to the supervision of bodies both internal and external to the GSS. The commission's recommendations were approved by the government.

The Petitions

17. Until now, it was not possible for the Court to hear the sort of arguments that would provide a complete normative picture, in all its complexity. At this time, in contrast, a number of petitions have properly laid out complete arguments. For this we thank them.

Some of the petitions are rather general or theoretical while others are quite specific. Even so, we have decided to deal with all of them, since we seek to clarify the state of the law in this most complicated question. To this end, we shall . . . examine whether a general power to investigate could potentially sanction the use of physical means – including mental suffering – the likes of which the GSS employs. Finally, we shall examine circumstances where such methods are immediately necessary to rescue human lives and shall decide whether such circumstances justify granting GSS investigators the authority to employ physical interrogation methods.

The Authority to Interrogate

18. The term "interrogation" takes on various meanings in different contexts. For the purposes of these petitions, we refer to the asking of questions which seek to elicit a truthful answer, subject to the privilege against self-incrimination. Generally, the investigation of a suspect is conducted at the suspect's place of detention. Any interrogation inevitably infringes the suspect's freedom – including his human dignity and privacy – even if physical means are not used. In a country adhering to the rule of law, therefore, interrogations are not permitted in absence of clear statutory authorization, whether such authorization is through primary or secondary legislation.

The Means Employed for Interrogation Purposes

21. As we have seen, GSS investigators are endowed with the authority to conduct interrogations. What is the scope of these powers and do they include the use of physical means in the course of the interrogation? Can use be made of the physical means presently employed by GSS investigators – such as shaking, the "Shabach" position, and sleep deprivation – by virtue of the investigating powers given the GSS investigators? Let us note that the state did not argue before us that all the means employed by GSS investigators are permissible by virtue of the "law of interrogation." Thus, for instance, the state did not make the argument that shaking is permitted simply because it is an "ordinary" method of investigation in Israel.

22. An interrogation, by its very nature, places the suspect in a difficult position. "The criminal's interrogation," wrote Justice Vitkon over twenty years ago, "is not a negotiation process between two open and honest merchants, conducting their affairs in mutual trust." An interrogation is a "competition of minds," in which the investigator attempts to penetrate the suspect's mind and elicit the information that the investigator seeks to obtain.

Indeed, the authority to conduct interrogations, like any administrative power, is designed for a specific purpose, and must be exercised in conformity with the basic principles of the democratic regime. In setting out the rules of interrogation, two values clash. On the one hand, lies the desire to uncover the truth, in accord with the public interest in exposing crime and preventing it. On the other hand is the need to protect the dignity and liberty of the individual being interrogated. This having been said, these values are not absolute. A democratic, freedom-loving society does not accept that investigators may use any means for the purpose of uncovering the truth. "The interrogation practices of the police in a given regime," noted Justice Landau, "are indicative of a regime's very character" At times, the price of truth is so high that a democratic society is not prepared to pay. To the same extent, however, a democratic society, desirous of liberty, seeks to fight crime and, to that end, is prepared to accept that an interrogation may infringe the human dignity and liberty of a suspect – provided that it is done for a proper purpose and that the harm does not exceed that which is necessary.

Our concern, therefore, lies in the clash of values and the balancing of conflicting values. The balancing process results in the rules for a "reasonable interrogation." These rules are based, on the one hand, on preserving the "human image" of the suspect, and on preserving the "purity of arms" used during the interrogation. On the other hand, these rules take into consideration the need to fight crime in general, and terrorist attacks in particular. These rules reflect "a degree of reasonableness, straight thinking, and fairness." The rules pertaining to investigations are important to a democratic state. They reflect its character. An illegal investigation harms the suspect's human dignity. It equally harms society's fabric.

23. Here we deal with the "law of interrogation" as a power of an administrative authority. The "law of interrogation" by its very nature, is intrinsically linked to the circumstances of each case. This having been said, a number of general principles are nonetheless worth noting.

First, a reasonable investigation is necessarily one free of torture, free of cruel, inhuman treatment, and free of any degrading conduct whatsoever. There is a prohibition on the use of "brutal or inhuman means" in the course of an investigation. Human dignity also includes the dignity of the suspect being interrogated. This conclusion is in accord with international treaties, to which Israel is a signatory, which prohibit the use of torture, "cruel, inhuman treatment" and "degrading treatment." *See* M. EVANS & R. MORGAN, PREVENTING TORTURE 61 (1998); N.S. RODLEY, THE TREATMENT OF PRISONERS UNDER INTERNATIONAL LAW 63 (1987). These prohibitions are "absolute." There are no exceptions to them and there is no room for balancing. Indeed, violence directed at a suspect's body or spirit does not constitute a reasonable investigation practice. The use of violence during investigations can lead to the investigator being held criminally liable.

Second, a reasonable investigation is likely to cause discomfort. It may result in insufficient sleep. The conditions under which it is conducted risk being unpleasant. Of course, it is possible to conduct an effective investigation without resorting to violence. Within the confines of the law, it is permitted to resort to various sophisticated techniques. Such techniques – accepted in the most progressive of societies – can be effective in achieving their goals. In the end result, the legality of an investigation is deduced from the propriety of its purpose and from its methods. Thus, for instance, sleep deprivation for a prolonged period, or sleep deprivation at night when this is not necessary to the investigation time-wise, may be deemed disproportionate.

From the General to the Particular

24. We shall now turn from the general to the particular. Clearly, shaking is a prohibited investigation method. It harms the suspect's body. It violates his dignity. It is a violent method which can not form part of a legal investigation. It surpasses that which is necessary. Even the state did not argue that shaking is an "ordinary" investigatory method which every investigator, whether in the GSS or the police, is permitted to employ. The argument before us was that the justification for shaking is found in the "necessity defense." That argument shall be dealt with below. In any event, there is no doubt that shaking is not to be resorted to in cases outside the bounds of "necessity" or as part of an "ordinary" investigation.

25. It was argued before the Court that one of the employed investigation methods consists of compelling the suspect to crouch on the tips of his toes for periods of five minutes. The state did not deny this practice. This is a prohibited investigation method. It does not serve any purpose inherent to an investigation. It is degrading and infringes an individual's human dignity.

26. The "Shabach" method is composed of several components: the cuffing of the suspect, seating him on a low chair, covering his head with a sack, and playing loud music in the area. [W]e accept that the suspect's cuffing, for the purpose of preserving the investigators' safety, is included in the general power to investigate. Even petitioners agree that it is permissible to cuff a suspect in such circumstances and that cuffing constitutes an integral part of an interrogation. The cuffing associated with the "Shabach" position, however, is unlike routine cuffing. The suspect is cuffed with his hands tied behind his back. One hand is placed inside the gap between the chair's seat and back support, while the other is tied behind him, against the chair's back support. This is a distorted and unnatural position. The investigators' safety does not require it. Similarly, there is no justification for handcuffing the suspect's hands with especially small handcuffs, if this is in fact the practice. The use of these methods is prohibited. As has been noted, "cuffing that causes pain is prohibited." Moreover, there are other ways of preventing the suspect from fleeing which do not involve causing pain and suffering.

27. The same applies to seating the suspect in question in the "Shabach" position. We accept that seating a man is inherent to the investigation. This is not the case, however, when the chair upon which he is seated is a very low one, tilted forward facing the ground, and when he is seated in this position for long hours. This sort of seating is not authorized by the general power to interrogate. Even if we suppose that the seating of the suspect on a chair lower than that of his investigator can potentially serve a legitimate investigation objective – for instance, to establish the "rules of the game" in the contest of wills between the parties, or to emphasize the investigator's superiority over the suspect – there is no inherent investigative need to seat the suspect on a chair so low and tilted forward towards the ground, in a manner that causes him real pain and suffering. Clearly, the general power to conduct interrogations does not authorize seating a suspect on a tilted chair, in a manner that applies pressure and causes pain to his back, all the more so when his hands are tied behind the chair, in the manner described. All these methods do not fall within the sphere of a "fair" interrogation. They are not reasonable. They infringe the suspect's dignity, his bodily integrity and his basic rights in an excessive manner. They are not to be deemed as included within the general power to conduct interrogations.

28. We accept that there are interrogation related concerns regarding preventing contact between the suspect under interrogation and other suspects, and perhaps even between the suspect and the interrogator. These concerns require means to prevent the said contact. The need to prevent contact may, for instance, flow from the need to safeguard the investigators' security, or the security of the suspects and witnesses. It can also be part of the "mind game" which pits the information possessed by the suspect, against that found in the hands of his investigators. For this purpose, the power to interrogate – in principle and according to the circumstances of each particular case – may include the need to prevent eye contact with a given person or place. In the case at bar, this was the explanation provided by the state for covering the suspect's head with a sack, while he is seated in the "Shabach" position. From what was stated in the declarations before us, the suspect's head is covered with a sack throughout his "wait" in the "Shabach" position. It was argued that the head covering causes the suspect to suffocate. The sack is large, reaching the shoulders of the suspect. All these methods are not inherent to an interrogation. They are not necessary to prevent eye contact between the suspect being interrogated and other suspects. Indeed, even if such contact is prevented, what is the purpose of causing the suspect to suffocate? Employing this method is not related to the purpose of preventing the said contact and is consequently forbidden. Moreover, the statements clearly reveal that the suspect's head remains covered for several hours, throughout his wait. For these purposes, less harmful means must be employed, such as letting the suspect wait in a detention cell. Doing so will eliminate any need to cover the suspect's eyes. In the alternative, the suspect's eyes may be covered in a manner that does not cause him physical suffering. For it appears that, at present, the suspect's head covering – which covers his entire head, rather than eyes alone – for a prolonged period of time, with no essential link to the goal of preventing contact between

the suspects under investigation, is not part of a fair interrogation. It harms the suspect and his dignity. It degrades him. It causes him to lose his sense of time and place. It suffocates him. All these things are not included in the general authority to investigate. In the cases before us, the State declared that it will make an effort to find a "ventilated" sack. This is not sufficient. The covering of the head in the circumstances described, as distinguished from the covering of the eyes, is outside the scope of authority and is prohibited.

29. Cutting off the suspect from his surroundings can also include preventing him from listening to what is going on around him. We are prepared to assume that the authority to investigate an individual may include preventing him from hearing other suspects under investigation or voices and sounds that, if heard by the suspect, risk impeding the interrogation's success. At the same time, however, we must examine whether the means employed to accomplish this fall within the scope of a fair and reasonable interrogation. In the case at bar, the detainee is placed in the "Shabach" position while very loud music is played. Do these methods fall within the scope or the general authority to conduct interrogations? Here too, the answer is in the negative. Being exposed to very loud music for a long period of time causes the suspect suffering. Furthermore, the entire time, the suspect is tied in an uncomfortable position with his head covered. This is prohibited. It does not fall within the scope of the authority to conduct a fair and effective interrogation. In the circumstances of the cases before us, the playing of loud music is a prohibited.

30. To the above, we must add that the "Shabach" position employs all the above methods simultaneously. This combination gives rise to pain and suffering. This is a harmful method, particularly when it is employed for a prolonged period of time. For these reasons, this method is not authorized by the powers of interrogation. It is an unacceptable method. "The duty to safeguard the detainee's dignity includes his right not to be degraded and not to be submitted to sub-human conditions in the course of his detention, of the sort likely to harm his health and potentially his dignity."

A similar – though not identical – combination of interrogation methods were discussed in the case of *Ireland v. United Kingdom*, 23 Eur. Ct. H.R. (ser. B) at 3 (1976). In that case, the Court examined five interrogation methods used by England to investigate detainees suspected of terrorist activities in Northern Ireland. The methods included protracted standing against a wall on the tip of one's toes, covering of the suspect's head throughout the detention (except during the actual interrogation), exposing the suspect to very loud noise for a prolonged period of time, and deprivation of sleep, food and drink. The Court held that these methods did not constitute "torture." However, since they subjected the suspect to "inhuman and degrading" treatment, they were nonetheless prohibited.

31. The interrogation of a person is likely to be lengthy, due to the suspect's failure to cooperate, the complexity of the information sought, or in light of the need to obtain information urgently and immediately. Indeed, a person undergoing interrogation cannot sleep like one who is not being interrogated. The suspect, subject to the investigators' questions for a prolonged period of

time, is at times exhausted. This is often the inevitable result of an interrogation. This is part of the "discomfort" inherent to an interrogation. This being the case, depriving the suspect of sleep is, in our opinion, included in the general authority of the investigator. Justice Shamgar noted as much in Cr. A. 485/76 *Ben Loulou v. The State of Israel* (unreported decision):

> The interrogation of crimes and, in particular, murder or other serious crimes, cannot be accomplished within an ordinary work day. . . . The investigation of crime is essentially a game of mental resistance. . . For this reason, the interrogation is often carried out at frequent intervals. This, as noted, causes the investigation to drag on . . . and requires diligent insistence on its momentum and consecutiveness.

The above described situation is different from one in which sleep deprivation shifts from being a "side effect" of the interrogation to an end in itself. If the suspect is intentionally deprived of sleep for a prolonged period of time, for the purpose of tiring him out or "breaking" him, it is not part of the scope of a fair and reasonable investigation. Such means harm the rights and dignity of the suspect in a manner beyond what is necessary.

32. All these limitations on an interrogation, which flow from the requirement that an interrogation be fair and reasonable, is the law with respect to a regular police interrogation. The power to interrogate granted to the GSS investigator is the same power the law bestows upon the ordinary police investigator. The restrictions upon the police investigations are equally applicable to GSS investigations. There is no statute that grants GSS investigators special interrogating powers that are different or more significant than those granted the police investigator. From this we conclude that a GSS investigator, whose duty it is to conduct the interrogation according to the law, is subject to the same restrictions applicable to police interrogators.

Physical Means and the "Necessity" Defense

33. We have arrived at the conclusion that GSS personnel who have received permission to conduct interrogations, as per the Criminal Procedure Statute [Testimony], are authorized to do so. This authority – like that of the police investigator – does not include most of the physical means of interrogation in the petition before us. Can the authority to employ these methods be anchored in a legal source beyond the authority to conduct an interrogation? This question was answered by the state in the affirmative. As noted, our law does not contain an explicit authorization permitting the GSS to employ physical means. An authorization of this nature can, however, in the state's opinion, be obtained in specific cases by virtue of the criminal law defense of "necessity," as provided in section 34(1) of the Penal Law. The statute provides:

> A person will not bear criminal liability for committing any act immediately necessary for the purpose of saving the life, liberty, body or property, of either himself or his fellow person, from substantial danger of serious harm, in response to particular circumstances during a specific time, and absent alternative means for avoiding the harm.

The state's position is that by virtue of this defense against criminal liability, GSS investigators are authorized to apply physical means – such as shaking –

in the appropriate circumstances and in the absence of other alternatives, in order to prevent serious harm to human life or limb. The state maintains that an act committed under conditions of "necessity" does not constitute a crime. Instead, the state sees such acts as worth committing in order to prevent serious harm to human life or limb. These are actions that society has an interest in encouraging, which should be seen as proper under the circumstances. In this, society is choosing the lesser evil. Not only is it legitimately permitted to engage in fighting terrorism, it is our moral duty to employ the means necessary for this purpose. This duty is particularly incumbent on the state authorities – and, for our purposes, on the GSS investigators – who carry the burden of safeguarding the public peace. As this is the case, there is no obstacle preventing the investigators' superiors from instructing and guiding them as to when the conditions of the "necessity" defense are fulfilled. This, the state contends, implies the legality of the use of physical means in GSS interrogations.

In the course of their argument, the state presented the "ticking bomb" argument. A given suspect is arrested by the GSS. He holds information regarding the location of a bomb that was set and will imminently explode. There is no way to diffuse the bomb without this information. If the information is obtained, the bomb may be neutralized. If the bomb is not neutralized, scores will be killed and injured. Is a GSS investigator authorized to employ physical means in order to obtain this information? The state answers in the affirmative. The use of physical means should not constitute a criminal offence, and their use should be sanctioned, according to the state, by the "necessity" defense.

34. We are prepared to assume, although this matter is open to debate, that the "necessity defense" is available to all, including an investigator, during an interrogation, acting in the capacity of the state. *See* A. Dershowitz, *Is it Necessary to Apply Physical Pressure 'to Terrorists – And to Lie About It?*, 23 ISRAEL L. REV. 193 (1989); K. Bernsmann, *Private Self-Defense and Necessity in German Penal Law and in the Penal Law Proposal – Some Remarks*, 30 ISRAEL L. REV. 171, 208-10 (1998). Likewise, we are prepared to accept – although this matter is equally contentious – that the "necessity defense" can arise in instances of "ticking bombs," and that the phrase "immediate need" in the statute refers to the imminent nature of the act rather than that of the danger. Hence, the imminence criteria is satisfied even if the bomb is set to explode in a few days, or even in a few weeks, provided the danger is certain to materialize and there is no alternative means of preventing it.

Consequently we are prepared to presume, as was held by the Report of the Commission of Inquiry, that if a GSS investigator – who applied physical interrogation methods for the purpose of saving human life – is criminally indicted, the "necessity defense" is likely to be open to him in the appropriate circumstances.

35. Indeed, we are prepared to accept that, in the appropriate circumstances, GSS investigators may avail themselves of the "necessity defense" if criminally indicted. This, however, is not the issue before this Court. We are not dealing with the criminal liability of a GSS investigator who employed physical interrogation methods under circumstances of "necessity." Nor are we addressing

the issue of the admissibility or probative value of evidence obtained as a result of a GSS investigator's application of physical means against a suspect. We are dealing with a different question. The question before us is whether it is possible, ex ante, to establish permanent directives setting out the physical interrogation means that may be used under conditions of "necessity." Moreover, we must decide whether the "necessity defense" can constitute a basis for the authority of a GSS investigator to investigate, in the performance of his duty. According to the state, it is possible to imply from the "necessity defense" – available post factum to an investigator indicted of a criminal offence – the ex ante legal authorization to allow the investigator to use physical interrogation methods. Is this position correct?

36. In the Court's opinion, the authority to establish directives respecting the use of physical means during the course of a GSS interrogation cannot be implied from the "necessity defense." The "necessity defense" does not constitute a source of authority, which would allow GSS investigators to make use physical means during the course of interrogations. The reasoning underlying our position is anchored in the nature of the "necessity defense." The defense deals with cases involving an individual reacting to a given set of facts. It is an improvised reaction to an unpredictable event. Thus, the very nature of the defense does not allow it to serve as the source of authorization. Authorization of administrative authority is based on establishing general, forward looking criteria, as noted by Professor Enker:

> Necessity is an after-the-fact judgment based on a narrow set of considerations in which we are concerned with the immediate consequences, not far-reaching and long-range consequences, on the basis of a clearly established order of priorities of both means and ultimate values. . . . The defense of necessity does not define a code of primary normative behavior. Necessity is certainly not a basis for establishing a broad detailed code of behavior such as how one should go about conducting intelligence interrogations in security matters, when one may or may not use force, how much force may be used and the like.

See A. Enker, *The Use of Physical Force in Interrogations and the Necessity Defense*, in ISRAEL AND INTERNATIONAL HUMAN RIGHTS LAW: THE ISSUE OF TORTURE 61, 62 (1995). In a similar vein, Kremnitzer and Segev note:

> The basic rationale underlying the necessity defense is the impossibility of establishing accurate rules of behavior in advance, appropriate in concrete emergency situations, whose circumstances are varied and unexpected. From this it follows, that the necessity defense is not well suited for the regulation of a general situation, the circumstances of which are known and may repeat themselves. In such cases, there is no reason for not setting out the rules of behavior in advance, in order that their content be determined in a thought out and well-planned manner, which would allow them to apply in a uniform manner to all.

The "necessity defense" has the effect of allowing one who acts under the circumstances of "necessity" to escape criminal liability. The "necessity defense" does not possess any additional normative value. It can not authorize the use of physical means to allow investigators to execute their duties in circumstances of necessity. The very fact that a particular act does not constitute a criminal act – due to the "necessity defense" – does not in itself authorize the act and the concomitant infringement of human rights. The rule of law, both as a formal and as a substantive principle, requires that an infringement of human rights be prescribed by statute. The lifting of criminal responsibility does not imply authorization to infringe a human right.

37. In other words, general directives governing the use of physical means during interrogations must be rooted in an authorization prescribed by law and not in defenses to criminal liability. The principle of "necessity" cannot serve as a basis of authority. If the state wishes to enable GSS investigators to utilize physical means in interrogations, it must enact legislation for this purpose. This authorization would also free the investigator applying the physical means from criminal liability. This release would not flow from the "necessity defense," but rather from the "justification" defense. This defense is provided for in section 34(13) of the Penal Law, which states:

> A person shall not bear criminal liability for an act committed in one of the following cases:

> (1) He was obliged or authorized by law to commit it.

This "justification" defense to criminal liability is rooted in an area outside the criminal law. This "external" law serves as a defense to criminal liability. This defense does not rest upon "necessity," which is "internal" to the Penal Law itself. Thus, for instance, where the question of when an officer is authorized to apply deadly force in the course of detention arises, the answer is found in the laws of detention, which is external to the Penal Law. If a man is killed as a result of this application of force, the "justification" defense will likely come into play. The power to enact rules and to act according to them requires legislative authorization. In such legislation, the legislature, if it so desires, may express its views on the social, ethical and political problems of authorizing the use of physical means in an interrogation. Naturally, such considerations did not come before the legislature when the "necessity" defense was enacted. The "necessity" defense is not the appropriate place for laying out these considerations.

38. We conclude, therefore, that, according to the existing state of the law, neither the government nor the heads of the security services have the authority to establish directives regarding the use of physical means during the interrogation of suspects suspected of hostile terrorist activities, beyond the general rules which can be inferred from the very concept of an interrogation itself. Similarly, the individual GSS investigator – like any police officer – does not possess the authority to employ physical means that infringe a suspect's liberty during the interrogation, unless these means are inherent to the very essence of an interrogation and are both fair and reasonable.

An investigator who employs these methods exceeds his authority. His responsibility shall be fixed according to law. His potential criminal liability shall be examined in the context of the "necessity defense." Provided the conditions of the defense are met by the circumstances of the case, the investigator may find refuge under its wings. Just as the existence of the "necessity defense" does not bestow authority, the lack of authority does not negate the applicability of the necessity defense or of other defenses from criminal liability. The Attorney-General can establish guidelines regarding circumstances in which investigators shall not stand trial, if they claim to have acted from "necessity." A statutory provision is necessary to authorize the use of physical means during the course of an interrogation, beyond what is permitted by the ordinary "law of investigation," and in order to provide the individual GSS investigator with the authority to employ these methods. The "necessity defense" cannot serve as a basis for such authority.

A Final Word

39. This decision opened with a description of the difficult reality in which Israel finds herself. We conclude this judgment by revisiting that harsh reality. We are aware that this decision does make it easier to deal with that reality [*sic-does not?*]. This is the destiny of a democracy – it does not see all means as acceptable, and the ways of its enemies are not always open before it. A democracy must sometimes fight with one hand tied behind its back. Even so, a democracy has the upper hand. The rule of law and the liberty of an individual constitute important components in its understanding of security. At the end of the day, they strengthen its spirit and this strength allows it to overcome its difficulties.

This having been said, there are those who argue that Israel's security problems are too numerous, and require the authorization of physical means. Whether it is appropriate for Israel, in light of its security difficulties, to sanction physical means is an issue that must be decided by the legislative branch, which represents the people. We do not take any stand on this matter at this time. It is there that various considerations must be weighed. The debate must occur there. It is there that the required legislation may be passed, provided, of course, that the law "befit[s] the values of the State of Israel, is enacted for a proper purpose, and [infringes the suspect's liberty] to an extent no greater than required." See article 8 of the Basic Law: Human Dignity and Liberty.

40. Deciding these petitions weighed heavily on this Court. True, from the legal perspective, the road before us is smooth. We are, however, part of Israeli society. Its problems are known to us and we live its history. We are not isolated in an ivory tower. We live the life of this country. We are aware of the harsh reality of terrorism in which we are, at times, immersed. The possibility that this decision will hamper the ability to properly deal with terrorists and terrorism disturbs us. We are, however, judges. We must decide according to the law. This is the standard that we set for ourselves. When we sit to judge, we ourselves are judged. Therefore, in deciding the law, we must act according to our purest conscience. We recall the words of Deputy President Landau, in HCJ 390/79 *Dawikat v. The State of Israel*, at 4:

> We possess proper sources upon which to construct our judgments and have no need – and, indeed, are forbidden – to allow our personal views as citizens to influence our decisions. Still, I fear that the Court will appear to have abandoned its proper role and to have descended into the whirlwind of public debate; that its decision will be acclaimed by certain segments of

the public, while others will reject it absolutely. It is in this sense that I see myself as obligated to rule in accordance with the law on any matter properly brought before the Court. I am forced to rule in accordance with the law, in complete awareness that the public at large will not be interested in the legal reasoning behind our decision, but rather in the final result. Conceivably, the stature of the Court as an institution that stands above the arguments that divide the public will be damaged. But what can we do, for this is our role and our obligation as judges?

The Commission of Inquiry pointed to the "difficult dilemma between the imperative to safeguard the very existence of the State of Israel and the lives of its citizens, and between the need to preserve its character – a country subject to the rule of law and basic moral values." The commission rejected an approach that would consign our fight against terrorism to the twilight shadows of the law. The commission also rejected the "ways of the hypocrites, who remind us of their adherence to the rule of law, even as they remain willfully blind to reality." Instead, the Commission chose to follow "the way of truth and the rule of law." In so doing, the Commission of Inquiry outlined the dilemma faced by Israel in a manner open to examination to all of Israeli society.

Consequently, it is decided that the order nisi be made absolute. The GSS does not have the authority to "shake" a man, hold him in the "Shabach" position (which includes the combination of various methods, as mentioned in paragraph 30), force him into a "frog crouch" position, and deprive him of sleep in a manner other than that which is inherently required by the interrogation. Likewise, we declare that the "necessity defense," found in the Penal Law, cannot serve as a basis of authority for interrogation practices, or for directives to GSS investigators, allowing them to employ interrogation practices of this kind. Our decision does not negate the possibility that the "necessity defense" will be available to GSS investigators – either in the choice made by the Attorney-General in deciding whether to prosecute, or according to the discretion of the court if criminal charges are brought.

Justice Y. KEDMI

I accept the conclusion reached by my colleague, the President, that the use of exceptional interrogation methods, according to the directives of the Ministerial Committee, "has not been authorized, and is illegal." I am also of the opinion that the time has come for this issue to be regulated by explicit, clear, and unambiguous legislation.

Even so, it is difficult for me to accept that, due to the absence of explicit legislation, the state should be helpless in those rare emergencies defined as "ticking bombs," and that the state would not be authorized to order the use of exceptional interrogation methods in such circumstances. As far as I am concerned, authority does exist under such circumstances, a result of the basic obligation of the state – like all countries of the world – to defend its existence, its well-being, and to safeguard the lives of its citizens. It is clear that, in those circumstances, the state – as well as its agents – will have the natural right of "self-defense," in the broad meaning of the term, against terrorist organizations that seek to take its life and the lives of its citizens.

Against this background, and in order to prevent a situation where the state stands helpless while the "bomb ticks" before our eyes, I suggest that this judgment be suspended for one year. During that year, the GSS will be allowed to employ exceptional interrogative methods in those rare cases of "ticking bombs," on the condition that explicit authorization is granted by the Attorney-General.

Such a suspension would not limit our present ruling that the use of exceptional interrogation methods – those that rely on directives of the Ministerial Committee – are illegal. The suspension of the judgment would not constitute authorization to continue acting according to those directives, and the authorization of the Attorney-General would not legalize the performance of an illegal action. This suspension would only affect the employment of exceptional interrogation methods under the emergency circumstances of a "ticking bomb."

During such a suspension period, the Knesset would be given an opportunity to consider the issue of exceptional interrogation methods in security investigations, both in general and in times of emergency. The GSS would be given the opportunity to cope with emergency situations until the Knesset considers the issue. Meanwhile, the GSS would also have an opportunity to adapt, after a long period during which the directives of the Ministerial Committee have governed.

I therefore join the judgment of the President, subject to my proposal to suspend the judgment for a period of one year.

NOTES AND QUESTIONS

1. The Center for the Defense of the Individual and the Public Committee Against Torture are both self-described independent human rights organizations providing representation for persons claiming mistreatment at the hands of Israeli authorities. They each have an elaborate web site devoted to the issues raised in this proceeding, among others.

2. Justice Kedmi would have the Court's judgment "suspended" for one year while the Knesset considers legislation, but he says that the suspension would not constitute authorization and would apply only under the circumstances of a "ticking bomb." But how would that differ from the very result the government wanted, which was advance authorization for interrogation methods under extreme circumstances?

3. The distinction between "necessity" and "justification" is an extremely sophisticated and complex problem in most of criminal law. In this situation, however, it turns out to be a reasonably straightforward proposition – the difference between advance authorization and the hope for later exoneration from something that is illegal. In a sense, the difference is something like the converse of the doctrine of prior restraint in First Amendment law – the distinction between punishing someone for speaking without permission and punishing that person for the nature of the speech or its consequences. U.S. law does not allow prior restraints absent a sufficiently strong governmental interest but it does allow punishment for harmful speech.

[B] ABU GHRAIB AND GUANTANAMO PRISONER ABUSE

The Abu Ghraib prisoner abuse scandal began surfacing in public around the first of May, 2004. Prior to that time, Army investigations had already disclosed widespread abuses and resulted in some sanctions. *See* SEYMOUR M. HERSH, CHAIN OF COMMAND (2004).

The first Army investigation of the situation by Major General Antonio M. Taguba, prepared before the scandal became public, summarized the principal abuses this way:

> Breaking chemical lights and pouring the phosphoric liquid on detainees; pouring cold water on naked detainees; beating detainees with a broom handle and a chair; threatening male detainees with rape; allowing a military police guard to stitch the wound of a detainee who was injured after being slammed against the wall in his cell; sodomizing a detainee with a chemical light and perhaps a broom stick, and using military working dogs to frighten and intimidate detainees with threats of attack, and in one instance actually biting a detainee.

As journalists and investigators probed further, it appeared that many of the "interrogation" techniques were the subject of high-level analysis if not approval. The most controversial document was the so-called "Bybee Memorandum," which described a very narrow reading of torture and outlined arguments by which torture or "inhuman or degrading treatment" of prisoners could be excused under U.S. law.

The Bybee Memorandum points out that the Convention on Torture (CAT) requires signatory nations to criminalize torture while merely committing to "undertake to prevent other acts of cruel, inhuman, or degrading treatment." Drawing on a variety of sources, the Memorandum concludes that torture consists of "severe" or "extreme" infliction of pain.

> The victim must experience intense pain or suffering of the kind that is equivalent to the pain that would be associated with serious physical injury so severe that death, organ failure, or permanent damage resulting in a loss of significant bodily function will likely result. If that pain or suffering is psychological, that suffering must result from one of the acts set forth in the statute. In addition, these acts must cause long-term mental harm.

> CAT not only defines torture as involving severe pain and suffering, but also it makes clear that such pain and suffering is at the extreme end of the spectrum of acts by reserving criminal penalties solely for torture. . . . [T]he treaty (and hence the statute) prohibits only the worst forms of cruel, inhuman, or degrading treatment or punishment.

After reviewing the *Ireland* case and cases in both U.S. and Israeli courts, the Memorandum emphasizes what it terms the torture/cruelty distinction:

> In sum, both the European Court on Human Rights and the Israeli Supreme Court have recognized a wide array of acts that constitute cruel,

inhuman, or degrading treatment or punishment, but do not amount to torture. Thus they appear to permit, under international law, an aggressive interpretation as to what amounts to torture, leaving that label to be applied only where extreme circumstances exist.

In this discussion, there is no recognition that the treaty requires a signatory nation to "undertake to prevent cruel, inhuman, or degrading treatment" and seems to say that international law condones many of the practices that were found to violate the ECHR, which were described in the Bowden article as part of the interrogation tools of U.S. agents, and which eventually surfaced as part of official policy for treatment of detainees at Guantanamo and Abu Ghraib.

The next section of the Memorandum considers whether the President of the United States can insulate interrogators from criminal responsibility.

Even if an interrogation method arguably were to violate Section 2340A, the statute would be unconstitutional if it impermissibly encroached on the President's constitutional power to conduct a military campaign. As Commander-in-Chief, the President has the constitutional authority to order interrogations of enemy combatants to gain intelligence information concerning the military plans of the enemy. The demands of the Commander-in-Chief power are especially pronounced in the middle of a war in which the nation has already suffered a direct attack. In such a case, the information gained from interrogations may prevent future attacks by foreign enemies. Any effort to apply Section 2340A in a manner that interferes with the President's direction of such core war matters as the detention and interrogation of enemy combatants thus would be unconstitutional.

Congress can no more interfere with the President's conduct of the interrogation of enemy combatants than it can dictate strategic or tactical decisions on the battlefield. Just as statutes that order the President to conduct warfare in a certain manner or for specific goals would be unconstitutional, so too are laws that seek to prevent the President from gaining the intelligence he believes necessary to prevent attacks upon the United States.

Under this reasoning, would the entire Uniform Code of Military Justice be unconstitutional? Congress has powers to declare war, to prescribe rules and regulations for governance of the armed forces, to define and punish offenses against the law of nations. Nor does the Memorandum address the lawmaking role highlighted in *Youngstown Sheet & Tube.*

Finally, the Memorandum attempts to set forth defenses under the headings of necessity and self-defense, ignoring entirely that international law regarding treatment of prisoners has been designed specifically for exigent situations, to control the use of force precisely when nations are under the most severe form of stress and emergency conditions. The whole point of these controls is to impose rules with such rigor that nobody even needs to think about whether inhumane treatment of a prisoner could be permissible. As the ECHR pointed out, the prohibition on torture is specifically exempt from the usual allowance for exigent circumstances.

Now, having soundly condemned the Bybee Memorandum, we need to consider honestly whether extreme methods of interrogation are going to be condemned in all circumstances. If, as Professor Dershowitz insists, anyone in the "ticking bomb" scenario will do whatever it takes to avoid mass casualties, what should be the legal system's response to this reality? If your child has been kidnapped and held under threat of death by terrorists, would you torture someone who knew the location and means of access to the child? If so, what would you expect the legal system to do with you after the safe return of your child? Is it really rational to expect our agents around the world to "play fair" in all the various settings in which they might have control over suspected terrorists with valuable knowledge?

As the scandal unfolded, it was learned that there were several memoranda of this type drafted in interaction among the White House, Justice Department, and Pentagon. The Pentagon responded with additional investigative reports, the most significant of which has been the Schlesinger Report from the "Independent Panel to Review DoD Detention Operations" chaired by James R. Schlesinger, a former Director of Central Intelligence and Secretary of Defense under Presidents Nixon and Ford. The Schlesinger Panel found "abuses occurred at the hands of both military police and military intelligence personnel. The pictured abuses, unacceptable even in wartime, were not part of authorized interrogations nor were they even aimed at intelligence targets. They represent deviant behavior and a failure of leadership and discipline."

With regard to the chain of command, the Report stated, "No approved procedures called for or allowed the kinds of abuse that occurred. There is no evidence of a policy of abuse promulgated by senior officials or military authorities. Still, the abuses were not just the failure of some individuals to follow known standards, and they are more than the failure of a few leaders to enforce proper discipline. There is institutional and personal responsibility at higher levels."

On December 29, 2004, the Justice Department released a memorandum "withdrawing" the Bybee Memorandum. Primarily, the new memorandum states that "we disagree with statements in the August 2002 Memorandum limiting 'severe' pain under the statute to 'excruciating and agonizing' pain or to pain 'equivalent in intensity to the pain accompanying serious physical injury, such as organ failure, impairment of bodily function, or even death.' . . . Because the discussion in that memorandum concerning the President's Commander-in-Chief power and the potential defenses to liability was – and remains – unnecessary, it has been eliminated."

§ 9.02 EMERGENCY POWERS & CIVIL LIBERTIES

A fitting conclusion to our study comes from the various opinions of the House of Lords in a case falling somewhere between *Hamdi* and *Rasul*. Although the case is important on its own terms, the opinions address several matters of more general interest such as the relative roles of the three branches of government, the applicability of international law, and the significance of national emergency.

To set the stage for what should be a general discussion of emergency powers and civil liberties, consider this argument:

The Extra-Legal Measures model proposed in this Article informs public officials that they may act extralegally when they believe that such action is necessary for protecting the nation and the public in the face of calamity, provided that they openly and publicly acknowledge the nature of their actions. It is then up to the people to decide . . . how to respond to such actions.

Oren Gross, *Chaos and Rules: Should Responses to Violent Crises Always Be Constitutional?* 112 YALE L.J. 1011, 1023 (2003). What happens to minority rights in this model? Does the model actually contemplate anything other than the normal political process in a democratic society?

[I]t should not be a surprise that courts have all too often deferred to unfounded assertions of government power on issues of national security; when the executive claims that the fate of the nation is at stake, it takes real courage to stand up to that assertion and subject it to careful scrutiny. . . . At the same time, the conventional wisdom that courts have failed during times of crisis is itself overstated. . . . Judicial decisions, while rarely providing relief to the initial victims of a crisis mentality, have played a role in restricting the options available to the government in the next emergency.

David Cole, *Judging the next Emergency: Judicial Review and Individual Rights in Times of Crisis*, 101 MICH. L. REV. 2565, 2594 (2003).

As you read the House of Lords opinions, reflect on how they differ from the U.S. Supreme Court's approach in *Hamdi*. The House of Lords is the highest appellate judicial tribunal in the United Kingdom. It acts through an Appellate Committee of appointed "Law Lords," a panel of which is chosen for each case. A proposal is pending to take the appellate judicial power out of the House of Lords and convert the Appellate Committee to a Supreme Court of the United Kingdom. In a way, that is the essence of the committee function at this time, but its opinions are still expressed as "speeches" to the House.

A v. SECRETARY OF STATE FOR THE HOME DEPARTMENT
[2004] UKHL 56, [2004] All ER (D) 271 (Dec 16, 2004)

PANEL: Lord Bingham of Cornhill, Lord Nicholls of Birkenhead, Lord Hoffmann, Lord Hope of Craighead, Lord Scott of Foscote, Lord Rodger of Earlsferry, Lord Walker of Gestingthorpe, Baroness Hale of Richmond and Lord Carswell

LORD BINGHAM OF CORNHILL:

My Lords,

[Nine aliens (Appellants) were detained as suspected terrorists or suspected of having links to terrorist organizations. The 2001 Anti-Terrorism Act contained in section 23 an authorization similar to section 412 of PATRIOT, allowing detention pursuant to a "Derogation Order" declaring a national emergency and derogating from certain provisions of the European Convention on Human Rights. Under a prior 1998 Human Rights Act, the UK courts had been given power to declare that a particular government action was "incompatible" with the ECHR.]

8. First, the Secretary of State might detain a non-British national pending the making of a deportation order against him. In *R. v Governor of Durham Prison, Ex parte Hardial Singh* [1984] 1 WLR 704 it was held, in a decision which has never been questioned, that such detention was permissible only for such time as was reasonably necessary for the process of deportation to be carried out. [ECHR] article 5(1) . . . guarantees the fundamental human right of personal freedom . . . [but] goes on to prescribe certain exceptions. One exception is crucial to these appeals:

(1) Everyone has the right to liberty and security of person. No one shall be deprived of his liberty save in the following cases and in accordance with a procedure prescribed by law:

(f) the lawful arrest or detention of . . . a person against whom action is being taken with a view to deportation

Thus there is . . . no warrant for the long-term or indefinite detention of a non-UK national whom the Home Secretary wishes to remove. Such a person may be detained only during the process of deportation. Otherwise, the Convention is breached and the Convention rights of the detainee are violated.

9. Secondly, reference must be made to the important decision of the European Court of Human Rights in *Chahal v United Kingdom* (1996) 23 EHRR 413. Mr Chahal was an Indian citizen who had been granted indefinite leave to remain in this country but whose activities as a Sikh separatist brought him to the notice of the authorities both in India and here. The Home Secretary of the day decided that he should be deported from this country because his continued presence here was not conducive to the public good for reasons of a political nature, namely the international fight against terrorism. He resisted deportation on the ground (among others) that, if returned to India, he faced a real risk of death, or of torture in custody contrary to article 3 of the European Convention, which provides that "No one shall be subjected to torture or to inhuman or degrading treatment or punishment." [The European Court] held that "Article 3 makes no provision for exceptions and no derogation from it is permissible under Article 15 even in the event of a public emergency threatening the life of the nation. Thus, whenever substantial grounds have been shown for believing that an individual would face a real risk of being subjected to treatment contrary to Article 3 if removed to another State, the responsibility of the Contracting State to safeguard him or her against such treatment is engaged in the event of expulsion."

In a case like Mr Chahal's, where deportation proceedings are precluded by article 3, article 5(1)(f) would not sanction detention because the non-national would not be "a person against whom action is being taken with a view to deportation." A person who commits a serious crime under the criminal law of this country may of course, whether a national or a non-national, be charged, tried and, if convicted, imprisoned. But a non-national who faces the prospect of torture or inhuman treatment if returned to his own country, and who cannot be deported to any third country and is not charged with any crime, may not under article 5(1)(f) of the Convention be detained here even if judged to be a threat to national security.

10. The European Convention gives member states a limited right to derogate from some articles of the Convention (including article 5, although not article 3).

ECHR article 15. Derogation in time of emergency

> 1. In time of war or other public emergency threatening the life of the nation any High Contracting Party may take measures derogating from its obligations under this Convention to the extent strictly required by the exigencies of the situation, provided that such measures are not inconsistent with its other obligations under international law.

A member state availing itself of the right of derogation must inform the Secretary General of the Council of Europe of the measures it has taken and the reasons for them. It was in exercise of his power under [the 1998 Act] that the Home Secretary, on 11 November 2001, made the Derogation Order, which came into force two days later.

15. The Act makes provision in section 25 for appeal to SIAC against certification by a certified suspected international terrorist.

Public emergency

16. The appellants repeated before the House a contention rejected by both SIAC and the Court of Appeal, that there neither was nor is a "public emergency threatening the life of the nation" within the meaning of article 15(1). Thus, they contended, the threshold test for reliance on article 15 has not been satisfied.

17. The European Court considered the meaning of this provision in *Lawless v Ireland* (No 3) (1961) 1 EHRR 15, a case concerned with very low-level IRA terrorist activity in Ireland and Northern Ireland between 1954 and 1957. The Irish Government derogated from article 5 in July 1957 in order to permit detention without charge or trial and the applicant was detained between July and December 1957. [EHR Court] ruled:

> 28. In the general context of Article 15 of the Convention, the natural and customary meaning of the words 'other public emergency threatening the life of the nation' is sufficiently clear; they refer to an exceptional situation of crisis or emergency which affects the whole population and constitutes a threat to the organised life of the community of which the State is composed. The Court, after an examination, finds this to be the case; the existence at the time of a 'public emergency threatening the life of the nation' was reasonably deduced by the Irish Government from a combination of several factors, namely: in the first place, the existence in the territory of the Republic of Ireland of a secret army engaged in unconstitutional activities and using violence to attain its purposes; secondly, the fact that this army was also operating outside the territory of the State, thus seriously jeopardising the relations of the Republic of Ireland with its neighbour; thirdly, the steady and alarming increase in

terrorist activities from the autumn of 1956 and throughout the first half of 1957.

28. The European Court decisions seem to me to be, with respect, clearly right. In each case the member state had actually experienced widespread loss of life caused by an armed body dedicated to destroying the territorial integrity of the state. To hold that the article 15 test was not satisfied in such circumstances, if a response beyond that provided by the ordinary course of law was required, would have been perverse.

29. I would accept that great weight should be given to the judgment of the Home Secretary, his colleagues and Parliament on this question, because they were called on to exercise a pre-eminently political judgment. It involved making a factual prediction of what various people around the world might or might not do, and when (if at all) they might do it, and what the consequences might be if they did. Any prediction about the future behaviour of human beings (as opposed to the phases of the moon or high water at London Bridge) is necessarily problematical. Reasonable and informed minds may differ, and a judgment is not shown to be wrong or unreasonable because that which is thought likely to happen does not happen. It would have been irresponsible not to err, if at all, on the side of safety. The more purely political (in a broad or narrow sense) a question is, the more appropriate it will be for political resolution and the less likely it is to be an appropriate matter for judicial decision. The smaller, therefore, will be the potential role of the court. It is the function of political and not judicial bodies to resolve political questions. Conversely, the greater the legal content of any issue, the greater the potential role of the court, because under our constitution and subject to the sovereign power of Parliament it is the function of the courts and not of political bodies to resolve legal questions. The present question seems to me to be very much at the political end of the spectrum. I conclude that the appellants have shown no ground strong enough to warrant displacing the Secretary of State's decision on this important threshold question.

Proportionality

31. The appellants' argument under this head can, I hope fairly, be summarised as involving the following steps:

(5) If the threat presented to the security of the United Kingdom by UK nationals suspected of being Al-Qaeda terrorists or their supporters could be addressed without infringing their right to personal liberty, it is not shown why similar measures could not adequately address the threat presented by foreign nationals.

(6) Since the right to personal liberty is among the most fundamental of the rights protected by the European Convention, any restriction of it must be closely scrutinised by the national court and such scrutiny involves no violation of democratic or constitutional principle.

36. In urging the fundamental importance of the right to personal freedom, as the sixth step in their proportionality argument, the appellants were able to draw on the long libertarian tradition of English law, dating back to chapter 39 of Magna Carta 1215, given effect in the ancient remedy of habeas corpus,

declared in the Petition of Right 1628, upheld in a series of landmark decisions down the centuries and embodied in the substance and procedure of the law to our own day.

37. [T]he Attorney General . . . directed the weight of his submission to challenging the standard of judicial review for which the appellants contended in this sixth step. He submitted that as it was for Parliament and the executive to assess the threat facing the nation, so it was for those bodies and not the courts to judge the response necessary to protect the security of the public. These were matters of a political character calling for an exercise of political and not judicial judgment. Just as the European Court allowed a generous margin of appreciation to member states, recognising that they were better placed to understand and address local problems, so should national courts recognise, for the same reason, that matters of the kind in issue here fall within the discretionary area of judgment properly belonging to the democratic organs of the state. It was not for the courts to usurp authority properly belonging elsewhere.

39. While any decision made by a representative democratic body must of course command respect, the degree of respect will be conditioned by the nature of the decision. In *R v Director of Public Prosecutions, Ex p Kebilene* [2000] 2 AC 326, 381, Lord Hope of Craighead said:

> It will be easier for such [a discretionary] area of judgment to be recognised where the Convention itself requires a balance to be struck, much less so where the right is stated in terms which are unqualified. It will be easier for it to be recognised where the issues involve questions of social or economic policy, much less so where the rights are of high constitutional importance or are of a kind where the courts are especially well placed to assess the need for protection.

In his dissenting judgment (cited with approval in *Libman*) in *RJR-MacDonald Inc v Attorney General of Canada* [1995] 3 SCR 199, para 68, La Forest J, sitting in the same court, said:

> Courts are specialists in the protection of liberty and the interpretation of legislation and are, accordingly, well placed to subject criminal justice legislation to careful scrutiny. However, courts are not specialists in the realm of policy-making, nor should they be.

Jackson J, sitting in the Supreme Court of the United States in *West Virginia State Board of Education v Barnette,* 319 U.S. 624 (1943), stated, speaking of course with reference to an entrenched constitution:

> The very purpose of a Bill of Rights was to withdraw certain subjects from the vicissitudes of political controversy, to place them beyond the reach of majorities and officials and to establish them as legal principles to be applied by the courts . . . . We cannot, because of modest estimates of our competence in such specialties as public education, withhold the judgment that history authenticates as the function of this Court when liberty is infringed.

42. It follows from this analysis that the appellants are in my opinion entitled to invite the courts to review, on proportionality grounds, the Derogation Order and the compatibility with the Convention of section 23 and the courts are not effectively precluded by any doctrine of deference from scrutinising the issues raised. It also follows that I do not accept the full breadth of the Attorney General's submissions. I do not in particular accept the distinction which he drew between democratic institutions and the courts. It is of course true that the judges in this country are not elected and are not answerable to Parliament. It is also of course true that Parliament, the executive and the courts have different functions. But the function of independent judges charged to interpret and apply the law is universally recognised as a cardinal feature of the modern democratic state, a cornerstone of the rule of law itself. The Attorney General is fully entitled to insist on the proper limits of judicial authority, but he is wrong to stigmatise judicial decision-making as in some way undemocratic. The effect is not, of course, to override the sovereign legislative authority of the Queen in Parliament, since if primary legislation is declared to be incompatible the validity of the legislation is unaffected and the remedy lies with the appropriate minister, who is answerable to Parliament. The 1998 Act gives the courts a very specific, wholly democratic, mandate.

43. The appellants' proportionality challenge to the Order and section 23 is, in my opinion, sound . . . . [I agree with] the central complaint made by the appellants: that the choice of an immigration measure to address a security problem had the inevitable result of failing adequately to address that problem (by allowing non-UK suspected terrorists to leave the country with impunity and leaving British suspected terrorists at large) while imposing the severe penalty of indefinite detention on persons who, even if reasonably suspected of having links with Al-Qaeda, may harbour no hostile intentions towards the United Kingdom. The conclusion that the Order and section 23 are, in Convention terms, disproportionate is in my opinion irresistible.

73. I would allow the appeals. There will be a quashing order in respect of the [Derogation Order]. There will also be a declaration that section 23 of the Act 2001 is incompatible with articles 5 and 14 of the European Convention insofar as it is disproportionate and permits detention of suspected international terrorists in a way that discriminates on the ground of nationality or immigration status.

LORD NICHOLLS OF BIRKENHEAD:

My Lords,

74. Indefinite imprisonment without charge or trial is anathema in any country which observes the rule of law. It deprives the detained person of the protection a criminal trial is intended to afford. Wholly exceptional circumstances must exist before this extreme step can be justified.

75. The government contends that these post-9/11 days are wholly exceptional. The circumstances require and justify the indefinite detention of non-nationals suspected of being international terrorists.

76. The principal weakness in the government's case lies in the different treatment accorded to nationals and non-nationals. The extended power of detention conferred by [the 2001 Act] applies only to persons who are not British citizens. It is difficult to see how the extreme circumstances, which alone would justify such detention, can exist when lesser protective steps apparently suffice in the case of British citizens suspected of being international terrorists.

81. In the present case I see no escape from the conclusion that Parliament must be regarded as having attached insufficient weight to the human rights of non-nationals. The subject matter of the legislation is the needs of national security. This subject matter dictates that, in the ordinary course, substantial latitude should be accorded to the legislature. But the human right in question, the right to individual liberty, is one of the most fundamental of human rights. Indefinite detention without trial wholly negates that right for an indefinite period. With one exception all the individuals currently detained have been imprisoned now for three years and there is no prospect of imminent release. It is true that those detained may at any time walk away from their place of detention if they leave this country. Their prison, it is said, has only three walls. But this freedom is more theoretical than real. This is demonstrated by the continuing presence in Belmarsh of most of those detained. They prefer to stay in prison rather than face the prospect of ill treatment in any country willing to admit them.

LORD HOFFMANN:

My Lords,

86. This is one of the most important cases which the House has had to decide in recent years. It calls into question the very existence of an ancient liberty of which this country has until now been very proud: freedom from arbitrary arrest and detention. The power which the Home Secretary seeks to uphold is a power to detain people indefinitely without charge or trial. Nothing could be more antithetical to the instincts and traditions of the people of the United Kingdom.

88. The technical issue in this appeal is whether such a power can be justified on the ground that there exists a "war or other public emergency threatening the life of the nation" within the meaning of article 15 of the European Convention on Human Rights. But I would not like anyone to think that we are concerned with some special doctrine of European law. Freedom from arbitrary arrest and detention is a quintessentially British liberty, enjoyed by the inhabitants of this country when most of the population of Europe could be thrown into prison at the whim of their rulers. It was incorporated into the European Convention in order to entrench the same liberty in countries which had recently been under Nazi occupation. The United Kingdom subscribed to the Convention because it set out the rights which British subjects enjoyed under the common law.

89. The exceptional power to derogate from those rights also reflected British constitutional history. There have been times of great national emergency in which habeas corpus has been suspended and powers to detain on suspicion conferred on the government. It happened during the Napoleonic Wars and during both World Wars in the twentieth century. These powers were conferred

with great misgiving and, in the sober light of retrospect after the emergency had passed, were often found to have been cruelly and unnecessarily exercised. But the necessity of draconian powers in moments of national crisis is recognised in our constitutional history. Article 15 of the Convention, when it speaks of "war or other public emergency threatening the life of the nation," accurately states the conditions in which such legislation has previously been thought necessary.

91. What is meant by "threatening the life of the nation"? The "nation" is a social organism, living in its territory (in this case, the United Kingdom) under its own form of government and subject to a system of laws which expresses its own political and moral values. When one speaks of a threat to the "life" of the nation, the word life is being used in a metaphorical sense. The life of the nation is not coterminous with the lives of its people. The nation, its institutions and values, endure through generations. In many important respects, England is the same nation as it was at the time of the first Elizabeth or the Glorious Revolution. The Armada threatened to destroy the life of the nation, not by loss of life in battle, but by subjecting English institutions to the rule of Spain and the Inquisition. The same was true of the threat posed to the United Kingdom by Nazi Germany in the Second World War.

94. The Home Secretary has adduced evidence, both open and secret, to show the existence of a threat of serious terrorist outrages. I am willing to accept that credible evidence of such plots exist. The events of 11 September 2001 in New York and Washington and 11 March 2003 in Madrid make it entirely likely that the threat of similar atrocities in the United Kingdom is a real one.

95. But the question is whether such a threat is a threat to the life of the nation. The Attorney General's submissions and the judgment of the Special Immigration Appeals Commission treated a threat of serious physical damage and loss of life as necessarily involving a threat to the life of the nation. But in my opinion this shows a misunderstanding of what is meant by "threatening the life of the nation." Of course the government has a duty to protect the lives and property of its citizens. But that is a duty which it owes all the time and which it must discharge without destroying our constitutional freedoms. There may be some nations too fragile or fissiparous to withstand a serious act of violence. But that is not the case in the United Kingdom. When Milton urged the government of his day not to censor the press even in time of civil war, he said:

> Lords and Commons of England, consider what nation it is whereof ye are, and whereof ye are the governours.

96. This is a nation which has been tested in adversity, which has survived physical destruction and catastrophic loss of life. I do not underestimate the ability of fanatical groups of terrorists to kill and destroy, but they do not threaten the life of the nation. Whether we would survive Hitler hung in the balance, but there is no doubt that we shall survive Al-Qaeda. The Spanish people have not said that what happened in Madrid, hideous crime as it was, threatened the life of their nation. Their legendary pride would not allow it. Terrorist violence, serious as it is, does not threaten our institutions of government or our existence as a civil community.

97. For these reasons I think that the Special Immigration Appeals Commission made an error of law and that the appeal ought to be allowed. Others of your Lordships who are also in favour of allowing the appeal would do so, not because there is no emergency threatening the life of the nation, but on the ground that a power of detention confined to foreigners is irrational and discriminatory. I would prefer not to express a view on this point. I said that the power of detention is at present confined to foreigners and I would not like to give the impression that all that was necessary was to extend the power to United Kingdom citizens as well. In my opinion, such a power in any form is not compatible with our constitution. The real threat to the life of the nation, in the sense of a people living in accordance with its traditional laws and political values, comes not from terrorism but from laws such as these. That is the true measure of what terrorism may achieve. It is for Parliament to decide whether to give the terrorists such a victory.

LORD HOPE OF CRAIGHEAD:

My Lords,

99. Although these appeals are concerned with general issues and not with the cases of each of the appellants individually, their importance to them is nevertheless very great. Two cardinal principles lie at the heart of the argument. It is the first responsibility of government in a democratic society to protect and safeguard the lives of its citizens. That is where the public interest lies. It is essential to the preservation of democracy, and it is the duty of the court to do all it can to respect and uphold that principle. But the court has another duty too. It is to protect and safeguard the rights of the individual. Among these rights is the individual's right to liberty.

100. It is impossible ever to overstate the importance of the right to liberty in a democracy. In the words of BARON HUME, COMMENTARIES ON THE LAW OF SCOTLAND RESPECTING CRIMES, 4th ed (1844), vol 2, p 98:

As indeed it is obvious, that, by its very constitution, every court of criminal justice must have the power of correcting the greatest and most dangerous of all abuses of the forms of law – that of the protracted imprisonment of the accused, untried, perhaps not intended ever to be tried, nay, it may be, not informed of the nature of the charge against him, or the name of the accuser.

These were not idle words. When Hume published the first edition of his Commentaries in 1797 grave abuses of the kind he described were within living memory. He knew the dangers that might lie in store for democracy itself if the courts were to allow individuals to be deprived of their right to liberty indefinitely and without charge on grounds of public interest by the executive. The risks are as great now in our time of heightened tension as they were then.

101. There is a third principle which the court must also recognise when it is called upon to perform its central function, which is to strike the balance between the public interest and the right to liberty. The basic principle is that the right belongs to everyone, whoever they may be and wherever they may have

come from, who happen to be within the Contracting State's territory. Everyone enjoys this right. It is a right, not a privilege. And it is accorded to everyone within the jurisdiction, as article 1 of the Convention declares. It is not given just to British citizens and those who have the right of abode in this country – not just to "British nationals".

105. The Secretary of State was, of course, entitled to discriminate between British nationals on the one hand and foreign nationals on the other for all the purposes of immigration control, subject to the limitations established by the *Chahal* case. What he was not entitled to do was to treat the right to liberty of foreign nationals as different in any respect from that enjoyed by British nationals.

114. [T]hat the European Court will accord a large margin of appreciation to the contracting states on the question whether the measures taken to interfere with the right to liberty do not exceed those strictly required by the exigencies of the situation cannot be taken as the last word on the matter so far as the domestic courts are concerned. Final responsibility for determining whether they do exceed these limits must lie with the courts.

The public emergency

115. The question whether there is a public emergency of the kind contemplated by article 15(1) requires the exercise of judgment. The primary meaning of the word is an occurrence that is sudden or unexpected. It has an extended meaning – a situation of pressing need. A patch of fog on the motorway or a storm which brings down power lines may create a situation of emergency without the life of the nation being under threat. It is a question of degree. The range of situations which may demonstrate such a threat will extend from the consequences of natural disasters of all kinds to the consequences of acts of terrorism. Few would doubt that it is for the executive, with all the resources at its disposal, to judge whether the consequences of such events amount to an emergency of that kind. But imminent emergencies arouse fear and, as has often been said, fear is democracy's worst enemy. So it would be dangerous to ignore the context in which the judgment is to be exercised. Its exercise needs to be watched very carefully if it is a preliminary to the invoking of emergency powers, especially if they involve actions which are incompatible with Convention rights.

116. I am content therefore to accept that the questions whether there is an emergency and whether it threatens the life of the nation are pre-eminently for the executive and for Parliament. The judgment that has to be formed on these issues lies outside the expertise of the courts. But in my opinion it is nevertheless open to the judiciary to examine the nature of the situation that has been identified by government as constituting the emergency, and to scrutinise the submission by the Attorney General that for the appellants to be deprived of their fundamental right to liberty does not exceed what is "strictly required" by the situation which it has identified. The use of the word "strictly" invites close scrutiny of the action that has been taken. Where the rights of the individual are in issue the nature of the emergency must first be identified, and then compared with the effects on the individual of depriving him of those rights.

In my opinion it is the proper function of the judiciary to subject the government's reasoning on these matters in this case to very close analysis.

119. The picture which emerges clearly from these statements is of a current state of emergency. It is an emergency which is constituted by the threat that these attacks will be carried out. It threatens the life of the nation because of the appalling consequences that would affect us all if they were to occur here. But it cannot yet be said that these attacks are imminent. It has to be recognised that, as the attacks are likely to come without warning, it may not be possible to identify a stage when they can be said to be imminent. This is an important factor, and I do not leave it out of account. But the fact is that the stage when the nation has to face that kind of emergency, the emergency of imminent attack, has not been reached.

120. The distinction which is to be drawn between these two situations is important. The situation which is said to require the derogation is the situation which we face now, not the situation that might arise at some unknown time in the future. The life of the nation is said to be threatened. But do the exigencies of the situation which we face now require that the appellants be deprived of their right to liberty? All the factual material which may provide an answer to this question is in the hands of the Home Secretary. But has he asked himself the right question in his analysis of this material? And did SIAC ask itself the right question when it was examining the decision of the Home Secretary?

Strictly required

121. In my opinion there were two questions that had to be addressed in order to determine whether or not the derogation that was proposed was strictly required. One was what its effects would be on the individuals who were to be affected by it. The other was whether, given those effects and the way British nationals who posed the same threat to the life of the nation were to be dealt with, derogating from the right to liberty of those individuals was strictly necessary. The second question is relevant to the discrimination issue, but I think that it also bears directly on the question whether the derogation went beyond what was strictly required.

129. The Attorney General, for understandable reasons, was not willing to elaborate on the measures that were being taken to contain the threat to the life of this nation from British nationals. But he said that a number of measures were in place for the protection of the public, and that those involved were being prosecuted where possible. He explained that any response which provided for the indefinite detention of those people would have had to have been a different response, as they were not subject to immigration control. The distinction which was drawn between their case and that of the foreign nationals was that the foreign nationals had no right to be here. For British nationals the measure would have had to have provided for a form of detention that had four walls. It would have had to have been more draconian. But that answer, while true, does not meet the objection that the indefinite detention without trial of foreign nationals cannot be said to be strictly required to meet the exigencies of the situation, if the indefinite detention without trial of those who present a threat to the life of the nation because they are suspected of involvement in

international terrorism is not thought to be required in the case of British nationals.

132. I would hold that the indefinite detention of foreign nationals without trial has not been shown to be strictly required, as the same threat from British nationals whom the government is unable or unwilling to prosecute is being met by other measures which do not require them to be detained indefinitely without trial. The distinction which the government seeks to draw between these two groups – British nationals and foreign nationals – proceeds on the misconception that it is a sufficient answer to the question whether the derogation is strictly required that the two groups have different rights in the immigration context. So they do. But the derogation is from the right to liberty. The right to liberty is the same for each group. If derogation is not strictly required in the case of one group, it cannot be strictly required in the case of the other group that presents the same threat.

LORD SCOTT OF FOSCOTE:

My Lords,

142. It has not been suggested, nor could it be suggested, that the 2001 Act is otherwise than an effective enactment made by a sovereign legislature. It was passed by both Houses of Parliament and received the Royal Assent. Whether the terms of the 2001 Act are consistent with the terms of the European Convention on Human Rights ("the ECHR") is, so far as the courts of this country are concerned, relevant only to the question whether a declaration of incompatibility under section 4 of the Human Rights Act 1998 should be made. The making of such a declaration will not, however, affect in the least the validity under domestic law of the impugned statutory provision. The import of such a declaration is political not legal.

143. So what is the point of these proceedings and these appeals, with nine of your Lordships sitting in judgment, with intervention from the National Council of Civil Liberties and from Amnesty International and with avid attention from the media?

145. The normal and proper function of the courts of this country is to adjudicate on the rights and liabilities under domestic law of citizens (or of institutions with legal personality) or to adjudicate on the validity of executive actions or omissions that may affect those rights and liabilities. It is not, normally, the function of the courts to entertain proceedings the purpose of which is to obtain a ruling as to whether an Act of Parliament is compatible with an international treaty obligation entered into by the executive. The executive cannot make laws for the United Kingdom otherwise than pursuant to and within the constraints imposed by an enabling Act of Parliament. The executive has extensive and varied prerogative powers that it can exercise in the name of the Crown but none that permit lawmaking. In being asked, therefore, to perform the function to which I have referred, the courts are, it seems to me, being asked to perform a function the consequences of which will be essentially political in character rather than legal. A ruling that an Act of Parliament is incompatible with the ECHR does not detract from the validity of the Act. It does

not relieve citizens from the burdens imposed by the Act. It provides, of course, ammunition to those who disapprove of the Act and desire to agitate for its amendment or repeal.

160. For the reasons . . . given by my noble and learned friends I conclude that the Order is not compliant with article 15 of the ECHR. I understand the Attorney General to have accepted that this conclusion would require the Order to be quashed. I venture to repeat my doubts about this. In the circumstances, however, I too would make the Order suggested by Lord Bingham of Cornhill.

LORD RODGER OF EARLSFERRY:

My Lords,

189. My Lords, I have anxiously considered all the evidential and other material, as well as the arguments which the Attorney General advanced to justify the legislation. Proceeding on the same basis as the Government and Parliament, that detention of the British suspects is not strictly required to meet the threat that they pose to the life of the nation, I have come, however, to the conclusion that the detention of the foreign suspects cannot be strictly required, either, to meet the comparable threat that they pose. The second requirement of article 15(1) is accordingly not satisfied.

LORD WALKER OF GESTINGTHORPE:

My Lords,

191. As all your Lordships recognise, these are very important and difficult appeals. Your Lordships have to consider the balancing of one of the most fundamental human freedoms – freedom from imprisonment for an indefinite period, without indictment, trial or conviction on a criminal charge – with one of the state's most basic and imperative duties – the duty of safeguarding the lives and well-being of its citizens and others resident in the United Kingdom. It is unnecessary to repeat citations as to the importance of these two principles.

192. The detention without trial of terrorist suspects is therefore a crucial instance – probably the most crucial instance of all-of the problems of reconciling individual human rights with the interests of the community, and of determining the proper functions, in this process, of different arms of government.

207. In these appeals attention has of course focused on Part 4 of the 2001 Act, since it contains the only provisions in respect of which the British Government thought it necessary to make a derogation from the Convention. Those are the measures which must be shown to be strictly required by the exigencies of the situation. But it would be a mistake, in my view, to divorce them entirely from their context, that is as part of a major enactment most of whose provisions are aimed impartially at British nationals and non-nationals, and some of whose provisions (those creating offences committed overseas) are aimed exclusively at nationals.

209. I have the misfortune to differ from most of your Lordships as to whether the derogating measures are proportionate, rational and non-discriminatory, or

are in the alternative disproportionate, irrational and offensively discriminatory. In the circumstances it would be inappropriate for me to add much to the already considerable volume of your Lordships' reasons; but it would also be inappropriate, in such an important case, not to set out briefly the reasons for my dissent. I hardly need add that having had the great advantage of reading and considering in draft all your Lordships' speeches, it is only with great diffidence that I have arrived at, and I still maintain, a different opinion. I do so for three main reasons:

(1) When this country is faced, as it is, with imminent threats from enemies who make use of secrecy, deception and surprise, the need for anti-terrorist measures to be "strictly necessary" must be interpreted in accordance with the precautionary principle recognised by the Strasbourg Court in *Ireland v. United Kingdom*.

(2) I agree with the Court of Appeal, and very respectfully disagree with SIAC and the majority of the House, on the issue of discrimination.

(3) SIAC is an independent and impartial tribunal of unquestioned standing and expertise. It carefully considers any appeal by a suspected terrorist, and periodically reviews any of its decisions which have been adverse to a detained suspect. I would in no way dissent from condemning the odiousness of indefinite detention at the will of the Executive, but such a description cannot be applied to detention under Part 4 of the 2001 Act without so much qualification as to amount almost to contradiction.

215. In this case a power of interning British citizens without trial, and with no option of going abroad if they chose to do so, would be far more oppressive, and a graver affront to their human rights, than a power to detain in "a prison with three walls" a suspected terrorist who has no right of abode in the United Kingdom, and whom the government could and would deport but for the risk of torture if he were returned to his own country. Detention of non-national suspects is still a cause of grave concern, and I share the anxieties expressed by [others]. But in my view Part 4 of the 2001 Act is not offensively discriminatory, because there are sound, rational grounds for different treatment.

217. As I have said, the detention without trial of non-national suspected terrorists is a cause of grave concern. But the judgment of Parliament and of the Secretary of State is that these measures were necessary, and the 2001 Act contains several important safeguards against oppression. The exercise of the Secretary of State's powers is subject to judicial review by SIAC, an independent and impartial court, which under sections 25 and 26 of the 2001 Act has a wide jurisdiction to hear appeals, and must also review every certificate granted under section 21 at regular intervals. Moreover the legislation is temporary in nature. Any decision to prolong it is anxiously considered by the legislature. While it is in force there is detailed scrutiny of the operation of sections 21 to 23 by the individual appointed under section 28. There is also a wider review by the Committee of Privy Councillors appointed under section 122. All these safeguards seem to me to show a genuine determination that the 2001 Act should not be used to encroach on human rights any more than is strictly necessary.

218. I think it is also significant that in a period of nearly three years no more than seventeen individuals have been certified under section 21. Of course every single detention without trial is a matter of concern, but in the context of national security the number of persons actually detained (now significantly fewer than 17) is to my mind relevant to the issue of proportionality. [*Amicus*] in its written submissions appears to rely on the small number of certifications as evidence that there is not a sufficiently grave emergency. That is, I think, a striking illustration of the dilemma facing a democratic government in protecting national security. I would dismiss these appeals.

BARONESS HALE OF RICHMOND:

My Lords,

226. The courts' power to rule on the validity of the derogation is another of the safeguards enacted by Parliament in this carefully constructed package. It would be meaningless if we could only rubber-stamp what the Home Secretary and Parliament have done. But any sensible court, like any sensible person, recognises the limits of its expertise. Assessing the strength of a general threat to the life of the nation is, or should be, within the expertise of the Government and its advisers. If a Government were to declare a public emergency where patently there was no such thing, it would be the duty of the court to say so. But we are here considering the immediate aftermath of the unforgettable events of 11 September 2001. The attacks launched on the United States on that date were clearly intended to threaten the life of that nation. SIAC were satisfied that the open and closed material before them justified the conclusion that there was also a public emergency threatening the life of this nation. I, for one, would not feel qualified or even inclined to disagree.

235. Are foreigners and nationals alike for this purpose? The Attorney General argued that they are not. The foreigners have no right to be here and we would expel them if we could. Hence, he argued, the true comparison is not with suspected international terrorists who are British nationals but with foreign suspected international terrorists who can be deported. This cannot be right. The foreigners who can be deported are not like the foreigners who cannot. These foreigners are only being detained because they cannot be deported. They are just like a British national who cannot be deported. The relevant circumstances making the two cases alike for this purpose are the same three which constitute the problem: a suspected international terrorist, who for a variety of reasons cannot be successfully prosecuted, and who for a variety of reasons cannot be deported or expelled.

237. Democracy values each person equally. In most respects, this means that the will of the majority must prevail. But valuing each person equally also means that the will of the majority cannot prevail if it is inconsistent with the equal rights of minorities. As Thomas Jefferson said in his inaugural address:

> Though the will of the majority is in all cases to prevail, that will to be rightful must be reasonable . . . . The minority possess their equal rights, which equal law must protect, and to violate would be oppression.

238. No one has the right to be an international terrorist. But substitute "black", "disabled", "female", "gay", or any other similar adjective for "foreign" before "suspected international terrorist" and ask whether it would be justifiable to take power to lock up that group but not the "white", "able-bodied", "male" or "straight" suspected international terrorists. The answer is clear.

LORD CARSWELL [concurred with Lord Bingham].

NOTES AND QUESTIONS

1. Is the presence of a national emergency a matter for political or judicial judgment? Compare the approaches and standards of review applied by Lord Bingham, Lord Hoffman, Lord Hope, and Baroness Hale. Then compare their approaches to the responses of the U.S. Justices when met with governmental claims for deference in the *Hamdi* and *Rasul* cases. When the next claim of emergency arises, which approach would you prefer to have in your bag of precedents?

2. On what basis does Lord Hoffman claim the power of judicial review over the findings of executive and legislative branches that an emergency exists in the UK?

3. Lord Bingham articulates a vision of strict scrutiny that sounds familiar to students of U.S. equal protection and First Amendment law. The reason the statute fails, in his view, is that its lack of application to UK nationals shows that other measures could be found to meet the emergency. What would he be likely to do if Parliament extended the power of detention without trial to UK nationals?

4. Lord Nicholls makes the point that most of the detainees could leave at any time but have chosen to remain in prison rather than go to any country that would have them. This is reminiscent of the dilemma faced in *Zadvydas*. What should a free society do about an alien who can't go home but who is a danger to the host country? Is monitoring that person's activities after release a sufficient answer? How long would it take to bankrupt a country, either economically or psychologically, if it were trying to monitor the activities of millions of suspected terrorists within its borders?

Some Concluding Thoughts and Questions

This course could conclude by spending some time ruminating on what all this means to us today and could mean in the future. There are many articles on the internet regarding the general themes of civil liberties and terrorism. Within academic writing, much effort is being spent on what constitutes an emergency and what powers government should be given in time of emergency.

> Experience shows that when grave national crises are upon us, democratic nations tend to race to the bottom as far as the protection of human rights and civil liberties, indeed of basic and fundamental legal principles, is concerned. . . . Speaking in Jerusalem in 1987, Justice Brennan stated:

> There is considerably less to be proud about, and a good deal to be embarrassed about, when one reflects on the shabby treatment civil liberties have received in the United States during times of war and perceived threats to its national security. . . . After each perceived security crisis ended, the United States has remorsefully realized that the abrogation of civil liberties was unnecessary. But it has proven unable to prevent itself from repeating the error when the next crisis came along.

Oren Gross, *Chaos and Rules: Should Responses to Violent Crises Always Be Constitutional?*, 112 YALE L.J. 1011 (2003).

The post-9/11 world epitomizes the constant need for law to assist in the elaboration of public policy issues. Toward that end, we should all be engaged in ongoing discussions of issues such as:

1. Do you dare take risks with the safety of your family given the avowed intent of some terrorists to kill Americans at any opportunity? Isn't the first responsibility of government to keep us alive?

2. How do you feel about the use of military force against non-state actors?

3. What is the law regarding the capture or killing of known terrorists hiding in other countries? Should we rethink our position on assassination of foreign persons in light of the difficulty of capture and prosecution?

4. Given threats to public safety, how important is the privacy of your
   a. communications and reading habits?
   b. bank accounts?
   c. membership or affinity with organizations?

5. Do you trust your government without knowing all it does? Do you want to know
   a. how many explosive devices and weapons have been confiscated at ports?
   b. who has been killed or captured in foreign lands?
   c. what communications have been recorded from satellite relays?

6. Do you trust the courts to protect your freedoms in time of crisis?

7. How important is it to you that we have the right to discuss these matters without fear of government reprisal?

SELECTED READINGS

General Interest:

▸ SEYMOUR HERSH, CHAIN OF COMMAND (2004).

▸ Russell J. Bruemmer, *Intelligence Community Reorganization: Declining the Invitation To Struggle*, 101 YALE L.J. 867 (1992).

Interrogation and Torture:

▸ Ian Brownlie, *Interrogation in Depth: The Compton and Parker Reports*, 35 MOD. L. REV. 501 (1972).

▸ JOHN LANGBEIN, TORTURE AND THE LAW OF PROOF: EUROPE AND ENGLAND IN THE ANCIENT REGIME (1977)

▸ John T. Parry, *What Is Torture, Are We Doing It, and What If We Are?* 64 U. PITT. L. REV. 237 (2003).

▸ Dawn J. Miller, *Holding States to Their Convention Obligations: The United Nations Convention Against Torture and the Need for a Broad Interpretation of State Action*, 17 GEO. IMMIGR. L.J. 299 (2003).

▸ Oren Gross, *Are Torture Warrants Warranted? Pragmatic Absolutism and Official Disobedience*, 88 MINN. L. REV. 1481 (2004).

Emergency Powers (in chronological order):

▸ PAUL L. MURPHY, THE CONSTITUTION IN CRISIS TIMES, 1918-1969 (1972).

▸ MARTHA CRENSHAW (ED.), TERRORISM, LEGITIMACY, AND POWER (1983).

▸ Pnina Lahav, *A Barrel Without Hoops: The Impact of Counterterrorism on Israel's Legal Culture*, 10 CARDOZO L. REV. 529 (1988).

▸ William J. Brennan, *The Quest To Develop a Jurisprudence of Civil Liberties in Times of Security Crisis*, 18 ISR. YB HUM. RTS. 11 (1988).

▸ Jules Lobel, *Emergency Power and the Decline of Liberalism*, 98 YALE L.J. 1385 (1989).

▸ Itzhak Zamir, *Human Rights and National Security*, 22 ISR. L. REV. 375 (1989).

▸ MICHAEL LINFIELD, FREEDOM UNDER FIRE: U.S. CIVIL LIBERTIES IN TIMES OF WAR (1990).

▸ Peter Rosenthal, *The New Emergencies Act: Four Times the War Measures Act*, 20 MAN. L.J. 563 (1991) (Canadian experience).

▸ Oren Gross, *"Once More Unto the Breach:" The Systemic Failure of Applying the European Convention on Human Rights to Entrenched Emergencies*, 23 YALE J. INT'L L. 437 (1998).

▸ WILLIAM H. REHNQUIST, ALL THE LAWS BUT ONE (1998).

▸ Keith E. Whittington, *Yet Another Constitutional Crisis?* 43 WM. & MARY L. REV. 2093 (2002).

▸ Rodney A. Smolla, *Terrorism and the Bill of Rights*, 10 WM. & MARY BILL OF RTS. J. 551 (2002).

▸ Oren Gross, *Chaos and Rules: Should Responses to Violent Crises Always Be Constitutional?* 112 YALE L.J. 1011, 1023 (2003).

▸ David Cole, *Judging the Next Emergency: Judicial Review and Individual Rights in Times of Crisis*, 101 MICH. L. REV. 2565, 2594 (2003).

▸ Oren Gross, *Providing for the Unexpected: Constitutional Emergency Provisions*, 33 ISR. Y.B. HUM. RTS. 13 (2003).

▸ Eric A. Posner & Adrian Vermeule, *Accommodating Emergencies*, 56 STAN. L. REV. 605 (2003).

▸ Bruce Ackerman, *The Emergency Constitution*, 113 YALE L.J. 1029 (2004).

- David Cole, *The Priority of Morality: The Emergency Constitution's Blind Spot*, 113 YALE L.J. 1753 (2004).
- Laurence H. Tribe & Patrick O. Gudridge, *The Anti-Emergency Constitution*, 113 YALE L.J. 1801 (2004).

Appendix

DOCUMENTS

A. U.S. STATUTES, RESOLUTIONS, AND ORDERS
1. General Federal Criminal Law

18 U.S.C. § 1111. Murder
(a) Murder is the unlawful killing of a human being with malice aforethought. Every murder perpetrated by poison, lying in wait, or any other kind of willful, deliberate, malicious, and premeditated killing; or committed in the perpetration of, or attempt to perpetrate, any arson, escape, murder, kidnaping, treason, espionage, sabotage, aggravated sexual abuse or sexual abuse, child abuse, burglary, or robbery; or perpetrated as part of a pattern or practice of assault or torture against a child or children; or perpetrated from a premeditated design unlawfully and maliciously to effect the death of any human being other than him who is killed, is murder in the first degree.

Any other murder is murder in the second degree.

(b) Within the special maritime and territorial jurisdiction of the United States,

Whoever is guilty of murder in the first degree shall be punished by death or by imprisonment for life;

Whoever is guilty of murder in the second degree, shall be imprisoned for any term of years or for life.

18 U.S.C. § 1114. Protection of officers and employees of the United States
Whoever kills or attempts to kill any officer or employee of the United States or of any agency in any branch of the United States Government (including any member of the uniformed services) while such officer or employee is engaged in or on account of the performance of official duties, or any person assisting such an officer or employee in the performance of such duties or on account of that assistance, shall be punished

(1) in the case of murder, as provided under section 1111;

(2) in the case of manslaughter, as provided under section 1112; or

(3) in the case of attempted murder or manslaughter, as provided in section 1113.

18 U.S.C. § 1119. Foreign murder of United States nationals
(a) Definition. In this section, "national of the United States" has the meaning stated in section 101(a)(22) of the Immigration and Nationality Act (8 U.S.C. 1101(a)(22)).

(b) Offense. A person who, being a national of the United States, kills or attempts to kill a national of the United States while such national is outside the

United States but within the jurisdiction of another country shall be punished as provided under sections 1111, 1112, and 1113.

(c) Limitations on prosecution.

(1) No prosecution may be instituted against any person under this section except upon the written approval of the Attorney General, the Deputy Attorney General, or an Assistant Attorney General, which function of approving prosecutions may not be delegated. No prosecution shall be approved if prosecution has been previously undertaken by a foreign country for the same conduct.

(2) No prosecution shall be approved under this section unless the Attorney General, in consultation with the Secretary of State, determines that the conduct took place in a country in which the person is no longer present, and the country lacks the ability to lawfully secure the person's return. A determination by the Attorney General under this paragraph is not subject to judicial review.

18 U.S.C. § 844 [Penalties for unlawful use of explosive materials]

(d) Whoever transports or receives, or attempts to transport or receive, in interstate or foreign commerce any explosive with the knowledge or intent that it will be used to kill, injure, or intimidate any individual or unlawfully to damage or destroy any building, vehicle, or other real or personal property, shall be imprisoned for not more than ten years, or fined under this title, or both; and if personal injury results to any person, including any public safety officer performing duties as a direct or proximate result of conduct prohibited by this subsection, shall be imprisoned for not more than twenty years or fined under this title, or both; and if death results to any person, including any public safety officer performing duties as a direct or proximate result of conduct prohibited by this subsection, shall be subject to imprisonment for any term of years, or to the death penalty or to life imprisonment.

(e) Whoever, through the use of the mail, telephone, telegraph, or other instrument of interstate or foreign commerce, or in or affecting interstate or foreign commerce, willfully makes any threat, or maliciously conveys false information knowing the same to be false, concerning an attempt or alleged attempt being made, or to be made, to kill, injure, or intimidate any individual or unlawfully to damage or destroy any building, vehicle, or other real or personal property by means of fire or an explosive shall be imprisoned for not more than 10 years or fined under this title, or both.

(f) (1) Whoever maliciously damages or destroys, or attempts to damage or destroy, by means of fire or an explosive, any building, vehicle, or other personal or real property in whole or in part owned or possessed by, or leased to, the United States, or any department or agency thereof, or any institution or organization receiving Federal financial assistance, shall be imprisoned for not less than 5 years and not more than 20 years, fined under this title, or both.

(2) Whoever engages in conduct prohibited by this subsection, and as a result of such conduct, directly or proximately causes personal injury or

creates a substantial risk of injury to any person, including any public safety officer performing duties, shall be imprisoned for not less than 7 years and not more than 40 years, fined under this title, or both.

(3) Whoever engages in conduct prohibited by this subsection, and as a result of such conduct directly or proximately causes the death of any person, including any public safety officer performing duties, shall be subject to the death penalty, or imprisoned for not less than 20 years or for life, fined under this title, or both.

2. Federal "Civil Rights" Statutes

18 U.S.C. § 241. Conspiracy against rights

If two or more persons conspire to injure, oppress, threaten, or intimidate any person in any State, Territory, Commonwealth, Possession, or District in the free exercise or enjoyment of any right or privilege secured to him by the Constitution or laws of the United States, or because of his having so exercised the same; or

If two or more persons go in disguise on the highway, or on the premises of another, with intent to prevent or hinder his free exercise or enjoyment of any right or privilege so secured;

They shall be fined under this title or imprisoned not more than ten years, or both; and if death results from the acts committed in violation of this section or if such acts include kidnapping or an attempt to kidnap, aggravated sexual abuse or an attempt to commit aggravated sexual abuse, or an attempt to kill, they shall be fined under this title or imprisoned for any term of years or for life, or both, or may be sentenced to death.

18 U.S.C. § 242 Deprivation of rights under color of law

Whoever, under color of any law, statute, ordinance, regulation, or custom, willfully subjects any person in [U.S. territory] to the deprivation of any rights, privileges, or immunities secured or protected by the Constitution or laws of the United States, . . . shall be fined under this title or imprisoned not more than one year, or both; and if bodily injury results from the acts committed in violation of this section or if such acts include the use, attempted use, or threatened use of a dangerous weapon, explosives, or fire, shall be fined under this title or imprisoned not more than ten years, or both; and if death results from the acts committed in violation of this section or if such acts include kidnaping or an attempt to kidnap, aggravated sexual abuse, or an attempt to commit aggravated sexual abuse, or an attempt to kill, shall be fined under this title, or imprisoned for any term of years or for life, or both, or may be sentenced to death.

18 U.S.C. § 245 Federally Protected Activities

(b) Whoever, whether or not acting under color of law, by force or threat of force willfully injures, intimidates or interferes with, or attempts to injure, intimidate or interfere with

(1) any person because he is or has been, or in order to intimidate such person or any other person or any class of persons from

(A) voting or qualifying to vote, qualifying or campaigning as a candidate for elective office, or qualifying or acting as a poll watcher, or any legally authorized election official, in any primary, special, or general election;

(B) participating in or enjoying any benefit, service, privilege, program, facility, or activity provided or administered by the United States; . . . or

(2) any person because of his race, color, religion or national origin and because he is or has been

(A) enrolling in or attending any public school or public college;

(B) participating in or enjoying any benefit, service, privilege, program, facility or activity provided or administered by any State or subdivision thereof; . . .

(E) traveling in or using any facility of interstate commerce, or using any vehicle, terminal, or facility of any common carrier by motor, rail, water, or air;

(F) enjoying the goods, services, facilities, privileges, advantages, or accommodations of any inn, hotel, motel, or other establishment which provides lodging to transient guests, or of any restaurant, cafeteria, lunchroom, lunch counter, soda fountain, or other facility which serves the public . . . or

. . .

shall be fined under this title, or imprisoned not more than one year, or both; and if bodily injury results from the acts committed in violation of this section or if such acts include the use, attempted use, or threatened use of a dangerous weapon, explosives, or fire shall be fined under this title, or imprisoned not more than ten years, or both; and if death results from the acts committed in violation of this section or if such acts include kidnapping or an attempt to kidnap, aggravated sexual abuse or an attempt to commit aggravated sexual abuse, or an attempt to kill, shall be fined under this title or imprisoned for any term of years or for life, or both, or may be sentenced to death.

3. U.S. Statutes Based on Extraterritoriality

18 USC § 7 (2002) Special maritime and territorial jurisdiction of the United States defined

The term "special maritime and territorial jurisdiction of the United States", as used in this title, includes:

(1) The high seas, any other waters within the admiralty and maritime jurisdiction of the United States and out of the jurisdiction of any particular

State, and any vessel belonging in whole or in part to the United States or any citizen thereof, or to any corporation created by or under the laws of the United States, or of any State, Territory, District, or possession thereof, when such vessel is within the admiralty and maritime jurisdiction of the United States and out of the jurisdiction of any particular State.

(2) Any vessel registered, licensed, or enrolled under the laws of the United States, and being on a voyage upon the waters of any of the Great Lakes, or any of the waters connecting them, or upon the Saint Lawrence River where the same constitutes the International Boundary Line.

(3) Any lands reserved or acquired for the use of the United States, and under the exclusive or concurrent jurisdiction thereof, or any place purchased or otherwise acquired by the United States by consent of the legislature of the State in which the same shall be, for the erection of a fort, magazine, arsenal, dockyard, or other needful building.

(4) Any island, rock, or key containing deposits of guano, which may, at the discretion of the President, be considered as appertaining to the United States.

(5) Any aircraft belonging in whole or in part to the United States, or any citizen thereof, or to any corporation created by or under the laws of the United States, or any State, Territory, district, or possession thereof, while such aircraft is in flight over the high seas, or over any other waters within the admiralty and maritime jurisdiction of the United States and out of the jurisdiction of any particular State.

(6) Any vehicle used or designed for flight or navigation in space and on the registry of the United States pursuant to the Treaty on Principles Governing the Activities of States in the Exploration and Use of Outer Space, Including the Moon and Other Celestial Bodies and the Convention on Registration of Objects Launched into Outer Space, while that vehicle is in flight, which is from the moment when all external doors are closed on Earth following embarkation until the moment when one such door is opened on Earth for disembarkation or in the case of a forced landing, until the competent authorities take over the responsibility for the vehicle and for persons and property aboard.

(7) Any place outside the jurisdiction of any nation with respect to an offense by or against a national of the United States.

(8) To the extent permitted by international law, any foreign vessel during a voyage having a scheduled departure from or arrival in the United States with respect to an offense committed by or against a national of the United States.

(9) With respect to offenses committed by or against a national of the United States as that term is used in section 101 of the Immigration and Nationality Act

(A) the premises of United States diplomatic, consular, military or other United States Government missions or entities in foreign States, including the buildings, parts of buildings, and land appurtenant or ancillary thereto or used for purposes of those missions or entities, irrespective of ownership; and

(B) residences in foreign States and the land appurtenant or ancillary thereto, irrespective of ownership, used for purposes of those missions or entities or used by United States personnel assigned to those missions or entities.

Nothing in this paragraph shall be deemed to supersede any treaty or international agreement with which this paragraph conflicts. This paragraph does not apply with respect to an offense committed by a person described in section 3261(a) of this title.

18 U.S.C. § 32. Destruction of aircraft or aircraft facilities

(a) Whoever willfully

(1) sets fire to, damages, destroys, disables, or wrecks any aircraft in the special aircraft jurisdiction of the United States or any civil aircraft used, operated, or employed in interstate, overseas, or foreign air commerce;

(2) places or causes to be placed a destructive device or substance in, upon, or in proximity to, or otherwise makes or causes to be made unworkable or unusable or hazardous to work or use, any such aircraft, or any part or other materials used or intended to be used in connection with the operation of such aircraft, if such placing or causing to be placed or such making or causing to be made is likely to endanger the safety of any such aircraft;

(3) sets fire to, damages, destroys, or disables any air navigation facility, or interferes by force or violence with the operation of such facility, if such fire, damaging, destroying, disabling, or interfering is likely to endanger the safety of any such aircraft in flight;

(4) with the intent to damage, destroy, or disable any such aircraft, sets fire to, damages, destroys, or disables or places a destructive device or substance in, upon, or in proximity to, any appliance or structure, ramp, landing area, property, machine, or apparatus, or any facility or other material used, or intended to be used, in connection with the operation, maintenance, loading, unloading or storage of any such aircraft or any cargo carried or intended to be carried on any such aircraft;

(5) performs an act of violence against or incapacitates any individual on any such aircraft, if such act of violence or incapacitation is likely to endanger the safety of such aircraft;

(6) communicates information, knowing the information to be false and under circumstances in which such information may reasonably be believed, thereby endangering the safety of any such aircraft in flight; or

(7) attempts or conspires to do anything prohibited under paragraphs (1) through (6) of this subsection;

shall be fined under this title or imprisoned not more than twenty years or both.

(b) Whoever willfully

(1) performs an act of violence against any individual on board any civil aircraft registered in a country other than the United States while such aircraft is in flight, if such act is likely to endanger the safety of that aircraft;

(2) destroys a civil aircraft registered in a country other than the United States while such aircraft is in service or causes damage to such an aircraft which renders that aircraft incapable of flight or which is likely to endanger that aircraft's safety in flight;

(3) places or causes to be placed on a civil aircraft registered in a country other than the United States while such aircraft is in service, a device or

substance which is likely to destroy that aircraft, or to cause damage to that aircraft which renders that aircraft incapable of flight or which is likely to endanger that aircraft's safety in flight; or

(4) attempts or conspires to commit an offense described in paragraphs (1) through (3) of this subsection;

shall be fined under this title or imprisoned not more than twenty years, or both. There is jurisdiction over an offense under this subsection if a national of the United States was on board, or would have been on board, the aircraft; an offender is a national of the United States; or an offender is afterwards found in the United States. For purposes of this subsection, the term "national of the United States" has the meaning prescribed in section 101(a)(22) of the Immigration and Nationality Act [8 U.S.C. § 1101(a)(22)].

(c) Whoever willfully imparts or conveys any threat to do an act which would violate any of paragraphs (1) through (5) of subsection (a) or any of paragraphs (1) through (3) of subsection (b) of this section, with an apparent determination and will to carry the threat into execution shall be fined under this title or imprisoned not more than five years, or both.

18 U.S.C. § 2340. [Torture Act] Definitions

As used in this chapter

(1) "torture" means an act committed by a person acting under the color of law specifically intended to inflict severe physical or mental pain or suffering (other than pain or suffering incidental to lawful sanctions) upon another person within his custody or physical control;

(2) "severe mental pain or suffering" means the prolonged mental harm caused by or resulting from

(A) the intentional infliction or threatened infliction of severe physical pain or suffering;

(B) the administration or application, or threatened administration or application, of mind-altering substances or other procedures calculated to disrupt profoundly the senses or the personality;

(C) the threat of imminent death; or

(D) the threat that another person will imminently be subjected to death, severe physical pain or suffering, or the administration or application of mind-altering substances or other procedures calculated to disrupt profoundly the senses or personality; and

(3) "United States" includes all areas under the jurisdiction of the United States including any of the places described in sections 5 and 7 of this title and section 46501(2) of title 49.

18 U.S.C. § 2340A. Torture

(a) Offense. Whoever outside the United States commits or attempts to commit torture shall be fined under this title or imprisoned not more than 20 years, or both, and if death results to any person from conduct prohibited by this subsection, shall be punished by death or imprisoned for any term of years or for life.

(b) Jurisdiction. There is jurisdiction over the activity prohibited in subsection (a) if

(1) the alleged offender is a national of the United States; or

(2) the alleged offender is present in the United States, irrespective of the nationality of the victim or alleged offender.

4. U.S. Statutes Referring to "Terrorism"

A. Designation of Organizations by State Department

8 USC § 1189. Designation of foreign terrorist organizations

(a) Designation.

(1) In general. The Secretary is authorized to designate an organization as a foreign terrorist organization in accordance with this subsection if the Secretary finds that

(A) the organization is a foreign organization;

(B) the organization engages in terrorist activity (as defined in [8 U.S.C. § 1182(a)(3)(B)]) or terrorism (as defined in [22 U.S.C. § 2656f(d)(2)]), or retains the capability and intent to engage in terrorist activity or terrorism; and

(C) the terrorist activity or terrorism of the organization threatens the security of United States nationals or the national security of the United States.

(2) Procedure.

(A) Notice.

(i) To congressional leaders. Seven days before making a designation under this subsection, the Secretary shall, by classified communication, notify the Speaker and Minority Leader of the House of Representatives, the President pro tempore, Majority Leader, and Minority Leader of the Senate, and the members of the relevant committees of the House of Representatives and the Senate, in writing, of the intent to designate an organization under this subsection, together with the findings made under paragraph (1) with respect to that organization, and the factual basis therefor.

(ii) Publication in Federal Register. The Secretary shall publish the designation in the Federal Register seven days after providing the notification under clause (i).

(B) Effect of designation.

(i) For purposes of section 2339B of title 18, United States Code, a designation under this subsection shall take effect upon publication under subparagraph (A)(ii).

(ii) Any designation under this subsection shall cease to have effect upon an Act of Congress disapproving such designation.

(C) Freezing of assets. Upon notification under paragraph (2)(A)(i), the Secretary of the Treasury may require United States financial institutions possessing or controlling any assets of any foreign organization included in the notification to block all financial transactions involving those assets until further directive from either the Secretary of the Treasury, Act of Congress, or order of court.

(3) Record.

(A) In general. In making a designation under this subsection, the Secretary shall create an administrative record.

(B) Classified information. The Secretary may consider classified information in making a designation under this subsection. Classified information shall not be subject to disclosure for such time as it remains classified, except that such information may be disclosed to a court ex parte and in camera for purposes of judicial review under subsection (b).

(4) Period of designation.

(A) In general. Subject to paragraphs (5) and (6), a designation under this subsection shall be effective for all purposes for a period of 2 years beginning on the effective date of the designation under paragraph (2)(B).

(B) Redesignation. The Secretary may redesignate a foreign organization as a foreign terrorist organization for an additional 2-year period at the end of [any] 2-year period.

(5) Revocation by Act of Congress. The Congress, by an Act of Congress, may block or revoke a designation made under paragraph (1).

(6) Revocation based on change in circumstances.

(A) In general. The Secretary may revoke a designation made under paragraph (1) or a redesignation made under paragraph (4)(B) if the Secretary finds that

(i) the circumstances that were the basis for the designation or redesignation have changed in such a manner as to warrant revocation; or

(ii) the national security of the United States warrants a revocation.

(B) Procedure. The procedural requirements of paragraphs (2) and (3) shall apply to a revocation under this paragraph. Any revocation shall take effect on the date specified in the revocation or upon publication in the Federal Register if no effective date is specified.

(7) Effect of revocation. The revocation of a designation under paragraph (5) or (6), or the revocation of a redesignation under paragraph (6), shall not affect any action or proceeding based on conduct committed prior to the effective date of such revocation.

(8) Use of designation in trial or hearing. If a designation under this subsection has become effective . . . , a defendant in a criminal action or an alien in a removal proceeding shall not be permitted to raise any question concerning the validity of the issuance of such designation or redesignation as a defense or an objection at any trial or hearing.

(b) Judicial review of designation.

(1) In general. Not later than 30 days after publication of the designation in the Federal Register, an organization designated as a foreign terrorist organization may seek judicial review of the designation in the United States Court of Appeals for the District of Columbia Circuit.

(2) Basis of review. Review under this subsection shall be based solely upon the administrative record, except that the Government may submit, for *ex parte* and *in camera* review, classified information used in making the designation.

(3) Scope of review. The Court shall hold unlawful and set aside a designation the court finds to be

(A) arbitrary, capricious, an abuse of discretion, or otherwise not in accordance with law;

(B) contrary to constitutional right, power, privilege, or immunity;

(C) in excess of statutory jurisdiction, authority, or limitation, or short of statutory right;

(D) lacking substantial support in the administrative record taken as a whole or in classified information submitted to the court under paragraph (2), or

(E) not in accord with the procedures required by law.

(4) Judicial review invoked. The pendency of an action for judicial review of a designation shall not affect the application of this section, unless the court issues a final order setting aside the designation.

8 U.S.C. § 1182(a)(3). Terrorist activity defined.

As used in [§ 1189], the term "terrorist activity" means any activity which is unlawful under the laws of the place where it is committed (or which, if it had been committed in the United States, would be unlawful under the laws of the United States or any State) and which involves any of the following:

(I) The highjacking or sabotage of any conveyance (including an aircraft, vessel, or vehicle).

(II) The seizing or detaining, and threatening to kill, injure, or continue to detain, another individual in order to compel a third person (including a governmental organization) to do or abstain from doing any act as an explicit or implicit condition for the release of the individual seized or detained.

(III) A violent attack upon an internationally protected person (as defined in 18 U.S.C. § 1116(b)(4)) or upon the liberty of such a person.

(IV) An assassination.

(V) The use of any

(a) biological agent, chemical agent, or nuclear weapon or device, or

(b) explosive, firearm, or other weapon or dangerous device (other than for mere personal monetary gain),

with intent to endanger, directly or indirectly, the safety of one or more individuals or to cause substantial damage to property.

(VI) A threat, attempt, or conspiracy to do any of the foregoing.

22 U.S.C. § 2256f(d) [definition of terrorism for purposes of designations]

(2) the term "terrorism" means premeditated, politically motivated violence perpetrated against noncombatant targets by subnational groups or clandestine agents.

B. Criminal Statutes Referring to Terrorism

18 USC § 2331. Definitions

As used in this chapter [18 U.S.C. §§ 2331 et seq.]

(1) the term "international terrorism" means activities that

(A) involve violent acts or acts dangerous to human life that are a violation of the criminal laws of the United States or of any State, or that would be a criminal violation if committed within the jurisdiction of the United States or of any State;

(B) appear to be intended

(i) to intimidate or coerce a civilian population;

(ii) to influence the policy of a government by intimidation or coercion; or

(iii) to affect the conduct of a government by mass destruction, assassination or kidnapping; and

(C) occur primarily outside the territorial jurisdiction of the United States, or transcend national boundaries in terms of the means by which they are accomplished, the persons they appear intended to intimidate or coerce, or the locale in which their perpetrators operate or seek asylum;

(2) the term "national of the United States" has the meaning given such term in section 101(a)(22) of the Immigration and Nationality Act [8 USCS § 1101(a)(22)];

(3) the term "person" means any individual or entity capable of holding a legal or beneficial interest in property;

(4) the term "act of war" means any act occurring in the course of

(A) declared war;

(B) armed conflict, whether or not war has been declared, between two or more nations; or

(C) armed conflict between military forces of any origin; and

(5) the term "domestic terrorism" means activities that

(A) involve acts dangerous to human life that are a violation of the criminal laws of the United States or of any State;

(B) appear to be intended

(i) to intimidate or coerce a civilian population;

(ii) to influence the policy of a government by intimidation or coercion; or

(iii) to affect the conduct of a government by mass destruction, assassination, or kidnapping; and

(C) occur primarily within the territorial jurisdiction of the United States.

18 U.S.C. § 2332. Criminal penalties

(a) *Homicide.* Whoever kills a national of the United States, while such national is outside the United States, shall,

(1) if the killing is murder (as defined in section 1111(a)), be fined under this title, punished by death or imprisonment for any term of years or for life, or both;

(2) if the killing is a voluntary manslaughter as defined in section 1112(a) of this title, be fined under this title or imprisoned not more than ten years, or both; and

(3) if the killing is an involuntary manslaughter as defined in section 1112(a) of this title, be fined under this title or imprisoned not more than three years, or both.

(b) *Attempt or conspiracy with respect to homicide.* Whoever outside the United States attempts to kill, or engages in a conspiracy to kill, a national of the United States shall

(1) in the case of an attempt to commit a killing that is a murder as defined in this chapter be fined under this title or imprisoned not more than 20 years, or both; and

(2) in the case of a conspiracy by two or more persons to commit a killing that is a murder as defined in section 1111(a) of this title, if one or more of such persons do any overt act to effect the object of the conspiracy, be fined under this title or imprisoned for any term of years or for life, or both so fined and so imprisoned.

(c) *Other conduct.* Whoever outside the United States engages in physical violence

(1) with intent to cause serious bodily injury to a national of the United States; or

(2) with the result that serious bodily injury is caused to a national of the United States;

shall be fined under this title or imprisoned not more that ten years, or both.

(d) *Limitation on prosecution.* No prosecution for any offense described in this section shall be undertaken by the United States except on written certification of the Attorney General or the highest ranking subordinate of the Attorney General with responsibility for criminal prosecutions that, in the judgment of the certifying official, such offense was intended to coerce, intimidate, or retaliate against a government or a civilian population.

18 USCS § 2332b Acts of terrorism transcending national boundaries

(a) Prohibited acts.

(1) Offenses. Whoever, involving conduct transcending national boundaries and in a circumstance described in subsection (b)

(A) kills, kidnaps, maims, commits an assault resulting in serious bodily injury, or assaults with a dangerous weapon any person within the United States; or

(B) creates a substantial risk of serious bodily injury to any other person by destroying or damaging any structure, conveyance, or other real or personal property within the United States or by attempting or conspiring to destroy or damage any structure, conveyance, or other real or personal property within the United States;

in violation of the laws of any State, or the United States, shall be punished as prescribed in subsection (c).

(2) Treatment of threats, attempts and conspiracies. Whoever threatens to commit an offense under paragraph (1), or attempts or conspires to do so, shall be punished under subsection (c).

(b) Jurisdictional bases.

(1) Circumstances. The circumstances referred to in subsection (a) are

(A) the mail or any facility of interstate or foreign commerce is used in furtherance of the offense;

(B) the offense obstructs, delays, or affects interstate or foreign commerce, or would have so obstructed, delayed, or affected interstate or foreign commerce if the offense had been consummated;

(C) the victim, or intended victim, is the United States Government, a member of the uniformed services, or any official, officer, employee, or agent of the legislative, executive, or judicial branches, or of any department or agency, of the United States;

(D) the structure, conveyance, or other real or personal property is, in whole or in part, owned, possessed, or leased to the United States, or any department or agency of the United States;

(E) the offense is committed in the territorial sea (including the airspace above and the seabed and subsoil below, and artificial islands and fixed structures erected thereon) of the United States; or

(F) the offense is committed within the special maritime and territorial jurisdiction of the United States.

(2) Co-conspirators and accessories after the fact. Jurisdiction shall exist over all principals and co-conspirators of an offense under this section, and accessories after the fact to any offense under this section, if at least one of the circumstances described in subparagraphs (A) through (F) of paragraph (1) is applicable to at least one offender.

(c) Penalties.

(1) Penalties. Whoever violates this section shall be punished

(A) for a killing, or if death results to any person from any other conduct prohibited by this section, by death, or by imprisonment for any term of years or for life;

(B) for kidnapping, by imprisonment for any term of years or for life;

(C) for maiming, by imprisonment for not more than 35 years;

(D) for assault with a dangerous weapon or assault resulting in serious bodily injury, by imprisonment for not more than 30 years;

(E) for destroying or damaging any structure, conveyance, or other real or personal property, by imprisonment for not more than 25 years;

(F) for attempting or conspiring to commit an offense, for any term of years up to the maximum punishment that would have applied had the offense been completed; and

(G) for threatening to commit an offense under this section, by imprisonment for not more than 10 years.

(2) Consecutive sentence. Notwithstanding any other provision of law, the court shall not place on probation any person convicted of a violation of this section; nor shall the term of imprisonment imposed under this section run concurrently with any other term of imprisonment.

(d)Proof requirements. The following shall apply to prosecutions under this section:

(1)Knowledge. The prosecution is not required to prove knowledge by any defendant of a jurisdictional base alleged in the indictment.

(2)State law. In a prosecution under this section that is based upon the adoption of State law, only the elements of the offense under State law, and not any provisions pertaining to criminal procedure or evidence, are adopted.

(e)Extraterritorial jurisdiction. There is extraterritorial Federal jurisdiction

(1) over any offense under subsection (a), including any threat, attempt, or conspiracy to commit such offense; and

(2) over conduct which, under section 3, renders any person an accessory after the fact to an offense under subsection (a).

(f) Investigative authority. In addition to any other investigative authority with respect to violations of this title, the Attorney General shall have primary investigative responsibility for all Federal crimes of terrorism, and any violation of section 351(e), 844(e), 844(f)(1), 956(b), 1361, 1366(b), 1366(c), 1751(e), 2152, or 2156 of this title, and the Secretary of the Treasury shall assist the Attorney General at the request of the Attorney General. Nothing in this section shall be construed to interfere with the authority of the United States Secret Service under section 3056.

(g)Definitions. As used in this section

(1) the term "conduct transcending national boundaries" means conduct occurring outside of the United States in addition to the conduct occurring in the United States;

(2) the term "facility of interstate or foreign commerce" has the meaning given that term in section 1958(b)(2);

(3) the term "serious bodily injury" has the meaning given that term in section 1365(g)(3);

(4) the term "territorial sea of the United States" means all waters extending seaward to 12 nautical miles from the baselines of the United States, determined in accordance with international law; and

(5) the term "Federal crime of terrorism" means an offense that

(A)is calculated to influence or affect the conduct of government by intimidation or coercion, or to retaliate against government conduct; and

(B) is a violation of

(i) section 32 (relating to destruction of aircraft or aircraft facilities), 37 (relating to violence at international airports), 81 (relating to arson within special maritime and territorial jurisdiction), 175 or 175b (relating to biological weapons), 229 (relating to chemical weapons), subsection (a), (b), (c), or (d) of section 351 (relating to congressional, cabinet, and Supreme Court assassination and kidnaping), 831 (relating to nuclear materials), 842(m) or (n) (relating to plastic explosives), 844(f)(2) or (3) (relating to arson and bombing of Government property risking or causing death), 844(i) (relating to arson and bombing of property used in interstate commerce), 930(c) (relating to killing or attempted killing during an attack on a Federal facility with a dangerous weapon), 956(a)(1) (relating to conspiracy to murder, kidnap, or maim persons abroad), 1030(a)(1) (relating to protection of computers), 1030(a)(5)(A)(i) resulting in damage as defined in 1030(a)(5)(B)(ii) through (v) (relating to protection of computers), 1114 (relating to killing or attempted killing of officers and employees of the United States), 1116 (relating to murder or manslaughter of foreign officials, official guests, or internationally protected persons), 1203 (relating to hostage taking), 1362 (relating to destruction of communication lines, stations, or systems), 1363 (relating to injury to buildings or property within special maritime and territorial jurisdiction of the United States), 1366(a) (relating to destruction of an energy facility), 1751(a), (b), (c), or (d) (relating to Presidential and Presidential staff assassination and kidnaping), 1992 (relating to wrecking trains), 1993 (relating to terrorist attacks and other acts of violence against mass transportation systems), 2155 (relating to destruction of national defense materials, premises, or utilities), 2280 (relating to violence against maritime navigation), 2281 (relating to violence against maritime fixed platforms), 2332 (relating to certain homicides and other violence against United States nationals occurring outside of the United States), 2332a (relating to use of weapons of mass destruction), 2332b (relating to acts of terrorism transcending national boundaries), 2332f (relating to bombing of public places and facilities), 2339 (relating to harboring terrorists), 2339A (relating to providing material support to terrorists), 2339B (relating to providing material support to terrorist organizations), 2339C (relating to financing of terrorism, or 2340A (relating to torture) of this title;

(ii) section 236 (relating to sabotage of nuclear facilities or fuel) of the Atomic Energy Act of 1954 *(42 U.S.C. 2284); or*

(iii) section 46502 (relating to aircraft piracy), the second sentence of section 46504 (relating to assault on a flight crew with a dangerous weapon), section 46505(b)(3) or (c) (relating to explosive or incendiary devices, or endangerment of human life by means of weapons, on aircraft), section 46506 if homicide or attempted homicide is involved (relating to application of certain criminal laws to acts on aircraft), or section 60123(b) (relating to destruction of interstate gas or hazardous liquid pipeline facility) of title 49.

18 U.S.C. § 2332f. Bombings of places of public use, government facilities, public transportation systems and infrastructure facilities
(a) Offenses.

(1) In general. Whoever unlawfully delivers, places, discharges, or detonates an explosive or other lethal device in, into, or against a place of public use, a state or government facility, a public transportation system, or an infrastructure facility

(A) with the intent to cause death or serious bodily injury, or

(B) with the intent to cause extensive destruction of such a place, facility, or system, where such destruction results in or is likely to result in major economic loss,

shall be punished as prescribed in subsection (c).

(2) Attempts and conspiracies. Whoever attempts or conspires to commit an offense under paragraph (1) shall be punished as prescribed in subsection (c).

(b) Jurisdiction. There is jurisdiction over the offenses in subsection (a) if

(1) the offense takes place in the United States and

(A) the offense is committed against another state or a government facility of such state, including its embassy or other diplomatic or consular premises of that state;

(B) the offense is committed in an attempt to compel another state or the United States to do or abstain from doing any act;

(C) at the time the offense is committed, it is committed

(i) on board a vessel flying the flag of another state;

(ii) on board an aircraft which is registered under the laws of another state; or

(iii) on board an aircraft which is operated by the government of another state;

(D) a perpetrator is found outside the United States;

(E) a perpetrator is a national of another state or a stateless person; or

(F) a victim is a national of another state or a stateless person;

(2) the offense takes place outside the United States and

(A) a perpetrator is a national of the United States or is a stateless person whose habitual residence is in the United States;

(B) a victim is a national of the United States;

(C) a perpetrator is found in the United States;

(D) the offense is committed in an attempt to compel the United States to do or abstain from doing any act;

(E) the offense is committed against a state or government facility of the United States, including an embassy or other diplomatic or consular premises of the United States;

(F) the offense is committed on board a vessel flying the flag of the United States or an aircraft which is registered under the laws of the United States at the time the offense is committed; or

(G) the offense is committed on board an aircraft which is operated by the United States.

(c) Penalties. Whoever violates this section shall be punished as provided under section 2332a(a) of this title.

(d) Exemptions to jurisdiction. This section does not apply to

(1) the activities of armed forces during an armed conflict, as those terms are understood under the law of war, which are governed by that law,

(2) activities undertaken by military forces of a state in the exercise of their official duties; or

(3) offenses committed within the United States, where the alleged offender and the victims are United States citizens and the alleged offender is found in the United States, or where jurisdiction is predicated solely on the nationality of the victims or the alleged offender and the offense has no substantial effect on interstate or foreign commerce.

18 U.S.C. § 2339A. Providing material support to terrorists

(a) Offense. Whoever, within the United States, provides material support or resources or conceals or disguises the nature, location, source, or ownership of material support or resources, knowing or intending that they are to be used in preparation for, or in carrying out, a violation of [specified federal crimes], or in preparation for, or in carrying out, the concealment or an escape from the commission of any such violation, shall be fined under this title, imprisoned not more than 10 years, or both.

(b) Definitions. As used in this section

(1) the term "material support or resources" means any property, tangible or intangible, or service, including currency or monetary instruments or financial securities, financial services, lodging, training, expert advice or assistance, safehouses, false documentation or identification, communications equipment, facilities, weapons, lethal substances, explosives, personnel (1 or more individuals who may be or include oneself), and transportation, except medicine or religious materials;

(2) the term "training" means instruction or teaching designed to impart a specific skill, as opposed to general knowledge; and

(3) the term "expert advice or assistance" means advice or assistance derived from scientific, technical or other specialized knowledge.

[Prior to Dec. 17, 2004, subsection (b) read: In this section, the term "material support or resources" means currency or other financial securities, financial services, lodging, training, safehouses, false documentation or identification, communications equipment, facilities, weapons, lethal substances, explosives, personnel, transportation, and other physical assets, except medicine or religious materials.]

18 U.S.C. § 2339B. Providing material support or resources to designated foreign terrorist organizations

(a) Prohibited Activities.

(1) Unlawful conduct. Whoever knowingly provides material support or resources to a foreign terrorist organization, or attempts or conspires to do so, shall be fined under this title or imprisoned not more than 10 years, or both. To violate this paragraph, a person must have knowledge that the organization is a designated terrorist organization (as defined in subsection (g)(6)), that the organization has engaged or engages in terrorist activity (as defined in 8 U.S.C. § 1182(a)(3)), or that the organization has engaged or engages in terrorism (as defined in 8 U.S.C. 2656f). [The last sentence was added by Pub. L. 108-458 Dec. 17, 2004]

(2) Financial institutions. Except as authorized by the Secretary, any financial institution that becomes aware that it has possession of, or control over, any funds in which a foreign terrorist organization, or its agent, has an interest, shall

(A) retain possession of, or maintain control over, such funds; and

(B) report to the Secretary the existence of such funds in accordance with regulations issued by the Secretary

(b) Civil Penalty. Any financial institution that knowingly fails to comply with subsection (a)(2) shall be subject to a civil penalty in an amount that is the greater of

(A) $50,000 per violation; or

(B) twice the amount of which the financial institution was required under subsection (a)(2) to retain possession or control.

(c) Injunction. Whenever it appears to the Secretary or the Attorney General that any person is engaged in, or is about to engage in, any act that constitutes, or would constitute, a violation of this section, the Attorney General may initiate civil action in a district court of the United States to enjoin such violation.

(d) Extraterritorial Jurisdiction.

(1) In general. There is jurisdiction over an offense under subsection (a) if

(A) an offender is a national of the United States or an alien lawfully admitted for permanent residence in the United States;

(B) an offender is a stateless person whose habitual residence is in the United States;

(C) after the conduct required for the offense occurs an offender is brought into or found in the United States, even if the conduct required for the offense occurs outside the United States;

(D) the offense occurs in whole or in part within the United States;

(E) the offense occurs in or affects interstate or foreign commerce; or

(F) an offender aids or abets any person over whom jurisdiction exists under this paragraph in committing an offense under subsection (a) or conspires with any person over whom jurisdiction exists under this paragraph to commit an offense under subsection (a).

(2) Extraterritorial jurisdiction. There is extraterritorial Federal jurisdiction over an offense under this section.

(e) Investigations.

(1) In general. The Attorney General shall conduct any investigation of a possible violation of this section, or of any license, order, or regulation issued pursuant to this section.

(2) Coordination with the department of the treasury. The Attorney General shall work in coordination with the Secretary in investigations relating to

(A) the compliance or noncompliance by a financial institution with the requirements of subsection (a)(2); and

(B) civil penalty proceedings authorized under subsection (b).

(3) Referral. Any evidence of a criminal violation of this section arising in the course of an investigation by the Secretary or any other Federal agency shall be referred immediately to the Attorney General for further investigation. The Attorney General shall timely notify the Secretary of any action taken on referrals from the Secretary, and may refer investigations to the Secretary for remedial licensing or civil penalty action.

(f) Classified Information in Civil Proceedings Brought by the United States.

(1) Discovery of classified information by defendants.

(A) Request by united states. - In any civil proceeding under this section, upon request made ex parte and in writing by the United States, a court, upon a sufficient showing, may authorize the United States to

(i) redact specified items of classified information from documents to be introduced into evidence or made available to the defendant through discovery under the Federal Rules of Civil Procedure;

(ii) substitute a summary of the information for such classified documents; or

(iii) substitute a statement admitting relevant facts that the classified information would tend to prove.

[omitted details on introduction of redacted classified information and interlocutory appeals]

(g) Definitions. As used in this section

. . . .

(4) the term ''material support or resources'' has the same meaning as in section 2339A;

. . . .

(6) the term ''terrorist organization'' means an organization designated as a terrorist organization under [8 U.S.C. § 1189].

(h) Provision of Personnel. No person may be prosecuted under this section in connection with the term "personnel" unless that person has knowingly provided, attempted to provide, or conspired to provide a foreign terrorist organization with 1 or more individuals (who may be or include himself) to work under that terrorist organization's direction or control or to organize, manage, supervise, or otherwise direct the operation of that organization. Individuals who act entirely independently of the foreign terrorist organization to advance its goals or objectives shall not be considered to be working under the foreign terrorist organization's direction and control. [added by Pub. L. 108-458, 12/17/04]

(i) Rule of Construction. Nothing in this section shall be construed or applied so as to abridge the exercise of rights guaranteed under the First Amendment to the Constitution of the United States.

(j) Exception. No person may be prosecuted under this section in connection with the term "personnel", "training", or "expert advice or assistance" if the provision of that material support or resources to a foreign terrorist organization was approved by the Secretary of State with the concurrence of the Attorney General.

18 U.S.C. § 2339D. Receiving military-type training from a foreign terrorist organization

[added by Pub. L. 108-458, Dec. 17, 2004]

(a) Offense. Whoever knowingly receives military-type training from or on behalf of any organization designated at the time of the training by the Secretary of State under section 219(a)(1) of the Immigration and Nationality Act as a foreign terrorist organization shall be fined under this title or imprisoned for ten years, or both. To violate this subsection, a person must have knowledge that the organization is a designated terrorist organization (as defined in subsection (c)(4)), that the organization has engaged or engages in terrorist activity (as defined in section 212 of the Immigration and Nationality Act), or that the organization has engaged or engages in terrorism (as defined in section 140(d)(2) of the Foreign Relations Authorization Act, Fiscal Years 1988 and 1989).

(b) Extraterritorial Jurisdiction. There is extraterritorial Federal jurisdiction over an offense under this section. There is jurisdiction over an offense under subsection (a) if

(1) an offender is a national of the United States (as defined in 101(a)(22) of the Immigration and Nationality Act) or an alien lawfully admitted for permanent residence in the United States (as defined in section 101(a)(20) of the Immigration and Nationality Act);

(2) an offender is a stateless person whose habitual residence is in the United States;

(3) after the conduct required for the offense occurs an offender is brought into or found in the United States, even if the conduct required for the offense occurs outside the United States;

(4) the offense occurs in whole or in part within the United States;

(5) the offense occurs in or affects interstate or foreign commerce; or

(6) an offender aids or abets any person over whom jurisdiction exists under this paragraph in committing an offense under subsection (a) or conspires with any person over whom jurisdiction exists under this paragraph to commit an offense under subsection (a).

(c) Definitions. As used in this section

(1) the term "military-type training" includes training in means or methods that can cause death or serious bodily injury, destroy or damage property, or disrupt services to critical infrastructure, or training on the use, storage, production, or assembly of any explosive, firearm or other weapon, including any weapon of mass destruction.

5. Statutes Providing for Civil Actions

18 U.S.C. § 2333. Civil remedies

(a) Action and jurisdiction. Any national of the United States injured in his or her person, property, or business by reason of an act of international terrorism, or his or her estate, survivors, or heirs, may sue therefor in any appropriate district court of the United States and shall recover threefold the damages he or she sustains and the cost of the suit, including attorney's fees.

(b) Estoppel under United States law. A final judgment or decree rendered in favor of the United States in any criminal proceeding under [designated statutes] shall estop the defendant from denying the essential allegations of the criminal offense in any subsequent civil proceeding under this section.

(c) Estoppel under foreign law. A final judgment or decree rendered in favor of any foreign state in any criminal proceeding shall, to the extent that such judgment or decree may be accorded full faith and credit under the law of the United States, estop the defendant from denying the essential allegations of the criminal offense in any subsequent civil proceeding under this section.

A. Alien Tort Claims Act and Torture Victim Prevention Act

28 U.S.C. § 1350 Alien's action for tort

The district courts shall have original jurisdiction of any civil action by an alien for a tort only, committed in violation of the law of nations or a treaty of the United States.

[The Torture Prevention Act is not codified. It appears as a "Note" to § 1350.]

Note

Sec. 2. Establishment of civil action

(a) Liability. An individual who, under actual or apparent authority, or color of law, of any foreign nation

(1) subjects an individual to torture shall, in a civil action, be liable for damages to that individual; or

(2) subjects an individual to extrajudicial killing shall, in a civil action, be liable for damages to the individual's legal representative, or to any person who may be a claimant in an action for wrongful death.

Sec. 3. Definitions

(a) Extrajudicial killing. For the purposes of this Act, the term "extrajudicial killing" means a deliberated killing not authorized by a previous judgment pronounced by a regularly constituted court affording all the judicial guarantees which are recognized as indispensable by civilized peoples. Such term, however, does not include any such killing that, under international law, is lawfully carried out under the authority of a foreign nation.

(b) Torture. For the purposes of this Act

(1) the term "torture" means any act, directed against an individual in the offender's custody or physical control, by which severe pain or suffering (other than pain or suffering arising only from or inherent in, or incidental to, lawful sanctions), whether physical or mental, is intentionally inflicted on that individual for such purposes as obtaining from that individual or a third

person information or a confession, punishing that individual for an act that individual or a third person has committed or is suspected of having committed, intimidating or coercing that individual or a third person, or for any reason based on discrimination of any kind; and

(2) mental pain or suffering refers to prolonged mental harm caused by or resulting from

(A) the intentional infliction or threatened infliction of severe physical pain or suffering;

(B) the administration or application, or threatened administration or application, of mind altering substances or other procedures calculated to disrupt profoundly the senses or the personality;

(C) the threat of imminent death; or

(D) the threat that another individual will imminently be subjected to death, severe physical pain or suffering, or the administration or application of mind altering substances or other procedures calculated to disrupt profoundly the senses or personality.

B. Foreign Sovereign Immunities Act

28 U.S.C. § 1603. Definitions

For purposes of this chapter

(a) A "foreign state", except as used in section 1608 of this title, includes a political subdivision of a foreign state or an agency or instrumentality of a foreign state as defined in subsection (b).

(b) An "agency or instrumentality of a foreign state" means any entity

(1) which is a separate legal person, corporate or otherwise, and

(2) which is an organ of a foreign state or political subdivision thereof, or a majority of whose shares or other ownership interest is owned by a foreign state or political subdivision thereof, and

(3) which is neither a citizen of a State of the United States . . . nor created under the laws of any third country.

(c) The "United States" includes all territory and waters, continental or insular, subject to the jurisdiction of the United States.

(d) A "commercial activity" means either a regular course of commercial conduct or a particular commercial transaction or act. The commercial character of an activity shall be determined by reference to the nature of the course of conduct or particular transaction or act, rather than by reference to its purpose.

(e) A "commercial activity carried on in the United States by a foreign state" means commercial activity carried on by such state and having substantial contact with the United States.

§ 1605. General exceptions to the jurisdictional immunity of a foreign state

(a) A foreign state shall not be immune from the jurisdiction of courts of the United States or of the States in any case

(1) in which the foreign state has waived its immunity either explicitly or by implication, notwithstanding any withdrawal of the waiver which the foreign state may purport to effect except in accordance with the terms of the waiver;

(2) in which the action is based upon a commercial activity carried on in the United States by the foreign state; or upon an act performed in the United States in connection with a commercial activity of the foreign state elsewhere; or upon an act outside the territory of the United States in connection with a commercial activity of the foreign state elsewhere and that act causes a direct effect in the United States;

(3) in which rights in property taken in violation of international law are in issue and that property or any property exchanged for such property is present in the United States in connection with a commercial activity carried on in the United States by the foreign state; or that property or any property exchanged for such property is owned or operated by an agency or instrumentality of the foreign state and that agency or instrumentality is engaged in a commercial activity in the United States;

(4) in which rights in property in the United States acquired by succession or gift or rights in immovable property situated in the United States are in issue;

(5) not otherwise encompassed in paragraph (2) above, in which money damages are sought against a foreign state for personal injury or death, or damage to or loss of property, occurring in the United States and caused by the tortious act or omission of that foreign state or of any official or employee of that foreign state while acting within the scope of his office or employment; except this paragraph shall not apply to

(A) any claim based upon the exercise or performance or the failure to exercise or perform a discretionary function regardless of whether the discretion be abused, or

(B) any claim arising out of malicious prosecution, abuse of process, libel, slander, misrepresentation, deceit, or interference with contract rights;

(6) in which the action is brought, either to enforce an agreement made by the foreign state with or for the benefit of a private party to submit to arbitration all or any differences which have arisen or which may arise between the parties with respect to a defined legal relationship, or

(7) not otherwise covered by paragraph (2), in which money damages are sought against a foreign state for personal injury or death that was caused by an act of torture, extrajudicial killing, aircraft sabotage, hostage taking, or the provision of material support or resources (as defined in section 2339A of title 18) for such an act if such act or provision of material support is engaged in by an official, employee, or agent of such foreign state while acting within the scope of his or her office, employment, or agency, except that the court shall decline to hear a claim under this paragraph

(A) if the foreign state was not designated as a state sponsor of terrorism . . . at the time the act occurred, unless later so designated as a result of such act or the act is related to Case Number 1:00CV03110(EGS) in the United States District Court for the District of Columbia; and

(B) even if the foreign state is or was so designated, if

(i) the act occurred in the foreign state against which the claim has been brought and the claimant has not afforded the foreign state a reasonable opportunity to arbitrate the claim in accordance with accepted international rules of arbitration; or

(ii) neither the claimant nor the victim was a national of the United States (as that term is defined in [8 U.S.C. § 1101(a)(22)]) when the act upon which the claim is based occurred.

(e) For purposes of paragraph (7) of subsection (a)

(1) the terms "torture" and "extrajudicial killing" have the meaning given those terms in section 3 of the Torture Victim Protection Act of 1991 [28 U.S.C. § 1350 note];

(2) the term "hostage taking" has the meaning given that term in Article 1 of the International Convention Against the Taking of Hostages; and

(3) the term "aircraft sabotage" has the meaning given that term in Article 1 of the Convention for the Suppression of Unlawful Acts Against the Safety of Civil Aviation.

6. Statutes Relating to Information and Investigations

18 U.S.C. § 793. Gathering, transmitting, or losing defense information

(a) Whoever, for the purpose of obtaining information respecting the national defense with intent or reason to believe that the information is to be used to the injury of the United States, or to the advantage of any foreign nation, goes upon, enters, flies over, or otherwise obtains information concerning any vessel, aircraft, . . . canal, railroad, . . . factory, mine, . . . telephone, wireless, . . . building, office, . . . or other place connected with the national defense owned . . . or under the control of the United States, . . . or any prohibited place so designated by the President by proclamation in time of war or in case of national emergency; or

(b) Whoever, for the purpose aforesaid, and with like intent or reason to believe, copies, takes, makes, or obtains, . . . any sketch, photograph, . . . plan, map, . . . writing, or note of anything connected with the national defense; or

(f) Whoever, being entrusted with or having lawful possession or control of any document . . . or information, relating to the national defense, (1) through gross negligence permits the same to be removed from its proper place of custody or delivered to anyone in violation of his trust, or to be lost, stolen, abstracted, or destroyed, or (2) having knowledge that the same has been illegally removed from its proper place of custody or delivered to anyone in violation of his trust, or lost, or stolen, abstracted, or destroyed, and fails to make prompt report of such loss, theft, abstraction, or destruction to his superior officer

Shall be fined under this title or imprisoned not more than ten years, or both.

18 U.S.C. § 794. Gathering or delivering defense information to aid foreign government

(a) Whoever, with intent or reason to believe that it is to be used to the injury of the United States or to the advantage of a foreign nation, communicates, delivers, or transmits, or attempts to communicate, deliver, or transmit, to any foreign government, or to any faction or party or military or naval force within a foreign country, whether recognized or unrecognized by the United States, or to any representative, officer, agent, employee, subject, or citizen thereof, either directly or indirectly, any document, writing, code book, signal book, sketch, photograph, photographic negative, blueprint, plan, map, model, note, instrument, appliance, or information relating to the national defense, shall be punished by death or by imprisonment for any term of years or for life, except that the sentence of death shall not be imposed unless the jury or, if there is no jury, the court, further finds that the offense resulted in the identification by a foreign power (as defined in section 101(a) of the Foreign Intelligence Surveillance Act of 1978) of an individual acting as an agent of the United States and consequently in the death of that individual, or directly concerned nuclear weaponry, military spacecraft or satellites, early warning systems, or other means of defense or retaliation against large-scale attack; war plans; communications intelligence or cryptographic information; or any other major weapons system or major element of defense strategy.

(b) Whoever, in time of war, with intent that the same shall be communicated to the enemy, collects, records, publishes, or communicates, or attempts to elicit any information with respect to the movement, numbers, description, condition, or disposition of any of the Armed Forces, ships, aircraft, or war materials of the United States, or with respect to the plans or conduct, or supposed plans or conduct of any naval or military operations, or with respect to any works or measures undertaken for or connected with, or intended for the fortification or defense of any place, or any other information relating to the public defense, which might be useful to the enemy, shall be punished by death or by imprisonment for any term of years or for life.

18 U.S.C. § 798. Disclosure of classified information

(a) Whoever knowingly and willfully communicates, furnishes, transmits, or otherwise makes available to an unauthorized person, or publishes, or uses in any manner prejudicial to the safety or interest of the United States or for the benefit of any foreign government to the detriment of the United States any classified information

(1) concerning the nature, preparation, or use of any code, cipher, or cryptographic system of the United States or any foreign government; or

(2) concerning the design, construction, use, maintenance, or repair of any device, apparatus, or appliance used or prepared or planned for use by the United States or any foreign government for cryptographic or communication intelligence purposes; or

(3) concerning the communication intelligence activities of the United States or any foreign government; or

(4) obtained by the processes of communication intelligence from the

communications of any foreign government, knowing the same to have been obtained by such processes

Shall be fined under this title or imprisoned not more than ten years, or both.

(b) As used in subsection (a) of this section

The term "classified information" means information which, at the time of a violation of this section, is, for reasons of national security, specifically designated by a United States Government Agency for limited or restricted dissemination or distribution;

The term "foreign government" includes in its meaning any person or persons acting or purporting to act for or on behalf of any faction, party, department, agency, bureau, or military force of or within a foreign country, . . . whether or not such government is recognized by the United States;

The term "communication intelligence" means all procedures and methods used in the interception of communications and the obtaining of information from such communications by other than the intended recipients;

The term "unauthorized person" means any person who, or agency which, is not authorized to receive information of the categories set forth in subsection (a) of this section, by the President, or by the head of a department or agency of the United States Government which is expressly designated by the President to engage in communication intelligence activities for the United States.

A. Classified Information Procedures Act, 18 U.S.C App

§ 1. Definitions

(a) "Classified information", as used in this Act, means any information or material that has been determined by the United States Government pursuant to an Executive order, statute, or regulation, to require protection against unauthorized disclosure for reasons of national security and any restricted data, as defined in paragraph r. of section 11 of the Atomic Energy Act of 1954.

(b) "National security", as used in this Act, means the national defense and foreign relations of the United States.

§ 3. Protective orders

Upon motion of the United States, the court shall issue an order to protect against the disclosure of any classified information disclosed by the United States to any defendant in any criminal case in a district court of the United States.

§ 4. Discovery of classified information by defendant

The court, upon a sufficient showing, may authorize the United States to delete specified items of classified information from documents to be made available to the defendant through discovery under the Federal Rules of Criminal Procedure, to substitute a summary of the information for such classified documents, or to substitute a statement admitting relevant facts that the classified information would tend to prove. The court may permit the United States to make a request for such authorization in the form of a written statement to be inspected by the court alone. If the court enters an order granting relief following such an ex parte showing, the entire text of the statement of the United States shall be sealed and preserved in the records of the court to be made available to the appellate court in the event of an appeal.

§ 5. Notice of defendant's intention to disclose classified information

(a) Notice by defendant. If a defendant reasonably expects to disclose or to cause the disclosure of classified information in any manner in connection with any trial or pretrial proceeding involving the criminal prosecution of such defendant, the defendant shall, within the time specified by the court or, where no time is specified, within thirty days prior to trial, notify the attorney for the United States and the court in writing. Such notice shall include a brief description of the classified information. Whenever a defendant learns of additional classified information he reasonably expects to disclose at any such proceeding, he shall notify the attorney for the United States and the court in writing as soon as possible thereafter and shall include a brief description of the classified information. No defendant shall disclose any information known or believed to be classified in connection with a trial or pretrial proceeding until notice has been given under this subsection and until the United States has been afforded a reasonable opportunity to seek a determination pursuant to the procedure set forth in section 6 of this Act, and until the time for the United States to appeal such determination under section 7 has expired or any appeal under section 7 by the United States is decided.

(b) Failure to comply. If the defendant fails to comply with the requirements of subsection (a) the court may preclude disclosure of any classified information not made the subject of notification and may prohibit the examination by the defendant of any witness with respect to any such information.

§ 6. Procedure for cases involving classified information

(a) Motion for hearing. Within the time specified by the court for the filing of a motion under this section, the United States may request the court to conduct a hearing to make all determinations concerning the use, relevance, or admissibility of classified information that would otherwise be made during the trial or pretrial proceeding. Upon such a request, the court shall conduct such a hearing. Any hearing held pursuant to this subsection (or any portion of such hearing specified in the request of the Attorney General) shall be held in camera if the Attorney General certifies to the court in such petition that a public proceeding may result in the disclosure of classified information. As to each item of classified information, the court shall set forth in writing the basis for its determination. Where the United States' motion under this subsection is filed prior to the trial or pretrial proceeding, the court shall rule prior to the commencement of the relevant proceeding.

(b) Notice.

(1) Before any hearing is conducted pursuant to a request by the United States under subsection (a), the United States shall provide the defendant with notice of the classified information that is at issue. Such notice shall identify the specific classified information at issue whenever that information previously has been made available to the defendant by the United States. When the United States has not previously made the information available to the defendant in connection with the case, the information may be described by generic category, in such form as the court may approve, rather

than by identification of the specific information of concern to the United States.

(2) Whenever the United States requests a hearing under subsection (a), the court, upon request of the defendant, may order the United States to provide the defendant, prior to trial, such details as to the portion of the indictment or information at issue in the hearing as are needed to give the defendant fair notice to prepare for the hearing.

(c) Alternative procedure for disclosure of classified information.

(1) Upon any determination by the court authorizing the disclosure of specific classified information under the procedures established by this section, the United States may move that, in lieu of the disclosure of such specific classified information, the court order

(A) the substitution for such classified information of a statement admitting relevant facts that the specific classified information would tend to prove; or

(B) the substitution for such classified information of a summary of the specific classified information.

The court shall grant such a motion of the United States if it finds that the statement or summary will provide the defendant with substantially the same ability to make his defense as would disclosure of the specific classified information. The court shall hold a hearing on any motion under this section. Any such hearing shall be held in camera at the request of the Attorney General.

(2) The United States may, in connection with a motion under paragraph (1), submit to the court an affidavit of the Attorney General certifying that disclosure of classified information would cause identifiable damage to the national security of the United States and explaining the basis for the classification of such information. If so requested by the United States, the court shall examine such affidavit in camera and ex parte.

(d) Sealing of records of in camera hearings. If at the close of an in camera hearing under this Act (or any portion of a hearing under this Act that is held in camera) the court determines that the classified information at issue may not be disclosed or elicited at the trial or pretrial proceeding, the record of such in camera hearing shall be sealed and preserved by the court for use in the event of an appeal. The defendant may seek reconsideration of the court's determination prior to or during trial.

(e) Prohibition on disclosure of classified information by defendant, relief for defendant when United States opposes disclosure.

(1) Whenever the court denies a motion by the United States that it issue an order under subsection (c) and the United States files with the court an affidavit of the Attorney General objecting to disclosure of the classified information at issue, the court shall order that the defendant not disclose or cause the disclosure of such information.

(2) Whenever a defendant is prevented by an order under paragraph (1) from disclosing or causing the disclosure of classified information, the court shall dismiss the indictment or information; except that, when the court

determines that the interests of justice would not be served by dismissal of the indictment or information, the court shall order such other action, in lieu of dismissing the indictment or information, as the court determines is appropriate. Such action may include, but need not be limited to

(A) dismissing specified counts of the indictment or information;

(B) finding against the United States on any issue as to which the excluded classified information relates; or

(C) striking or precluding all or part of the testimony of a witness.

An order under this paragraph shall not take effect until the court has afforded the United States an opportunity to appeal such order under section 7, and thereafter to withdraw its objection to the disclosure of the classified information at issue.

(f) Reciprocity. Whenever the court determines pursuant to subsection (a) that classified information may be disclosed in connection with a trial or pretrial proceeding, the court shall, unless the interests of fairness do not so require, order the United States to provide the defendant with the information it expects to use to rebut the classified information. The court may place the United States under a continuing duty to disclose such rebuttal information. If the United States fails to comply with its obligation under this subsection, the court may exclude any evidence not made the subject of a required disclosure and may prohibit the examination by the United States of any witness with respect to such information.

§ 7. Interlocutory appeal

(a) An interlocutory appeal by the United States taken before or after the defendant has been placed in jeopardy shall lie to a court of appeals from a decision or order of a district court in a criminal case authorizing the disclosure of classified information, imposing sanctions for nondisclosure of classified information, or refusing a protective order sought by the United States to prevent the disclosure of classified information.

(b) An appeal taken pursuant to this section either before or during trial shall be expedited by the court of appeals. Prior to trial, an appeal shall be taken within ten days after the decision or order appealed from and the trial shall not commence until the appeal is resolved. If an appeal is taken during trial, the trial court shall adjourn the trial until the appeal is resolved and the court of appeals (1) shall hear argument on such appeal within four days of the adjournment of the trial, (2) may dispense with written briefs other than the supporting materials previously submitted to the trial court, (3) shall render its decision within four days of argument on appeal, and (4) may dispense with the issuance of a written opinion in rendering its decision. Such appeal and decision shall not affect the right of the defendant, in a subsequent appeal from a judgment of conviction, to claim as error reversal by the trial court on remand of a ruling appealed from during trial.

B. Foreign Intelligence Surveillance Act

[50 U.S.C. §§ 1801-1862, as amended by USA PATRIOT Act]

§ 1801. Definitions

As used in this title:

(a) "Foreign power" means

(1) a foreign government or any component thereof whether or not recognized by the United States;

(2) a faction of a foreign nation or nations, not substantially composed of United States persons;

(3) an entity that is openly acknowledged by a foreign government or governments to be directed and controlled by such foreign government or governments;

(4) a group engaged in international terrorism or activities in preparation therefor;

(5) a foreign-based political organization, not substantially composed of United States persons; or

(6) an entity that is directed and controlled by a foreign government or governments.

(b) "Agent of a foreign power" means

(1) any person other than a United States person, who

(A) acts in the United States as an officer or employee of a foreign power, or as a member of a foreign power as defined in subsection (a)(4);

(B) acts for or on behalf of a foreign power which engages in clandestine intelligence activities in the United States contrary to the interests of the United States, when the circumstances of such person's presence in the United States indicate that such person may engage in such activities in the United States, or when such person knowingly aids or abets any person in the conduct of such activities or knowingly conspires with any person to engage in such activities; or

(C) engages in international terrorism or activities in preparation therefor [paragraph (C) was added on Dec. 17, 2004 and is scheduled to "sunset" on Dec. 31, 2005]; or

(2) any person who

(A) knowingly engages in clandestine intelligence gathering activities for or on behalf of a foreign power, which activities involve or may involve a violation of the criminal statutes of the United States;

(B) pursuant to the direction of an intelligence service or network of a foreign power, knowingly engages in any other clandestine intelligence activities for or on behalf of such foreign power, which activities involve or are about to involve a violation of the criminal statues of the United States;

(C) knowingly engages in sabotage or international terrorism, or activities that are in preparation therefor, for or on behalf of a foreign power;

(D) knowingly enters the United States under a false or fraudulent identity for or on behalf of a foreign power or, while in the United States, knowingly assumes a false or fraudulent identity for or on behalf of a foreign power; or

(E) knowingly aids or abets any person in the conduct of activities described in subparagraph (A), (B), or (C) or knowingly conspires with any person to engage in activities described in subparagraph (A), (B), or (C).

(c) "International terrorism" means activities that

(1) involve violent acts or acts dangerous to human life that are a violation of the criminal laws of the United States or of any State, or that would be a criminal violation if committed within the jurisdiction of the United States or any State;

(2) appear to be intended

(A) to intimidate or coerce a civilian population;

(B) to influence the policy of a government by intimidation or coercion; or

(C) to affect the conduct of a government by assassination or kidnapping; and

(3) occur totally outside the United States or transcend national boundaries in terms of the means by which they are accomplished, the persons they appear intended to coerce or intimidate, or the locale in which their perpetrators operate or seek asylum.

(d) "Sabotage" means activities that involve a violation of [18 U.S.C. §§ 2151 *et seq.*], or that would involve such a violation if committed against the United States.

(e) "Foreign intelligence information" means

(1) information that relates to, and if concerning a United States person is necessary to, the ability of the United States to protect against--

(A) actual or potential attack or other grave hostile acts of a foreign power or an agent of a foreign power;

(B) sabotage or international terrorism by a foreign power or an agent of a foreign power; or

(C) clandestine intelligence activities by an intelligence service or network of a foreign power or by an agent of a foreign power; or

(2) information with respect to a foreign power or foreign territory that relates to, and if concerning a United States person is necessary to

(A) the national defense or the security of the United States; or

(B) the conduct of the foreign affairs of the United States.

(i) "United States person" means a citizen of the United States, an alien lawfully admitted for permanent residence, an unincorporated association a substantial number of members of which are citizens of the United States or aliens lawfully admitted for permanent residence, or a corporation which is incorporated in the United States, but does not include a corporation or an association which is a foreign power, as defined in subsection (a)(1), (2), or (3).

§ 1804. Applications for court orders [for electronic surveillance – essentially the same procedures apply to searches under § 1823 by substituting "premises" for "target"]

(a) Submission by Federal officer; approval of Attorney General; contents. Each application for an order approving electronic surveillance under this title shall be made by a Federal officer in writing upon oath or affirmation to a judge having jurisdiction under section 1803. Each application shall require the approval of the Attorney General based upon his finding that it satisfies the criteria and requirements of such application as set forth in this title. It shall include

(1) the identity of the Federal officer making the application;

(2) the authority conferred on the Attorney General by the President of the United States and the approval of the Attorney General to make the application;

(3) the identity, if known, or a description of the target of the electronic surveillance;

(4) a statement of the facts and circumstances relied upon by the applicant to justify his belief that--

(A) the target of the electronic surveillance is a foreign power or an agent of a foreign power; and

(B) each of the facilities or places at which the electronic surveillance is directed is being used, or is about to be used, by a foreign power or an agent of a foreign power;

(5) a statement of the proposed minimization procedures;

(6) a detailed description of the nature of the information sought and the type of communications or activities to be subjected to the surveillance;

(7) a certification or certifications by the Assistant to the President for National Security Affairs or an executive branch official or officials designated by the President from among those executive officers employed in the area of national security or defense and appointed by the President with the advice and consent of the Senate--

(A) that the certifying official deems the information sought to be foreign intelligence information;

(B) that a significant purpose of the surveillance is to obtain foreign intelligence information;

(C) that such information cannot reasonably be obtained by normal investigative techniques;

(D) that designates the type of foreign intelligence information being sought according to the categories described in section 1801(e); and

(E) including a statement of the basis for the certification that

(i) the information sought is the type of foreign intelligence information designated; and

(ii) such information cannot reasonably be obtained by normal investigative techniques;

(8) a statement of the means by which the surveillance will be effected and a statement whether physical entry is required to effect the surveillance;

§ 1805. Issuance of order

(a) Necessary findings. Upon an application made pursuant to section 1804, the judge shall enter an ex parte order as requested or as modified approving the electronic surveillance if he finds that--

(3) on the basis of the facts submitted by the applicant there is probable cause to believe that--

(A) the target of the electronic surveillance is a foreign power or agent of a foreign power: Provided, That no United States person may be considered a foreign power or an agent of a foreign power solely upon the basis of activities protected by the first amendment to the Constitution of the United States; and

(B) each of the facilities or places at which the electronic surveillance is directed is being used, or is about to be used, by a foreign power or an agent of a foreign power;

(4) the proposed minimization procedures meet the definition of minimization procedures under section 1804(h); and

(5) the application which has been filed contains all statements and certifications required by section 1804 and, if the target is a United States person, the certification or certifications are not clearly erroneous on the basis of the statement made under section 1804(a)(7)(E) and any other information furnished under section 1804(d).

§ 1806. Use of information

(a) *Compliance with minimization procedures; privileged communications; lawful purposes.* Information acquired from an electronic surveillance conducted pursuant to this title concerning any United States person may be used and disclosed by Federal officers and employees without the consent of the United States person only in accordance with the minimization procedures required by this title. No otherwise privileged communication obtained in accordance with, or in violation of, the provisions of this title shall lose its privileged character. No information acquired from an electronic surveillance pursuant to this title may be used or disclosed by Federal officers or employees except for lawful purposes.

(b) *Statement for disclosure*. No information acquired pursuant to this title shall be disclosed for law enforcement purposes unless such disclosure is accompanied by a statement that such information, or any information derived therefrom, may only be used in a criminal proceeding with the advance authorization of the Attorney General.

(c) *Notification by United States*. Whenever the Government intends to enter into evidence or otherwise use or disclose in any trial, hearing, or other proceeding in or before any court, department, officer, agency, regulatory body, or other authority of the United States, against an aggrieved person, any information obtained or derived from an electronic surveillance of that aggrieved person pursuant to the authority of this title, the Government shall, prior to the trial, hearing, or other proceeding or at a reasonable time prior to an effort to so disclose or so use that information or submit it in evidence, notify the aggrieved person and the court or other authority in which the information is to be disclosed or used that the Government intends to so disclose or so use such information.

(e) *Motion to suppress*. Any person against whom evidence obtained or derived from an electronic surveillance to which he is an aggrieved person is to be, or has been, introduced or otherwise used or disclosed in any trial, hearing, or other proceeding in or before any court, department, officer, agency, regulatory body, or other authority of the United States, a State, or a political subdivision thereof, may move to suppress the evidence obtained or derived from such electronic surveillance on the grounds that

(1) the information was unlawfully acquired; or

(2) the surveillance was not made in conformity with an order of authorization or approval.

Such a motion shall be made before the trial, hearing, or other proceeding unless there was no opportunity to make such a motion or the person was not aware of the grounds of the motion.

(f) *In camera and ex parte review by district court*. Whenever a court or other authority is notified pursuant to subsection (c) or (d), or whenever a motion is made pursuant to subsection (e), or whenever any motion or request is made by an aggrieved person pursuant to any other statute or rule of the United States of any State before any court or other authority of the United States or any state to discover or obtain applications or orders or other materials relating to electronic surveillance or to discover, obtain, or suppress evidence or information obtained or derived from electronic surveillance under this Act, the United States district court or, where the motion is made before another authority, the United States district court in the same district as the authority, shall, notwithstanding any other law, if the Attorney General files an affidavit under oath that disclosure or an adversary hearing would harm the national security of the United States, review in camera and ex parte the application, order, and such other materials relating to the surveillance as may be necessary to determine whether the surveillance of the aggrieved person was lawfully authorized and conducted. In making this determination, the court may disclose to the aggrieved person, under appropriate security procedures and protective orders, portions of the application, order, or other materials relating to the surveillance only where such disclosure is necessary to make an accurate determination of the legality of the surveillance.

(k) *Coordination with law enforcement.*

(1) Federal officers who conduct electronic surveillance to acquire foreign intelligence information under this title may consult with Federal law enforcement officers or law enforcement personnel of a State or political subdivision of a State (including the chief executive officer of that State or political subdivision who has the authority to appoint or direct the chief law enforcement officer of that State or political subdivision) to coordinate efforts to investigate or protect against

(A) actual or potential attack or other grave hostile acts of a foreign power or an agent of a foreign power;

(B) sabotage or international terrorism by a foreign power or an agent of a foreign power; or

C) clandestine intelligence activities by an intelligence service or network of a foreign power or by an agent of a foreign power.

(2) Coordination authorized under paragraph (1) shall not preclude the certification required by section 1804(a)(7)(B) or the entry of an order under section 1805.

§ 1861. Access to certain business records for foreign intelligence and international terrorism investigations

(a) (1) The Director of the Federal Bureau of Investigation or a designee of the Director (whose rank shall be no lower than Assistant Special Agent in Charge) may make an application for an order requiring the production of any tangible things (including books, records, papers, documents, and other items) for an investigation to obtain foreign intelligence information not concerning a United States person or to protect against international terrorism or clandestine intelligence activities, provided that such investigation of a United States person is not conducted solely upon the basis of activities protected by the first amendment to the Constitution.

(2) An investigation conducted under this section shall

(A) be conducted under guidelines approved by the Attorney General under Executive Order 12333 [50 U.S.C. § 401 note] (or a successor order); and

(B) not be conducted of a United States person solely upon the basis of activities protected by the first amendment to the Constitution of the United States.

(b) Each application under this section

(1) shall be made to

(A) a judge of the [FISA] court; or

(B) a United States Magistrate Judge who is publicly designated by the Chief Justice of the United States to have the power to hear applications and grant orders for the production of tangible things under this section on behalf of a judge of that court; and

(2) shall specify that the records concerned are sought for an authorized investigation conducted in accordance with subsection (a)(2) to obtain foreign intelligence information not concerning a United States person or to protect against international terrorism or clandestine intelligence activities.

(c) (1) Upon an application made pursuant to this section, the judge shall enter an ex parte order as requested, or as modified, approving the release of records if the judge finds that the application meets the requirements of this section.

(2) An order under this subsection shall not disclose that it is issued for purposes of an investigation described in subsection (a).

(d) No person shall disclose to any other person (other than those persons necessary to produce the tangible things under this section) that the Federal Bureau of Investigation has sought or obtained tangible things under this section.

(e) A person who, in good faith, produces tangible things under an order pursuant to this section shall not be liable to any other person for such production. Such production shall not be deemed to constitute a waiver of any privilege in any other proceeding or context.

7. Military Provisions
A. Uniform Code of Military Justice

10 U.S.C. § 821 Jurisdiction of courts-martial not exclusive

The provisions of this chapter [10 U.S.C. §§ 801 *et seq.*] conferring jurisdiction upon courts-martial do not deprive military commissions, provost courts, or other military tribunals of concurrent jurisdiction with respect to offenders or offenses that by statute or by the law of war may be tried by military commissions, provost courts, or other military tribunals.

10 U.S.C. § 836 President may prescribe rules

(a) Pretrial, trial, and post-trial procedures, including modes of proof, for cases arising under this chapter [10 U.S.C. §§ 801 *et seq.*] triable in courts-martial, military commissions and other military tribunals, and procedures for courts of inquiry, may be prescribed by the President by regulations which shall, so far as he considers practicable, apply the principles of law and the rules of evidence generally recognized in the trial of criminal cases in the United States district courts, but which may not be contrary to or inconsistent with this chapter.

(b) All rules and regulations made under this article shall be uniform insofar as practicable.

B. Resolutions and Orders

MILITARY ORDER #1

PUBLIC PAPERS OF THE PRESIDENTS (Vol 37 - Number 46, 11/19/01)

(Fed. Reg. 11/16/01)

November 13, 2001

By the authority vested in me as President and as Commander in Chief of the Armed Forces of the United States by the Constitution and the laws of the United States of America, including the Authorization for Use of Military Force Joint Resolution (Public Law 107-40, 115 Stat. 224) and sections 821 and 836 of title 10, United States Code, it is hereby ordered as follows:

Section 1. Findings.

(a) International terrorists, including members of al Qaida, have carried out attacks on United States diplomatic and military personnel and facilities abroad and on citizens and property within the United States on a scale that has created a state of armed conflict that requires the use of the United States Armed Forces.

(b) In light of grave acts of terrorism and threats of terrorism, including the terrorist attacks on September 11, 2001, on the headquarters of the United States Department of Defense in the national capital region, on the World Trade Center in New York, and on civilian aircraft such as in Pennsylvania, I proclaimed a national emergency on September 14, 2001 (Proc. 7463, Declaration of National Emergency by Reason of Certain Terrorist Attacks).

(e) To protect the United States and its citizens, and for the effective conduct of military operations and prevention of terrorist attacks, it is necessary for individuals subject to this order pursuant to section 2 hereof to be detained, and, when tried, to be tried for violations of the laws of war and other applicable laws by military tribunals.

(f) Given the danger to the safety of the United States and the nature of international terrorism, and to the extent provided by and under this order, I find consistent with section 836 of title 10, United States Code, that it is not practicable to apply in military commissions under this order the principles of law and the rules of evidence generally recognized in the trial of criminal cases in the United States district courts.

Sec. 2. Definition and Policy.

(a) The term "individual subject to this order" shall mean any individual who is not a United States citizen with respect to whom I determine from time to time in writing that:

(1) there is reason to believe that such individual, at the relevant times,

(i) is or was a member of the organization known as al Qaida;

(ii) has engaged in, aided or abetted, or conspired to commit, acts of international terrorism, or acts in preparation therefor, that have caused, threaten to cause, or have as their aim to cause, injury to or adverse effects on the United States, its citizens, national security, foreign policy, or economy; or

(iii) has knowingly harbored one or more individuals described in subparagraphs (i) or (ii) of subsection 2(a)(1) of this order; and

(2) it is in the interest of the United States that such individual be subject to this order.

(b) It is the policy of the United States that the Secretary of Defense shall take all necessary measures to ensure that any individual subject to this order is detained in accordance with section 3, and, if the individual is to be tried, that such individual is tried only in accordance with section 4.

(c) It is further the policy of the United States that any individual subject to this order who is not already under the control of the Secretary of Defense but who is under the control of any other officer or agent of the United States or any State shall, upon delivery of a copy of such written determination to such officer or agent, forthwith be placed under the control of the Secretary of Defense.

Sec. 3. Detention Authority of the Secretary of Defense. Any individual subject to this order shall be

(a) detained at an appropriate location designated by the Secretary of Defense outside or within the United States;

(b) treated humanely, without any adverse distinction based on race, color, religion, gender, birth, wealth, or any similar criteria;

(c) afforded adequate food, drinking water, shelter, clothing, and medical treatment;

(d) allowed the free exercise of religion consistent with the requirements of such detention; and

(e) detained in accordance with such other conditions as the Secretary of Defense may prescribe.

Sec. 4. Authority of the Secretary of Defense Regarding Trials of Individuals Subject to this Order.

(a) Any individual subject to this order shall, when tried, be tried by military commission for any and all offenses triable by military commission that such individual is alleged to have committed, and may be punished in accordance with the penalties provided under applicable law, including life imprisonment or death.

(b) As a military function and in light of the findings in section 1, including subsection (f) thereof, the Secretary of Defense shall issue such orders and regulations, including orders for the appointment of one or more military commissions, as may be necessary to carry out subsection (a) of this section.

(c) Orders and regulations issued under subsection (b) of this section shall include, but not be limited to, rules for the conduct of the proceedings of military commissions, including pretrial, trial, and post-trial procedures, modes of proof, issuance of process, and qualifications of attorneys, which shall at a minimum provide for

(1) military commissions to sit at any time and any place, consistent with such guidance regarding time and place as the Secretary of Defense may provide;

(2) a full and fair trial, with the military commission sitting as the triers of both fact and law;

(3) admission of such evidence as would, in the opinion of the presiding officer of the military commission (or instead, if any other member of the commission so requests at the time the presiding officer renders that opinion, the opinion of the commission rendered at that time by a majority of the commission), have probative value to a reasonable person;

(4) in a manner consistent with the protection of information classified or classifiable under Executive Order 12958 of April 17, 1995, as amended, or any successor Executive Order, protected by statute or rule from unauthorized disclosure, or otherwise protected by law, (A) the handling of, admission into evidence of, and access to materials and information, and (B) the conduct, closure of, and access to proceedings;

(5) conduct of the prosecution by one or more attorneys designated by the Secretary of Defense and conduct of the defense by attorneys for the individual subject to this order;

(6) conviction only upon the concurrence of two-thirds of the members of the commission present at the time of the vote, a majority being present;

(7) sentencing only upon the concurrence of two-thirds of the members of the commission present at the time of the vote, a majority being present; and

(8) submission of the record of the trial, including any conviction or sentence, for review and final decision by me or by the Secretary of Defense if so designated by me for that purpose.

Joint Resolution to authorize the use of United States Armed Forces against those responsible for the recent attacks launched against the United States

PUB. L. 107-40 [S.J. Res. 23] (Sept. 18, 2001)

Whereas, on September 11, 2001, acts of treacherous violence were committed against the United States and its citizens; and

Whereas, such acts render it both necessary and appropriate that the United States exercise its rights to self-defense and to protect United States citizens both at home and abroad; and

Whereas, in light of the threat to the national security and foreign policy of the United States posed by these grave acts of violence; and

Whereas, such acts continue to pose an unusual and extraordinary threat to the national security and foreign policy of the United States; and

Whereas, the President has authority under the Constitution to take action to deter and prevent acts of international terrorism against the United States: Now, therefore, be it

Resolved by the Senate and House of Representatives of the United States of America in Congress assembled,

SECTION 1. SHORT TITLE.

This joint resolution may be cited as the "Authorization for Use of Military Force".

SEC. 2. AUTHORIZATION FOR USE OF UNITED STATES ARMED FORCES.

(a) In General. That the President is authorized to use all necessary and appropriate force against those nations, organizations, or persons he determines planned, authorized, committed, or aided the terrorist attacks that occurred on September 11, 2001, or harbored such organizations or persons, in order to prevent any future acts of international terrorism against the United States by such nations, organizations or persons.

(b) War Powers Resolution Requirements

(1) Specific statutory authorization. Consistent with section 8(a)(1) of the War Powers Resolution, the Congress declares that this section is intended to constitute specific statutory authorization within the meaning of section 5(b) of the War Powers Resolution.

(2) Applicability of other requirements. Nothing in this resolution supercedes any requirement of the War Powers Resolution.

Joint Resolution to authorize the use of United States Armed Forces against Iraq

PUB. L. 107-243 [H.J. Res. 114] (Oct. 16, 2002).

Whereas in 1990 in response to Iraq's war of aggression against and illegal occupation of Kuwait, the United States forged a coalition of nations to liberate Kuwait and its people in order to defend the national security of the United States and enforce United Nations Security Council resolutions relating to Iraq;

Whereas after the liberation of Kuwait in 1991, Iraq entered into a United Nations sponsored cease-fire agreement pursuant to which Iraq unequivocally agreed, among other things, to eliminate its nuclear, biological, and chemical weapons programs and the means to deliver and develop them, and to end its support for international terrorism;

Whereas the efforts of international weapons inspectors, United States intelligence agencies, and Iraqi defectors led to the discovery that Iraq had large stockpiles of chemical weapons and a large scale biological weapons program, and that Iraq had an advanced nuclear weapons development program that was much closer to producing a nuclear weapon than intelligence reporting had previously indicated;

Whereas Iraq, in direct and flagrant violation of the cease-fire, attempted to thwart the efforts of weapons inspectors to identify and destroy Iraq's weapons of mass destruction stockpiles and development capabilities, which finally resulted in the withdrawal of inspectors from Iraq on October 31, 1998;

. . . .

Whereas United Nations Security Council Resolution 678 (1990) authorizes the use of all necessary means to enforce United Nations Security Council Resolution 660 (1990) and subsequent relevant resolutions and to compel Iraq to cease certain activities that threaten international peace and security, including the development of weapons of mass destruction and refusal or obstruction of United Nations weapons inspections in violation of United Nations Security Council Resolution 687 (1991), repression of its civilian population in violation of United Nations Security Council Resolution 688 (1991), and threatening its neighbors or United Nations operations in Iraq in violation of United Nations Security Council Resolution 949 (1994);

. . . .

SEC. 3. AUTHORIZATION FOR USE OF UNITED STATES ARMED FORCES.

(a) Authorization. The President is authorized to use the Armed Forces of the United States as he determines to be necessary and appropriate in order to

(1) defend the national security of the United States against the continuing threat posed by Iraq; and

(2) enforce all relevant United Nations Security Council resolutions regarding Iraq.

(b) Presidential Determination. In connection with the exercise of the authority granted in subsection (a) to use force the President shall, prior to such exercise or as soon thereafter as may be feasible, but no later than 48 hours after exercising such authority, make available to the Speaker of the House of Representatives and the President pro tempore of the Senate his determination that

(1) reliance by the United States on further diplomatic or other peaceful means alone either (A) will not adequately protect the national security of the United States against the continuing threat posed by Iraq or (B) is not likely to lead to enforcement of all relevant United Nations Security Council resolutions regarding Iraq; and

(2) acting pursuant to this joint resolution is consistent with the United States and other countries continuing to take the necessary actions against international terrorist and terrorist organizations, including those nations, organizations, or persons who planned, authorized, committed or aided the terrorist attacks that occurred on September 11, 2001.

(c) War Powers Resolution Requirements.

(1) Specific statutory authorization. Consistent with section 8(a)(1) of the War Powers Resolution, the Congress declares that this section is intended to constitute specific statutory authorization within the meaning of section 5(b) of the War Powers Resolution.

(2) Applicability of other requirements. Nothing in this joint resolution supersedes any requirement of the War Powers Resolution.

SEC. 4. REPORTS TO CONGRESS.

(a) Reports. The President shall, at least once every 60 days, submit to the Congress a report on matters relevant to this joint resolution, including actions taken pursuant to the exercise of authority granted in section 3 and the status of planning for efforts that are expected to be required after such actions are completed, including those actions described in section 7 of the Iraq Liberation Act of 1998 (Public Law 105-338).

(b) Single Consolidated Report. To the extent that the submission of any report described in subsection (a) coincides with the submission of any other report on matters relevant to this joint resolution otherwise required to be submitted to Congress pursuant to the reporting requirements of the War Powers Resolution (Public Law 93-148), all such reports may be submitted as a single consolidated report to the Congress.

(c) Rule of Construction. To the extent that the information required by section 3 of the Authorization for Use of Military Force Against Iraq Resolution (Public Law 102-1) is included in the report required by this section, such report shall be considered as meeting the requirements of section 3 of such resolution.

B. INTERNATIONAL CONVENTIONS

1. Geneva Conventions (1949)

[Note: There are four 1949 Geneva Conventions. Convention I deals with "Wounded and Sick Members of Armed Forces in the Field," II with "Wounded, Sick and Shipwrecked Members of Armed Forces at Sea," and IV with "Protection of Civilian Persons in Time of War." Convention IV is "Relative to the Treatment of Prisoners of War." Article 3 is identical in all four conventions and is known as "Common Article 3."]

III

Convention Relative to the Treatment of Prisoners of War

Article 2

In addition to the provisions which shall be implemented in peace time, the present Convention shall apply to all cases of declared war or of any other armed conflict which may arise between two or more of the High Contracting Parties, even if the state of war is not recognized by one of them.

The Convention shall also apply to all cases of partial or total occupation of the territory of a High Contracting Party, even if the said occupation meets with no armed resistance.

Although one of the Powers in conflict may not be a party to the present Convention, the Powers who are parties thereto shall remain bound by it in their mutual relations. They shall furthermore be bound by the Convention in relation to the said Power, if the latter accepts and applies the provisions thereof.

Article 3

In the case of armed conflict not of an international character occurring in the territory of one of the High Contracting Parties, each party to the conflict shall be bound to apply, as a minimum, the following provisions:

1. Persons taking no active part in the hostilities, including members of armed forces who have laid down their arms and those placed hors de combat by sickness, wounds, detention, or any other cause, shall in all circumstances be treated humanely, without any adverse distinction founded on race, colour, religion or faith, sex, birth or wealth, or any other similar criteria.

To this end the following acts are and shall remain prohibited at any time and in any place whatsoever with respect to the above-mentioned persons:

(a) Violence to life and person, in particular murder of all kinds, mutilation, cruel treatment and torture;

(b) Taking of hostages;

(c) Outrages upon personal dignity, in particular, humiliating and degrading treatment;

(d) The passing of sentences and the carrying out of executions without previous judgment pronounced by a regularly constituted court affording all the judicial guarantees which are recognized as indispensable by civilized peoples.

2. The wounded and sick shall be collected and cared for.

An impartial humanitarian body, such as the International Committee of the Red Cross, may offer its services to the Parties to the conflict.

The Parties to the conflict should further endeavour to bring into force, by means of special agreements, all or part of the other provisions of the present Convention.

The application of the preceding provisions shall not affect the legal status of the Parties to the conflict.

Article 4

A. Prisoners of war, in the sense of the present Convention, are persons belonging to one of the following categories, who have fallen into the power of the enemy:

1. Members of the armed forces of a Party to the conflict as well as members of militias or volunteer corps forming part of such armed forces.

2. Members of other militias and members of other volunteer corps, including those of organized resistance movements, belonging to a Party to the conflict and operating in or outside their own territory, even if this territory is occupied, provided that such militias or volunteer corps, including such organized resistance movements, fulfil the following conditions:

(a) That of being commanded by a person responsible for his subordinates;

(b) That of having a fixed distinctive sign recognizable at a distance;

(c) That of carrying arms openly;

(d) That of conducting their operations in accordance with the laws and customs of war.

3. Members of regular armed forces who profess allegiance to a government or an authority not recognized by the Detaining Power.

4. Persons who accompany the armed forces without actually being members thereof, such as civilian members of military aircraft crews, war correspondents, supply contractors, members of labour units or of services responsible for the welfare of the armed forces, provided that they have received authorization from the armed forces which they accompany, who shall provide them for that purpose with an identity card similar to the annexed model.

5. Members of crews, including masters, pilots and apprentices, of the merchant marine and the crews of civil aircraft of the Parties to the conflict, who do not benefit by more favourable treatment under any other provisions of international law.

6. Inhabitants of a non-occupied territory, who on the approach of the enemy spontaneously take up arms to resist the invading forces, without having had time to form themselves into regular armed units, provided they carry arms openly and respect the laws and customs of war.

B. The following shall likewise be treated as prisoners of war under the present Convention:

1. Persons belonging, or having belonged, to the armed forces of the occupied country, if the occupying Power considers it necessary by reason of such allegiance to intern them, even though it has originally liberated them while hostilities were going on outside the territory it occupies, in particular where such persons have made an unsuccessful attempt to rejoin the armed forces to which they belong and which are engaged in combat, or where they fail to comply with a summons made to them with a view to internment.

2. The persons belonging to one of the categories enumerated in the present Article, who have been received by neutral or non-belligerent Powers on their territory and whom these Powers are required to intern under international law, without prejudice to any more favourable treatment which these Powers may choose to give and with the exception of Articles 8, 10, 15, 30, fifth paragraph, 58-67, 92, 126 and, where diplomatic relations exist between the Parties to the conflict and the neutral or non-belligerent Power concerned, those Articles concerning the Protecting Power. Where such diplomatic relations exist, the Parties to a conflict on whom these persons depend shall be allowed to perform towards them the functions of a Protecting Power as provided in the present Convention, without prejudice to the functions which these Parties normally exercise in conformity with diplomatic and consular usage and treaties.

C. This Article shall in no way affect the status of medical personnel and chaplains as provided for in Article 33 of the present Convention.

Article 5

The present Convention shall apply to the persons referred to in Article 4 from the time they fall into the power of the enemy and until their final release and repatriation.

Should any doubt arise as to whether persons, having committed a belligerent act and having fallen into the hands of the enemy, belong to any of the categories enumerated in Article 4, such persons shall enjoy the protection of the present Convention until such time as their status has been determined by a competent tribunal.

Article 99

No prisoner of war may be tried or sentenced for an act which is not forbidden by the law of the Detaining Power or by international law, in force at the time the said act was committed.

No moral or physical coercion may be exerted on a prisoner of war in order to induce him to admit himself guilty of the act of which he is accused.

No prisoner of war may be convicted without having had an opportunity to present his defence and the assistance of a qualified advocate or counsel.

Article 100

Prisoners of war and the Protecting Powers shall be informed as soon as possible of the offences which are punishable by the death sentence under the laws of the Detaining Power.

Other offences shall not thereafter be made punishable by the death penalty without the concurrence of the Power upon which the prisoners of war depend.

The death sentence cannot be pronounced on a prisoner of war unless the attention of the court has, in accordance with Article 87, second paragraph, been particularly called to the fact that since the accused is not a national of the Detaining Power, he is not bound to it by any duty of allegiance, and that he is in its power as the result of circumstances independent of his own will.

Article 102

A prisoner of war can be validly sentenced only if the sentence has been pronounced by the same courts according to the same procedure as in the case of members of the armed forces of the Detaining Power, and if, furthermore, the provisions of the present Chapter have been observed.

Article 105

The prisoner of war shall be entitled to assistance by one of his prisoner comrades, to defence by a qualified advocate or counsel of his own choice, to the calling of witnesses and, if he deems necessary, to the services of a competent interpreter. He shall be advised of these rights by the Detaining Power in due time before the trial.

Failing a choice by the prisoner of war, the Protecting Power shall find him an advocate or counsel, and shall have at least one week at its disposal for the purpose. The Detaining Power shall deliver to the said Power, on request, a list of persons qualified to present the defence. Failing a choice of an advocate or counsel by the prisoner of war or the Protecting Power, the Detaining Power shall appoint a competent advocate or counsel to conduct the defence.

Article 118

Prisoners of war shall be released and repatriated without delay after the cessation of active hostilities.

IV

Convention Relative to the Protection of Civilian Persons in Time of War

Article 2

In addition to the provisions which shall be implemented in peace-time, the present Convention shall apply to all cases of declared war or of any other armed conflict which may arise between two or more of the High Contracting Parties, even if the state of war is not recognized by one of them.

The Convention shall also apply to all cases of partial or total occupation of the territory of a High Contracting Party, even if the said occupation meets with no armed resistance.

Article 3

In the case of armed conflict not of an international character occurring in the territory of one of the High Contracting Parties, each Party to the conflict shall be bound to apply, as a minimum, the following provisions:

(1) Persons taking no active part in the hostilities, including members of armed forces who have laid down their arms and those placed hors de combat by sickness, wounds, detention, or any other cause, shall in all circumstances be treated humanely, without any adverse distinction founded on race, colour, religion or faith, sex, birth or wealth, or any other similar criteria.

To this end the following acts are and shall remain prohibited at any time and in any place whatsoever with respect to the above-mentioned persons:

(a) violence to life and person, in particular murder of all kinds, mutilation, cruel treatment and torture;
(b) taking of hostages;
(c) outrages upon personal dignity, in particular humiliating and degrading treatment;
(d) the passing of sentences and the carrying out of executions without previous judgment pronounced by a regularly constituted court, affording all the judicial guarantees which are recognized as indispensable by civilized peoples.

Article 4

Persons protected by the Convention are those who, at a given moment and in any manner whatsoever, find themselves, in case of a conflict or occupation, in the hands of a Party to the conflict or Occupying Power of which they are not nationals.

Nationals of a State which is not bound by the Convention are not protected by it. Nationals of a neutral State who find themselves in the territory of a belligerent State, and nationals of a co-belligerent State, shall not be regarded as protected persons while the State of which they are nationals has normal diplomatic representation in the State in whose hands they are.

Article 5

Where in the territory of a Party to the conflict, the latter is satisfied that an individual protected person is definitely suspected of or engaged in activities hostile to the security of the State, such individual person shall not be entitled to claim such rights and privileges under the present Convention as would, if exercised in the favour of such individual person, be prejudicial to the security of such State.

Where in occupied territory an individual protected person is detained as a spy or saboteur, or as a person under definite suspicion of activity hostile to the security of the Occupying Power, such person shall, in those cases where absolute military security so requires, be regarded as having forfeited rights of communication under the present Convention.

In each case, such persons shall nevertheless be treated with humanity and, in case of trial, shall not be deprived of the rights of fair and regular trial prescribed by the present Convention. They shall also be granted the full rights and privileges of a protected person under the present Convention at the earliest date consistent with the security of the State or Occupying Power, as the case may be.

Section III. Occupied territories

Article 64

The penal laws of the occupied territory shall remain in force, with the exception that they may be repealed or suspended by the Occupying Power in cases where they constitute a threat to its security or an obstacle to the application of the present Convention.

Subject to the latter consideration and to the necessity for ensuring the effective administration of justice, the tribunals of the occupied territory shall continue to function in respect of all offences covered by the said laws.

The Occupying Power may, however, subject the population of the occupied territory to provisions which are essential to enable the Occupying Power to fulfil its obligations under the present Convention, to maintain the orderly government of the territory, and to ensure the security of the Occupying Power, of the members and property of the occupying forces or administration, and likewise of the establishments and lines of communication used by them.

Article 72

Accused persons shall have the right to present evidence necessary to their defence and may, in particular, call witnesses. They shall have the right to be assisted by a qualified advocate or counsel of their own choice, who shall be able to visit them freely and shall enjoy the necessary facilities for preparing the defence.

Failing a choice by the accused, the Protecting Power may provide him with an advocate or counsel. When an accused person has to meet a serious charge and the Protecting Power is not functioning, the Occupying Power, subject to the consent of the accused, shall provide an advocate or counsel.

2. STATUTES OF THE INTERNATIONAL CRIMINAL TRIBUNALS

[Note: The two ICT's were established for slightly different circumstances. The assumption at the time seems to have been that Yugoslavia presented an "international armed conflict" while Rwanda was an "armed conflict not of an international character," thus producing slightly different statements of substantive law to be applied with respect to the Geneva Conventions. The substantive law portions of the two statutes are rearranged for ease of comparison.]

STATUTE OF THE INTERNATIONAL CRIMINAL TRIBUNAL FOR YUGOSLAVIA

Article 1
Competence of the International Tribunal

The International Tribunal shall have the power to prosecute persons responsible for serious violations of international humanitarian law committed in the territory of the former Yugoslavia since 1991 in accordance with the provisions of the present Statute.

Article 2
Grave breaches of the Geneva Conventions of 1949

The International Tribunal shall have the power to prosecute persons committing or ordering to be committed grave breaches of the Geneva Conventions of 12 August 1949, namely the following acts

STATUTE OF THE INTERNATIONAL CRIMINAL TRIBUNAL FOR RWANDA

Article 1: Competence of the International Tribunal for Rwanda

The International Tribunal for Rwanda shall have the power to prosecute persons responsible for serious violations of international humanitarian law committed in the territory of Rwanda and Rwandan citizens responsible for such violations committed in the territory of neighbouring States between 1 January 1994 and 31 December 1994, in accordance with the provisions of the present Statute.

Article 4: Violations of Article 3 Common to the Geneva Conventions and of Additional Protocol II

The International Tribunal for Rwanda shall have the power to prosecute persons committing or ordering to be committed serious violations of Article 3 common to the Geneva Conventions of 12 August

[ICTY cont.]

against persons or property protected under the provisions of the relevant Geneva Convention:

(a) wilful killing;
(b) torture or inhuman treatment, including biological experiments;
(c) wilfully causing great suffering or serious injury to body or health;
(d) extensive destruction and

appropriation of property, not justified by military necessity and carried out unlawfully and wantonly;
(e) compelling a prisoner of war or a civilian to serve in the forces of a hostile power;
(f) wilfully depriving a prisoner of war or a civilian of the rights of fair and regular trial;
(g) unlawful deportation or transfer or unlawful confinement of a civilian;
(h) taking civilians as hostages.

[ICTR cont.]

1949 for the Protection of War Victims, and of Additional Protocol II thereto of 8 June 1977. These violations shall include, but shall not be limited to:
(a) Violence to life, health and physical or mental well-being of persons, in particular murder as well as cruel treatment such as torture, mutilation or any form of corporal punishment;
(b) Collective punishments;
(c) Taking of hostages;
(d) Acts of terrorism;
(e) Outrages upon personal dignity, in particular humiliating and degrading treatment, rape, enforced prostitution and any form of indecent assault;
(f) Pillage;
(g) The passing of sentences and the carrying out of executions without previous judgement pronounced by a regularly constituted court, affording all the judicial guarantees which are recognized as indispensable by civilised peoples;
(h) Threats to commit any of the foregoing acts.

Article 4
Genocide

1. The International Tribunal shall have the power to prosecute persons committing genocide as defined in paragraph 2 of this article or of committing any of the other acts enumerated in paragraph 3 of this article.

2. Genocide means any of the following acts committed with intent to destroy, in whole or in part, a national, ethnical, racial or religious group, as such:

(a) killing members of the group;
(b) causing serious bodily or mental harm to members of the group;

Article 2
Genocide

1. The International Tribunal for Rwanda shall have the power to prosecute persons committing genocide as defined in paragraph 2 of this Article or of committing any of the other acts enumerated in paragraph 3 of this Article.

2. Genocide means any of the following acts committed with intent to destroy, in whole or in part, a national, ethnical, racial or religious group, such as:

(a) Killing members of the group;
(b) Causing serious bodily or mental harm to members of the group;

[ICTY cont.]

(c) deliberately inflicting on the group conditions of life calculated to bring about its physical destruction in whole or in part;

(d) imposing measures intended to prevent births within the group;

(e) forcibly transferring children of the group to another group.

3. The following acts shall be punishable:

(a) genocide;

(b) conspiracy to commit genocide;

(c) direct and public incitement to commit genocide;

(d) attempt to commit genocide;

(e) complicity in genocide.

Article 5
Crimes against humanity

The International Tribunal shall have the power to prosecute persons responsible for the following crimes when committed in armed conflict, whether international or internal in character, and directed against any civilian population:

(a) murder;

(b) extermination;

(c) enslavement;

(d) deportation;

(e) imprisonment;

(f) torture;

(g) rape;

(h) persecutions on political, racial and religious grounds;

(i) other inhumane acts.

Article 3
Violations of the laws or customs of war

The International Tribunal shall have the power to prosecute persons violating the laws or customs of war. Such violations shall include, but not

[ICTR cont.]

(c) Deliberately inflicting on the group conditions of life calculated to bring about its physical destruction in whole or in part;

(d) Imposing measures intended to prevent births within the group;

(e) Forcibly transferring children of the group to another group.

3. The following acts shall be punishable:

(a) Genocide;

(b) Conspiracy to commit genocide;

(c) Direct and public incitement to commit genocide;

(d) Attempt to commit genocide;

(e) Complicity in genocide.

Article 3
Crimes against Humanity

The International Tribunal for Rwanda shall have the power to prosecute persons responsible for the following crimes when committed as part of a widespread or systematic attack against any civilian population on national, political, ethnic, racial or religious grounds:

(a) Murder;

(b) Extermination;

(c) Enslavement;

(d) Deportation;

(e) Imprisonment;

(f) Torture;

(g) Rape;

(h) Persecutions on political, racial and religious grounds;

(i) Other inhumane acts.

be limited to:

(a) employment of poisonous weapons or other weapons calculated to cause unnecessary suffering;

(b) wanton destruction of cities, towns or villages, or devastation not justified by military necessity;

(c) attack, or bombardment, by whatever means, of undefended towns, villages, dwellings, or buildings;

(d) seizure of, destruction or wilful damage done to institutions dedicated to religion, charity and education, the arts and sciences, historic monuments and works of art and science;

(e) plunder of public or private property.

3. Convention Against Torture and Other Cruel, Inhuman or Degrading Treatment or Punishment

Article 1

1. For the purposes of this Convention, torture means any act by which severe pain or suffering, whether physical or mental, is intentionally inflicted on a person for such purposes as obtaining from him or a third person information or a confession, punishing him for an act he or a third person has committed or is suspected of having committed, or intimidating or coercing him or a third person, or for any reason based on discrimination of any kind, when such pain or suffering is inflicted by or at the instigation of or with the consent or acquiescence of a public official or other person acting in an official capacity. It does not include pain or suffering arising only from, inherent in or incidental to lawful sanctions.

2. This article is without prejudice to any international instrument or national legislation which does or may contain provisions of wider application.

Article 2

1. Each State Party shall take effective legislative, administrative, judicial or other measures to prevent acts of torture in any territory under its jurisdiction.

2. No exceptional circumstances whatsoever, whether a state of war or a threat or war, internal political instability or any other public emergency, may be invoked as a justification of torture.

3. An order from a superior officer or a public authority may not be invoked as a justification of torture.

Article 3

1. No State Party shall expel, return ("refouler") or extradite a person to another State where there are substantial grounds for believing that he would be in danger of being subjected to torture.

2. For the purpose of determining whether there are such grounds, the competent authorities shall take into account all relevant considerations including, where applicable, the existence in the State concerned of a consistent pattern of gross, flagrant or mass violations of human rights.

Article 4

1. Each State Party shall ensure that all acts of torture are offences under its criminal law. The same shall apply to an attempt to commit torture and to an act by any person which constitutes complicity or participation in torture.

2. Each State Party shall make these offences punishable by appropriate penalties which take into account their grave nature.

Article 5

1. Each State Party shall take such measures as may be necessary to establish its jurisdiction over the offences referred to in article 4 in the following cases:

> When the offences are committed in any territory under its jurisdiction or on board a ship or aircraft registered in that State;

> When the alleged offender is a national of that State;

> When the victim was a national of that State if that State considers it appropriate.

2. Each State Party shall likewise take such measures as may be necessary to establish its jurisdiction over such offences in cases where the alleged offender is present in any territory under its jurisdiction and it does not extradite him pursuant to article 8 to any of the States mentioned in Paragraph 1 of this article.

3. This Convention does not exclude any criminal jurisdiction exercised in accordance with internal law.

Article 6

1. Upon being satisfied, after an examination of information available to it, that the circumstances so warrant, any State Party in whose territory a person alleged to have committed any offence referred to in article 4 is present, shall take him into custody or take other legal measures to ensure his presence. The custody and other legal measures shall be as provided in the law of that State but may be continued only for such time as is necessary to enable any criminal or extradition proceedings to be instituted.

Article 7

1. The State Party in territory under whose jurisdiction a person alleged to have committed any offence referred to in article 4 is found, shall in the cases contemplated in article 5, if it does not extradite him, submit the case to its competent authorities for the purpose of prosecution.

Article 8

1. The offences referred to in article 4 shall be deemed to be included as extraditable offences in any extradition treaty existing between States Parties. States Parties undertake to include such offences as extraditable offences in every extradition treaty to be concluded between them.

4. Such offences shall be treated, for the purpose of extradition between States Parties, as if they had been committed not only in the place in which they occurred but also in the territories of the States required to establish their jurisdiction in accordance with article 5, paragraph 1.

4. International Convention for the Suppression of the Financing of Terrorism

Article 2

1. Any person commits an offence within the meaning of this Convention if that person by any means, directly or indirectly, unlawfully and wilfully, provides or collects funds with the intention that they should be used or in the knowledge that they are to be used, in full or in part, in order to carry out:

(a) An act which constitutes an offence within the scope of and as defined in one of the treaties listed in the annex; or

(b) Any other act intended to cause death or serious bodily injury to a civilian, or to any other person not taking an active part in the hostilities in a situation of armed conflict, when the purpose of such act, by its nature or context, is to intimidate a population, or to compel a government or an international organization to do or to abstain from doing any act.

3. For an act to constitute an offence set forth in paragraph 1, it shall not be necessary that the funds were actually used to carry out an offence referred to in paragraph 1.

4. Any person also commits an offence if that person attempts to commit an offence as set forth in paragraph 1 of this article.

5. Any person also commits an offence if that person:

(a) Participates as an accomplice in an offence as set forth in paragraph 1 or 4 of this article;

(b) Organizes or directs others to commit an offence as set forth in paragraph 1 or 4of this article;

(c) Contributes to the commission of one or more offences as set forth in paragraphs 1 or 4 of this article by a group of persons acting with a common purpose. Such contribution shall be intentional and shall either:

(i) Be made with the aim of furthering the criminal activity or criminal purpose of the group, where such activity or purpose involves the commission of an offence as set forth in paragraph 1 of this article; or

(ii) Be made in the knowledge of the intention of the group to commit an offence as set forth in paragraph 1 of this article.

Article 3

This Convention shall not apply where the offence is committed within a single State, the alleged offender is a national of that State and is present in the territory of that State and no other State has a basis under article 7, paragraph 1, or article 7, paragraph 2, to exercise jurisdiction, except that the provisions of articles 12 to 18 shall, as appropriate, apply in those cases.

Article 4

Each State Party shall adopt such measures as may be necessary:

(a) To establish as criminal offences under its domestic law the offences set forth in article 2;

(b) To make those offences punishable by appropriate penalties which take into account the grave nature of the offences.

Article 5

1. Each State Party, in accordance with its domestic legal principles, shall take the necessary measures to enable a legal entity located in its territory or organized under its laws to be held liable when a person responsible for the management or control of that legal entity has, in that capacity, committed an offence set forth in article 2. Such liability may be criminal, civil or administrative.

2. Such liability is incurred without prejudice to the criminal liability of individuals having committed the offences.

3. Each State Party shall ensure, in particular, that legal entities liable in accordance with paragraph 1 above are subject to effective, proportionate and dissuasive criminal, civil or administrative sanctions. Such sanctions may include monetary sanctions.

Article 6

Each State Party shall adopt such measures as may be necessary, including, where appropriate, domestic legislation, to ensure that criminal acts within the scope of this Convention are under no circumstances justifiable by considerations of a political, philosophical, ideological, racial, ethnic, religious or other similar nature.

Article 7

1. Each State Party shall take such measures as may be necessary to establish its jurisdiction over the offences set forth in article 2 when:

(a) The offence is committed in the territory of that State;

(b) The offence is committed on board a vessel flying the flag of that State or an aircraft registered under the laws of that State at the time the offence is committed;

(c) The offence is committed by a national of that State.

2. A State Party may also establish its jurisdiction over any such offence when:

(a) The offence was directed towards or resulted in the carrying out of an offence referred to in article 2, paragraph 1, subparagraph (a) or (b), in the territory of or against a national of that State;

(b) The offence was directed towards or resulted in the carrying out of an offence referred to in article 2, paragraph 1, subparagraph (a) or (b), against a State or government facility of that State abroad, including diplomatic or consular premises of that State;

(c) The offence was directed towards or resulted in an offence referred to in article 2, paragraph 1, subparagraph (a) or (b), committed in an attempt to compel that State to do or abstain from doing any act;

(d) The offence is committed by a stateless person who has his or her habitual residence in the territory of that State;

(e) The offence is committed on board an aircraft which is operated by the Government of that State.

[The "prosecute or extradite" provisions are essentially the same as in other Conventions, such as the Torture Convention.]

5. UN Security Council Resolution 1373

Sept. 28, 2001

The Security Council,

Reaffirming its resolutions 1269 (1999) of 19 October 1999 and 1368 (2001) of 12 September 2001,

Reaffirming also its unequivocal condemnation of the terrorist attacks which took place in New York, Washington, D.C. and Pennsylvania on 11 September 2001, and expressing its determination to prevent all such acts,

Reaffirming further that such acts, like any act of international terrorism, constitute a threat to international peace and security,

Reaffirming the inherent right of individual or collective self-defence as recognized by the Charter of the United Nations as reiterated in resolution 1368 (2001),

Reaffirming the need to combat by all means, in accordance with the Charter of the United Nations, threats to international peace and security caused by terrorist acts,

Deeply concerned by the increase, in various regions of the world, of acts of terrorism motivated by intolerance or extremism,

Calling on States to work together urgently to prevent and suppress terrorist acts, including through increased cooperation and full implementation of the relevant international conventions relating to terrorism,

Recognizing the need for States to complement international cooperation by taking additional measures to prevent and suppress, in their territories through all lawful means, the financing and preparation of any acts of terrorism,

Reaffirming the principle established by the General Assembly in its declaration of October 1970 (resolution 2625 (XXV)) and reiterated by the Security Council in its resolution 1189 (1998) of 13 August 1998, namely that every State has the duty to refrain from organizing, instigating, assisting or participating in terrorist acts in another State or acquiescing in organized activities within its territory directed towards the commission of such acts,

Acting under Chapter VII of the Charter of the United Nations,

1. *Decides* that all States shall:

(a) Prevent and suppress the financing of terrorist acts;

(b) Criminalize the wilful provision or collection, by any means, directly or indirectly, of funds by their nationals or in their territories with the intention that the funds should be used, or in the knowledge that they are to be used, in order to carry out terrorist acts;

(c) Freeze without delay funds and other financial assets or economic resources of persons who commit, or attempt to commit, terrorist acts or participate in or facilitate the commission of terrorist acts; of entities owned or controlled directly or indirectly by such persons; and of persons and entities acting on behalf of, or at the direction of such persons and entities, including funds derived or generated from property owned or controlled directly or indirectly by such persons and associated persons and entities;

(d) Prohibit their nationals or any persons and entities within their territories from making any funds, financial assets or economic resources or financial or other related services available, directly or indirectly, for the benefit of persons who commit or attempt to commit or facilitate or participate in the commission of terrorist acts, of entities owned or controlled, directly or indirectly, by such persons and of persons and entities acting on behalf of or at the direction of such persons;

2. *Decides also* that all States shall:

(a) Refrain from providing any form of support, active or passive, to entities or persons involved in terrorist acts, including by suppressing recruitment of members of terrorist groups and eliminating the supply of weapons to terrorists;

(b) Take the necessary steps to prevent the commission of terrorist acts, including by provision of early warning to other States by exchange of information;

(c) Deny safe haven to those who finance, plan, support, or commit terrorist acts, or provide safe havens;

(d) Prevent those who finance, plan, facilitate or commit terrorist acts from using their respective territories for those purposes against other States or their citizens;

(e) Ensure that any person who participates in the financing, planning, preparation or perpetration of terrorist acts or in supporting terrorist acts is brought to justice and ensure that, in addition to any other measures against them, such terrorist acts are established as serious criminal offences in domestic laws and regulations and that the punishment duly reflects the seriousness of such terrorist acts;

(f) Afford one another the greatest measure of assistance in connection with criminal investigations or criminal proceedings relating to the financing or support of terrorist acts, including assistance in obtaining evidence in their possession necessary for the proceedings;

(g) Prevent the movement of terrorists or terrorist groups by effective border controls and controls on issuance of identity papers and travel documents, and through measures for preventing counterfeiting, forgery or fraudulent use of identity papers and travel documents;

3. *Calls* upon all States to:

(a) Find ways of intensifying and accelerating the exchange of operational information, especially regarding actions or movements of terrorist persons or networks; forged or falsified travel documents; traffic in arms, explosives or sensitive materials; use of communications technologies by terrorist groups; and the threat posed by the possession of weapons of mass destruction by terrorist groups;

(b) Exchange information in accordance with international and domestic law and cooperate on administrative and judicial matters to prevent the commission of terrorist acts;

(c) Cooperate, particularly through bilateral and multilateral arrangements and agreements, to prevent and suppress terrorist attacks and take action against perpetrators of such acts;

(d) Become parties as soon as possible to the relevant international conventions and protocols relating to terrorism, including the International Convention for the Suppression of the Financing of Terrorism of 9 December 1999;

(e) Increase cooperation and fully implement the relevant international conventions and protocols relating to terrorism and Security Council resolutions 1269 (1999) and 1368 (2001);

(f) Take appropriate measures in conformity with the relevant provisions of national and international law, including international standards of human rights, before granting refugee status, for the purpose of ensuring that the asylum-seeker has not planned, facilitated or participated in the commission of terrorist acts;

(g) Ensure, in conformity with international law, that refugee status is not abused by the perpetrators, organizers or facilitators of terrorist acts, and that claims of political motivation are not recognized as grounds for refusing requests for the extradition of alleged terrorists;

4. *Notes* with concern the close connection between international terrorism and transnational organized crime, illicit drugs, money-laundering, illegal armstrafficking, and illegal movement of nuclear, chemical, biological and other potentially deadly materials, and in this regard emphasizes the need to enhance coordination of efforts on national, subregional, regional and international levels in order to strengthen a global response to this serious challenge and threat to international security;

5. *Declares* that acts, methods, and practices of terrorism are contrary to the purposes and principles of the United Nations and that knowingly financing, planning and inciting terrorist acts are also contrary to the purposes and principles of the United Nations;

6. *Decides* to establish, in accordance with rule 28 of its provisional rules of procedure, a Committee of the Security Council, consisting of all the members of the Council, to monitor implementation of this resolution, with the assistance of appropriate expertise, and calls upon all States to report to the Committee, no later than 90 days from the date of adoption of this resolution and thereafter according to a timetable to be proposed by the Committee, on the steps they have taken to implement this resolution;

7. *Directs* the Committee to delineate its tasks, submit a work programme within 30 days of the adoption of this resolution, and to consider the support it requires, in consultation with the Secretary-General;

8. *Expresses* its determination to take all necessary steps in order to ensure the full implementation of this resolution, in accordance with its responsibilities under the Charter;

9. *Decides* to remain seized of this matter.

6. Draft Comprehensive Convention on International Terrorism

Article I

For the purposes of this Convention:

1. "State or government facility" includes any permanent or temporary facility or conveyance that is used or occupied by representatives of a State, members of Government, the legislature or the judiciary or by officials or employees of a State or any other public authority or entity or by employees or officials of an intergovernmental organization in connection with their official duties.

2. "Military forces of a State" means the armed forces of a State which are organized, trained and equipped under its internal law for the primary purpose of national defence or security, and persons acting in support of those armed forces who are under their formal command, control and responsibility.

3. "Infrastructure facility" means any publicly or privately owned facility providing or distributing services for the benefit of the public, such as water, sewerage, energy, fuel or communications, and banking services, telecommunications and information networks.

4. "Place of public use" means those parts of any building, land, street, waterway or other location that are accessible or open to members of the public, whether continuously, periodically or occasionally, and encompasses any commercial, business, cultural, historical, educational, religious, governmental, entertainment, recreational or similar place that is so accessible or open to the public.

5. "Public transportation system" means all facilities, conveyances and instrumentalities, whether publicly or privately owned, that are used in or for publicly available services for the transportation of persons or cargo.

Article 2

1. Any person commits an offence within the meaning of this Convention if that person, by any means, unlawfully and intentionally, does an act intended to cause:

(a) Death or serious bodily injury to any person; or

(b) Serious damage to a State or government facility, a public transportation system, communication system or infrastructure facility with the intent to cause extensive destruction of such a place, facility or system, or where such destruction results or is likely to result in major economic loss;

when the purpose of such act, by its nature or context, is to intimidate a population, or to compel a Government or an international organization to do or abstain from doing any act. [In some versions of the draft, this last clause is printed at the end of, as if part of, subsection (b). If placed there, then (a) would stand alone without a requirement of political motivation and thus cover virtually any act of violence.]

2. Any person also commits an offence if that person attempts to commit an offence or participates as an accomplice in an offence as set forth in paragraph 1.

3. Any person also commits an offence if that person:

(a) Organizes, directs or instigates others to commit an offence as set forth in paragraph 1 or 2; or

(b) Aids, abets, facilitates or counsels the commission of such an offence; or

(c) In any other way contributes to the commission of one or more offences referred to in paragraphs 1, 2 or 3(a) by a group of persons acting with a common purpose; such contribution shall be intentional and either be made with the aim of furthering the general criminal activity or purpose of the group or be made in the knowledge of the intention of the group to commit the offence or offences concerned.

Article 3

This Convention shall not apply where the offence is committed within a single State, the alleged offender is a national of that State and is present in the territory of that State and no other State has a basis under article 6, paragraph 1, or article 6, paragraph 2, to exercise jurisdiction, except that the provisions of articles 10 to 22 shall, as appropriate, apply in those cases.

Article 4

Each State Party shall adopt such measures as may be necessary:

(a) To establish as criminal offences under its domestic law the offences set forth in article 2;

(b) To make those offences punishable by appropriate penalties which take into account the grave nature of those offences.

Article 5

Each State Party shall adopt such measures as may be necessary, including, where appropriate, domestic legislation, to ensure that criminal acts within the scope of this Convention are under no circumstances justifiable by considerations of a political, philosophical, ideological, racial, ethnic, religious or other similar nature.

Article 6

1. Each State Party shall take such measures as may be necessary to establish its jurisdiction over the offences referred to in article 2 in the following cases.

(a) When the offence is committed in the territory of that State or on board a ship or aircraft registered in that State;

(b) When the alleged offender is a national of that State or is a person who has his or her habitual residence in its territory;

(c) When the offence is committed wholly or partially outside its territory, if the effects of the conduct or its intended effects constitute or result, within its territory, in the commission of an offence referred to in article 2.

2. A State may also establish its jurisdiction over any such offence when it is committed:

(a) By a stateless person whose habitual residence is in that State; or

(b) With respect to a national of that State; or

(c) Against a State or government facility of that State abroad, including an embassy or other diplomatic or consular premises of that State; or

(d) In an attempt to compel that State to do or to abstain from doing any act;

(e) On board a ship or aircraft which is operated by the Government of that State.

3. Each State Party shall take such measures as may be necessary to establish its jurisdiction over the offences referred to in article 2 in cases where the alleged offender is present in its territory and where it does not extradite such person to any of the States Parties that have established their jurisdiction in accordance with paragraphs 1 or 2.

4. When more than one State Party claims jurisdiction over the offences set forth in article 2, the relevant States Parties shall strive to coordinate their actions appropriately, in particular concerning the conditions for prosecution and the modalities for mutual legal assistance.

5. This Convention does not exclude any criminal jurisdiction exercised in accordance with national law.

Article 7

States Parties shall take appropriate measures, before granting asylum, for the purpose of ensuring that asylum is not granted to any person in respect of whom there are reasonable grounds indicating his involvement in any offence referred to in article 2.

Article 8

States Parties shall cooperate in the prevention of the offences set forth in article 2, particularly:

(a) By taking all practicable measures, including, if necessary, adapting their domestic legislation, to prevent and counter preparations in their respective territories for the commission, by whomsoever and in whatever manner, of those offences within or outside their territories, including:

(i) Measures to prohibit in their territories the establishment and operation of installations and training camps for the commission, within or outside their territories, of offences referred to in article 2; and

(ii) Measures to prohibit the illegal activities of persons, groups and organizations that encourage, instigate, organize, knowingly finance or engage in the commission, within or outside their territories, of offences referred to in article 2;

(b) By exchanging accurate and verified information in accordance with their national law, and coordinating administrative and other measures taken as appropriate to prevent the commission of offences as referred to in article 2.

Article 9

1. Each State Party, in accordance with its domestic legal principles, shall take the necessary measures to enable a legal entity located in its territory or organized under its laws to be held liable when a person responsible for the management or control of that legal entity has, in that capacity, committed an offence referred to in article 2. Such liability may be criminal, civil or administrative.

2. Such liability is incurred without prejudice to the criminal liability of individuals having committed the offences.

3. Each State Party shall ensure, in particular, that legal entities liable in accordance with paragraph (i) above are subject to effective, proportionate and dissuasive criminal, civil or administrative sanctions. Such sanctions may include monetary sanctions.

Article 10

1. Upon receiving information that a person who has committed or who is alleged to have committed an offence referred to in article 2 may be present in its territory, the State Party concerned shall take such measures as may be necessary under its domestic law to investigate the facts contained in the information.

2. Upon being satisfied that the circumstances so warrant, the State Party in whose territory the offender or alleged offender is present shall take the appropriate measures under its domestic law so as to ensure that person's presence for the purpose of prosecution or extradition.

6. When a State Party, pursuant to the present article, has taken a person into custody, it shall immediately notify, directly or through the Secretary-General of the United Nations, the States Parties which have established jurisdiction in accordance with article 6, paragraph 1 or 2, and if it considers it advisable, any other interested States Parties, of the fact that such person is in custody and of the circumstances which warrant that person's detention. The State which

makes the investigation contemplated in paragraph 1 shall promptly inform the said States Parties of its findings and shall indicate whether it intends to exercise jurisdiction.

Article 11

1. The State Party in whose territory the alleged offender is found shall, if it does not extradite the person, be obliged, without exception whatsoever and whether or not the offence was committed in its territory, to submit the case to its competent authorities for the purpose of prosecution through proceedings in accordance with the laws of that State. Those authorities shall take their decision in the same manner as in the case of any ordinary offence of a grave nature under the law of that State.

2. Whenever a State Party is permitted under its domestic law to extradite or otherwise surrender one of its nationals only upon the condition that the person will be returned to that State to serve the sentence imposed as a result of the trial or proceeding for which the extradition or surrender of the person was sought, and that State and the State seeking the extradition of the person agree with this option and other terms they may deem appropriate, such a conditional extradition or surrender shall be sufficient to discharge the obligation set forth in paragraph 1.

TABLE OF CASES